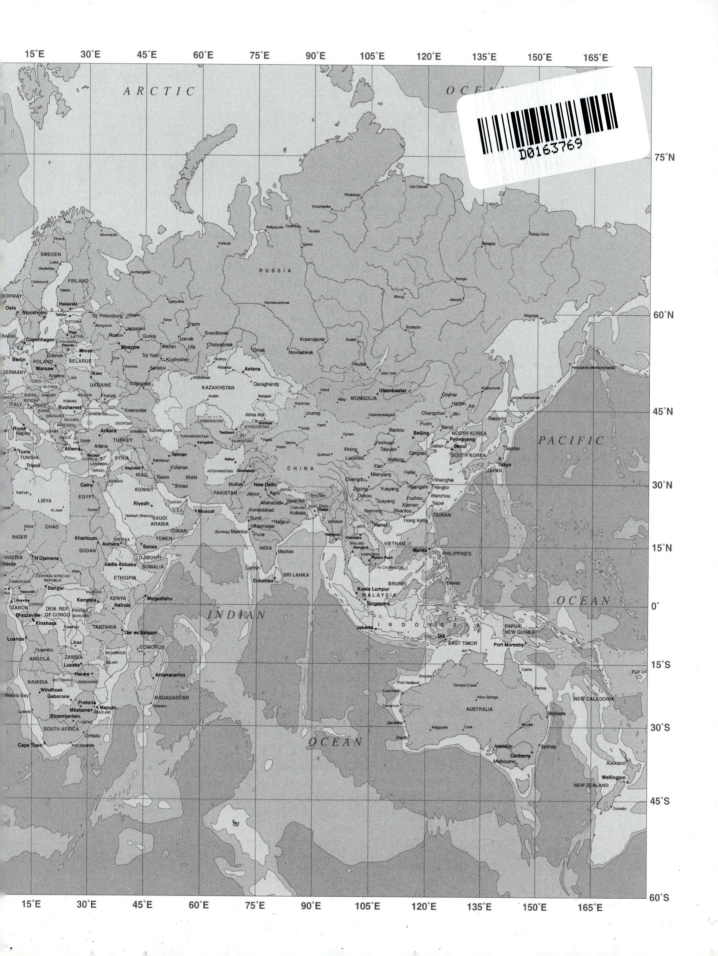

Table of Cases

THE WORLD ECONOMY

INTERNATIONAL TRADE

SEVENTH EDITION

Beth V. Yarbrough
Amherst College

Robert M. Yarbrough
Amherst College

THOMSON
SOUTH-WESTERN

Australia · Canada · Mexico · Singapore · Spain · United Kingdom · United States

THOMSON

SOUTH-WESTERN

The World Economy: International Trade, Seventh Edition
Beth V. Yarbrough and Robert M. Yarbrough

VP/Editorial Director:
Jack W. Calhoun

VP/Editor-in-Chief:
Dave Shaut

Senior Developmental Editor:
Sarah Dorger

Marketing Manager:
John Carey

Senior Production Editor:
Kara ZumBahlen

Manager of Technology, Editorial:
Vicky True

Technology Project Editor:
Peggy Buskey

Web Coordinator:
Karen Schaffer

Senior Manufacturing Coordinator:
Sandee Milewski

Production House:
Stratford Publishing Services, Inc.

Compositor:
Integra

Art Director:
Michelle Kunkler

Internal Designer:
Paul Neff Design

Cover Designer:
Tippy McIntosh

Cover Images:
© Getty Images, Inc.

Printer:
Courier
Kendalville, IN

Library of Congress Control Number:
2005920272

For more information about our products, contact us at:

Thomson Learning Academic Resource Center

1-800-423-0563

Thomson Higher Education
5191 Natorp Boulevard
Mason, OH 45040
USA

Asia (including India)
Thomson Learning
5 Shenton Way
#01-01 UIC Building
Singapore 068808

Australia/New Zealand
Thomson Learning Australia
102 Dodds Street
Southbank, Victoria 3006
Australia

Canada
Thomson Nelson
1120 Birchmount Road
Toronto, Ontario
M1K 5G4
Canada

Latin America
Thomson Learning
Seneca, 53
Colonia Polanco
11560 Mexico
D.F.Mexico

UK/Europe/Middle East/Africa
Thomson Learning
High Holborn House
50/51 Bedford Row
London WC1R 4LR
United Kingdom

Spain (including Portugal)
Thomson Paraninfo
Calle Magallanes, 25
28015 Madrid, Spain

To Y. Y.

Preface

The success of earlier editions of *The World Economy: Trade and Finance* owes much to developments outside the classroom. Specific episodes come and go, but the pace of world events continues to remind us all of the big role international issues play in our economic lives. Zimbabwe slips into economic crisis as Argentina attempts to crawl out, and Japan teeters between economic recovery and continued stagnation. The United States and China make progress on intellectual property rights disputes, while the European Union and the United States bicker and test the World Trade Organization's ability to resolve disputes over U.S. tax and antidumping policies. The global textile and apparel industries scramble to adjust to the January 1, 2005, end of the complex web of import quotas that dominated the industries for 40 years. Ten Central and Eastern European countries, most only recently released from decades of central planning, celebrate their new membership in the European Union; but others, such as Belarus and Turkmenistan, remain mired in isolation, erratic reform, and recurrent political and economic crisis. After decades of hope and years of planning, the euro finally arrives as a real currency, promptly plummets in value relative to the dollar, then reverses course. The entire Iraqi economy needs rebuilding, amid significant turmoil in its major export market—oil. And several of the poorest countries in the world face the daunting and expensive task of recovering from a tsunami that ranks among the worst natural disasters in the past 100 years.

WHAT ARE WE TRYING TO DO IN *THE WORLD ECONOMY: INTERNATIONAL TRADE?*

The pace, scale, and scope of such events underscore the widespread perception of the increased importance of international economics for understanding world events. Luckily, just a few simple tools of economic analysis can provide a great deal of insight into the ever-changing world economy. The goals of this seventh edition of *The World Economy* remain unchanged from those of the first six:

- Present the *basic tools* of international economic analysis clearly, consistently, and comprehensively;
- Provide lots of applications to actual events so students can learn to *use* the tools soundly and confidently to analyze the world economy; and
- Give a sense of the broad range of *challenging and exciting issues* (as well as some humorous and quirky ones) that arise in the international economic arena.

Integrated Theory and Applications

By combining up-to-date theory with current events and policy debates, we emphasize learning how to use international economics as a tool for understanding. By the end of the course, students can analyze problems independently, not just those that happen to dominate the headlines at the time of the book's writing. *The World Economy* has never glorified theory for its own sake. The rule we endeavor to follow remains that *any theory worth presenting is worth teaching students to use; if it's not useful in understanding the world economy, it doesn't belong in the book.*

The World Economy is self-contained; it defines all necessary concepts and doesn't rely on students' memories from other economics courses. Frequent data tables tie abstract concepts to their concrete empirical counterparts. *We believe that an international economics course should familiarize students with the empirical reality of the world economy as well as with abstract models of it*, so we present data more frequently than is typical in other texts. We refer often to common errors or misinterpretations in the popular press, because learning how to read the newspaper or listen to the television news with a keen eye and ear is at least as important as learning how to read the scholarly literature.

The integration of clear, concise theory with up-to-date examples and cases has always set *The World Economy* apart from its competitors. One example of this integration is our focus throughout the book on policy's distributional consequences. These consequences represent the crux of most international economic policy controversies, but many texts shortchange them with a flurry of tangency conditions. We make extensive use of examples from diverse areas of the world economy—Iceland, Central Asia, Africa, Singapore, and North Korea, not just the United States and Western Europe. We highlight the relevance of international economic theory for understanding front-page microeconomic issues such as trends in trade and wages, intellectual property protection and piracy in pharmaceuticals, distance and trade, the role of science in trade policy, agricultural subsidies, regionalism, the "resource curse," Russia's efforts to join the World Trade Organization, and the effect of aid on growth.

Careful, Clear Pedagogy

We employ a number of pedagogical devices to assist students in their reading. We number major sections within each chapter of *The World Economy* for easy reference. And to encourage *active* reading, at crucial points in an argument, we ask students in a parenthetic insertion, *"Why?"* These queries stop the reader from moving passively through the argument without confronting its underlying logic. Comments from our students indicate that the queries achieve their goal.[1] *The World Economy's* generous use of graphs, as well as their color format, make the arguments easy to follow. All graphs are fully integrated into the text and accompanied by self-contained legends. We encourage students to practice active translation between graphs and legends (*Can you cover the graph and draw your own, given the legend? Can you cover the legend and write your own explanation of the graph?*). Again, the emphasis is on learning to *use* the graphs as tools for understanding, not on memorization or rote manipulation.

Each chapter contains several cases, a summary, a "Looking Ahead" section that links the chapter to the next one, a list of key terms (boldfaced in the text), review questions and problems (including new ones in every chapter of the seventh edition), and a list of supplementary readings. The cases provide examples of the economic concepts and models developed in the chapter as well as extensive empirical information about the countries that make up the world economy. The end-of-chapter

---

1. Several students have reported making a game of the queries by trying to read each chapter without being "caught" unprepared to answer a query.

"Problems and Questions for Review" highlight major concepts from the chapter and relate those concepts to current policy debates. Many of the end-of-chapter questions from earlier editions now appear in the *Study Guide* (a new version of which accompanies this new edition). Unlike the bibliographies in many textbooks, the readings suggested in *The World Economy* include short, up-to-date articles as well as classic treatises and survey articles; and we note readings as appropriate for introductory, intermediate, or advanced students.

WHAT'S NEW TO THE SEVENTH EDITION?

Our basic goals, philosophy, and pedagogy remain unchanged, but this seventh edition incorporates many improvements. We've thoroughly updated and revised the book, including the text of each chapter as well as figures, tables, and cases. We've also made the language, headings, figure titles, and case titles more student friendly.

New Cases

We've added many new cases to reflect current events and issues. The new cases include:

- Which Plants Export?
- Lights-Out Factories
- A Rare Opportunity: Learning from Japanese Economic History
- Trade and Sir Isaac Newton's Apples
- Are There Economies of Scale?
- Binding Policy Makers' Hands
- Shooting Down the Byrd Amendment
- Cotton Pits Farmer Versus Farmer
- Sticky Business in Singapore
- All in the Family
- Is Japan Being Left Out?
- How Big Are They?
- WTO Member or Market Economy?

We've also updated and expanded many of the cases carried over from the sixth edition.

INTENDED AUDIENCE

By presenting the fundamentals of international economics clearly but rigorously, *The World Economy* becomes adaptable for a variety of courses. Our correspondence with adopters of earlier editions indicates that they use the book successfully in many different ways. Students with only a one-semester introductory economics course as background have no trouble mastering the material; in fact, we use the text extensively in classes at that level. Simply omit the appendixes and choose supplementary reading from the articles denoted as appropriate for beginning students. For students who've completed courses in intermediate micro, add the appendixes along with a wider range of supplementary reading. The flexibility of the book also serves beginning graduate students with no specific background in international economics and provides a stepping stone to more advanced texts and the professional literature. The book appeals to students of political science, international relations, and international business by providing economics' unique perspective on international issues.

ALTERNATE COURSE OUTLINES

In a one-semester course, we use Chapters One through Eleven, but users can omit any combination of Chapters Five, Nine, Ten, and Eleven to permit more extensive use of supplementary readings. No doubt many other permutations are possible.

ANCILLARIES BY THE TEXT AUTHORS

Study Guide

The seventh edition of *The World Economy* has its own *Study Guide*, available from Thomson Business and Professional Publishing through your local or college bookstore or from your Thomson Business and Professional Publishing representative. We wrote the *Study Guide* ourselves, coordinating it with the text and using the same careful pedagogy. The *Study Guide* contains:

- A "Quick Quiz" of multiple-choice questions for each chapter, designed to test whether students understood the chapter's main points
- Additional "Problems and Questions for Review" with answers
- Answers to chapter italicized queries
- Matching exercises for key terms in each chapter
- List of key points for each chapter
- Hints for writing a successful term paper on the world economy
- List of source materials for international information and data
- List of Web resources

Instructor's Manual

The *Instructor's Manual*, which we also wrote, contains:

- Answers to the italicized queries in the text
- Suggested test questions for each chapter
- Answers to the end-of-chapter "Problems and Questions for Review," including those new to the seventh edition
- Chapter-by-chapter key points
- Information on alternate course structures

PowerPoint Slides

PowerPoint slides are available for use by instructors for enhancing their lectures. The slides are available for download from the book's Web site at http://yarbrough.swlearning.com.

Online Quizzes

Students can test their comprehension of text readings by taking the online quizzes available at the book's Web site at http://yarbrough.swlearning.com.

e-con @pps

Thomson Business and Professional Publishing has included an innovative technology supplement with this edition: the e-con @pps Web site (http://econapps.swlearning.com). This site provides some valuable Web features: EconNews Online, EconDebate Online, and EconData Online. These features, which are organized by pertinent economic topics, are easy to integrate into classroom discussion. EconNews, EconDebate, and EconData should help motivate students, by taking them out of their usual passive mode and prompting them to analyze the latest economic news stories, policy debates, and data. These features are updated on a regular basis. The e-con @pps Web site is complimentary via an access card included with each new edition of *The World Economy*.

ACKNOWLEDGMENTS

The staffs at Thomson Business and Professional Publishing and Stratford Publishing deserve all the credit for the beautiful book that's emerged at the end of a long production process. The stalwart team of Sarah Dorger, Kara ZumBahlen, and Simone Payment, in particular, cheerfully kept things afloat even when their authors were sinking.

Thanks go also to our reviewers: Basanta Chaudhuri, *Rutgers University*, Tolga Koker, *Hamilton College*, Wetinee Matsathit, *University of Hawaii-Manoa*, Marc Melitz, *Harvard University*, Devashish Mitra, *Syracuse University*, Emanual Ornelas, *University of Georgia*, Raymond Robertson, *Macalester College*, Udayan Roy, *Long Island University*, Jeffery Steagall, *University of North Florida*, and Michael Szenberg, *Pace University*. We're grateful to all, and we appreciate the comments we didn't use as much as those we did. Compliments, suggestions, and criticisms from *The World Economy* users continue to play an essential role in the book's edition-to-edition improvement, so do contact us if you have comments.

Suggestions and questions—and, yes, even occasional blank stares—from students in the International Trade courses at Amherst College constantly help us improve. One of those students, Rajashree Datta, helped compile the original list of Web resources now included in the *Study Guide*. Our long-time friend and administrative assistant, Jeanne Reinle, graciously tolerates us even when a tight production schedule occasionally puts us in a cranky mood.

Beth V. Yarbrough
Robert M. Yarbrough
Amherst, Massachusetts
January 2005

Contents

CHAPTER 9
The Political Economy of Trade Policy and Borders   244

CHAPTER 10
Growth, Immigration, and Multinationals   279

CHAPTER 11
Development, Transition, and Trade   325

CHAPTER 1

Introduction to *International Trade* in the World Economy

1 WHY STUDY INTERNATIONAL TRADE?

Chances are at least some of the clothing you're wearing right now bears a "Made in China" label. Software programmers in India probably wrote or debugged parts of the computer software you'll use for your studies this semester. If you ate a banana as a before-class snack, it probably came from Central America (if you ate the snack in the United States) or from Africa or the Caribbean (if you ate the snack in the European Union). And, even if you think you drive a domestically produced car, at least some of the car's components almost certainly were produced in far-flung locations. So you already have lots of day-to-day experience with international trade, even if you've never studied it before. International trade has a big effect on your everyday life—probably bigger than you realize. Trade provides you a wider variety of goods and services plus lower prices for those products than you could possibly enjoy without trade. It also makes you interdependent in complex ways with clothing workers in China, programmers in India, banana growers in Ecuador, Cameroon, and St. Lucia, and automobile producers from Mexico to the Philippines.

Understanding international trade—what it is, how it works, why we do it, and how policy makers treat it—is absolutely essential to understanding today's world economy. Discussions of new degrees and even new types of international economic interdependence fill the news, and rapidly expanding international trade is one important reason. The fact that no nation is an economic island has never been more obvious. Citizens of many countries feel increasingly affected by external economic events over which they, and sometimes their national policy makers, exert less-than-total control. Many of the major economic stories that occupy newspaper headlines are stories about trade-related interdependence, its ramifications, and policy makers' and citizens' attempts to come to terms with it.

Sometimes the stories about international trade and interdependence have a long-run focus: Would completely free trade mean the end of the U.S. industries such as steel, apparel, and sugar? What will happen to developed-country wages if trade with developing countries continues to grow? How long will it take for the countries in transition from central planning to develop well-functioning market economies? Have Africa's and the Middle East's relatively closed trade policies contributed to those regions' slow growth over the past several decades? Will exports continue to dominate growth in the Chinese economy, or will domestic demand become more important? Sometimes the stories emerge in an instant: Should the United States loosen its restrictions on Pakistani textile exports to repay that country for its support in the war on terror? Does Russia's sudden arrest of an oil oligarch signal improved economic governance or a shift toward economic authoritarianism; how will the answer affect world oil prices? Will North Korea try to use nuclear weapons to engage in economic blackmail; and, if so, is there a useful role for trade sanctions?

All these questions make studying international trade more important than ever before, whether you are (or hope to be) a national policy maker, a business owner planning corporate strategy, or simply an informed citizen, voter, and participant in the world economy. *International Trade* provides a basic tool kit. It presents simple models to explain how international trade works in the world economy, empirical evidence to evaluate the models' predictions, dozens of case studies and applications from both historical and current events around the globe, and lots of useful trade-related information and data about the world economy and the diverse countries that constitute it. When you finish the book, you should feel confident weighing politicians' statements about international trade policy, evaluating the key international influences on a firm or industry, and analyzing the linkages between the trade policies followed by your home country and those followed by the rest of the world.

2 WHAT DO WE MEAN BY INTERNATIONAL INTERDEPENDENCE?

It's hard to pick up a newspaper or listen to the news these days without hearing about *globalization*. But the term itself usually goes undefined. Does it refer to the fact that consumers in dozens of countries can now buy McDonald's Big Macs—although the burgers, in fact, differ according to local tastes and culinary customs? Or that consumers in Mongolia can buy goods from abroad without having to pay any taxes (called *tariffs*) to import them? Or that the World Trade Organization can tell the United States that it can't subsidize its cotton producers? Or that many citizens in remote corners of the globe admire and strive for "Western" values of individual freedom, democracy, and economic growth? The diversity of these issues suggests that the term *globalization* may be so broad and subject to varying connotations that it loses its ability to communicate effectively. So, marketing considerations aside, most economists prefer to speak instead in terms of **international interdependence** and **international economic integration**. These terms refer to the degree to which economic events in one country affect others and the extent to which markets for goods, services, labor, and capital can operate freely across national boundaries. In other words, to what extent do national boundaries matter; do they block the flow of economic transactions or the effects of economic events and policies?

The term *international interdependence* entered the newspaper-headline vocabulary during the 1970s when the industrialized countries, along with oil-importing developing ones, helplessly endured two rounds of sudden and dramatic oil-price increases by the Organization of Petroleum Exporting Countries (OPEC).[1] By the early 1980s, countries' roles reversed. OPEC watched the price of oil tumble as demand fell because of a policy-induced recession in the industrialized countries. Most industrial and oil-importing developing countries welcomed the fall in oil prices (although not the recession that triggered it); but the decline also heightened the debt problem of several developing-country oil exporters, most notably Mexico. The resulting debt crisis among developing countries, in turn, generated financial uncertainty and a loss of export markets for the developed world and threatened the solvency of several major U.S. commercial banks.[2]

---

1. We'll analyze the trade policies of OPEC and similar groups in Chapter Six.

2. Chapter Eleven outlines the history and lessons of the 1980s debt crisis.

By the 1980s, key industries such as steel and automobiles, once dominated by a handful of U.S. firms, spanned the globe. Many U.S. industries struggled against increasingly potent foreign competition, and one by one those industries sought protection in the form of policy barriers against imports. But industries are themselves interdependent; so one industry's import barriers, which raise the price of that industry's output, can make it more difficult for related industries to remain competitive.[3] For example, when the U.S. steel industry won protection from its foreign rivals, U.S. automobile manufacturers had to pay higher prices for steel and became more vulnerable to competition from foreign car producers. As U.S. auto producers lost their dominance in their home market, they pressured policy makers for their own protection from foreign competition.

Policy makers responded to the auto industry's demands by placing a "voluntary" export restraint on Japanese automobiles. The restraint, which limited Japanese firms' ability to export cars produced in Japan to the United States, prompted a dramatic international relocation of much of the world's auto production.[4] Japanese firms such as Honda and Toyota now produce cars in the United States and export them to Europe, to Asia, and even back to Japan. Figure 1 documents one example: the worldwide pattern of production and sales of Hondas. In fact, it no longer makes much sense to talk about "American" cars or "Japanese" cars. Auto-industry analysts speak instead of "captive imports" (vehicles such as the Geo, made by a foreign-based company but sold through domestic dealerships) and "transplants" (for example, the Honda Accord, built domestically by a foreign-based company). Today, Chinese factories assemble "German" Volkswagens, "Japanese" Hondas, and "American" Chevrolets.

Even though consumers can no longer easily define cars' nationality, firms recognize that as long as domestic interests dominate the policy-making process, it's to the firms' advantage to appear domestic. So advertising often emphasizes firms' links to the domestic economy. For example, a 1997 Toyota advertisement in *Newsweek* highlighted the firm's "homegrown success" at its U.S. plants, such as the original one in Georgetown, Kentucky, and implicitly linked the firm to a quintessentially American event, the Kentucky Derby horse race.

A product's nationality becomes even more difficult to determine once we recognize that firms now assemble their products from components manufactured around the world. Ford, for example, assembles its Escort in Germany from parts produced in 15 countries, from Austria to Canada to Japan. Such production linkages represent one type of economic interdependence, a type increasingly prevalent in the world economy. Occasionally, the result is embarrassment—for policy makers intent on giving preference to domestic products to win favor with domestic special-interest groups. For example, a small town in New York, determined to "buy American," bought a $55,000 John Deere excavator in preference over a comparable $40,000 Komatsu model. Town decision makers soon discovered that Komatsu built its machine in Illinois and that Deere built its in Japan.[5]

The debates over international trade and interdependence that heated up in the 1970s and 1980s haven't cooled, but some of the details have changed. For example, one of the most important trends of recent years is developing countries' expanding involvement in international trade. After decades of attempting to isolate themselves from world markets, many developing countries now open their borders and pursue policies designed to integrate themselves into international trade activity. This trend produces new patterns of international interdependence that bring new debates to the fore. What are the implications

---

3. See the discussions of trade barriers in Chapters Six and Seven and of the effective rate of protection in Chapter Six.

4. Chapter Ten explains the implications of international capital mobility.

5. *The Economist*, February 1, 1992, p. 26.

Figure 1   Honda Automobiles Produced and Exported by Region, January–September 2004

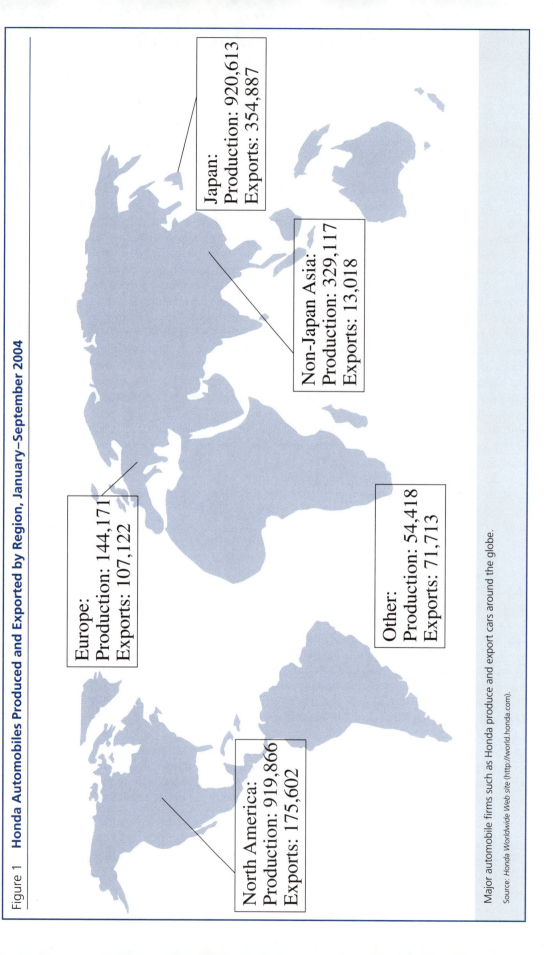

Japan:
Production: 920,613
Exports: 354,887

Non-Japan Asia:
Production: 329,117
Exports: 13,018

Europe:
Production: 144,171
Exports: 107,122

Other:
Production: 54,418
Exports: 71,713

North America:
Production: 919,866
Exports: 175,602

Major automobile firms such as Honda produce and export cars around the globe.

Source: *Honda Worldwide Web site* (http://world.honda.com).

for developed countries of trade with developing ones? Is the "common sense" conclusion—that trade with low-wage countries lowers wages for American workers—correct? In other words, as the title of one article put it, "Are Your Wages Set in Beijing?"[6] As we'll see in Chapter Four, most international economists agree, based on mounting empirical evidence, that trade with low-wage countries has *not* lowered U.S. wages significantly. But the debate continues and many of the loudest antiglobalization activists simply ignore the empirical evidence.

International trade and interdependence aren't limited to the markets for goods and services. International financial markets—bonds, stocks, and banks loans—provide mechanisms for **international investment**, which plays a vital role in the world economy. From a lender's perspective, these markets allow individuals, firms, and governments with funds to lend to find the most productive investment projects to fund, regardless of the projects' locations. From a borrower's perspective, international financial markets allow individuals, firms, and governments with promising investment projects to seek lenders willing to fund the projects on attractive terms, regardless of the lenders' nationalities or places of residence.

The growth of international flows of goods and services, financial assets such as stocks and bonds, and information reflects, in part, declines in international transportation and communication costs. Sea cargo, air transport, and telephone calls all have become dramatically cheaper (see Figure 2), and these trends facilitate and encourage international trade.[7] However, government policies also exert an important influence. Since World War II, more and more governments have recognized the importance of open international markets for goods, services, and investment and reduced their restrictions on international transactions. These policy changes facilitate the increases in international economic integration encouraged by falling transport and communication costs.

2.1 Trade-Policy Implications of International Interdependence

The increase in international economic activity, in turn, has far-flung implications for the world political economy. Policy makers in issue areas once considered domestic—such as antitrust policy, environmental policy, and taxation—now must reckon with those policies' international ramifications. U.S. antitrust policy makers, who approved a merger between General Electric and Honeywell, fumed when the merger failed because European Union antitrust policy makers blocked it. In the North American Free Trade Agreement (NAFTA), U.S. and Canadian environmental interests still fear that firms will exploit Mexico's allegedly lower environmental standards and enforcement by moving to Mexico and exporting goods produced under the laxer standards to U.S. and Canadian markets, although existing empirical evidence doesn't support those fears.[8] With increased international mobility of labor and capital, countries that try to tax their citizens or firms at rates far above those in other nations risk losing some of their most productive citizens and enterprises.[9] In all these cases, policies that at first glance appear to have primarily domestic effects turn out to be linked to important international questions as well. Effective economic policy making requires that these international linkages be taken into account.

---

6. Richard B. Freeman, "Are Your Wages Set in Beijing?" *Journal of Economic Perspectives*, 1995, pp. 15–32.

7. Unfortunately, increased costs associated with the need for improved security against terrorism at least partially offset the transport-cost declines made possible by technological advances.

8. We'll see more on the environment and trade in Chapters Eight and Eleven.

9. See the discussion of taxation and factor mobility in Chapter Ten.

Figure 2   **Transport and Communication Costs, 1930–1990 (Index: 1930 = 100)**

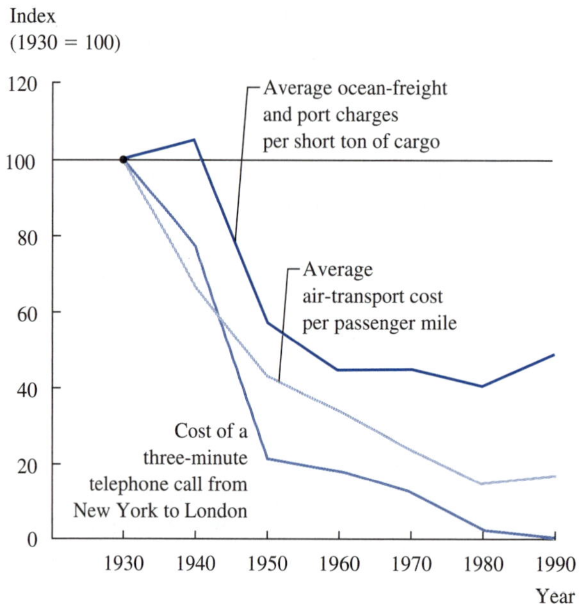

Declines in transport and communication costs during the twentieth century encouraged increased international economic activity.

Source: Data from Institute for International Economics.

2.2 Symptoms of International Interdependence

It's not easy to measure international economic interdependence, but we can examine some trade-related symptoms. The first is simply the trend in the extent of trade, or the volume of goods exchanged across national boundaries, illustrated in Figure 3. The volume of world merchandise trade has expanded rapidly over the past half-century; in fact, since 1950, merchandise *trade* has grown more than twice as fast as merchandise *production.* Panel (b) focuses on the past decade, during which trade volume continued to grow much faster (almost 7 percent per year) than production (about 3 percent per year). These trends indicate an increasingly vital role of international trade in allocating the world's resources. Economics is the study of the allocation of scarce resources among alternative uses, so the importance of international issues in the study of economics also has increased.

As we'll see in Chapters Two and Three, international trade improves individuals' potential well-being by raising incomes and increasing the quantity of goods and services available to consume. Nevertheless, interdependence, of which trade is a symptom, often is viewed as a mixed blessing. For U.S. consumers, trade makes available sugar from Brazil, apparel from China, steel from South Korea, and wine from France. However, U.S. sugar producers, clothing manufacturers, steel producers, and wine growers demand protection from competition by foreign rivals, even though we'll see that the costs of such protection rest squarely on domestic consumers.

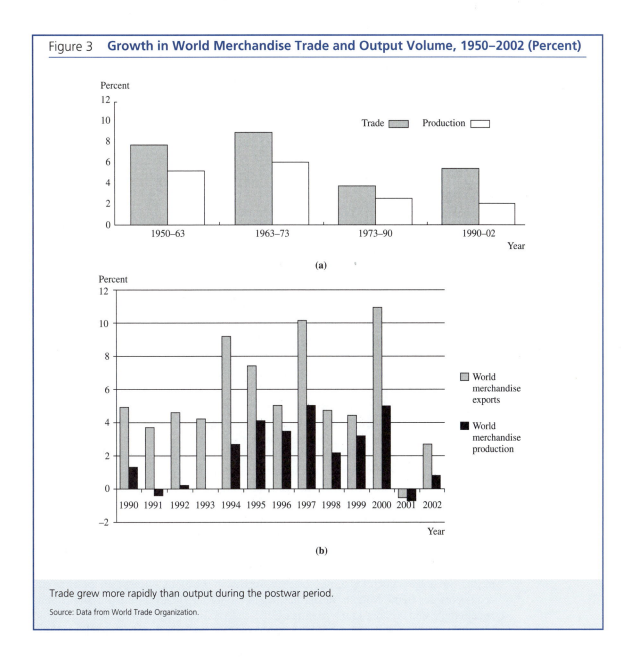

Figure 3   Growth in World Merchandise Trade and Output Volume, 1950–2002 (Percent)

Trade grew more rapidly than output during the postwar period.

Source: Data from World Trade Organization.

Despite dramatic increases in trade worldwide, countries continue to differ significantly in the extent to which they engage in trade. Figure 4 presents some examples; it measures a country's involvement in trade by merchandise exports (horizontal axis) and imports (vertical axis) as shares of total output or gross national product (GNP). The 2002 export shares range from a low of 8 percent for Rwanda to a high of 151 percent for Hong Kong, a specialist in trade-middleman services.[10] Import percentages range from Japan's 10 percent to Hong Kong's 142 percent, again reflecting that country's specialization in assembly and re-export tasks.

---

10. How can a country's trade exceed its production? Economies such as Hong Kong, Malaysia, and Singapore import inputs, assemble them, and then export finished goods. In a multistage production process, measures of output such as GDP and GNP count only the value of the final good, but measures of trade count all imports and exports.

Figure 4   **Merchandise Exports and Imports, 2002 (Percent of GDP)**

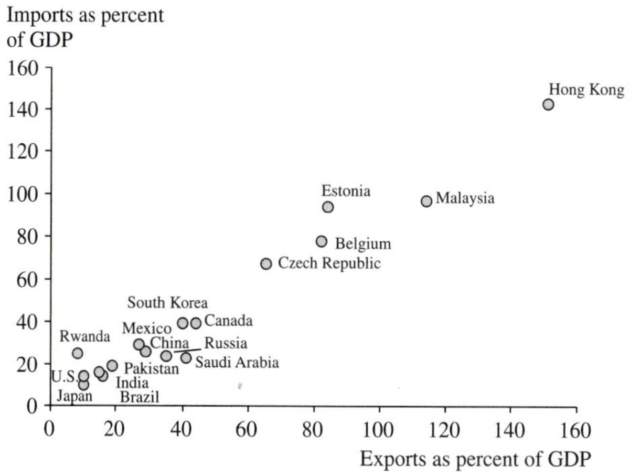

Imports as percent
of GDP

Countries vary widely in the extent to which they engage in international trade.

Source: Data from World Bank.

Other things being equal, large countries such as the United States tend to engage in less trade, as a share of their production, than do smaller ones. The main reason is easy to see: The size and diversity of the United States mean that domestic markets can efficiently satisfy many needs. On the import side, residents of Rhode Island get corn from Iowa, oil from Alaska, and lettuce from California; they go beachcombing in Florida, mountain climbing in Colorado, and bird watching in Hawaii. They execute financial deals in New York and watch Hollywood movies. On the export side, U.S. firms enjoy access to a huge domestic market; historically, very few small and medium-sized U.S. firms exported, but this is slowly changing. Although still modest by world standards, as indicated in Figure 4, U.S. involvement in international trade has increased rapidly in recent years. Figure 5, which reports the dollar value of U.S. merchandise imports and exports through the postwar era, documents this trend. Note, however, that Figure 4 indicates that U.S. imports and exports remain quite small relative to the country's GNP.

Not only do countries engage in trade to differing extents, but their trade tends to cluster with different sets of trading partners. This isn't surprising because transportation costs, while now low by historical standards, still play a role in determining trade patterns. Figure 6 highlights this clustering by dividing trade flows into seven major groups or blocs of countries: North America, Asia, Western Europe, Latin America, the Middle East, Africa, and the areas of Central and Eastern Europe along with the Baltic states and the Commonwealth of Independent States (most of the former Soviet Union). Recently, policy makers have expressed concern over the risk that trade patterns will evolve more in the direction of trade blocs—with open intrabloc trade but high barriers to trade between blocs. This concern underlies some economists' criticisms of the European Union and NAFTA and other regional trade agreements, which offer special, favorable terms for intragroup trade. However, Figure 6 clarifies that large trade flows continue between North America and Asia and between Western Europe and Asia, despite the EU and NAFTA preferences.

Historical evidence can suggest many interesting patterns in economic behavior, including those illustrated in Figures 3, 4, 5, and 6, but can't explain the reasons behind

Figure 5   U.S. Merchandise Imports and Exports, 1950–2002 (Billions $)

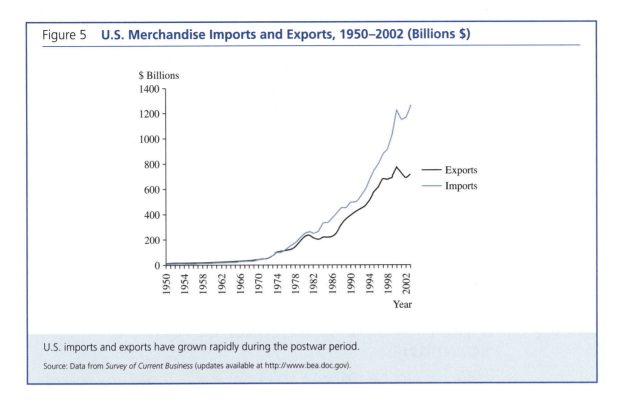

U.S. imports and exports have grown rapidly during the postwar period.

Source: Data from *Survey of Current Business* (updates available at http://www.bea.doc.gov).

Figure 6   Regional Flows of Merchandise Trade, 2002 (Billions $)

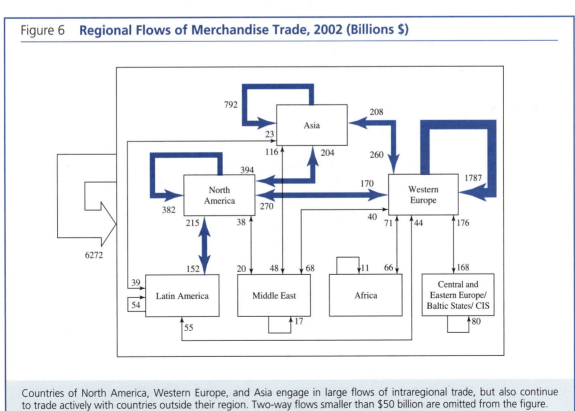

Countries of North America, Western Europe, and Asia engage in large flows of intraregional trade, but also continue to trade actively with countries outside their region. Two-way flows smaller than $50 billion are omitted from the figure.

Source: Data from World Trade Organization.

them. Because of the inability of empirical evidence alone to explain observed patterns, we need *theories* of economic behavior to answer questions such as: What are the nature and consequences of the trade ties among the countries of the world economy? How should policy makers respond to particular cases of international economic interdependence?

International Trade addresses these fundamental questions from the perspective of economics. Within the sphere of countries' international relationships, political and economic elements are difficult, if not impossible, to separate. However, the basic concepts of economic theory can be surprisingly helpful in untangling the maze of issues that constitutes the world economy. Millions of firms produce hundreds of thousands of commodities in approximately 200 countries, so we need a systematic framework for analysis—and this is what economic theory can provide. Thus, it is this book's perspective more than its subject matter that marks it as a text in international *economics*. The subjects covered—such as comparative advantage, protectionism, growth, the transition from central planning, multinational enterprises, immigration, relations between developed and developing countries, and developing-country debt—are also of direct interest to political scientists, as well as to specialists in international relations, international business, and public policy.

3 THE ECONOMIC SIGNIFICANCE OF POLITICAL BOUNDARIES

International economics traditionally has been the subject of special books and courses, separate from the rest of economics. At the same time, the interaction between international economics and the remainder of economic theory has been rich and, like international trade itself, beneficial to both parties. Economists working specifically on international problems developed many of the analytical techniques now used in all areas of the discipline. Similarly, many recent advances in international economics have built on developments in other areas of economics.

Why does the separate study of international questions persist? The main reason is that the **economic significance of political boundaries** persists. Most people would agree that life in a small New England college town differs radically from life in Los Angeles. From an economist's point of view, however, residents of the two places share a great deal. All use U.S. dollars as a currency or means of payment. All live under a common set of federal laws and a common political and economic system, and many communicate in a common language. All share in the fortunes of the U.S. economy, benefiting from the country's resource endowment and feeling the effects of U.S. policy decisions. Because of all these shared features, most economic transactions between the New Englander and the Californian face a smaller set of barriers than do economic transactions between a U.S. resident and a resident of a foreign country. The Californian can relocate in New England if he or she chooses, and the New Englander is free to migrate to California. If the pattern of interest rates makes deposits in California banks or bonds issued by California firms or government agencies attractive, the New Englander can choose to buy those assets; and vice versa for the Californian buying assets in New England.

National boundaries are economically relevant not only in determining the extent of legal, language, and currency barriers to transactions but in determining economic policy. In other words, the nature of the policy-making process also tends to make international economics a separate field of study. Despite the growing internationalization of many markets, economic policy making remains largely a matter of national sovereignty. In fact, many national governments respond to the perception of increased international interdependence by guarding their sovereign policy-making powers even more jealously. As a result, the policy process typically favors the interests of domestic residents over the interests of the world as a whole. This tendency is easy to understand given the realities of policy making. Decisions on policies that are either universally beneficial or universally harmful are easy—but, unfortunately for policy makers, such easy decisions are rare. The more typical policy decision involves evaluating a policy that benefits some individuals and harms others. In such a situation, we shouldn't be surprised that consideration given to the policy's effect on domestic residents usually outweighs that given to the effect on individuals abroad.

At the same time, it's important to realize that the major popular misconception about international trade policy is that policy choices pit the interests of one country against those of the other. In fact, trade-policy choices rarely take this form. Instead, trade policy primarily affects the distribution of income *within* each country. If the United States blocks imports of Chinese apparel, the main result isn't to help the United States at China's expense; rather, the main effect is to help *American* apparel *producers* at the expense of *American* apparel *consumers.* Similarly, if the U.S. steel industry wins protection from its South Korean competitors, the main losers are American steel consumers, such as the U.S. automobile industry and American car buyers. Economists think that individuals typically act in their own self-interest, so evaluating the effects of various international trade policies on different interest groups will be one of our major tasks. By understanding a policy's effects on different groups within the economy, we can better understand the observed pattern of political support for and opposition to the policy.

4 STUDYING INTERNATIONAL ECONOMICS

Economists traditionally divide the subject matter of international economics into two parts. This book covers the first, called the **theory of international trade**, which extends *micro*economic analysis to international questions. Here we consider decisions concerning the quantities of various goods produced, consumed, and traded by different countries. We'll see that the goods and services available for consumers to enjoy are at a maximum when each country specializes in producing those goods that it can produce relatively efficiently. Trade then allows each country's residents to import a variety of other goods to consume. These production and consumption decisions collectively determine the relative prices both of goods and of factors of production such as labor, capital, and land. These prices, in turn, determine the distribution of income among individuals in the economy.

Like microeconomics, trade theory traditionally ignores monetary issues by expressing all costs and prices in terms of other goods rather than a monetary unit such as dollars. In other words, goods exchange directly for other goods (one bushel of corn for two bushels of wheat, or four computers for one car). By examining trade's effect on the relative prices of different goods and factors of production, trade theory highlights the distributional impact of trade. Unrestricted international trade can change relative prices, so it also can alter the distribution of income among various groups within each country. An understanding of this interrelationship between trade and income distribution is essential to making sense of the political pressures for **protectionist policies**, which restrict international trade to "protect" domestic producers from foreign competition.

The second major branch of international economics, called **open-economy macroeconomics**, applies *macro*economic analysis to aggregate international problems and is covered in this book's companion volume, *The World Economy: Open-Economy Macroeconomics and Finance.* Major concerns there include the level of employment and output in each economy as well as changes in the price level, balance of payments, and **exchange rates** or relative prices of different national currencies. The most basic issue addressed by open-economy macroeconomics is the interaction of international goals and influences with domestic ones in determining a country's macroeconomic performance and policy. Can a country that engages in international transactions (called an **open economy**) pursue the same macroeconomic policies as a country that engages in no international transactions (a **closed economy**) and achieve the same results? The answer is no; so, understanding the implications of openness turns out to be essential to effective macroeconomic policy making.

As in microeconomic analysis of international trade policy, macroeconomic policies have distributional consequences. Policy choices typically stated in terms of domestic interests versus foreign ones actually involve differences in the interests of various groups *within* each economy. For example, journalists, commentators, and politicians often speak of any currency depreciation (that is, a rise in the exchange rate expressed as the domestic currency price of a unit of foreign currency) as an economic problem in need of a remedy. Indeed, sound economic policy making does require that any country experiencing a chronic currency depreciation consider adjusting its macroeconomic policies. We also must recognize, however, that depreciations *help* some groups within the domestic economy, especially import-competing and export industries. Those same currency depreciations also *hurt* other domestic groups, particularly importers and consumers of imported goods.

We begin our study of international trade by building a simple model and then elaborate on it and apply it to many historical and current events in the world economy. The models are just road maps to describe the way the world economy works. They may seem overly simple and "unrealistic." However, that's the whole point of building models. After all, a road map would be of little practical use if it faithfully illustrated every bump, anthill, grain of sand, pothole, and roadside sign. We need models like good road maps: as *simple* as possible while still capturing the *key features* necessary to understand the world economy. Once you master the basic models of international trade covered in this book, you can use them to analyze not only the applications considered in the text but the constantly changing international economic news.

Economists call models that describe in a simplified way how the world economy works *positive models*. For the most part, we'll employ **positive analysis** in this book, using models to understand how the world economy is structured and how it functions. This approach focuses primarily on explanation and prediction. The goal is to understand the world economy well enough to be able to say, "If event X happens, event Y will follow." For example, after reading Chapter Four we might predict that, given the opportunity to choose between unrestricted trade and protectionism, farmers in Japan would tend to choose protectionism. This prediction *doesn't* depend on whether we, as economists or citizens, believe protectionism is desirable; the prediction follows directly from our model of how the world economy works. We can then look at Japanese farmers' political behavior and see if they do in fact support protectionist policies. (To jump ahead a bit, the answer is *yes*.)

Another type of analysis, **normative analysis**, *does* depend on our judgments about what is and isn't desirable. For example, if we think trade is desirable because it maximizes the quantity of goods and services available to consumers, we might conclude that Japanese policy makers should pursue open trade policies in the agricultural sector even though Japanese farmers oppose them. Normative analyses rely on our values to determine what types of international economic goals and policies we think policy makers should pursue.

From our discussion of the differences between positive and normative economic analysis, we can see that disagreements over international policy issues can come from at least two sources. First, there may be disagreement about the way the world works. One individual may think that if event X happens, event Y will follow, while another may think that if event X happens, event Z will follow. For example, one person might argue that opening international trade (X) will reduce economic growth (Y) because imported goods will replace domestic production, while someone else claims that opening trade (X) will increase economic growth (Z) by moving resources into their most productive uses. Analysts usually can resolve such disagreements by conducting further empirical research to determine whether Y or Z follows X.[11]

Disagreements based on normative judgments typically prove more difficult to resolve. Two policy makers may agree that "If we pursue policy X, result Y will follow." But if the two disagree about whether Y is desirable, they will disagree about whether they should pursue policy X. For example, most economists acknowledge that policies of unrestricted international trade would result in the decline of several U.S. industries, including nonspecialty steel, some types of automobiles, footwear, and many types of textiles and apparel, because those U.S. industries are relatively inefficient compared with their foreign counterparts. Whether one supports policies of unrestricted trade thus depends in part on one's evaluation of the trade-offs among trade's efficiency benefits, the short-run costs of resource reallocation associated with the decline of certain industries, the costs to consumers of protecting inefficient industries, and the increased interdependence that comes from relying on foreign suppliers.

Throughout this book, both positive and normative issues arise. Although the distinction isn't always sharp, we must keep in mind the conceptual difference between the two. Debates over the desirability of various trade policies can be useful only when it's clear where the disagreement originates—in our views of the way the world works or in our views of how we would like the world to be.

Throughout the book, we present data on many aspects of the world economy, ranging from Russia's WTO accession negotiations, Japanese economic history, gravity and trade, Singapore's restrictions on chewing-gum sales, the effect of regionalism on Japan, the China–Hong Kong free-trade agreement, African countries' cotton-subsidy complaints against the United States, new factory technologies, and the U.S.'s controversial Byrd amendment. A rich variety of sources of additional information about the world economy exists. We've included many in the references at the end of each chapter. In addition, the *Study Guide* written to accompany this book suggests useful leads, including many Web resources, if you want to pursue a particular trade topic in more detail. If you don't yet have a copy of the *Study Guide,* check with your instructor or bookstore. Along with data sources on the world economy, the *Study Guide* contains study aids and questions with answers for each chapter in the text, helpful hints for writing economics papers, and much more.

KEY TERMS

international interdependence	open-economy macroeconomics
international economic integration	exchange rates
international investment	open economy
economic significance of political boundaries	closed economy
theory of international trade	positive analysis
protectionist policies	normative analysis

---

11. On the trade–growth connection, the empirical evidence suggests that countries with open markets experience faster growth, although direct causality is difficult to establish definitely. Sebastian Edwards, "Openness, Productivity and Growth: What Do We Really Know?" *Economic Journal*, March 1998, pp. 383–398, summarizes the evidence. See also Jeffrey A. Frankel and David Romer, "Does Trade Cause Growth?" *American Economic Review*, June 1999, pp. 379–399, and David Dollar and Aart Kraay, "Trade, Growth, and Poverty," World Bank Policy Research Working Paper No. 2199, 2001 (available at http://www.worldbank.org).

PROBLEMS AND QUESTIONS FOR REVIEW

1. For each of the types of cost illustrated in Figure 2 (air transport, sea transport, telephone costs), explain why a decline in the cost might lead to an increase in international trade. Why might a decline in the cost lead to an increase in international investment?
2. Look at the data in Figure 4. Why might some countries choose to engage more in international trade than other countries?
3. Name some trade-related examples of the economic significance of political boundaries.
4. Firms often buy advertising to lobby support for their positions on international trade issues. Suppose that you represent Acme Thingamajigs, a major producer of thingamajigs. What kinds of trade policies for the thingamajig market might you support, and why? What would you consider in deciding whether buying an advertisement to lobby for your position would be worthwhile?
5. Name three recent events in international microeconomics that you hope to understand better after mastering Chapters Two through Eleven.
6. Some economists have argued that increased liberalization of international trade is allowing geographically smaller countries to be economically viable. The number of recognized independent nation-states rose from 74 in 1946 to 192 in 1995.[12] Why might small countries be especially reliant on the availability of open international trade?
7. Suppose we divided developing countries into two groups: those that have followed policies to integrate themselves into the world economy ("globalizers") and those that have followed policies to insulate themselves from the world economy ("nonglobalizers").[13] How would you expect the groups' economic performances to compare?
8. Look at the data in Figure 6, especially the volume of North American exports to North America and Western European exports to Western Europe. How do the sizes of the two trade flows compare? The size of Western Europe's economy is approximately the same size as the U.S. economy. How might you explain the observation that intra-Western Europe international trade is more than four times the size of intra-North American international trade? [*Hint: Think about what is required for a transaction to be recorded as* international *trade.*]

REFERENCES AND SELECTED READINGS

Bhagwati, Jagdish. *Protectionism.* Cambridge, Mass.: MIT Press, 1988.
A lively treatment of the history and status of protectionism; for all students.

Cohen, Tyler. *Creative Destruction: How Globalization is Changing the World's Cultures.* Princeton: Princeton University Press, 2002.
Readable introduction to the cultural effects of international economic integration.

Destler, I. M. *American Trade Politics.* Washington, D.C.: Institute for International Economics, 1995.
Excellent treatment of the historical evolution of U.S. trade policy-making institutions; for all students.

European Bank for Reconstruction and Development. *Annual Transition Report.* Paris: EBRD, annual.
Excellent source of up-to-date information and analysis of the transitional economies.

Fieleke, Norman S. "Popular Myths about the World Economy." *New England Economic Review* (July–August 1997): 17–26.
Introductory overview of popular misconceptions about trade.

Irwin, Douglas A. *Free Trade Under Fire.* Princeton: Princeton University Press, 2002.
Excellent overview of trade policy issues.

James, Harold. *The End of Globalization: Lessons from the Great Depression.* Cambridge, Mass.: Harvard University Press, 2001.
Historian's treatment of the end of the earlier era of international economic integration.

Krugman, Paul. "Growing World Trade: Causes and Consequences." *Brookings Papers on Economic Activity* 1 (1995): 327–377.
Survey of recent trends in world trade; for intermediate students.

---

12. See Alberto Alesina et al., "Economic Integration and Political Disintegration," *American Economic Review* 90 (December 2000), p. 1276.

13. See David Dollar and Aart Kraay, "Trade, Growth, and Poverty," World Bank Policy Research Working Paper No. 2199, 2001 (available at http://www.worldbank.org).

Legrain, Philippe. *One World: The Truth About Globalization.* Chicago: Ivan R. Dee, 2002.
Nontechnical introduction to the many aspects of international economic integration.

Symposium on "The Shape of Global Integration." *Finance and Development* 39 (March 2002): 4–43.
Collection of accessible papers on the meaning and effects of globalization.

United Nations. *World Investment Report.* New York: UN, annual.
Excellent source of data and analysis of recent trends in international capital flows.

World Bank. *Globalization, Growth, and Poverty.* Washington, D.C.: World Bank, 2002.
Easy-to-read overview of what economists know about the relationship between international economic integration and poverty.

World Bank. *World Development Indicators.* Washington, D.C.: World Bank, annual.
Excellent source of recent economic data, as well as analysis of development-related events by the World Bank staff.

World Trade Organization. *Annual Report.* Geneva: WTO, annual.
Excellent source of information on WTO activities.

World Trade Organization. *International Trade Statistics.* Geneva: WTO, annual.
Excellent source of trade statistics for WTO members.

World Trade Organization. *World Trade Report.* Geneva: WTO, annual.
New annual report on trade policy.

Yarbrough, Beth V., and Robert M. Yarbrough. "The 'Globalization' of Trade: What's Changed and Why?" In *Studies in Globalization and Development,* edited by S. Gupta and N. K. Choudry. Norwell, Mass.: Kluwer Academic Publishers, 1997.
Trends in international trade; for all students.

INTERNATIONAL
MICROECONOMICS

2

Comparative Advantage I: Labor Productivity and Trade

1 INTRODUCTION

Countries engage in international trade because they benefit from doing so.[1] The gains from trade arise because trade allows countries to specialize their production in a way that allocates resources to their most productive uses. Trade plays an essential role in achieving this allocation by freeing each country's residents from having to consume goods in the same combination in which the domestic economy can produce them. If the United States specialized its production but didn't engage in international trade, U.S. residents would have lots of wheat and soybeans, airplanes, and medical equipment, but no coffee or bananas and few shoes or textiles. Residents of Japan, on the other hand, would find themselves well stocked with automobiles and consumer electronics but without gasoline to run the automobiles and confined to a diet consisting largely of fish.

We can easily see the benefits from productive specialization and trade at the individual level. Most individuals *specialize* in producing one good (for example, teaching economics) and then *trade* some of that good for other goods to consume (such as food, clothing, and housing). Suppose, instead, you generated your own electricity and made your clothes along with growing your food and building your house. Providing yourself with these "necessities" would require so much time and effort that there'd be none left to produce the luxuries, such as skis, cell phones, and personal digital assistants, to which you're accustomed. The same holds true for countries that forgo the opportunities provided by specialization and trade. The fact that political boundaries divide the world into nation-states doesn't alter trade's potential for expanding output by allocating the world's scarce resources to their most productive uses. But policy makers and political economists didn't completely understand this simple point until around 1817, and many still forget or ignore it today.

This chapter demonstrates the existence of gains from trade in the simplest possible context; later chapters extend the analysis to fit reality more closely. The fundamental ideas in this chapter—simple though they are—represent both the heart of international trade theory and perhaps economics' most enduring contribution to improving the well-being of citizens of the world economy.

---

1. For convenience, we speak of "countries" engaging in international trade and making production and consumption decisions. In fact—at least in market-oriented economies—individual firms and consumers, not "countries" or their governments, make most production and consumption decisions and conduct most trade. In nonmarket economies, government enterprises conduct a large percentage of trade as well as control production patterns.

2 EARLY THINKING ABOUT TRADE: THE MERCANTILISTS

During the seventeenth and eighteenth centuries, **mercantilism** represented the dominant attitude toward international trade. The period was one of nation-building and consolidation of power by newly formed states. Gold and silver circulated as money, and the quantity of these precious metals a country held symbolized that nation's wealth and power. National leaders wanted to accumulate as much gold and silver as possible. When a nation's exports (goods produced domestically and sold abroad) proved more than sufficient to pay for its imports (purchases of foreign goods), flows of precious metals settled the account balance; so any country that exported more than it imported experienced an inflow of gold and silver. The policy prescription based on this mercantilist view was to encourage exports and restrict imports, since mercantilists viewed trade primarily as a way to accumulate gold.

Mercantilists assumed trade was a **zero-sum game**—that it couldn't benefit all parties. (Poker is a zero-sum game: Whatever one player wins, the other players lose.) Mercantilists assumed that fixed amounts of goods and gold existed in the world and that trade merely determined their distribution among nations.[2]

3 THE DECLINE OF MERCANTILISM (AND THE BIRTH OF ECONOMICS)

Late in the eighteenth century, mercantilism came under attack by leaders of the new science of political economy. In 1752, David Hume pointed out two weaknesses in mercantilists' logic.

First, it isn't the quantity of gold and silver a nation holds that matters; it's the quantity of goods and services that the gold and silver can buy. Individuals get satisfaction from consuming goods, not from accumulating precious metals for their own sake. Mercantilists wanted to export as many goods, and import as few, as possible. This implied that other nations would accumulate goods while the mercantilist nation accumulated gold. (*Would you want to live in a country that successfully pursued mercantilist policies?*)

Second, a country can't accumulate gold and silver forever, so mercantilist policies aren't effective in the long run. Suppose a country ran a trade surplus (that is, the value of the country's exports exceeded the value of its imports) and so experienced an inflow of gold. Gold formed nations' money supplies during the mercantilist period, so the gold inflow would raise both the money supply and prices.[3] As prices of the nation's goods rose relative to prices of other nations' goods, the change in relative prices would make the nation's exports less attractive to foreign buyers and imports more attractive to domestic residents. Exports would fall, and imports would rise. Thus, the price effects of the gold inflow would automatically eliminate the nation's initial trade surplus. Economists call this effect the **specie-flow mechanism**.

A second political economist to question mercantilist policies was Adam Smith, writing in 1776. Smith focused on mercantilists' assumption that trade constituted a zero-sum game. Smith showed this assumption to be wrong. If each country could produce

---

2. The debate over the causes and consequences of mercantilism can be found in references by Smith, Heckscher, Viner, Ekelund and Tollison, and Irwin in the references at the end of the chapter.

3. Recall one of the most fundamental relationships in macroeconomics: Other things being equal, a change in the money stock moves the price level in the same direction.

some commodities using less labor than its trading partners, *all* parties to international trade could benefit. How? According to Smith, trade improved the allocation of labor, ensuring that production of each good occurred in the country where production required the least labor. The result would be a larger total quantity of goods produced in the world. With more goods available for distribution among nations, each could be made better off. Trade would be a positive-sum game, like a hypothetical poker game in which all players could win.

In 1817, David Ricardo showed that even Smith's optimistic view failed to capture all of trade's benefits. Ricardo's work provided the basis for our modern understanding of the importance of trade. We're now ready to examine a modern version of Adam Smith's and David Ricardo's revolutionary views of trade. First we'll discuss some simplifying assumptions of our analysis. We could relax most of these, at the expense of additional complexity, without altering the basic results.[4]

4 KEEPING THINGS SIMPLE: SOME ASSUMPTIONS

First, we assume that **perfect competition** prevails in both output and factor markets. Each buyer and seller is small enough relative to the market to take the market-determined price as given. Each commodity is homogeneous (that is, all units of each good are identical), and buyers and sellers have good information about market conditions. Market entry and exit are easy. The perfect-competition assumption is important because it implies that the price of each good will equal its **marginal cost** of production, or the change in total cost due to production of one additional unit of output.

Second, we assume that each country has a fixed endowment of resources that are fully employed and homogeneous. So the problem each country faces involves how to allocate this fixed quantity of resources among production of the many goods residents want to consume.

Third, we assume that firms' technologies don't vary. Different countries may use different technologies, but all firms within each country employ a common production method for each good.

Fourth, we assume that transportation costs are zero. This implies that consumers will be indifferent between the domestically produced and imported versions of a good when their prices are the same. We also ignore, for now, other barriers to trade.

Fifth, we assume that factors of production (or inputs) such as labor and capital are completely mobile among industries within each country and completely immobile among countries. Obviously, this assumption is too strong to represent an accurate description of the world, and we'll relax the assumption in Chapter Ten. However, resources that are much more mobile within than among countries capture an essential element of the economic significance of political boundaries. Perfect mobility of resources among industries implies that the price of each factor must be equal in all industries within each country. Otherwise, resources would move from low-paying to high-paying industries. But the price of each factor generally will differ across countries without trade because factors are immobile among countries.

Finally, we'll operate in a world with two countries, each using a single input to produce two goods. For simplicity, we'll refer to the countries as A and B, the single input as L (for *labor*), and the two goods as X and Y.

---

4. Chapters Five and Eight relax the perfect-competition assumption. For the implications of factor mobility, see Chapter Ten. Theories of trade that focus on technology can be found in Chapters Five, Eight, and Ten. Chapter Five contains a discussion of transportation costs. Chapters Six and Seven concentrate on trade restrictions and their effects. The specific-factors model in Chapter Four captures the effects of an input that can't move across industries.

5 THE RICARDIAN WORLD WITHOUT TRADE

To answer the question "Does international trade benefit its participants?" we must compare a world without trade to one with trade and show that more goods are available to consume in the latter. Economists call the case of self-sufficiency, or no trade, **autarky**. In autarky each nation must produce whatever its residents consume because there's no other way to obtain goods. In other words, the resource-allocation decision made by a country in autarky is simultaneously a production decision *and* a consumption decision. This decision depends on two sets of information. First, the *production* trade-offs between goods X and Y that are possible given the available resources and technology determine what the country can produce. Second, residents' preferences, that is, their subjective trade-offs between *consumption* of goods X and Y, determine which of the possible combinations is most preferred.

5.1 Production in Autarky

We can characterize the various combinations of goods X and Y that countries A and B can produce by developing a production possibilities frontier (or transformation curve) for each country. The **production possibilities frontier** represents all the alternate combinations of goods X and Y a country could produce. To sketch country A's production possibilities frontier, we must know A's resource endowment—the quantity of labor available in A—and the technology available to transform those labor inputs into outputs. We denote country A's labor endowment as L^A. Two **input coefficients**, a_{LX} and a_{LY}, summarize the production technology. The input coefficients tell us how many units of labor are required to produce one unit of each of the two outputs. In country A, production of one unit of good X requires a_{LX} units of labor, and production of one unit of good Y requires a_{LY} units of labor.

It helps to have a memory aid for the meaning of the input coefficients. The first letter refers to the *country*, the first subscript to the *input*, and the second subscript to the *output* produced. For example, a_{LX} might be the number of units of labor required to produce a Xerox machine in America, while b_{LY} could denote the number of units of labor needed to produce a yo-yo in Britain. The best way to become comfortable with the input coefficients is to practice reading them in terms of what they mean rather than the letters themselves. The statement $a_{LX} = 2$ reads "the number of units of labor required to produce 1 unit of good X in country A is 2." With a little patience and practice, the input coefficients will become familiar and convenient ways to represent the productive technology available in different countries.

Note the relationship between country A's input coefficients, or technology, and the country's labor productivity. The *more* productive country A's labor is in producing good X, the *fewer* units of labor will be required to produce 1 unit of X, so the *lower* a_{LX} will be. Similarly, *high* labor productivity in the Y industry translates into a *low* value of a_{LY}. Ricardo's model contains only one input (labor), so a country's technology simply reflects the country's labor productivity in the two industries.

If country A chose to use all its labor making good X, it could produce L^A/a_{LX} units of X and zero units of Y. Consider country A with 100 units of labor ($L^A = 100$) where 2 units of labor are required to produce 1 unit of good X ($a_{LX} = 2$) and 5 units of labor are required to produce 1 unit of good Y ($a_{LY} = 5$). If country A chose to use all the available labor producing good X, it could produce 50 units ($L^A/a_{LX} = 100/2 = 50$). If it chose instead to use all its labor producing Y, it could produce 20 units of Y and zero units of X. (*Why?*)

Alternatively, country A could produce one of a variety of combinations containing some of *both* goods. For every unit of X forgone, A can produce a_{LX}/a_{LY} (or 2/5 in our numerical example) additional units of good Y. Producing 1 fewer X releases 2 units of labor ($a_{LX} = 2$)—enough labor to produce 2/5 units of Y, since 5 units of labor ($a_{LY} = 5$) are required to produce 1 unit of Y. All the possible production choices can be represented

---

Figure 1   **What Can Country *A* Produce?**

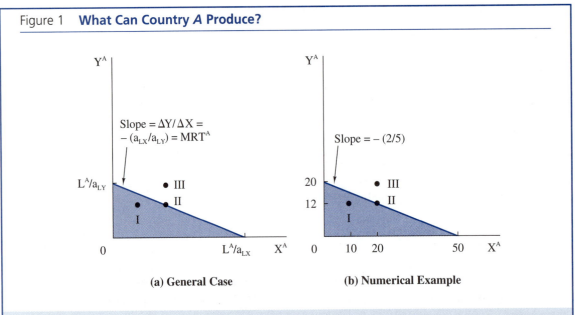

(a) General Case   **(b) Numerical Example**

Country A's production possibilities frontier illustrates the different combinations of goods X and Y the country can produce, given its labor endowment and technology. Country A can use its labor endowment (L^A, or 100) to produce L^A/a_{LX} (100/2 = 50) units of good X, L^A/a_{LY} (100/5 = 20) units of good Y, or any intermediate combination. The slope of the frontier ($-[a_{LX}/a_{LY}]$ or $-2/5$) equals the opportunity cost of good X, or the rate at which good X can be "transformed" into good Y.

---

graphically as country A's production possibilities frontier, illustrated in Figure 1, where ΔY denotes "change in Y" and similarly for ΔX.

The negative slope of the production possibilities frontier reflects the fact that labor is scarce. Only L^A is available, and it is fully employed; the only way to produce more of one good is to produce less of the other. The rate at which one good can be transformed into the other is a_{LX}/a_{LY}, which defines the (absolute value of the) slope of the production possibilities frontier.[5] In economic terminology, the slope gives the **opportunity cost** of good X, or the number of units of good Y forgone to produce an additional unit of good X. This is called the **marginal rate of transformation (MRT)**, because it is the rate at which the economy can "transform" good X into good Y—by transferring labor out of the X industry and into the Y industry.

In autarky, residents of country A can choose to produce any one of the combinations of goods X and Y on the production possibilities frontier. It's also possible to produce at a point inside the frontier, such as point I in Figure 1. In the numerical example, country A could produce 10 units of X and 12 units of Y using a total of $2 \cdot 10 + 5 \cdot 12 = 80$ units of labor. However, the country wouldn't choose to locate at an interior point such as I, because it could produce (and consume) more by moving to an on-the-frontier point such as II. At each interior point, some resources either aren't being used at all or aren't being used to their full productive potential. Points such as III that lie outside the production possibilities frontier are desirable but unattainable due to the constraint

---

5.   The production possibilities frontier is defined by full employment. This can be expressed as $L^A = a_{LX} \cdot X + a_{LY} \cdot Y$; in words, the total quantity of labor must equal the quantity employed in producing good X plus the quantity employed in producing good Y. Along a production possibilities frontier, the total quantity of labor available, L^A, is constant. For the full-employment condition to continue to hold when output levels of goods X and Y are varied, it must be true that $\Delta L^A = a_{LX} \cdot \Delta X + a_{LY} \cdot \Delta Y = 0$, where Δ, the upper-case Greek letter delta, is a shorthand notation for "change in." Rearranging this expression, $\Delta Y/\Delta X = -(a_{LX}/a_{LY})$ represents the slope of the production possibilities frontier.

imposed by the fixed quantity of labor available. For example, country A couldn't produce 20 units of good X along with 20 units of good Y, because such a combination would require 140 units of labor ($2 \cdot 20 + 5 \cdot 20 = 140$) but only 100 units are available.

The **Ricardian model** implies a straight-line production possibilities frontier. The frontier's slope represents the opportunity cost of good X, given by a_{LX}/a_{LY}; and this opportunity cost is independent of the particular output combination being produced. For this reason, the Ricardian model sometimes is referred to as a **constant-cost model**. In autarky, the shaded triangle formed in Figure 1 by the two axes and the production possibilities frontier represents both the **production opportunity set** (the set of all possible combinations of X and Y the country could produce) and the **consumption opportunity set** (the set of all possible combinations of X and Y its residents could consume). The two sets coincide in autarky, because domestic production is the only source of goods for consumption.

5.2 **Consumption in Autarky**

The production possibilities frontier tells only half the autarky story by revealing all the combinations of goods X and Y it's possible to produce given the available labor and technology. To determine which of these possible points will be chosen, we must introduce the tastes, or preferences, of the country's residents. We assume that the level of satisfaction or **utility** enjoyed by residents depends on the quantities of goods X and Y available for consumption and that the production/consumption decision is made in such a way as to maximize utility. A graphical technique called an **indifference curve** shows all the different combinations of goods X and Y that generate a given level of utility.

Indifference curves have four basic properties. First, indifference curves are downward sloping. Panel (a) of Figure 2 shows why. Initially, the country is at point 1, consuming X_1 units of good X and Y_1 units of good Y. Which other points would generate the same level of consumer satisfaction as point 1? Surely not any points in area III, because they contain less of each good. We can also rule out points in area II, because they contain more of each good and therefore would be preferred to point 1. We're left with areas I and IV. Area I points contain less good X than point 1 but also more good Y. Area IV points contain less good Y than point 1 but more good X. Therefore, areas I and IV represent the possibility of consumers *substituting* more of one good for less of the other with no change in overall utility. The fact that residents must be compensated for the loss of one good by more of the other good to maintain the same utility implies that indifference curves slope downward.

A second requirement is that indifference curves be convex, or bowed in toward the graph's origin. The slope of an indifference curve represents the rate at which residents willingly trade off consumption of the two goods; economists call this rate the **marginal rate of substitution (MRS)**. Convexity of the indifference curve implies that this rate of trade-off changes along the curve. As consumers have more X and less Y (moving down an indifference curve), they start to value good Y more highly relative to good X; in other words, the amount of additional X required to compensate for further reducing consumption of Y increases.

Suppose, for example, that good X represents food and good Y clothing. At a point high and to the left on an indifference curve, consumers have a large amount of clothing and very little food. In such a situation, individuals probably would willingly trade a substantial amount of their clothing to obtain a small amount of additional food. The marginal rate of substitution between food and clothing would be high, and the indifference curve steep. At a point low and to the right on the same indifference curve, consumers have a large amount of food and very little clothing. Individuals then would willingly give up very little clothing to obtain additional food. The marginal rate of substitution between food and clothing

Figure 2   Indifference Curves

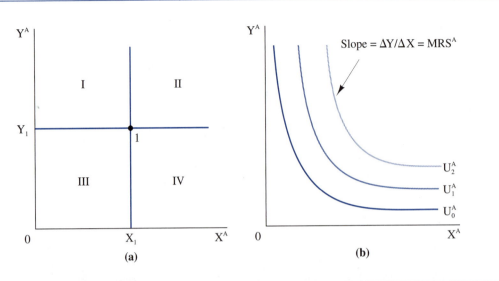

An indifference curve shows all combinations of goods X and Y that give consumers a given level of utility. Panel (a) illustrates why indifference curves are downward sloping. Residents wouldn't be indifferent between point 1 and any point in areas II or III. Points in area II are preferred to point 1 because they contain more of each good. Points in area III are inferior to point 1 because they contain less of each good. All points that generate a level of utility equal to that at point 1 must lie in area I or IV. The indifference curves in panel (b) exhibit four necessary characteristics: each is downward sloping and convex, the curves do not intersect, and higher curves are preferred to lower ones.

would be low, and the indifference curve relatively flat. Therefore, as we move down and to the right along an indifference curve, it becomes flatter as good X becomes less highly valued relative to good Y. The result is a convex, or bowed-in, indifference curve.

A third characteristic of indifference curves is that they never intersect. Each point represents a single combination of goods X and Y and lies on one—and only one—indifference curve. Each consumption bundle generates a unique level of utility, although we'll discuss some potential problems surrounding this requirement shortly.

Finally, indifference curves further from the origin represent higher levels of utility and, therefore, are preferred to lower indifference curves. This simply reflects consumers' preference for more goods over fewer goods. The indifference curves in panel (b) of Figure 2 satisfy the four requirements discussed.

Economists originally developed indifference curves to represent one individual's tastes. Here we're using **community indifference curves** to represent the tastes of a country's residents as a group. This obviously is a much more complicated problem than dealing with a single consumer's tastes. We'll use community indifference curves exactly as if they were individual indifference curves. However, be aware that this sidesteps some questions that arise from the issue of **income distribution**. For example, suppose a country has X_1 units of X and Y_1 units of Y. How does the country's utility compare if (1) one individual owns all the X_1 and Y_1 and all other residents have nothing, or (2) the X_1 and Y_1 are divided evenly among all individuals? Without making interpersonal comparisons of utility, it's impossible to say. We can't just assume that case 2 implies higher utility because more people gained than lost in moving there from case 1. There's no "objective" way to compare one individual's loss of utility with another individual's gain. We'll ignore these questions temporarily and return to them in Chapter Four, where we discuss the effects of trade and trade restrictions on a country's distribution of income. For now, notice that increased availability of goods always raises **potential utility**; whether actual utility increases depends on the distribution of income. Whenever a larger quantity of goods becomes available, it's possible to make every individual better off (in terms of dessert, if the pie's bigger, everyone can have a bigger piece).

5.3 Equilibrium in Autarky

In autarky, a country makes its production and consumption decision to maximize utility subject to the constraint imposed by the production possibilities frontier. Panel (a) of Figure 3 illustrates this decision by country A by combining Figure 1's production possibilities frontier with the indifference curves from panel (b) of Figure 2. Point A* puts residents on indifference curve U_1^A, the highest level of satisfaction attainable given the country's resource endowment (L^A) and available technology (a_{LX} and a_{LY}). Point A* is the country's **autarky equilibrium**. If country A doesn't trade with other countries, point A* represents the allocation of resources between industries X and Y that produces the highest level of utility for country-A residents. Points along lower indifference curves (illustrated by U_0^A) are less preferred than A*. Points along higher indifference curves (such as U_2^A) aren't attainable because of the resource and technology constraint.

At the autarky equilibrium, the marginal rate of transformation (the rate at which the country *can* transform good X into good Y along the production possibilities frontier) equals the marginal rate of substitution (the rate at which residents *willingly* give up some of one good to get more of the other good along an indifference curve). The common slope of the production possibilities frontier and the indifference curve also represents the opportunity cost of good X expressed in terms of good Y. All markets are perfectly competitive, so the

---

Figure 3   What Would Country *A* and Country *B* Do in Autarky?

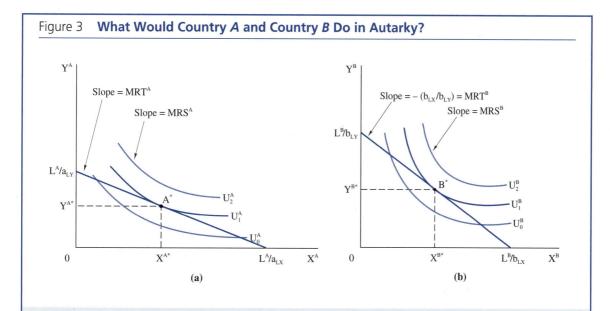

(a)   **(b)**

Country A makes its production and consumption decision to maximize utility subject to the constraint imposed by the availability of resources and technology. This decision is represented graphically in panel (a) by the point of tangency between the (highest attainable) indifference curve and the production possibilities frontier at point A*. At that point—and only at that point—the rate at which it is possible to transform good X into good Y (MRT^A) equals the rate at which residents of A are willing to trade off goods X and Y in consumption (MRS^A). In autarky, country B produces and consumes at B* in panel (b), the point of tangency between its production possibilities frontier and the (highest attainable) indifference curve, U_1^B.

relative price of each good equals its opportunity cost.[6] Therefore, we can also identify the (absolute value of the) slope of the production possibilities frontier with the relative price of good X in country A, or $(P_X/P_Y)^A$, which denotes the rate at which units of goods X and Y exchange in the domestic market. This relative price is called the **autarky relative price** of good X in country A. In the numerical example (with $L^A = 100$, $a_{LX} = 2$, and $a_{LY} = 5$), the relative price of good X in country A equals 2/5 units of good Y because production of an additional unit of good X requires that Y production fall by 2/5 units.

We can also calculate country A's wage rate in autarky. We'll use three pieces of information. First, labor's the only input; so the marginal costs of producing goods X and Y must equal $a_{LX} \cdot w^A$ and $a_{LY} \cdot w^A$, respectively, where w^A denotes the wage rate per unit of labor. Second, all markets exhibit perfect competition, so the price of each good equals its marginal cost, or $P_X^A = a_{LX} \cdot w^A$ and $P_Y^A = a_{LY} \cdot w^A$. Third, the wage rate must be equal in the two industries. Otherwise, workers would all want to work in the high-wage industry and production of the other good would fall to zero. Consumers want to consume *both* goods, so wages must be equal to induce some workers to employment in each industry. Combining these three facts, we arrive at the conclusion: All workers in autarky in country A earn a wage equal to $w^A = P_X^A/a_{LX} = P_Y^A/a_{LY}$.

6 THE RICARDIAN WORLD WITH TRADE

We've seen that in autarky a country's production opportunity set and consumption opportunity set coincide. International trade relaxes this restriction on consumption opportunities; residents can consume combinations of the two goods that couldn't possibly be produced domestically. To understand the source of this result, we need to introduce country B, a trading partner for country A.

Country B's autarky situation resembles country A's. The consumption possibilities of country B are limited to B's production possibilities, defined by the resource endowment (L^B) and the available technology $(b_{LX}$ and $b_{LY})$. The two input coefficients again define the number of units of labor required to produce a unit of good *X* in country B (b_{LX}) and the number of units of labor required to produce a unit of good *Y* in country B (b_{LY}). Of course, there's no reason to expect that countries A and B will have identical quantities of labor available or use the same technology. If technologies differ, the two countries' production possibilities frontiers generally will have different slopes. In fact, these differences form the basis for mutually beneficial trade. We'll see later that if two countries' production possibilities frontiers have the same slope, trade between the two would be pointless. (*Explain why different relative labor productivity in the two industries across countries generates different slopes of the two countries' production possibilities frontiers.*)

Country B's preferences for goods X and Y can be represented by a set of indifference curves. These must satisfy the four restrictions discussed earlier in this chapter (see section 5.2), but there's no reason to expect country-B residents' preferences to be identical to those of country A's.

Combining the production possibilities frontier and indifference curves for country B, panel (b) of Figure 3 shows B's autarky equilibrium at B*. The slope of B's production possibilities frontier gives the marginal rate of transformation between goods X and Y (MRT^B), or the opportunity cost of good X; the slope of B's indifference curve represents the marginal rate of substitution (MRS^B), or the rate at which residents of B willingly trade

---

6. Remember the two-step logic behind this statement: Firms maximize profit by choosing to produce the output at which marginal revenue (MR) equals marginal cost (MC), and a perfectly competitive firm's marginal revenue equals price (P); therefore, P = MC.

off consumption of the two goods. In autarky equilibrium, when country B makes its production/consumption decision to maximize utility subject to the production constraint, these two slopes are equal. The (absolute value of the) slope of country B's production possibilities frontier also equals the autarky relative price of good X in B, or $(P_X/P_Y)^B$. In autarky, country-B workers earn a wage of $w^B = P_X^B/b_{LX} = P_Y^B/b_{LY}$ per unit of labor, regardless of whether they work in the X or the Y industry. (*Why?*)

To demonstrate international trade's potential to improve the welfare of both countries' residents, it's first necessary to show that the allocation of resources implied by the two autarky equilibria, A* and B* in Figure 3, does *not* maximize total world output. More precisely, by moving away from A* and B*, more of one of the two goods can be produced *without* decreasing production of the other. In other words, we must show that it's possible to produce more output by having countries A and B produce combinations of X and Y different from those represented by A* and B*. Adam Smith first demonstrated this fundamental result using the concept of absolute advantage.

6.1 Adam Smith and Absolute Advantage

Country A has an **absolute advantage** in production of good X if $a_{LX} < b_{LX}$, that is, if it takes fewer units of labor to produce a unit of good X in country A than in B. Adam Smith asserted that international trade between two countries would be *mutually* beneficial whenever one country had an absolute advantage in production of one good and the other country an absolute advantage in production of the other good. For example, if $a_{LX} < b_{LX}$ and $a_{LY} > b_{LY}$, country A has an absolute advantage in production of good X and country B has an absolute advantage in good Y; fewer units of labor are required to produce a unit of good X in country A than in B, and fewer units of labor are required to produce a unit of good Y in B than in A. According to Smith, it would benefit each country to specialize in producing the good in which it has an absolute advantage and to import the good in which it has an **absolute disadvantage**.

To illustrate how specialization and trade between two countries, one of which has an absolute advantage in each of the two goods, can increase world output and utility, we summarize the countries' input coefficients in Table 1 in both general terms and a specific numerical example. Starting from the autarky positions, A* and B*, let country A produce one less Y (the good in which A has an absolute *dis*advantage); this frees up a_{LY} (or 5) units of labor. Let country B replace the lost output by producing one more Y; this requires b_{LY} (or 4) units of labor. Total world production of good Y hasn't changed. But a_{LY} units of labor have been freed up in A, while only b_{LY} additional units of labor are required in B. Since $a_{LY} > b_{LY}$, this implies $5 - 4 = 1$ unit of labor available for production of *additional* X or Y. The greater the extent of B's absolute advantage, the more labor available for additional production. (*Why?*) The reader can use a similar exercise to show that switching a unit of X production from country B to country A produces a similar gain. These gains from specializing according to absolute advantage happen because such specialization involves producing each good in the country where it can be produced with less labor. By producing each unit of output using the minimum quantity of labor, the world's scarce labor ($L^W = L^A + L^B$) can produce a larger total of goods X and Y.[7]

---

7. With two goods, the phrase "a larger total of goods X and Y" is not well defined, because it's possible to produce more of one good *by producing less of the other.* We use the phrase to refer to the fact that it's impossible to produce more of one good *without* reducing production of the other. Moving from a position of autarky to one of productive specialization allows more of one good to be produced without reducing production of the other good. Once countries are completely specialized, further such gains aren't possible.

Table 1	COUNTRIES' PRODUCTIVE TECHNOLOGIES			
	General Case		Numerical Example	
	Country A	Country B	Country A	Country B
Labor units to produce one X	a_{LX}	b_{LX}	2	3
Labor units to produce one Y	a_{LY}	b_{LY}	5	4

The technologies, summarized by the input coefficients for each country, relate the number of units of labor required to produce one unit of each of the outputs.

Adam Smith's discussion represented a giant step forward in understanding the nature and potential of international trade. His main contribution was the idea that trade *isn't* a zero-sum game. International trade policy between the United States and China or the European Union isn't like a giant poker game in which one player wins at the other's expense. However, according to Smith, mutually beneficial trade required each country to have an absolute advantage in one of the goods. This requirement rules out many potential trading relationships in which one of the two countries has an absolute advantage in *both* goods (for example, if $a_{LX} = 2$, $a_{LY} = 5$, $b_{LX} = 8$, $b_{LY} = 10$). David Ricardo soon demonstrated that even Smith's optimistic view of trade was not optimistic enough.[8]

6.2 David Ricardo and Comparative Advantage

Perhaps the greatest of David Ricardo's many contributions to economics was his demonstration that mutually beneficial trade is possible even if one of the trading partners has an absolute advantage in production of *both* goods. Failure to understand this simple but important point leads to one of the most common fallacies in modern discussions of international trade and trade policy: the claim that developing economies with low labor productivity relative to the rest of the world should isolate themselves from international trade.

To expose this fallacy, Ricardo articulated the concept of **comparative advantage**, a simple extension of the concept of opportunity cost. Country A has a comparative advantage in production of good X if $(a_{LX}/a_{LY}) < (b_{LX}/b_{LY})$. This simply says that country A has a comparative advantage in production of good X if, to produce an additional unit of good X in A, it is necessary to forgo fewer units of *good Y* than would be necessary to produce the additional unit of good X in country B.[9] This is equivalent to saying that the opportunity cost of good X in country A (measured in units of good Y) is lower than in B.

Table 2 reports the opportunity cost of each good in each country in both general form and a numerical example. In country A, $a_{LX} = 2$ units of labor are required to

---

8. Historians of economic thought disagree whether Adam Smith intended his discussion to cover cases of comparative advantage. Regardless of one's view on this debate, Smith's achievement in communicating the potential benefits of international trade was monumental.

9. To see that (a_{LX}/a_{LY}) is measured in units of good Y per unit of good X, note that a_{LX} is measured in units of labor per unit of X (or L/X) while a_{LY} is measured in units of labor per unit of Y (or L/Y). Therefore, a_{LX}/a_{LY} is in units of Y per unit of X (or Y/X).

Table 2	**OPPORTUNITY COSTS OF PRODUCING GOODS X AND Y**			
	General Case		Numerical Example	
	Country A	Country B	Country A	Country B
Good X	a_{LX}/a_{LY}	b_{LX}/b_{LY}	$(2/5)Y$	$(8/10)Y$
Good Y	a_{LY}/a_{LX}	b_{LY}/b_{LX}	$(5/2)X$	$(10/8)X$

The opportunity cost of producing each good in each country equals the number of units of labor required to produce a unit of the good divided by the number of units of labor required to produce a unit of the other good. For example, to produce 1 additional unit of good X in country B requires $b_{LX} = 8$ units of labor. To obtain those 8 units of labor, Y production in B would have to be cut by 8/10 units, because each unit of Y produced uses $b_{LY} = 10$ units of labor. Therefore, the opportunity cost of 1 additional unit of X is 8/10 units of Y.

produce 1 unit of good X, and $a_{LY} = 5$ units of labor are required to produce 1 unit of good Y. Therefore, production of 1 additional unit of X means forgoing 2/5 units of Y; in other words, the opportunity cost of producing good X in country A is 2/5 units of Y. Similarly, production of an additional unit of Y in country A is possible only if X production is cut by 5/2. (*Why?*) In country B, $b_{LX} = 8$ units of labor are required to produce 1 unit of good X and $b_{LY} = 10$ to produce 1 unit of Y. This implies that the opportunity cost of producing X in country B is 8/10 units of Y, and the opportunity cost of producing Y is 10/8 units of X. In the numerical example, country A has an absolute advantage in *both* goods. (*Why?*) Nonetheless, we'll demonstrate that trade according to comparative advantage can benefit both countries.

Note that one country *can't* have a comparative advantage in both goods. (*Why?*)[10] Note too that tastes are irrelevant in determining comparative advantage under constant costs because the slopes of the production possibilities frontiers are constants. Tastes do affect the particular point at which a country chooses to produce in autarky, but the comparison of opportunity costs in the two countries (the determinant of comparative advantage) is the same regardless of tastes.

The principle of comparative advantage states that it will be beneficial for a country to specialize in production of the good in which it has a comparative advantage and to trade for the good in which it has a comparative disadvantage. Such specialization and trade make both countries potentially better off by expanding their consumption opportunity sets. In other words, specialization and trade allow a country's *consumption* opportunity set to expand beyond its *production* opportunity set. Residents can choose to consume combinations of goods impossible to produce domestically. In autarky, the domestic production possibilities frontier defines both the production and consumption opportunity sets, and its slope defines both the opportunity costs and the relative prices of goods X and Y. We can now demonstrate that specialization and trade along the lines of comparative advantage can increase the total world quantities of the two goods available for consumption and, therefore, expand the consumption opportunity sets beyond the production opportunity sets.[11]

---

10. By definition, country A has a comparative advantage in good X if $(a_{LX}/a_{LY}) < (b_{LX}/b_{LY})$ or in good Y if $(a_{LY}/a_{LX}) < (b_{LY}/b_{LX})$. These two statements can't both be true. (*Use the numerical example from Table 1 to see why. If one example isn't convincing, make up others by using different numerical values for the input coefficients.*)

11. The appendix to this chapter presents another way to demonstrate this effect of trade, based on the world production possibilities frontier.

Figure 4   **How Countries Specialize According to Comparative Advantage**

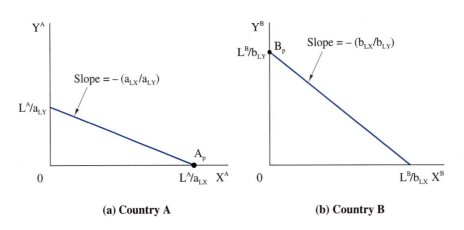

(a) Country A   **(b) Country B**

Because the opportunity cost of producing good X is lower in country A than in country B, total output of X can be increased without reducing production of good Y by switching X production from B to A. Once A is completely specialized in producing X (at point A_p), further increases in X production require reductions in Y production. Because country B has a comparative advantage in production of good Y, total output of Y can be increased without reducing production of X when B specializes completely in Y (at point B_p).

In Table 2, country A has a comparative advantage in good X and country B has a comparative advantage in good Y. *(Why?)* Suppose that beginning at its autarky equilibrium, A*, country A produces 1 additional unit of good X. A's production of good Y must fall by a_{LX}/a_{LY} (or 2/5 in the numerical example), the opportunity cost of good X in A. Now suppose that from its autarky equilibrium, B*, country B produces 1 fewer unit of good X. B's production of good Y rises by b_{LX}/b_{LY} (or 8/10), the opportunity cost of good X in B. By the definition of comparative advantage in our example, $(a_{LX}/a_{LY}) <$ (b_{LX}/b_{LY}), so the same fixed quantity of total labor is now producing the same quantity of good X and a *larger* quantity of good Y than were being produced in autarky. In fact, the increased production of good Y is equal to the difference in opportunity costs $[(b_{LX}/b_{LY}) - (a_{LX}/a_{LY})]$, or $(8/10 - 2/5 = 4/10)$; therefore, the stronger the pattern of comparative advantage, the greater the gains from specialization.

We can repeat the same switching technique (that is, switching production of each good from its comparative-disadvantage country to its comparative-advantage country) until each country is completely specialized in the good in which it has a comparative advantage.[12] This is true in the constant-cost model because, as countries specialize according to comparative advantage, changes in production don't alter the pattern of costs or comparative advantage, represented by the constant slopes of the production possibilities frontiers. At points A_p and B_p in Figure 4, the total quantity of goods X and Y produced in the world is maximized given the available resources and technology; additional units of either good can be produced *only* by decreasing production of the other.

---

12. Each country will specialize completely as long as tastes for the two goods and countries' sizes don't differ too much. If tastes are strongly biased toward one good (say, everyone likes to consume lots of X but only a little Y), both countries may continue to produce some X; but the country with a comparative advantage in X will specialize completely. If the countries are very different in size, the small country may not be able to satisfy the large country's demand for the good in which the small country has a comparative advantage. In this case, the small country will specialize completely while the large country will produce some of both goods.

If the countries can produce more by specializing, why did they choose not to specialize in autarky? Because in autarky residents of each country must consume only the goods produced domestically. If country A specialized completely in production of good X in autarky, its residents would be forced to consume L^A/a_{LX} units of X and none of good Y. However, consumers generally want to diversify their consumption, consuming some of many different goods. This characteristic of tastes rules out production specialization without trade. With trade, a country can specialize its production and then trade some of its domestically produced good (produced at relatively low opportunity cost) for some of the goods produced in other countries (which could be produced domestically only at a relatively high opportunity cost).

6.3 International Equilibrium with Trade

Once both countries have opened trade and specialized production according to comparative advantage, at what relative price ratio will trade occur? How many units of its export good (X) will country A have to give up to obtain a unit of its import good (Y)? And how many units of its export good (Y) will country B have to give up to get a unit of its import good (X)? First, we can see that the price ratio at which trade occurs (written as $[P_X/P_Y]^{tt}$ and called the **terms of trade**) must lie between the two countries' autarky price ratios, or $(P_X/P_Y)^A < (P_X/P_Y)^{tt} < (P_X/P_Y)^B$. To see why, consider that each country now has two possible methods for turning good X into good Y or vice versa. The first is by altering its domestic production (at a rate defined by the domestic opportunity cost, which equals the autarky price ratio). The second is through international trade (at a rate defined by the international price ratio or terms of trade). Having this choice, a country would never trade voluntarily at terms of trade less favorable than its own autarky price ratio.

For example, from the point of productive specialization, A_p in panel (a) of Figure 4, country A can transform good X into good Y through domestic production at a rate of $a_{LX}/a_{LY} = (P_X/P_Y)^A$ units of Y obtained per unit of X forgone. In order for country A to choose instead to continue to specialize in production of good X and trade some of it to country B in exchange for some good Y, trade with B must give A at least $a_{LX}/a_{LY} = (P_X/P_Y)^A$ units of Y imports for each unit of X exported. Graphically, beginning at point A_p country A will find it beneficial to trade with country B only if trade occurs at a relative price represented by the slope of a line from point A_p that is *steeper* than A's production possibilities frontier. Residents of A will purchase Y from B if they can do so at a price below the autarky price of Y, or $(P_X/P_Y)^A$. (Note that a low autarky relative price of X is equivalent to a high autarky relative price of Y.) Panel (a) of Figure 5 illustrates this restriction imposed by country A on the terms of trade.

Country B faces a similar choice of ways to get good X to consume. From the point of productive specialization, B_p in panel (b) of Figure 4, country B can obtain good X through domestic production by forgoing good Y at a rate of $b_{LX}/b_{LY} = (P_X/P_Y)^B$ per unit of X produced. If country B can obtain X at a more favorable rate through international trade, it will choose to specialize in production of Y and trade with A to get X for consumption. Residents of B will be willing to purchase X from country A at any price below country B's autarky price, $(P_X/P_Y)^B$. Examples of terms of trade at which B would choose to trade are illustrated in panel (b) of Figure 5 by lines from point B_p that are *flatter* than B's production possibilities frontier.

For trade to occur, the terms of trade must satisfy both partners. Therefore, the terms of trade must be equal to the slope of a line that is both steeper than country A's production possibilities frontier and flatter than country B's (that is, $[P_X/P_Y]^A < [P_X/P_Y]^{tt} < [P_X/P_Y]^B$).

The international terms of trade must satisfy one additional condition beyond those in Figure 5: The equilibrium terms of trade also must be the **market-clearing price** for the two goods. In other words, the quantity of good X that country A wants to *export* at

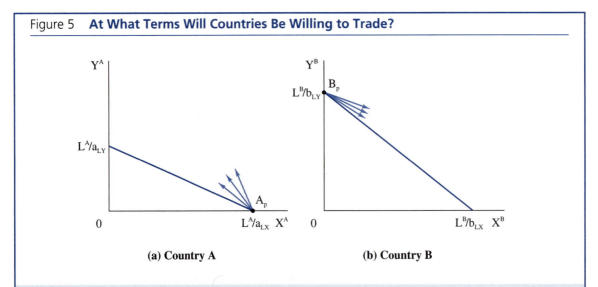

Figure 5   At What Terms Will Countries Be Willing to Trade?

(a) Country A   **(b) Country B**

For country A to trade voluntarily with country B, the terms of trade must be more favorable to A than are its own production possibilities or domestic opportunity costs. For any terms of trade represented in panel (a) as a line from point A_p that is *steeper* than the production possibilities frontier, country A can obtain more units of good Y for each unit of good X forgone through trade than through domestic production. Because B can get 1 unit of X through domestic production by forgoing b_{LX}/b_{LY} units of Y, B will trade voluntarily only if it can obtain 1 unit of X for fewer than b_{LX}/b_{LY} units of Y. Therefore, all the terms of trade at which country B would willingly trade can be represented in panel (b) by lines from point B_p that are *flatter* than B's production possibilities frontier.

the terms of trade must equal the quantity of X that country B wants to *import* at the same terms of trade. Simultaneously, the quantity of good Y that country B wants to export at the terms of trade must equal the quantity of Y that country A wants to import. To incorporate this requirement into our graphical framework, we must go beyond Figure 5 to see how each country decides how much of goods X and Y to consume under unrestricted trade.

Each country chooses its consumption point to maximize utility. We saw the consumption decisions under autarky in Figure 3. With trade, however, the consumption opportunity set no longer coincides with the production opportunity set. Once country A specializes in producing good X and opens up trade with country B, residents of A can consume any combination of X and Y that lies on the terms-of-trade line through the production point, A_p. From panel (a) of Figure 5, we see that this is a clear improvement over autarky for country-A residents. With specialization and trade, they can consume larger quantities of both X and Y than under autarky; country A's consumption opportunity set has expanded. From panel (b) of Figure 5, we see that residents of country B enjoy a similar expansion of their consumption opportunity set due to specialization and trade. Each country takes advantage of the new opportunities by locating at the point of tangency between the highest possible indifference curve and the terms-of-trade line.

Figures 6 and 7 show the results for each country. Country A *produces* at point A_p and *consumes* at point A_c. Country B *produces* at point B_p and *consumes* at point B_c. The shaded triangles in the figures, known as **trade triangles**, summarize each country's imports and exports as well as the terms of trade. For country A, the base of triangle AA_cA_p, line AA_p, represents exports of good X; the height, line AA_c, gives imports of Y. The slope of line A_cA_p measures the equilibrium terms of trade. Triangle BB_pB_c in Figure 7

Figure 6   What Would Country *A* Do Under Free Trade?

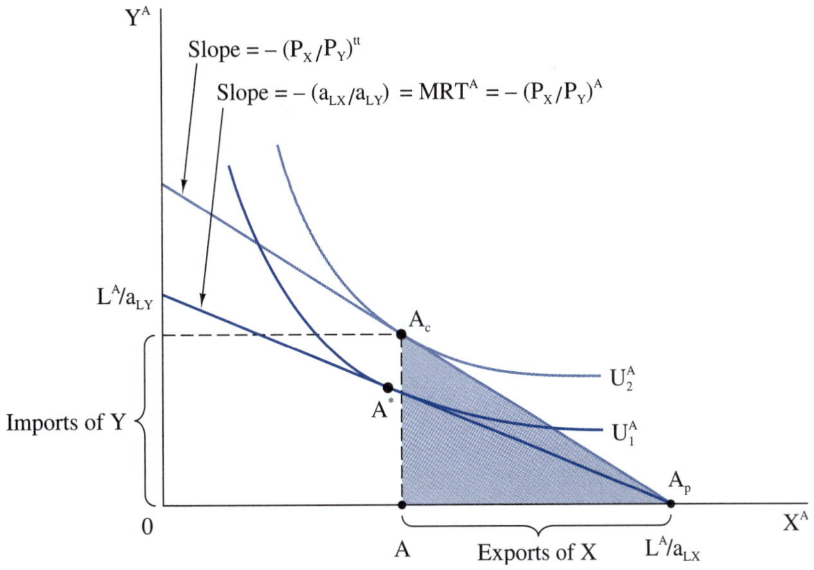

Country A produces at A_p and consumes at A_c, the point of tangency of the indifference curve with the equilibrium terms-of-trade line. At the equilibrium terms of trade, country A's exports of good X equal country B's imports, and A's imports of good Y equal B's exports. Country A's trade triangle is AA_cA_p.

summarizes the analogous information for country B. (*What relationship must hold between the lengths of AA_p and BB_c? AA_c and BB_p? The slopes of A_cA_p and B_pB_c? Why?*)

Notice that country B partakes of the gains from trade by specializing according to comparative advantage *even though* B suffers an absolute disadvantage in both goods or, equivalently, even though country B's labor is less productive than country A's in both industries. Often-heard claims that countries with low labor productivity need to isolate themselves from trade with more productive economies represent a serious and fundamental fallacy based on a failure to understand comparative advantage. Unfortunately, policies based on this fallacy have proven costly to many developing economies over the last half century.

We can also conclude that real wages rise in both countries with the opening of trade. Simply put, this happens because trade allows each country's labor to specialize in producing the good in which it is relatively more productive. Recall that in autarky, $w^A = P_X^A/a_{LX} = P_Y^A/a_{LY}$ and $w^B = P_X^B/b_{LX} = P_Y^B/b_{LY}$, because workers in each country had to produce some of both goods. With trade, country A no longer needs to produce any good Y, in which country-A labor is *relatively* unproductive; country B no longer has to produce any good X, in which country-B labor is relatively unproductive. Therefore, with trade, the conditions defining equilibrium wages in the two countries simplify to $w^{A*} = P_X^{tt}/a_{LX}$ and $w^{B*} = P_Y^{tt}/b_{LY}$. Figures 6 and 7 show that the relative price of each country's export good has risen with the opening of trade. Each country no longer produces its import good, so the declines in those relative prices that accompany the opening of trade exert no negative effect on real wages.

Table 3 summarizes trade's effects on production, consumption, prices, and wages in each country. Each produces more of its comparative-advantage good and less of its

Figure 7   What Would Country *B* Do Under Free Trade?

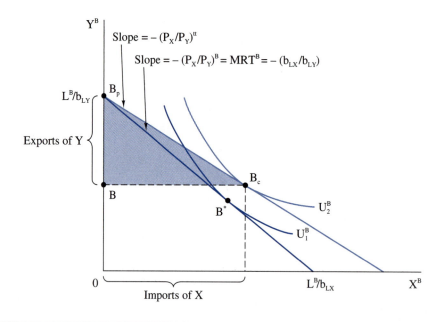

Country B *produces at point* B$_p$ *and consumes at point* B$_c$, *exporting good Y and importing good X. This free-trade equilibrium produces a higher level of utility* (U$_2^B$) *than was attainable under autarky* (U$_1^B$). *Country B's trade triangle is* BB$_p$B$_c$.

Table 3   WHAT ARE THE EFFECTS OF TRADE?

	Autarky	Free Trade	Effect of Trade
Country A:			
Production	Point A* in Figure 6	Point A$_p$ in Figure 6	X⇑, Y⇓
Consumption	Point A* in Figure 6	Point A$_c$ in Figure 6	X⇑, Y⇑
Prices	$(P_X/P_Y)^A = (a_{LX}/a_{LY})$	$(P_X/P_Y)^{tt} > (a_{LX}/a_{LY})$	(P_X/P_Y)⇑
Wages	$w^A = P_X^A/a_{LX} = P_Y^A/a_{LY}$	$w^{A*} = P_X^{tt}/a_{LX}$	w^A⇑
Country B:			
Production	Point B* in Figure 7	Point B$_p$ in Figure 7	X⇓, Y⇑
Consumption	Point B* in Figure 7	Point B$_c$ in Figure 7	X⇑, Y⇑
Prices	$(P_X/P_Y)^B = (b_{LX}/b_{LY})$	$(P_X/P_Y)^{tt} < (b_{LX}/b_{LY})$	(P_X/P_Y)⇓
Wages	$w^B = P_X^B/b_{LX} = P_Y^B/b_{LY}$	$w^{B*} = P_Y^{tt}/b_{LY}$	w^B⇑

comparative-disadvantage good. Consumption of both goods can rise in both countries, because productive specialization according to comparative advantage increases the total quantities that can be produced using the two countries' limited resources. In each country, the relative price of the export good rises, and the relative price of the import good falls as imports from the lower-cost country become available. Real wages rise in both countries as labor shifts to the industry in which it is relatively more productive.

6.4 Who Gains, and by How Much?

We've demonstrated that trade can be mutually beneficial as long as the countries possess a comparative advantage. This *doesn't* mean that the gains from trade necessarily will be shared equally by the trading partners. Specifying the precise division of the gains from trade between the two countries requires additional information. Figure 5 clearly shows that trade expands each country's consumption opportunity set by allowing the country to trade at terms that differ from the autarky price ratio. The implication is that a country captures a larger share of the gains from trade when the equilibrium terms of trade differ significantly from the country's autarky price ratio (or are very close to the trading partner's autarky price ratio). The importance of this statement lies in its implications for the relationship between country size and the division of the gains from trade.

Economists define a small country as one whose participation in a market is small relative to the overall size of that market, so that the country's decisions don't affect the market price. A large country, in contrast, does affect the market price through its production and consumption decisions, because its activity constitutes a larger share of the market. In trade between a large country and a small country, the *small* country captures the gains—because the terms of trade will be the same as the large country's autarky price.

7 THE GAINS FROM TRADE: EXCHANGE AND SPECIALIZATION

Thus far, we've discussed the gains from trade rather abstractly, implying that all the gains come from specialization according to comparative advantage. In this section, we focus more explicitly on the gains from trade and distinguish two sources.

7.1 Gains from Exchange

One portion of the gains from trade, called the **gains from exchange**, comes from allowing unrestricted exchange of goods between countries *without* altering autarky production patterns. In autarky, the relative prices of the two goods differ between countries, as shown in Figures 6 and 7. Because the relative price in each country equals the marginal rate of substitution there, the rates at which consumers in the two countries are willing to trade off consumption of the two goods also differ in autarky. In country B, consumers are willing to give up as many as $(P_X/P_Y)^B$ units of good Y for an additional unit of good X; in country A, consumers are willing to give up a unit of good X for as few as $(P_X/P_Y)^A$ units of good Y. By the definition of comparative advantage in our example, $(P_X/P_Y)^A < (P_X/P_Y)^B$. Therefore, a simple exchange of good X for good Y between countries A and B could be mutually beneficial: Country A values the Y it can get from B more highly than the X it must give up; likewise, country B values the X it can get from A more highly than the Y it must forgo. Panel (a) of Figure 8 illustrates these gains from exchange for country A.

Each country continues to *produce* at its autarky point; but rather than consuming the goods produced domestically, residents of A can then exchange with residents of B. Firms in country A will be willing to export good X at any price higher than the autarky price in A, $(P_X/P_Y)^A$; consumers in country B will be willing to import good X at any price lower than the autarky price in B, $(P_X/P_Y)^B$. (*Why?*) As we've seen, for both countries to trade voluntarily, the terms of trade must fall between these limits—$(P_X/P_Y)^A < (P_X/P_Y)^{tt} < (P_X/P_Y)^B$. At any terms of trade within this range, the two countries will find exchange mutually beneficial. The precise equilibrium terms of trade at which exchange will occur also require that

Figure 8   **What Does a Country Gain from Exchange and Specialization?**

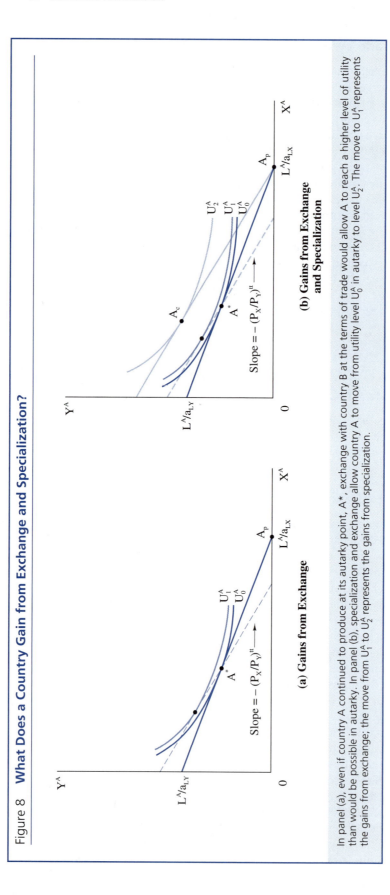

In panel (a), even if country A continued to produce at its autarky point, A*, exchange with country B at the terms of trade would allow A to reach a higher level of utility than would be possible in autarky. In panel (b), specialization and exchange allow country A to move from utility level U_0^A in autarky to level U_2^A. The move to U_1^A represents the gains from exchange; the move from U_1^A to U_2^A represents the gains from specialization.

markets for the two goods clear. The quantity of good X that country A is willing to export in exchange for a quantity of good Y from country B must match the quantity of X that B is willing to import in exchange for its exports of Y. Through this exchange, each country attains a higher level of utility than was possible in autarky, even though each country's production pattern remains unchanged.

In panel (a) of Figure 8, the move from U_0^A to U_1^A represents the gains from exchange for country A. (*Test your understanding by drawing the corresponding diagram for country B.*) These gains come from simply reallocating the same quantities of goods X and Y produced in autarky between the two countries based on their residents' tastes for each good.

7.2 Gains from Specialization

The gains from exchange illustrated in panel (a) of Figure 8 obviously don't constitute all of country A's gains from trade. The remainder come from specializing production according to comparative advantage and are called the **gains from specialization**. With open trade, countries no longer choose to produce the same combination of goods they did in autarky. Each country adjusts its production along the production possibilities frontier, producing more of the good in which it has a comparative advantage and less of the good in which it has a comparative disadvantage.

Panel (b) of Figure 8 reproduces country A's unrestricted-trade equilibrium from Figure 6, but also illustrates how we can break down the total gains from trade (the move from U_0^A to U_2^A) into gains from exchange (U_0^A to U_1^A) and gains from specialization (U_1^A to U_2^A).

8 USING DEMAND AND SUPPLY TO ANALYZE TRADE

The autarky and trade results we've developed within the production possibilities frontier-indifference curve framework also can be presented using demand and supply curves. The demand-supply framework is useful because it allows us to see more directly the determination of the equilibrium terms of trade; the demand-supply approach also will prove convenient for analyzing the effects of trade restrictions in Chapters Six and Seven.

8.1 Demand and Supply in Autarky

In autarky, the market for each good in each country is isolated from the market for the same good in the other country; therefore, there are four markets (one for each of the two goods in each of the two countries) represented by the four panels of Figure 9. In each market, the interaction of domestic demand and domestic supply determines the good's autarky relative price.

A downward-sloping demand curve for each good represents the tastes of each country's residents. The quantity demanded of each good depends negatively on the good's autarky price, other things being equal. The opportunity costs of producing the goods determine the shape of the supply curves. In this chapter's constant-cost model, the opportunity cost of producing each good in each country is constant out to the maximum amount of the good the country can produce. This gives the supply curves a 90-degree angle: horizontal then suddenly vertical. The level of output at which the supply curve of good X becomes vertical in panel (a) corresponds to the point at which country A's production possibilities frontier intersects the X axis (that is, L^A/a_{LX}); a similar relationship holds for A's production of good Y in panel (b).

In competitive markets, the price of each good equals its opportunity cost. The equilibria in the four separate markets represent the same situation as autarky points

---

Figure 9   **Domestic Markets for Goods X and Y in Autarky under Constant Costs**

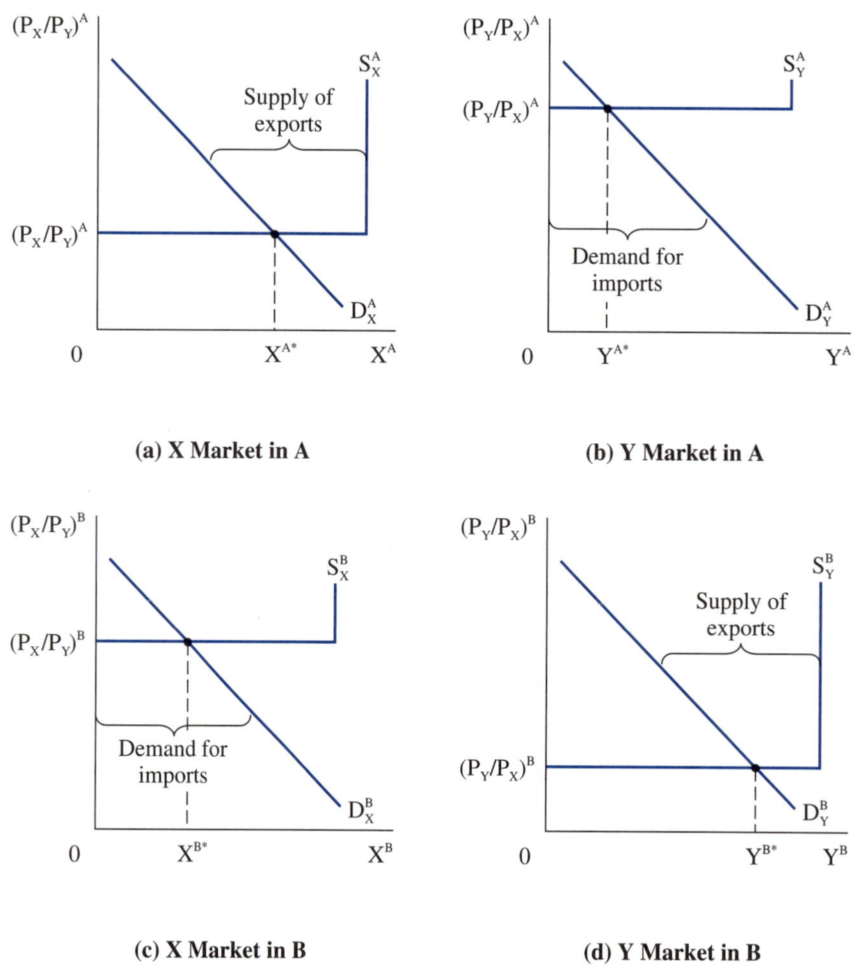

(a) X Market in A

(b) Y Market in A

(c) X Market in B

(d) Y Market in B

In autarky, goods' relative prices are determined by equality of quantity demanded domestically and quantity supplied domestically. Domestic demand for each good depends negatively on the good's relative price. A country can produce each good at a constant opportunity cost to the point where the country's entire labor endowment is employed producing the one good; at that point, it becomes impossible to produce more of the good domestically, so the domestic supply curve becomes vertical. At relative prices at which domestic quantity demanded exceeds quantity supplied of a good, the domestic shortage would result in a demand for imports, as noted in panels (b) and (c). At relative prices at which domestic quantity supplied exceeds quantity demanded of a good, the domestic surplus would result in a supply of exports, as noted in panels (a) and (d).

A^* and B^* in Figure 3. Country A, where the autarky relative price is $(P_X/P_Y)^A$, produces X^{A*} units of X and Y^{A*} units of Y. Country B, with an autarky relative price of $(P_X/P_Y)^B$, produces X^{B*} units of X and Y^{B*} units of Y. Comparison of the two countries' markets for good X in panels (a) and (c) of Figure 9 reveals that country A has a comparative advantage in production of good X. Similarly, country B has a comparative advantage in production of good Y, as shown by comparing panels (b) and (d). (*Why?*)

8.2 Demand and Supply with Trade

Opening trade allows countries A and B to participate in a common international market for each good. The two separate markets for good X in panels (a) and (c) of Figure 9 combine to become the international market for good X in panel (a) of Figure 10. Similarly, panels (b) and (d) from Figure 9 form the basis for panel (b) of Figure 10.

Panel (a) of Figure 9 demonstrates that country A is willing to export good X at any price greater than $(P_X/P_Y)^A$. The horizontal distance between the domestic demand and supply curves measures the supply of exports offered at each price. The "Supply of exports$_X^A$" line in panel (a) of Figure 10 depicts this supply of exports of good X by country A. Note that Figure 10's horizontal axis measures the quantity of good X *traded,* not the quantity produced or consumed as in earlier diagrams. Panel (c) of Figure 9 shows that country B's residents demand to import good X from A at any price below $(P_X/P_Y)^B$ in quantities given by the horizontal distance between the domestic demand and supply curves. This demand for imports of good X by country B becomes the "Demand for imports$_X^B$" line in panel (a) of Figure 10.

Combining the export-supply and import-demand curves yields the unrestricted trade equilibrium in the international market for good X. The international market is in equilibrium when the quantity of the good that one country (A in the case of good X) wants to export at the terms of trade equals the quantity that the other country (here, B) wants to import on those same terms. The equilibrium price of good X is $(P_X/P_Y)^{tt}$, and country A exports X^{tt} to country B. (*We argued in the production possibilities frontier-indifference curve framework that the international terms of trade would lie between the two countries' autarky price ratios. How does the demand and supply framework in Figure 10 reflect this restriction?*)

We can use the same procedure to derive the international market for good Y (panel (b) of Figure 10) from panels (b) and (d) of Figure 9. The demand for imports of good Y

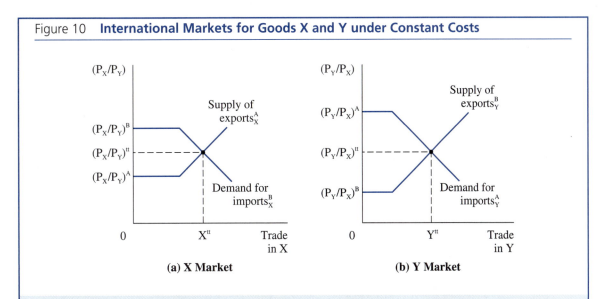

Figure 10 International Markets for Goods X and Y under Constant Costs

(a) X Market

(b) Y Market

Each country is willing to import its good of comparative disadvantage at prices below its autarky price. At each price, the quantity demanded of imports equals the difference between quantity demanded and quantity produced domestically. Each country also is willing to export its good of comparative advantage at prices above its autarky price. At each price, the quantity of exports supplied equals the difference between quantity supplied and quantity demanded domestically. The equilibrium terms of trade lie between the two countries' autarky prices. At the equilibrium terms of trade, the quantity one country wants to import matches the quantity the other country wants to export.

by country A comes from panel (b) of Figure 9, and the supply of exports of good Y by country B comes from panel (d). (*What determines the vertical intercepts of "Demand for imports$_Y^A$" and "Supply of exports$_Y^B$"?*) The international equilibrium price of good Y is $(P_Y/P_X)^{tt}$, and country B exports Y^{tt} to country A. These results correspond to the information summarized in the trade triangles in Figures 6 and 7.

In the remainder of the book, we'll use both the demand-supply and production possibilities-indifference curve frameworks. Although the two methods of analysis convey the same basic information, each is more convenient for answering certain questions. As each issue arises, we'll address it with the more appropriate method. Translating back and forth between the two methods also provides practice in working with the basic ideas of international trade theory.[13]

This completes our development of the basic Ricardian model and the demonstration of the gains from specialization and trade. We now turn to two cases that report the results of several attempts to test empirically the major implications of the Ricardian theory of trade. Can differences in technology or labor productivity among countries actually explain trade patterns observed in the world economy? Cases One and Two suggest that the answer is yes: Countries *do* tend to export goods in which their labor is relatively productive and to import those in which their labor is relatively unproductive. Case Three extends the Ricardian approach to see what happens when different plants in an industry have different labor productivities.

CASE 1: CAN THE RICARDIAN MODEL *REALLY* EXPLAIN TRADE?

U.S./U.K.

G. D. A. MacDougall undertook the first and best-known effort to test empirically the major implication of the Ricardian model in 1951.[14] MacDougall used 1937 data on U.S. and U.K. exports in 25 industries. Recall that the Ricardian model implies that each country tends to export those goods in which it has a comparative advantage. Its comparative advantage lies in those goods in which its labor is highly productive compared to the trading partner's labor.[15] MacDougall combined these two aspects of the Ricardian model to formulate the following testable hypothesis: Other things being equal, the higher the U.S. output per worker relative to the U.K. output per worker in a given industry, the higher the exports by the United States relative to those by the United Kingdom in that industry. Figure 11 reports MacDougall's findings, and they clearly

support the major implication of the Ricardian model: High relative labor productivity in a given industry accompanied a high market share. Later studies confirmed MacDougall's findings using data for different time periods.

Notice how Figure 11 confirms the importance of *comparative* as opposed to absolute advantage. U.S. labor productivity exceeded that of the United Kingdom in all 25 industries MacDougall examined. On average, U.S. productivity was approximately twice U.K productivity, as illustrated by the pale horizontal line in Figure 11. If absolute advantage determined trade patterns, the United Kingdom wouldn't have exported in any of the industries. But because comparative advantage determines trade patterns, the United Kingdom did export—in those industries in which U.K. labor productivity was closer to that of the United States

---

13. Appendix B to Chapter Three covers a third graphical technique, called the *offer curve* or *reciprocal demand curve*. We can obtain all the information conveyed by offer-curve analysis using either the production possibilities-indifference curve or the demand-supply technique.

14. G. D. A. MacDougall, "British and American Exports: A Study Suggested by the Theory of Comparative Costs," *Economic Journal* 61 (December 1951), pp. 697–724.

15. Highly productive labor in an industry is equivalent to a low input coefficient. The input coefficient (for example, a_{LX}) measures how many units of labor are needed to produce 1 unit of output, while labor productivity (or, $1/a_{LX}$) asks how many units of output 1 unit of labor can produce.

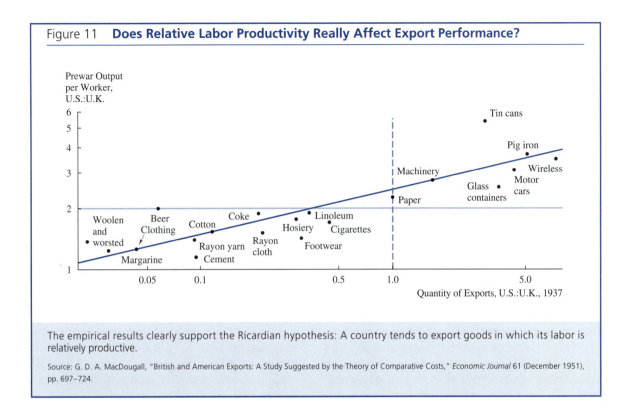

Figure 11 **Does Relative Labor Productivity Really Affect Export Performance?**

The empirical results clearly support the Ricardian hypothesis: A country tends to export goods in which its labor is relatively productive.

Source: G. D. A. MacDougall, "British and American Exports: A Study Suggested by the Theory of Comparative Costs," *Economic Journal* 61 (December 1951), pp. 697–724.

(for example, woolens, beer, and clothing). The United States exported more in the industries where U.S. labor productivity most significantly exceeded that of the United Kingdom (for example, pig iron and tin cans).

Does Ricardo's basic prediction still hold? A 2000 study suggests that the answer is yes. Stephen S. Golub and Chang-Tai Hsieh calculated the relationship between relative labor productivity and relative exports for 39 industries and for four trading partner pairs: U.S.–Japan, U.S.–Germany, U.S.–U.K., and U.S.–France, using data from the late 1970s to the early 1990s.[16] They found an industry's relatively high labor productivity to be associated with relatively high exports. For example, focusing on U.S.–Japan trade, a one percent rise in an industry's labor productivity relative to that in the other country led to a 0.3 percent increase in that industry's relative exports.

Ricardo originally intended his model as a simple framework for highlighting the principle of comparative advantage rather than as a full explanation for observed trade patterns in the world economy. Both the theoretical

model and the empirical tests ignore many relevant issues, such as the presence of nonlabor inputs, tariffs, transportation costs, economies of scale, and product differentiation, each of which will be a focus in later chapters. The theoretical version of Ricardo's model implies that relative labor productivity (represented by the pattern of input coefficients) determines opportunity costs, which in turn determine autarky price ratios, which in turn determine trade patterns. However, autarky prices typically are unobservable because trade is occurring; thus, empirical tests must seek a direct relationship between labor productivity and trade patterns, bypassing the unobservable autarky prices.[17] That this problem in implementing the model empirically can't disguise the comparative advantage/export relationship is a tribute to the power of Ricardo's insight.

In the two centuries since Ricardo wrote, economists have come to appreciate many explanations for trade patterns. However, in recent years, Ricardo's insights, particularly the importance of cross-country differences in technology and labor productivity, once again have come

---

16. Stephen S. Golub and Chang-Tai Hsieh, "Classical Ricardian Theory of Comparative Advantage Revisited," *Review of International Economics* 8 (May 2000), pp. 221–234.

17. Occasionally, rare historical circumstances do reveal autarky prices—for example, the case of the opening of Japan to trade during the nineteenth century.

to the forefront. Two major issues in the world economy—the need to integrate developing countries and the formerly centrally planned countries into the world economy—help explain this new appreciation of Ricardo's insights. When a country isolates its economy from the rest of the world, as many developing and centrally planned nations did for decades of the twentieth century,

and then reemerges and tries to integrate itself into the world economy, the years of isolation leave a legacy of backward technology and low labor productivity. Policy makers must evaluate the implications of this legacy and design policies for confronting it. Two centuries after his original contribution, David Ricardo continues to lend a powerful helping hand in this task.

CASE 2: DOES LABOR PRODUCTIVITY *REALLY* VARY?

U.S./Germany/Japan

We'll see in Chapters Three and Five that differences in relative labor productivity form only one of several possible bases of comparative advantage and that, in turn, comparative advantage is only one of several possible foundations for mutually beneficial international trade. Nonetheless, we can explore at this point whether significant cross-country differences in relative labor productivity exist. Table 4 reports recent estimates of value-added per hour worked for several major manufacturing sectors in Germany and Japan relative to the United States. Value-added is a measure of output, so value-added per hour worked corresponds to the inverse of our input coefficients; a_{LX} reports the number of units of labor required to produce 1 unit of X, so its inverse, $1/a_{LX}$, measures output per unit of labor.

The top half of Table 4 compares labor productivity in Germany and the United States in each of six manufacturing sectors. Each number in the table reports value-added per hour of labor in Germany ($1/g_{LX}$ in terms of our input coefficients) divided by value-added per hour worked in the United States ($1/a_{LX}$), or (a_{LX}/g_{LX}). To determine the countries' comparative advantages across two sectors, X and Y, we need to compare (a_{LX}/a_{LY}) and (g_{LX}/g_{LY}). When the former exceeds the latter, Germany has a comparative advantage in good X and the United States in good Y; when the latter exceeds the former, the United States has a comparative advantage in good X and Germany in good Y. The condition (a_{LX}/a_{LY}) > (g_{LX}/g_{LY}) is algebraically equivalent to (a_{LX}/g_{LX}) > (a_{LY}/g_{LY}).[18] So, within each column in the top half of Table 4, industries with the highest numbers (that is, sectors with the highest values of [a_{LX}/g_{LX}]) correspond to industries of German comparative advantage relative to the United States, and industries with the lowest numbers (that is, sectors with the lowest values of [a_{LX}/g_{LX}]) correspond to industries of U.S. comparative advantage relative to Germany.

The data suggest that German labor productivity overall improved relative to that of the United States between 1950 and 1990, but still lagged behind in 1990. After solid gains during most of the postwar period, German productivity lost ground relative to that of the United States in several sectors between 1979 and 1990. Note also that the pattern of comparative advantage shifted. During the early postwar years, German comparative advantage relative to the United States was in food, beverages, and tobacco, along with textiles, apparel, and leather, while the United States exhibited an advantage in chemicals and metals. By 1990, metals showed the strongest German comparative advantage. *(Based on the data in the table, what patterns of imports and exports would you expect between Germany and the United States based on comparative advantage? If trade were based on absolute advantage, what would you predict about U.S.–German trade based on the table? Which fits better with what you know about trade?)*

The bottom half of Table 4 performs the same exercise for Japan and the United States. Japan's productivity catch-up during the postwar years was even more impressive than Germany's. In 1950, Japan showed a comparative advantage relative to the United States in food and textiles, and a comparative disadvantage in machinery and other manufacturing. By 1990, Japanese comparative advantage had shifted to metals and to machinery, where Japanese productivity surpassed that of the United States. *(Based on the data in the table, what patterns of imports and exports would you expect between Japan and the United States based on comparative advantage? If trade were based on absolute advantage, what would you predict about U.S.–Japan trade based on the table? Which fits better with what you know about trade?)*

---

18. To obtain the second inequality from the first, multiply through by (a_{LY}/g_{LX}).

Table 4 **VALUE-ADDED PER HOUR WORKED IN MANUFACTURING, 1950–1990 (U.S. = 100)**

	1950	1965	1973	1979	1990
Germany/United States: $(1/g_{LX})/(1/a_{LX}) = (a_{LX}/g_{LX})$					
Food, beverages, tobacco	53.1	76.9	68.4	74.1	75.8
Textiles, apparel, leather	44.0	78.1	81.0	85.9	88.2
Chemicals, allied products	32.4	64.3	90.5	106.0	76.7
Basic, fabricated metals	30.9	53.6	67.2	90.1	98.8
Machinery, equipment	43.7	77.1	90.0	110.7	87.6
Other manufacturing	34.2	56.6	68.8	80.1	79.3
Japan/United States: $(1/j_{LX})/(1/a_{LX}) = (a_{LX}/j_{LX})$					
Food, beverages, tobacco	26.7	25.8	39.5	39.8	37.0
Textiles, apparel, leather	24.7	37.5	53.2	54.9	48.0
Chemicals, allied products	13.0	32.1	60.4	78.0	83.8
Basic, fabricated metals	12.5	23.1	61.4	84.3	95.6
Machinery, equipment	8.0	23.5	50.6	79.6	114.4
Other manufacturing	9.7	20.0	34.0	39.8	54.9

Source: Bart Van Ark and Dirk Pilat, "Productivity Levels in Germany, Japan, and the United States: Differences and Causes," *Brookings Papers on Economic Activity: Microeconomics* 2 (1993), p. 17.

CASE 3: WHICH PLANTS EXPORT?

David Ricardo's remarkable insight into labor productivity as a source of comparative advantage provided a clear testable prediction: If a country permits trade, its exports will come from industries with relatively high labor productivity (and, therefore, comparative advantage) and its imports from industries with relatively low labor productivity (and, therefore, comparative disadvantage). Case One provided evidence in favor of this simple but powerful prediction.

Ricardo's basic framework assumed equal labor productivity across all plants in an industry in a given country. But, in a complex modern economy, things aren't so simple; labor productivity can vary significantly between plants even in the same industry in the same country. This fact suggests a follow-up inquiry still very much in the spirit of Ricardo. If we separated plants into those that export and those that don't, would we find that exporting plants

have higher labor productivity than nonexporting ones? A group of economists recently used data from the *1992 U.S. Census of Manufactures,* which covers approximately 200,000 manufacturing plants, to find out.[19] What they discovered wouldn't have surprised Ricardo. Exporters exhibited a 33 percent labor productivity advantage over nonexporters overall and a 15 percent advantage over nonexporters within their same industry.

Figure 12 illustrates the relationship between labor productivity and exports. The research team calculated each plant's labor productivity relative to the average productivity of all plants. For example, a plant whose labor was half as productive as the average got a score of 0.50, and a plant whose labor was twice as productive as average got a score of 2.00. Plants on the left-hand side of Figure 12—those with a score lower than one—have labor productivity below

19. Andrew B. Bernard, et al., "Plants and Productivity in International Trade," *American Economic Review* 93 (September 2003), pp. 1268–1290.

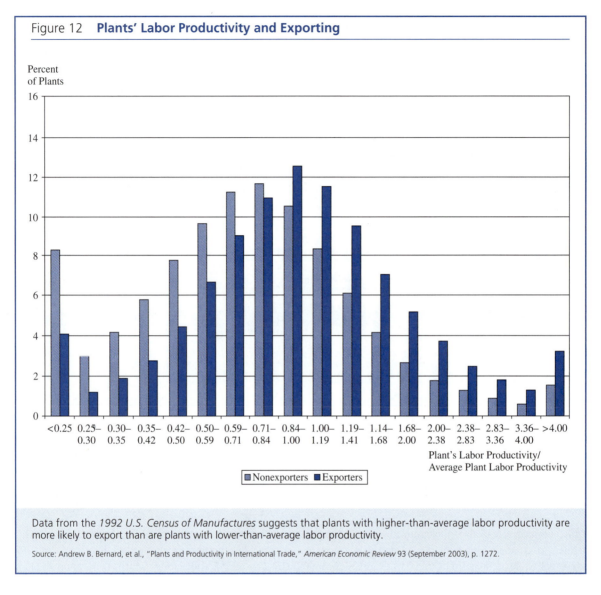

Figure 12   **Plants' Labor Productivity and Exporting**

Data from the *1992 U.S. Census of Manufactures* suggests that plants with higher-than-average labor productivity are more likely to export than are plants with lower-than-average labor productivity.

Source: Andrew B. Bernard, et al., "Plants and Productivity in International Trade," *American Economic Review* 93 (September 2003), p. 1272.

the average of all plants. Plants on the right-hand side of Figure 12—those with a score higher than one—have labor productivity above the average. Notice that the nonexporting plants tend to lie on the low-productivity (left) side of the figure and exporting plants tend to lie on the high-productivity (right) side of the figure.

Not only was Ricardo correct in his argument that industries with relatively high labor productivity would constitute a country's export industries; economists have now extended the argument to show that plants with relatively high labor productivity are more likely to constitute an industry's export plants.

SUMMARY

Early trade policies reflected mercantilism, which set a trade-policy goal of accumulating gold. Mercantilists viewed trade as a zero-sum game that distributed the available gold among countries; whatever one country gained came at the expense of another.

Adam Smith and David Ricardo forcefully challenged the zero-sum view of trade. Following the insights of Smith and Ricardo, this chapter demonstrated how trading internationally allows a country to separate its production decision from its consumption decision. Gains from trade arise when a country can specialize its production according to comparative advantage—based on differences in technology or labor productivity—and then trade with other countries to obtain its preferred set of goods for consumption. The gains in efficiency allow trade to be *mutually* beneficial.

LOOKING AHEAD

The complete production specialization predicted by the Ricardian model rarely occurs. The two-country, two-good model drastically simplifies the many-country, many-good world economy. In a more realistic setting, most countries produce more than one good, and most goods are produced in more than one country. There are at least three reasons. First, even in a two-country, two-good world, complete specialization would occur only if there were no restrictions on trade, no transportation costs, and no product differentiation, and if each country were large enough to satisfy world demand for its comparative-advantage good. Second, there are many more goods than there are countries in the world economy. If all the goods that consumers want are to be produced, at least some countries must produce more than one good. This chapter's model can easily be expanded to include many goods. We would simply rank goods according to the extent of a country's comparative advantage, and the country would produce goods high on the list and import goods low on the list. Third, and probably most important, the complete-specialization result follows directly from the assumption of constant costs; we've assumed that comparative advantage never shifts from one country to another—regardless of the degree of productive specialization. Economists observe that constant opportunity cost is the exception rather than the rule. For most production technologies, the opportunity cost of producing a good rises with the level of production. In Chapter Three, we expand our model of trade to include increasing costs. We'll also see a second major source of comparative advantage: differences in countries' factor endowments. In the process, we'll discover why trade policy has proven so enduringly controversial.

KEY TERMS

mercantilism
zero-sum game
specie-flow mechanism
perfect competition
marginal cost
autarky
production possibilities frontier
input coefficient
opportunity cost
marginal rate of transformation (MRT)
Ricardian model
constant-cost model
production opportunity set
consumption opportunity set
utility

indifference curve
marginal rate of substitution (MRS)
community indifference curve
income distribution
potential utility
autarky equilibrium
autarky relative price
absolute advantage
absolute disadvantage
comparative advantage
terms of trade
market-clearing price
trade triangles
gains from exchange
gains from specialization

PROBLEMS AND QUESTIONS FOR REVIEW

1. Let country A's endowment of labor equal 200 and country B's endowment of labor equal 200. The number of units of labor required to produce 1 unit of good X in country A equals 5, and the number of units of labor required to produce 1 unit of good Y in

country A equals 4. The number of units of labor required to produce 1 unit of good X in B equals 4, and the number of units of labor required to produce 1 unit of good Y in B equals 8.

a. Draw the production possibilities frontier for each country. Be sure to label carefully.

b. Which country has an absolute advantage in which good(s)? Why? What would a theory of absolute advantage imply about the direction of trade? Why?

c. If free trade according to absolute advantage were allowed, what degree of productive specialization would occur? Why? How much of each good would be produced?

d. Answer the questions in parts (b) and (c) for the principle of comparative advantage rather than absolute advantage.

e. How do your answers in (b) and (c) differ from those in (d)? Why?

2. Consider a world consisting of two countries, Continentia and Islandia. Each country has 500 units of labor, the only input. In Continentia, it takes 5 units of labor to produce a computer and 10 units of labor to produce a unit of textiles. In Islandia, it takes 10 units of labor to produce a computer and 5 units of labor to produce a unit of textiles.

a. Sketch each country's production possibilities frontier. Label the vertical and horizontal intercepts and the slopes.

b. What is the opportunity cost of producing a computer in Continentia? Why? What is the opportunity cost of producing a unit of textiles in Continentia? Why? What is the opportunity cost of producing a computer in Islandia? Why? What is the opportunity cost of producing a unit of textiles in Islandia? Why?

c. In autarky, what would be the relative price of computers in Continentia? In Islandia? Why?

d. Which country has a comparative advantage in producing which good? Why?

e. If Continentia and Islandia specialize according to comparative advantage, how many computers and how many units of textiles will Continentia produce? Islandia? Why?

f. After several years of trade, Continentia and Islandia pass new laws stating that half of each country's labor force must be used in each industry. In other words, half of Continentia's labor must produce computers and half must produce textiles. The same is true in Islandia. Under the new laws, how many computers and how many units of textiles will Continentia produce? Islandia? Why?

g. How big is the economic cost of the laws that restrict specialization and trade between Continentia and Islandia?

3. "There is no country whose economic circumstances prevent it from engaging in mutually beneficial trade with other countries."[20] Does this statement apply to countries with an absolute disadvantage in all goods? Why, or why not?

4. Assume that $L^A = 1,000$; $a_{LX} = 10$; $a_{LY} = 20$; $L^B = 1,000$; $b_{LX} = 20$; and $b_{LY} = 10$.

a. Sketch and label each country's production possibilities frontier.

b. Which country has a comparative advantage in which good, and why? Would trade between country A and country B be mutually beneficial? Why, or why not?

c. Now suppose that researchers in country A discover a way to produce both good X and good Y using only half as much labor as before, so now $a_{LX} = 5$ and $a_{LY} = 10$. Sketch and label the new production possibilities frontier. Which country has a comparative advantage in which good, and why? Would trade between country A and country B be mutually beneficial? Why or why not?

5. Assume that initially $L^A = 1,000$; $a_{LX} = 10$; $a_{LY} = 20$; $L^B = 1,000$; $b_{LX} = 20$; and $b_{LY} = 10$ as in question 4.

a. Suppose that researchers in country A discover a way to produce good X using only half as much labor as before, so now $a_{LX} = 5$ and $a_{LY} = 20$. Sketch and label the new production possibilities frontier. Which country has a comparative advantage in which good, and why? Would trade between country A and country B be mutually beneficial? Why or why not?

Compare your answer with that in question 4, part (c).

20. See Irwin (2002, p. 28).

b.   Now suppose, instead, that researchers in country A discover a way to produce good Y using only one-quarter as much labor as before, so now $a_{LX} = 10$ and $a_{LY} = 5$. Sketch and label the new production possibilities frontier. Which country has a comparative advantage in which good, and why? Would trade between country A and country B be mutually beneficial? Why or why not? Compare your answer with those in question 4, part (c), and in part (a) of this question.

6.   "An absolute productive advantage is not required to participate in international trade and reap the benefits of trade. But an absolute productive advantage is enormously beneficial for another reason: it translates into higher per capita income."[21] Explain. Note that per capita income is determined by the wage rate.

7.   Country A can produce 1,000 bushels of corn if it uses all its resources in the corn industry or 2,000 bushels of wheat if it uses all its resources in the wheat industry; costs are constant. Currently, country A doesn't trade and consumes 500 bushels of corn and 1,000 bushels of wheat.

a.   Draw country A's production possibilities frontier, placing corn on the horizontal axis and wheat on the vertical axis.

b.   Illustrate country A's autarky equilibrium.

c.   A trading partner offers to trade corn and wheat with country A at a price ratio of 1. Show that, even if country A continues to *produce* 500 bushels of corn and 1,000 bushels of wheat, residents of country A would be better off if they exchanged with the trading partner. Would country A export wheat or corn? Would country A import wheat or corn?

d.   Compared with part (c), how would the amount of trade change if country A specialized its production according to comparative advantage? Would country A specialize in wheat or corn? Would the country specialize partially or completely?

8.   Comment on the following statement. "The Ricardian model of trade assumes that each country's fixed endowment of labor is fully employed both in autarky and under unrestricted trade. The model also assumes that technology (labor productivity) does not change. Therefore, the world economy cannot produce more output with trade than in autarky."

REFERENCES AND SELECTED READINGS

Dornbusch, Rudiger, Stanley Fischer, and Paul Samuelson. "Comparative Advantage, Trade, and Payments in a Ricardian Model with a Continuum of Goods." *American Economic Review* 67 (December 1977): 823–839.
A modern version of the Ricardian model, with many goods; for intermediate and advanced students.

Ekelund, Robert B., Jr., and Robert D. Tollison. *Mercantilism as a Rent-Seeking Society: Economic Regulation in Historical Perspective.* College Station, Tex.: Texas A&M Press, 1981.
A modern reinterpretation of mercantilism emphasizing rent seeking; for all students.

Heckscher, Eli F. *Mercantilism.* London: Allen and Unwin, 1934.
Along with Viner (see below), one of the two classic treatises on mercantilism; for all students.

Hume, David. "Of the Balance of Trade." In *Essays, Moral, Political, and Literary.* London, 1752.
Hume's classic critique of mercantilism.

Irwin, Douglas A. *Free Trade Under Fire.* Princeton: Princeton University Press, 2002.
Highly recommended overview of the free-trade versus protection issue; for all students.

Krugman, Paul. "Ricardo's Difficult Idea: Why Intellectuals Don't Understand Comparative Advantage." In *The Economics and Politics of International Trade*, Vol. 2, edited by Gary Cook. London: Routledge, 1998.
Entertaining and informative examination of why so many otherwise-smart people still don't understand comparative advantage 200 years after Ricardo.

Krugman, Paul. "What Do Undergrads Need to Know about Trade?" *American Economic Review Papers and Proceedings* 83 (May 1993): 23–26.
An entertaining tour of the many fallacies in supposedly enlightened discussions of international trade policy. Essential reading for all students.

Ricardo, David. *The Principles of Political Economy and Taxation.* Baltimore: Penguin, 1971 (Originally published 1817).
Chapter 7 contains the original, classic version of comparative advantage. Appropriate for all students.

---

21.   See Irwin (2002, p. 28).

Smith, Adam. *An Inquiry into the Nature and Causes of the Wealth of Nations*. New York: Random House, 1937 (Originally published 1776).
The book often credited with founding economics as a discipline. The whole book is accessible to students at all levels; Books I and IV contain the specialization argument.

Sykes, Alan O. "Comparative Advantage and the Normative Economics of International Trade Policy." *Journal of International Economic Law* 1 (March 1998): 49–82.
Readable overview of the economist's insights into international trade and trade policy.

Viner, Jacob. *Studies in the Theory of International Trade.* Clifton, N.J.: Kelley, 1965 (Originally published 1937).
Along with Heckscher, one of the two classic treatises on mercantilism; for all students.

APPENDIX

WHAT CAN THE WORLD PRODUCE? THE WORLD PRODUCTION POSSIBILITIES FRONTIER

We can see the gains from trade by constructing a world production possibilities frontier that illustrates all the combinations of goods X and Y that can be produced using the world's labor according to the pattern of comparative advantage. The technique for constructing the frontier is similar to that used in section 5.1. If all the world's labor $(L^W = L^A + L^B)$ were devoted to producing good X, $[(L^A/a_{LX}) + (L^B/b_{LX})]$ units could be produced; this marks the intersection of the world production possibilities frontier and the horizontal axis at point 1 in Figure A.1. Similarly, devoting all labor to producing good Y would permit $[(L^A/a_{LY}) + (L^B/b_{LY})]$ units to be produced, representing the intersection of the world production possibilities frontier with the vertical axis at point 3 in the figure.

Even though costs of production are constant within each country, giving each *country's* production possibilities frontier a straight-line shape, the *world* production possibilities frontier *isn't* a straight line. This is true because the opportunity cost of each good differs between countries. We'll assume for the remainder of this appendix that country A has a comparative advantage in good X and country B in good Y. Any X produced should be produced first in country A, and any Y produced should come first from country B. *(Why?)* In Figure A.1, moving upward and to the left from point 1, where only good X is produced, country B begins to produce good Y; the opportunity cost is b_{LY}/b_{LX}. At point 2, country B can't produce any more good Y *(why?)*, so if we continue to move further upward and to the left, the additional good Y must be produced in country A, where the opportunity cost is $(a_{LY}/a_{LX}) > (b_{LY}/b_{LX})$. Similarly, moving downward to the right from point 3, where only good Y is being produced, country A begins to produce good X at an opportunity cost of a_{LX}/a_{LY} per unit.

Figure A.1 **What Can the World Produce?**

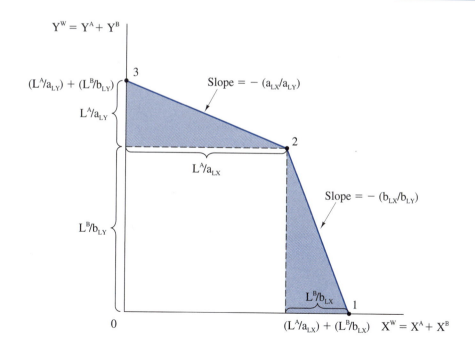

The world production possibilities frontier illustrates the combinations of goods X and Y that can be produced if countries specialize according to comparative advantage. The slopes of the two segments of the world production possibilities frontier represent opportunity costs in the two countries. Moving from point 1 toward point 3, good Y is produced first by country B (from 1 to 2) and then by country A (from 2 to 3). Moving from point 3 toward point 1, good X is produced first by country A (at opportunity cost a_{LX}/a_{LY}) and then by country B (at opportunity cost b_{LX}/b_{LY}).

At point 2, country A is completely specialized and can't produce more X. Therefore, any additional X must be produced in country B at an opportunity cost of (b_{LX}/b_{LY}). Note that the two shaded triangles in the figure correspond to the production possibilities frontiers of the two countries, A on the upper left and B on the lower right. *(Suppose the two countries specialize according to their comparative disadvantage rather than their comparative advantage. Construct the world production possibilities frontier under this assumption. How does it compare with the frontier in Figure A.1? Why?)*

3

Comparative Advantage II: Factor Endowments and Trade

1 INTRODUCTION

Chapter Two's Ricardian model of production, consumption, and trade is very useful in showing how and why trade based on differences in technology or labor productivity can be mutually beneficial. Case One in that chapter showed that repeated empirical tests support the major implication of the Ricardian model—a positive relationship between countries' relative labor productivities and relative market shares in various industries. However, another implication of the constant-cost model—complete productive specialization—fails to match what we typically observe in the world economy.[1]

Detailed studies of many industries indicate that the opportunity costs of production increase with output rather than remain constant for most goods. In this chapter, we focus on this phenomenon of increasing costs and its implications for trade. We'll see that incorporating increasing costs into the basic trade model can both explain countries' partial rather than complete specialization and reveal sources of comparative advantage beyond the differences in relative labor productivity emphasized by Ricardo. Comparative advantage merely reflects differences in opportunity costs between two countries. But why should opportunity costs differ? In the context of the Ricardian model, the only explanation is differences in the productive technologies, captured by the input coefficients that reflect labor productivity. If relative labor productivity were the same in the two countries, then goods' opportunity costs and autarky relative prices would also be the same in both countries, and there would be no potential gains from trade. Thus, although the Ricardian model powerfully demonstrates the gains from trade, we want to look for additional explanations of *why* opportunity costs might differ.

The increasing-cost model also has a second advantage: its ability to explain why international trade policy is so persistently controversial. Strong feelings on both sides of the issue always accompany trade-policy decisions; in each country, some groups advocate unrestricted trade, while others support tight restrictions on trade.

---

1. As mentioned in Chapter Two, differences in country size can result in partial specialization by one of the two countries (the large one) even with constant costs. We'll see later that two other circumstances can produce complete specialization in the increasing-cost model: highly dissimilar factor endowments across countries and highly similar factor intensities across industries.

2 THE NEOCLASSICAL WORLD WITHOUT TRADE

In this chapter, we continue to use the simplifying assumptions introduced in section 4 of Chapter Two. Again our goal is to compare the availability of goods in autarky with that under unrestricted trade. In autarky, each country must make a decision concerning the allocation of its available resources between production of two goods. This decision decides not only the country's production but also its consumption.

2.1 Production in Autarky

To incorporate the idea of increasing costs, we need a new element in the model, that is, a second factor of production. Chapter Two's constant-cost model contained only one factor of production, which we called labor; and each unit of labor was a perfect substitute for any other unit. Here, in the **Neoclassical** or **increasing-cost model**, there are two factors of production—we'll call them labor (L) and capital (K)—and they aren't equally effective in producing the two outputs, X and Y. The word *capital*, when used in trade theory, refers to durable inputs such as machines, buildings, assembly lines, and tools.

How can we represent the production technology when there are two inputs? A few products may require the two inputs in **fixed proportions**. In such cases, the technology resembles a recipe that calls for ingredients in certain proportions. A cake recipe that specifies two cups of flour and one cup of milk won't produce a cake if you reverse the proportions to one cup of flour and two of milk. Most production processes, however, offer a fairly wide range of opportunities for substituting one input for another. For example, automobiles can be built using mechanized assembly lines and robots (that is, capital) and very little labor. Automobiles also can be built almost entirely by hand, using a large quantity of labor and very little capital in the form of simple tools. The textile industry provides another example. Japan and the United States both produce textiles using sophisticated, computerized equipment and relatively little labor. At the same time, many developing countries continue to use large quantities of labor along with simple hand looms to make textiles. Economists capture these possibilities for substitution with tools called production functions and isoquants.

PRODUCTION FUNCTIONS AND ISOQUANTS   For each industry, a recipe called the **production function** specifies the maximum output firms can produce with given quantities of inputs. We denote the production functions for the X and Y industries in country A by $X^A = f_X^A(L_X^A, K_X^A)$ and $Y^A = f_Y^A(L_Y^A, K_Y^A)$. Plugging the quantities of resources used in each industry into the right-hand side of the production functions, we can determine the output of each industry. For example, if f_X^A is defined as $X^A = 2L_X^A K_X^A$, employment of 3 units of labor and 2 units of capital will produce $X^A = 2 \cdot 3 \cdot 2 = 12$ units of good X. With this production function, firms can produce a given quantity of output using a variety of combinations of labor and capital, because the two inputs are substitutes for each other. The 12 units of good X produced using 3 units of labor and 2 of capital could also be produced using, for example, 6 units of labor and 1 of capital (because $X^A = 2 \cdot 6 \cdot 1 = 12$) or 2 units of labor and 3 of capital (because $X^A = 2 \cdot 2 \cdot 3 = 12$). The graphical technique that represents these substitution possibilities is called an **isoquant** (or *same-quantity*) map. Each isoquant shows all the combinations of labor and capital with which it's possible to produce a given amount of output. Figure 1 presents an isoquant map for production of good X in country A.

Each isoquant is downward sloping and convex, and higher isoquants correspond to higher levels of output. Isoquants are downward sloping because using less of one input implies that a firm must use more of the other input to maintain the same level of output

Figure 1   **Isoquant Map for an X-Producing Firm in Country *A***

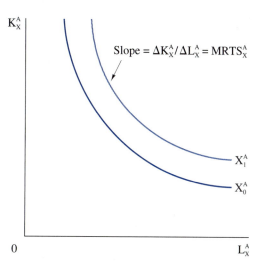

$$\text{Slope} = \Delta K_X^A / \Delta L_X^A = MRTS_X^A$$

Each isoquant depicts all the combinations of labor and capital that can produce a given level of output of good X in country A. Each isoquant is downward sloping, reflecting substitutability of inputs, and convex. Higher isoquants represent higher levels of output (for example, $X_1^A > X_0^A$).

(that is, to stay on the same isoquant). In other words, the negative slope of an isoquant represents the fact that the two inputs are substitutes—using less of one requires using more of the other. The slope of an isoquant represents the rate at which producers can substitute one input for the other; this rate is called the **marginal rate of technical substitution (MRTS)**. The convexity of the isoquant implies that this rate changes along the curve. As the firm uses more labor and less capital (moving down and to the right along an isoquant), it becomes more difficult to substitute additional labor for capital. The amount of additional labor required to compensate for a given reduction in capital increases.

Given all the possible combinations of labor and capital for producing a given level of good X in country A, we must specify how X-producing firms choose a particular production process. Firms' profits equal total revenue minus total cost; so a firm wants to produce its output at minimum cost. Assuming there are only two inputs, total costs for an X-producing firm in country A equal the wage rate in A (w^A) times the quantity of labor employed (L_X^A) plus the rental rate for capital (r^A) times the quantity of capital employed (K_X^A). The wage rate and the rental rate for capital are called **factor prices** or **factor rewards**.[2] Total costs can be represented as $C = w^A L_X^A + r^A K_X^A$. For example, if the wage rate in country A equals $10 per unit of labor and the rental rate for capital is $15 per unit, the total cost for a firm that employs 3 units of labor and 2 units of capital would be $C = \$10 \cdot 3 + \$15 \cdot 2 = \$60$.

2. Capital inputs provide productive services for more than one period. For example, a machine may last many years even though a firm must purchase it only once. The cost of using such a machine for one period isn't its purchase price but only a portion of that price. Economists refer to the cost of using the machine for one period as the *rental rate, r*, because it corresponds to the cost of renting the machine for one period rather than purchasing it. Of course, the same holds true for labor, since the wage rate represents the cost of "renting" a unit of labor for a specified period, not the price of buying a worker!

Figure 2   **Costs of Different Input Combinations for an X-Producing Firm in Country *A***

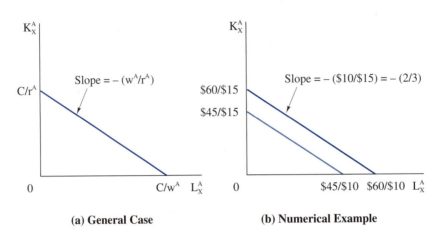

(a) General Case   **(b) Numerical Example**

An isocost line depicts all combinations of labor and capital a firm could hire with a given total cost of C. The (absolute) slope of each isocost equals the ratio of the input prices, –(w/r). Higher isocost lines correspond to higher levels of total costs.

Using the expression for total cost, we can draw a line that represents all the combinations of L and K a firm could hire for a given level of total cost, as in Figure 2. If the firm hired only capital, how many units could it hire? The answer is given by the amount of total cost (C) divided by the rental rate (for example, $C/r^A = \$60/\$15 = 4$); this defines the vertical intercept of an isocost line (or *same-cost* line). Similarly, if the firm hired only labor, the maximum number of units it could hire for a total cost of C would be C/w^A, or $\$60/\$10 = 6$. (*Why?*) Connecting these two points yields the **isocost line**, which comprises all the possible combinations of labor and capital the firm could hire for a total cost of C given factor prices of w^A and r^A. The slope of the isocost line is $-(w^A/r^A)$, or $-(2/3)$. (*Why?*)[3] The isocost line for a lower level of total cost (such as $45) would lie parallel to the one drawn for C = $60 in Figure 2, but shifted in toward the origin.

We can combine Figures 1 and 2 to illustrate the profit-maximizing firm's choice of production process. For any specified level of output, the firm produces it at minimum cost by choosing the point on the isoquant that lies on the lowest possible isocost line. This occurs at the point of tangency between the isoquant and the isocost line in Figure 3. The firm produces output X_0^A using L_X^{A*} units of labor and K_X^{A*} units of capital at a total cost of $C^* = w^A L_X^{A*} + r^A K_X^{A*}$. At the chosen point, the relative factor prices (given by the absolute slope of the isocost line) just equal the rate at which the firm can substitute the two inputs while maintaining a constant level of output (given by the absolute slope of the isoquant, or the marginal rate of technical substitution). In other words, at this point the rate at which the two inputs can be

---

3. The slope of a line is defined as the rise, or vertical change, divided by the run, or horizontal change. Between the vertical and horizontal intercepts of the isocost line, the vertical change, or change in capital purchased, is $-(C/r^A)$; the horizontal change, or change in labor purchased, is (C/w^A). Therefore, the slope is $-(C/r^A)/(C/w^A) = -(w^A/r^A)$. With a wage rate of $10 and a rental rate of $15, the slope of the isocost would be $-(2/3)$. Hiring an additional unit of labor would require the firm to hire two-thirds units less capital to keep total cost unchanged.

Figure 3   How Will a Firm in Country _A_ Produce Good X?

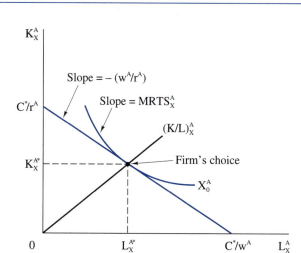

The profit-maximizing firm produces its output at the minimum possible total cost. The point of tangency of an isoquant with an isocost line represents this decision. The firm uses L_X^{A*} units of labor and K_X^{A*} units of capital to produce X_0^A units of output. The slope of the straight line from the origin through the production point indicates the capital-labor ratio.

---

substituted while keeping total _cost_ constant equals the rate at which they can be substituted while keeping _output_ constant.

THE CAPITAL-LABOR RATIO   The ratio of capital to labor the firm chooses to use, K_X^{A*}/L_X^{A*}, is called the **capital-labor ratio**. The slope of a ray through the origin and the chosen production point gives the capital-labor ratio in Figure 3.[4] We can easily relate the capital-labor ratio to the input coefficients from Chapter Two.[5] Dividing both K_X^{A*} and L_X^{A*} by the number of units of X being produced gives the number of units of capital and labor used to produce each unit of good X. This corresponds to the definition of the input coefficients from Chapter Two, except that now there are _two_ coefficients for the X industry in country A: $a_{KX} = K_X^{A*}/X_0^A$ and $a_{LX} = L_X^{A*}/X_0^A$. The first coefficient represents the number of units of capital used to produce a unit of good X in country A, and the second the number of units of labor used to produce a unit of X in A. Note that $K_X^{A*}/L_X^{A*} = a_{KX}/a_{LX}$.

The major difference between these coefficients and the ones in Chapter Two is that these aren't constants but depend on the relative prices of the two factors of production.

---

4. At any point along the ray, the vertical distance from the origin measures the amount of capital used, while the horizontal distance from the origin measures the quantity of labor. Using the rise/run formula for the slope of a line, the slope of a ray from the origin is K_X^A/L_X^A.

5. We'll restrict our attention to production processes in which the firm would choose the same capital-labor ratio regardless of the level of output as long as factor prices remained the same. Production functions that satisfy this condition are called _homothetic_. In economic terms, the marginal rate of technical substitution depends only on the capital-labor ratio, not on the level of output. Graphically, this implies that the tangencies of all isoquants with the corresponding isocost lines lie along a straight line from the origin as long as factor prices don't change. We also assume that constant returns to scale characterize production. This means that changing the usage of both inputs by a certain proportion changes output by that same proportion; we'll relax this assumption in Chapter Five.

The input coefficients have become economic choices. In the constant-cost model, a firm in country A had only one way to produce a unit of good X: Use a_{LX} units of labor. Now the firm can choose from among all the combinations of labor and capital along an isoquant, and the profit-maximizing firm will choose based on the relative prices of the two inputs. For example, a fall in the wage rate relative to the rental rate causes the firm to use more labor and less capital to produce any given output—that is, the capital-labor ratio falls. (*How can you demonstrate this graphically in Figure 3?*)

New General Motors plants around the world provide an example of how a firm's capital-labor ratio responds to different factor prices. Ninety-five percent of the tasks performed at GM's state-of-the-art facility in Eisenach, Germany, are automated (that is, performed using large quantities of capital and little labor) because of Germany's very high labor costs, the highest in the world by most measures. But at GM's even newer facility in Rosario, Argentina, where labor costs are relatively low, only 45 percent of tasks are automated.[6]

Firms that produce good Y in country A go through the same type of decision process as X-producing firms. Each firm chooses its production process to minimize costs, and the choice can be summarized by the ratio of the input coefficients, a_{KY}/a_{LY}. The important point is that the ratios of input coefficients generally will *differ* for the two industries even if the two industries face the *same* relative factor prices, as they will due to mobility of factors within the country. For example, in Figure 4, steel-producing firms choose a production technique that uses a large quantity of capital relative to labor, and

---

Figure 4 Industries Differ in Their Capital-Labor Ratios

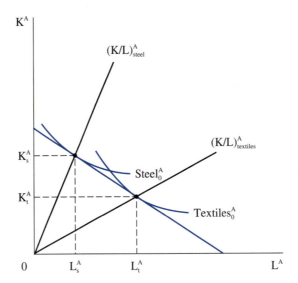

Although both industries in an economy face the same relative factor prices because factors are mobile between industries, industries generally choose different capital-labor ratios. This tendency for industries to utilize factors in different proportions or intensities carries important implications for international trade.

---

6. "GM Is Building Plants in Developing Nations to Woo New Markets," *The Wall Street Journal*, August 4, 1997.

textile firms choose one using more labor relative to capital, even though both industries face the same relative prices for labor and capital.

If $(a_{KX}/a_{LX}) > (a_{KY}/a_{LY})$, good X is the **capital-intensive good**. Note that what matters is the amount of capital used *relative* to labor, not just the amount of capital. Perhaps good Y requires more of both labor and capital than does good X (for example, $a_{LX} = 2$, $a_{KX} = 4$, $a_{LY} = 3$, and $a_{KY} = 5$). Nevertheless, if good X requires *relatively* more capital ($4/2 > 5/3$), good X is capital intensive. With only two goods and two factors of production, the statement that good X is capital intensive is equivalent to the statement that good Y is **labor intensive**. (*Why?*)[7] In Figure 4, steel is the capital-intensive industry and textiles the labor-intensive one.

Table 1 illustrates differences among industries' factor intensities by reporting the ten most capital-intensive and ten most unskilled-labor-intensive industries in the United States in the early 1990s. Notice in the table that seven of the ten most-capital-intensive industries (in italics) also appear on the least-unskilled-labor-intensive list; and six of the most-unskilled-labor-intensive industries, again in italics, also appear on the least-capital-intensive list. If the

---

Table 1 FACTOR INTENSITIES OF U.S. INDUSTRIES

Ten Most-Capital-Intensive Industries	Ten Most-Unskilled-Labor-Intensive Industries
Cigarettes	*Gray iron foundries*
Flavoring extracts and syrups	*Industrial patterns*
Cereal breakfast foods	*Textile goods*
Wet corn milling	*Schiffli machine embroideries*
Dog and cat food	Footwear, except rubber
Agricultural chemicals	Leather gloves and mittens
Roasted coffee	Wood TV and radio cabinets
Distilled liquor, except brandy	Textile bags
Pharmaceutical preparations	*Special dyes, tools, jigs, and fixtures*
Industrial gases	*Ship building and repairing*

Ten Least-Capital-Intensive Industries	Ten Least-Unskilled-Labor-Intensive Industries
Textile goods	*Flavoring extracts and syrups*
Elevators and moving stairways	*Cigarettes*
Gray iron foundries	Periodicals
Industrial patterns	Book publishing
Rolling mill machinery	*Pharmaceutical preparations*
Ship building and repairing	*Agricultural chemicals*
Machine tools, metal forming types	*Industrial gases*
Special dyes, tools, jigs, and fixtures	*Wet corn milling*
Schiffli machine embroideries	*Roasted coffee*
Electronic computers	Electronic computers

Source: John Romalis, "Factor Proportions and the Structure of Commodity Trade," *American Economic Review* (March 2004), p. 79.

---

7. The inequality that defines good X as capital intensive directly implies that $(a_{LY}/a_{KY}) > (a_{LX}/a_{KX})$, the definition of labor intensity of good Y.

data used to create the lists in Table 1 included just two factors, unskilled labor and capital, then the "most" and "least" lists would correspond exactly: the most-capital-intensive industries would be the least-unskilled-labor-intensive ones, and vice versa. The reason that Table 1 contains a few exceptions to the rule is that the data on which the table is based include a third factor of production, skilled labor; so, for example, the highly capital-intensive cereal breakfast foods industry also appears on the least-skill-intensive list, which is omitted from Table 1 because we're restricting our attention to two factors of production.

The production technologies summarized by the four input coefficients provide one of the two pieces of information necessary to sketch country A's production possibilities frontier. The other required information is A's endowment of labor and capital. We assume that country A has L^A units of labor and K^A units of capital. The fact that firms will produce the two outputs using the two factors in different proportions (or different *intensities*) implies that the production possibilities frontier is no longer a straight line as in Chapter Two's constant-cost model; rather, it's concave, or bowed out from the origin. Suppose good X is capital intensive, good Y is labor intensive, and country A is currently at point 1 in Figure 5, producing a large amount of Y and a small amount of X. As the country changes its production along the frontier from point 1 toward point 2, reduced production of good Y (the labor-intensive good) releases relatively large amounts of labor and small amounts of capital. These released resources are in the "wrong" proportion for the X industry, which is capital intensive. The further the country moves toward point 2, the greater the adjustment that industry X must make in its production process to absorb the resources released by the shrinking Y industry. This increasingly difficult adjustment implies that successive reductions in Y production lead to smaller and smaller increases in the output of good X. This phenomenon is represented graphically by the concavity of the production possibilities frontier.

Figure 5   What Can a Country Produce under Increasing Costs?

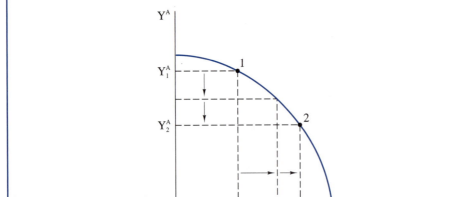

With two factors of production unequally suited to producing the two outputs, the production possibilities frontier bows out from the origin. Reduced production of good Y releases resources in the "wrong" proportion for the X industry. Adjustment becomes increasingly difficult as more and more X is produced, causing X's opportunity cost to rise.

The (absolute value of the) slope of the production possibilities frontier at each point along the curve represents the opportunity cost of good X in terms of forgone good Y. (*Why?*) As country A produces more and more X along with less and less Y, the opportunity cost of X rises. Similarly, the opportunity cost of producing Y (= 1/absolute slope of the production possibilities frontier) increases as A produces more and more Y along with less and less X. The marginal rate of transformation (MRT^A) no longer is constant as in the constant-cost model of Chapter Two; it now depends on the particular combination of X and Y that country A produces. Opportunity costs rise with production because the two factors of production aren't perfect substitutes for each other; they aren't equally well suited to producing both goods. Efficient production of goods X and Y requires that the two inputs be used with differing intensities in the two industries.

2.2 Equilibrium in Autarky

The indifference-curve technique used in Chapter Two to represent tastes for the two goods also applies under conditions of increasing costs. The production possibilities frontier defines the production opportunity set. In autarky, the country's consumption possibilities are limited to these same combinations of X and Y. Residents will choose the point in the opportunity set that lies on the highest attainable indifference curve, thereby maximizing utility subject to the constraint imposed by resource availability and technology. Figure 6 illustrates this result.

Country A reaches the highest attainable level of utility at point A*, the tangency of indifference curve U$_0^A$ with the production possibilities frontier. The autarky equilibrium involves production and consumption of X^{A*} units of good X and Y^{A*} units of good Y. At the

Figure 6   What Would Countries *A* and *B* Produce and Consume in Autarky with Increasing Costs?

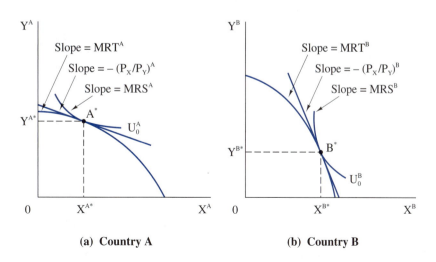

(a) Country A   (b) Country B

Country A locates at the tangency of the highest attainable indifference curve and the production possibilities frontier. The absolute slope of the production possibilities frontier at A* gives the opportunity cost and the relative price of good X. In autarky, country B produces and consumes at B*, thereby achieving the highest level of utility attainable given the constraint imposed by the availability of resources and technology.

equilibrium, the opportunity cost of X in terms of Y is given by the (absolute) slope of the production possibilities frontier at point A*. All markets are perfectly competitive, so the relative price of good X must equal its opportunity cost; thus, the relative price of X in autarky is given by the (absolute) slope of a line tangent to the production possibilities frontier at A*. Therefore, *in autarky equilibrium, $MRT^A = MRS^A = -(P_X/P_Y)^A$*. These conditions ensure that country A produces so as to achieve the highest possible level of satisfaction given its available resources and technology. The rate at which it's possible to transform good X into good Y in country A (along the production possibilities frontier) equals the rate at which residents of A willingly trade off consumption of the two goods (along the indifference curve). However, by introducing country B as a potential trading partner for country A, we can demonstrate that trade will allow A to achieve an outcome superior to A*, the best possible in autarky.

Country B has L^B units of labor and K^B units of capital to allocate between production of goods X and Y. Firms in each industry in country B choose among all the possible production techniques and select the combination of labor and capital that minimizes the cost of production. The chosen production processes can be summarized by the input coefficients (b_{LX} and b_{KX} for the X industry and b_{LY} and b_{KY} for the Y industry), which, like the coefficients in country A, aren't constants but choices that depend on the relative prices of the two factors of production in country B. The factor endowment and the production technology in B combine to determine the production possibilities frontier. In Figure 6, country B's autarky equilibrium lies at B*, where the production possibilities frontier is tangent to the highest attainable indifference curve. The (absolute) slope of the production possibilities frontier at B* equals the opportunity cost of producing good X in country B. The (absolute) slope of the indifference curve at B* gives the MRS^B, or the rate at which residents of country B willingly trade off consumption of the two goods. All markets are perfectly competitive, so the relative price of each good must equal its opportunity cost; thus, the (absolute) slope of a line tangent to the production possibilities frontier at B* measures the relative price of good X in autarky in country B.

3 THE NEOCLASSICAL WORLD WITH TRADE

In autarky, each country's production opportunity set coincides with its consumption opportunity set. Opening up the possibility of trade between countries A and B creates an opportunity for residents of each country to consume combinations of the two goods that lie *outside* the respective production possibilities frontiers. Once again, the key to increased consumption with trade is found in the difference between the autarky relative prices in the two countries.

3.1 Productive Specialization

In the Neoclassical model, country A is defined as having a **comparative advantage** in production of good X if the relative price of X in A, $(P_X/P_Y)^A$, is lower than that in B, $(P_X/P_Y)^B$. Because all markets are perfectly competitive, this condition also implies that good X's opportunity cost is lower in A than in B. Graphically, country A has a comparative advantage in good X if the slope of the relative price line in Figure 6 representing A's autarky equilibrium is flatter than that representing B's.

Just as in Chapter Two's constant-cost model, comparative advantage here is a natural extension of the concept of opportunity cost. However, in the increasing-cost model, comparative advantage is defined by comparing autarky relative *prices* (which reflect opportunity costs) rather than by directly comparing opportunity *costs*. The reason is that, under increasing costs, opportunity costs vary along the production possibilities frontier. By using autarky relative prices, we specify at what points along the two production possibilities frontiers to compare the opportunity costs. This observation points out an important difference between the constant- and increasing-cost models. In both models, determining the direction of comparative advantage involves comparing the slopes of the production possibilities frontiers. Under constant costs, the slope of each frontier is a constant; thus, the determination of comparative advantage doesn't depend on the country's particular location along the frontier. This implies that tastes play no role in the constant-cost model in determining comparative advantage *(why?)*; advantage is determined on the "supply" side of the model by technology rather than on the "demand" side by tastes. Under increasing costs, the determination of comparative advantage requires that we specify the exact points on the production possibilities frontiers at which to compare the opportunity costs, because costs change along the frontiers. As we'll see later in section 4.2, this fact allows tastes a role in determining comparative advantage.

In Figure 6, country A has a comparative advantage in production of good X. *(Why?)* This implies that country B has a comparative advantage in production of good Y. *(Why?)* Suppose each country begins to produce more of its comparative-advantage good and less of its comparative-disadvantage good. Each additional unit of good X produced in country A requires forgoing fewer units of good Y than when that unit of X was produced in country B. Similarly, each additional unit of good Y produced in country B requires forgoing fewer units of good X than when that unit of Y was produced in country A. Therefore, specialization according to comparative advantage allows total output to expand; more of one good can be produced *without* producing less of the other good.

In Chapter Two's constant-cost model, this process of specialization continued until each country produced *only* its good of comparative advantage. Will the complete-specialization result continue to hold under increasing costs? Probably not. Figure 7 illustrates why. As each country begins to specialize by moving along its

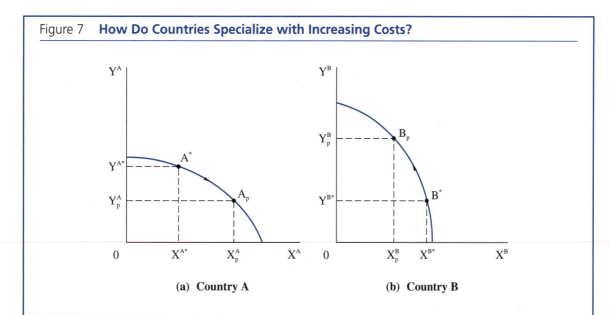

Figure 7 **How Do Countries Specialize with Increasing Costs?**

(a) Country A

(b) Country B

From the autarky equilibrium, A^*, country A specializes in its comparative-advantage good, X. As country A produces more X and less Y, the opportunity cost and relative price of good X rise while those of good Y fall. From the autarky equilibrium at B^*, country B increases production of good Y until the opportunity cost of each of the two goods equalizes with that in country A. Specialization continues to point A_p, where the slope of A's production possibilities frontier equals the slope of country B's at B_p.

production possibilities frontier in the direction of its comparative-advantage good, the opportunity cost of producing that good rises and the cost of producing the comparative-disadvantage good falls. As the cost of producing good X rises in country A and falls in country B, eventually costs in the two countries equalize. Similarly, as the cost of producing good Y rises in country B and falls in country A, costs in the two countries eventually converge. When the cost of producing each good becomes equal in the two countries, the advantage to *further* productive specialization disappears. The optimal degree of productive specialization occurs at points A_p and B_p (the p subscripts denote *production*), where the slopes of the two production possibilities frontiers are equal.[8] Country A produces X_p^A and Y_p^A, and country B produces X_p^B and Y_p^B. Notice that if the two countries' autarky prices (and therefore opportunity costs) were equal, there would be no comparative advantage and no reason to specialize.

The condition illustrated in Figure 7 ensures that production is allocated efficiently between the two countries or according to comparative advantage. However, this condition alone isn't sufficient to determine exactly which combinations of goods X and Y the two countries will produce. After all, there are many potential pairs of points at which the slopes of the two production possibilities frontiers are equal; points A_p and B_p in the figure constitute only one possible pair that satisfies the equal-slope requirement. At which of these pairs will production actually occur? To answer this question, we must bring tastes back in.

3.2 International Equilibrium with Trade

Once productive specialization has occurred so that each good's opportunity costs are equalized between the two countries, the goods' relative prices also will be equal in A and B. (*Why?*) Of all the possible sets of relative prices, at which one will trade actually occur? The market-clearing or equilibrium terms of trade will be the one at which the quantity of good X that country A wants to export equals the quantity of X that country B wants to import, and the quantity of Y that B wants to export equals the quantity that A wants to import. This is the international version of the definition of the **equilibrium price** of any good: the price at which quantity demanded equals quantity supplied. In panel (a) of Figure 8, country A can trade along the common relative price line representing the international terms of trade to the point of tangency with the highest attainable indifference curve. This occurs at point A_c, which is A's optimal consumption point under unrestricted trade (the c subscript denotes *consumption*). Country A produces at A_p, exports $(X_p^A - X_c^A)$ units of good X to country B, and imports $(Y_c^A - Y_p^A)$ units of Y from country B.

Panel (b) of Figure 8 represents country B's equilibrium. Residents of B can trade with those of A along the terms-of-trade line. The utility-maximizing consumption choice is B_c. Country B imports $(X_c^B - X_p^B)$ from country A in exchange for exporting $(Y_p^B - Y_c^B)$ to A.

Unrestricted trade expands each country's consumption opportunity set by allowing residents to trade at the international terms of trade and to obtain consumption combinations that lie outside the production possibilities frontiers and therefore couldn't be produced domestically. It would be impossible for country A to produce X_c^A units of good X and Y_c^A

---

8. It is theoretically possible for two countries to have factor endowments *so* different that no pair of points exists at which the two countries' production possibilities frontiers have the same slope. In this case, each country will specialize completely in its good of comparative advantage (as in the Ricardian model). Countries may also specialize completely if the two industries have very similar factor intensities. In this case, opportunity costs are increasing only slightly, so the production possibilities frontier will be only slightly concave (that is, almost a straight line); and the outcome is like that of the Ricardian model.

Figure 8 What Do Countries Produce and Consume under Free Trade with Increasing Costs?

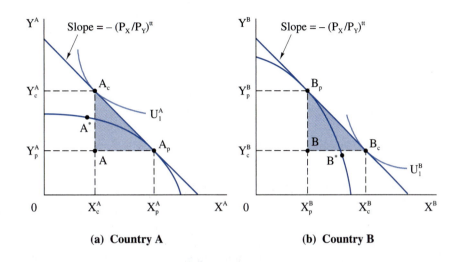

(a) Country A   (b) Country B

Country A specializes production in its comparative-advantage good, X, until the opportunity cost of X equalizes in the two countries. Trade occurs along the terms-of-trade line until country A reaches its highest attainable indifference curve at point A_c. The trade triangle is AA_cA_p. Country B specializes in producing good Y until the cost of Y equalizes in the two countries at B_p. Trade occurs along the international terms-of-trade line until country B reaches its highest attainable indifference curve at B_c. The trade triangle for B is BB_pB_c.

Table 2 EFFECTS OF TRADE

	Autarky	Free Trade	Effect of Trade
Labor-Abundant Country A:			
Production	Point A* in Figure 8(a)	Point A_p in Figure 8(a)	X⇑, Y⇓
Consumption	Point A* in Figure 8(a)	Point A_c in Figure 8(a)	X⇑, Y⇑
Prices	$(P_X/P_Y)^A$ = slope of ppf at A*	$(P_X/P_Y)^{tt}$ = slope of ppf at A_p	(P_X/P_Y)⇑
Exports	None	$(X_p^A - X_c^A)$	Exports X
Imports	None	$(Y_c^A - Y_p^A)$	Imports Y
Capital-Abundant Country B:			
Production	Point B* in Figure 8(b)	Point B_p in Figure 8(b)	X⇓, Y⇑
Consumption	Point B* in Figure 8(b)	Point B_c in Figure 8(b)	X⇑, Y⇑
Prices	$(P_X/P_Y)^B$ = slope of ppf at B*	$(P_X/P_Y)^{tt}$ = slope of ppf at B_p	(P_X/P_Y)⇓
Exports	None	$(Y_p^b - Y_c^B)$	Exports Y
Imports	None	$(X_c^B - X_p^B)$	Imports X

units of good Y, and country B couldn't produce X_c^B and Y_c^B. Trade also equalizes the opportunity cost of each good across countries by increasing production of each good in the low-cost (comparative-advantage) country and decreasing production in the high-cost (comparative-disadvantage) one. Table 2 summarizes trade's effects on production, consumption, prices, exports, and imports for each good in each country.

4 SOURCES OF COMPARATIVE ADVANTAGE

Under increasing costs, a country has comparative advantage in production of goods whose relative prices are lower there in autarky than in the other country. So, to locate the sources of comparative advantage, it's necessary to examine the determinants of relative prices. As illustrated in Figure 6, the interaction of supply (resource availability and technology as summarized in the production possibilities frontier) and demand (tastes as summarized by the indifference curves) determines relative prices in each country. So differences in relative prices can originate from differences in resource availability, technology, tastes, or some combination thereof. We examined the role of technology or labor productivity differences in Chapter Two. Here we restrict our attention to the possible effects of differences in resource endowments and tastes in determining comparative advantage by assuming that the two countries use the same technologies.

4.1 The Role of Factor Endowments

Two Swedish economists, Eli Heckscher and Bertil Ohlin, pointed out the importance of differences between countries' endowments of various factors of production in determining patterns of opportunity costs. To demonstrate the role of factor endowments, Heckscher and Ohlin used several simplifying assumptions. In addition to the basic assumptions we've used throughout the first two chapters (see section 4 of Chapter Two), they assumed that tastes and technology did not differ between countries, that countries differed in factor abundance, and that goods differed in factor intensity.

FACTOR ABUNDANCE First, we must define what Heckscher and Ohlin meant by the assumption that countries differ in **factor abundance**. Country A is **capital abundant** if $(K^A/L^A) > (K^B/L^B)$—that is, if A has more capital per unit of labor than does country B. Note that A could actually have *less* capital than B yet still be capital abundant (for example, if $K^A = 50$, $L^A = 50$, $K^B = 100$, and $L^B = 150$, so that $K^A/L^A = 1$ and $K^B/L^B = 2/3$). What matters is a comparison of capital *per unit of labor*, or the *ratio* of capital to labor, in the two countries. Given two factors and two countries, if country A is capital abundant, country B must be **labor abundant**. *(Why?)* Table 3 highlights the significant differences among countries' factor endowments. *(Which country is most capital abundant? Least capital abundant?)*

THE HECKSCHER-OHLIN THEOREM Heckscher and Ohlin combined the notion of factor *abundance* with the idea that different goods involve different factor *intensities* to infer that a country will have a comparative advantage in the good whose production involves intensive use of that country's abundant factor.[9] Further, under unrestricted trade, the country will export the good in which it has a comparative advantage and import the good whose production involves intensive use of the factor that the country possesses in relative scarcity. We assume that if good X is the capital-intensive good in country A (that is, if $[a_{KX}/a_{LX}] > [a_{KY}/a_{LY}]$), it also will be capital intensive in country B ($[b_{KX}/b_{LX}] > [b_{KY}/b_{LY}]$).[10]

As an example, assume that country A is labor abundant ($[L^A/K^A] > [L^B/K^B]$) and good X is labor intensive ($[a_{KX}/a_{LX}] < [a_{KY}/a_{LY}]$ and $[b_{KX}/b_{LX}] < [b_{KY}/b_{LY}]$). These two

---

9. Don't make the mistake of confusing factor abundance and factor intensity. Abundance refers to *countries' endowments* of factors of production. Intensity refers to *industries' usage* of factors of production. For example, the Philippines is (compared with the United States) labor abundant, and the textile industry is (compared with the aircraft industry) labor intensive.

10. The case in which a good is capital intensive in one country but labor intensive in the other is known as a *factor-intensity reversal*. We assume that such reversals do not occur.

Table 3	**CAPITAL-PER-WORKER ENDOWMENTS, 1990**				
Country	Capital/Labor ($1,000/L)	Country	Capital/Labor ($1,000/L)	Country	Capital/Labor ($1,000/L)
Argentina	$ 8	Greece	$24	Norway	$60
Australia	58	Guatemala	4	Panama	9
Austria	48	India	3	Philippines	5
Belgium	52	Ireland	37	Portugal	19
Bolivia	3	Israel	32	South Africa	12
Brazil	14	Italy	50	Spain	46
Canada	66	Japan	56	Sri Lanka	5
Chile	18	Jordan	13	Sweden	49
Colombia	10	Kenya	1	Thailand	9
Costa Rica	10	Korea	32	Turkey	13
Denmark	43	Malaysia	23	United Kingdom	39
Ecuador	13	Mauritius	7	Uruguay	10
Finland	64	Mexico	18	United States	63
France	57	Netherlands	50	Venezuela	19
Germany	54	New Zealand	46	Zimbabwe	2

Source: Peter K. Schott, "One Size Fits All? Heckscher-Ohlin Specialization in Global Production," *American Economic Review* (June 2003), p. 693.

conditions imply that A has a resource endowment relatively well suited to production of good X, and B a resource endowment relatively well suited to production of Y. For example, the United States has a resource endowment well suited to the production of wheat; the country is farmland abundant, and wheat is a farmland-intensive good. China has a resource endowment well suited to the production of apparel; China is labor abundant, and apparel is a labor-intensive industry. The production possibilities frontier of each country reflects a **production bias** toward the good of comparative advantage, as shown in the two panels of Figure 9.

If tastes were identical in the two countries, as Heckscher and Ohlin assumed, the autarky price of wheat would be lower in the United States and that of apparel lower in China.[11] Each country would be the low-cost producer of the good that used its abundant factor intensively. Under unrestricted trade, each country would specialize in and export the good that used the abundant factor intensively because of that good's low autarky price. This result is known as the **Heckscher-Ohlin theorem**. (*Using Table 3 and the Heckscher-Ohlin theorem, name a country you would expect to export capital-intensive goods. Name a country you would expect to export labor-intensive goods. What do you know about the trade of the countries you named? Does it fit your predictions?*)

A theory of trade based *solely* on production bias due to factor endowments is somewhat artificial. Under conditions of increasing costs, tastes and productive possibilities

---

11. The assumption of identical tastes in the two countries does *not* imply that residents of each will consume the two goods in equal quantities or in equal proportions. Identical tastes are defined as identical sets of indifference curves. Imagine a set of homothetic indifference curves drawn on a piece of transparent plastic and placed over two graphs, one containing each country's production possibilities frontier. Even though the indifference curves are identical, the actual consumption point chosen in each graph might differ because of the differences between production possibilities. Only when consumers in both countries face the same output prices, as they would under free trade, would identical indifference-curve maps imply identical or proportional consumption choices.

Figure 9   How Do Differences in Factor Abundance Affect What Countries Can Produce?

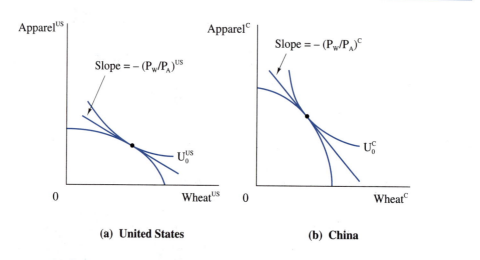

(a) United States   **(b) China**

Each country's production possibilities frontier exhibits a bias toward the axis representing the good whose production involves *intensive* use of that country's *abundant* factor of production. This production bias creates a tendency for each country to have a comparative advantage in the good that uses the abundant factor intensively.

interact to determine comparative advantage. What ultimately matters is the comparison of autarky price ratios in the two countries. This is distinct from the constant-cost case, in which comparative advantage is determined on the supply side (by the production possibilities frontier) with demand conditions (tastes) determining the volume of trade.

4.2 The Role of Tastes

Although the simplest Heckscher-Ohlin model assumes that the production bias resulting from differences in factor endowments forms the basis for trade, there are other possibilities.[12] For example, two countries could have identical production possibilities frontiers (that is, identical factor endowments and technology) but very different tastes. The taste differences could produce different autarky price ratios, as shown in Figure 10, and a basis for mutually beneficial trade.

In Figure 10, residents of country A have tastes biased toward consumption of good Y, and residents of country B have tastes biased toward consumption of good X. With identical production possibilities, the strong demand for Y in A and for X in B result in different relative prices in each country. This **taste bias** gives country A a comparative advantage in production of good X. Under unrestricted trade, A would specialize in X and B in Y even though the countries' production possibilities are identical. When Heckscher-Ohlin's identical-taste assumption is relaxed and both factor endowments and tastes are allowed to differ, the taste bias can reinforce, partially offset, or totally

---

12. Chapter Two covered technology as a source of comparative advantage. In Chapter Five, we'll add economies of scale as a basis for mutually beneficial trade not based on comparative advantage.

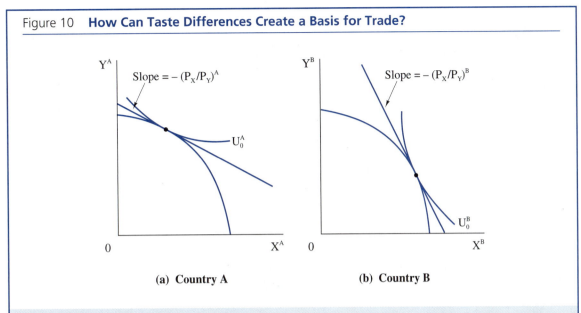

Figure 10 **How Can Taste Differences Create a Basis for Trade?**

(a) Country A

(b) Country B

If tastes differ between countries A and B, the autarky price ratios will differ even if the production possibilities are identical, and a basis for mutually beneficial trade will exist.

offset the production bias. Unlike in the constant-cost case, tastes can play a significant role in determining the direction of comparative advantage. Most empirical studies indicate that tastes exhibit a **home bias**; that is, residents of a country tend to consume relatively large quantities of goods produced there and relatively small quantities of goods produced only abroad.

CASE 1: LIGHTS-OUT FACTORIES

Changes in technology can alter firms' options for substituting capital and labor in their production processes. Lights-out factories—where machines produce for hours in the dark with little or no human intervention—provide one dramatic example.[13] In some cases, computer-operated machines are reliable enough to run without human monitors. In other cases, machines are linked to the Internet so monitors can check performance or make needed repairs from a distance.

These technologies change firms' factor intensities in two ways. First, capital usage rises relative to labor. Second, the labor used switches from less skilled to more skilled as

workers' jobs change from actually making or assembling the final product to monitoring, maintaining, and repairing the complex machines that perform the production and assembly.

When the recently completed $300 million Steel Dynamics plant in Indiana reaches its full output capacity of 1.3 million tons of steel, it will do so using fewer than 400 workers, including the office staff—only 10–20 percent of the workforce that would have been required using earlier steel technology. Workers on the plant floor monitor computers that run the machines that pour molten steel into molds, measure the steel's chemical content, and finally create steel rails and beams.

13. See Timothy Aeppel, "Workers Not Included," *The Wall Street Journal*, November 19, 2002; Clare Ansberry, "Less Sweat, More Tech," *The Wall Street Journal*, June 30, 2003; and Robert Guy Matthews, "A Steelworker's Lonely Life," *The Wall Street Journal*, June 30, 2003.

CASE 2: **FROM FISH TO INFORMATION TECHNOLOGY**

Iceland

What would the Heckscher-Ohlin model predict about the comparative advantage of Iceland, a small (population 283,000), geographically isolated island in the rugged North Atlantic, just south of the Arctic Circle? For decades, the economy depended heavily on a predictable industry: fishing. The island sits near some of the world's richest fishing grounds. Overfishing reduced fish stocks; but, perhaps due to its small size, Iceland had better success than most other countries in using government restrictions both to reduce the catch sufficiently for stocks to recover and to support sustainable fishing and fish-processing industries.

What other industries might the country's factor abundance promote? Abundant cheap energy from hydroelectric and geothermal sources provides heat in the cold climate and supports a large aluminum industry. Aluminum producers, among the most energy-intensive firms in the world economy, routinely locate in low-cost energy areas; for example, most U.S. producers are found in Washington state, home of the lowest U.S. electricity prices.

New technologies have opened up new possibilities for Iceland, reducing the impact of its geographical remoteness. New biotech firms hope to find bases for new medicines among the island's unique ecosystems.[14] The country boasts the highest per-capita Internet and cellular-phone usage in the world, at 70 percent and 73 percent, respectively. The number of software firms doubled between 1995 and 2000. Even the most remote areas, such as tiny Hrisey Island off Iceland's north coast, now enjoy technology links to the rest of the world; residents there operate a call center, placing public-opinion-poll calls.[15]

Iceland's three largest trading partners are the United Kingdom, Germany, and the United States. Despite heavy trade with members of the European Union, Iceland has resisted joining the EU, because membership would require adherence to the group's Common Fisheries Policy and limit Iceland's ability to manage what Heckscher and Ohlin would have predicted to be its most important industry.

CASE 3: **SOCKS: MADE IN USA**

United States

The Heckscher-Ohlin theorem provides the key insight into why the United States imports about two-thirds of its apparel. Most apparel production relies heavily on unskilled labor, a factor relatively scarce in the United States. Major apparel exporters to the United States include Mexico, countries of the Caribbean, and China, all of which possess abundant unskilled labor (see Case Four for more on China's factor endowment and trade). We'll see later that the U.S. textile and apparel markets are subject to complex trade restrictions, so the trade pattern observed doesn't necessarily strictly reflect comparative advantage. In

particular, Mexico, a member of the North American Free Trade Agreement, and the countries of the Caribbean Basin Economic Recovery Act group enjoy less-restricted access to U.S. markets than do other countries. But even though trade restrictions distort the pattern of exports and imports from what we would observe under free trade, the Heckscher-Ohlin model explains why we still observe large-scale apparel exports to the United States from countries such as Mexico, China, and the Dominican Republic.

So why does the United States manufacture 90 percent of its own socks?[16] Americans buy 3.5 billion pairs of socks

14. "A Country Which Defies the Elements," *Financial Times*, September 19, 2000; and "Iceland Transforms Itself into a Hotbed of New Industries," *The Wall Street Journal*, March 13, 2001. Visit the Web site of the Trade Council of Iceland at http://www.icetrade.is/english.

15. "Who Needs Fish? Villagers in Iceland Cast Bets on the Net," *The Wall Street Journal*, August 1, 2000.

16. See "Socks Are Odd: Made in America," *The Wall Street Journal*, May 3, 2001.

each year; most are made in North Carolina and Alabama. Again, the trade restrictions that limit textile and apparel imports play a role, but the Heckscher-Ohlin framework can help us understand why the U.S. sock industry has outlasted other sectors of U.S. apparel production. Sock production, compared with other apparel manufacturing, uses more capital and skilled labor and less unskilled labor. So sock production better matches the U.S. factor endowment.

The knitting of yarn into socks occurs on computer-controlled knitting machines that run with little human intervention. Unskilled labor tasks involve seaming the toes, stretching and ironing the sock, and packaging; but these labor costs constitute only a small share of the total cost of sock production. The more important and more costly labor involves the small number of skilled "fixers" who work with the computer-controlled knitting machines and whose main job is to spot machine malfunctions or production imperfections and stop the machines for adjustment—before they waste yarn and turn out thousands of unusable socks. Producers sometimes ship unfinished socks to Mexico or Honduras for the unskilled finishing work; but, so far, there aren't enough skilled "fixers" abroad. So for now, the capital- and skilled-labor-intensive parts of the production process keep most socks "Made in USA."

CASE 4: CAN HECKSCHER-OHLIN EXPLAIN CHINA'S TRADE?

China

The Heckscher-Ohlin theorem predicts that a country will specialize in and export goods that use the country's abundant factors intensively, while importing goods intensive in the country's scarce factors. The United States possesses human capital and arable farmland in abundance, and unskilled labor is the United States' scarce factor. China, on the other hand, possesses unskilled labor in great abundance, but has little arable farmland in comparison with its large population. Therefore, the Heckscher-Ohlin theorem predicts that the United States would export to China products whose production involves intensive use of skilled labor (embodying the country's human capital) and land and that China would export to the United States products intensive in unskilled labor.

From the late 1950s until the mid-1970s, China's economic policies allowed very little role for markets and largely ignored the country's comparative advantage. Beginning in the late 1970s, China's economic policies began to move, slowly and erratically, in the direction of larger roles for markets and for international trade. The sum of China's total imports and exports has grown from less than 20 percent of the country's output in 1979 to more than 50 percent today. Have the changes in China's pattern of trade been consistent with the predictions of Heckscher-Ohlin? Several pieces of information suggest that the answer is yes. First, since 1975, the overall role of food and agricultural products in China's exports has declined dramatically, as reported in Figure 11. This is what we should expect, given the country's relative scarcity of arable farmland. Second, the role of manufactured exports, especially labor-intensive ones such as apparel, has grown dramatically. Again, this fits the predictions of Heckscher-Ohlin, given China's abundant unskilled labor endowment. The data in Figure 11 indicate that, consistent with Heckscher-Ohlin, China has begun to specialize in and export labor- instead of land-intensive products.

Despite the broad trend illustrated in Gigure 11, China continues to grow agricultural goods, but production has shifted away from land-intensive products such as soybeans, cotton, and grains (which pre-reform government restrictions had forced farmers to grow to keep the country self-sufficient in food) toward labor-intensive crops such as garlic, mushrooms, sweet corn, peppers, leeks, cut flowers, apples, and pears.[17] China successfully exports these products to the European Union, the United States, and much of Southeast Asia.

Now let's turn to the manufacturing sector and use another piece of information about China's factor endowment—that its abundance lies in unskilled rather than skilled labor—to examine further the fit between China's experience and the predictions of the Heckscher-Ohlin model. Table 4 reports data from a recent study. That study's authors divided a sample of 131 industries into 10 groups (or deciles) according to their skill intensity. Group 1 includes the most skill-intensive industries, and group 10 the least skill intensive. Table 4 lists sample industries for each group, along with the group's share of Chinese exports to the United States and of U.S. exports to China in 1990.

17. See "Foreign Investors Eye Chinese Farming," *Financial Times*, September 30, 2003; and "China's New Crop of Exports," *The Wall Street Journal*, December 17, 2003.

Figure 11 How Did China's Exports Change, 1975–1990?

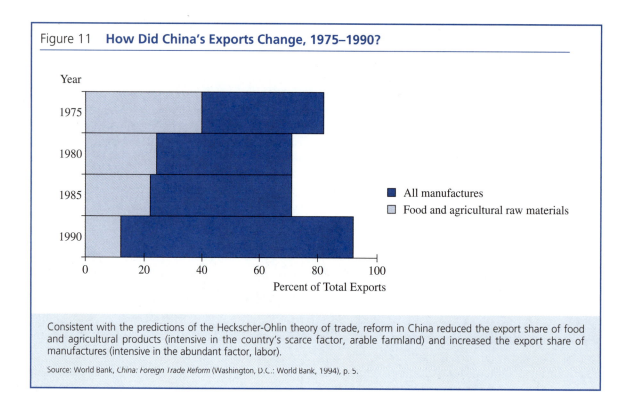

Consistent with the predictions of the Heckscher-Ohlin theory of trade, reform in China reduced the export share of food and agricultural products (intensive in the country's scarce factor, arable farmland) and increased the export share of manufactures (intensive in the abundant factor, labor).

Source: World Bank, *China: Foreign Trade Reform* (Washington, D.C.: World Bank, 1994), p. 5.

Table 4 SKILL COMPOSITION OF U.S.–CHINA TRADE, 1990

Skill Group (Industry Examples)	Percent of Chinese Exports to U.S.	Percent of U.S. Exports to China
Most Skilled		
1 (Periodicals, office and computing machines)	4.8%	**7.7%**
2 (Aircraft and parts, industrial inorganic chemicals)	2.6	**48.8**
3 (Engines and turbines, fats and oils)	3.9	**21.3**
4 (Concrete, nonelectric plumbing and heating)	11.5	4.3
5 (Watches, clocks, toys, sporting goods)	18.9	6.3
6 (Wood buildings, blast furnaces, basic steel)	8.2	1.3
7 (Ship building and repair, furniture and fixtures)	4.1	2.8
8 (Cigarettes, motor vehicles, iron and steel foundries)	5.2	1.8
9 (Weaving, wool, leather tanning and finishing)	**17.2**	0.4
10 (Children's outerwear, nonrubber footwear)	**23.5**	5.2
Least Skilled		

Source: Data from Jeffrey D. Sachs and Howard J. Shatz, "Trade and Jobs in U.S. Manufacturing," *Brookings Papers on Economic Activity* 1 (1994), pp. 18, 53.

The pattern of U.S.–China trade in 1990 fits closely with Heckscher-Ohlin predictions. U.S. exports to China are concentrated in the high-skill sectors; deciles 1–3 (high-lighted in the table) account for 78 percent of U.S. exports to China. Chinese exports to the United States fall into the lower skill categories; the highlighted groups 9 and 10, the least skilled, constitute more than 40 percent of the total. Chinese exports in groups 4 and 5 include mostly labor-intensive assembly tasks in the radio, television, and toy industries.

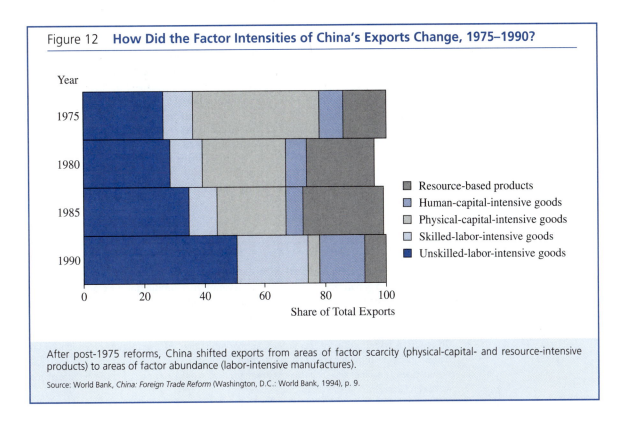

Figure 12 **How Did the Factor Intensities of China's Exports Change, 1975–1990?**

After post-1975 reforms, China shifted exports from areas of factor scarcity (physical-capital- and resource-intensive products) to areas of factor abundance (labor-intensive manufactures).

Source: World Bank, *China: Foreign Trade Reform* (Washington, D.C.: World Bank, 1994), p. 9.

Finally, Figure 12 summarizes how the factor intensity of Chinese exports has changed during the reform period since 1975. The figure clearly demonstrates the rapid growth of labor-intensive exports, especially unskilled ones, and the corresponding decline of physical-capital-intensive manufactures along with natural-resource-based products. Overall, the Heckscher-Ohlin model clearly *can* explain the broad patterns of Chinese trade.

SUMMARY

When firms produce goods using two inputs that aren't perfect substitutes for each other, the opportunity cost of producing each good rises as more of the good is produced. A country has a comparative advantage in production of a good when the opportunity cost of that good is lower there than in the trading partner. When trade is possible, each country will specialize in and export the good in which it has a comparative advantage. We've now encountered three bases for comparative advantage and mutually beneficial trade: (1) differences in technology or labor productivity, as in Chapter Two's Ricardian model, (2) differences in factor endowments, emphasized in this chapter's Heckscher-Ohlin theorem, and (3) differences in tastes under increasing costs.

LOOKING AHEAD

Chapters Two and Three demonstrated the potential of international trade based on comparative advantage for increasing the welfare of residents of participating countries. Nevertheless, decisions on trade policy always generate controversy, leading us to suspect that the case for trade must be more complicated than we've seen so far. In Chapter Four, we introduce an effect of trade we've ignored up to now: its effect on the distribution of income *within* each country.

KEY TERMS

Neoclassical (increasing-cost) model
fixed proportions
production function
isoquant
marginal rate of technical
   substitution (MRTS)
factor prices (factor rewards)
isocost line
capital-labor ratio
capital-intensive good

labor-intensive good
comparative advantage
equilibrium price
factor abundance
capital abundance
labor abundance
production bias
Heckscher-Ohlin theorem
taste bias
home bias

PROBLEMS AND QUESTIONS FOR REVIEW

1. Assume that tastes and technology are identical in China and Japan. Assume that China is labor abundant and Japan is capital abundant. Assume that production of clothing is labor intensive and production of automobiles is capital intensive.
   a. Sketch the production possibilities frontiers for China and Japan. Explain briefly why you drew them as you did.
   b. In autarky, which country has a comparative advantage in production of which good? Show how you know, or why you don't know.
   c. What does the Heckscher-Ohlin theorem predict would happen if trade were opened between China and Japan?
   d. Show and label the autarky and unrestricted-trade equilibria, production and consumption points, imports and exports, autarky price ratios, and terms of trade.
2. Under increasing costs, will two countries find it beneficial to trade if they have:
   a. identical production possibilities and different tastes?
   b. identical tastes and different production possibilities?
   c. identical tastes and identical production possibilities?
   Explain and illustrate.
3. In Table 3, divide the countries into those with capital endowments greater than $35,000 per worker and those with capital endowments less than $35,000 per worker. Is there a locational pattern between the two groups? Does the Heckscher-Ohlin model imply that only the former groups would gain from trade? Why, or why not?
4. In terms of the production possibilities frontier/indifference curve diagram, explain the effects on North Korea's economy of:
   a. the country's isolation from new technologies.
   b. residents' inability to exchange goods with residents of other countries.
   c. firms' inability to specialize according to comparative advantage.
5. A firm's production function is $X = 5LK$. Name three input combinations that would allow the firm to produce 100 units of output. In each case, what is the firm's capital-labor ratio? If the wage rate is $10 per unit and the rental rate on capital is $20 per unit, what are the firm's costs for each of the three input combinations?
6. What determines the capital-labor ratio for each good in each country? Why might both industries use a higher capital-labor ratio in one country than in another? Can you think of circumstances in which each industry would exhibit the same capital-labor ratio in both countries? Explain.
7. Which of the goods in Table 1 would you expect the United States to export? To import? Why?
8. Suppose that tastes exhibit a home bias in the sense that each country's residents consume relatively large quantities of goods produced domestically and relatively small quantities of goods that must be imported. Would the home bias strengthen or weaken the pattern of production bias based on differing factor endowments? Why? Would the result be more trade or less trade than in the identical-taste case?

REFERENCES AND SELECTED READINGS

Bernhofen, Daniel M., and John C. Brown. "A Direct Test of the Theory of Comparative Advantage: The Case of Japan." *Journal of Political Economy* 112 (February 2004): 48–67.
A study of a rare opportunity to test the theory of comparative advantage, the opening of Japan to trade in 1859.

Coughlin, Cletus C., and Patricia S. Pollard. "Comparing Manufacturing Export Growth across States: What Accounts for the Differences?" Federal Reserve Bank of St. Louis *Review* 83 (January/February 2001): 25–40.
Introduction to the roles of trade in different U.S. states' economies.

Heckscher, Eli. "The Effect of Foreign Trade on the Distribution of Income." *Ekonomisk Tidskrift* 21 (1919). Reprinted in American Economic Association, *Readings in the Theory of International Trade*. Philadelphia: Blakiston, 1949, Chap. 13.
The original statement of the Heckscher-Ohlin results.

Irwin, Douglas A. *Free Trade Under Fire.* Princeton: Princeton University Press, 2002.
Readable overview of the links between the Heckscher-Ohlin model and current trade-policy debates.

Jones, Ronald W. "The Structure of Simple General Equilibrium Models." *Journal of Political Economy* 73 (December 1965): 557–572.
For advanced students, the classic mathematical presentation of the basic trade model.

Noland, Marcus, et al. "The Economics of Korean Unification." *Journal of Policy Reform* 3 (1999): 255–299.
Empirical estimates of the benefits and costs of unification of North and South Korea.

Ohlin, Bertil. *Interregional and International Trade.* Cambridge, Mass.: Harvard University Press, 1933.
Ohlin's elaboration of Heckscher's earlier work on the factor-proportions model.

Prasad, Eswar, and Thomas Rumbaugh. "Beyond the Great Wall." *Finance and Development* 40 (December 2003): 46–49.
Introduction to China's changing trade patterns.

Romalis, John. "Factor Proportions and the Structure of Commodity Trade." *American Economic Review* 94 (March 2004): 67–97.
A modern investigation of the links between factor intensities and trade; for intermediate and advanced students.

Samuelson, Paul A. "The Gains from International Trade." *Canadian Journal of Economics and Political Science* 9 (1939): 195–205.
Early, readable demonstration of how international trade improves potential welfare.

Samuelson, Paul A. "The Gains from International Trade Once Again." *Economic Journal* 72 (1962): 820–829.
Update of the preceding paper.

Trefler, Daniel. "The Case of the Missing Trade and Other Mysteries." *American Economic Review* (December 1995): 1029–1046.
Tests of the Heckscher-Ohlin model find that home bias in consumption and technological differences, along with factor endowments, affect trade patterns; for advanced students.

THE EDGEWORTH BOX

One of the inconveniences of studying the world economy as opposed to a single domestic economy is the need to keep track of so many things at once. Even with our simplifying assumption of only two countries and two industries, the analysis usually requires using at least two graphs, such as those in Figure 6, representing the situations in countries A and B. Some tasks would be easier if we could combine information about the two countries in a single graph. One convenient tool to do this is called an *Edgeworth box* (named after, but apparently not invented by, economist and mathematician Francis Edgeworth). Simply put, an Edgeworth box combines two two-axis diagrams (such as those for our two countries or for two industries within a single country) into a single, box-shaped diagram.

First, let's develop an Edgeworth box that combines information about two industries in a single country (the X and Y industries in country A), where each industry uses two inputs: labor (L) and capital (K). Each industry is characterized by a set of isoquants, as illustrated in Figure A.1. The lengths of the axes in Figure A.1 are defined by the quantities of labor and capital available in country A; it's impossible to use more than L^A units of labor or more than K^A units of capital.

To form an Edgeworth box, we take the Y-industry diagram and rotate it 180 degrees so that the origin lies in its upper right-hand rather than lower left-hand corner. Next, we move the X-industry and Y-industry diagrams toward each other until the two touch to form a box, as in Figure A.2.

The horizontal dimension of the box measures the total quantity of labor available in A to be allocated between the X and Y industries. The vertical dimension captures the same information about capital. Each point in the box, then, represents an allocation of labor and capital between X production and Y production. For example, point I implies that L^A_{X0} units of labor are being used in the X industry and L^A_{Y0} units (read from right to left from the Y origin) in the Y industry. Similarly, point I involves allocating K^A_{X0} units of capital to the X industry and K^A_{Y0} to the Y industry.

Each point in or on the Edgeworth box represents a point inside or on country A's production possibilities frontier. The points lying *on* the production possibilities frontier can be distinguished by the fact that they are tangencies between the X-industry and Y-industry isoquants in the Edgeworth box. This must be true because at any point in Figure A.2 that isn't such a tangency, country A could produce more of one good without producing less of the other. For example, from point I (a nontangency point), A can produce more good Y without reducing production of X by moving to point II (a tangency point) *or* produce more X without reducing production of Y by moving to point III (another tangency point). Points II and III, therefore, lie on country A's production possibilities frontier, while point I is an interior point, as illustrated in Figure A.3.

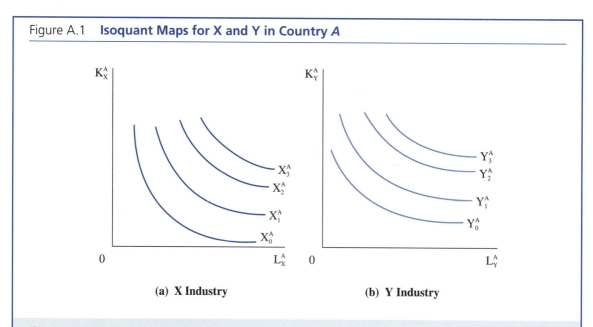

Figure A.1 **Isoquant Maps for X and Y in Country *A***

(a) **X Industry**

(b) **Y Industry**

The country's resource endowment defines the length of each axis. L^A determines the lengths of the horizontal axes, and K^A the lengths of the vertical axes.

Figure A.2 Edgeworth Box for X and Y Production in Country *A*

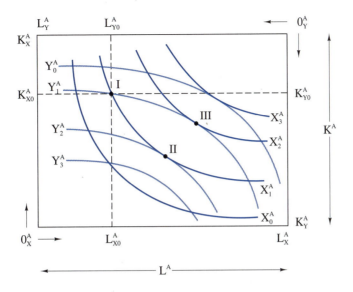

Each point in the box describes an allocation of the total available labor and capital between the X and Y industries. Industry X values are read from left to right and from bottom to top from the 0^A_X origin. Industry Y values are read from right to left and from top to bottom from the 0^A_Y origin.

Figure A.3 Country *A*'s Production Possibilities Frontier

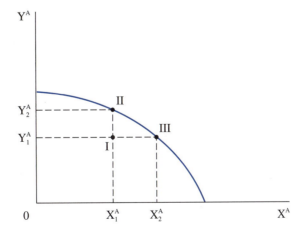

Points I, II, and III correspond to the matching points from Figure A.2. All points *on* the production possibilities frontier correspond to points of tangency between an X isoquant and a Y isoquant in the Edgeworth box. All points *inside* the production possibilities frontier correspond to nontangency points in the Edgeworth box, that is, to points from which it is possible to increase production of one good without decreasing production of the other.

Now let's use the Edgeworth-box technique to consider the gains from specialization and exchange. Let $X^W = X^A + X^B$ represent the total world quantity of good X produced and $Y^W = Y^A + Y^A$ represent the total world quantity of good Y produced. These two quantities form the dimensions of a second type of Edgeworth box. By allowing more of one good to be produced without producing less of the other, productive specialization according to comparative advantage can increase the size of the box. Using the production possibilities frontiers from Chapter Three, Figure A.4 illustrates the increase in the size of the box due to productive specialization. Under autarky, $X^W = X^{A*} + X^{B*}$ and $Y^W = Y^{A*} + Y^{B*}$ from Figure 6, while with specialization according to comparative advantage, $X^W = X^A_p + X^B_p > X^{A*} + X^{B*}$ and $Y^W = Y^A_p + Y^B_p > Y^{A*} + Y^{B*}$ from Figure 8.

Once productive specialization has increased the quantity of goods available, residents of A exchange with residents of B according to their tastes for the two goods. In Figure A.5, we represent tastes by a set of community indifference curves for each country. Beginning at point p (for *production*), the two countries trade along a line (whose slope measures the international terms of trade) to a point of tangency between two indifference curves, one for each country. From such a point (denoted c for *consumption*), it's impossible to move residents of one country onto a higher indifference curve without moving residents of the other onto a lower curve.

Figure A.4   Edgeworth Box for Total World Production of Goods X and Y

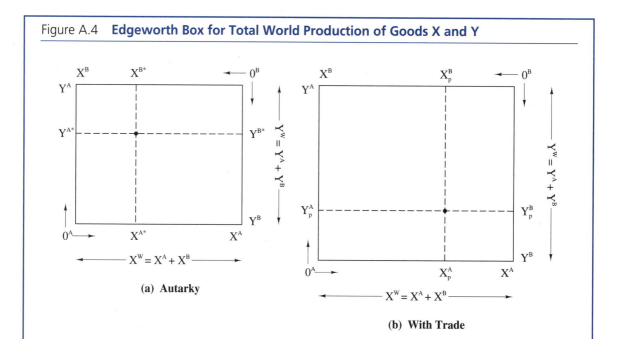

Production at the autarky production points (A* and B* from Figure 6) defines the dimensions of the box in panel (a). The larger dimensions of the box in panel (b) reflect increased production brought about by productive specialization according to comparative advantage (as illustrated in Figure 8).

Figure A.5   Edgeworth Box Depiction of Trade between Countries *A* and *B*

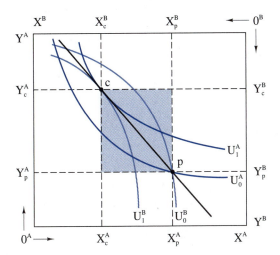

Beginning from the point of productive specialization (p), residents of both countries can make themselves better off through trade, which occurs at the international terms of trade to consumption point c. There it becomes impossible to improve the welfare of residents of one country without reducing the welfare of residents of the other. The two countries' trade triangles constitute the shaded rectangle. Its length represents A's exports (and B's imports) of good X, its height represents B's exports (and A's imports) of good Y, and the (absolute) slope of the line that bisects it indicates the equilibrium terms of trade. Points p and c are equivalent to, respectively, points A_p and B_p and points A_c and B_c in Figure 8.

OFFER CURVES

Recall from section 3.2 that the equilibrium terms of trade between countries A and B must satisfy two conditions: (1) The terms of trade must lie between the two autarky price ratios, or $(P_X/P_Y)^A < (P_X/P_Y)^{tt} < (P_X/P_Y)^B$ if country A has a comparative advantage in production of X; and (2) the amount of a good one country wants to export at the terms of trade must equal the amount of that good the other country wants to import (that is, markets must clear). Finding the equilibrium terms of trade in a production possibilities frontier/indifference curve graph like Figure 8 is a matter of artistic trial and error. An alternate graphical technique, known as *offer curves* or *reciprocal demand curves*, has two advantages: Offer curves clearly show the equilibrium terms of trade, while also presenting information about countries A and B in a single graph.

The term *offer curve* refers to the curve's illustration of the "offer" one country would make for trade with another at any given terms of trade—that is, country A's offer curve answers the question "At each relative price of goods X and Y, what quantities would residents of A want to export and import?" Country B's offer curve presents the same information about the trade offers B would make. The other designation, *reciprocal demand curve*, refers to the curve's

emphasis on the reciprocity between exports and imports; a country exports to receive imports in return. For each relative price or terms of trade, an offer curve shows how much of its export good a country is willing to give up in exchange for a given amount of its import good. Therefore, an offer curve combines the information in an import demand curve *and* an export supply curve, or in an indifference curve map *and* a production possibilities frontier.

We draw offer curves in a two-dimensional space with the amount of good X traded measured on the horizontal axis and the amount of good Y traded measured on the vertical axis. Note that this differs from most of the graphs we've used so far, which measure the quantities of the two goods produced or consumed on the axes rather than the internationally *traded* quantities.

Figure B.1 illustrates the offer curves for countries A and B. The slope of any ray from the origin measures one possible relative price of good X or one possible value for the terms of trade. This is true because the slope of the ray is given by the line's rise (ΔY) divided by the run (ΔX), or how much good Y must be given up to obtain an additional unit of good X through exchange. Steeper rays represent relatively high prices for good X (and relatively low prices for good Y), while flatter rays represent relatively low prices for X (or relatively high prices for Y).

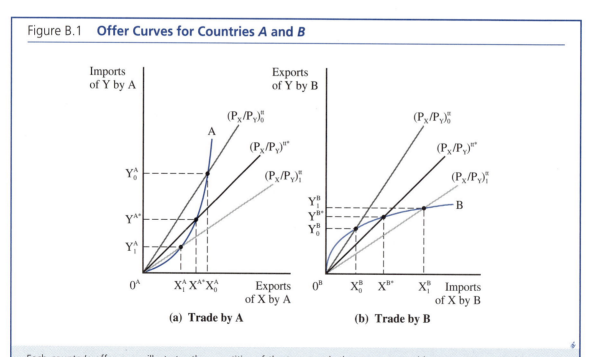

Figure B.1 **Offer Curves for Countries *A* and *B***

Each country's offer curve illustrates the quantities of the two goods that country would want to export and import at different terms of trade, represented by the slopes of rays from the origin.

In panel (a) of Figure B.1, A's offer curve reflects A's willingness to export larger quantities of good X as the relative price of X rises. The rising relative price of X means that A can obtain more imported Y for each unit of exported X, making exporting more attractive to A. The curve also reveals A's willingness to import larger quantities of good Y as the relative price of Y falls. The falling price of Y (rising price of X) means Y is less costly in terms of the amount of X that must be exported in exchange. Each point on the curve represents A's desired exports and imports for the terms of trade given by a ray from the origin through that point.

Panel (b) of Figure B.1 depicts country B's offer curve. Given our assumption that B has a comparative advantage in good Y, B exports Y and imports X. A steep terms-of-trade line implies that country B's imports of X are expensive in terms of exported Y. As a result, the volume of trade in which B wants to engage is relatively small. Along a flatter terms-of-trade line, the price of B's export good is higher relative to the price of its import good, and B wants to engage in a larger volume of trade.

Now we can see the convenience of the offer-curve technique for finding the *equilibrium* terms of trade. Equilibrium occurs at the terms of trade for which A's desired exports of X equal B's desired imports of X, and B's desired exports of Y equal A's desired imports of Y. Obviously, the intersection of the two countries' offer curves meets this condition; $(P_X/P_Y)^{tt*}$ represents the equilibrium relative price at which the markets for goods X and Y clear.

Figure B.2 illustrates the adjustment that brings the terms of trade to equilibrium. If the relative price of good X were too high for market clearing, such as $(P_X/P_Y)^{tt}_0$, A would want to export more X than B would want to import, while B would be willing to export less Y than A would want to import. The excess supply of good X and the excess demand for good Y would cause P_X/P_Y to fall toward equilibrium. On the other hand, if the relative price of good X were too low, such as $(P_X/P_Y)^{tt}_1$, B would want to import more X than A would want to export, and A would want to import less Y than B would want to export. The

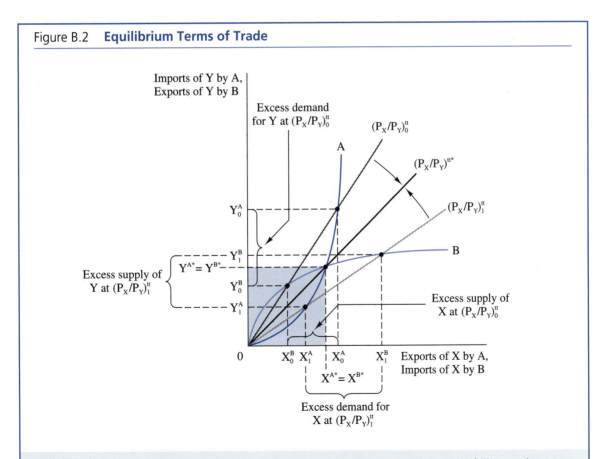

Figure B.2   Equilibrium Terms of Trade

At the equilibrium terms of trade, $(P_X/P_Y)^{tt*}$, the quantity of good X country A wants to export equals the quantity country B wants to import, and the quantity of good Y country B wants to export equals the quantity A wants to import. At any other terms of trade, there is excess supply of one good and excess demand for the other. The shaded rectangle combines the two countries' trade triangles from Figure 8.

excess demand for good X and the excess supply of good Y would cause P_X/P_Y to rise.

Finally, note the graphical relationship between the offer-curve diagram in Figure B.2 and the production possibilities frontier/indifference curve diagram in Figure 8. Each point on an offer curve can be thought of as defining a trade triangle. Recall that the base and height of a trade triangle represent imports and exports of the two goods and that the slope of the third side (hypotenuse) of the triangle measures the terms of trade. In Figure B.2, the shaded rectangle depicts the same two trade triangles as in Figure 8. The origin in Figure B.2 corresponds to the production points, A_p and B_p. The intersection of the two countries' offer curves corresponds to the consumption points, A_c and B_c. The point on the horizontal axis directly below the offer-curve intersection corresponds to point A from Figure 8(a), and the point on the vertical axis directly to the left of the offer-curve intersection corresponds to point B from Figure 8(b). The slope of the terms-of-trade line, $(P_X/P_Y)^{tt*}$, which bisects the rectangle into the two countries' trade triangles, measures the equilibrium terms of trade.

4

Trade, Distribution, and Welfare

1 INTRODUCTION

We need to understand why so much controversy still surrounds the issue of free trade versus protection more than two hundred years after David Hume, Adam Smith, and David Ricardo. In Chapters Two and Three, we learned that the mechanism by which trade produces a more efficient outcome than does autarky involves the reallocation of production so that relative output prices (which reflect opportunity costs) equalize across countries. This reallocation ensures that each good gets produced in the country where its production requires forgoing less in terms of other goods; this is the essence of efficient production. So far, we've treated this change in relative output prices and resource allocation as the end of the story. But, to understand the enduring controversy that surrounds trade policy, we must consider that changes in relative output prices and production will generate changes in other variables, particularly in the rewards or wages paid to factors of production. In other words, *the relative price changes that occur when countries open trade alter the distribution of income within each country*. Any policy that alters income distribution will generate controversy, because individuals whose positions improve will support the policy, and those harmed will oppose it.

2 HOW DO OUTPUT PRICES AFFECT FACTOR PRICES? THE STOLPER-SAMUELSON THEOREM

The changes in relative output prices that accompany the opening of trade follow from changes in the two goods' production levels in each country. To capture the gains from trade, countries specialize production according to comparative advantage. Production of each good involves using the two inputs in different proportions, so changing the *output* combination alters relative demands for the two *inputs*.[1] This change in relative input demands causes changes in relative input prices and, therefore, in the distribution of income. If production shifts from steel (a capital-intensive good) to textiles (a labor-intensive good), the demand for capital decreases and the demand for labor increases. The pattern of factor rewards within the economy will reflect these shifts in demand;

---

1. For a review, see section 2.1, especially Figure 4, in Chapter Three.

the price of capital falls, and the wage rate rises, hurting capital owners and helping workers. Notice the distinct steps in the logic:

Comparative advantage ⟶ Production specialization and trade ⟶
Change in relative outputs of goods X and Y ⟶ Change in relative demands for inputs L and K ⟶
Change in input prices w and r ⟶ Change in distribution of income.

If we assume, along with Heckscher and Ohlin, that comparative advantage reflects the interaction of goods' factor intensity and countries' factor abundance, opening trade increases production of the good that uses a country's abundant factor intensively, which increases demand for that factor. Similarly, production of the good that uses the scarce factor intensively falls with the opening of trade, decreasing demand for that factor. Remember that each country's endowment of each factor is fixed, so a vertical line represents the supply of each factor. Increased demand for the abundant factor bids up its price, and decreased demand for the scarce factor bids down its price. Again, follow the steps in the logic once we incorporate Heckscher and Ohlin's assumption about the source of comparative advantage:

Comparative advantage in abundant-factor-intensive good/disadvantage in scarce-factor-intensive good ⟶
Produce more of abundant-factor-intensive good/less of scarce-factor-intensive good and trade ⟶
Increase in demand for abundant factor/decrease in demand for scarce factor ⟶
Increase in price of abundant factor/decrease in price of scarce factor ⟶
Change in distribution of income in favor of abundant factor and against scarce factor.

As an example, assume that country A is labor abundant and good X is the labor-intensive good. According to the Heckscher-Ohlin theorem, under unrestricted trade country A will specialize in good X. Production of good X involves intensive use of labor, so the demand for labor in A will increase. Of course, country A will, at the same time, decrease production of good Y. (*Why?*) Falling Y production will release some labor previously used in the Y industry; but production of Y is capital intensive, so the amount of labor released will be relatively small.

Panel (a) of Figure 1 illustrates these effects of trade on labor demand in country A. D_{L0}^A represents the demand for labor in autarky. Once trade begins, increased production of good X increases demand to D_{L1}^A, and decreased production of good Y decreases demand to D_{L2}^A. The vertical supply curve, L^A, represents the country's fixed endowment of labor; so trade raises the equilibrium wage from w_0^A to w_2^A.

The effects that occur simultaneously in country A's capital market appear in panel (b) of Figure 1. In autarky, the production pattern results in a demand for capital given by D_{K0}^A and an equilibrium rental rate of r_0^A. When trade opens, country A reduces production of good Y, the capital-intensive good, causing demand to shift down to D_{K1}^A. Production of good X increases; but X is labor intensive, so this involves only a small increase in the demand for capital, to D_{K2}^A. The new equilibrium rental rate is r_2^A. The wage rate has risen and the rental rate has fallen; so the new equilibrium wage-rental ratio, w_2^A/r_2^A, exceeds the ratio that prevailed in autarky, w_0^A/r_0^A. The output price changes that occur when trade opens have redistributed income toward owners of the abundant factor, labor in our example, and away from owners of the scarce factor, capital. These changes in relative factor prices must accompany any change in relative output prices.[2]

In fact, we can make an even stronger statement about the relationship between output prices and factor prices: Each factor price changes in the same direction but *more than proportionally* with the price of the output that uses that factor intensively. For example, if the

---

2. We'll see in Chapter Ten that, while changes in output prices lead to changes in factor prices, changes in factor quantities (that is, in countries' endowments) do *not* lead to changes in factor prices. The reason that endowment changes *do not* affect factor prices is the mirror image of the reason that output prices *do*: both lead to changes in output mix.

Figure 1   **How Does Trade Affect the Demand for Inputs in a Labor-Abundant Country?**

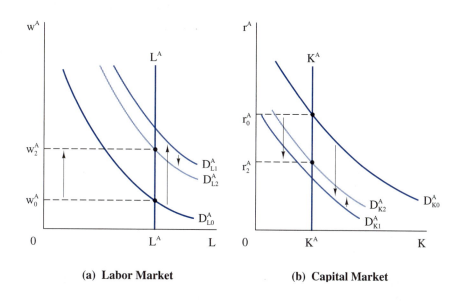

(a) Labor Market   **(b) Capital Market**

As production of the labor-intensive good increases, opening trade generates a net increase in demand for labor. The net effect on demand for capital is negative, because production of the capital-intensive good falls. With fixed factor endowments, the reward paid to the abundant factor (here, labor) rises and that paid to the scarce factor (capital) falls. The wage-rental ratio under unrestricted trade exceeds the ratio under autarky.

price of the labor-intensive good rises by 10 percent, the wage rate rises by more than 10 percent.[3] If the price of the capital-intensive good remains unchanged when the price of the labor-intensive good rises by 10 percent, the price of capital must fall. To see why, recall that under perfect competition the price of a good must equal its marginal cost, or the change in total cost from producing an additional unit. With two inputs, this requirement can be expressed as $P_X = a_{LX} \cdot w + a_{KX} \cdot r = MC_X$ for good X and $P_Y = a_{LY} \cdot w + a_{KY} \cdot r = MC_Y$ for good Y, because the marginal cost of one unit of output equals the number of additional units of labor used times the wage rate plus the number of additional units of capital used times the rental rate. In other words, the price of a good can be written as a weighted sum of the input prices, where the weights are the input coefficients. The expression for P_Y reveals that if P_Y doesn't change when w rises (due to a rise in P_X), r must fall.[4]

This **magnification effect**—the fact that changes in output prices have a magnified or more-than-proportional effect on factor prices—carries important implications for evaluating the effects of international trade policy. Suppose labor-abundant country A opens trade. The price of labor-intensive good X rises while the price of good Y falls, and

---

3. Similarly, if the price of the labor-intensive good falls by 10 percent, the wage falls by more than 10 percent.

4. This result is easy to see if we assume that the input coefficients don't change. Then we can take percentage rates of change of both sides of the price-equals-marginal-cost expressions, which gives $(a_{LX}/MC_X) \cdot \hat{w} + (a_{KX}/MC_X) \cdot \hat{r} = \hat{P}_X$ and $(a_{LY}/MC_Y) \cdot \hat{w} + (a_{KY}/MC_Y) \cdot \hat{r} = \hat{P}_Y$, where "hats" denote percentage rates of change in a variable. If $\hat{w} > \hat{P}_X > \hat{P}_Y = 0$, then $\hat{r}$ must be negative; the marginal cost of Y, which must equal P_Y, can remain unchanged when the wage rate rises only if the price of capital falls. This result continues to hold without the assumption of fixed input coefficients, although the demonstration requires a more advanced technique.

the wage rate rises while the rental rate falls. (*Why?*) Now suppose you're a worker in country A. You now earn a higher wage, but you also must pay a higher price for any good X you consume. Are you better off? That is, has your purchasing power or your *real* wage risen? The magnification-effect analysis allows you to answer yes (even if you spend all your income on the now more-expensive good X), because wages have risen proportionally more than the price of good X (that is, $\hat{w}^A > \hat{P}^A_X$, so w^A/P^A_X has risen).

On the other hand, suppose you're a capital owner in country A. The rental rate earned on your capital has fallen, but so has the price you must pay for any good Y you consume. Are you better off or worse off in terms of your purchasing power or *real* return? The magnification effect implies that you are worse off (even if you spend all your income on the now-cheaper good Y), because the rental rate earned on your capital has fallen proportionally more than the price of good Y (that is, $\hat{r}^A < \hat{P}^A_Y$, so r^A/P^A_Y has fallen).

In discussing this link between changes in output prices and changes in factor prices, we've loosely stated one of the basic theorems of international trade theory, the **Stolper-Samuelson theorem**, named after Wolfgang Stolper and Paul Samuelson who co-authored the 1941 paper that first demonstrated it. In its most general form the theorem states that, under the assumptions of our model, a change in the price of a *good* changes, in the same direction and more than proportionally, the price of the *factor* used intensively in that good's production.[5]

If we add the assumptions of the Heckscher-Ohlin model, the Stolper-Samuelson theorem means that opening trade raises the real reward of the abundant factor and lowers the real reward of the scarce factor. This follows because trade boosts production of the comparative-advantage good and increases that good's opportunity cost and relative price. The Heckscher-Ohlin model defines comparative advantage in terms of intensive use of the abundant factor; so trade raises the price of the good that uses the abundant factor intensively, thereby raising the abundant factor's real price. Table 1 summarizes trade's

Table 1	THE STOLPER-SAMUELSON THEOREM: OPENING TRADE CHANGES OUTPUT PRICES *AND* REAL FACTOR PRICES	
	Effect of Opening Trade	
Labor-Abundant Country A:		
Production	$X\Uparrow$, $Y\Downarrow$	
Output prices	$P_X\Uparrow$, $P_Y\Downarrow$	
Factor prices	$w\Uparrow\Uparrow$, $r\Downarrow\Downarrow$[a]	
Capital-Abundant Country B:		
Production	$X\Downarrow$, $Y\Uparrow$	
Output prices	$P_X\Downarrow$, $P_Y\Uparrow$	
Factor prices	$w\Downarrow\Downarrow$, $r\Uparrow\Uparrow$	

[a]Double arrows denote the magnification effect, or changes in *real* factor prices.

5. A different statement of the same result: An increase in the relative price of a good increases the *real* return to the factor used intensively in that good's production and decreases the *real* return to the other factor. Statement of the result in real terms captures the magnification effect, or the fact that factor prices change proportionally more than output prices.

effects on production, output prices, and factor prices, assuming country A is labor abundant and good X is labor intensive.

The Stolper-Samuelson theorem clarifies one reason for the controversial nature of trade policy. Opening trade leads to output price changes that alter real factor rewards, creating incentives for owners of the abundant input to support trade and for owners of the scarce input to resist it. It's important to remember that the country *as a whole* is made potentially better off by trade; that is, the winners from trade (owners of the abundant factor) gain enough from trade to allow them to compensate the losers (owners of the scarce factor) and still be better off. However, such compensation, though theoretically possible, may not occur. Therefore, the Stolper-Samuelson theorem clearly pinpoints at least one constituency for protectionist policies or restrictions on trade: owners of a country's scarce factor. Later, when we discuss various protectionist measures and their effects, we'll also examine some policies that aim to eliminate this natural protectionist constituency by redistributing the gains from trade to compensate the losers.

The Stolper-Samuelson theorem highlights the relationship between *output prices* and *factor prices* within a single country. The next result to emerge from the basic trade model deals with the relationship between relative factor prices across countries.

3 HOW DO FACTOR PRICES VARY ACROSS COUNTRIES? THE FACTOR PRICE EQUALIZATION THEOREM

It's easy to see that trade tends to equalize across countries the price of each good traded. Countries' different autarky output prices converge to the international terms of trade once countries open trade. But what about *factor* prices? If factors of production moved freely across national borders, we'd expect the price of each factor to equalize across countries. Labor would flow from countries with low wages to those with high wages, thereby raising wages in the low-wage countries and lowering wages in the high-wage ones until $w^A = w^B$. Similarly, capital would flow from countries where it received a low reward to those where it received a high reward until $r^A = r^B$. But recall that we're assuming factors of production *aren't* mobile among countries.[6] In Chapter One, we argued that restricted factor mobility between countries constitutes one aspect of the economic significance of political boundaries.[7] While factors aren't actually completely immobile, it is true that factors are much less mobile among countries than within them. Some barriers, such as language or cultural ones, are "natural"; and policy makers impose other artificial barriers, including immigration restrictions and capital controls. Factor immobility implies that there's no obvious mechanism by which unrestricted trade in *outputs* can equalize *factor* prices across countries; but one important role for economic models is to allow us to see things that aren't obvious.

When trade begins, a country increases its output of the good in which it possesses a comparative advantage. According to Heckscher and Ohlin, production of this good involves intensive use of the country's abundant factor. Thus, according to the Stolper-Samuelson theorem, moving from autarky to unrestricted trade raises the real reward of the abundant factor (which was low in autarky because of the factor's abundance); similarly, such a move lowers the real reward of the scarce factor (which was high without trade because of scarcity). The same adjustment process also occurs in the second country, but with the roles of the two factors reversed. (*Could the same factor be abundant in both countries?*

---

6. We'll relax this assumption in Chapter Ten.

7. The degree of factor mobility is an important distinction between interregional and international trade, as we'll see in section 5.1 of Chapter Nine.

Table 2	THE FACTOR PRICE EQUALIZATION THEOREM: FREE TRADE IN OUTPUTS EQUALIZES EACH *FACTOR'S* PRICE ACROSS COUNTRIES		
	Autarky	Effect of Trade	Free Trade
Labor-Abundant Country A:			
Output prices	$(P_X/P_Y)^A < (P_X/P_Y)^B$	$(P_X/P_Y)^A \Uparrow$	$(P_X/P_Y)^{tt}$
Wage	$w^A < w^B$	$w^A \Uparrow \Uparrow \uparrow a$	$w^A = w^B$
Rental rate	$r^A > r^B$	$r^A \Downarrow \Downarrow$	$r^A = r^B$
Capital-Abundant Country B:			
Output prices	$(P_X/P_Y)^B > (P_X/P_Y)^A$	$(P_X/P_Y)^B \Downarrow$	$(P_X/P_Y)^{tt}$
Wage	$w^B > w^A$	$w^B \Downarrow \Downarrow$	$w^B = w^A$
Rental rate	$r^B < r^A$	$r^B \Uparrow \Uparrow$	$r^B = r^A$

aDouble arrows denote the magnification effect, or changes in *real* factor prices.

Why or why not?) So trade raises a factor's real reward in the country where that factor is abundant and lowers its real reward in the country where it's scarce. Therefore, *even when factors are immobile between countries, unrestricted trade in goods equalizes the price of each factor across countries*. With free trade in goods, even with no international factor mobility, $w^A = w^B$ and $r^A = r^B$.[8] This is the logic behind the **factor price equalization theorem**, which Paul Samuelson demonstrated in 1948. Table 2 summarizes the theorem's implications, assuming that country A is labor abundant and good X is labor intensive.

The preceding discussion focused on the economy-wide adjustment that results in equalization across countries of each factor's price. We also can view the process of factor price equalization from the viewpoint of how a firm adjusts to trade.

As the world economy moves from autarky to unrestricted trade in outputs, each country increases production of the good that uses the country's abundant factor intensively. Suppose for a moment that firms in each country tried to continue to use capital and labor in the same proportions as they'd been used in autarky (that is, suppose that firms' input coefficients didn't change). The different output combination produced under trade then would imply more total use of the abundant factor and less total use of the scarce factor in each country. But total usage of each factor in each country (adding usage in the two industries, X and Y) must equal the country's fixed endowment of the input. In other words, it must be true, both in autarky and with trade, that

$$L^A = L_X^A + L_Y^A = a_{LX} \cdot X^A + a_{LY} \cdot Y^A,$$
$$K^A = K_X^A + K_Y^A = a_{KX} \cdot X^A + a_{KY} \cdot Y^A,$$
$$L^B = L_X^B + L_Y^B = b_{LX} \cdot X^B + b_{LY} \cdot Y^B,$$
$$K^B = K_X^B + K_Y^B = b_{KX} \cdot X^B + b_{KY} \cdot Y^B.$$

Therefore, a country can't produce a *different* combination of the two outputs while continuing to use the *same* production techniques (that is, capital-labor ratios or input coefficients) as before.

---

8. Avoid making the common mistake of thinking that factor price equalization implies w = r; it does not. The *equalization* in "factor price equalization" refers to the prices of a single factor in different countries, not to the prices of different factors.

Consider the case in which labor-abundant country A opens trade and wants to specialize in labor-intensive good X. To increase production of X, country A must decrease production of good Y. This releases a package of inputs composed of capital and labor in the proportion currently used in the Y industry. This package of inputs includes a relatively large amount of capital and a small amount of labor, because Y is the capital-intensive good. The package of resources needed to produce an additional unit of good X using current production techniques includes a relatively large quantity of labor and a small amount of capital. This scenario implies that opening trade causes an excess supply of capital—as shrinking firms in the Y industry release more capital than expanding X firms want to hire. There also is an excess demand for labor—as shrinking Y firms release less labor than growing X firms want to hire.

Something must happen to cause the firms to adjust their production techniques. What occurs is a change in the relative prices of the two factors. Capital becomes relatively cheaper, causing Y firms to release less of it and X firms to hire more. Labor becomes relatively more expensive, causing Y firms to release more of it and X firms to hire less.

The isoquant diagram in Figure 2 illustrates how firms' cost-minimizing production techniques change. Recall that firms in each industry choose their capital-labor ratio by equating the marginal rate of technical substitution (the absolute value of the slope of the isoquant) to the ratio of the factor prices (the absolute value of the slope of the isocost line).[9] We can represent a rise in w/r from $(w/r)_0$ to $(w/r)_1$ as a clockwise rotation of the isocost line, or an increase in (the absolute value of) its slope. Firms respond by choosing a *higher* capital-labor ratio, $(K/L)_{X1}$ rather than $(K/L)_{X0}$. This adjustment occurs in both industries.

Figure 2   Changes in Factor Prices Cause Firms to Change Their Capital-Labor Ratios

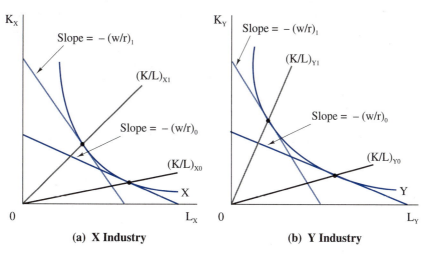

(a) X Industry   **(b) Y Industry**

For the country to increase production of the labor-intensive good (X), firms in both industries must increase their capital-labor ratios. The rise in the wage-rental ratio from $(w/r)_0$ to $(w/r)_1$ brings about this adjustment. Firms choose to use less labor and more capital as labor becomes more expensive relative to capital.

---

9. For a review, see section 2.1 in Chapter Three.

Why would the labor-abundant country need to use a higher capital-labor ratio in production of both goods? When the country engages in trade, it specializes its production according to comparative advantage. This means specializing in the good that uses the abundant factor intensively—but the country has available only a fixed quantity of that factor. To produce more of the good that uses the abundant factor intensively, production of each unit of both goods must use somewhat less of that factor than before so there will be enough of it to go around. The factor price changes described by the factor price equalization theorem provide firms an incentive to undertake the necessary changes in production techniques. Profit-maximizing firms will choose to use more of the scarce factor as it becomes relatively cheaper and less of the abundant factor as it becomes more expensive. This "economizing" on use of the abundant factor allows the country to specialize in producing the comparative-advantage good, which uses the abundant factor intensively.

3.1 An Alternate View of Factor Price Equalization

Even economists initially found the factor price equalization theorem—that is, that trade in outputs could equalize each factor's price across countries even when factors were completely immobile internationally—a surprising result. Robert Mundell provided an intuitive and insightful explanation. According to Mundell, trade in outputs serves as a "substitute" for trade in factors of production.

For example, when a labor-abundant country exports a labor-intensive good, the country indirectly exports labor to a labor-scarce country. Similarly, when a labor-abundant country imports a capital-intensive good, the country indirectly imports capital from a capital-abundant country. Mundell went even further to "turn the model on its head" and show that if factors of production were freely traded and outputs immobile among countries, rather than vice versa, trade in inputs would equalize output prices. Unrestricted trade in either output or input markets can substitute for trade in the other markets. It's easy to find examples of policy makers responding to this linkage between trade policy and immigration policy. NAFTA's improved access for Mexican goods to the U.S. market, for example, reduced pressure for Mexican workers to migrate illegally to the United States; instead, they can work in Mexico and benefit from U.S. sales of the labor-intensive goods they produce.[10] Similarly, supporters of European Union enlargement to include the countries of Central and Eastern Europe hope that better access for those countries' goods in Western European markets will reduce incentives for workers to migrate west.

3.2 Why Don't We Observe Full Factor Price Equalization?

We don't observe full factor price equalization, and it's important to understand why.[11] Figure 3 reports one measure of hourly compensation for production workers in manufacturing for 26 countries. Compensation differs by a factor of 10; that is, those in the highest-wage country (Norway) are more than 10 times as high as those in the lowest-wage country (Mexico), where wages are still far above those in the lowest-wage countries in the world. Given these data, a reasonable question about the factor price equalization theorem would be: Why aren't factor prices equalized? There are several reasons why full factor price equalization isn't observed.

First, much of the observed inequality of income and wealth across countries comes from uneven ownership of human and nonhuman capital. Our basic trade model

---

10. "A New Future for Mexico's Work Force," *The Wall Street Journal*, April 14, 2000.

11. The Leamer and Levinsohn and the Rassekh and Thompson articles in the chapter references survey the empirical literature on factor price equalization.

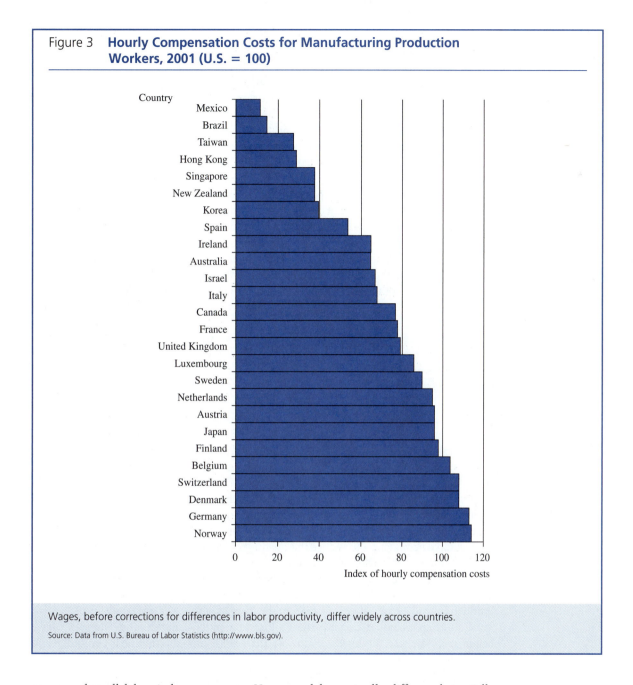

Figure 3   **Hourly Compensation Costs for Manufacturing Production Workers, 2001 (U.S. = 100)**

Wages, before corrections for differences in labor productivity, differ widely across countries.

Source: Data from U.S. Bureau of Labor Statistics (http://www.bls.gov).

assumes that all labor is homogeneous. However, labor actually differs substantially across countries in terms of human capital—skill, training, education, nutrition, and a variety of other attributes. Wage differences reflect these variations; we wouldn't expect a nuclear physicist with 20 years' experience in Norway to earn the same wage as an unskilled laborer entering the workforce for the first time in Mexico. Also, most individuals in developed countries earn part of their incomes from ownership of capital in addition to what they earn by selling their labor services.

Second, we've assumed that each good is produced using the same technology in all countries. When someone develops a new and better technology, it tends to spread and replace older, less effective technologies; but the process can be slow, particularly between developed and developing countries. When two countries produce a good using different technologies, the rewards paid to the factors of production won't equalize across countries, even in the presence of trade, although the rewards will move closer together than without trade.

Both differences in ownership of human capital and differences in technology cause factor productivity to vary across countries. Under such circumstances, we wouldn't expect actual factor prices to equalize, but rather factor prices *corrected for productivity differences* to equalize. For example, we would expect countries with labor productivity higher than that of the United States to exhibit wages higher than those in the United States and vice versa. Figure 4 presents evidence of this relationship. The horizontal axis in panel (a) measures each country's labor productivity relative to that in the United States, and the vertical axis measures the country's wage compared to that in the United States. The data points for 30 diverse developing and developed countries cluster around a 45-degree line, just as we would expect. Panel (b) presents the corresponding information for capital. These data indicate that factor prices, once corrected for productivity differences, do tend toward equality across countries.

Recall that we've argued that countries generally specialize their production only partially under conditions of increasing costs; in other words, both countries continue to produce some of both goods. It turns out that factor prices equalize in the basic trade model only when this is true, not when countries specialize completely. So, if countries' factor endowments are so very different that countries specialize completely in their good of comparative advantage, factor price equalization won't occur.

Also, remember that factor price equalization follows from output price equalization. But complete output price equalization doesn't always occur, for reasons that can include transportation costs, policy barriers to trade, and the existence of goods (for example, haircuts or health care) not easily traded.

Despite these hindrances to actual complete factor price equalization, the factor price equalization theorem is useful in understanding trade liberalization's effects. From a theoretical point of view, the theorem highlights the interrelatedness of the various markets in our basic trade model and the importance of a rigorous formulation to derive all its implications. From a policy point of view, the theorem points out that trade in outputs and trade in inputs can be substitutes in terms of their effects on the world economy. Consider the case of an extremely labor-abundant country. In autarky, wages would tend to be very low, and policy makers might be tempted to prescribe policies such as forced emigration to reduce the quantity of labor and raise wages. But the costs of mobility for some factors of production, especially labor, can be very high in both economic and psychological terms. The factor price equalization theorem suggests an important policy alternative: Allow free trade in outputs, specialize in labor-intensive production, and export labor indirectly in the form of labor-intensive goods.[12]

Countries including Ireland, the Philippines, India, Jamaica, and Singapore have begun using new technologies to do just that. With new international computer and telecommunication networks, labor-abundant countries such as those mentioned can perform labor-intensive data-processing tasks for foreign firms. Entering data into computers for new databases, creating telephone directories, maintaining computer files for magazine subscriptions, processing computer records for health-insurance companies, and telephone call-center operations are just a few of the jobs, not all of which are low-skill occupations.

---

12. For our purposes, understanding the mechanism that pushes toward factor price equalization—changes in output mix—is, in fact, much more important than the empirical question of whether factor prices fully equalize. Some recent disagreements between labor economists and trade economists over measuring trade's effect on the wages of skilled and unskilled workers hinge on the output-mix issue. Work by labor economists tends to ignore changes in the product mix, while work by trade economists recognizes those changes as the very channel by which trade affects factor prices. See Case Two.

Figure 4 **Factor Prices Reflect Productivity**

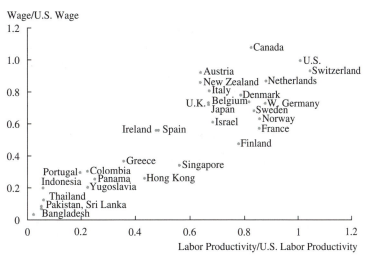

(a) Labor Productivity and Wages

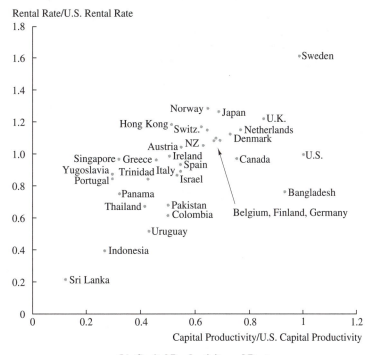

(b) Capital Productivity and Rents

Relative factor price differences across countries match relative productivity differences. Countries with high (low) labor productivity relative to that of the United States tend to have high (low) wages relative to the United States. Countries with high (low) capital productivity relative to that of the United States tend to have high (low) rental rates relative to the United States.

Source: Data from Daniel Trefler, "International Factor Price Differences: Leontief Was Right!" *Journal of Political Economy* 101 (1993), p. 972.

4 WHAT IF FACTORS ARE IMMOBILE IN THE SHORT RUN? THE SPECIFIC-FACTORS MODEL[13]

The Stolper-Samuelson and factor price equalization theorems summarize the effects of opening trade on real factor prices under the assumption that factors are completely mobile among industries within a country and completely immobile among countries. In the short run, however, the mobility of factors among industries may be imperfect. When factors can't move easily or quickly among industries, the short-run effects of opening trade differ from the long-run effects captured by the Stolper-Samuelson and factor price equalization theorems.

4.1 What Are the Reasons for Short-Run Factor Immobility?

Factor mobility among industries may be less than perfect for several reasons. In the case of physical capital, such as machines and factories, one cause of limited mobility is clear. A machine designed to manufacture shoes can't suddenly manufacture computers. At any moment, a significant share of a country's capital stock takes the form of specialized equipment—equipment suited only for the specific purpose for which it was designed.

How, then, does a country's capital stock change over time to reflect various industries' rising and falling fortunes? As machines, buildings, and other physical capital wear out from use and age, firms set aside funds to replace the equipment when the time comes. These funds are called **depreciation allowances** and comprise a form of saving by firms. Just as an individual might save to be able to buy a new car when the old one wears out, a firm saves to accumulate funds to replace worn-out capital equipment. Although a particular piece of equipment often can't be switched to use in a different production process, depreciation funds can be used to buy a different type of capital. In other words, as the economy's capital equipment wears out and is replaced, firms can change the character of the capital stock in response to changes in relative demands for and supplies of various goods. If firms want to produce fewer shoes, some of the machines used in shoe production won't be replaced when they wear out. On the other hand, if firms want to produce more computers, they will not only replace machines worn out in computer production but will invest in additional computer-producing equipment as well.

The preceding arguments for the capital stock also apply, with appropriate modifications, to the country's workforce. Individuals learn certain skills suited for specific occupations. Some general skills, of course, apply in a wide range of industries; oral and written communication skills, good interpersonal skills, and desirable work habits such as punctuality prove useful in almost any job. Other skills are more specific. A welder can't become a mathematics professor overnight in response to a decline in the construction industry and a boom in education. Similarly, a mathematics professor can't suddenly become a welder in response to the opposite trend. Individuals can learn new skills, but the process takes time. As older workers retire and new ones enter the labor force, the skill distribution across the labor force slowly changes in favor of growing industries and away from shrinking ones. This captures the labor-force version of the depreciation of the capital stock.

In the long run, the process of depreciation, retraining, and replacement allows both capital and labor to flow from declining industries to rising ones; but such mobility may be limited in the short run. The more specialized the capital equipment and skills and the slower the rate of depreciation in a given industry, the more slowly that industry will adjust to change—including change generated by trade.

---

13. Paul Samuelson, "Ohlin Was Right," *Swedish Journal of Economics* 73 (1971), pp. 365–384, and Ronald W. Jones, "A Three-Factor Model in Theory, Trade, and History," in *Trade, Balance of Payments, and Growth*, eds., Jagdish Bhagwati, et al. (Amsterdam: North-Holland, 1971), pp. 3–21, developed the specific-factors model.

4.2 Effects of Short-Run Factor Immobility

Suppose country A uses labor and capital to produce shoes (s) and computers (c). Labor is perfectly mobile between the shoe and computer industries, but capital is industry specific. Shoe capital (SK) can't produce computers, and computer capital (CK) can't produce shoes. As a result, the wage paid to labor will be equal in the two industries, but the rental rates paid to the two types of capital may differ. (*Why?*)

Figure 5 illustrates equilibrium in country A's factor markets. In panel (a), the length of the horizontal axis $(0_s 0_c)$ measures the total quantity of labor available in country A, or L^A. The two vertical axes measure the wage paid to labor in the two industries (w_s on the left axis and w_c on the right). We measure labor used in the shoe industry from left to right from the shoe origin (0_s), and labor used in the computer industry from right to left from the computer origin (0_c). Any point along the horizontal axis represents an allocation of the available labor between the two industries.

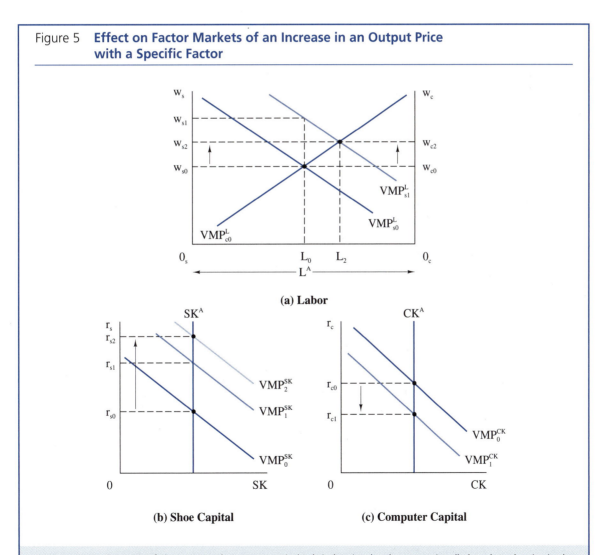

Figure 5   Effect on Factor Markets of an Increase in an Output Price with a Specific Factor

(a) Labor

(b) Shoe Capital

(c) Computer Capital

An increase in the price of shoes raises the wage rate in both industries, but by proportionally less than the rise in the price of shoes. The return to capital specific to the shoe industry rises more than proportionally with the price of shoes, and the return to capital specific to the computer industry falls.

The curves VMP^L_{s0} and VMP^L_{c0} represent the value *marginal product* of *labor* in the two industries, respectively. The value marginal product of labor equals the increase in revenue to a firm that hires an additional unit of labor, or the marginal product of labor (the additional output produced when the firm employs one additional unit of labor) multiplied by the price of the good produced, $\text{VMP}^L \equiv \text{MP}^L \cdot P$. As the quantity of labor employed in an industry rises, the marginal productivity of labor falls, and with it the value marginal product of labor; therefore, the VMP curves slope downward when viewed from their respective axes.[14] We assume the labor market to be perfectly competitive, so labor earns a wage in each industry equal to the value of the productivity of the marginal unit of labor in that industry.[15] In the figure, $0_s L_0$ workers work in the shoe industry and $0_c L_0$ workers in the computer industry, the allocation that equalizes wages at $w_{s0} = w_{c0}$. (*Explain why mobility of labor between industries ensures this division of labor between the industries. What would happen if* $w_s > w_c$ *or vice versa?*)

Panels (b) and (c) of Figure 5 illustrate equilibrium in the markets for shoe capital and for computer capital. Country A's endowments of these two inputs are fixed at SK^A and CK^A, respectively; so the supply curve of each is a vertical line. The demand for each type of capital reflects the value of its marginal product, or the additional revenue to a firm hiring one more unit of the capital. The VMP curves slope downward because the marginal product of each type of capital falls as more is used. Each type of capital earns the rental rate at which the quantity available equals the quantity firms want to hire; the equilibrium rental rates are r_{s0} and r_{c0}.

What happens if the price of shoes (P_s) rises? The value marginal product of labor in the shoe industry rises proportionally with P_s, since $\text{VMP}^L_s \equiv \text{MP}^L_s \cdot P_s$. The VMP^L_s curve in panel (a) shifts upward. At the initial allocation of labor between the two industries (the vertical line, L_0), $w_{s1} > w_{c0}$. Workers move from the computer industry to the shoe industry until wages again equalize at $w_{s2} = w_{c2}$; L_2 represents the new allocation of labor between industries.

Notice that wages rise *less* than proportionally with the price of shoes (reflected in Figure 5 by the fact that $w_{s2} < w_{s1}$); the magnification effect does *not* apply to the mobile factor when one of the factors is immobile between industries. The rise in the price of shoes exerts an ambiguous effect on workers' real wages or purchasing power. Wages rise, but by less than the rise in the price of shoes. If a worker spent all of his or her income on shoes, that worker's purchasing power would fall because w/P_s falls; but a worker who spent most of his or her income on computers (whose price hasn't changed) would enjoy an increase in purchasing power because w/P_c rises.

Even though capital can't move between industries, the rise in the price of shoes still affects capital markets. The marginal product of any factor of production depends positively on the quantity of other factors with which the factor works. As labor moves into the shoe industry, shoe capital has more labor to work with and the marginal product of shoe capital rises; the $\text{VMP}^{SK} \equiv \text{MP}^{SK} \cdot P_s$ line shifts up to VMP^{SK}_1. The exodus of labor from the computer industry, on the other hand, reduces the marginal product of computer capital and shifts $\text{VMP}^{CK} \equiv \text{MP}^{CK} \cdot P_c$ down to VMP^{CK}_1. The rise in the price of shoes also causes a proportional shift up in $\text{VMP}^{SK} \equiv \text{MP}^{SK} \cdot P_s$ to VMP^{SK}_2. The net result is that the rental rate earned by shoe capital *rises more than proportionally* with the price of shoes, while the rental rate earned by computer capital *falls*. The rise in

---

14. The marginal product of labor eventually falls as the firm uses more labor, because the marginal product of a factor is defined as the change in output resulting from a one-unit change in use of that factor *with the quantities of all other factors held constant*. As more labor is combined with a fixed amount of capital, additional workers eventually become less productive (*think of a simple example*); therefore, the marginal product of labor declines.

15. Competitive profit-maximizing firms hire labor until the additional revenue from hiring a worker (VMP^L) equals the additional cost incurred by hiring the worker (w).

Table 3 EFFECT OF A RISE IN THE PRICE OF SHOES ON FACTOR PRICES WHEN CAPITAL IS IMMOBILE

The wage rate rises in both industries, but by less than the increase in the price of shoes. The effect on workers' purchasing power (that is, the *real* wage) depends on the shares of shoes and computers in workers' consumption. The return to shoe capital rises more than the price of shoes, so owners of shoe capital enjoy an increase in buying power regardless of their consumption pattern. The return to computer capital falls, so owners of computer capital suffer a loss of purchasing power regardless of their consumption pattern.

Effect on

w	$\Uparrow$
Purchasing power of w	$?^a$ ($w/P_s \Downarrow$, $w/P_c \Uparrow$)
r_s	$\Uparrow$
Purchasing power of r_s	$\Uparrow^b$ ($r_s/P_s \Uparrow$, $r_s/P_c \Uparrow$)
r_c	$\Downarrow$
Purchasing power of r_c	$\Downarrow^b$ ($r_c/P_s \Downarrow$, $r_c/P_c \Downarrow$)

[a]No magnification effect.

[b]Magnification effect.

the price of shoes improves the purchasing power of owners of shoe capital, even if they spend all their incomes on now-more-expensive shoes (because r_s/P_s rises), and reduces the purchasing power of owners of computer capital, even if they spend all of their incomes on computers, whose price hasn't changed. Therefore, the magnification effect *does* hold for the immobile factor. Table 3 summarizes these results.

4.3 Trade with an Industry-Specific Factor

Short-run factor immobility among industries implies that the short-run effects of opening trade on the distribution of income differ from the predictions of the Stolper-Samuelson theorem, which applies only when both factors can move between industries. To highlight the importance of factor mobility in determining trade's effects on income, we'll continue to consider the case in which labor is highly mobile among industries but capital is immobile in the short run. Suppose a country with a comparative advantage in labor-intensive shoe production and a comparative disadvantage in capital-intensive computer production opens trade. Shoe production rises and computer production falls as the country specializes its production according to comparative advantage.

If both labor and capital were mobile between the two industries, newly unemployed workers from the computer industry would flow into the shoe industry, and the shoe industry would buy unused capital from the computer industry. Given our assumption of mobile labor and immobile capital, workers do flow from the computer to the shoe industry, but the machines formerly used in producing computers are useless in making shoes.

What happens to wages and to the rates of return earned by capital owners? First, note that the price of shoes rises and the price of computers falls as the production pattern shifts. The price of computers falls because more efficiently produced imports replace relatively inefficient and costly domestic production. The price of shoes rises with the level of production, a reflection of increasing costs. The net effect on wages depends on the magnitudes of the fall in P_c and the rise in P_s. (*How could you illustrate this in Figure 5(a)? What would happen to VMP_s^L and VMP_c^L?*) Regardless of whether wages rise or fall, the effect on workers' purchasing power depends on the combination of goods they consume, because w/P_s falls and w/P_c rises. If a worker spends a large share of income on computers (whose price has fallen) and a small share on shoes (whose price has risen), that individual definitely will enjoy an increase in purchasing power, or ability to buy goods. Another worker will be worse off if he or she buys no computers but does buy new shoes, because the price of shoes rises by a greater proportion than do wages. (*Why?*)[16]

The effect on the returns to capital is clearer. Owners of capital designed to produce computers are definitely worse off, since the rate of return to computer-specific capital falls and does so by more than the price of computers. Owners of capital designed to produce shoes definitely are better off, because the return to shoe-specific capital rises and by more than the price of shoes. In the short run, therefore, the mobile factor's *consumption pattern* and the *industry* that employs the immobile factor determine trade's effect on each factor's real reward. Only in the long run, when all factors can move between industries, does a factor's *relative scarcity or abundance* determine the impact of opening trade.

Table 4 illustrates the distinction between trade's short-run and long-run effects on factor prices in terms of our shoe-computer example. In the short run, the returns to capital employed in the expanding shoe industry rise. This creates an incentive to invest in capital designed to produce shoes. The other side of the adjustment process is a fall in the returns to capital specifically employed in the computer industry, creating incentives not to replace that capital as it wears out. Again, wages may rise or fall, but the effect on workers' purchasing power will depend on whether workers buy primarily (now-cheaper) computers or (now-more-expensive) shoes.

In the long run, both workers and capital can move between industries, and the Stolper-Samuelson theorem holds. Wages rise throughout the economy, because the expanding shoe industry is more labor intensive than the contracting computer industry. The return to all capital falls as the economy cuts production of the capital-intensive good, computers.

The existence of factors specific to single industries creates a short-run rigidity, or limitation on the economy's ability to reallocate production among industries quickly. The more industry-specific the factors of production, the slower and more costly will be any adjustment to relative price changes in terms of temporary unemployment or underutilization of capital. These short-term adjustment costs can cause policy problems as individuals attempt to insulate themselves from the effects of unfavorable price changes.

Whenever relative prices change and some industries decline, political pressure for protection builds from resources tied to those industries; but interference with relative price changes and the resulting factor price changes can be dangerous to the health of the economy as a whole. As we noted in the shoe-computer example, the temporary fall in the reward to capital in the computer industry and rise in the reward to capital in the shoe industry create the incentives needed for the economy to adjust to trade by specializing according to comparative advantage. Trade, in turn, improves potential welfare by increasing the total quantity of goods and services available for consumption.

---

16. When capital is immobile, an increase in the price of a good causes wages to rise less-than-proportionally with the good's price, as demonstrated for shoes in section 4.2. Here the addition of a decline in the price of the second good (computers) causes wages to rise even less. If the decline in the price of computers more than offsets the rise in the price of shoes, wages may fall; but the effect on labor's purchasing power will remain ambiguous, because wages can neither rise proportionally more than P_s nor fall proportionally more than P_c.

Table 4   **SHORT- AND LONG-RUN EFFECTS OF TRADE ON FACTOR PRICES AND PURCHASING POWER**

The country has a comparative advantage in shoes. In the short run, owners of capital employed in the shoe industry and workers who buy more computers than shoes gain from opening trade. Owners of capital employed in the computer industry and workers who buy more shoes than computers lose. In the long run, workers, the factor used intensively in expanding shoe production, gain from the opening of trade; owners of capital, the factor used intensively in shrinking computer production, lose.

	Effect of Trade in	
	Short Run	Long Run
w_s	?	⇑
Purchasing power of w_s	?[a]	⇑[b]
w_c	?	⇑
Purchasing power of w_c	?[a]	⇑[b]
r_s	⇑	⇓
Purchasing power of r_s	⇑[b]	⇓[b]
r_c	⇓	⇓
Purchasing power of r_c	⇓[b]	⇓[b]

[a]No magnification effect.

[b]Magnification effect.

5 TRADE AND WELFARE: GAINERS, LOSERS, AND COMPENSATION

The Stolper-Samuelson theorem and the specific-factors model explain why various groups in the economy may feel quite differently about trade. Under the assumptions of the Heckscher-Ohlin theorem, a country indirectly "exports" its abundant factor through trade, thereby increasing demand for that factor and raising its real reward. Likewise, the country indirectly "imports" its scarce factor, decreasing demand and lowering the factor's real reward. In the short run, when some factors are industry specific, (1) the real rewards of factors specific to the comparative-advantage industry rise, (2) the real rewards to factors specific to the comparative-disadvantage industry fall, and (3) the real reward to the mobile factor rises (falls) if its owner purchases mainly the comparative-disadvantage (advantage) good. In the long run, the real reward of the abundant factor rises and that of the scarce factor falls. But, in Chapter Three we demonstrated that opening trade increases the *total* quantity of goods available and makes it possible for *everyone* to gain. In order for everyone to gain—despite the changes in factor rewards implied by the Stolper-Samuelson theorem and the specific-factors model—a portion of the gains enjoyed by some groups would have to be used to compensate other groups for their losses. If this were done, trade could make every person, and therefore society as a whole, better off. In general, however, no automatic mechanism exists to make this compensatory redistribution.

These issues of income distribution and trade's different impacts on various groups within a country didn't arise in the Ricardian model in Chapter Two. The reason is that the Ricardian model contained only one input, which we called *labor*. In each country, opening trade raised the relative price of the output that the country's labor produced relatively efficiently. Real wages rose, and everyone was made better off (see Table 3 in

Chapter Two). In reality, however, things aren't so simple.[17] Policy makers usually must deal with decisions involving policies that help some groups and harm others.

5.1 Potential versus Actual Utility

In Chapters Two and Three, we demonstrated that unrestricted international trade increases the output that the world's endowment of scarce resources can produce. With more goods available for consumption, we can see a potential increase in world welfare or utility. Figure 6 illustrates this potential increase.[18]

Why must we speak of an increase in *potential* world welfare or utility? We can't say that a move from point 1 (representing autarky) to point 2 (representing unrestricted trade) in Figure 6 necessarily increases *actual* utility. After all, we know nothing about the distribution of goods at either point. At point 1, society produces X_1 units of good X and Y_1 units of good Y. One individual may have all the X and all the Y while everyone else has nothing, or the X and Y may be evenly distributed. The same holds true at point 2: There are X_2 units of X and Y_2 units of Y available, but we don't know how these goods are distributed. The fact that point 2 lies on a higher indifference curve than point 1 merely implies that moving from 1 to 2 has the *potential* to make every individual better off (for example, if the additional goods were distributed among all individuals).

Figure 6   **Trade Increases Potential Welfare**

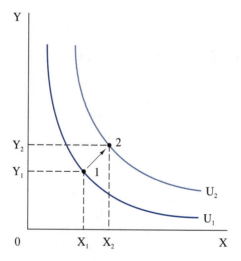

Trade allows production of larger quantities of goods, making a higher indifference curve attainable.

---

17.   The result from the Ricardian model carries over to the case of two inputs only if both industries use those inputs in the same proportions. (*Why would the adjustment of production techniques illustrated in Figure 2 be unnecessary in this special case?*)

18.   For a review of the basics of indifference curves and some hints at the distributional problems involved in using community indifference curves, see section 5.2 in Chapter 2. The distributional issues central to the analysis of community indifference curves don't arise in the case of individual indifference curves because all goods belong to the same individual.

5.2 Comparing Utility: The Pareto Criterion

Suppose that in moving from point 1 to point 2 in Figure 6, we distributed the additional goods ([$X_2 - X_1$] units of X and [$Y_2 - Y_1$] units of Y) so that everyone ended up with more of each good. In such a case, we might say that the move from point 1 to 2 increased actual welfare or utility. The **Pareto criterion** (named after economist Vilfredo Pareto) formalizes this idea. According to the Pareto criterion, any change that makes at least one person better off *without* making any individual worse off increases welfare. The example in which increased production was distributed among all residents clearly satisfies this requirement.

The Pareto criterion provides a useful benchmark for assessing various economic policies' welfare effects. Unfortunately, it sidesteps the really tough policy questions. In Chapter One, we suggested that policy makers rarely are lucky enough to evaluate policies that either benefit everyone or harm everyone. Decisions on such policies are relatively easy; both common sense and the Pareto criterion recommend pursuing the former class of policies and avoiding the latter. Far more common are policy questions that involve benefits to some individuals and costs to others. In these cases, neither common sense nor the Pareto criterion provides much assistance.

5.3 Comparing Utility: The Compensation Criterion

Clearly, the Pareto criterion can't answer some questions that arise in evaluating international trade's effect on world welfare. The changes in factor prices predicted by the Stolper-Samuelson and factor price equalization theorems and by the specific-factors model imply that opening trade will harm some groups. In the short run, these groups include owners of any specific factors employed in the country's comparative-disadvantage industry. In the long run, the losers include owners of the factor used intensively in the country's comparative-disadvantage industry.

Several economists have suggested ways to evaluate the welfare effects of policies that benefit some individuals and harm others, thereby circumventing the boundaries of the issues the Pareto criterion can address. The specific proposals vary; however, a simple common idea underlies each. The key question is whether the gainers from a policy gain enough to allow them to compensate the losers for their losses and still enjoy a net gain.

Opening international trade satisfies this **compensation criterion** for a welfare improvement. The world economy can produce more goods with trade, so gainers can, in principle, compensate losers and still be better off. The remaining problems arise because such compensation, though possible, may not occur.

5.4 Adjustment Costs and Compensation in Practice: Trade Adjustment Assistance

Specialization and trade according to comparative advantage are dynamic processes. Countries gain and lose comparative advantage as demand and supply conditions in various output and factor markets change. Efficiency requires that industries adapt to these changes, but such adjustment imposes costs. Resources employed in a shrinking industry may suffer losses due to temporary unemployment, relocation, or retraining. The more specifically resources are designed for certain industries, the larger the dislocation costs are likely to be, because specialized resources, by definition, are ill suited for movement among industries. There can be little doubt that these costs and the associated redistributions of income are an important cause of political pressures for protectionist policies, which rob countries of potential gains from trade. Industries have every incentive to lobby for protection to avoid the adjustment costs associated with changing patterns of comparative advantage.

Adjustment costs create three distinct but related policy problems. The first concerns equity in dealing with individuals adversely affected by trade. We've seen that unrestricted international trade maximizes world welfare. We've also seen that certain groups in the economy are harmed by trade. The extent to which society should compensate those groups represents an important policy question. The second issue concerns how to prevent individuals harmed by trade from successfully lobbying for protectionist policies that reduce total world welfare. The third question is how policy makers can promote the adjustments necessary to realize the full potential gains from international trade.

Many countries have government-administered programs to aid individuals who've lost jobs because of changing patterns of comparative advantage. These programs have the triple purpose of more equitably distributing the adjustment costs incurred to capture the gains from trade, placating the most potent constituency for protectionism, and encouraging and facilitating the necessary adjustments.

The U.S. government administers the **Trade Adjustment Assistance (TAA)** program. The Trade Expansion Act of 1962 contained the first provision for a program aimed specifically at workers displaced for trade-related reasons (in particular, by increased imports resulting from tariff reductions negotiated through the General Agreement on Tariffs and Trade—predecessor to today's World Trade Organization). The act provided extended unemployment benefits plus retraining and relocation funds for workers in industries that could prove liberalization of international trade as the cause of their displacement. Requirements for such proof were quite stringent, and no workers qualified for assistance until 1969. Gradually, Congress eased the requirements, and more workers became eligible for benefits.

The Trade Act of 1974 mandated that imports need only "contribute importantly" to displacement rather than be the direct cause. More important, the 1974 act changed the nature of the link between trade and displacement. Congress had designed the 1962 act with the idea that workers injured *by a government policy* (that is, internationally negotiated reductions in tariffs) should receive compensation. The 1974 act altered the purpose of the program to include compensation of workers injured by increases in imports *regardless of the cause* of those increases. The number of workers receiving assistance grew slowly through the 1970s before exploding in 1980, when automobile workers qualified. Table 5 reports cash payments to workers under the TAA program.

Controversy surrounds the TAA program because its three goals, to some extent, inevitably conflict. The goal of compensating workers displaced by international trade can interfere with the goal of facilitating the adjustments required by trade according to comparative advantage. Many economists feel that TAA's heavy emphasis on extended unemployment benefits and weak focus on retraining and relocation assistance may actually hinder adjustment. The extra year of unemployment benefits may encourage workers to remain unemployed and await recall to their old jobs rather than seek employment in growing industries. Between 1975 and 1987, about $4,400 million went to Trade Readjustment Allowances, or extended unemployment benefits, while only $228 million was spent on retraining, job search, and relocation.

In response to these criticisms, the Omnibus Trade and Competitiveness Act of 1988 added the requirement that workers participate in a job-training program to be eligible for TAA payments. About one-third of total program expenditures in 1999 went to training, job-search, and relocation allowances, while two-thirds went to extended unemployment benefits. However, skepticism persists about the effectiveness of the job-training provisions since several studies have found no difference in ultimate employment and wage outcomes between workers who received training and those who did not.

In 2002, Congress altered the TAA program again, this time to include a "wage insurance" component that older workers can choose in place of the training-based program. If a TAA-eligible displaced worker aged 50 or older takes a new full-time job within

Table 5 TRADE-READJUSTMENT-ALLOWANCE EXPENDITURES ($ MILLIONS)

Year	Total Outlays	Year	Total Outlays	Year	Total Outlays
1976	$ 79	1986	$116	1996	$166
1977	148	1987	198	1997	188
1978	257	1988	186	1998	152
1979	256	1989	125	1999	213
1980	1,622	1990	92	2000	258
1981	1,440	1991	116	2001	260
1982	103	1992	43	2002	229
1983	37	1993	50	2003	327
1984	35	1994	120		
1985	43	1995	153		

Source: Data from U.S. Department of Labor.

26 weeks of displacement, but at a wage less than $50,000 per year and less than that earned in the original job, government funds pay the worker half of the shortfall between the old wage and the new one (up to $10,000) for two years. The wage-insurance policy encourages workers who have lost their jobs because of trade to find new jobs quickly and limits the risks faced by older workers who might be displaced into lower-wage jobs.

In 2002, Congress also extended TAA benefit availability to new categories of workers and added a tax credit to help eligible workers buy health insurance. One large group of workers remains ineligible under the TAA program: service workers such as those employed in information-technology services and software development. As comparative advantage in many service jobs shifts from the United States to labor-abundant countries such as India, political pressure rises to expand the TAA program to cover these workers. On the other hand, empirical evidence suggests that workers displaced because of import competition fare at least as well in terms of reemployment as do similar workers displaced for non-trade-related reasons (for example, shifts in consumer tastes, changes in technology, or increased domestic competition). These findings bring into question the fairness of a special program that treats workers displaced by trade more favorably than workers who lose jobs for other reasons.

CASE 1: TRADE AND WAGES I: ASIA

Countries of Asia

Our basic trade model, although a simplified view of the world economy, highlights some common fallacies in discussions of international trade policy. One of the model's most important lessons is the fact that factor prices and the pattern of trade are determined *jointly*. Each affects and is affected by the other. Failure to recognize this two-way interaction can result in nonsensical arguments and poor predictions.

For example, many so-called experts argue that an economy's openness to imports from lower-wage countries will result in massive employment shifts to those countries. You may recall Ross Perot's often-quoted 1992 prediction of a "giant sucking sound" that would shift hundreds of thousands of jobs from the United States to Mexico under NAFTA. Such an argument has many problems (not the least of which is that the prediction didn't come true!), but a pivotal one is its failure to recognize that wages *rise* in low-wage countries as production of labor-intensive goods moves there in response to the initially low wages. Thailand, South Korea,

Singapore, and Taiwan, for example, all have experienced dramatic wage increases as they removed trade barriers and integrated themselves into the world economy, specializing at first in relatively low-skill labor-intensive goods. Between 1975 and 1999, wages in the newly industrializing Asian economies rose by an average of 11.2 percent each year, despite the effects of the Asian crisis that struck in 1997.[19] In China, the increased demand for labor also forces firms to do more to keep their workers. In addition to raising wages, firms have responded by providing perks such as on-site free cafeterias, gyms, bowling alleys, roller-skating rinks, libraries, discos, movies, Internet access, and karaoke machines to keep turnover down among their mostly young workers.[20]

As wages begin to rise, several adjustments occur. First, firms have less incentive, other things being equal, to move their labor-intensive production to the country; so the increase in demand for labor moderates. Korean workers at automaker Hyundai now earn $21.05 an hour, close to the U.S. auto industry average wage of $25.63. So, fewer auto,

steel, ship, electronics, and chemicals producers move to South Korea now than in the 1980s; instead, production relocates to countries where wages remain low, especially Indonesia, China, and Vietnam.[21] Rising wages in China, especially along the export-oriented southern coast, are pushing firms to look elsewhere (including the Chinese interior) for unskilled workers.[22] Second, firms in the countries where wages have risen shift into new, less unskilled-labor-intensive lines of production. For example, in the early 1990s, Korean shoe producers changed from producing simple sneakers to hiking boots and in-line skates, products that lower-wage countries such as China still lacked the skill to produce reliably. More recently, Korean shoe-makers have shifted into custom, made-to-measure shoes produced using digital technology.[23] Similarly, Malaysian apparel firms have moved their basic sewing work abroad to Sri Lanka and China, choosing to use their more-skilled Malaysian workers to make clothing from expensive high-tech fabrics such as those that provide ultraviolet-ray protection.[24]

CASE 2: TRADE AND WAGES II: THE UNITED STATES

United States

Much has been written about the possible relationship among three trends in the U.S. economy during the past quarter century. First, the U.S. merchandise trade deficit (that is, the excess of the total value of imported goods over the total value of exported goods) grew. Second, the upward trend in average U.S. real wages, exhibited through the earlier postwar period, stalled. And third, the wage differential between skilled, well-educated U.S. workers and unskilled, poorly educated U.S. workers expanded. Some obvious questions arise: Did international trade, reflected in the trade deficit, slow the growth in U.S. real wages? And did international trade, especially with low-wage countries such as China, cause the real

incomes of low-skilled and poorly educated U.S. workers to fall?

Attempts at empirical tests to answer these questions face many obstacles. One is the fact that so many things change simultaneously in the world economy that attempts to identify causality always run the risk of misattributing the cause.[25] A second hurdle follows from the discussion in Case One. Changes in trade patterns may affect wages, but changes in wages also affect trade patterns; and many empirical tests fail to use statistical techniques that can handle the two-way relationship.[26]

Most economists tentatively agree that the trends in wages in the United States reflect primarily changes in

19. Data from the U.S. Bureau of Labor Statistics Web site at http://www.bls.gov.

20. "Chinese Factories Roll Out More Perks to Woo Workers," *Financial Times*, March 19, 2004.

21. Andrew Ward, "South Korea Feels the Chill in China's Growing Shadow," *Financial Times*, September 25, 2003; "South Korea's Competitiveness Eroded by Costs," *Financial Times*, November 3, 2003.

22. "China's Increasing Costs of Labor Start to Deter Japanese Businesses," *The Wall Street Journal*, December 14, 1999.

23. Kim Jung Min, "South Korea's Shoe Industry Steps Up to Stay in the Running," *The Wall Street Journal*, February 12, 2002.

24. Cris Prystay, "Textile Makers Shift Strategy," *The Wall Street Journal*, October 7, 2003.

25. The Bhagwati and Kosters reference discusses this problem.

26. This is one reason for the different conclusions about the trade–wage relationship often drawn by labor economists and by trade economists. See the discussion by Leamer and Levinsohn, especially pp. 1349 and 1360–1362.

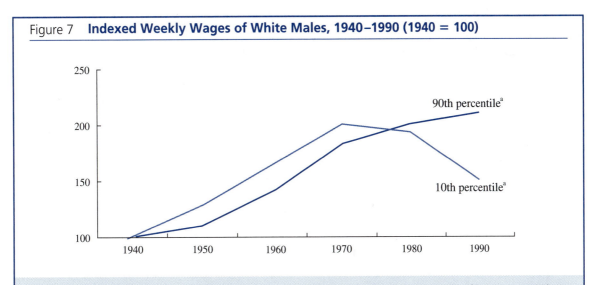

Figure 7 **Indexed Weekly Wages of White Males, 1940–1990 (1940 = 100)**

From the mid-1970s through the mid-1990s, wages of high-income workers rose relative to those of low-income workers.

[a]Percentiles refer to percentiles of the wage distribution, where workers in the 99th percentile have the highest earnings.

Source: Elaine Buckberg and Alun Thomas, "Wage Dispersion and Job Growth in the United States," *Finance and Development* (June 1995), p. 17; data from C. Huhn, "Wage Inequality and Industrial Change," National Bureau of Economic Research Working Paper No. 4684, March 1994.

technology rather than international trade. The increased importance of knowledge-intensive skills has increased demand for workers who possess those skills and decreased demand for less-educated workers who lack them. Today, even entry-level factory jobs require advanced math and computer skills.[27] The result has been rapidly rising real wages for skilled, educated workers and stagnant or falling real wages for unskilled, poorly educated ones, a trend captured in Figure 7.

Why do most economists who have studied this trend carefully attribute it primarily to technological change rather than trade? First, the basic trade model implies that the mechanism through which trade could cause a decline in wages for unskilled labor would be a fall in the price of unskilled-labor-intensive goods (remember the Stolper-Samuelson theorem). Data on this point are somewhat mixed, but most analysts agree that little evidence of such a price trend exists. Second, if trade reduced the wages of unskilled workers in skill-abundant countries such as the United States, that same trade should *increase* the earnings of unskilled workers in unskilled-labor-abundant developing countries.

(*Why?*) But evidence suggests the opposite: Many unskilled-labor-abundant developing countries (for example, Chile, Colombia, Costa Rica, Mexico, and Uruguay) have experienced the same pattern as in the United States—an increase in the relative wages of skilled workers.[28] Third, if trade depressed the wages of unskilled workers, we should be observing all industries substituting toward using more of those now-cheaper workers. (*Use a diagram similar to Figure 2, but with skilled labor on one axis and unskilled labor on the other, to explain why.*) That substitution hasn't happened; instead, most industries now use more skilled labor relative to unskilled labor. Finally, U.S. trade with low-wage developing countries, although it has grown significantly, remains small relative to the size of the economy. U.S. imports from Taiwan, Hong Kong, China, Malaysia, the Philippines, Singapore, and Thailand *combined* equaled only 1.95 percent of U.S. GDP in 1996, up from 0.82 percent in 1982.[29] It's difficult to see how such a small trade share could comprise the primary cause of the trend illustrated in Figure 7.

Despite the evidence that technological change rather than trade provides the main explanation for recent wage

27. "Manufacturers Decry a Shortage of Workers While Rejecting Many," *The Wall Street Journal,* September 8, 1995, p. A1; Clare Ansberry, "Less Sweat, More Tech," *The Wall Street Journal*, June 30, 2003.

28. Donald Robbins, "Evidence on Trade and Wages in the Developing World," *OECD Development Center Technical Paper* No. 119, December 1996.

29. OECD, *Economic Outlook*, December 1997, p. A70.

trends, technological change need not be totally independent of developments on the trade front. Firms that face or anticipate increased competition from imports from low-wage economies may choose either to invest in technology that reduces their use of labor or to outsource low-skill aspects of their production abroad.

Regardless of the final outcome of the debate on the causes of recent wage trends, virtually all economists agree that protection *doesn't* represent a fruitful approach for combating any decline in real wages of low-skill workers.[30] Even if increased openness to international trade were the cause of that decline (despite current evidence that suggests otherwise), protection would impose costs on the economy that would far exceed any benefits to low-skill workers. This doesn't mean that low-wage workers must bear all the costs of opening trade. We know that unrestricted international trade allows the economy to produce a larger total quantity of goods and services. We also know that some groups gain and others lose when a country opens trade. But the gains from trade guarantee that winners from trade can compensate losers, allowing all to share in the gains.

Since the mid-1990s, some evidence suggests the gap between wages of educated and uneducated U.S. workers may have stopped growing. Workers have responded to the gap by attending college and getting more training.

CASE 3: DÉJÀ VU: LEARNING FROM THE HISTORY OF THE WORLD ECONOMY

Most studies of trade and wages, like those summarized in Cases One and Two, focus on recent events. However, economic history offers richer opportunities to observe this important relationship. During the second half of the nineteenth century, declining transportation costs encouraged international trade. What happened to wages?

Economists Kevin O'Rourke and Jeffrey Williamson indicate that the real wage rates of unskilled urban workers in the United States, Sweden, Britain, Germany, Ireland, and Australia converged.[31] This is exactly what our basic trade model predicts. As the United States and Australia expanded trade, they specialized in goods intensive in their abundant factor, land, while European countries specialized in goods intensive in their abundant factor, labor. The ratio of wages to land rents fell in the United States and Australia, where they had been high in the absence of trade; the wage-rent ratio rose in Europe, where it had been low. The factor price changes were most dramatic in countries that were most open to trade. Around 1895, the move toward free trade stalled, and so did the international convergence of wages; the trend wouldn't resume until the 1950s.

Japan

CASE 4: A RARE OPPORTUNITY: LEARNING FROM JAPANESE ECONOMIC HISTORY

Almost all economies engage in international trade, so economists rarely get to observe a country shift suddenly from virtually no trade to completely open trade. Luckily, Meiji Japan's dramatic 1859 trade-policy shift provides a rare exception, although reliable data from the 150-year-old episode are much less plentiful than we'd like. Does what we know about the period support or refute our expectations from comparative advantage, the Heckscher-Ohlin theorem, and the Stolper-Samuelson theorem?

If opening trade allowed Japan to specialize in its comparative-advantage goods (such as silk and silkworms) and to import its comparative-disadvantage ones (such as

---

30. See, in particular, the Deardorff article in the chapter references.

31. This case draws on the O'Rourke and Williamson book in the chapter references.

Figure 8   Testing the Theory of Comparative Advantage: Nineteenth-Century Japan

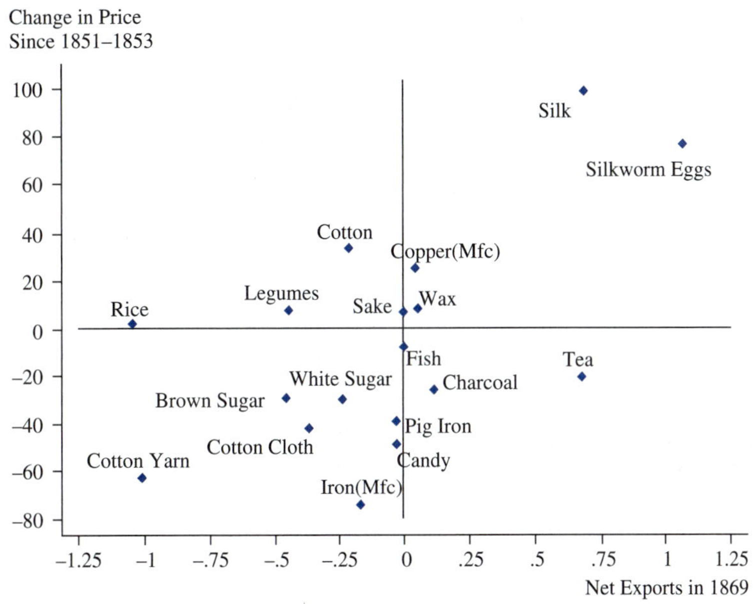

In 1859, Japan suddenly shifted from complete closure to trade to almost unrestricted trade. As the theory of comparative advantage predicts, relative prices rose for Japan's export goods and fell for the country's import goods.

Source: Daniel M. Bernhofen and John C. Brown, "A Direct Test of the Theory of Comparative Advantage: The Case of Japan," *Journal of Political Economy* 112 (February 2004), p. 63.

cotton yarn, cotton cloth, and sugar), we'd expect the prices of the former goods to rise relative to the price of the latter ones following Japan's shift from closure to open trade. In other words, we would expect Japanese relative prices to rise for goods of which Japan became a net exporter once the country opened trade. Similarly, we would expect Japanese relative prices to fall for goods of which Japan became a net importer. This is exactly the pattern that Daniel Bernhofen and John Brown found; Figure 8 illustrates their conclusions.

The horizontal axis measures Japan's net exports for an industry in 1869 (in millions of ryō, the Japanese currency of the time), about ten years after the policy change. The vertical axis measures the percent change in each industry's relative price between 1851–1853 and 1869. If trade occurred according to comparative advantage, we'd observe exactly what we do observe—relative price

increases for most industries with positive net exports and relative price declines for most industries with negative net exports (or net imports).

What about the Heckscher-Ohlin and Stolper-Samuelson theorems? Japan was (and is) labor abundant and land scarce, which according to Heckscher and Ohlin would explain a comparative advantage in labor-intensive goods such as silk and a comparative disadvantage in land-intensive goods such as sugar. What happened to wages and land prices when the country opened trade? The Stolper-Samuelson theorem predicts a rise in the wage-rental ratio when labor-abundant, land-scarce Japan opened trade. Estimates suggest that real wages for unskilled workers rose by 60–70 percent. Direct information on land rents doesn't exist, but plausible inferences from available data indicate that land rents fell by around 80 percent. Overall, the wage-rental ratio rose by over 700 percent.[32]

32. See the O'Rourke and Williamson book in the chapter references, especially p. 74.

SUMMARY

This chapter explicitly introduced the concept of general-equilibrium analysis to emphasize some of the many interrelated changes within an economy that result from opening international trade. Figure 9 illustrates the key relationships among the various markets.

The basic information the trade model takes as exogenous includes tastes, technology, and factor endowments. These three ingredients form the basis for the demand for outputs and the demand for and supply of factors of production. Factor prices, determined by supply and demand, in turn influence incomes, which feed back through the demand for outputs. Factor prices are linked to output prices (which depend on factor endowments according to the Heckscher-Ohlin theorem) through the Stolper-Samuelson theorem and to factor prices in the other country through the factor price equalization theorem. Finally, relative output prices in the two countries determine the pattern of comparative advantage and productive specialization. The equilibrium terms of trade resulting from this process determine the size and allocation of the gains from trade.

Figure 9   **General-Equilibrium Linkages in the Basic Trade Model**

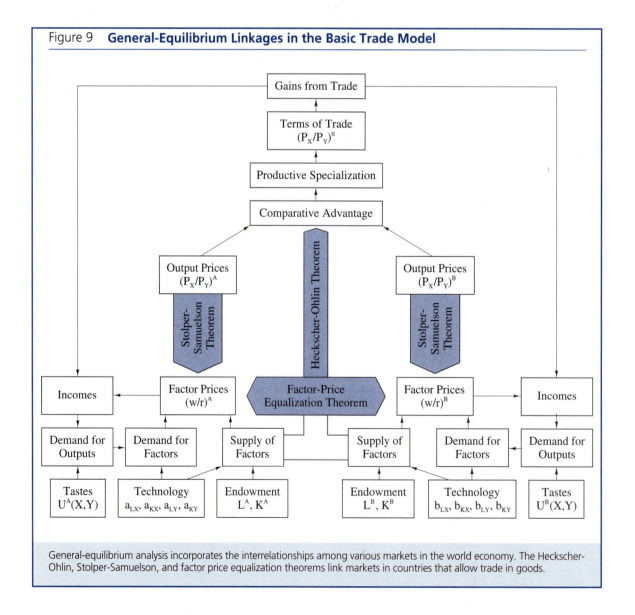

General-equilibrium analysis incorporates the interrelationships among various markets in the world economy. The Heckscher-Ohlin, Stolper-Samuelson, and factor price equalization theorems link markets in countries that allow trade in goods.

LOOKING AHEAD

In this chapter, we explored the wide-ranging effects of opening international trade, particularly those on factor prices and the distribution of income. In Chapter Five, we'll examine attempts to test the Heckscher-Ohlin explanation of trade patterns and outline some of the resulting refinements and modifications of the theory. Then we'll turn to trade based on economies of scale rather than on comparative advantage.

KEY TERMS

magnification effect

Stolper-Samuelson theorem

factor price equalization theorem

depreciation allowances

Pareto criterion

compensation criterion

Trade Adjustment Assistance (TAA)

PROBLEMS AND QUESTIONS FOR REVIEW

1. Suppose that $P_X = a_{LX} \cdot w + a_{KX} \cdot r = 60 \cdot w + 40 \cdot r$ and that $P_Y = a_{LY} \cdot w + a_{KY} \cdot r = 75 \cdot w + 25 \cdot r$.
    a. If $P_X = P_Y = 100$, what are the equilibrium values for the wage rate and the rental rate?
    b. If P_Y rose to 120 and the input coefficients didn't change, what would be the new equilibrium values of w and r?[33]
    c. After the change in part (b), would workers' wages buy more or less good X? More or less good Y? Would capital-owners' rent buy more or less good X? More or less good Y? Have *real* wages risen or fallen? The real rental rate?
    d. Of what trade theorem is your answer to part (c) an example?
2. Farmia is a labor-abundant country that grows coffee and wheat. Assume that labor and land are the only two inputs. Coffee production is labor intensive, and wheat production is land intensive. Labor can work in either the coffee or the wheat industry and can move easily back and forth between the two. But land is specialized; land on the plains is suited to produce wheat and land in the mountains to produce coffee. "Wheat land" is useless in producing coffee, and "coffee land" is useless in producing wheat. If Farmia opens trade with a country with identical tastes, what will happen in the short run to
    a. Farmia's production of wheat and coffee? What information or theorem did you use as the basis for your answer?
    b. Prices of wheat and coffee in Farmia? How do you know?
    c. Wages in Farmia? How do you know?
    d. The price of wheat land in Farmia? How do you know?
    e. The price of coffee land in Farmia? How do you know?
    f. The welfare or purchasing power of workers, owners of wheat land, and owners of coffee land in Farmia? How do you know?
3. This question continues question 1 from Chapter Three.
    a. If both factors of production are mobile between industries, how would the following groups feel about opening trade: capital owners in China, labor in China, capital owners in Japan, and labor in Japan?
    b. Now assume that labor is perfectly mobile between industries, but that capital is immobile between industries. That is, some capital is suitable for producing automobiles, but not suitable for producing clothing and vice versa. How would the following groups feel about opening trade: owners of auto capital in China, owners of clothing capital in China, owners of auto capital in Japan, owners of clothing capital in Japan, labor in China, and labor in Japan?

---

33. In fact, as we argued in this chapter, the input coefficients *would* change. Using techniques beyond the scope of this book, it's possible to show that the qualitative results derived in this question still hold if the input coefficients change; see, for example, the Jones article in the chapter references.

4. Suppose two countries allow both free trade in goods and free flows of factors (such an arrangement is called a *common market*). Why would it be difficult to predict the extent and pattern of trade in goods between them?

5. In debates over international trade policy, workers and capital owners in a given industry often take the same side (for example, U.S. auto producers and the United Auto Workers union, or U.S. steel producers and the United Steelworkers union). However, the Stolper-Samuelson theorem predicts that owners of capital and labor would be affected differently by trade. How can international trade theory explain the observation?

6. The invention of ATM machines and personal computers reduced demand for bank tellers and typists. This is just one example of technological change that altered demand for various types of labor.
   a. Suppose that bank tellers and typists, facing declining employment prospects and wages, pressured policy makers to ban ATMs and personal computers. Would the likely effect on the overall economy of such bans be positive or negative?
   b. After the 1960s, consumers lost interest in hula hoops and moved on to other toys. Suppose that hula-hoop workers, facing declining employment prospects and wages, pressured policy makers to ban non-hula-hoop toys. Would the likely effect on the overall economy of such bans be positive or negative?
   c. Opening trade reduced demand in the United States for textile and apparel workers. Suppose that textile and apparel workers, facing declining employment prospects and wages, pressured policy makers to ban textile and apparel imports. Would the likely effect on the overall economy of such bans be positive or negative?

7. Briefly explain why the magnification effect plays an important role in predicting whether various groups in the economy will support or oppose international trade.

8. The labor-abundant countries of Asia have experienced rapidly rising wages since those economies liberalized their international trade policies. Does this observation match the predictions of international trade theory? Explain.

REFERENCES AND SELECTED READINGS

Aghion, Philippe, and Jeffrey G. Williamson. *Growth, Inequality, and Globalization: Theory, History, and Policy*. Cambridge: Cambridge University Press, 1998.
Advanced treatment of the historical relationship between inequality and support for open international markets.

Baicker, Katherine, and M. Marit Rehavi. "Trade Adjustment Assistance." *Journal of Economic Perspectives* 18 (Spring 2004): 239–255.
Survey of TAA's history and recent changes in the program.

Bhagwati, Jagdish. *Free Trade Today*. Princeton: Princeton University Press, 2002.
Very readable responses to the standard antitrade arguments.

Bhagwati, Jagdish, and Marvin H. Kosters, eds. *Trade and Wages*. Washington, D.C.: American Enterprise Institute, 1994.
Accessible overview of theory and empirical evidence on the relationship between changes in international trade and wages.

Coughlin, Cletus. "The Controversy over Free Trade: The Gap Between Economists and the General Public." *Federal Reserve Bank of St. Louis Review* 84 (January/February 2002): 1–22.
Accessible discussion of the sources of differences in opinion about trade policy.

Deardorff, Alan V. "Technology, Trade, and Increasing Inequality: Does the Cause Matter for the Cure?" *Journal of International Economic Law* 1 (September 1998): 353–376.
Argues that the right policies to address income inequality don't hinge on its causes.

Deardorff, Alan V., and Robert M. Stern, eds. *The Stolper-Samuelson Theorem: A Golden Jubilee*. Ann Arbor, Mich.: University of Michigan Press, 1994.
Collection of papers celebrating the 50th anniversary of the Stolper-Samuelson theorem. The papers vary in level of difficulty.

Fishow, Albert, and Karen Parker, eds. *Growing Apart*. New York: Council on Foreign Relations, 1999.
Collection of readable papers on nontrade sources of inequality trends.

Grossman, Gene M. "Partially Mobile Capital: A General Approach to Two-Sector Trade Theory." *Journal of International Economics* 15 (1983): 1–117.
For intermediate and advanced students; a model that includes the standard and specific-factor models as special cases.

Irwin, Douglas A. *Free Trade Under Fire*. Princeton: Princeton University Press, 2002.
Excellent explanations of the follies of protectionist policies.

Jones, Ronald W. "The Structure of Simple General Equilibrium Models." *Journal of Political Economy* 73 (December 1965): 557–572.
The classic algebraic demonstration of the magnification effect and related ideas.

Leamer, Edward, and James Levinsohn. "International Trade Theory: The Evidence." In *Handbook of International Economics*, Vol. 3, edited by G. M. Grossman and K. Rogoff, 1339–1394. Amsterdam: North-Holland, 1995.
Advanced survey of empirical evidence on international trade theories.

Mundell, Robert A. "International Trade and Factor Mobility." *American Economic Review* 47 (June 1957): 321–335.
Presents the argument that trade in goods and mobility of factors are substitutes. Although the basic argument is highly readable, the graphical proofs may be difficult to follow.

Noussair, Charles N., et al. "An Experimental Investigation of the Patterns of International Trade." *American Economic Review* (June 1995): 462–491.
Experimental results that suggest that factor price equalization arises in laboratory experiments; for advanced students.

O'Rourke, Kevin H., and Jeffrey G. Williamson. *Globalization and History.* Cambridge, Mass.: MIT Press, 1999.
Fascinating applications of the basic trade models to the nineteenth-century Atlantic economy.

Rassekh, F., and H. Thompson. "Factor Price Equalization: Theory and Evidence." *Journal of International Economic Integration* 8 (1993): 1–32.
Useful survey of the literature on factor price equalization.

Samuelson, Paul A. "International Factor-Price Equalization Once Again." *Economic Journal* (June 1949): 181–197.
Clarified version of the original demonstration of the factor price equalization theorem. With the exception of a brief mathematical section, the paper is appropriate for students of all levels.

Stolper, Wolfgang, and Paul A. Samuelson. "Protection and Real Wages." *Review of Economic Studies* 9 (November 1941): 58–73.
Original presentation of the Stolper-Samuelson theorem; accessible to intermediate students.

Williamson, Jeffrey G. "Globalization, Labor Markets and Policy Backlash in the Past." *Journal of Economic Perspectives* 12 (Fall 1998): 51–72.
Earlier episodes of the trade-and-wages debate; for all students.

Winters, L. Alan, et al. "Trade Liberalization and Poverty: The Evidence So Far." *Journal of Economic Literature* 52 (March 2004): 72–115.
Up-to-date survey of the empirical evidence on the relationship between trade liberalization and poverty; for intermediate students.

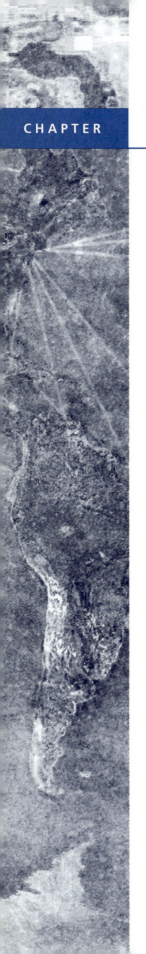

Beyond Comparative Advantage: Empirical Evidence and New Trade Theories

1 INTRODUCTION

Chapters Two through Four explored why nations trade, the direction and volume of trade, and its impact on output prices and factor prices. Economists have suggested several theories to explain international trade patterns, including the Ricardian, Neoclassical, and Heckscher-Ohlin models. It's now time to confront the question of which (if any) of these theories is *the* model that best explains observed trade patterns. First, we'll review just what we're trying to explain. Must we adopt a single theory of trade, or might different theories best explain various aspects of trade? Next, after a brief discussion of the role of empirical testing, we'll review the empirical evidence concerning the various models. Finally, we'll discuss some suggested modifications and important recent extensions of international trade theories.

2 QUESTIONS TO BE ANSWERED

The models in Chapters Two through Four focus on the determinants of trade patterns. Why does Colombia export coffee, Taiwan semiconductor chips, the United States airplanes, Japan digital cameras, China apparel, or Brazil steel? Is one explanation sufficient for all these observations? This chapter argues that the answer to the second question probably is no: Various types of international trade likely require different explanations. Trade in manufactured goods may respond to influences different from those that affect trade in primary products. The importance of factor endowments in determining trade patterns in oil or diamonds seems much more obvious than in the case of bicycles or shoes. Differences in relative labor productivity probably play a larger role in U.S. exports of computer software than in Saudi Arabian exports of oil.

A large and growing share of trade in manufactured goods is **intra-industry trade**—trade in which each country *both* imports and exports in the same industry. Explaining this component of trade requires modifying our basic trade model. Some countries tend to trade largely with others of a similar income, particularly in manufactured goods; this provides the basis for an alternate theory of trade. The United States and a few other countries typically produce and export new or high-technology products; this observation gives rise to yet another theory of trade. All these considerations are important to a full explanation of international trade patterns. Simple extensions of the basic model already introduced can incorporate some of these; others require complementary models.

A second set of questions concerns how the pattern of trade changes over time. In the case of the preceding export examples, Colombia has exported large amounts of coffee for a long time, but all the other exports are recent. Steel, semiconductor chips, and apparel now produced in Brazil, Taiwan, and China were, not long ago, produced primarily in the United States. The huge international market in aircraft is relatively new, and digital cameras didn't even exist until a few years ago. Trade patterns can change significantly over time. This carries important implications for trade policy because, as we saw in Chapter Four, such changes can generate significant policy controversy and political pressure for protection.

3 HOW DO WE KNOW IF A THEORY ABOUT TRADE IS CORRECT?

In the previous section, we argued intuitively that some considerations are likely more important than others in explaining various aspects of world trade patterns. In some cases these intuitive arguments seem very persuasive—for example, the importance of factor endowments in explaining trade patterns in primary products such as oil or diamonds. In other cases, the arguments may seem less compelling. To strengthen our arguments about the important influences on various types of trade, we must turn to empirical tests of the different possible explanations.

Empirical work on international trade, both formal and informal, has a long and distinguished history. Adam Smith used his observation that income levels tended to be higher in coastal cities (which engaged actively in trade) than in inland areas (which engaged in little trade) to support his argument that trade increased income. David Ricardo used his observations of differing opportunity costs in the production of wine and cloth in Portugal and England to argue that unrestricted trade between the two countries could increase the output of both wine and cloth. Certainly these early examples fail the rigorous standards by which economists judge empirical work today. With the development of the science of statistics, the capacity of modern computers, and the vast amount of available (albeit imperfect) data on production, consumption, and world trade, the empirical testing of trade theories has grown into a highly technical and exacting field. Nonetheless, the Smith and Ricardo examples remind us that the vital interaction between trade theory and empirical observation has been going on for centuries.

Empirical testing helps economists separate theories with real explanatory power from those that, though plausible, can't really explain observed phenomena. However, we must keep in mind the difficulties inherent in such testing. The fact that the available empirical evidence supports a theory can't prove that theory true. A second and as-yet undiscovered explanation may be the true one despite apparent empirical support for the existing theory. Empirical testing can never prove a theory true, but repeated testing can increase our confidence in the theory. Similarly, empirical results that contradict a theory's implications can't prove the theory false. Such contradictions should weaken our confidence in the theory and lead us to consider alternatives, but there always is a chance that the test itself was faulty in design or execution. Compromises are necessary in translating a theory's implications into a form suitable for empirical implementation, and these compromises may introduce logical flaws that invalidate the test. Often the most useful outcome of an empirical test is not so much clear validation nor invalidation of the theory in question but refinement of both the theory and the test. In the next section, we discuss attempts to test the Heckscher-Ohlin or factor-endowment theory of trade.

4 TESTING THE HECKSCHER-OHLIN MODEL

4.1 Early Tests

The key testable implication of the Heckscher-Ohlin model is that a country will export goods whose production involves intensive use of its relatively abundant factor and import goods whose production involves intensive use of its scarce factor. This implies that exports as a group should be more intensive in use of the abundant factor than imports as a group. For several decades after development of the Heckscher-Ohlin model, it wasn't possible to test the theory empirically using anything more than the simplest observations. England doesn't specialize in wheat, or the United States in bananas, or France in diamonds. All these observations are consistent with Heckscher and Ohlin's proposal of factor endowments as the basis of comparative advantage; but the observations hardly constitute definitive evidence.

Wassily Leontief performed the first real tests of Heckscher and Ohlin's key proposition. During the period immediately following World War II, when Leontief performed these tests using 1947 data for the United States, no one questioned the relative capital abundance of the United States. The country had possessed a highly developed, capital-intensive manufacturing sector before the war; and the war's destruction of much of the rest of the world's capital stock made the United States even more relatively capital abundant. This implied that goods the United States exported should be capital intensive relative to goods it imported.

Much to everyone's surprise, Leontief found the opposite: The United States exported labor-intensive goods and imported capital-intensive ones. Leontief's calculations, reported in Table 1, showed U.S. exports to be about 30 percent more labor intensive than U.S. imports. This result was so puzzling that it earned a name: the **Leontief paradox**. A flurry of research activity emerged to explain the paradox. Economists performed tests for different countries and for different time periods. For some countries and time periods, the implications of the Heckscher-Ohlin model seemed consistent with observed trade patterns; in other cases, the Leontief paradox recurred.

In general, it's fair to say that the simplest version of the Heckscher-Ohlin model does a poor job of explaining overall trade patterns, particularly in manufactured goods. These results have prompted some analysts to abandon the basic notions of factor abundance and factor intensity as explanations for trade. Others have retained the basic Heckscher-Ohlin framework, incorporated extensions, and relaxed assumptions to

---

Table 1   THE LEONTIEF PARADOX

Given the country's apparent capital abundance, everyone expected the United States to export capital-intensive goods. Instead, Leontief found U.S. exports to be about 30 percent more labor intensive than U.S. imports. The numbers reported are inputs per $1 million of exports and import substitutes.[a]

	Exports	Import Substitutes[a]
Capital (1947 $)	$2,550,780	$3,091,339
Labor (person-years)	182	170
Capital-labor ratio ($ per person-year)	$ 14,015	$ 18,184

[a]Lack of data on the factor intensity of actual U.S. imports forced Leontief to rely on data for import substitutes, the U.S.-produced versions of the goods the country imported.

Source: W. W. Leontief, "Domestic Production and Foreign Trade," *Proceedings of the American Philosophical Society*, 1953.

produce a more general model of trade still in the spirit of Heckscher-Ohlin. The continuing empirical work on these questions indicates that modified versions of the Heckscher-Ohlin model can explain many aspects of trade quite well. Other aspects, however, seem to require more substantive changes and the introduction of considerations outside the Heckscher-Ohlin framework and, in fact, beyond comparative advantage.

In the next section, we present several modifications of the Heckscher-Ohlin model and evaluate their ability to explain trade patterns. Later we consider alternate and complementary theories that help us understand aspects of trade poorly explained by the Heckscher-Ohlin model.

4.2 Fine-Tuning the Heckscher-Ohlin Model

The primary modifications of the Heckscher-Ohlin model suggested as possible explanations of the Leontief paradox include incorporating a role for taste differences, categorizing inputs in more details than the simple capital-labor dichotomy, and allowing for technology and productivity differences (à la Ricardo), in addition to adjusting for the fact that a country's trade may not be "balanced" (that is, the value of imports and the value of exports may be unequal).[1]

CROSS-COUNTRY TASTES DIFFERENCES   Recall from Chapter Three that Heckscher and Ohlin assumed that tastes were identical across countries in order to focus on factor endowments' role in comparative advantage. When tastes are identical, the production bias from countries' different factor endowments implies that a country will have a comparative advantage in the good that uses its abundant factor intensively. Section 4.2 in Chapter Three showed that large differences in tastes among countries can introduce a taste bias that, in principle, can dominate the production bias. Should this occur, a country will have a comparative advantage in production of the good that uses its scarce factor intensively.

Logically, taste bias might explain the Leontief paradox. If residents of the United States had tastes very strongly biased toward consumption of capital-intensive goods relative to tastes in the rest of the world, the U.S. price of capital-intensive goods would be high; so the United States would import capital-intensive goods and export labor-intensive ones. Such a finding wouldn't violate the spirit of the Heckscher-Ohlin model, which states that different factor endowments create a production bias toward the good intensive in the abundant factor.

How likely are tastes differences to be the true source of the Leontief paradox? Evidence does exist for a "home bias" in consumption; that is, consumers tend to consume more domestically produced goods and fewer imports than we might expect. But, for most countries, the observed home bias in consumption is unlikely to overwhelm factor-endowment-based differences in production possibilities. Home bias in consumption does seem to play some role in explaining trade patterns; but it can't single-handedly explain the Leontief result.[2]

CLASSIFICATION OF INPUTS   Attempts to test the Heckscher-Ohlin model of trade revealed the shortcomings of the traditional two-way classification of inputs as capital or

---

1. Another possible explanation—factor-intensity reversals—occurs when a good is labor intensive in one country but capital intensive in the other. We'll assume such reversals don't occur.

2. See Trefler (1995).

labor.[3] Most modern production processes involve many inputs, some not easily grouped into the capital or labor category. A five-way categorization of inputs can capture the major differences among the factor endowments of various countries much more successfully than can the capital-labor breakdown. Authors have classified inputs in several ways, but the most common includes arable farmland, raw materials or natural resources, human capital or skilled labor, man-made or nonhuman capital, and unskilled labor. Given this more precise categorical breakdown, the United States' factor abundance lies in human capital and arable farmland. This explains U.S. export success in high-technology and research-and-development-intensive industries, such as large-scale computers, and in agricultural products, a seemingly peculiar combination. Once we incorporate this more comprehensive breakdown of inputs, Heckscher and Ohlin's fundamental notion of comparative advantage based on differing factor endowments and factor intensities does a much better job of explaining trade patterns for many goods.

TECHNOLOGY, PRODUCTIVITY, AND SPECIALIZATION   Recall that Heckscher and Ohlin assumed not only identical tastes, but also identical technologies across countries when they predicted countries would export those goods that used their abundant factors intensively. The identical-technology assumption implies that, with completely unrestricted trade, equalized output and factor prices would lead firms in all countries to adopt identical production processes. (*Why?*)

But we clearly observe technology differences across countries. Some are easy to understand. Warm, sunny countries have access to a technology for producing tropical fruits that colder, less sunny countries can't match. Firms that undertake the research-and-development expenditures necessary to discover an innovative production process typically apply for patents that restrict other firms' abilities to use that process—including firms in other countries. Workers in wealthy countries with adequate food supplies and effective health-care systems may be more productive than workers in poor countries who may lack adequate nutrition and health care.

Other sources of technological differences across countries, while just as important, are harder to explain. The former Soviet Union trained many talented scientists and engineers. Yet those highly skilled individuals failed to attain the levels of productivity in the Soviet Union that they have since emigrating to the West. One likely reason is that the incentive system in the Soviet Union and other centrally planned economies failed to encourage individual productivity. When considerations such as these result in different countries using different technologies of production, the simple predictions of Heckscher and Ohlin, based on identical technologies, may not follow directly, but must be amended to take account of the cross-country differences in production processes. In fact, most recent empirical work finds that both the factor-endowment differences emphasized by Heckscher-Ohlin and the technology differences emphasized by Ricardo have important roles to play in determining actual trade patterns.

ADJUSTING FOR UNBALANCED TRADE   Edward Leamer has shown that Leontief's technique for testing the Heckscher-Ohlin model failed to adjust for the fact that in 1947 U.S. trade was unbalanced because the value of U.S. exports exceeded the value of imports. To make the necessary adjustment, Leamer reformulated the test to compare the factor content of U.S. production and U.S. consumption. If the United States was capital abundant and if Heckscher-Ohlin's basic factor-endowment argument was correct, then

---

3. Table 3 in Chapter Three reports estimates of countries' factor endowments using the simple capital-labor breakdown.

Table 2	**LEAMER'S REFORMULATION OF LEONTIEF TEST, CORRECTED FOR UNBALANCED U.S. TRADE**	
	U.S. Production	U.S. Consumption
Capital ($ billions)	$ 327	$ 305
Labor (million person-years)	47	45
Capital-labor ratio ($ per person-year)	$6,949	$6,737

Source: Edward E. Leamer, "The Leontief Paradox, Reconsidered," *Journal of Political Economy* 88: 495–503.

U.S. production should embody more capital relative to labor than U.S. consumption.[4] Table 2 reports Leamer's results, which support the key implication of the Heckscher-Ohlin model and exhibit no paradox.

The preceding modifications to the Heckscher-Ohlin model, taken together, appear to produce a framework capable of explaining a significant portion of world trade. Some aspects of trade, however, require alternate, complementary models—including some not based on comparative advantage—to which we now turn.

5 INTRA-INDUSTRY TRADE

5.1 What Is It, and How Big Is It?

Intra-industry trade—trade in which a single country both imports and exports products in the same industry—comprises a significant share of world trade, particularly in manufactures. How can we estimate the extent of intra-industry trade in a given industry? The most commonly used measure is the *intra-industry trade* (IIT) index,

$$IIT_X = 1 - \frac{|Exports_X - Imports_X|}{Exports_X + Imports_X}, \qquad [1]$$

where the vertical bars in the numerator denote absolute value.[5] The IIT index varies from 0 to 1 as intra-industry trade in industry X increases. If a country *only* imports or *only* exports the good in question (no intra-industry trade), the index equals 0. (*Why?*) If a country's X-industry imports and exports are *equal* (maximum intra-industry trade), the IIT index takes a value of 1.

One warning: intra-industry trade measures are very sensitive to the definitions of products or industries used. For example, early estimates suggested that two-thirds of trade in chemicals was intra-industry. The chemical industry is large and diverse; so, we would expect different countries to have comparative advantages in different specific chemicals, and it isn't surprising that most industrialized countries import some types of chemicals and export others. If, instead of calculating the IIT index for

4. We leave the derivation of the appropriate test to more advanced textbooks. Note, however, the general lesson that subtle mistakes in implementing empirical tests can invalidate their results. In this case, failing to adjust for unbalanced trade in the original Leontief tests seems to have created the famous paradox.

5. If the country's trade is not balanced (if total imports do not equal total exports), each export and import term in Equation 1 should be replaced by industry exports or imports as a share of total exports or imports.

chemicals as a whole, we calculated the index for a narrower product category, such as sulphuric acid, we would expect a smaller IIT index value. In general, the more narrowly defined the industry classifications used, the lower the resulting estimates of intra-industry trade.

In addition to the intra-industry trade index for a particular industry, we can define an analogous index for a country's trade as a whole. This involves calculating the ratio on the right side of Equation 1 for each industry, summing those ratios across industries, and using the summation in place of the industry ratios as indicated in Equation 2, where the symbol Σ represents summation across industries:

$$IIT = 1 - \frac{\Sigma|\text{Exports} - \text{Imports}|}{\Sigma(\text{Exports} + \text{Imports})}. \qquad [2]$$

Calculating the IIT index for a country's overall trade allows comparison across countries of the degree of intra-industry trade. Table 3 lists intra-industry trade indexes for a large sample of countries. The values reported in Table 3 are low relative to some other IIT estimates for two reasons; the study's authors included all trade rather than just manufacturing, and the estimates use trade data for narrow rather than broad product

Table 3   **INTRA-INDUSTRY TRADE INDEXES, 1985**

High-Income Countries	IIT Index	Middle-Income Countries	IIT Index	Low-Income Countries	IIT Index
United States	.1371	Israel	.0721	Thailand	.0286
Canada	.0550	Spain	.0807	Jamaica	.0050
Switzerland	.1227	Ireland	.0746	Dominican Republic	.0120
Norway	.0537	Venezuela	.0078	Guatemala	.0079
Australia	.0306	Greece	.0304	Paraguay	.0021
Sweden	.1163	Mexico	.0239	Sri Lanka	.0186
Denmark	.0923	Taiwan	.0569	Morocco	.0067
West Germany	.1473	Argentina	.0201	Bolivia	.0006
Belgium-Luxembourg	.1347	Portugal	.0473	Ivory Coast	.0076
Iceland	.0064	Syria	.0011	Philippines	.0240
France	.1377	Mauritius	.0106	Honduras	.0028
Finland	.0625	South Korea	.0644	Zimbabwe	.0033
Japan	.0640	Iran	.0033	Nigeria	.0024
Netherlands	.1283	Panama	.0074	India	.0305
New Zealand	.0189	Chile	.0081	Nepal	.0031
United Kingdom	.1495	Turkey	.0195	Sierra Leone	.0029
Austria	.1031	Colombia	.0092	Zambia	.0053
Italy	.1111	Ecuador	.0031	Kenya	.0052
Hong Kong	.0805	Peru	.0077	Madagascar	.0059
				Malawi	.0028
Average	**.0876**	**Average**	**.0274**	**Average**	**.0089**

Source: Data from Simon J. Evenett and Wolfgang Keller, "On Theories Explaining the Success of the Gravity Equation," *Journal of Political Economy* 110 (April 2002), pp. 290–292.

categories. The table reveals that IIT indexes tend to be substantially higher for high-income countries than for middle- or low-income ones, reflecting the formers' more extensive manufacturing sectors.

Intra-industry trade represents a growing share of total trade, especially among the high-income industrial economies. But why would a country choose to export and import similar goods?

5.2 Intra-Industry Trade in Homogeneous Goods

Transportation costs and seasonal trade patterns can explain intra-industry trade in nondifferentiated or **homogeneous goods**. Figure 1 illustrates the transportation-cost case. Homogeneous goods most likely to be involved in intra-industry trade include items that are heavy or for some other reason expensive to transport. In Figure 1, firm F^A in country A and firm F^B in country B, spatially located as shown, produce such a product. Consumers C^A and C^B buy the product. Because of the firms' and consumers' locations, it may be the case that consumer C^A buys from firm F^B and consumer C^B from firm F^A to minimize transportation costs. As a result, countries A and B both import and export the good. Later in this chapter, we'll look in more detail at transportation costs and the location of industry as explanations for the pattern of trade.

Seasonal considerations also can cause intra-industry trade in homogeneous goods. Agricultural growing seasons provide a clear example. A country in the Northern Hemisphere might export agricultural products during the summer and import those same goods from a Southern Hemisphere trading partner during the winter. Governments report most trade statistics on an annual basis, so summer exports and winter imports appear in the statistics as simultaneous exports and imports of the same goods.

Figure 1   Location Can Cause Intra-Industry Trade in Homogeneous Goods

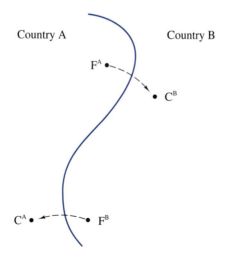

Each country imports *and* exports the product because of consumers' greater proximity to the foreign than to the domestic producer.

5.3 Intra-Industry Trade in Differentiated Goods

The basic trade model assumes that goods are homogeneous; this is one of the assumptions required for perfectly competitive markets. Homogeneity implies (in the presence of transportation costs) that a single good typically wouldn't be both imported and exported by the same country. Rather than import the good from abroad, a country would simply choose to consume more of its domestic production and reduce its exports. However, many manufactured goods don't satisfy the homogeneity assumption very well.[6] The example most often cited is automobiles. Firms produce a variety of types and models of automobiles, and all the major industrialized economies both import and export cars.[7] American consumers buy Mercedes and Hyundais, while German consumers buy Chevrolets and Saabs. The English drive Fords, and Japanese drive Volkswagens. Obviously firms incur substantial costs to ship all these automobiles among countries. This is worthwhile only because consumers don't view the various types of cars as perfect substitutes. An American who buys a BMW or Toyota isn't indifferent between that car and a Ford or Chevrolet. To explain trade in many manufactured goods we must take into account such **product differentiation** and the intra-industry trade it generates.

Product differentiation takes us one step toward understanding intra-industry trade, but a real explanation of the phenomenon requires an additional step. Suppose that most Japanese are content to drive Toyotas and Hondas, while most Germans are happy with their Volkswagens and BMWs. Nonetheless a few Japanese want BMWs, and a few Germans want Hondas. Why don't Japanese auto producers just make a few close BMW substitutes and Germans a few good Honda substitutes? To explain why this adjustment to minority tastes sometimes doesn't occur and intra-industry trade occurs instead, we will need to incorporate the idea of increasing returns to scale, the subject of section 6. But first, we need to understand a second type of intra-industry trade and why the difference between inter-industry and intra-industry trade matters for trade policy.

5.4 Vertical Specialization, or Breaking Up the Production Chain

Most industrialized economies both import and export finished automobiles so that domestic consumers can buy their preferred varieties. But a second type of intra-industry trade, often called *vertical specialization*, may be even more important in complex manufacturing industries such as automobile production. Increasingly, the various components of cars are produced in different locations around the world and then brought together for final assembly. This type of intra-industry trade is very much in the spirit of Heckscher and Ohlin. After all, the factor intensities of making floor mats, tires, transmission subassemblies, airbags, and computerized controllers for antilock braking systems differ widely; so we should expect countries to have comparative advantages in different aspects of car production. Honda makes transmissions in Indonesia, engine

---

6. Markets with differentiated products but that otherwise satisfy the requirements for perfect competition are called *monopolistically competitive markets*.

7. The automobile industry, as well as other industries, actually engages in two types of intra-industry trade. The first—the focus here—is bidirectional trade in differentiated but similar finished goods. The second, explored later, is vertical specialization or trade in component parts; for example, a car may be assembled in Korea from parts produced in 15 different countries. Since components typically are classified within the automotive-industry category for purposes of trade statistics, such trade in components shows up, along with bidirectional trade in finished automobiles, as intra-industry trade. Some intra-industry trade also is due to cross-hauling—the fact that once a loaded ship carries goods from country A to country B, the cost of shipping goods back from B to A rather than sending an empty ship is low.

parts in China, and assembles its City subcompact in Thailand.[8] Household appliances provide another example; Maytag dishwashers contain Chinese motors and Mexican wiring harnesses, and are assembled in the United States.[9] Low transportation and communication costs make it feasible for firms to perform each task in the most efficient location. Low transportation costs are essential to vertical specialization, which can involve multiple ocean crossings for each partially assembled unit. Cheap communication technologies such as faxes and e-mail are also important because vertical specialization requires that managers maintain close contact with plants around the world to keep the production process coordinated and on schedule.

Most analysts date the take-off of vertical specialization to the 1960s. The U.S. and Canadian automobile industries, clustered in Detroit and Toronto respectively, integrated their production. Around the same time, Hong Kong, Thailand, Malaysia, and Singapore developed large electronics assembly industries. Experts agree that the importance of vertical specialization has grown. One measure involves calculating the ratio of international trade to value-added. As the name suggests, value-added is the increase in a product's value as it moves through the various stages of production. For example, if $1,000 worth of steel is processed into a car body worth $3,000, the value-added for that stage of production equals $3,000 − $1,000 = $2,000. With more vertical specialization, production processes are divided into longer chains of smaller pieces, and components are shipped back and forth across national boundaries to be processed further. As firms become more vertically specialized internationally, the ratio of trade to value-added rises. Table 4 provides some recent estimates. Notice that this type of intra-industry trade plays a particularly large role in the newly industrialized economies of Asia and Mexico.

Consider a Kia Sorento automobile's CD player; in the process of production, it goes from China to Thailand to Mexico to California to South Korea (where it's installed in the car) to the United States![10]

5.5 Why Does Intra-Industry Trade Matter?

Unlike trade based on comparative advantage, intra-industry trade in finished products occurs in greatest volume between developed industrial economies with similar factor endowments, skill levels, and stages of development. The industries most likely to report high intra-industry trade in finished products include sophisticated manufactured goods that exhibit product differentiation and whose production processes are characterized by economies of scale.

Intra-industry trade in finished products based on transportation costs, seasonal trade, or product differentiation often presents fewer pressures for protection and less political controversy than does inter-industry trade or intra-industry vertical specialization based on comparative advantage. Recall that the redistribution of income caused by inter-industry trade or vertical specialization occurs because the *different* factor intensities of industries imply that opening trade alters relative demands for different factors and thereby changes their relative prices. Intra-industry trade in finished products, on the other hand, involves trade in goods in the same industry and produced using *similar* factor intensities. Therefore, the changes in factor demands and relative factor prices from such trade tend to be smaller. This may provide one explanation for the pattern of observed trade liberalization since World War II. The greatest success in lowering trade barriers has

8. Todd Zaun, "In Asia, Honda Employs New Tactic in Building Cars," *The Wall Street Journal*, April 28, 2003.

9. Timothy Aeppel, "Three Countries, One Dishwasher," *The Wall Street Journal*, October 6, 2003.

10. Sarah McBride, "Kia's Audacious Sorento Plan," *The Wall Street Journal*, May 2003.

Table 4   **RATIO OF MERCHANDISE TRADE TO MERCHANDISE VALUE-ADDED, 1980, 1990, 2000 (PERCENT)**

Country	1980	1990	2000
Major industrialized economies	46.2%	51.6%	76.3%
Canada	63.7	70.6	108.8
France	50.6	62.0	90.0
Germany	52.0	63.7	96.7
Italy	45.7	46.9	76.7
Japan	28.7	20.6	24.2
United Kingdom	52.0	62.4	83.5
United States	30.9	35.1	54.6
Emerging market economies			
Asia	93.8	115.6	168.5
China	12.1	23.7	32.9
India	11.3	12.4	21.6
Hong Kong, Korea, Singapore, Taiwan	216.5	259.3	365.5
Bangladesh, Indonesia, Malaysia, Pakistan, Philippines, Thailand	39.4	52.4	84.3
Western Hemisphere	37.2	42.6	58.6
Argentina	25.3	13.2	29.7
Brazil	19.4	14.6	34.1
Chile	42.8	55.8	60.9
Mexico	22.8	48.3	102.6
Bolivia, Colombia, Costa Rica, Panama, Paraguay, Uruguay, Venezuela	44.4	52.3	63.0

Source: International Monetary Fund, *World Economic Outlook September 2002*, Washington D.C.: International Monetary Fund, p. 128.

occurred in manufactured-goods industries in which the developed industrial countries engage in large amounts of *intra*-industry trade in finished products. In contrast, barriers to trade have been slower to come down in agriculture, primary products, and other sectors in which we would expect resource-based comparative advantage to result in *inter*-industry trade between developed and developing countries.

6 TRADE WITH ECONOMIES OF SCALE

For some goods, the average cost of production depends on the scale of output, or the number of units produced. If average cost falls as the scale of production rises, production exhibits **decreasing costs**, **increasing returns to scale**, or **economies of scale**. Some types of economies of scale can make it difficult for small firms to compete with large ones. Whether economies of scale give an advantage to large firms depends on whether the scale economies are internal or external to the firm.

Internal scale economies occur when the firm's average costs fall as the *firm's* output rises, as in panel (a) of Figure 2. The primary source of internal economies of scale is large fixed costs that can be spread over all the firm's output; examples include research-and-development expenditures and assembly-line production techniques such as robotics. In an industry characterized by internal scale economies, a firm that produces a small output, X^S in Figure 2, faces relatively high average costs of AC^S. A large firm in

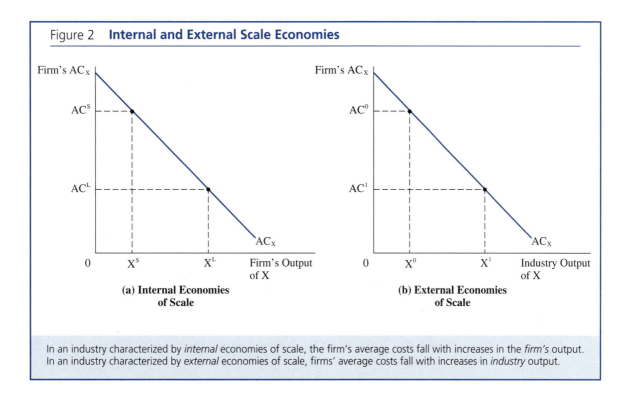

Figure 2   **Internal and External Scale Economies**

(a) Internal Economies of Scale

(b) External Economies of Scale

In an industry characterized by *internal* economies of scale, the firm's average costs fall with increases in the *firm's* output. In an industry characterized by *external* economies of scale, firms' average costs fall with increases in *industry* output.

the same industry produces more output, X^L, can spread its fixed costs over more units, and therefore achieves lower per unit costs, AC^L. These lower costs allow the large firm to sell its product at a lower price, so we wouldn't expect the small firm to survive in the long run.[11] The automobile industry provides a classic example of an industry characterized by internal economies of scale. Most studies suggest that a small automobile plant that produced only a few cars per year would have much higher average costs per car than would a giant firm such as General Motors or Toyota.[12] If economies of scale in a particular industry are internal to the firm, large firms have a cost advantage over small ones. The perfectly competitive market structure, in which many small firms take the market price as given, tends to give way to an imperfectly competitive one, in which each firm is large and acts as if it has some control over the price of its product.

External scale economies, on the other hand, occur when the firm's average costs fall as the *industry's* output rises, as in Figure 2, panel (b). When the output of the computer industry rises, for example, computer firms' costs fall because the industry becomes large enough to support a pool of skilled labor, along with input suppliers such as semiconductor-chip manufacturers. Therefore, AC^0 represents the average costs of a typical computer firm when the industry is small (industry output X^0), while AC^1 denotes the typical firm's average costs when the industry reaches output level X^1. (*How might this phenomenon explain why so many computer-related firms concentrate in regional centers such as California's Silicon Valley or Bangalore, India?*)

---

11. In the long run, with entry and exit, a firm's price must equal its average costs, and the firm earns zero economic profit.

12. Internal economies of scale can include plant economies (declining average costs as production in a given *plant* rises) or firm economies (declining average costs as the production of a given *firm* rises, perhaps in multiple plants). The auto industry exhibits both types.

Economies of scale, whether internal or external, have important implications for international trade. Such economies create an additional incentive for production specialization. Rather than producing a few units of each good domestic consumers want to buy, a country can specialize in producing large quantities of a small number of goods (in which the industries achieve scale economies) and trade for the remaining goods. Therefore, economies of scale provide a basis for trade *even between countries with identical production possibilities and tastes*. (Recall from Chapters Two and Three that under constant or increasing costs, mutually beneficial trade requires that two countries *differ* in production possibilities, tastes, or both, to generate a pattern of comparative advantage.)

Figure 3, which assumes that countries A and B are identical in both tastes and production possibilities, shows the potential of mutually beneficial trade based solely on economies of scale rather than comparative advantage. Gains from trade occur because scale economies place a special premium (in the form of cost reductions) on specialization. Just as increasing opportunity costs produced a concave production possibilities frontier in Chapter Three, decreasing opportunity costs result in a *convex* or bowed-in production possibilities frontier. At each point, the (absolute) slope of the frontier reflects the opportunity cost of good X; along a convex frontier such as that in Figure 3, this cost *decreases* as a country produces more good X. Without trade, the two identical countries would produce and consume at their autarky equilibria, A* and B*, placing them on indifference curves U_0^A and U_0^B. Each industry in each country fails to achieve economies of scale because domestic consumers demand some of *both* goods. Alternatively, each country can take advantage of economies of scale by specializing in production of one of the goods. Note an important difference from trade based on comparative advantage: The two countries are identical, so *it doesn't matter which country produces which good.* Suppose A specializes in good X (at point A_p) and B in good Y

Figure 3   Mutually Beneficial Trade Based Solely on Scale Economies

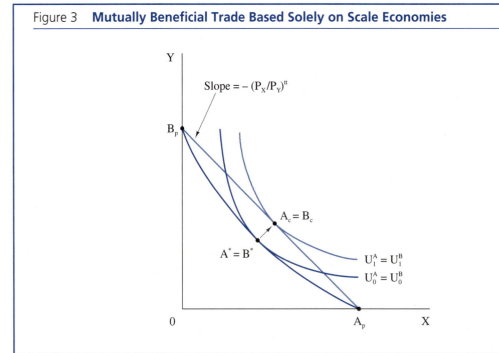

Productive specialization provides an additional benefit—lower costs—with economies of scale.

(at point B_p). The two countries can then trade along the terms-of-trade line to points A_c and B_c, reaching indifference curves U_1^A and U_1^B—a clear improvement for both over the autarky equilibria. Consumers in each economy can have a variety of goods to consume while still enjoying the cost savings from specialized large-scale production.

We'll see that whether trade in the presence of economies of scale will be unambiguously beneficial depends on whether the economies are internal or external to the firm and on the presence or absence of comparative advantage.

6.1 Internal Economies of Scale

With internal economies of scale, trade allows consumers to consume a larger variety of goods at lower prices.[13] Generally, we associate more varieties with higher levels of consumer welfare or satisfaction for one of two reasons. For some goods, individual consumers may want to consume several varieties; clothing provides one obvious example. If trade increases the number of styles and fabrics available, most consumers enjoy the expanded choices for variety in their wardrobes. For other goods, each individual may consume a single variety, but different individuals may prefer different varieties. Although each individual may own only one car at a time, some individuals prefer BMW sports cars while others prefer Honda minivans or Ford pickups, so the availability of different varieties improves welfare.

But why should trade increase variety? Without trade, firms produce only for the domestic population. That population may value variety; but, because of the population's limited size, firms may limit the number of variations in order to achieve economies of scale. For example, if the domestic population buys a million cars per year, domestic firms may choose to produce, say, a half million each of two varieties, not a hundred thousand each of ten varieties. To produce ten varieties for such a small population would result in high per-unit cost—because of failure to achieve economies of scale. Trade can help by expanding the consuming population for any firm's product. Firms in one country specialize in one set of varieties, and firms in the other in another set. Consumers then have access to all the varieties through trade, while each firm achieves economies of scale by specializing.

Figure 4 illustrates. The four panels represent the markets for goods X and Y in countries A and B. We assume that the costs of producing each good don't vary across countries, so the average-cost curves for good X in panels (a) and (c) match, as do those for good Y in panels (b) and (d). In other words, we assume that the two countries do *not* exhibit a pattern of comparative advantage. To focus on the effect of scale economies, we also assume that demands for the two goods in the two countries are identical. Curve D_X^A represents country A's demand for good X in panel (a), and D_X^{A+B} shows the total demand for good X, including both countries A and B.[14]

With no international trade, firms in each country would produce for domestic consumers only. Outputs would be X_0^A, Y_0^A, X_0^B, and Y_0^B in the four markets, respectively, where domestic demand intersects the average-cost curve in each case, because long-run equilibrium requires that price equal average cost. The relatively small levels of output would cause firms to forgo economies of scale, so average costs would be relatively high (with superscript zeroes in Figure 4); and consumers would pay correspondingly high prices. If the two countries opened trade, each could specialize in producing just

---

13. We'll demonstrate that opening trade reduces average costs. As long as entry and exit remain unrestricted, price will equal average costs in the long run because any differential between the two would reflect either positive economic profit (causing entry) or negative economic profit (causing exit).

14. The horizontal distance between these two demand curves at any price measures country B's quantity demanded.

Figure 4   Internal Scale Economies as a Basis for Trade between Identical Countries

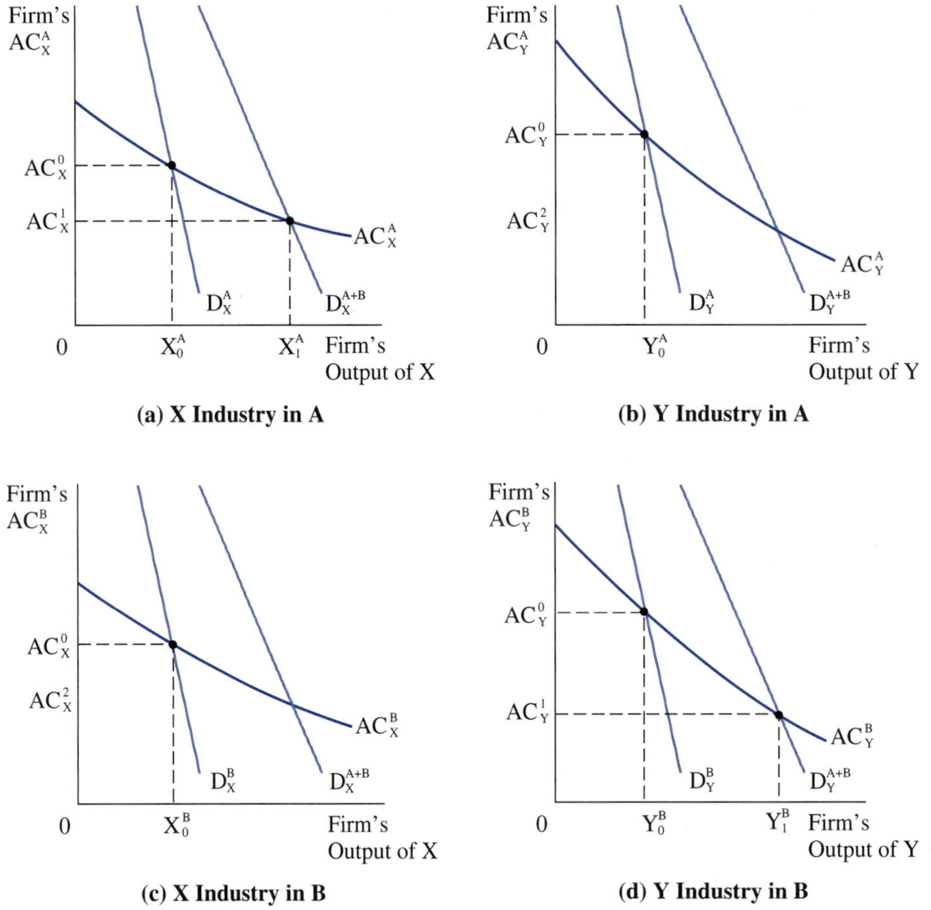

(a) X Industry in A

(b) Y Industry in A

(c) X Industry in B

(d) Y Industry in B

With internal economies of scale and no comparative advantage, international trade permits production of higher levels of output (X_1^A and Y_1^B) at lower costs (AC_X^1 and AC_Y^1) than does autarky (X_0^A, Y_0^A, X_0^B, and Y_0^B at costs AC_X^0 and AC_Y^0). Consumers enjoy both a variety of goods and the cost savings from production specialization.

one of the two goods. The countries are identical, so which country produces which good doesn't matter. Assume that country A specializes in good X and country B in Y. Country A would produce X_1^A in panel (a) and serve the entire market for X; its average costs and price would fall to AC_X^1. Country B would produce Y_1^B in panel (d), serve the entire world market for Y, and achieve economies of scale that lower average cost and price to AC_Y^1. (*Explain why, if country A specialized in Y and B in X rather than vice versa, average costs would be AC_X^2 and AC_Y^2.*) Note that the smaller the home market relative to the world market, the bigger the gain from opening trade in goods whose production exhibits internal economies of scale.

Economies of scale contribute a key element to our understanding of intra-industry trade in differentiated products. In industries that exhibit such economies, domestic firms have an incentive to produce for the majority or mass domestic market and to ignore small domestic consumer groups with tastes for different types of products. The costs of small-scale production to satisfy minority tastes would result in very high-priced products. However, if minority tastes in country A match majority tastes in country B, then imports from country B, produced there with economies of scale, can satisfy those tastes. At the same time, a few consumers in country B probably will have "type A" tastes that imports from country A can satisfy at low cost.

6.2 External Economies of Scale

External economies of scale can help explain the widely observed phenomenon of industrial agglomeration, or the tendency of firms in an industry to cluster geographically. Examples include the watch industry in Switzerland, the high-fashion apparel industry in Italy, the movie industry in Hollywood, the financial industry in New York and London, and the software industry in Bangalore. Recall that external economies arise when firms' average costs fall as the *industry's* output rises. Such a scenario typically happens when the clustered industry reaches a size adequate to support specialized services such as skilled labor markets and makers of specialized inputs. (*Suppose you own a computer software firm, and your star programmer just quit to start her own firm. Do you think you could find a suitable replacement more quickly if you were located in Palo Alto, California, or in Peoria, Illinois? Why? How would this affect your costs?*) Small firms can remain viable in industries characterized by external economies, unlike the internal-economies case, because industry rather than firm output generates the cost reductions. Even the tiniest technology firm in Silicon Valley benefits from the rich pools of specialized workers and components available nearby as a result of the industry's agglomeration.

The agglomeration effects generated by external scale economies can give "historical accident" an important role in production and trade patterns. It's easy to see why. Suppose that a few high-fashion firms just happen to locate in northern Italy. Then the next few firms will have lower average costs if they also locate in northern Italy—where they can take advantage of the specialized input markets supported by the earlier firms. This location pattern becomes self-perpetuating and reinforcing. Eventually, no one may even remember the details of how or why the cluster got started in a particular place.

The interaction between external scale economies and international trade can be either beneficial or harmful, depending on the presence or absence of comparative advantage. Consider first the pure case in which an industry's costs exhibit external economies but are identical in two countries (that is, there is no comparative advantage). Then Figure 4's analysis of the benefits from opening trade carries over; we just need to relabel the horizontal axes to measure industry rather than firm output. In this case, external economies provide the *only* basis for trade because no comparative advantage exists, and trade benefits both countries by providing more output at lower costs.

However, things aren't always so simple. Consider Figure 5. Now external economies of scale characterize industry X, *and* country A has a comparative advantage in X—in the sense that the average costs of producing good X, *at any given level of industry output*, are lower in country A than in country B. To keep things simple, we continue to assume that the two countries' demands for good X are identical. If the two countries begin in autarky, they will produce X_0^A and X_0^B at average costs of AC^A and AC^B, respectively. (*Why?*) From this autarky starting point, opening trade would benefit each country. Country A, with its cost advantage, would produce X_1 units at cost AC_1, at the point where the total demand curve (D^{A+B}) intersects A's average-cost curve. Consumers in both countries benefit from lower prices and more good X to consume. (*Would consumers in A or B gain more? Why?*)

Figure 5   **External Scale Economies and Comparative Advantage**

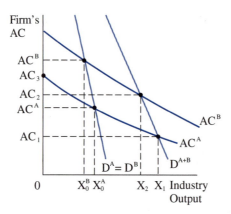

In autarky, country A produces X_0^A at cost AC^A and country B produces X_0^B at cost AC^B. International trade will be mutually beneficial if the country with comparative advantage (here, A) gets a head start in the industry; firms in country A would produce X_1 at cost AC_1. However, if the comparative-disadvantage country (B) gets a head start, firms in the comparative-advantage country may not be able to enter because of their high initial costs (AC_3), and country B firms will produce X_2 at cost AC_2.

What if the two countries start out, not in autarky, but trading with each other? If, for some historical reason, country A got started in the X industry first, the outcome would be the same as in the case where the countries move from autarky to trade. Country A will produce X_1 units at cost AC_1, and country B will produce other goods. Here, external scale economies reinforce country A's comparative advantage, and both countries benefit from trade.

However, if the industry's history is such that country B happened to get an early start, firms from B would end up servicing the entire market, producing X_2 at cost AC_2, under unrestricted trade. In this case, firms from country A might have a hard time breaking into the market *despite their lower average-cost curve* because B's head start gives it the advantage of large scale. A firm in A, wanting to enter the industry, would incur initial average costs of AC_3 and couldn't compete with established firms from country B who can sell at AC_2. This presents a case in which trade may be harmful—in the sense that it allowed country B firms to achieve economies of scale and foreclose entry to country A firms, which have a comparative advantage. Consumers in both countries pay a higher price (AC_2 versus AC_1) for a smaller quantity of good X (X_2 versus X_1) as a result. Historical accident, in the form of country B's head start in the X industry, has combined with external scale economies to dominate comparative advantage in determining the pattern of trade.

Might protection help in cases such as the one in Figure 5, where economies of scale result in trade that runs counter to comparative advantage? Maybe, and maybe not. Figure 6 illustrates the two cases. In panel (a), if country A's government prohibited imports of X and kept A's market for domestic firms, those firms could achieve partial economies of scale and produce X_4 at AC_4. This would allow them to undersell the country B firms (who under free trade sell at a price equal to AC_2) and capture the rest of the market from the initially advantaged country B firms. Consumers in both countries eventually might benefit from lower prices and increased availability of good X (at AC_5 and X_5) as country A served both markets.[15] But in some cases such a strategy may not work. Panel (b) shows why. There, even a completely protected home market in good X may not allow country A firms to move far enough down their average-cost curve to undersell country B firms; the best A firms can do is output X_6 at a price equal to AC_6, which may not be good enough to displace the B firms, whose initial price equals AC_2. Eventually, if country A did impose protection, the loss of A's market would push B firms upward and to the left along their average-cost curves as industry output fell. The extent to which this occurs and the time horizon over which it happens depend on the exact source of the industry's external economies. In general, existing skilled-labor pools or specialized input markets probably wouldn't disappear very quickly in B, so any increase in B firms' costs due to A's protection of its home market could be slow to materialize. The smaller and slower the increase in B firms' costs, the less likely A's protection would be to allow A firms to capture the market and realize their comparative advantage.

Which case occurs, (a) or (b), depends on a combination of the strength of external economies in the industry (that is, how *steep* are the AC curves?) and the extent of comparative advantage (that is, how large is the *vertical distance* between the two countries' average-cost curves?). With small economies of scale and a strong pattern of comparative advantage, as in Figure 6 panel (a), protection of A's home market can permit country A firms to displace the already-established country B firms. But with large economies of scale and a weak pattern of comparative advantage, as in panel (b), even protection of their home market may not allow country A firms to catch up with their country B rivals.

Figure 6 **Interaction of External Scale Economies and Comparative Advantage**

(a) Small Scale Economies, Large Comparative Advantage

(b) Large Scale Economies, Small Comparative Advantage

Panel (a) combines weak scale economies and strong comparative advantage. Temporary protection of A's market could allow country A firms to capture the market even if country B firms enjoyed a head start. Panel (b) combines strong scale economies and weak comparative advantage. Temporary protection of A's market would not necessarily allow country A firms to capture the market from already established B firms, despite A's comparative advantage.

---

15. In Chapter Eight, we'll discuss some potential problems with these protectionist policies.

6.3 Dynamic External Economies

In some cases, firms' average costs depend not on the industry's *current* output but on its *cumulative* output, that is, the total of all past industry production. This occurs when the learning process plays a large role in achieving cost reductions. The downward-sloping curve that captures the negative relationship between cumulative industry output and firms' average costs, illustrated as LC in Figure 7, is called the **learning curve**, and the associated economies are called **dynamic external economies**. When these dynamic effects are present, they can reinforce or work against comparative advantage, just like other external economies. In Figure 7, where country A has a comparative advantage, learning and comparative advantage could work together under free trade to give consumers the most output at the best price (X_0 and AC_0), but only if the industry got underway first in country A. If a quirk of history gave the industry a head start in country B, free trade would generate X_1 at price AC_1, definitely an inferior outcome. Despite their comparative advantage, country A firms, with no history of production to let them generate dynamic external economies, might not be able to break into the B-dominated market because of their high initial costs (AC_2), even though they could eventually produce more at lower cost than country B firms. (*Show that trade must be beneficial with a learning curve and no comparative advantage.*)

6.4 The Scope of Economies and Learning

Note that all our discussion of external scale economies has assumed that the industry output of relevance is the *domestic* industry. The other possibility is the case in which firms' costs depend on the output of the *worldwide* industry, either current or cumulative. If this were the case, arguments for protection based on external economies of scale, like the one in Figure 6, panel (a), would disappear. To see why, look again at Figure 7, and assume that country B has captured the market through historical accident. If country

Figure 7 **Dynamic External Economies and the Learning Curve**

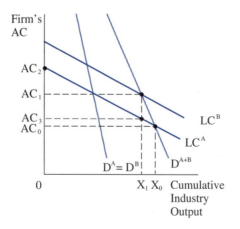

With a learning curve based on the domestic industry's output, country A firms can be shut out of the market if country B firms get a head start, despite A firms' comparative advantage. The outcome would be output X_1 produced at cost AC_1. However, if domestic firms can learn from foreign firms' experience, the learning curve won't block entry by firms from country A, whose initial average cost will equal AC_3. The outcome then will be output X_0 at cost AC_0.

A firms can learn from country B firms' production experience as well as they could learn from domestic firms' experience, then A firms can start producing at cost AC_3, not AC_2. (*Why?*) This allows A firms to undersell their B rivals and capture the market, building on their comparative advantage. They then produce X_0 at a price equal to AC_0.

Because policy recommendations can hinge on whether dynamic economies of scale depend on output of the domestic or the worldwide industry, answering this question is a high priority. Unfortunately, external economies have proven very difficult to identify and measure. However, in one industry thought to be characterized by strong external economies—the semiconductor industry—recent evidence suggests that effective learning may take place based on foreign as well as domestic production experience.[16] If so, any case for protection disappears.

In summary, scale economies can provide a basis for trade, even in the absence of comparative advantage. In markets characterized by *internal* economies of scale, international trade allows consumers to enjoy a greater variety of goods while still achieving the cost savings that come with large-scale production. The resulting trade is intra-industry and may generate fewer political pressures for protection than inter-industry trade because of its smaller impact on relative factor demands, factor prices, and the distribution of income. Trade based on *external* economies of scale can be beneficial or harmful depending on (1) the importance of scale economies relative to comparative advantage, (2) whether historical production patterns follow or run counter to comparative advantage, and (3) whether domestic or worldwide industry output provides the basis for the external scale economies.

Economies of scale as basis for trade is just one of several ways in which the characteristics of available production technologies affect international trade. The next section introduces the idea that changes in technology over time can change the pattern of imports and exports.

7 TECHNOLOGY-BASED THEORIES OF TRADE: THE PRODUCT CYCLE

The Heckscher-Ohlin trade model assumes that all countries have access to and use the same technologies. Remember that this implies that the isoquant map for each industry is the same across countries. Even though the isoquant maps are identical, firms in different countries may use different capital-labor ratios in their production processes because of different factor prices that reflect differences in factor endowments. However, with unrestricted trade, factor prices equalize across countries, and all firms use identical production techniques.[17]

Some industries probably satisfy the assumption of identical technologies reasonably well; for others, the assumption seems less viable. Consider, for example, the electric-power industry. Countries endowed with large, flowing rivers have access to a technology for production of electric power not available to desert countries. The natural endowment of resources such as rivers is just one possible source of differences in the technologies available in various countries. Other sources include technologies kept secret for security reasons (such as nuclear power and some computer capabilities) and legal restrictions such as patents that prohibit imitation of proprietary technologies. History provides many examples of technological innovations that allowed firms in one country to make significant advances over others at least in the short run, most notably England's

---

16. See the Irwin and Klenow paper in the chapter references.

17. The reader may want to review section 2.1 in Chapter Three and section 3 in Chapter Four.

textile-based industrial revolution of the late eighteenth century, the mass-production-based "second industrial revolution" in late-nineteenth- and early-twentieth-century America, and the late-twentieth-century "computer revolution."

Economists have suggested a number of ways that cross-country differences in technology affect international trade. Here we'll concentrate on one particular technology-based explanation for temporal changes in the observed pattern of trade: the **product-cycle hypothesis**, first articulated by Raymond Vernon in the 1960s. The basic idea underlying the product cycle is that certain countries tend to specialize in making new technologically innovative products, while other countries specialize in producing already well-established goods. One important implication of the theory is that, as each product moves through its life cycle, the geographic location of its production changes.

Vernon argued that technological innovation and new-product development tend to occur in a few major industrialized economies, particularly the United States. This reflects those countries' highly educated and skilled workforces and the relatively high level of expenditures on research and development. Early production of a new product typically occurs on a small scale as the innovating firm debugs and refines both the product and the production process. Firms usually aim this early, small-scale production at the domestic rather than the export market. At first, actual production needs to be located close to consumers so they can provide feedback. Only the technologically innovative firm owns the new technology, so production occurs only in that firm's home country.

Eventually, the firm perfects the product and production accelerates, first for the domestic market and then for export. Domestic consumption and domestic production rise, but production rises more rapidly to accommodate growing export demand. The innovating firm still controls the new technology.

As the production technology becomes standardized (no longer a matter of trial and error and experimentation), the innovating firm may find it profitable to license the technology to other firms both domestically and abroad. It then becomes feasible to relocate production to other countries in which the cost of standardized production is lower. The cost of such production in the innovating country remains relatively high because of its highly skilled labor force. Once production no longer requires the research-and-development and engineering skills of that labor force, relocation of production becomes economical. Some domestic production of the good continues in the innovating country; but exports level off as new, low-cost foreign producers licensed by the innovating firm capture export markets.

Next, imports rather than domestic production begin to serve the innovating country's domestic market. The technology has diffused completely, and any patents or other proprietary restrictions that once limited its use have expired. Domestic production falls rapidly as the domestic industry loses both its domestic and export markets.

Finally, the product completes its cycle. Although domestic consumption of the good may continue, imports satisfy that consumption. Attention in the innovating country concentrates on new technological innovations, leading to new products in the early stage of their product cycles. Examples of products that appear to have experienced a typical product cycle include radios, black-and-white and then color televisions, and semiconductor chips.[18]

The textile industry provides a long-term example of the product-cycle scenario at work. The industrial revolution gave England a huge technological advantage in textile production. As the new technologies spread, the textile industry moved to the United States (first to New England, then to the South) and then on to other countries where

---

18. For evidence that the product cycle doesn't characterize most industries, see Joseph Gagnon and Andrew Rose, "Dynamic Persistence of Industry Trade Balances: How Pervasive Is the Product Cycle?" *Oxford Economic Papers,* 1995.

abundant low-skilled labor permitted production of low-cost textiles using a standardized technology. Today the major centers of textile production are in the labor-abundant countries of Asia. The industry's migration continues; as wages rose in established textile centers such as Hong Kong and Singapore, production shifted to new Asian centers including Malaysia, the Philippines, and China (first along the coast, then shifting to the interior).

The product-cycle hypothesis and other related explanations of trade focus on characteristics of the production process. An alternate theory focuses on the importance of demand characteristics in various countries.

8 OVERLAPPING DEMANDS AS A BASIS FOR TRADE

The Ricardian and Heckscher-Ohlin theories of trade imply that a country will find it most beneficial to trade with countries very *different* from itself. Differences in production possibilities, tastes, or both can form a basis for trade, as we learned in Chapter Three. This would lead us to expect large volumes of trade between dissimilar countries, particularly between the capital- and human-capital-abundant developed countries and the mineral- and unskilled-labor-abundant developing countries. World trade figures, however, don't bear out this expectation. The largest share of world trade, particularly in manufactured goods, occurs among the group of developed countries, which have high incomes and similar factor endowments. One explanation of this phenomenon focuses on economies of scale (section 6) rather than comparative advantage as the source of trade.

Alternatively, economist Staffan Linder suggested that similarities in *demand* between two countries also can form a basis for trade, especially for manufactured goods.[19] This argument rests on the idea that firms typically don't produce goods solely for export; most produce goods for which domestic demand exists. If a country develops only those industries for which a viable domestic market exists, trade will occur in those products for which domestic consumers and foreign consumers share similar tastes.

To formulate empirically testable implications, we must state the hypothesis more precisely. Linder argues that for many manufactured goods, the *quality* of the good that consumers in a particular country demand depends primarily on their income. Consumers with higher incomes demand manufactured goods of higher quality. Panel (a) in Figure 8, with income measured on the horizontal axis and quality measured on the vertical one, represents this hypothesized relationship as an upward-sloping line. Of course, the income levels of consumers in any given country vary. In Figure 8, panel (a), incomes for country A range from a low of I_{min}^A to a high of I_{max}^A. Given these incomes, consumers in country A demand goods of *quality* range Q_{min}^A to Q_{max}^A. If, as Linder suggests, a domestic market is necessary for an industry to develop, country A will produce manufactured goods in the Q_{min}^A to Q_{max}^A quality range.

Figure 8, panel (b), introduces a second country with income range I_{min}^B to I_{max}^B and demand for goods in quality range Q_{min}^B to Q_{max}^B. Industries in country B will develop to provide goods in the quality range demanded by B consumers. The overlap in the quality ranges demanded by consumers in countries A and B (Q_{min}^B to Q_{max}^A in panel (b)) represents the goods in which trade between the two countries might occur. The more similar the two countries' income ranges, the larger the overlap in the demanded qualities and the greater the potential for trade.

19. Staffan B. Linder, *An Essay on Trade and Transformation* (New York: Wiley, 1961).

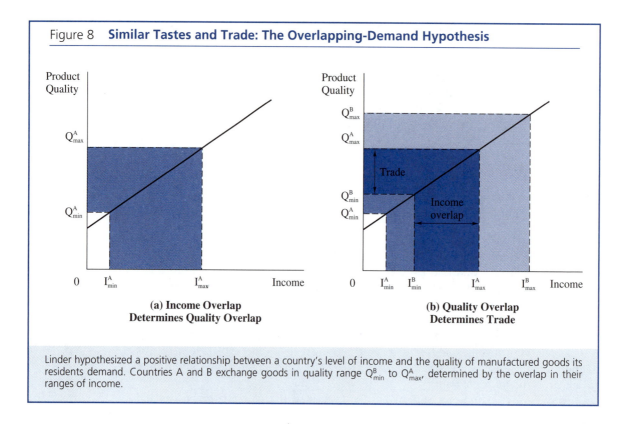

Figure 8   Similar Tastes and Trade: The Overlapping-Demand Hypothesis

**(a) Income Overlap
Determines Quality Overlap**

**(b) Quality Overlap
Determines Trade**

Linder hypothesized a positive relationship between a country's level of income and the quality of manufactured goods its residents demand. Countries A and B exchange goods in quality range Q^B_{min} to Q^A_{max}, determined by the overlap in their ranges of income.

Empirical evidence on the validity of the overlapping-demands hypothesis is mixed. As mentioned earlier, the large share of trade that occurs among the high-income developed countries provides informal evidence in support. In 2001, 61 percent of all world merchandise exports went from one high-income economy to another, as illustrated in Figure 9. Only 36 percent of exports went from a high-income economy to a developing one or vice versa.

More precise tests of the overlapping-demands hypothesis have been less encouraging. However, in evaluating tests of the model, we must remember the problems introduced by differences in the distribution of income across countries. Consider an extreme example. Let all but one consumer in country A have income level I^A_{min}, and let the remaining individual have income level I^A_{max}; and let all country B individuals but one have income level I^B_{max}, and let the remaining individual have income level I^B_{min}. The potential for trade is much lower than the illustrated range of overlap in qualities suggests. Because of this problem, tests of the overlapping-demands hypothesis require careful corrections for the distribution of income; reliable, internationally comparable data on the distribution of income are difficult to obtain. An additional problem in testing the hypothesis arises because the model's predictions closely match that of a model of intra-industry trade based on economies of scale—both predict high levels of trade in manufactured goods between similar trading partners. The similarity of the models' predictions presents a problem for empirical researchers trying to sort out the relative merits of the two for explaining the pattern of trade observed in the world economy.

Besides theories of trade based on the characteristics of production or of demand, several rely heavily on characteristics of the trade process itself. One consideration we've ignored so far is the role of transportation costs.

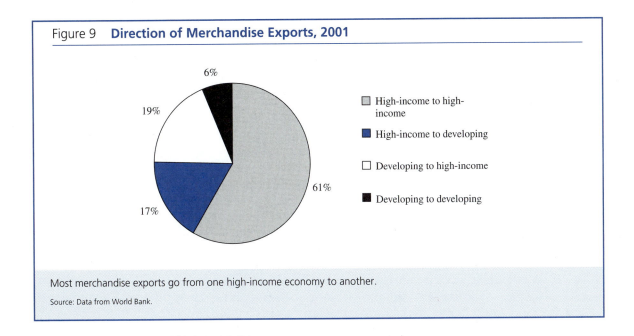

Figure 9 **Direction of Merchandise Exports, 2001**

Legend:
- High-income to high-income
- High-income to developing
- Developing to high-income
- Developing to developing

Most merchandise exports go from one high-income economy to another.

Source: Data from World Bank.

9 TRANSPORT COSTS AS A DETERMINANT OF TRADE

Some goods typically aren't traded internationally. Called **nontraded goods**, the reason for their special status usually involves a prohibitive cost of transporting them. The classic example is haircuts (actually a service rather than a good). Substantial differences exist in the prices of haircuts across countries, but trade doesn't develop exporting haircuts from low-price to high-price countries. The cost of transporting the customer to take advantage of the low price in another country would far outweigh the price differential.

For other classes of goods, **transport costs** may not be prohibitive (that is, high enough to prevent any trade) but still may be high enough to significantly affect the pattern of trade. Heavy goods tend to be more costly to transport; and the relationship between the item's weight and value affects whether the good will be traded. Automobiles, heavy but of high value, are traded; gravel, on the other hand, typically isn't traded internationally because its low value doesn't warrant the high transport costs implied by its weight. We learned in section 5.2 that transport costs could generate intra-industry trade in heavy homogeneous goods, but only if the placement of national borders put consumers in country A near producers in country B. Also, perishable items must be moved quickly, and rapid means of transportation usually are more expensive than slower means.

Traditionally, economists devoted little attention to transport costs' effect on trade. The volume of trade in the world economy certainly is smaller than would be the case if firms could transport goods costlessly and instantaneously from country to country. In fact, since many developing countries have lowered some of their policy barriers to trade, high transport costs now represent the major impediment to trade. High transport costs limit firms' ability to vertically specialize by performing different stages of production in different countries depending on their comparative advantages. Landlocked countries, particularly those in Africa, have transport costs approximately three times as high as those in industrial countries; part of this cost differential reflects

African countries' poor transportation infrastructures (for example, roads and port facilities). Africa's high transport costs contribute to the continent's inability to grow through development of assembly-oriented manufacturing facilities.

As long as transport costs remain fairly constant over time, their incorporation adds little explanatory power to the models already developed. When *changes* occur in transport costs, things become more interesting. Often such changes result from an advance in technology. Dramatic late-nineteenth-century examples include introduction of steamships and railroads, along with construction of the Suez and Panama canals to shorten shipping distances. A more recent example is development of refrigerated truck and ship transportation. This innovation reduced spoilage by enough to make international trade in many products feasible for the first time. In the northeastern United States, many of the fresh fruits and vegetables available in stores during the winter come from Latin America. Fresh cut flowers in European stores come from Kenya, while those in U.S. stores are grown in Colombia. Before refrigerated transport, spoilage costs would have prohibited such trade. Containerized intermodal cargo shipping provides another example of a trade-enhancing technological change that lowered transport cost. By prepacking goods in very large, uniformly sized containers that giant cranes can load quickly and efficiently onto ships, trucks, and railroad cars, the cost of hauling many large items long distances has been substantially reduced. Approximately 80 percent of all sea-cargo trade between industrialized countries now travels in intermodal containers. And development of jet engines and wide-body aircraft created the first means of fast transport for large items; more than 30 percent of the value of all U.S. imports now arrive in the country by air.

Transport costs also play an important role in trade with external economies of scale. High transport costs can contribute to the agglomeration effects common in industries characterized by external economies. Also, past high transport costs may have caused an industry to spring up in a particular location to be near customers, and external economies of scale may perpetuate that locational pattern long after the initial transport-cost reason for it disappears.

Another interesting issue concerning transport costs is the question of who pays them—the importer or the exporter. In general, the two share the costs. Other things being equal, the less price responsive the demand for the good by the importing country, the larger the share of transport costs the importer will bear; and the less price responsive the supply of the good by the exporting country, the greater the share of transport costs the exporter will bear.

Panel (a) in Figure 10 illustrates the international market for good X. Country A is assumed to have a comparative advantage in production of X and is willing to export X at any price above its autarky price, P_X^A.[20] The supply curve for exports, $Exports_X^A$, shows how many units of good X country A is willing to export at various prices. Country B has a comparative disadvantage in good X and is willing to import X at any price below its autarky price, P_X^B. The demand curve for imports, $Imports_X^B$, shows how many units of good X country B is willing to import at various prices. The equilibrium outcome with no transport costs involves X* units of good X traded at international terms of trade P_X^{tt}.

Next, consider the effect of transportation costs of T per unit of good X transported between countries A and B, as shown in panel (b) of Figure 10. T includes the cost of packing and transporting the good as well as insurance premiums for the trip and related

---

20. To simplify notation, we show the price of good X simply as P_X rather than as the relative price, P_X/P_Y.

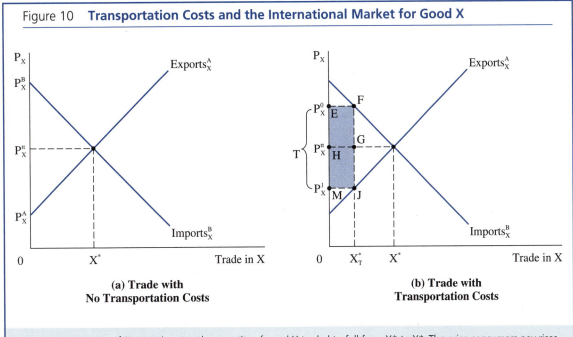

Figure 10   Transportation Costs and the International Market for Good X

(a) Trade with No Transportation Costs

(b) Trade with Transportation Costs

Transportation costs of T per unit cause the quantity of good X traded to fall from X* to X^*_T. The price consumers pay rises from P^{tt}_X to P^0_X, and the price producers receive falls from P^{tt}_X to P^1_X.

expenses. The price consumers in country B pay for good X must cover *both* the price paid to producers in A and the transport costs. If $T = P^0_X - P^1_X$, the new equilibrium volume of good X traded is X^*_T. Consumers in country B pay price P^0_X, and producers in country A get price P^1_X. The difference of T per unit, or $T \cdot X^*_T$ in total, goes to pay the costs of transport. Transport costs reduce the volume of trade in good X, just as we would expect.

Producers in country A pay a share of the transportation costs by accepting the lower price P^1_X rather than the price P^{tt}_X that prevailed without these costs; the area of rectangle HGJM in Figure 10, panel (b), shows producers' contribution toward the costs. Consumers in country B share in the burden of the transport costs by paying the higher price P^0_X; the area of rectangle EFGH represents their contribution. The graphical demonstration that the division of the total transport costs, area EFJM, between the share borne by producers and that borne by consumers depends on the particular shapes of the demand and supply curves is left to the reader. (*Hint: Draw two graphs with identical demand curves, one with a very steep supply curve and the other with a very flat supply curve.*)

If transport costs are an important determinant of the pattern of international trade, the choices of firms and industries concerning where to locate also must be significant, because distance from consumers affects transport costs. In fact, one of the most robust empirical findings in trade is that, other things being equal, the extent to which two countries trade is negatively related to the distance between them.[21]

---

21. Models that incorporate distance between countries as a determinant of their trade are called *gravity models*. We'll see more about these models in Case One.

Here we suggest a few basic industry characteristics that play a role in firms' locational choices.

10 LOCATION OF INDUSTRY

A firm's decision about where to locate depends on, among other things, the characteristics of the production process in the industry. Industries can be classified as resource oriented, market oriented, or footloose.

Resource-oriented industries locate near sources of their inputs or raw materials. One obvious example is mining operations. Once the ore is out of the ground, the location of each stage of the refining process must be decided. Should the ore be refined into its final form next to the mine, or should the raw material be shipped to another location for refining? The answer largely depends on how the ore's weight changes as it moves through the refining stages. Transport costs increase with weight, so firms have an incentive to avoid moving the good long distances until it is refined to a lighter form. Industries in which the good becomes lighter as it moves through the production stages tend to locate near the raw-material source to avoid having to move the good in its heavy form.

An example of a **market-oriented industry** is retail-sales operations. It wouldn't make sense to locate all bakeries in Iowa just to be near the wheat fields. Bakeries locate near their customers to sell fresh goods made in small batches. Other industries may be market oriented because they involve goods that become heavier or more difficult to move during the production process. It generally is less costly to gather the inputs to construct a building on the site and then assemble the parts than to build the building and then move it to its site (some small modular buildings provide an exception to the rule); hence, the construction industry locates near its markets. The soft-drink industry provides another example. Most soft-drink companies manufacture a concentrated syrup in a centralized location and ship it to local bottling companies, which add carbonated water and distribute the soft drinks to retailers. Shipping the small volume of concentrated syrup is cheaper than shipping the much larger volume of soft drink.

A third category of industry has no need to locate near either raw material sources or markets; these industries are characterized as **footloose** or **light industries**. Their products typically neither gain nor lose a significant amount of weight or volume as they move through the stages of production. Goods such as semiconductor chips and electronics components fall into this category because of their high value-to-weight ratios. Such light industries are free to move around the world in response to changes in the prices of inputs and assembly. The product-cycle idea may be important in the locational choices of footloose industries. As a product matures, the type of labor and other resources required to produce it may change, causing the industry to relocate. Both the semiconductor and consumer-electronics industries followed this pattern.

Economies of scale also play a role in determining firms' and industries' locations. A firm with substantial internal economies needs a large market to achieve those economies. If transport costs are low, the firm can serve a large dispersed market and be flexible in its location. But if transport costs are high, a geographically dispersed market becomes prohibitively expensive to serve, and the firm needs to locate near a large concentration of its customers. We've already seen how external scale economies can dictate that firms concentrate geographically; but high transport costs for a firm's final product may counteract the tendency toward agglomeration if the good's consumers are spread over a large area.

CASE 1: TRADE AND SIR ISAAC NEWTON'S APPLES

For the past half century, one class of very simple empirical models has performed remarkably well to explain the volume of bilateral trade between country pairs. The models are called *gravity models*. Yes, the same type of gravity as in Sir Isaac Newton and his famous apple; but the models don't exactly predict that the physical force of gravity pulls apparel from China to the United States and Boeing aircraft from the United States to Japan. Gravity models of trade predict that the larger the product of two countries' GDPs (that is, the total when we multiply one country's output by the other country's), the more bilateral trade between the two countries, other things being equal. Economic size increases countries' tendency to trade with one another just as objects' physical mass increases their tendency to be pulled together by Newton's gravitational force. Why? Because consumers in richer economies demand variety, which leads to more intra-industry trade in differentiated products, along with comparative-advantage-based inter-industry trade.

The physical force of gravity faces resistance, and so does trade in gravity models. In both cases, distance is the primary source of resistance. Just as distant bodies create a weaker gravitational force in physics, distant economies tend, other things being equal, to trade less with one another. Other considerations economists have found to affect countries' bilateral trade include landlocked status (which raises transport cost), historical linkages and cultural similarities, and policy-induced issues such as trade barriers and the ease with which traders can exchange the countries' currencies.

One recent study by a team of economists at the International Monetary Fund (IMF) found that country pairs experienced on average a 0.94 percent increase in their bilateral trade for each 1.0 percent increase in the product of their GDPs and experienced a 1.17 percent decrease in their bilateral trade for each 1.0 percent increase in distance between them.[22] Other variables that increased bilateral trade in the IMF study included the product of trading partners' per capita incomes, as well as sharing a land border, language, colonizer, past or present colonial relationship, or currency. Variables that decreased bilateral trade included landlocked locations, and restrictive trade and balance-of-payments policies.

CASE 2: ARE THERE ECONOMIES OF SCALE?

Industries that exhibit economies of scale provide an incentive to specialize and trade even without comparative advantage. So, to understand actual trade patterns, we must combine two bases for mutually beneficial trade: (1) scale economies for industries in which average costs fall as output rises and (2) comparative advantage for constant-returns-to-scale industries. This raises the question: Which industries are which? Measuring an industry's scale economies is a difficult task, but economists Werner Antweiler and Daniel Trefler recently calculated some useful estimates.

Figure 11 summarizes some of their findings, based on data from 71 countries, 1972–1992. For each industry, Antweiler and Trefler estimated an "elasticity of scale." A value of one means that a one-percent increase in output has no effect on average cost in the industry (total costs, of course, rise). The value of 1.403 for the Petroleum and Coal Products industry implies that a one-percent increase in output lowers average cost by 0.403 percent—the largest case of scale economies found in the study.

The lightly shaded bars on the left in Figure 11 represent manufacturing industries that exhibit scale economies. Darkly shaded bars in the middle of the figure represent natural-resource industries that exhibit scale economies. For all these industries, economies of scale provide a basis for mutually advantageous trade even without comparative advantage. Textured bars on the right in the figure represent constant-returns-to-scale industries, in which we would expect comparative advantage to form the basis for mutually beneficial trade.

---

22. International Monetary Fund, *World Economic Outlook,* September 2002, Chapter III.

Figure 11   Elasticities of Scale by Industry

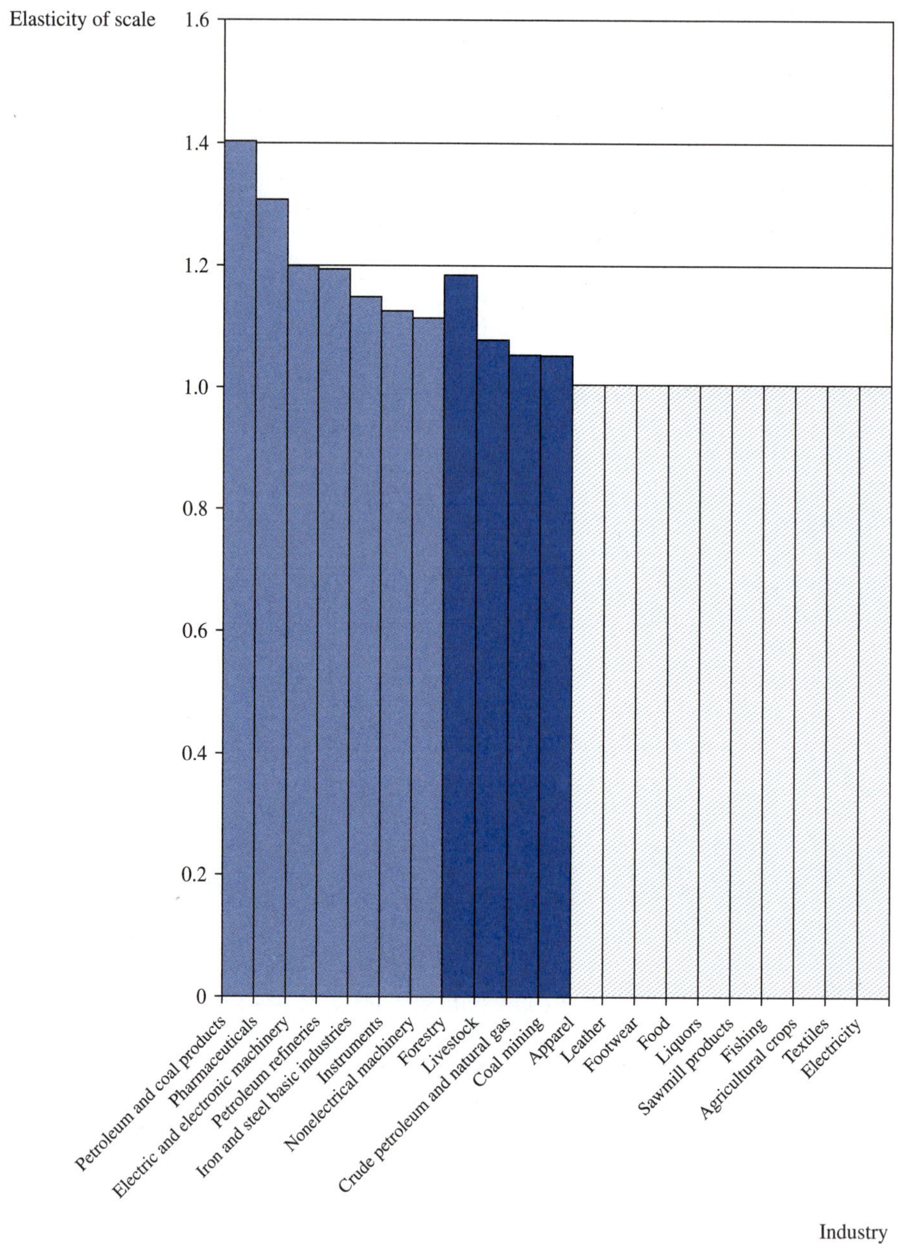

Industries with an elasticity of scale greater than 1.0 experience a decline in average cost as output rises. For example, the pharmaceutical industry's elasticity of 1.30 implies that when pharmaceutical output rises by one percent, average cost falls by approximately 0.30 percent.

Source: Data from Werner Antweiler and Daniel Trefler, "Increasing Returns and All That: A View from Trade," *American Economic Review* 92 (March 2002).

CASE 3: AROUND THE WORLD IN 22 DAYS

Transportation costs add from 5 to 10 percent to the prices of most internationally traded consumer goods. Air freight costs three to ten times as much as moving containers by sea. Until the mid-1970s, most U.S. imports from Asia came across the Pacific Ocean, through the Panama Canal, and up to East Coast ports such as New York. Then the arrival of intermodal transport, which coordinates containerized shipments by ship, rail, and truck, shifted Asia–U.S. trade toward the West Coast ports of Long Beach–Los Angeles, Oakland, Tacoma, and Seattle. Goods arrived there by ship, where giant cranes loaded the bus-sized containers onto railroads and trucks for the trip east, along the route illustrated in Figure 12 panel (a); the total trip was five or six days faster than the Panama Canal route. During the 1990s, routes shifted again—9,000 miles across the Indian Ocean, through the Suez Canal, and across the Atlantic to East Coast ports, along the route shown in panel (b).

The times involved in the Pacific and Suez routes are similar: about 25 days by ship and rail and about 22 days by ship, respectively, made possible by recent improvement in ship speeds relative to rail. The Suez route is more convenient for Southeast Asian exporters such as Malaysia, Singapore, and Thailand; the direct Pacific route, on the other hand, better suits Northern Asian exporters Japan and South Korea. Moving an average cargo container from Asia to the United States in 2003 cost between $3,500 and $5,000. The Suez Canal Authority, which sets rates for the canal, is charged with raising maximum revenue for the Egyptian government (which nationalized the canal in 1952), so the canal authority sets rates to make the Suez trip just cheaper than alternate routes. But as of 2001, the canal carried only about half of its 80-ship-per-day capacity.[23]

Meanwhile, traffic through the Panama Canal, much of it from China and headed for East Coast U.S. ports, has started to grow rapidly, even though the canal is too narrow to handle today's largest container ships. A new reservation system installed several years ago cut the time for a ship to get through the canal from two days to 16 hours, making the Panama route more attractive relative to the two alternatives. Studies are underway on the feasibility of widening the canal and installing new locks twice as large as the existing ones so the new super-cargo container ships could fit through. Cost estimates are $8 billion for the expansion; and experts view the scale and logistics of the project as comparable to the building of the canal itself during the early twentieth century.

Several economic factors affect exporters' route choices. The shipping lines that operate on each route belong to a cartel that controls shipping rates and other terms. Shipping is one of the few industries in which such cartels are legal in the United States; Congress exempted them from antitrust action in the Shipping Act of 1916. In 1999 Congress weakened the cartels' power to keep rates high by changing the law to permit shipping firms to reach confidential deals with customers rather than requiring all rates to be posted publicly. Under the old rules, once rates were posted, cargo had to be carried at that price on a first-come, first-serve basis; shipping firms "overbooked," and the resulting waits could be long and costly for customers. Under the new rules, a firm with fresh shrimp to move can simply agree to pay a higher price for immediate service. The shipping cartels were also weakened during the 1990s by entry of new Asian fleets that didn't join the cartels; about 85 percent of U.S.–Asia shipping capacity belongs to cartel members. As the relative strengths of the cartels on different routes (the Trans-Atlantic Conference Agreement and the Transpacific Stabilization Agreement) fluctuate, relative shipping rates change; and exporters respond by shifting to the cheaper route. For example, between 1995 and 1997, Atlantic shipping prices remained steady while Pacific prices fell by 12 percent; then, with the onset of the Asian financial crisis in late 1997, Pacific prices plummeted.

East and West Coast U.S. ports are worked by union stevedores—the International Longshoremen's Association and the International Longshore and Warehouse Union (ILWU), respectively. Fluctuations in the two unions' strength, like that of the shipping cartels, alters the cost of unloading goods on the two coasts. For example, in 1999, West Coast longshore workers' entry wage was almost double that of East Coast workers;[24] handling a single container cost about $300 at the port of Los Angeles. Port

---

23. "Too Big for World Trade Demands," *Financial Times*, May 9, 2001.

24. "West Coast Cargo Firms Plan Stingy Labor Talks," *The Wall Street Journal*, May 12, 1999.

Figure 12   **Asia–U.S. Trade Routes**

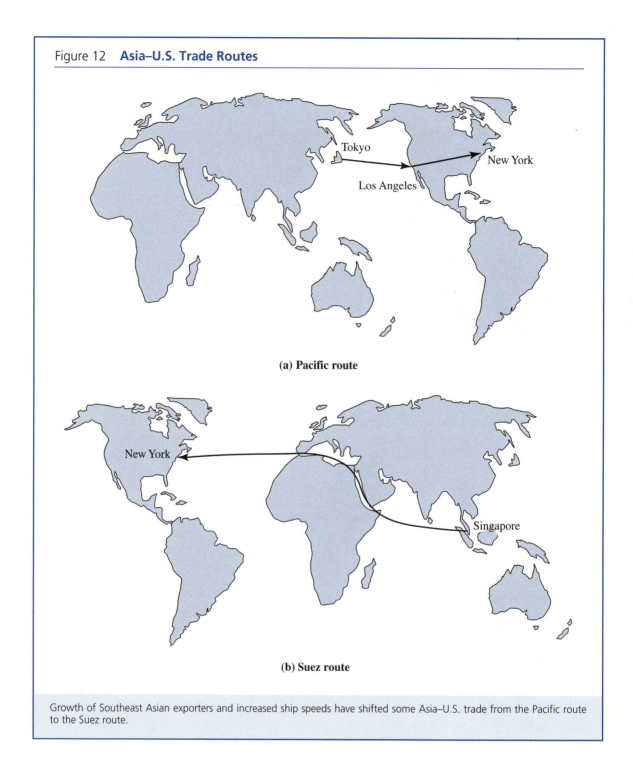

(a) Pacific route

(b) Suez route

Growth of Southeast Asian exporters and increased ship speeds have shifted some Asia–U.S. trade from the Pacific route to the Suez route.

cities watch shifts in these costs closely, because building and modernizing a port requires billions of dollars of investment, and facilities go underutilized if longshore wages drive shippers to other ports. For more than a decade, the ILWU blocked efforts to automate both container tracking and worker scheduling at West Coast ports; instead of electronically scanning container data, as happens at most big ports, union marine clerks (who earn about $128,000 per year) still copied container numbers by hand and entered them manually into computers.

And, rather than operating around the clock like most ports, West Coast ones operated just eight hours per day.[25] When the ILWU's contract expired in 2002, the union went on strike to block the new container-management technologies demanded by employers. The president of the United States ordered federal negotiators to mediate the dispute. In the end, employers got their new technology, but only by guaranteeing lifetime employment for all the current union marine clerks who write numbers on their clipboards.[26]

The increased transportation costs caused by shipping cartels, longshore unions, and many harbor-service restrictions have a significant impact on world trade. A World Bank study found that breaking up shipping cartels could cut transport costs for U.S. trade by up to 25 percent and that deregulating port services could lower costs by 9 percent.[27]

Technology is changing traditional port practices around the world. The largest ports are Hong Kong, a local cargo port for containers coming from and going to China by truck, and Singapore, a transshipment hub where most containers both arrive and leave by boat. In the newest facilities, loading, unloading, and container tracking are automated and computerized, requiring little labor. Singapore's PSA Corporation handled 17 million containers in 2000, using its proprietary computer software to track each container and ensure that ships remained stable as they're loaded with thousands of containers each of a different weight. Only one container per million shipped through Singapore was damaged or misplaced.[28] Such high-tech ports can unload and reload a container ship in about half the time required at older-style U.S. ports (40 versus 76 hours). The Hong Kong port facility can handle 20,000 TEUs (*twenty-foot equivalent units*, the standard unit of container measurement) per acre per year, compared with only 4,500 TEUs per acre per year at Los Angeles and 2,300 at New York.[29] In Asia, intense competition between 25-mile-apart ports in Singapore and Tanjung Pelepas, Malaysia, has cut prices for container unloading and associated port services. Shanghai, China, recently passed Pusan, South Korea, to become the world's third-largest port, in part because of labor unrest at the Pusan docks.

In Africa, a lack of modern port facilities hampers trade even for countries that aren't landlocked. Mozambique recently privatized it long-neglected facility at Maputo and hopes both to lure business from Durban, South Africa, and to facilitate more trade between African countries and the rest of the world.

SUMMARY

International trade is too complex a phenomenon to be explained fully by one simple theory. This chapter explored the ability of the Heckscher-Ohlin model to explain observed trade patterns, along with several alternate theories useful for understanding particular aspects of trade. The Heckscher-Ohlin model does a good job of explaining a large share of trade, with refined definitions of inputs to account for modern production processes. However, growing intra-industry trade in manufactures requires that we move beyond comparative advantage and add scale economies to our list of bases for mutually beneficial trade. Alternate, complementary explanations include the product cycle, overlapping demands, transportation costs, and location of industry.

LOOKING AHEAD

Chapter Six examines the simplest form of trade restriction: the tariff. By altering relative prices, tariffs change consumption and production decisions as well as

25. "Slinging Their Hooks," *The Economist,* September 14, 2002, p. 32; "Dock Lockout Spurs Shortages Concern," *The Wall Street Journal*, October 1, 2002.

26. "Dock Around the Clock," *The Economist*, November 30, 2002, p. 28.

27. Carsten Fink, et al., "Trade in International Maritime Services: How Much Does Policy Matter?" World Bank Development Research Group.

28. "Singapore Port Positions Itself for IPO This Year," *Financial Times*, February 19, 2001.

29. "U.S. Ports Are Losing the Battle to Keep Up with Overseas Trade," *The Wall Street Journal*, July 9, 2001.

redistribute income. The overall welfare effect of a tariff in a small country is negative, but a large country may be able to gain at the expense of its trading partners by imposing a tariff on imports. International negotiations since World War II have significantly lowered overall tariff levels, but high tariffs still distort trade in several important industries.

KEY TERMS

intra-industry trade	internal scale economies	transport costs
Leontief paradox	external scale economies	resource-oriented
homogeneous good	learning curve	industries
product differentiation	dynamic external	market-oriented
decreasing costs	economies	industries
(increasing returns to	product-cycle hypothesis	footloose (light)
scale, economies of scale)	nontraded goods	industries

PROBLEMS AND QUESTIONS FOR REVIEW

1. a. According to *The Economist* (August 9, 2003), civil war stopped transport along Congo's main transportation artery, the Congo River. For the five years prior to 2003, goods reached the town of Kisangani (1,500 kilometers from the capital city of Kinshasa) only by airplane because the country has very few paved roads. *The Economist* explains that, while the river was closed, "Kisangani got less for its own products, notably palm oil, and had to pay more for everything it bought." Use a diagram to explain why, when closure of the river forced traders to use more-costly air transport, Kisangani residents received lower prices for the products they sold and had to pay higher prices for products they bought.

   b. The *Financial Times* reported (October 13, 2003) that Mexican television-set assemblers in Tijuana, Mexico, find it increasingly difficult to compete with Chinese firms that can assemble televisions at lower cost "even though they lack the benefits of scale Tijuana has gained from concentrating so much of the industry in one place." Analyze this statement from the perspective of the relationship between scale economies and comparative advantage. Use an appropriate diagram.

2. a. Write the formula for the intra-industry trade index. Explain why the index takes a value of 0 in industries with no intra-industry trade and a value of 1 in industries with maximal intra-industry trade.

   b. If country A exports $10 million worth of semiconductor chips per year and imports $20 million worth of semiconductor chips per year, what is country A's intra-industry trade index for semiconductor chips? Suppose you had data to calculate the IIT index for 256K DRAMs. How would you expect the two IIT indices to compare? Explain.

3. Use a figure similar to Figure 4 to show that international trade is particularly important for small countries in the presence of scale economies. (*Hint: Alter Figure 4 so that country A's demand for each good is half the size of country B's demand.*) Explain.

4. How can international trade theory explain intra-industry trade?

5. The product-cycle theory of trade argues that the economically efficient geographic location of production changes as a good moves through its life cycle. In what sense is this consistent with the Heckscher-Ohlin theory of trade? Why might the kinds of locational shifts suggested by the product-cycle theory result in pressures for protectionist policies?

6. Assume that (1) the computer software industry exhibits external scale economies, (2) India has a comparative advantage over the United States in computer software, (3) the Indian market for software is one-tenth the size of the U.S. market, and (4) the United States has a head start in the industry and currently produces for both the U.S. and Indian markets. Illustrate in a diagram similar to Figure 5. What would happen if India protected its software market? On what does your answer depend?

7. Before the Soviet Union collapsed in 1991, Soviet economic planners were famous for keeping transport costs within the Union artificially low. The Soviet Union was also known for its massive industrial plants, often designed to serve the entire Soviet Union plus its satellite states in Eastern and Central Europe. Explain the relationship between the two policies, and how you would expect the policies to affect the level of trade among the Soviet republics.

8. Why might we expect intra-industry trade based on scale economies to be less politically controversial than inter-industry trade based on comparative advantage?

REFERENCES AND SELECTED READINGS

Antweiler, Werner, and Daniel Trefler. "Increasing Returns and All That: A View From Trade." *American Economic Review* 92 (March 2002): 93–119.
Divides industries into those with constant and increasing returns to scale; for advanced students.

Debaere, Peter. "*Relative* Factor Abundance." *Journal of Political Economy* 111 (June 2002): 589–610.
Tests of Heckscher-Ohlin using bilateral factor abundance; for intermediate and advanced students.

Evenett, Simon, and Wolfgang Keller. "On Theories Explaining the Success of the Gravity Equation." *Journal of Political Economy* 110 (April 2002): 281–316.
Linkages between theories of trade and the gravity equation; for advanced students.

Feenstra, Robert C. "Integration of Trade and Disintegration of Production in the Global Economy." *Journal of Economic Perspectives* 12 (Fall 1998): 31–50.
Relationship between trade patterns and production patterns; for all students.

Freund, Caroline, and Diana Weinhold. "The Internet and International Trade in Services." *American Economic Review Papers and Proceedings* 92 (May 2002): 236–240.
The Internet as a source of growth of trade in services; for all students.

Grossman, Gene M., and Elhanan Helpman. "Technology and Trade." In *Handbook of International Economics,* Vol. 3, edited by G. M. Grossman and K. Rogoff, 1279–1338. Amsterdam: North-Holland, 1995.
Advanced survey of technology-related aspects of international trade and trade theory.

Helpman, Elhanan. "The Structure of Foreign Trade." *Journal of Economic Perspectives* 13 (Spring 1999): 121–144.
Interaction between traditional trade models and more modern developments; for intermediate students.

Hummels, David, et al. "Vertical Specialization and the Changing Nature of World Trade." Federal Reserve Bank of New York *Economic Policy Review* (June 1998): 79–99.
How firms' location of the different stages of their production processes affect trade patterns; for intermediate students.

Irwin, Douglas A., and Peter J. Klenow. "Learning-by-Doing Spillovers in the Semiconductor Industry." *Journal of Political Economy* 102 (December 1994): 1200–1227.
Empirical estimation of learning curves in the semiconductor industry; for advanced students.

Krugman, Paul R. *Development, Geography, and Trade.* Cambridge, Mass.: MIT Press, 1995.
How increasing returns affect locational choice, development, and trade; for all students.

Leamer, Edward, and James Levinsohn. "International Trade Theory: The Evidence." In *Handbook of International Economics,* Vol. 3, edited by G. M. Grossman and K. Rogoff, 1339–1394. Amsterdam: North-Holland, 1995.
Advanced survey of empirical evidence on international trade theories.

Leontief, Wassily. "Domestic Production and Foreign Trade: The American Capital Position Reexamined." *Economia Internazionale* 7 (February 1954): 3–32.
Presents the empirical evidence that became known as the Leontief paradox; for introductory or intermediate students.

Murphy, K. M., and A. Schleifer. "Quality and Trade." *Journal of Development Economics* (June 1997): 1–15.
More on the overlapping-demands story.

Romalis, John. "Factor Proportions and the Structure of Commodity Trade." *American Economic Review* 94 (March 2004): 67–97.
Advanced tests of Heckscher-Ohlin.

Schott, Peter K. "One Size Fits All? Heckscher-Ohlin Specialization in Global Production." *American Economic Review* 93 (June 2003): 686–708.
Advanced empirical tests of Heckscher-Ohlin.

Session on "Empirical Testing of Trade Theories." *American Economic Review Papers and Proceedings* 90 (May 2000): 145–160.
Advanced treatment of testing trade theories; emphasis on the role of technology.

Trefler, Daniel. "International Price Differences." *Journal of Political Economy* 101 (December 1993): 961–987.
Empirical test of the factor price equalization theorem emphasizing productivity differences; for advanced students.

Trefler, Daniel. "The Case of the Missing Trade and Other Mysteries." *American Economic Review* (December 1995): 1029–1046.
Tests of Heckscher-Ohlin; for advanced students.

Vernon, Raymond. "The Product Cycle Hypothesis in a New International Environment." *Oxford Bulletin of Economics and Statistics* 41 (November 1979): 255–267.
Updated perspective on the product cycle from its original proponent; for introductory or intermediate students.

Westhoff, Frank H., Beth V. Yarbrough, and Robert M. Yarbrough. "Complexity, Organization, and Stuart Kauffman's *The Origins of Order.*" *Journal of Economic Behavior and Organization* 29 (January 1996): 1–25.
Application of complexity theory to the role of "historical accident" in economic history; for advanced students.

World Bank. *Global Economic Prospects 2002.* Washington, D.C.: World Bank, 2002.
Chapter 4 contains a useful discussion of the role of transport costs in trade.

Yarbrough, Beth V., and Robert M. Yarbrough. "International Contracting and Territorial Control: The Boundary Question." *Journal of Institutional and Theoretical Economics* 150 (March 1994): 239–264.
Application of the new economics of organization to the problem of why national boundaries change; for all students.

6

Tariffs

1 INTRODUCTION

Up to this point, we've explored the benefits of international trade. Although we've used methods from the modern economist's tool kit, the benefits of trade have been known for more than two centuries, at least since the work of David Hume, Adam Smith, and David Ricardo. Nonetheless, no historical period has been free of trade restrictions. Chapter Four presented several reasons for the controversial nature of trade, particularly its effect of redistributing income within each participating country. The policies countries use to restrict trade are called **barriers to trade**, one of which is the tariff. In this chapter, we explore tariffs' effects on production, consumption, prices, trade volume, and welfare.

A **tariff** is a tax imposed on a good as it crosses a national boundary. Historically, tariffs were the most commonly used type of trade restriction; in recent years, however, use of tariffs has declined, and use of a variety of other trade restrictions has increased. Average tariff levels have fallen both in the United States and abroad, largely as a result of international negotiations conducted under the General Agreement on Tariffs and Trade (GATT), now called the World Trade Organization (WTO), a forum created after World War II for international negotiation of trade issues.

2 WHY WOULD A COUNTRY IMPOSE A TARIFF?

A country might impose a tariff for any of four reasons. First, a tariff, like any tax, discourages consumption of a particular good. Placing a tariff on an imported good makes that good relatively more costly to consumers. For example, during the OPEC oil price increases of the 1970s, many policy makers proposed a tariff on oil imports; proponents argued that the United States needed to reduce its consumption of oil, particularly foreign oil, and that a tariff presented one possible incentive.

A second reason for imposing a tariff, like any tax, is to generate government revenue. Developed countries rarely impose tariffs specifically to raise revenue, because those countries have the infrastructure necessary to administer other taxes, such as personal and corporate income taxes. Figure 1, panel (a) traces the dramatic historical decline in tariffs' share of U.S. government revenue. Many developing countries, however, still use tariffs to raise a significant share of the revenue to finance their

Figure 1   Tariff Revenue as Share of Government Revenue

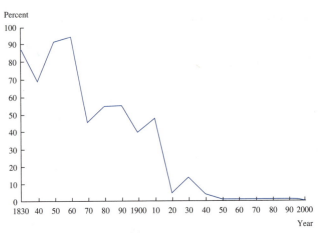

**(a) U.S. Tariff Revenue as Share of Total
U.S. Federal Government Receipts, 1830–2000**

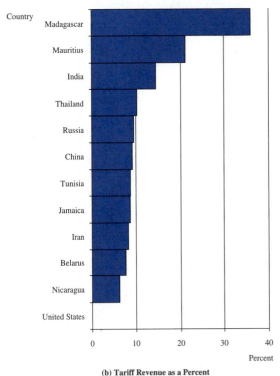

**(b) Tariff Revenue as a Percent
of Central Government Revenue, 2002**

Tariff revenue has fallen from about 90 percent of total U.S. government receipts to far less than 1 percent. Some countries still rely more heavily on tariffs as a source of central government revenue.

Sources: Data for panel (a) from U.S. Department of Commerce; data for panel (b) from International Monetary Fund, *Government Finance Statistics Yearbook 2003*.

governments' activities; Figure 1, panel (b) provides some examples. Administration of an income tax requires a well-developed and effective bureaucracy as well as a literate and settled population; countries lacking one or more of these requisites find it easier to administer tariffs by patrolling ports and national borders.

A third reason for imposing import tariffs is to discourage imports to eliminate a balance-of-trade deficit (that is, a situation in which payments to foreigners for imports exceed receipts from foreigners for exports). A country designing a tariff to reduce a trade deficit would apply the tariff to all imports, or at least to a broad range of goods, rather than to a single good or a narrow range of goods. This motive involves tariffs as a tool of *macro*economic rather than *micro*economic policy, so we won't focus on this motive here; but tariffs aren't likely to be an effective method to reduce a balance-of-trade deficit, and proper use of other macroeconomic policy tools makes tariffs for balance-of-trade purposes unnecessary.

The fourth—and most common—purpose of tariffs, and the one on which we'll focus, is as a **protectionist policy**—a way to "protect" or insulate a domestic industry from competition by foreign producers of the same good. An import tariff allows domestic producers to both capture a larger share of the domestic market and charge a higher price than would otherwise be possible.

Countries impose many more tariffs on imports than on exports, especially developed countries that don't use tariffs as a major source of government revenue. In fact, the U.S. Constitution makes export taxes illegal in the United States. So, we'll focus our discussion on import tariffs and, at the end of the chapter, briefly examine the effects of export taxes and the history behind the U.S. prohibition on them.

3 TYPES OF TARIFFS AND WAYS TO MEASURE THEM

Like any tax, tariffs can be classified as specific or ad valorem.[1] **Specific tariffs** charge a specified amount for each unit imported of the tariffed good. For example, the United States charges a tariff of $0.68 per live goat. **Ad valorem tariffs** charge a specified percentage of the value of the tariffed good; for example, the United States imposes a tariff of 2.4 percent of a dog leash's value. The basic economic effects of tariffs apply to both specific and ad valorem ones. Specific tariffs will be more convenient for most of our analysis because they're easier to depict graphically.

Countries apply tariffs on a detailed product-by-product basis; for example, the U.S. tariff code contains more than eight thousand categories, on which tariffs range from 0 percent to 458 percent.[2] However, economists and policy makers often want a measure of a country's *overall* tariff level. That is, we often want to know about the general level of trade restriction a country imposes in the form of tariffs rather than the amount of the tariff on a narrow product category such as "grapefruit, imported during October" (*yes*, grapefruit imported during October are tariffed at a rate [$0.015 per kilogram] different from the rate applied to grapefruit imported during either August or September [$0.019 per kilogram] or November through July [$0.025 per kilogram]!).

This idea appears simple enough, but measuring a country's overall tariff level turns out to be more complicated than it seems. Tariff rates differ across goods (for example, separate U.S. tariff rates apply to more than 200 different types of watches and clocks),

1. Compound tariffs combine a specific and an ad valorem tariff on the same good. You can find examples in the U.S. *Harmonized Tariff Schedule,* at http://www.usitc.gov/taffairs.htm.

2. See the U.S. *Harmonized Tariff Code* at http://www.usitc.gov/taffairs.htm.

so characterizing the overall level of a country's tariff protection requires combining these rates into some type of average. There are two basic approaches; each has advantages and disadvantages.

The first technique involves a simple unweighted average of industry tariff rates. Consider country A, which imports two goods, X and Y, with imports of X subject to a 25 percent tariff and imports of good Y to a 50 percent tariff. Country A's unweighted average tariff equals $(0.25 + 0.50)/2 = 0.375$ or 37.5 percent. This unweighted-average technique works well for countries that import approximately equal amounts of different goods—for example, if country A imported $50 worth of X and $50 worth of Y.

But what if country A imported $80 worth of X and only $20 of Y? In this case, simply averaging the two tariff rates without taking into account the goods' relative importance in overall imports seems less informative. This is why the more common measure of tariffs is a weighted-average measure. It involves weighting each industry's tariff rate by that industry's share of total imports. If country A imported $50 worth of X and $50 worth of Y, the weighted-average tariff rate would equal $(\$50/\$100) \cdot 0.25 + (\$50/\$100) \cdot 0.50 = 0.375 = 37.5$ percent. Note that with equal imports in both industries, the unweighted and weighted tariff measures give the same result. However, if A imports $80 worth of X and only $20 worth of Y, the weighted-average measure equals $(\$80/\$100) \cdot 0.25 + (\$20/\$100) \cdot 0.50 = 0.30$, considerably below the unweighted figure of 0.375. This difference occurs because the more prevalent import, X, has the low tariff rate. In this case, the weighted-average tariff gives a more accurate picture of country A's overall tariff.

For the purpose of measuring a country's overall trade restrictiveness, both types of average tariffs have a serious problem: They ignore trade foreclosed by the tariff. In other words, neither measure takes into account that the country might have imported $100 *million* (rather than $100) worth of the two goods had there been no tariffs. The easiest way to see this problem is to consider the extreme case of a **prohibitive tariff**, that is, one high enough to halt trade in the product. Consider again the case where country A imports $50 worth each of goods X and Y. Now suppose country A raises its tariff on good Y from 50 percent to 100 percent, high enough to cause Y imports to fall to zero. Total imports fall to $50, all good X. The average tariff (weighted or not) now equals 25 percent because the tariff on good Y disappears from the calculation. Ironically, the *increase* in the tariff on good Y caused a *decrease* in country A's average tariff. But we wouldn't want to conclude that country A has become more open to trade!

Despite impressive liberalization since World War II, some products remain subject to much higher-than-average tariff rates. In the markets for these products, tariffs (and, in some cases, nontariff barriers as well) continue to distort trade. Even after the WTO Uruguay Round of tariff reductions, approximately 5 percent of developed-country imports remain subject to "peak" tariffs—those in excess of 15 percent. For example, the United States cut its average tariffs on apparel as part of the Uruguay Round, but only from 19.3 to 17.5 percent.[3] In addition, the United States doesn't grant the negotiated tariff reductions, either from the Uruguay Round or from earlier rounds, to some countries for political or security reasons. Countries that in 2004 didn't receive U.S. normal-trading-relations status, which grants access to the lower tariffs, include Cuba, Laos, and North Korea.

Peak tariffs (that is, those greater than 15 percent) affect a much higher share of products in many developing countries than in developed ones. South African peak

3. Jeffrey J. Schott, *The Uruguay Round: An Assessment* (Washington, D.C.: Institute for International Economics, 1994), p. 62.

tariffs apply to 32 percent of products, Brazilian peak tariffs to 41 percent, Bangladeshi peak tariffs to 55 percent of goods, and Indian peak tariffs to 93 percent of goods.[4]

Most of the tariff reductions since World War II have taken place in the context of GATT/WTO negotiations, so nonmember countries often retain high tariffs relative to the members. However, WTO membership has grown rapidly. In 2003, 145 countries were members and 26 more had requested accession to the group; the newest WTO members include Chinese Taipei (Taiwan) and Armenia. Even among WTO members, tariff rates vary widely by country, by source of imports, and by product. Only three WTO members—Hong Kong, Chinese Taipei, and Singapore—impose no tariffs. Figure 2 indicates regional variations in tariff levels. The industrial economies of North America and western Europe have the lowest tariffs, and the developing economies of South Asia the highest; but tariffs in all regions have fallen since the early 1980s. Variation in tariffs across products is as important as variation across regions. Table 1 reports average tariffs in effect at the end of the Uruguay Round on industrial products.

Notice two patterns in Table 1: Developing-country tariffs are much higher than industrial-country ones, and the textile and clothing industries have unusually high rates of protection. We'll see more about both issues later.

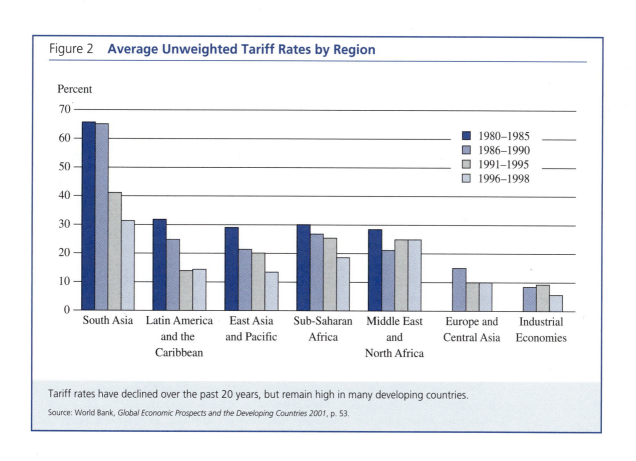

Figure 2 **Average Unweighted Tariff Rates by Region**

Tariff rates have declined over the past 20 years, but remain high in many developing countries.

Source: World Bank, *Global Economic Prospects and the Developing Countries 2001*, p. 53.

4. World Trade Organization, *Annual Report 2003* (Geneva: World Trade Organization, 2003), p. 15.

Table 1   **POST–URUGUAY ROUND TARIFF RATES ON INDUSTRIAL PRODUCTS**

Industrial Product	Average Trade-Weighted Tariff Rate (Percent)		
	Industrial-Economy Imports from Developing Economies	Developing-Economy Imports from Industrial Economies	Developing-Economy Imports from Developing Economies
Fish and fish products	5.0%	8.7%	15.9%
Wood, pulp, paper, and furniture	1.5	9.6	7.3
Textiles and clothing	11.1	20.7	21.1
Leather, rubber, footwear, and travel goods	6.1	18.5	8.2
Metals	0.8	13.5	8.5
Chemicals and photographic supplies	2.7	13.0	9.2
Transport equipment	3.9	21.8	10.6
Nonelectric machinery	1.2	14.4	10.2
Electric machinery	2.4	16.0	14.0
Mineral products	1.0	9.4	8.1
Other manufactured articles	2.0	13.9	8.8
All industrial products (excluding petroleum)	3.9	14.7	10.3

Source: Data from Marcelo de Paiva Abreu, "Trade in Manufactures: The Outcome of the Uruguay Round and Developing Country Interests," in Will Martin and L. Alan Winters, eds., *The Uruguay Round and the Developing Countries* (Cambridge: The World Bank, 1996), pp. 66, 75, 79.

4 WHAT HAPPENS WHEN A SMALL COUNTRY IMPOSES AN IMPORT TARIFF?

In analyzing a tariff's effects, the size of the country imposing it matters. We begin with the case of a small country. *Small* refers not to geographic size but to economic size in world markets. A small country is a price taker in world markets; that is, its activity comprises such a small share of total purchases and sales of a good that the country's actions have no perceptible effect on the world price. In other words, a small country's terms of trade are determined exogenously (outside the country), and the country makes its production and consumption decisions based on those given terms of trade.

4.1 Effects on Production, Consumption, and Price

We begin by analyzing the partial-equilibrium effects of a small country's imposition of an import tariff. The analysis is a partial-equilibrium one because it focuses on the tariff's effects in the market for the tariffed good and in the country imposing the tariff. Let D^d and S^d in Figure 3 represent *domestic demand* and *domestic supply*, respectively, of good Y in the small country. (We omit country superscripts because the analysis refers to a single country.) In autarky, point E represents equilibrium in the market for Y, with Y^0 units produced and sold at price P_Y^0. With unrestricted trade, the equilibrium world price of good Y equals P_Y^1, which is less than P_Y^0. This relationship between the autarky and world prices implies that the country has a comparative disadvantage in good Y, consistent with good Y being the country's imported good.

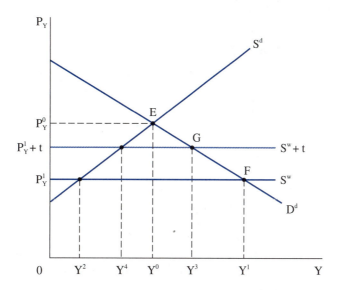

Figure 3 **What Happens When a Small Country Imposes an Import Tariff?**

The tariff increases the domestic price of the good by the amount of the tariff, reduces domestic consumption, increases domestic production, and decreases imports.

The country is small, so it can buy as much good Y as it chooses on the world market at price P_Y^1. The perfectly elastic (horizontal) supply of the good available to the country from the rest of the world, S^w, represents graphically the country's smallness. Under unrestricted trade, the economy would locate at point F, consume Y^1 units of good Y, produce Y^2 units domestically, and import $Y^1 - Y^2$ units, all at price P_Y^1. Even though residents consume more good Y at a lower price under unrestricted trade than in autarky, domestic producers sell fewer units and at a lower price. This effect of trade on domestic producers creates pressure for protection from foreign competition. Given the situation depicted in Figure 3, unrestricted trade doesn't eliminate the domestic Y industry, but lowers both industry output and the price domestic firms can charge. The cost of domestic production is such that domestic firms can produce units of good Y up to Y^2 more cheaply than they could be imported. Figure 3 reflects this, because the domestic supply curve (which represents the domestic cost of production) lies below the world export supply curve (which represents the foreign cost of production or, from a domestic perspective, the cost of importing) out to Y^2. For all units of good Y beyond Y^2, however, foreign production is less costly than domestic production; thus, the country imports those units if policy makers allow unrestricted trade.

Suppose the country imposes a specific tariff of t per unit on imported Y to improve the position of domestic Y producers. A horizontal line at $P_Y^1 + t$ illustrates the new world export supply curve the country faces. The small country can't affect its terms of trade, so the tariff is simply an addition to the domestic price of imports. To import a unit of Y, domestic consumers now must pay P_Y^1 to the foreign producer plus t to the domestic government. Point G represents the new equilibrium. Consumers demand Y^3 units of Y at price $P_Y^1 + t$; domestic producers supply Y^4 units; and $Y^3 - Y^4$ units are imported. The tariff raises the good's effective domestic price, reduces consumption of good Y, increases domestic production, and cuts imports. Domestic producers of good Y now produce more and can sell at a higher price, but domestic consumers consume less and must pay a higher price.

4.2 Effects on Welfare

A tariff's impact on production, prices, and consumption translates into an effect on the small country's welfare. To analyze the change in welfare caused by the tariff, it's useful to separate the effects on consumers from those on producers. For each group we need a measure of welfare, called *consumer surplus* and *producer surplus*, respectively.

CONSUMER SURPLUS **Consumer surplus** measures the satisfaction consumers receive from a good beyond the amount they must pay to obtain it. In panel (a) of Figure 4, the shaded triangle under the demand curve and above the price of the good illustrates the consumer surplus. (*Why?*) The height of a demand curve measures the maximum amount consumers are willing and able to pay for each successive unit of the good. No one would pay more for a good than the satisfaction gained from its consumption, so the height of the demand curve represents the satisfaction derived from each unit. If consumers demand Y^0 units, the total satisfaction must equal the area under the demand curve for good Y out to Y^0, or the sum of the satisfactions generated by each unit. But consumers must pay P_Y^0 for each unit; in other words, consumers' expenditures on Y equal the area of rectangle $0P_Y^0CY^0$. This implies that the satisfaction from consumption of Y^0 units net of their cost is the area under the demand curve out to Y^0 and above P_Y^0, or triangle P_Y^0EC.

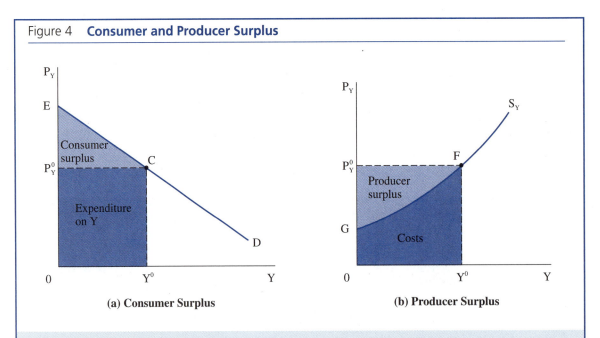

Figure 4   Consumer and Producer Surplus

(a) Consumer Surplus

(b) Producer Surplus

The consumer surplus generated by consumption of a good equals the value of the satisfaction from that consumption over and above the expenditures necessary to obtain the good. Graphically, panel (a) represents consumer surplus as the area under the demand curve out to the level of consumption and above the good's price. Producer surplus equals the revenue producers receive over and above the minimum necessary to cover production costs. Graphically, panel (b) represents producer surplus by the area above the supply curve and below the good's price.

PRODUCER SURPLUS   **Producer surplus** measures the revenue producers receive beyond the minimum required to induce them to supply the good.[5] In panel (b) of Figure 4, the area above the supply curve and below the good's price represents producer surplus. The height of the supply curve represents the minimum price at which producers would willingly supply each unit of the good. The minimum price rises with the level of production because of increasing opportunity costs. If the market price equals P_Y^0 and firms supply Y^0 units, producer surplus equals the area above the supply curve out to Y^0 and below P_Y^0. Producers receive total revenue equal to area $0P_Y^0FY^0$. The minimum revenue they must receive to produce Y^0 is area $0GFY^0$, which would just cover their production costs. The difference, GP_Y^0F, captures producer surplus.

A TARIFF'S EFFECT ON CONSUMER AND PRODUCER SURPLUS   Figure 5 shows the welfare effects of an import tariff by a small country in terms of changes in consumer and producer surplus. In autarky, area P_Y^0HE represents consumer surplus. Under unrestricted trade, consumer surplus rises to P_Y^1HF. When the country imposes a tariff, consumer surplus falls to $(P_Y^1 + t)HG$. Therefore, imposition of the tariff reduces consumer surplus by the area bounded by $P_Y^1(P_Y^1 + t)GF$. We can divide this loss of consumer surplus into revenue, redistribution, production, and consumption effects.

   In Figure 5, rectangle n is the tariff's **revenue effect**, a transfer from consumer surplus to the government that collects the tariff revenue. The amount of revenue raised by the tariff equals the quantity of imports with the tariff, $Y^3 - Y^4$, times the tariff per

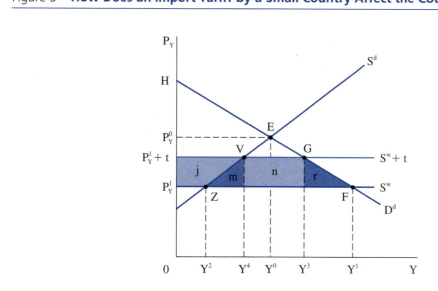

Figure 5   How Does an Import Tariff by a Small Country Affect the Country's Welfare?

Areas j and n represent transfers of consumer surplus to domestic producers and the domestic government, respectively. Areas m and r represent deadweight losses due to production and consumption inefficiencies generated by the tariff.

---

5. The minimum revenue required to induce production is a short-run concept; that is, it includes variable but not fixed costs.

unit, t. The tariff transfers this revenue from consumers to the government, and most analyses assume that the government uses the revenue to finance spending it otherwise would finance with some type of domestic tax. Therefore, the tariff's revenue effect represents not a net welfare loss to the country but merely a transfer.[6] Consumers of good Y suffer a loss of consumer surplus, but residents of the country also enjoy a reduction in their other tax bills made possible by the tariff revenue.

Area j in Figure 5 is the tariff's **redistribution effect**—the consumer surplus that the tariff transfers to domestic producers. (*What area in Figure 5 represents domestic producer surplus in autarky? With unrestricted trade? With the tariff?*) Like the revenue effect, the tariff's redistribution effect isn't lost to society, but rather transferred from consumers to domestic producers of good Y. The transfer takes place through the higher prices consumers pay and domestic producers receive with the tariff. Under unrestricted trade, the revenue domestic Y producers receive is $0P_Y^1ZY^2$. With the tariff, domestic producers receive $0(P_Y^1 + t)VY^4$ in revenue. Increased costs offset a portion of the increased revenue as production rises from Y^2 to Y^4; these increased costs are measured by the area under the domestic supply curve between Y^2 and Y^4.[7] The excess of increased revenue over increased cost, area j, is the increase in producer surplus.

Triangle m in Figure 5 is the tariff's **production effect**.[8] With the tariff, units Y^2 through Y^4 are now produced domestically rather than imported. Producing each of those units domestically involves production costs (represented by the height of the domestic supply curve) that exceed the cost of importing the units (represented by the height of the world export supply curve, S^w). Area m is a **deadweight loss** to the small country, that is, a loss of consumer surplus *not* transferred to another group in the country but lost through inefficient domestic production. Efficiency requires each unit of a good to be produced by the low-opportunity-cost supplier. This condition was satisfied under unrestricted trade, at point F, but isn't satisfied under the tariff. The domestic production of units Y^2 through Y^4 caused by the tariff is inefficient because the small country is the high-opportunity-cost producer; foreign firms can produce those units at lower opportunity cost. By causing inefficiently high domestic production of good Y, the tariff reduces welfare in the small country by an amount equal to the area of triangle m. The high opportunity cost of domestic production of units Y^2 through Y^4 signals that those resources could be used more productively elsewhere in the economy.

Triangle r in Figure 5 represents another deadweight loss to the small country. This **consumption effect** is the loss of consumer surplus that occurs because consumers no longer can obtain units Y^3 through Y^1 at price P_Y^1 with the tariff.[9] For each unit of Y between Y^3 and Y^1, consumers value the good by an amount (measured by the height of the demand curve, D^d) greater than the cost of importing (measured by the height of the world export supply curve, S^w). Efficiency requires that each good be consumed to the point at which the marginal benefit from consuming an additional unit just equals the marginal cost of

---

6. One branch of international trade theory suggests that this assumption may not be realistic. Rent-seeking or directly unproductive profit-seeking (DUP) analysis argues that individuals and groups in society lobby to capture the available revenue. Resources will be spent in lobbying up to an amount equal to the reward from lobbying (the tariff revenue), making the revenue a loss to society rather than a transfer. See the Magee, Brock, and Young reference at the end of the chapter.

7. These costs include wages paid to workers retained in the industry because of the tariff; gains to those workers are offset by losses to consumers.

8. Don't make the mistake of confusing producer surplus (the area above the domestic supply curve and below the price) with the production effect (the negative welfare effect of the inefficient increase in domestic production that occurs as a result of the tariff).

9. Don't confuse consumer surplus with the consumption effect of a tariff.

producing it. The unrestricted trade equilibrium, point F, satisfied this condition. The tariff causes consumption to be inefficiently low, thereby lowering welfare.

A TARIFF'S NET WELFARE EFFECTS   The net welfare loss to the small country as a whole from the import tariff equals the sum of areas m and r in Figure 5. The remainder of the loss of consumer surplus (areas j and n) is a transfer from domestic consumers to domestic producers (j) and to the government (n). The small country enjoys no gain in welfare to offset the loss of areas m and r. The tariff clearly benefits domestic producers of good Y—but at the direct expense of domestic consumers.

The tariff taxes trade, encourages domestic production, and discourages domestic consumption and imports. The volume of trade falls under the tariff; and the sum of areas m and r is often called the volume-of-trade effect. Imposition of a tariff wipes out a portion of the potential gains from trade by artificially limiting the extent to which a country can specialize production according to its comparative advantage and import goods in which it has a comparative disadvantage. In fact, a tariff set at a high enough rate can stop trade completely, returning countries to autarky and eliminating all the gains from trade. Such a prohibitive tariff would equal $P_Y^0 - P_Y^1$ in Figure 5.

Notice that in our analysis of a tariff's welfare effects, we've implicitly used the compensation criterion from section 5.3 in Chapter Four. Domestic producers gain area j from a tariff, and the government gains area n. Domestic consumers lose area $j + m + n + r$. Can the gainers compensate the losers and still be better off? Clearly the answer is no: The gainers from a tariff gain less than the losers lose, making compensation impossible. This is just another way of saying that the tariff imposes a *net* welfare loss on the country equal to area $m + r$.

Under some circumstances, residents of a country may want to create a transfer from consumers to producers and the government. Chapter Eight discusses this possibility as a potential justification for tariffs. In general, however, if a society wants to make such a transfer, there are more efficient ways to do so than through a tariff. This is because a tariff not only creates the transfer but causes deadweight losses $(m + r)$. We'll see in Chapter Eight that other means of accomplishing the transfer can avoid the inefficient production and consumption that create the deadweight losses and, therefore, can effect the desired transfer at a lower opportunity cost to society.

4.3 Estimating the Effects of High U.S. Tariffs

We've seen that, while overall tariff levels have fallen dramatically during the past half-century, tariffs remain high in some industries. As of 1990, there were 13 major U.S. industries for which tariffs exceeded 9 percent.[10] The protection of 12 of those 13 industries dates from 1930 or before; the exception is canned tuna, whose protection dates from 1951. Table 2 reports estimates of the welfare effects of each industry's tariffs. Areas j, m, n, and r in the table refer to the areas highlighted in Figure 5. Consumers in each case lose consumer surplus equal to the total of columns 3, 4, and 5 (or areas $j + m + n + r$). Producers gain the amount in column 3 (area j); and the U.S. government collects tariff revenue equal to the amount in column 4 (area n). Column 5 reports the deadweight efficiency losses (areas $m + r$), which equal the net welfare effect in column 6.[11]

---

10. The Hufbauer and Elliott study restricts attention to industries with U.S. consumption of at least $1 billion per year and potential imports (if tariffs were eliminated) of $100 million or more.

11. The exception is canned tuna, where a tariff-rate quota imposes additional welfare losses, so the amount in column 6 exceeds that in column 5.

Table 2   **WELFARE EFFECTS OF U.S. TARIFFS, 1990 (MILLIONS $ PER YEAR)**

Product Category	Tariff Rate (% of P_Y^1)	Redistribution Effect (Area j)	Revenue Effect (Area n)	Production and Consumption Effects (Areas m + r)	Net Welfare Effect on U.S. (−[Area m + r])
Ball bearings	11.0%	$ 13	$ 50	$ 1	−$1
Benzenoid chemicals	9.0	127	172	10	−10
Canned tuna	12.5	31	31	4	−10
Ceramic articles	11.0	18	81	2	−2
Ceramic tiles	19.0	45	92	2	−2
Costume jewelry	9.0	46	51	5	−5
Frozen concentrated orange juice	30.0	101	145	35	−35
Glassware	11.0	162	95	9	−9
Luggage	16.5	16	169	26	−26
Polyethylene resins	12.0	95	60	20	−20
Rubber footwear	20.0	55	141	12	−12
Women's footwear, except athletic	10.0	70	295	11	−11
Women's handbags	13.5	16	119	13	−13

Source: Data from Gary Clyde Hufbauer and Kimberley Ann Elliott, *Measuring the Costs of Protection in the United States* (Washington, D.C.: Institute for International Economics, 1994), p. 8.

5 WHAT HAPPENS WHEN A LARGE COUNTRY IMPOSES AN IMPORT TARIFF?

A *large* country constitutes a share of the world market sufficient to enable it to affect its terms of trade. When this condition is satisfied, the country may be able to use an import tariff to improve its terms of trade. Therefore, a large country can in some cases improve its welfare by imposing a tariff, an outcome impossible for a small country. The United States plays a large enough role in many markets to affect world prices through its trade policy. However, many other countries are also large in a few markets. Some developing countries, for example, produce a large share of the world total of some products and therefore possess some market power.

5.1 Effects on Production, Consumption, and Price

The supply curve of good Y facing the large country is the summation of domestic supply and export supply from the rest of the world. In Figure 6, S^d represents the *domestic* supply, S^w the export supply from the rest of the world, and S^{d+w} the total supply. At each price for good Y, we find the total quantity supplied by adding the quantity supplied domestically (read off the domestic supply curve) to the quantity supplied to the domestic economy by the rest of the world (read off the rest-of-world export supply curve). The total supply curve slopes upward because the large country, as it buys more Y in world markets, pushes up the world price.

Figure 6   Total Supply Equals Domestic Supply Plus Export Supply from the Rest of the World

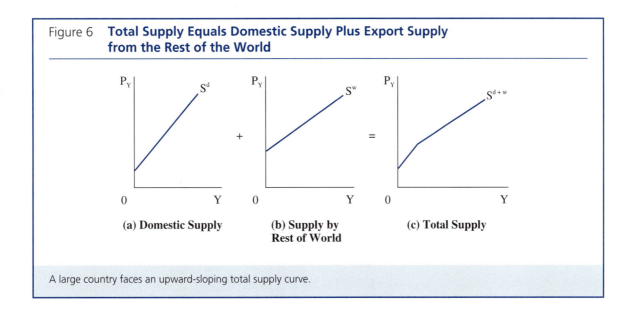

(a) Domestic Supply   **(b) Supply by Rest of World**   **(c) Total Supply**

A large country faces an upward-sloping total supply curve.

Figure 7 combines the total supply curve, S^{d+w}, with the domestic demand curve, D^d, to determine the unrestricted trade equilibrium at point C. Domestic residents consume Y^0 units of good Y, of which Y^1 units are produced domestically and $Y^0 - Y^1$ units imported, at the equilibrium price P_Y^0. For the first Y^1 units of output, domestic production involves a lower cost than importing; beyond Y^1, the domestic country becomes the high-cost producer. Consumer and producer surplus under unrestricted trade equal the areas P_Y^0EC and GP_Y^0F, respectively.

Now the country imposes an import tariff of t per unit on good Y. The total supply curve shifts upward by t to $S^{d+w} + t$. For each unit imported, domestic consumers must pay the price charged by foreign producers *plus* the tariff. Point H represents the new equilibrium. The domestic price of good Y rises to P_Y^1; Y^2 units are consumed, Y^3 produced domestically, and $Y^2 - Y^3$ imported. Consumer surplus now is P_Y^1EH, and domestic producer surplus is GP_Y^1I. Areas j, m, n, and r represent, respectively, the transfer from consumer to producer surplus (redistribution effect), the deadweight loss from inefficiently high domestic production (production effect), the tariff revenue transferred from domestic consumers to the government (revenue effect), and the deadweight loss due to inefficiently low domestic consumption (consumption effect). Thus far, the analysis exactly parallels that of the small-country case from section 4.2.

Notice, however, that area n can't represent all the tariff revenue. Total tariff revenue must equal the quantity of imports ($Y^2 - Y^3$) times the amount of the tariff (the vertical distance between the S^{d+w} and $S^{d+w} + t$ curves). The revenue effect, area n, is only a portion of the total revenue—the share paid by domestic consumers in higher prices for good Y (that is, P_Y^1 rather than P_Y^0). Area s represents the remainder of the revenue, the portion of the tariff borne by foreign producers of good Y who must accept a lower price for their product. Before the tariff, foreign producers received P_Y^0 for each unit of good Y they exported. With the tariff, they receive only P_Y^2, or the price paid by domestic consumers (P_Y^1) *minus* the tariff, because the tariff goes to the domestic government, not to foreign producers.

How does the tariff force foreign producers to accept a lower price? The tariff raises the price paid by domestic consumers, lowering the quantity of good Y demanded. The tariff-imposing country is large enough, by assumption, for this decline in quantity

Figure 7   How Does an Import Tariff by a Large Country Affect the Country's Welfare?

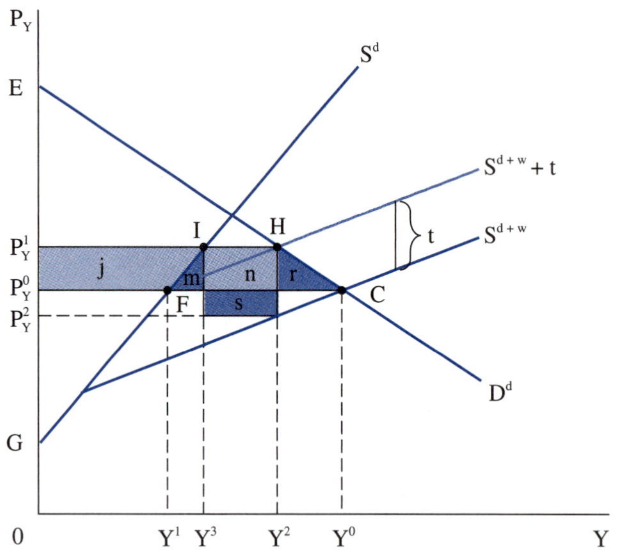

The tariff reduces consumption from Y^0 to Y^2, increases domestic production from Y^1 to Y^3, and decreases imports. The price domestic consumers pay rises from P_Y^0 to P_Y^1, and the price foreign producers receive falls from P_Y^0 to P_Y^2. Area j is a transfer from domestic consumers to domestic producers. Areas m and r are deadweight losses reflecting inefficient production and consumption, respectively. Area n is a transfer from domestic consumers to the government. Area s is a transfer from foreign producers to the domestic government.

demanded to have a significant impact on the market. When foreign producers face a substantially lower quantity demanded for their product, their opportunity costs of production fall, and so does the minimum price they are willing to accept. This effect of the tariff is called the **terms-of-trade effect**.

The welfare analyses of areas j, m, n, and r are precisely the same as in the small-country case. Areas j and n represent transfers within the country, and m and r are deadweight welfare losses caused by inefficient domestic production and consumption. The large-country case introduces a gain to the tariff-imposing country: the tariff revenue paid to the domestic government by foreign producers, area s. If the deadweight losses m and r (the production and consumption effects) exceed this revenue gain s (the terms-of-trade effect), imposing the tariff harms the large country. If the revenue gain from foreign producers exceeds the deadweight losses, the large country may improve its welfare by imposing the import tariff. Table 3 summarizes these results.

Of course, the tariff also affects the domestic distribution of income. Domestic producers of good Y gain at consumers' expense. In the long run, when resources are free to move among industries, the Stolper-Samuelson theorem implies that owners of resources used intensively in production of good Y gain from the tariff, while owners of resources used intensively in production of other goods lose (see section 2 in Chapter Four).

The tariff also exerts a redistributive effect among countries. Even if conditions are such that the large tariff-imposing country gains, all its gains come at the expense of its trading partners, which must accept a lower price for their exports. In other words,

Table 3	**POSSIBLE NET WELFARE EFFECTS OF A TARIFF BY A LARGE COUNTRY**
If:	Then:
$m + r = s$	No net effect on domestic welfare Negative net effect on world welfare
$m + r < s$	Positive net effect on domestic welfare Negative net effect on world welfare
$m + r > s$	Negative net effect on domestic welfare Negative net effect on world welfare

a tariff has a negative impact on world welfare regardless of the size of the countries involved. Tariffs cause inefficient production and consumption patterns and a loss of part of the gains from trade. If the industries involved exhibit economies of scale, tariffs can impose additional costs on the economy by limiting firms' abilities to specialize and capture those scale economies.

5.2 Optimal Tariffs and the Threat of Retaliation

We've seen that imposition of an import tariff by a large country has two effects on the country's welfare. The first, called the **volume-of-trade effect**, occurs when the tariff lowers welfare by discouraging trade. Second, by lowering the price foreign producers receive, the tariff causes a terms-of-trade effect that enhances welfare in the tariff-imposing country. The tariff's net effect on the large country's welfare depends on the relative magnitudes of the volume-of-trade and terms-of-trade effects, as noted in Table 3. The tariff rate that maximizes the net benefits to the country $(s - [m + r])$ is called the **optimal tariff**. Note that the optimal tariff for a small country always equals zero because of the absence of any terms-of-trade effect $(s = 0)$. For a large country beginning from unrestricted trade, increasing the tariff raises welfare up to a point beyond which welfare begins to decline.

The concept of an optimal tariff deserves some skepticism. Imposition of a tariff reduces *world* welfare regardless of the size of the countries involved. The source of a large country's ability to affect its terms of trade is simply its ability to force its trading partners to accept a lower price for their exports. Any improvement in its terms of trade that a large country generates by imposing an import tariff also causes a deterioration in the terms of trade of the country's trading partners. The trading partners' losses exceed the tariff-imposing country's gains, because the tariff causes an inefficient pattern of production and consumption. Policies such as optimal tariffs that try to improve the welfare of the domestic country at the expense of others are called **beggar-thy-neighbor policies**.

The beggar-thy-neighbor character of tariffs implies that they risk retaliation by trading partners. The so-called optimal tariff is the one that maximizes the imposing country's welfare, *assuming* that trading partners do nothing in response to having their exports tariffed and their terms of trade harmed. This seems like a rather unrealistic assumption, since the tariff definitely reduces exporting countries' welfare. A tariff by one country invites retaliation, which invites counter-retaliation, and so on. A tariff war that progressively lowers the volume of trade and welfare for all combatants may result.

6 HOW DOES A TARIFF AFFECT FACTOR PRICES? SPECIFIC FACTORS AND STOLPER-SAMUELSON

Imposition of an import tariff by a small country raises the domestic price of the imported good by the tariff amount. If one or more factors can't move among industries in the short run, the factor specific to the import-competing industry will gain from the tariff, while the factor specific to the export industry will lose, as suggested by the specific-factors model (see section 4.3 in Chapter Four). The short-run effect on any factor able to move among industries will depend on the factor owner's consumption pattern. The tariff's welfare effect will be positive if he or she consumes mainly the now-cheaper export good and negative if he or she consumes mainly the now-more-expensive import good.

In the long run, when all factors can move between industries, the tariff has the effects predicted by the Stolper-Samuelson theorem (see section 2 in Chapter Four). That theorem states that a rise in the price of a good will cause a more-than-proportional rise in the price of the input used intensively in that good's production and a fall in the price of the other input. Under the assumptions of the Heckscher-Ohlin theorem, production of the import good will involve intensive use of the scarce factor. Therefore, a tariff, by raising the domestic price of the import good, raises the real reward to the scarce factor and lowers the real reward to the abundant factor.

7 TARIFFS AND ECONOMIES OF SCALE

Thus far, our analysis of tariffs' effects has assumed that comparative advantage—differences in production possibilities or in tastes—forms the basis for trade. In this case, tariffs interfere with the allocation of production to low-cost locations, causing a loss of gains from trade. Recall from Chapter Five, section 6, that economies of scale provide another potential basis for mutually beneficial trade, one applicable even if two countries have identical production possibilities and tastes. Tariffs also can interfere with this type of trade. With widespread tariffs, each country must produce small quantities of all the goods domestic consumers want to consume, instead of specializing in the export good and producing a large quantity of it, thereby achieving economies of scale. This implies that the costs of tariffs can be even higher in industries characterized by economies of scale. Recent empirical work suggests that a large share of the actual gains from international trade come from exploiting economies of scale, a point of great importance to countries with domestic markets too small to allow their industries to achieve those economies without access to foreign markets.[12]

8 THE EFFECTIVE RATE OF PROTECTION

It's tempting to assume that all domestic producers in industries with high import tariffs receive extensive protection from foreign competition. However, such a simple relationship between tariff rates and degrees of protection doesn't necessarily hold. To determine the actual degree of protection for any domestic industry, we must consider not only tariffs on the industry's own output but also any tariffs on inputs the industry uses. The relationship among tariffs in related industries is called **tariff structure**.

Although tariff structure differs across sectors of the economy, tariffs generally rise as products move through the stages of production as illustrated in Figure 8, which includes both developed and developing countries. Raw materials typically have lower tariffs than the finished products ultimately produced with them, a phenomenon known as **cascading tariffs**.

---

12. See section 6 in Chapter Five and the discussion of strategic trade policy in Chapter Eight, section 4.3.

Figure 8 Tariffs Increase with the Level of Processing, 2000–2002

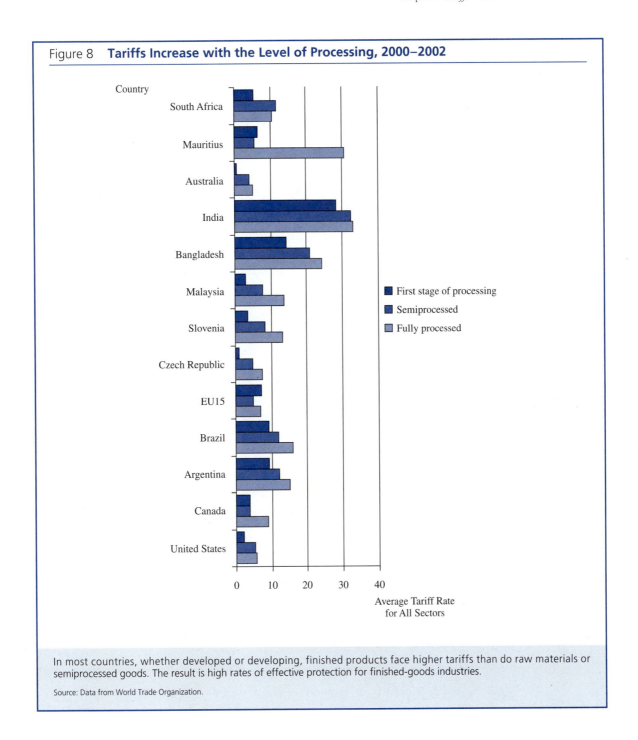

In most countries, whether developed or developing, finished products face higher tariffs than do raw materials or semiprocessed goods. The result is high rates of effective protection for finished-goods industries.

Source: Data from World Trade Organization.

If we ignore the effect of tariff structure, the tariff rate on a final good may provide an inaccurate measure of the effective protection provided to domestic producers. An alternative measure that accounts for the role of tariff structure is the **effective rate of protection (ERP)**. To illustrate, suppose a domestically produced television sells at the world price of $500 under unrestricted trade. The domestic producer uses $300 worth of imported inputs (picture tube, chassis, tuner, and various electronic components). The $200 difference between the world price of the finished television and the cost of the imported components represents **domestic value-added (V)**. Domestic value-added includes the payments made to domestic labor and capital inputs for assembling the imported components into a finished television. Under unrestricted trade, domestic value-added can't exceed $200, or the price of domestically produced televisions will exceed that of imported ones and the domestic TVs won't sell.

An ad valorem tariff of 10 percent on imported televisions would raise the domestic price of an imported TV to $550 (= $500[1 + 0.10]). The price of the domestically produced TV then could rise as high as $550 and still compete against imported sets in the domestic market. The nominal tariff rate is 10 percent—but what is the effective rate of protection? The ERP answers the question, "What percentage increase in domestic value-added does the tariff make possible?" Domestic value-added under unrestricted trade (V_0) was $200; a higher level of value-added would have rendered domestically produced televisions non-competitive by raising their price above the $500 world price. Domestic value-added with a 10 percent tariff on imported televisions (V_1) can rise to $250 (or $550 − $300 worth of imported inputs) and still allow domestic TVs to compete. The effective rate of protection provided for domestic television producers by the 10 percent tariff on imports of finished televisions is ERP = $(V_1 − V_0)/V_0$ = ($250 − $200)/$200 = 25 percent. The 10 percent nominal tariff allows domestic value-added to rise by 25 percent, and this measures the degree of protection for domestic producers.

A 10 percent nominal tariff doesn't always imply an effective rate of protection of 25 percent. The relationship between the nominal tariff rate and the effective rate of protection depends on (1) the share of imported inputs in the production process and (2) the presence or absence of tariffs on imported inputs. To examine the impact on the effective rate of protection of a tariff on imported inputs, consider once again the 10 percent tariff on finished televisions—now accompanied by a 5 percent tariff on imported components used in domestic production of TVs. The 5 percent tariff on inputs implies that domestic producers now must pay $300(1 + 0.05) = $315 for their inputs. Domestic value-added with the tariff package can be as high as V_1 = $500(1 + 0.10) −$300(1 + 0.05) = $550 − $315 = $235 before domestic TVs become noncompetitive. This new value-added is the difference between the tariffed price of imported televisions and the tariffed price of imported inputs used in domestic production. The effective rate of protection is ERP = $(V_1 − V_0)/V_0$ = ($235 − $200)/$200 = 17.5 percent. Imposition of the 5 percent tariff on imported inputs lowers the ERP provided by a 10 percent nominal tariff on finished televisions from 25 to 17.5 percent. The tariff on finished TVs taxes imports of both foreign inputs and foreign assembly costs (foreign value-added). If imported inputs used domestically don't face a tariff, domestic value-added can absorb all the differential.

The general formula for the effective rate of protection is

$$ERP = \frac{t_f − at_i}{1 − a},$$

where t_f is the nominal tariff rate on the imported *finished* good (imported televisions), a is the value of imported inputs as a share of the final good's price under free trade ($300/$500 = 0.6), and t_i is the tariff on imported inputs used by domestic producers.[13] From the general expression for ERP, we can see that whenever the tariff rate on finished goods exceeds the rate on imported inputs ($t_f > t_i$), the ERP is greater than the tariff on

---

13. With more than one input, the sum of the shares and tariff rates for all inputs replaces the at_i term. It is easy to show that $(V_1 − V_0)/V_0 = (t_f − at_i)/(1 − a)$. Letting P denote the price of the finished product, $(V_1 − V_0)/V_0 = [P(1 + t_f) − Pa(1 + t_i) − P(1 − a)]/P(1 − a) = (t_f − at_i)/(1 − a)$.

Table 4	**EFFECTIVE RATES OF PROTECTION FOR EXPORT SECTORS, 1986 AND 1997**							
	Brazil		China		India		Malawi	
	1986	1997	1986	1997	1986	1997	1986	1997
Agriculture	−43%	−5%	−28%	−15%	−14%	−5%	−9%	−7%
Agricultural processing	−83	−28	−72	−54	−64	−39	−20	−16
Resources	−45	−6	−14	−7	−9	−3	−6	−5
Labor-intensive manufacturing	−72	−17	−54	−35	−45	−23	−18	−15
Capital-intensive manufacturing	−79	−22	−46	−28	−60	−35	−11	−9
Services	−31	−3	−26	−14	−16	−6	−5	−4

Source: Data from World Bank, *Global Economic Prospects 2004*. Washington, D.C.: The World Bank, p. 77.

finished goods (ERP > t_f). When imported finished goods and imported inputs are tariffed at the same rate ($t_f = t_i$), that rate accurately measures the protection provided for the domestic industry (ERP = $t_f = t_i$). When a country tariffs imported inputs at a rate exceeding that on finished goods ($t_f < t_i$), the effective rate of protection is lower than the tariff rate on finished goods (ERP < t_f). In fact, the ERP can be negative even though t_f is positive! A negative ERP implies that the tariff structure actually makes it harder for domestically produced goods to compete against foreign ones.

Negative effective rates of protection are more than just a theoretical curiosity. Export sectors in many developing economies that place high tariffs on the inputs used by those sectors face negative ERPs. Table 4 provides some examples. Notice that the export sectors' 1997 ERPs, while still negative, are less so than in 1986. This improvement in export sectors' ability to compete in world markets reflects the countries' reductions in import tariffs during 1986–1997, a period that spanned completion of the Uruguay Round of trade-liberalization negotiations.

Other things being equal, the effective rate of protection is higher (1) the higher the nominal tariff rate on finished goods, (2) the lower the tariff rate on imported inputs, and (3) the larger the share of imported inputs in the value of the good (if $t_f > t_i$).[14] Effective rates of protection differ greatly from actual or nominal tariff rates for many industries. Actual tariff rates significantly underestimate the effective protection received by many industries in the United States as well in other countries. The effective-rate-of-protection idea carries over to nontariff barriers as well; trade barriers on inputs always lower the effective protection given to finished-goods producers.

9 OFFSHORE ASSEMBLY PROVISIONS

We've seen that tariffs differ by industry and by country. However, many countries, including the United States, have special tariff provisions that make things even more complicated.[15] Some of the most common are **offshore assembly provisions (OAPs)**,

14. You can verify results (1) through (3) by taking the partial derivatives of the ERP equation with respect to t_f, t_i, and a, respectively.

15. Look at the general statistics chapter of the U.S. *Harmonized Tariff Schedule* at http://www.usitc.gov/taffairs.htm.

which allow reduced or waived tariffs on goods assembled abroad from domestically produced components.

Suppose, for example, that the United States imposed a 50 percent tariff on imported cigars and that the Dominican Republic developed an industry that assembled cigars from U.S.-made tobacco.[16] With no offshore assembly provision, a Dominican cigar with a free-trade price of $2 would sell for $3 in the United States, since $3 = $2(1 + 0.50); in other words, the tariff would equal $1. One simple form of offshore assembly provision would state that cigars imported into the United States from the Dominican Republic must pay the 50 percent tariff *only* on Dominican value-added, not on the item's full value. If we assume that each $2 cigar uses $1.50 worth of U.S. tobacco, making Dominican value-added $0.50, then the cigars would sell in the United States for $2 + ($0.50)(0.50) = $2.25. The OAP reduces the tariff from $1 to $0.25 per cigar, although the nominal tariff rate remains 50 percent, by restricting the tariff to foreign value-added and allowing U.S.-made components (in this case, tobacco) to re-enter the United States tariff free. An alternative form of OAP would waive the cigar tariff completely so long as a specified percentage of the cigar's value reflected U.S.-grown tobacco.

Many countries export to the United States under OAP arrangements, among them the 24 members of the Caribbean Basin Economic Recovery Act, which includes the Dominican Republic. OAP provisions aren't limited to developing countries, but most OAP imports into the United States do come from developing economies, because they tend to have comparative advantages in the labor-intensive assembly tasks that make OAP provisions attractive in industries such as apparel.

10 TAXING EXPORTS

In some cases, countries place trade restrictions on exports as well as imports. Export taxes violate the Constitution in the United States, although other export restrictions are legal. During the framing of the U.S. Constitution, southern states, fearful that protectionist-minded northern interests would tax the South's cotton and tobacco exports, successfully pressured for the export-tax ban.

The goal of an export tax obviously wouldn't be to protect domestic producers from foreign competition. Why might a country tax its own exports? There are two basic reasons.[17] The first is in response to pressure by domestic consumer groups to keep the domestic price of a good low; goods such as food and oil are particularly susceptible to these political pressures. The second reason for an export tax applies only to large countries, which may try to exploit their market power by using export taxes to raise the prices foreign buyers must pay. Such a mechanism allowed the Organization of Petroleum Exporting Countries (OPEC) to engineer the infamous oil price increases of the 1970s.

10.1 An Export Tax Imposed by a Small Country

Consider the effect of an export tax imposed by a small country—that is, a country that can export all it wants without lowering the world price. In Figure 9, point E represents equilibrium under unrestricted trade in the market for good X. The small country

---

16. The cigar industry, along with various clothing sectors, is one of the biggest users of the U.S. offshore assembly provision with the Caribbean countries.

17. A third set of reasons, which underlie many U.S. export restrictions, include national security, weapons nonproliferation, and foreign policy. For an excellent summary of U.S. export restrictions, including economically and politically motivated ones, see the Richardson book in the chapter references.

Figure 9   What Happens When a Small Country Imposes an Export Tax?

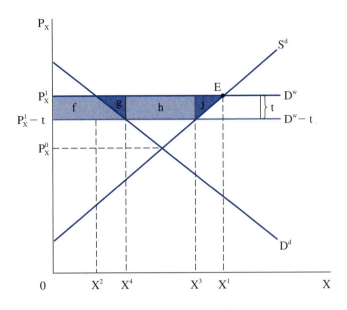

The export tax encourages domestic consumption and discourages domestic production and exports. Consumers gain at the expense of domestic producers.

---

produces X^1 units, consumes X^2 units, and exports $X^1 - X^2$ at the world price P_X^1. Note that the world price of good X lies *above* the country's autarky price (P_X^0) because X is the export good in which the country has a comparative advantage.

The country levies a specific tax of t per unit on exports of good X. For each unit exported, domestic producers still receive the world price (P_X^1) from consumers; but producers must pay t to the domestic government, leaving a *net* price to the producer of $P_X^1 - t$. Domestic production falls from X^1 to X^3, and domestic consumption rises from X^2 to X^4. Exports fall to $X^3 - X^4$.

Domestic producers of good X lose producer surplus equal to f + g + h + j because of the export tax. Area f is a transfer to domestic consumers, who now can buy good X at price $P_X^1 - t$ rather than P_X^1. Area g is a deadweight loss from the inefficient increase in domestic consumption caused by the tax. Too much X is consumed domestically because the marginal benefit of domestic consumption at X^4 (given by the height of D^d) is less than the marginal benefit of foreign consumption of X (measured by the world price foreign consumers are willing to pay for the country's exports). Foreign consumers value the units of good X between X^2 and X^4 more highly than do domestic consumers; but the export tax causes those units to go to domestic consumers. Area h is a transfer from producer surplus to the domestic government in the form of tax revenue. Area j is the deadweight loss from curtailment of domestic production to X^3. For all units of good X between X^1 and X^3, the cost of producing domestically is less than the value foreign consumers place on the good. So long as consumers somewhere in the world are willing to pay P_X^1 for good X, efficiency requires that domestic production be X^1, not X^3.

Some small, very open economies use export taxes primarily as a revenue-generating mechanism; but the most common reason for export taxes is to "protect" domestic consumers from competition by foreign consumers. An export tax by a small country transfers welfare from domestic producers to domestic consumers. The tax causes inefficient production and consumption decisions, so the tax-imposing country suffers a net welfare loss. Domestic producers lose more than domestic consumers gain; therefore, small-country export taxes fail the test of whether gainers can compensate losers.

10.2 An Export Tax Imposed by a Large Country

The second reason for export taxes applies only to countries large in the market for the export good. An export tax may allow such countries to exploit their market position by charging higher prices for their exports than otherwise would be possible. Consider the case of a country that produces a large share of total world output of a particular product, good X. In Figure 10, S^d represents the country's domestic supply curve, D^d its domestic demand curve, and D^{d+w} the total demand curve facing domestic producers of good X (this includes both domestic demand and demand by the rest of the world for the country's exports). The distance between D^d and D^{d+w} at each price measures the rest of the world's demand for imports of good X from the domestic country. Under unrestricted trade, the country would produce X^0 units, of which X^1 would be sold domestically and $X^0 - X^1$ exported; price P_X^0 would apply to both domestic sales and exports.

Figure 10 **What Happens When a Large Country Imposes an Export Tax?**

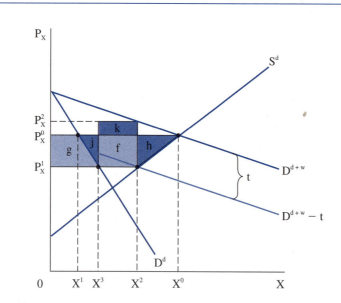

The tax-imposing country suffers deadweight losses equal to area h + j and enjoys a gain in revenue from foreign consumers equal to area k. If (h + j) > k, the country suffers a net welfare loss from the tax. If (h + j) < k, the country enjoys a net welfare gain. The export tax reduces world welfare regardless of the relative sizes of h, j, and k.

If:	Then:
$h + j = k$	No net effect on domestic welfare Negative net effect on world welfare
$h + j < k$	Positive net effect on domestic welfare Negative net effect on world welfare
$h + j > k$	Negative net effect on domestic welfare Negative net effect on world welfare

Table 5 POSSIBLE NET WELFARE EFFECTS OF AN EXPORT TAX BY A LARGE COUNTRY

Now suppose the country imposes a tax of t per unit on X exports; units sold domestically are exempt from the tax. The total demand curve facing domestic producers shifts down by the amount of the tax to $D^{d+w} - t$. Production falls to X^2, with X^3 sold in the domestic market and $X^2 - X^3$ exported. Producers receive price P_X^1 for each unit sold, and the government receives t for each unit exported. Domestic consumers pay P_X^1, but foreign consumers pay P_X^2, with P_X^1 going to producers and t to the exporting-country government.

Domestic consumer surplus rises by area g, as domestic consumers can now buy the good at P_X^1 rather than P_X^0. Domestic producer surplus falls by area $f + g + h + j$, of which f is a transfer to the government (revenue effect), g is a transfer to domestic consumers (redistribution effect), h is a deadweight loss from the inefficient cut in production (production effect), and j is a deadweight loss caused by the inefficient expansion of domestic consumption (consumption effect). So far, the analysis parallels that of the small-country case. However, area f in Figure 10, the transfer from domestic producers to the domestic government, can't represent all the revenue from the tax. Total tax revenue must equal area $f + k$, whose length is the quantity exported and whose height is the per-unit tax. Area k is paid to the domestic government by *foreign* consumers, who now must pay P_X^2 for each unit of good X. Thus, k is a gain to the country imposing the export tax that comes at the expense of trading partners. If this transfer from abroad exceeds the deadweight losses $(h + j)$ from the tax, the tax-imposing country will enjoy a net welfare gain, as Table 5 summarizes. The magnitude of the tax that maximizes the net gain $(k - [h + j])$ is the optimal export tariff.

Any net gain to the tax-imposing country comes from foreign consumers, so the export tax's effect on world welfare is always negative. Attempts to use beggar-thy-neighbor export taxes can backfire. Such policies create an incentive for foreign consumers to find new suppliers, and those suppliers have an enhanced incentive (the higher world price) to enter the market. Ghana and Nigeria suffered such a fate in the cocoa market, and Nigeria and Zaire in palm oil.[18] OPEC's use of export taxes during the 1970s spurred a dramatic decrease in the growth of petroleum use as well as increased production by non-OPEC suppliers such as Britain, the United States, Mexico, Russia, and several new oil producers in Africa. OPEC produced almost half of the world's oil in 1975 but only about 38 percent in 2004.

18. World Bank, *World Development Report 1988* (New York: Oxford University Press), p. 91.

CASE 1: MAKING CHEAP MEDICINE EXPENSIVE

Countries of Africa

The *Anopheles* mosquito carries the protozoan parasite that causes malaria. Experts estimate that between one million and two million Africans, mostly children, die of malaria each year. In fact, 90 percent of worldwide deaths from malaria occur in sub-Saharan Africa. No effective malaria vaccine exists; most treatments work only in the short run and have serious side effects. Insecticide-treated bed nets provide one of the few effective precautions against contracting malaria. Studies conducted in Africa conclude that bed-net use can reduce childhood malaria deaths by almost one-third.

Bed nets sell in world markets for about $2.50, so surely everyone in malaria-prone areas uses nets. Right?

Wrong. Governments tariffed imported bed nets, raising their price out of reach of many residents of Africa's poorest countries. Fourteen sub-Saharan governments tariffed bed nets at rates of 30 percent or higher, up to Senegal's 65 percent tariff—even though there were no domestic bed-net producers to "protect." The World Trade Organization has pressured governments to lower their tariffs on bed nets in an effort to control the spread of malaria.[19]

CASE 2: BINDING POLICY MAKERS' HANDS

When member countries of the World Trade Organization negotiate to reduce tariffs against one another's products, the rates under negotiation are countries' bound tariff rates rather than applied tariff rates. What's the difference? Applied tariffs are, as the name suggests, the tariff rates countries actually *apply* to imports. Bound tariffs refer to commitments made by WTO-member countries not to raise tariffs above a specified (bound) rate. For example, country A might currently apply a 10 percent ad valorem tariff to imported clothing but have a bound apparel tariff of 20 percent. This situation would allow country A to raise its tariff on imported apparel without violating its WTO commitments.

For industrial countries, bound and applied tariff rates typically correspond closely if not exactly for manufactured goods; that is, these countries have made WTO commitments not to raise their tariffs on these products above the currently applied rates. For most developing countries, bound rates on many goods remain well above applied rates. And for some developing countries outside of Latin America, tariff rates remain unbound. Figure 11 illustrates some of these differences at the end of the Uruguay Round negotiations. Compare, for example, the

United States and Uruguay. Both countries have bound 100 percent of their tariffs; however, 86 percent of U.S. imports but only 3.7 percent of Uruguayan imports have rates bound at the applied rates. Neighbors Argentina and Brazil exhibit a similar contrast. Sri Lanka has bound tariffs on only 9.2 percent of its imports and of these, 1.4 percent are bound at above-applied rates.

Can bound rates ever exceed applied ones? Yes, for two reasons. First, policy makers may give in to domestic political pressure for protection and act in violation of the country's WTO commitments, although doing so makes the country subject to complaints filed by trading partners with the WTO. Second, the agreements reached in WTO negotiations typically are phased in gradually over a several-year period. During the phase-in period, while countries are in the process of lowering their applied tariffs, some applied rates may still be above the bound rate promised in the negotiations. For example, tariff data for 1995, just after the end of the Uruguay Round of negotiations, show several countries still in the process of lowering their applied tariffs to reach compliance with the bound-tariff commitments they made in the negotiations.

---

19. "Jamming the Net Work," *The Economist*, August 1, 1998, p. 69.

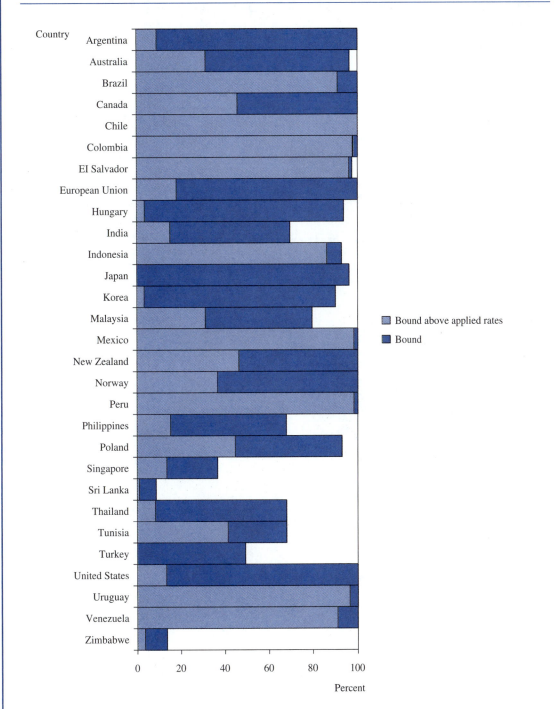

Figure 11   **Share of GATT Imports Covered by Bound Tariff Rates, End of Uruguay Round**

The longer bar for each country represents the share of the country's GATT trade covered by bound tariffs. The shorter bar represents the share of the country's GATT trade covered by tariffs bound at rates above applied rates.

Source: Data from World Bank.

CASE 3: **CHINA, TARIFFS, AND THE WTO**

China, one of the fastest-growing parties to trade, wanted to join the World Trade Organization and began trying to gain entry in 1986. China had helped found the GATT (predecessor to the WTO) in 1947, but the Taiwan-based government had withdrawn in 1950 after the Communists took power on the mainland. In 1986, China applied to "resume" membership. GATT members ruled that membership couldn't be resumed, but that China could negotiate for accession as a new member. The negotiations proved long (15 years) and acrimonious, in part because of the nonmarket-based nature of China's economy. China wanted to complete accession before January 1, 1995, so it could be a founding member of the new WTO, which took effect on that date; but negotiators failed to make the deadline. The results of the Uruguay Round enhanced

China's incentive to achieve membership. Member countries agreed to phase out by 2005 the Agreement on Textiles and Clothing, which severely restricted China's textile and apparel exports; but the change would apply only to trade with WTO members.[20]

WTO members claimed that Chinese tariffs were too high, too variable across products, and too opaque for China to become a member. Chinese tariffs rose between 1987 and 1992. The government cut tariffs on more than 3,000 products in 1992, but only to an average rate of about 36 percent. Then Beijing raised tariffs in early 1995 on a list of goods bought primarily by foreigners. Chinese tariff reforms in 1996, shortly after formal WTO accession talks began, lowered average tariff rates from 36 percent to 23 percent; but the new rates remained above those of most members

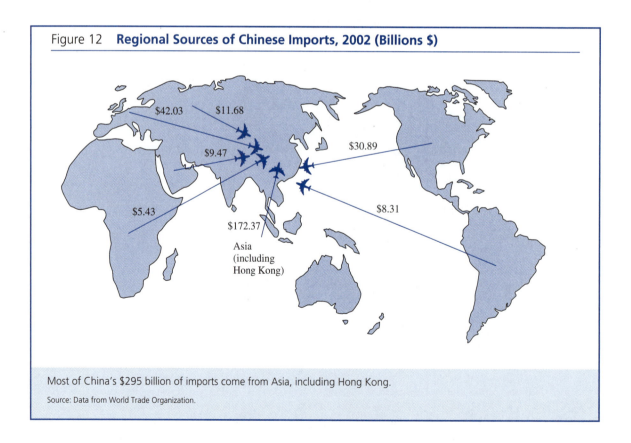

Figure 12   **Regional Sources of Chinese Imports, 2002 (Billions $)**

$42.03

$11.68

$9.47

$30.89

$5.43

$172.37

Asia
(including
Hong Kong)

$8.31

Most of China's $295 billion of imports come from Asia, including Hong Kong.

Source: Data from World Trade Organization.

---

20. A World Bank study predicted a 375 percent increase in Chinese textile and apparel exports in the first 10 years after WTO entry (see "China Textiles Braced for WTO Pain as Well as Gain," *Financial Times*, August 16, 2001).

and even of most developing countries. Some sectors, such as cars, still carried tariffs of 100 percent or more. And the tariff schedule's opacity remained. For example, the new system required wheat importers, up to "a certain level" of imports, to pay tariffs of 1 percent to 35 percent, while imports above "a certain level" had to pay tariffs of up to 180 percent; but the law failed to disclose the "certain level"![21]

Late in 1997, China made additional concessions to try to win WTO membership. The government reduced its weighted-average tariff from 23 percent to 17 percent by cutting rates on more than five thousand items, and promised to lower tariffs on all industrial goods to an average of no more than 10 percent by 2005. WTO accession negotiations between China and the United States continued erratically through 1999, and in November of that year the two countries announced successful completion of their bilateral negotiations.[22] China would reduce its tariffs to an average of 9.4 percent

overall and to 7.1 percent on U.S. priority products. Auto tariffs, then at 80 to 100 percent, would fall to 25 percent by 2006; tariffs on telecom equipment would end; and agricultural tariffs would be cut from 31.5 percent to 14.5 percent. When the entire package of accession talks finally ended successfully in late 2001, China had promised to cut its tariffs on many products by 2004. By 2010, Chinese bound tariff rates will average 8.9 percent for industrial goods and 14.5 percent for farm products. Chinese consumers will enjoy significant increases in their consumer surplus from the approximately 80-percent drop in tariffs from their levels at the time the country began trying to join the WTO in 1986.

Figure 12 illustrates the regional sources of China's imports for 2002. Imports from Asia include those from Hong Kong, which officially became a special administrative region of China in 1997 but continues to collect and report separate economic and trade statistics.

SUMMARY

This chapter analyzed tariffs' effects on resource allocation and income distribution. Tariffs have a negative effect on welfare in a small country, although a large country may be able to improve its terms of trade and produce an increase in welfare through an import tariff. Even when imposed by a large country, however, a tariff reduces world welfare and invites retaliation by trading partners.

When imported inputs as well as imports of finished products are considered, nominal tariff rates fail to measure accurately the degree of protection a particular tariff structure provides. The effective rate of protection corrects this problem by taking into account the relationship between tariffs on inputs and those on finished products.

LOOKING AHEAD

The international negotiations sponsored by the GATT/WTO since World War II have produced significant reductions in tariff rates, although trade in certain industries remains subject to high tariffs. Recently, other types of trade barriers—so-called nontariff barriers—have received increasing attention. These barriers, the subject of Chapter Seven, have effects at least as harmful as those of tariffs and have proven much less amenable to international liberalization efforts.

KEY TERMS

barriers to trade
tariff
protectionist policy

specific tariff
ad valorem tariff
prohibitive tariff

consumer surplus
producer surplus
revenue effect

21. "Under New Laws," *The Economist*, April 13, 1996, p. 62.

22. Countries negotiating accession to the WTO must reach agreement with all member countries; bilateral negotiations with the United States and the European Union typically take the longest and determine the final outcome.

redistribution effect	volume-of-trade effect	effective rate of
production effect	optimal tariff	protection (ERP)
deadweight loss	beggar-thy-neighbor policy	domestic value-added (V)
consumption effect	tariff structure	offshore assembly
terms-of-trade effect	cascading tariff	provision (OAP)

PROBLEMS AND QUESTIONS FOR REVIEW

1. If the world price of automobiles is $10,000 under free trade and domestic producers of automobiles use $5,000 worth of imported inputs, what is domestic value-added under free trade?
   a. What rate of effective protection would be provided to the domestic auto industry by a 25 percent tariff on imported autos with no tariff on inputs?
   b. What rate of effective protection would be provided to the domestic auto industry by a 25 percent tariff on imported autos with a 25 percent tariff on inputs?
   c. What rate of effective protection would be provided to the domestic auto industry by a 25 percent tariff on imported autos with a 50 percent tariff on inputs?
   d. What rate of effective protection would be provided to the domestic auto industry by a 25 percent tariff on imported autos with a 100 percent tariff on inputs?

2. The United States has a comparative disadvantage in furniture production; and much of the furniture sold in the United States comes from abroad, especially from China. A multiyear housing boom has increased demand for furniture as families have moved into new and bigger houses. Assuming that the United States is a small country in the world furniture market, what would you expect to be the effect of the housing boom on the U.S. price of furniture, the quantity produced and consumed domestically, and the quantity imported? Why?

3. This question asks you to analyze the effects of *removal* of a tariff on imported oranges. The following table summarizes situations in the orange market with and without the tariff. The first column describes the situation with a $4.00-per-bushel tariff on oranges. The second column represents the situation after the tariff is removed. You may assume that transportation costs are zero and that the supply and demand curves are straight lines.

	With $4.00 Tariff	With Free Trade
World price of oranges ($/bushel)	$12.00	$12.00
Tariff per bushel ($/bushel)	$4.00	$0.00
Domestic price of oranges ($/bushel)	$16.00	$12.00
Oranges consumed domestically (million bushels/year)	24	28
Oranges produced domestically (million bushels/year)	8	6

   a. Illustrate the effects of *removal* of the tariff. (You may find graph paper useful.) Label the free-trade and tariff equilibria in terms of consumption, domestic production, imports, and domestic and world prices.
   b. Estimate the amount domestic consumers gain from removal of the tariff. Show and explain your work.
   c. Estimate the amount of the *net* effect on the country's welfare from removal of the tariff. Show and explain your work.
   d. In this case, would the optimal import tariff on oranges be negative, zero, or positive? Why? Under what assumptions is the "optimal" tariff really optimal?

4. Country A is labor abundant and practices unrestricted trade with the rest of the world. The country's new minister for trade proposes an import tariff, claiming that such a policy would raise wages relative to the return to capital. Do you agree? Why, or why not?

5. For each of the following, how do tariffs affect the distribution of income?[23]

---

23. Data for this problem come from "The Truth About Industrial Country Tariffs," *Finance and Development* 39 (September 2002), pp. 14–15.

a. According to the World Bank, per-capita incomes in France and Bangladesh in 2001 were $24,080 and $1,600, respectively. The United States imported approximately $30 billion worth of goods from France and $2.4 billion from Bangladesh. The United States collected $330 million in tariff revenue from its imports from France and $331 million on those from Bangladesh.

b. A single-parent family in the United States has an average income of $25,095 per year and pays approximately 1.2 percent of that income in tariffs, primarily on clothing and shoes—goods that face unusually high tariff rates and which comprise a relatively large share of spending for low-income families. The average income of a U.S. two-parent family is $66,913, and those families pay approximately 0.7 percent of that income in import tariffs, in part because they spend a much lower share of their income on high-tariff goods such as clothing and shoes.

c. The U.S. import tariff on silk shirts is 1.9 percent, while the tariff on polyester shirts is 32.5 percent.

6. The domestic demand for good X is $D^d = 100 - 20P$. The domestic supply of good X is $S^d = 20 + 20P$.

a. Draw the domestic demand and supply curves for good X. (Remember that price appears on the vertical axis in the graph.)

b. If the country allows no trade in good X, what are the equilibrium price, quantity produced, and quantity consumed?

c. Imports of good X are available in the world market at $P_X = 1$. Draw the total supply curve. If the country allows free trade in good X, what are the equilibrium price, quantity produced domestically, quantity consumed domestically, and quantity imported?

d. If the country imposes a specific tariff of $t = 0.5$ per unit of imported X, what are the equilibrium price, quantity produced domestically, quantity consumed domestically, and quantity imported?

e. Who gains and who loses from the tariff? Does national welfare rise or fall?

7. Assume that small country Usia, because of its abundant endowment of forests, has a comparative advantage in producing both logs and lumber (that is, processed logs).

a. Usia imposes a *prohibitive* export tax on logs. Illustrate the effects of such a tax. Label the effects on consumption, production, exports, world and domestic prices, consumer and producer surplus, and economic efficiency. Explain.

b. Usia's lumber industry uses logs as its major input. Illustrate the effect of the prohibitive export tax on *logs* on Usia's *lumber* industry. What will happen to consumption, production, price, and exports of lumber because of the tax on log exports? Explain.

8. U.S. presidential candidate and ardent protectionist Patrick Buchanan argues that "Tariffs are taxes, but . . . you don't have to pay them . . . if you Buy American" ("Letters to the Editor," *The Wall Street Journal*, June 2, 1998). Do you agree? Why or why not? Support your argument with an appropriate graph.

REFERENCES AND SELECTED READINGS

Bhagwati, Jagdish. *Free Trade Today.* Princeton: Princeton University Press, 2002.
Very readable responses to the standard antitrade arguments.

Francois, Joseph F., and Will Martin. "Binding Tariffs: Why Do It?" In *Development, Trade, and the WTO,* edited by B. Hoekman, et al., 540–547. Washington, D.C.: The World Bank, 2002.
How and why countries bind their tariffs within the WTO.

Hufbauer, Gary Clyde, and Kimberley Ann Elliott. *Measuring the Costs of Protection in the United States.* Washington, D.C.: Institute for International Economics, 1994.
Attempt to quantify the cost to U.S. consumers and the U.S. economy as a whole of the structure of protection.

Irwin, Douglas A. *Free Trade Under Fire.* Princeton: Princeton University Press, 2002.
Highly recommended overview of the free-trade versus protection issue; for all students.

Irwin, Douglas A. "Interpreting the Tariff-Growth Correlation of the Late 19th Century." *American Economic Review Papers and Proceedings* 92 (May 2002): 165–169.
Overview of nineteenth-century tariff policy; for all students.

Magee, Stephen P., William A. Brock, and Leslie Young. *Black Hole Tariffs and Endogenous Policy Theory.* Cambridge: Cambridge University Press, 1989.

Path-breaking contribution to analysis of tariffs as the outcome of special-interest-group politics; for intermediate and advanced students.

Michalopoulos, Constantine. "WTO Accession." In *Development, Trade, and the WTO,* edited by B. Hoekman, et al., 61–70. Washington, D.C.: The World Bank, 2002.
Easy summary of the process involved in joining the World Trade Organization.

Olarreaga, Marcelo, and Francis Ng. "Tariff Peaks and Preferences." In *Development, Trade, and the WTO,* edited by B. Hoekman, et al., 105–113. Washington, D.C.: The World Bank, 2002.
Overview of variation in tariff rates across industries and countries.

Organization for Economic Cooperation and Development. *Indicators of Tariff and Non-Tariff Barriers.* Paris: OECD, 1997.
Good source of data on trade barriers.

Panagariya, Arvind. "Costs of Protection: Where Do We Stand?" *American Economic Review Papers and Proceedings* 92 (May 2002): 175–179.
Why even small tariffs can have relatively large welfare effects; for intermediate students.

Panagariya, Arvind. "Formula Approaches to Reciprocal Tariff Liberalization." In *Development, Trade, and the WTO,* edited by B. Hoekman, et al., 535–539. Washington, D.C.: The World Bank, 2002.
Overview of the effects of various approaches to negotiated reductions in tariff rates.

Richardson, J. David. *Sizing Up U.S. Export Disincentives.* Washington, D.C.: Institute for International Economics, 1993.
Readable survey of policies that discourage U.S. exports, along with empirical estimates of the policies' importance.

Sazanami, Yoko, Shujiro Urata, and Kiroki Kawai. *Measuring the Costs of Protection in Japan.* Washington, D.C.: Institute for International Economics, 1995.
Attempt to quantify the cost to Japanese consumers and the Japanese economy as a whole of the structure of protection; for intermediate students.

Schott, Jeffrey J. *The Uruguay Round: An Assessment.* Washington, D.C.: Institute for International Economics, 1994.
Excellent accessible survey of the issues and results of the Uruguay Round, including tariff reductions.

Smith, Dustin. "The Truth About Industrial Country Tariffs." *Finance and Development* 39 (March 2002): 14–15.
Readable summary of the patterns typical of industrial country tariffs.

Tarr, David G. "Arguments for and against Uniform Tariffs." In *Development, Trade, and the WTO,* edited by B. Hoekman, et al., 526–534. Washington, D.C.: The World Bank, 2002.
The effects of variation in tariff rates across industries.

Trebilcock, Michael J., and Robert Howse. *The Regulation of International Trade.* London: Routledge, 1995.
Comprehensive overview of the world trading system, including tariffs; for all students.

Yi, Kei-Mu. "Can Vertical Specialization Explain the Growth of World Trade?" *Journal of Political Economy* 111 (March 2003): 52–102.
Even low tariffs can have a big effect when goods cross borders multiple times during the production process; for intermediate and advanced students.

OFFER CURVES AND TARIFFS

An import tariff's effect on the terms of trade (or lack of effect in the small-country case) is easily seen using offer curves. Recall from Appendix B to Chapter Three that an offer curve represents how much of its export good a country is willing to give up to obtain a unit of its import good. The slope of a straight line through the origin and the intersection of two countries' offer curves captures the equilibrium, or market-clearing, terms of trade.

Figure A.1, panel (a), illustrates an offer curve (denoted A) for country A, assuming unrestricted trade. Country A has a comparative advantage in production of good X and exports X to country B in exchange for good Y. Point C, for example, illustrates A's willingness to export X_0 units of X in exchange for Y_0 units of Y. Now suppose country A imposes a tariff on imports of good Y. The effect on A's offer curve is shown by the shift from curve A to curve A_t, where the t subscript denotes *tariff*. The offer curve drawn for a tariff-imposing country is called a *tariff-ridden offer curve*.

Why does A's offer curve shift inward toward the origin as a result of the tariff? One way to answer this is to recall from the analysis of tariffs in Chapter Six that a tariff *reduces* the volume of trade in which the tariff-imposing country wants to engage. This implies that country A will be willing to export a smaller quantity of X in exchange for any given quantity of Y (for example, only X_1 rather than X_0 units in exchange for Y_0).

A second way to consider the shift in A's offer curve caused by the tariff is to note that consumers of Y in country A now must pay *both* the producers of Y in country B and the domestic government for each unit of Y imported. To consume Y_0 units of Y, consumers must pay X_1 units of X to country B and $X_0 - X_1$ to the domestic government. Thus, in total, the price consumers in A are willing to pay for Y_0 units of Y is still X_0 units of X, but now that price is divided between foreign producers and the government. The tariff reduces the amount of good X that country A is willing to offer to country B by the amount of the tariff; and the new offer curve reflects this new lower quantity of goods traded. Therefore, country A's offer curve shifts inward, or to the left, by a proportion equal to the tariff rate.

Now that we know the tariff's effect on the offer curve, we can use it to examine the tariff's effect on the equilibrium terms of trade and the importance of country size in determining that effect. First, we assume that country A is small in the markets for goods X and Y; it possesses no market power. In an offer-curve diagram, A's smallness is represented by drawing the trading partner's (country B's) offer curve as a straight line, as in Figure A.1, panel (b). The slope of B's offer curve measures the equilibrium terms of trade that, by assumption, A cannot affect. If A imposes an import tariff, shifting its offer curve to A_t, the volume of trade declines (from X_2 and Y_2 to X_3 and Y_3) but the terms of trade aren't affected. The decline in the volume of trade has a negative welfare effect on country A (and on B), so the overall welfare effect of a tariff by a small country is negative.

Next, we assume that country A is large enough to possess some degree of market power in the markets for goods X and Y. In this case, the trading partner's (B's) offer curve no longer is a straight line but curved, as in panel (a) of Figure A.2. Imposition of an import tariff by A improves A's terms of trade, as shown by the increase in the slope of the relative price line. Since the slope of the price line measures the relative price of good X, country A's export good, an increase in the line's slope represents an improvement in A's terms of trade and a deterioration in B's. In other words, country A now gets more imported Y for each unit of X the country exports; and B now gets less imported X for each unit of Y it exports. The imposition of a tariff reduces the volume of trade, just as in the small-country case, but now the terms of trade are affected as well. The net effect of the tariff on country A's welfare depends on the two effects' relative magnitudes.

It's important to note that the improvement in country A's terms of trade through the tariff is synonymous with a deterioration in country B's. Country B is unambiguously harmed by A's tariff and may retaliate by imposing an import tariff of its own on country A's exports.

Figure A.2, panel (b), illustrates the possibility of retaliation by B. Should this occur, B's offer curve shifts inward to B_t, further reducing the volume of trade and again shifting the terms of trade—this time in B's favor. Whether the *net* effect on the terms of trade favors A or B depends, of course, on the magnitudes of the original and retaliatory tariffs and on the precise shapes of the countries' offer curves. As drawn, the terms of trade following B's retaliation remain more favorable to A than the pre-tariff terms of trade (omitted from the figure). Country B could restore the original terms of trade by imposing a higher retaliatory tariff. However, the stronger retaliation would reduce further the volume of trade. If a trade war of retaliation and counter-retaliation erupted, the countries could be driven back to autarky, represented by the origin in Figure A.2.

Figure A.1 **Effects of an Import Tariff by Country A**

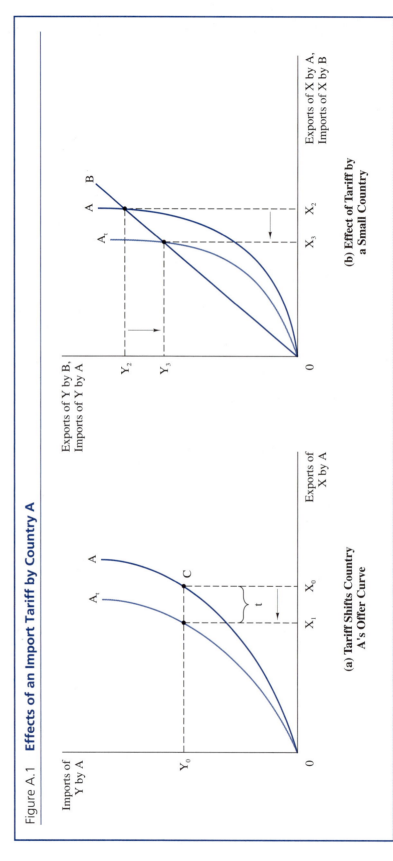

(a) Tariff Shifts Country A's Offer Curve

(b) Effect of Tariff by a Small Country

An import tariff of t imposed by country A reduces the volume of trade in which A wants to engage and shifts A's offer curve inward to A_t in panel (a). In exchange for Y_0 units of imports, country A reduces the amount of good X it is willing to export from X_0 to X_1. The difference, $X_0 - X_1$, goes to A's government as tariff revenue. In panel (b), country A's smallness is represented by the straight-line shape of trading partner B's offer curve. The slope of B's offer curve determines the equilibrium terms of trade regardless of A's action. The tariff imposed by A reduces the volume of trade from X_2 and Y_2 to X_3 and Y_3 but has no effect on the equilibrium terms of trade.

Figure A.2 **Effects of an Import Tariff by a Large Country**

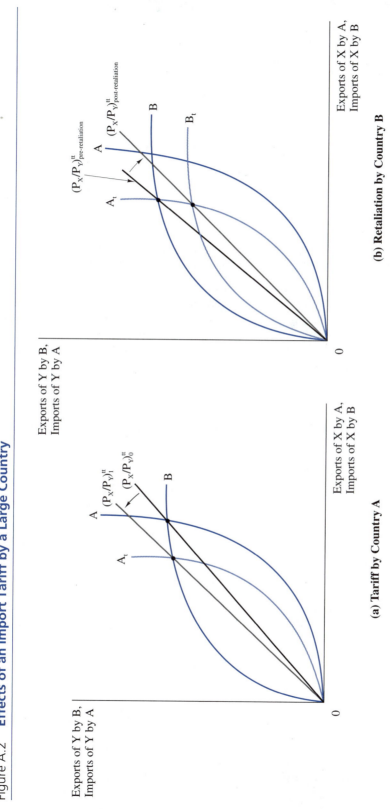

Country A's large size is represented by the curved shape of trading partner B's offer curve. In panel (a), imposition of a tariff by A raises the relative price of good X, A's export good, as shown by the increased slope of the straight line from the origin through the new intersection of the two countries' offer curves. Country A's tariff worsens country B's terms of trade and reduces the volume of trade. In response to the damage caused by A's tariff, B may choose to impose its own import tariff, shifting its offer curve to B_t in panel (b). Such retaliation further reduces the volume of trade; the net effect on the terms of trade depends on the relative sizes of the two countries' tariffs and on the shapes of their offer curves. As drawn, B's retaliatory tariff is too low to restore the terms of trade to their pre-tariff level.

APPENDIX B

GENERAL-EQUILIBRIUM TARIFF EFFECTS IN A SMALL COUNTRY

General-equilibrium analysis allows a tariff's effects on consumption and production of *both goods* to be investigated. In addition, it illustrates more directly the tariff's negative impact on the imposing country's welfare. We assume that the country is small and has a comparative advantage in production of good X.

In Figure B.1, the *production* and *consumption* points under free trade are p^0 and c^0, respectively. We omit the autarky equilibrium and the country superscripts for simplicity. The equilibrium terms of trade are given by the world price ratio, $(P_X/P_Y)^w$, and the country's utility is U_0. Now suppose the country imposes a tariff of t on each unit of good Y imported. The tariff doesn't affect the world price of good Y, P_Y^w, because of the country's small size. The domestic price of Y in the small country rises to $P_Y^w + t$. The new relative price ratio relevant for individual domestic producers is $[P_X^w/(P_Y^w + t)]$, which is less than $(P_X/P_Y)^w$. Production occurs at the point where the production possibilities frontier is tangent to the price line

relevant for domestic producers; and this production point with the tariff is p^1 in Figure B.1.

The country can trade on world markets to obtain the combination of goods its residents want to consume. At which price ratio does this trade occur? It must occur at $(P_X/P_Y)^w$, because that's the only price ratio at which trade occurs in world markets; the small country's tariff can't affect world prices. Another way to see that $(P_X/P_Y)^w$ is the relevant price ratio for international trade is to note that out of the new domestic price of good Y, only P_Y^w goes to the foreign country while t goes to the domestic government as tariff revenue. Thus, for the importing country as a whole, the price of the import still is only P_Y^w.

At first glance, we might expect the country to trade along the price line going through the tariff production point p^1 to the point tangent to the highest attainable indifference curve (U_1). If consumption point c^1 were the final equilibrium, there would be only one source of welfare loss from the tariff: the loss caused by inefficient production (p^1 rather than p^0) and represented by the move from utility level U_0 to U_1. However, the actual outcome involves a second welfare loss due to inefficient

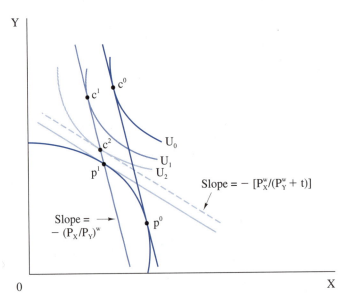

Figure B.1   **General-Equilibrium Effects of an Import Tariff by a Small Country**

The tariff shifts production from p^0 to p^1, causing a loss of efficiency and a decrease in welfare represented by the move from indifference curve U_0 to U_1. Consumption is based on the domestic price ratio ($P_X^w/[P_Y^w + t]$) and also is inefficient, causing a further reduction in welfare from U_1 to U_2.

consumption. The price ratio relevant for individual domestic consumers is $P_X/(P_Y^w + t)$ because for each imported unit of good Y, a consumer must pay P_Y^w to the producer *and* t to the domestic government. The final equilibrium involves trading along the world price line to a point where an indifference curve is tangent to the domestic price line. The final consumption point with the tariff is c^2 on indifference curve U_2. The move from U_1 to U_2 represents the welfare loss due to inefficient consumption.

7

Nontariff Barriers

1 INTRODUCTION

Nontariff barriers (NTBs) include import and export quotas, export subsidies, and a variety of other regulations and restrictions covering international trade. International economists and policy makers have grown increasingly concerned about such barriers in recent years for three reasons. First, success in reducing tariffs through international negotiations has made NTBs all the more visible. Nontariff barriers have proven less amenable than tariffs to international negotiation. In fact, until recently, most agreements to lower trade barriers more or less explicitly excluded the two major industry groups most affected by NTBs, agriculture and textiles/apparel. Second, countries sometimes use nontariff barriers precisely because the main body of international trade rules, the World Trade Organization, doesn't discipline many NTBs as effectively as it does tariffs. Countries can circumvent WTO rules by using loopholes in the agreements and imposing types of barriers over which negotiations have failed. The fears aroused by nontariff barriers reflect not only the negative welfare effects of specific restrictions already imposed, but also the potential damage done to the framework of international agreements when countries intentionally circumvent the specified rules of conduct. Third, countries often apply NTBs in a discriminatory way; that is, the barriers often apply to trade with some countries but not others. In particular, exports from developing countries appear especially vulnerable to nontariff barriers. NTBs by the European Union, the United States, and Japan apply to a higher percentage of exports from developing countries than from industrial countries. Such barriers can only make the development process more difficult.

2 QUOTAS

The simplest and most direct form of nontariff trade barrier is the import **quota**, a direct restriction on the quantity of a good imported during a specified period. Countries impose quotas for the same reasons as those for imposing import tariffs (see section 2 in Chapter Six). As in the case of tariffs, we'll focus on the protection issue: Quotas can protect a domestic industry from foreign competition. Developed countries (for example, Japan, the United States, and the members of the European Union) have used import quotas primarily to protect agricultural producers. Developing countries, on the other hand, have used quotas on imported manufactured goods to try to stimulate growth of their domestic manufacturing sectors; but we'll see in Chapter Eleven that protection's repeated failure to stimulate manufacturing has finally persuaded many developing countries to move toward more open trade policies.

Figure 1 **What Are the Effects of an Import Quota on Good Y?**

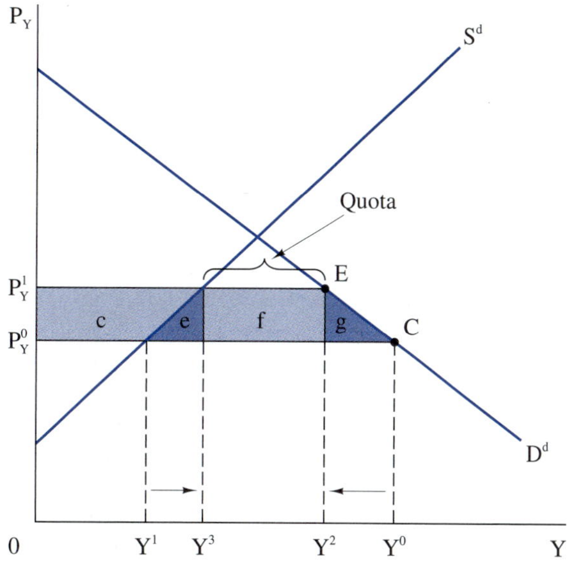

By restricting imports, a quota increases domestic production from Y^1 to Y^3 and decreases domestic consumption from Y^0 to Y^2. The net welfare loss from the quota is shown as the sum of the areas of triangles e and g. Area c represents a transfer from domestic consumers to producers; area f represents the quota rents.

Analysis of an import quota's effects closely resembles that for a tariff. In Figure 1, D^d and S^d represent, respectively, the *domestic* demand and supply for good Y, the import good of the country imposing the quota. For simplicity, the figure omits the total supply curve of good Y that faces the country. Assume that the unrestricted trade equilibrium is at point C. Residents consume Y^0 units, of which Y^1 units are produced domestically and $Y^0 - Y^1$ imported. The price of the good, both domestically and in world markets, is P_Y^0.

Now suppose policy makers decide that availability of low-cost imports is limiting sales by domestic producers to Y^1. One method to protect the domestic industry from foreign competition is to impose an import quota. To find the effect, we define a horizontal line whose length represents the quota (for example, 1 million tons of sugar per year). Then we "slide" this line that represents the quota up until it fits horizontally between the domestic demand and supply curves. Point E in Figure 1 denotes equilibrium with the quota. The new domestic price of good Y is P_Y^1; at this psice, the quantity produced domestically (Y^3) plus the imports allowed under the quota ($Y^2 - Y^3$) equals the quantity demanded by domestic consumers (Y^2).

Area $c + e + f + g$ represents the loss of consumer surplus due to the quota, much as in the case of an import tariff. (You can review the concepts of consumer and producer surplus in section 4.2 of Chapter Six.) The basic interpretations of areas c, e, f, and g are the same as the analogous areas in the tariff analysis. Area c is a transfer from domestic consumers to domestic producers now able to sell more of their product at a higher price. Consumers pay the amount represented by c in a higher price (P_Y^1 rather than P_Y^0). Triangle e is a deadweight welfare loss. The quota causes the country to produce units between Y^1 and Y^3 domestically rather than importing them; however, each of those units cost more to produce domestically (represented by the height of the domestic supply curve) than to import (represented by P_Y^0). Triangle g is the other deadweight loss, this one caused by inefficient consumption. The quota reduces domestic consumption from Y^0 to Y^2. For each unit of consumption forgone, the value to consumers (represented by the height of the domestic demand curve) exceeds the cost of importing the good (represented by P_Y^0). Therefore, the reduction in consumption caused by the quota is inefficient.

Area f symbolizes a type of "revenue" generated by the quota, called the **quota rents**. For each unit imported under the quota ($Y^2 - Y^3$), domestic consumers now pay a higher price. But to whom do the rents go? Under a tariff, the answer was clear: The tariff revenue went to the tariff-imposing government.[1] Under a quota, the answer is less certain; rents generated by the quota may go to any of several groups, depending on their relative bargaining strengths and the institutional arrangements the government uses to administer the quota. Importers or exporters, foreign producers, or the quota-imposing government may capture the rents; or they may become an additional deadweight loss.

The rents go to importers if they have the bargaining power to buy $Y^2 - Y^3$ units on world markets at price P_Y^0 and sell them domestically at P_Y^1. This occurs if importers have monopoly power. If importing is a competitive industry, importers will bid against one another to buy good Y, and the price producers or exporters charge will rise above P_Y^0. In that case, the sellers of good Y, either producers or exporters, will capture the quota rents represented by area f in Figure 1.

Administration of an import quota is less simple than it first appears. The government issues a statement that no more than $Y^2 - Y^3$ units of good Y may be imported. To enforce the restriction, the government must devise a scheme both to keep track of how many units enter the country and to allocate the quota among importers. The government may choose to auction import licenses. Under such a system, the rents from the quota go to the government, because an importer able to buy Y on the world market for P_Y^0 would willingly pay approximately $P_Y^1 - P_Y^0$ for a license to import 1 unit. (*Why?*) The total amount for which the government could sell the import licenses equals the area of rectangle f. Quotas administered under such a scheme are called *auction quotas*.

A third possibility is that area f may end up as an additional deadweight loss; that is, the rents may go to no one. Suppose, for example, that the government doesn't sell import licenses but gives them away on a first-come, first-served basis. Importers then have an incentive to lobby to obtain licenses and otherwise spend resources to obtain them; for example, importers might be willing to wait in line for hours, an allocation method economists refer to as *queuing*. The value of a license to import 1 unit of Y is approximately $(P_Y^1 - P_Y^0)$, so importers would willingly expend resources equal to that amount to obtain a license. The total resources spent on lobbying or waiting in line equal area f. The process of competition for licenses "uses up" the quota rents, which, in this case, represent an additional deadweight loss from society's viewpoint.

The final possibility is that foreign producers or exporters will capture the rents from the quota. Administration of the quota by the exporting country rather than the importing one increases the likelihood that foreign producers or exporters will capture a large share of the rents. Usually the exporting-country government administers the quota by assigning an export limit to each firm. This method of administration prohibits competition among the firms and allows them to charge a higher price (P_Y^1 rather than P_Y^0).

The effects of quotas include a tendency for exporters to raise the average quality of their exported goods.[2] In 1981, Japan agreed under U.S. pressure to restrict its passenger-car

---

1. Most economic analyses assume that governments use tariff revenue in place of domestic taxes. However, rent-seeking behavior by producers may use up the revenue, adding an additional deadweight loss due to trade restrictions (see footnote 6 in Chapter Six).

2. This quality-adjustment effect also applies to specific, but not ad valorem, tariffs.

exports to the United States to 1.68 million per year. Japanese automobile firms responded by stopping shipments of plain, low-priced models in favor of higher-priced ones with more add-on features. This effect implies that quotas impose especially high welfare costs on the poor, because the imports such policies eliminate include the lower-priced items bought primarily by low-income families.

Thus far, with the exception of the rents issue, the effects of import quotas appear identical to those of tariffs. Nonetheless, economists generally think quotas cause larger losses of welfare than do equivalent tariffs. Section 3 examines the reasoning behind this belief.

3 COMPARISON OF IMPORT TARIFFS AND QUOTAS

We've seen one major difference between the effects of an import tariff and those of an import quota: The revenue from a tariff goes to the tariff-imposing government, but the quota rent can go to different groups depending on how the government administers the quota. Several other, more subtle differences matter in evaluating the overall effects of the two policies.

Domestic firms in an industry seeking protection typically prefer a quota to other types of import restrictions. One explanation for this preference is the greater certainty associated with a quota's protective effects. A quota assures the domestic industry a ceiling on imports *regardless of changing market conditions*. Even if the domestic industry's comparative disadvantage grows more severe, the quota prohibits consumers from switching to the imported good. Note, however, that the quota does cause a decline in quantity demanded by raising the good's domestic price; therefore, a quota can't keep the domestic industry from facing a shrinking market.

Beyond increasing their market share, domestic firms also seek protection from foreign competition to gain and exploit monopoly power in the domestic market.[3] Suppose an industry following this strategy gains protection in the form of an import tariff. Firms in the industry can raise their prices. However, if they raise prices too much, consumers will switch to the imported good even though they have to pay the tariff. In particular, if domestic firms try to charge a price that exceeds the world price plus the tariff, consumers won't buy from domestic firms. If the industry's protection takes the form of a quota, however, the attempt to gain monopoly power by restricting foreign competition will more likely succeed. Under a quota, domestic consumers *don't* have the option of switching to the imported good. If domestic firms try to exploit a monopoly position by raising prices, consumers face just one choice: pay the higher prices or consume less of the good. Successful monopolization of an industry reduces efficiency, so economists think the tendency of quotas to facilitate firms' efforts to gain monopoly power makes quotas more damaging than tariffs.[4]

Setting aside the issue of who gets the associated rents, it's possible, given any tariff, to define a quota with precisely the same effects on prices, production, consumption, and trade. Similarly, given any quota, it's possible to set a tariff with exactly the same effects. Economists call this result the **equivalence of tariffs and quotas**.[5] We've hinted, however, that as market conditions change, tariffs and quotas cease to have identical effects. Figure 2 illustrates this for a large country. Panel (a) analyzes an increase in demand for good Y under a tariff; panel (b) examines the effect of the same increase in demand under a quota. We define the tariff and quota so that at the initial level of demand (D^d), Y^0 units are consumed under both systems, Y^1 units are produced domestically, and $Y^0 - Y^1$ units are imported at price P_Y^0.

---

3. Monopoly power may allow a profit-maximizing firm to price above marginal cost and earn a positive economic profit.

4. Monopoly power reduces efficiency by allowing profit-maximizing firms to restrict output and charge prices above marginal cost.

5. This result provides the basis for the process of *tariffication*, through which countries replace their quotas with equivalent tariffs, as required by the Uruguay Round. Equivalence also underlies one technique for measuring or quantifying NTBs; see section 8.

Figure 2 **What Happens in Response to Increased Demand under a Tariff and under a Quota?**

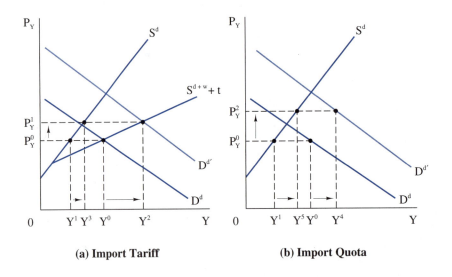

(a) Import Tariff　　　　　**(b) Import Quota**

An import quota is more restrictive than an equivalent tariff when demand increases. Under a tariff, imports cover a portion of the increased demand; in panel (a), increased demand causes a larger increase in consumption than in domestic production. A quota forces all increased demand to be matched by increases in (inefficient) domestic production, as panel (b) illustrates. An equal increase in demand causes a larger price increase under a quota than under a tariff.

In panel (a), with an increase in demand to $D^{d'}$, the quantity of good Y consumed rises to Y^2, of which domestic firms produce Y^3 units under the tariff. Note that domestic production rises by *less* than consumption rises; part of the increased consumption comes from increased imports. The tariff allows increased imports by permitting consumers to either buy domestically or import at a price equal to the world price plus the tariff.

In panel (b), the same increase in demand raises consumption to Y^4 and domestic production to Y^5 under the quota. Increased domestic production exactly *matches* increased consumption, because the quota prohibits any increase in imports. The increased domestic production is inefficient (that is, more costly than imports); therefore, the domestic price of good Y rises more under the quota (to P_Y^2) than under the tariff (to P_Y^1). The quota forbids additional imports no matter what price domestic consumers are willing to pay for them. (*Compare the effects of a reduction in domestic supply under a tariff and under a quota.*)

Table 1 presents empirical estimates of the effects of several U.S. quotas in 1990. Areas c, e, f, and g in the table correspond to the redistribution, production, quota rent, and consumption effects from Figure 1. All U.S. quotas except the dairy-products program were administered by exporting countries; so the estimates in Table 1 assume that foreign exporters captured the quota rents, making area f part of the U.S.'s net welfare loss from the quotas.

4 EXPORT QUOTAS

Restrictions on exports are much less common than those on imports, but the former do exist. We analyzed export taxes in section 10 of Chapter Six, and policy makers can achieve similar effects by imposing an **export quota** that restricts the number of units of

Table 1 **COSTS OF U.S. IMPORT QUOTAS, 1990 (MILLIONS $)**

Product Category (Tariff Equivalent)	Redistribution Effect (Area c)	Quota Rent Effect (Area f)[a]	Production and Consumption Effects (Areas e + g)	Net Welfare Effect on U.S. (−[Area e + f + g])[a]
Protected by import quotas:				
Dairy products (50%)	$ 835	$244	$104	−$104
Peanuts (50%)	32	0	22	−22
Sugar (66%)	776	396	185	−581
Maritime (85%)	1,275	0	556	−556

[a]In all cases except dairy products, quota rents are assumed captured by foreign exporters (and, therefore, a net U.S. welfare loss), because all other quotas are administered by the exporting country. In dairy products, the rents are assumed captured by licensed U.S. importers (and, therefore, not a net U.S. welfare loss).

Source: Data from Gary Clyde Hufbauer and Kimberley Ann Elliott, *Measuring the Costs of Protection in the United States* (Washington, D.C.: Institute for International Economics, 1994), pp. 8–9.

a good that can be exported. As in the export-tax case, small countries have one primary reason to impose an export quota: to make the good cheaper for domestic consumers. Large countries have an additional reason; they can force foreign consumers to pay a higher price for their product by restricting the amount they offer for sale on the world market. Figure 3 depicts both cases.

Figure 3 **What Are the Effects of an Export Quota?**

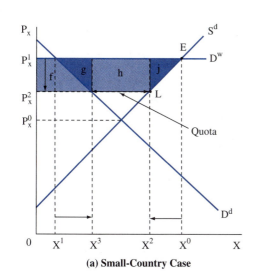
(a) Small-Country Case

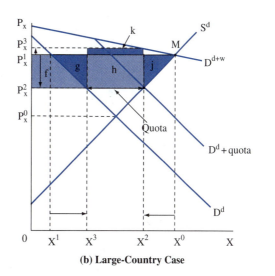
(b) Large-Country Case

When imposed by a small country (panel (a)), an export quota decreases domestic production, increases domestic consumption, and pushes down the domestic price. When imposed by a large country (panel (b)), an export quota decreases domestic production, increases domestic consumption, pushes down the domestic price, and pushes up the world price.

4.1 Small-Country Case

In panel (a), point E represents equilibrium under unrestricted trade in a small country's market for its export good, X. Demand for the small country's exports by the rest of the world, D^w, sets the world price. The country is small in the X market, so it can't affect the world price by altering its trade policy; this small-country assumption is reflected in the horizontal shape of the demand curve the country faces for its exports. Note that the world price of good X lies *above* the country's autarky price (P_X^0), because X is the export good in which the country has a comparative advantage. Under unrestricted trade, the small country produces X^0 units, consumes X^1, and exports $X^0 - X^1$ at the world price P_X^1.

Now the country imposes an export quota of $(X^2 - X^3)$. To find the effect, we define a horizontal line whose length represents the size of the quota (for example, 1 million tons of steel per year). Then we "slide" this line down until it fits horizontally between the domestic demand (D^d) and domestic supply (S^d) curves. Point L represents the new equilibrium. The domestic price of good X falls to P_X^2. Domestic production falls from X^0 to X^2, and domestic consumption rises from X^1 to X^3. Exports fall to $X^2 - X^3$, as required by the export quota.

Domestic producers of good X lose producer surplus equal to f + g + h + j because of the export quota. Area f is transferred to domestic consumers, who now can buy good X at price P_X^2 rather than P_X^1. Area g is a deadweight loss from the inefficient increase in domestic consumption. Too much X is now consumed domestically because the marginal benefit of domestic consumption at X^3 (given by the height of D^d) is less than the marginal benefit of foreign consumption of X (given by the height of D^w, which measures the amount foreign consumers are willing to pay for the small country's exports). Foreign consumers value the units of good X between X^1 and X^3 more highly than do domestic consumers; but the export quota causes those units to go to domestic consumers. Area j is the deadweight loss from curtailment of domestic production to X^2. For all units of good X between X^0 and X^2, the cost of producing domestically (indicated by the height of S^d) is less than the value foreign consumers place on the good (indicated by the height of D^w). So long as foreign consumers are willing to pay P_X^1 for good X, efficiency requires that domestic production be X^0, not X^2.

Area h represents the quota rents. Like in the import-quota case, which group gets the rents from an export quota depends on market conditions and on how policy makers administer the quota program. For example, if policy makers auction licenses that convey the right to export, firms will pay an amount up to the area of rectangle h for the export licenses. This system allows a government to capture the quota rents, much as would happen in the case of an export tax. But, if policy makers give away the export licenses, export firms may expend resources up to the area of rectangle h in a lobbying effort to win the licenses, making h a deadweight loss to the economy. If domestic firms can costlessly obtain licenses that allow them to export and sell on the world market for the world price P_X^1, then those firms capture the quota rents represented by area h.

An export quota by a small country transfers welfare from domestic producers to domestic consumers (area f). The quota causes inefficient production and consumption decisions, so the export-quota-imposing country suffers a net welfare loss (area [g + j]). Domestic producers lose more (f + g + h + j) than domestic consumers gain (f); therefore, small-country export quotas fail the test of whether gainers can compensate losers. The net welfare loss equals either (g + j) or (g + j + h) depending on whether the method of administering the export quota transfers the rents to some group in the economy or makes them an additional deadweight loss.

4.2 Large-Country Case

Panel (b) in Figure 3 depicts imposition of an export quota by a large country. Such a country faces a downward-sloping total demand curve for good X (D^{d+w}), which includes both domestic demand (D^d) and demand by the rest of the world for the country's exports.[6] The country is large in the X market, reflected in the downward-sloping curve the country faces for its exports. Point M represents equilibrium under unrestricted trade in a large country's market for good X. The world price of good X is above the autarky price (P_X^0) because X is the country's comparative-advantage good. Under unrestricted trade, the large country produces X^0 units, consumes X^1, and exports $X^0 - X^1$ at the world price P_X^1.

If the large country imposes an export quota equal to ($X^2 - X^3$), exporters can no longer sell as much as they want in response to demand by the rest of the world. The new demand curve firms face is D^d + quota, which includes domestic demand plus just the permitted quantity of exports. Domestic price falls to P_X^2. The loss of producer surplus is the same as in the small-country case: Producers of good X lose f + g + h + j of surplus; and the analysis of each of these areas is the same as in the small-country case in section 4.1. Notice, however, that area h doesn't include all of the quota rents. The quota-imposing country is large, so its policy pushes the world price of good X up to P_X^3. Foreign consumers are willing to pay a higher price for good X because the export quota by a large country makes the good more scarce. The area of rectangle k represents the portion of the quota rents that foreign consumers pay in the form of a higher price. If (1) domestic producers or the domestic government can capture this portion of the rents, k, and (2) the rents represented by area k exceed the deadweight losses (area [g + j]), then the export quota may produce a net welfare gain for the large country.

Export quotas often involve markets in which the "consumers" are actually firms. If firms in an industry can persuade policy makers to impose an export quota on a product they use as an input, they can then buy that input at a lower price. Of course, as we've seen, the gains to the "consumer" firms (f) from an export quota are smaller than the losses to the "producer" firms (f + g + h + j). Steel scrap is an industry periodically subject to export quotas. Ukraine imposed a quota in 2003, and the U.S. is considering one.[7] Steel producers called mini-mills use steel scrap as an input to make new steel products, so mini-mills represent the "consumers" who would gain from U.S. export quotas on steel scrap. The scrap-recycling industry, on the other hand, would lose.

Sometimes export quotas generate trade disputes when one country claims to be harmed by another's quota. China imposes export quotas on coke, an input in steel production. In 2004, the country announced plans to tighten the quota in order to keep domestic coke prices low and help domestic steel producers. These events in China pushed up the world price of coke, which imposed higher input costs on steel producers in the rest of the world, especially Japan and the European Union. The European Union responded by threatening to file a complaint with the World Trade Organization, to which China gained entry in 2001. The Chinese government allocates export licenses for coke to state-owned firms that can then sell the licenses, so these state-owned firms capture most of the quota rents, area (h + k).[8]

Until recently, most attention devoted to trade barriers focused on tariffs and quotas. In the last few years, subtler, more complex restrictions have proliferated. In the following sections, we examine several of these barriers, including export subsidies and countervailing duties, dumping, domestic-content rules and rules of origin, government procurement, and technical standards.

---

6. At each price, the horizontal distance between the total demand (D^{d+w}) and the domestic demand (D^d) represents demand by the rest of the world for the country's exports.

7. Paul Glader, "Steelmakers, Buyers Consider Cap on Scrap Exports," *The Wall Street Journal*, February 12, 2004.

8. "Chinese Set to Debate Changes to Restrictions on Coke Exports," *Financial Times*, May 14, 2004.

5 SUBSIDIES AND COUNTERVAILING DUTIES

Subsidies are, in effect, negative taxes, or payments from a government for undertaking an activity. Policy makers can choose to subsidize anything—education, fuel-efficient cars, or research and development—they want firms or consumers to do more of. Two categories of subsidies affect international trade patterns and sometimes lead to trade disputes: export subsidies and production subsidies for a country's export good.

5.1 Export Subsidies

An **export subsidy** is a government's financial contribution to a firm for export of a commodity; the exporting firm receives the government subsidy along with the price paid by foreign consumers. Note that this definition restricts subsidies to *exports* rather than the country's *export good*. For example, if American Steel Company produces 5 million tons of steel of which it exports 2 million tons, a subsidy of $10 per ton on *exports* implies a total subsidy of $20 million, while a $10-per-ton subsidy on *production* implies a total subsidy of $50 million. Both types of subsidies are important in international trade, but more controversy surrounds export subsidies because they involve differential or discriminatory treatment of domestic sales versus exports. Such subsidies create incentives for firms to export larger shares of their production and sell smaller shares domestically, since the latter don't receive the subsidy payment.

THE IMPORTING-COUNTRY VIEW   Given the jealousy with which industries guard their domestic markets from foreign competition, it isn't surprising that government subsidization of exports is one of the most controversial issues in international trade policy. Domestic industries often argue that they face "unfair" competition from rivals subsidized by foreign governments.

Our initial examination of export subsidies' effects takes the perspective of the importing country, which we assume to be small in the market for good Y. (Note that desirability of subsidies from the exporting country's standpoint also is an issue, the subject of upcoming section 5.1.2.) The importing country's trading partners subsidize exports of good Y by s per unit.[9] A subsidy is just a negative tax, so it lowers the price at which importing-country consumers can buy the good.

In Figure 4, the subsidy shifts the supply curve facing the importing country for good Y, the country's import good, down by the amount of the subsidy from S^{d+w} to $S^{d+w} - s$, because the country can now buy all the imports it wants at the world price minus the subsidy, s. The overall effect is to increase consumption of good Y from Y^0 to Y^2, decrease importing-country production from Y^1 to Y^3, and increase imports from $Y^0 - Y^1$ to $Y^2 - Y^3$. The domestic price of good Y falls from the free-trade price, P_Y^0, to P_Y^1; exporting-country producers willingly sell at a lower price because they now receive the subsidy from their government in addition to the price they receive from consumers. Importing-country consumers gain an amount represented by area e + f + g + h in consumer surplus. (*Why?*) The subsidy harms importing-country producers, as lower-priced imports reduce sales by domestic firms and dictate a lower price. Area e captures this loss of producer surplus, which is transferred to domestic consumers. The remainder of domestic consumers' gains

---

9. We assume that all exporting countries subsidize, so the importing country can purchase all the good Y it wants at the subsidized price. If a single small country subsidized, buyers would compete for that country's exports, driving the price back up to the initial world price and allowing the subsidizing country's exporters to earn the world price *plus* the subsidy for each unit exported.

Figure 4   **What Are the Effects of an Export Subsidy? Importing-Country Perspective**

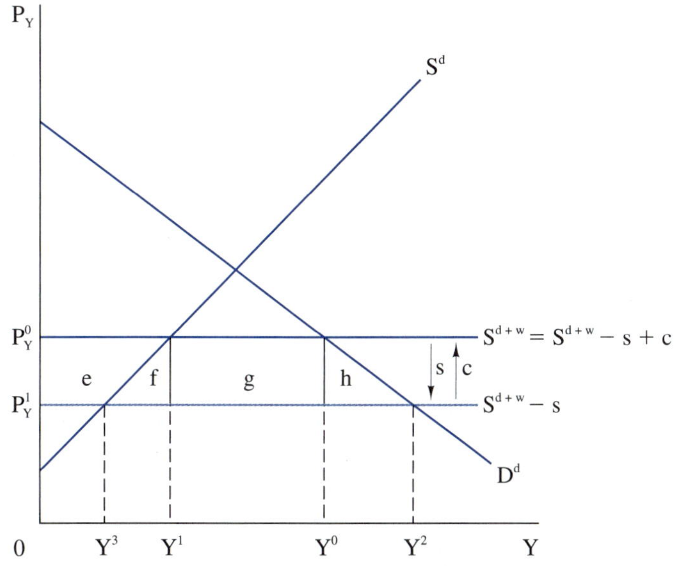

An export subsidy of s per unit increases domestic consumption from Y^0 to Y^2 and reduces domestic production from Y^1 to Y^3. The difference is made up by increased imports now available at a lower price (P_Y^1 rather than P_Y^0). Importing-country producers are harmed (area e), but by less than the gains to importing-country consumers (area e + f + g + h) in the form of lower prices and increased availability of imports. A countervailing duty (c) can offset the subsidy's effects on trade and consumption but will not eliminate the transfer (area g) from exporting-country to importing-country taxpayers.

(area f + g + h) come at the expense of exporting countries' taxpayers, who must pay taxes to finance the subsidy.

Importing-country producers of good Y are likely to lobby for protection from "unfair" subsidized exports to prevent the loss of area e. WTO rules allow for **countervailing duties (CVDs)**, or import tariffs designed specifically to offset the competitive advantage provided by trading partners' export subsidies. A countervailing duty of c ($= s$) per unit in Figure 4 eliminates the subsidy's effect on trade by shifting the supply curve facing the importing country back up to $S^{d+w} - s + c$. Importing-country consumption returns to Y^0 and production to Y^1. Note, however, that one important effect of the subsidy remains, even with the countervailing duty: The importing country continues to gain area g at the expense of exporting-country taxpayers, who still pay a subsidy of s per unit on units Y^1 through Y^0. With the countervailing duty, importing-country consumers don't reap the subsidy directly through lower prices, but the importing-country government collects the countervailing duty and can lower domestic taxes accordingly. Therefore, area g represents a transfer from exporting-country taxpayers (who finance the subsidy) to importing-country taxpayers (who enjoy lower domestic taxes).

Figure 4 makes clear that the importing country as a whole loses from a countervailing duty. The duty imposes costs on importing-country consumers (area e + f + g + h) that outweigh the gains to producers (area e) and the government (area g). So why would a country ever impose a countervailing duty rather than just reaping the benefit of cheaper imports made possible by another country's export subsidy? From the importing-country perspective, a countervailing duty represents a victory of protectionist pressures by domestic producers. But from a worldwide view, a countervailing duty improves total welfare because the cost of the subsidy to exporting countries outweighs the benefits to the importing country. The countervailing duty cancels the production and consumption inefficiencies introduced by the subsidy; only the transfer from taxpayers in the exporting countries to those in the importing country remains.

U.S. law requires firms that allege foreign export subsidies to file complaints with the Department of Commerce and the International Trade Commission. Commerce investigates to determine whether a subsidy in fact exists, and the Commission determines whether the subsidy, if any, harms or threatens to harm domestic firms. If both findings are affirmative, the United States imposes a countervailing duty. Sometimes, a subsidy investigation leads to a protectionist outcome other than a countervailing duty. A "suspension agreement" occurs if the accused exporter agrees to stop exporting to the United States or to charge higher prices to eliminate the alleged harm to the U.S. industry. In effect, suspension agreements work like quotas: They limit U.S. imports and facilitate noncompetitive pricing among domestic and foreign firms. The Uruguay Round Agreement requires countries to conduct "sunset" reviews of outstanding countervailing-duty orders when those orders have been in effect for five years; these reviews can result in revocation or continuation of the duty.

Table 2 summarizes the history of U.S. investigations. As of the end of 2002, the United States had 59 countervailing duties in effect, some of which dated from the 1970s and 1980s, that covered goods ranging from steel to pistachio nuts to cotton shop towels, with countries from Argentina to Iran to the United Kingdom.

Table 2	**U.S. COUNTERVAILING-DUTY INVESTIGATIONS**			
			Sunset Investigations	
	Investigations Initiated	CVDs Imposed	CVD Revoked	CVD Continued
1986	28	13	n.a.	n.a.
1987	8	14	n.a.	n.a.
1988	17	7	n.a.	n.a.
1989	7	6	n.a.	n.a.
1990	7	2	n.a.	n.a.
1991	11	2	n.a.	n.a.
1992	22	4	n.a.	n.a.
1993	5	16	n.a.	n.a.
1994	7	1	n.a.	n.a.
1995	2	2	n.a.	n.a.
1996	1	2	n.a.	n.a.
1997	6	0	n.a.	n.a.
1998	11	1	n.a.	n.a.
1999	10	6	n.a.	n.a.
2000	7	6	8	22
2001	18	6	1	5
2002	3	0	0	0
2003	5	2	0	0

Source: Data from U.S. International Trade Commission, *Trade Policy Agenda and Annual Report.*

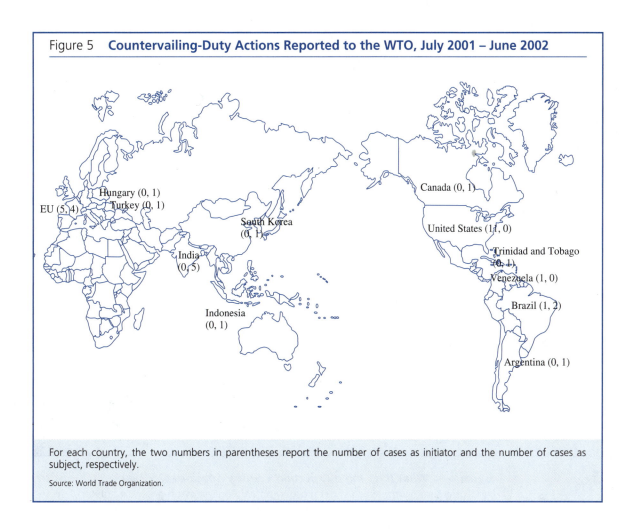

Figure 5 **Countervailing-Duty Actions Reported to the WTO, July 2001 – June 2002**

For each country, the two numbers in parentheses report the number of cases as initiator and the number of cases as subject, respectively.

Source: World Trade Organization.

Figure 5 illustrates the geographic pattern of new countervailing-duty investigations reported to the WTO by member countries in 2002; for each country, the first number in parentheses gives the number of countervailing-duty investigations that country *initiated* in 2002 and the second number reports the number of new countervailing-duty investigations to which that country was *subject* in 2002. The United States initiated the largest number of investigations (11); India was the subject of the largest number of investigations (5).

THE EXPORTING-COUNTRY VIEW   From the importing country's perspective, foreign export subsidies produce a net welfare gain but impose losses on domestic producers who must compete with the subsidized foreign products. The situation in the exporting country is quite different. There, subsidized producers gain at the expense of consumers and/or taxpayers, depending on how many countries in the market subsidize exports.

Figure 6 represents the market for good Y in the exporting country. We continue to assume that the country is small in the world market. Point C represents the unrestricted-trade equilibrium. The country produces Y^0 units, consumes Y^1, and exports $Y^0 - Y^1$. Domestic consumer surplus is $P_Y^0 MZ$, and domestic producer surplus is $NP_Y^0 C$.

Figure 6   **What Are the Effects of an Export Subsidy? Exporting-Country Perspective**

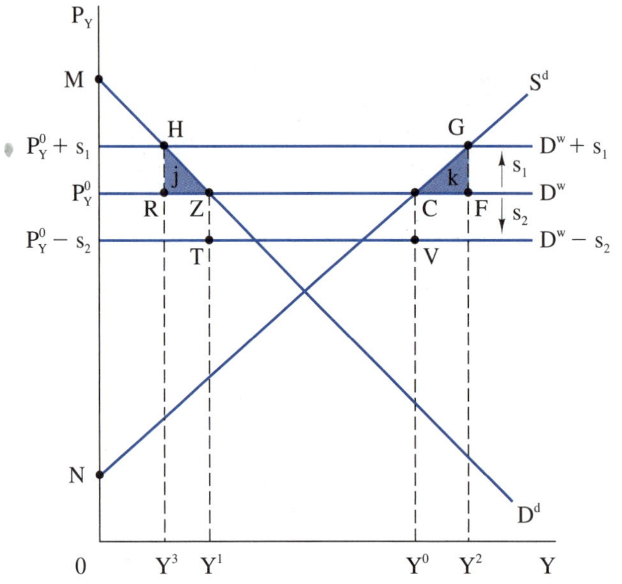

If a small country is the only exporter subsidizing (Scenario 1), its export firms receive the world price *plus* the subsidy $(P_Y^0 + s_1)$, and the net welfare effect on the exporting country is a loss equal to areas j and k. If all exporters subsidize (Scenario 2), the world price is bid down by the amount of the subsidy (s_2). Exporting firms receive only P_Y^0, and the net welfare loss to the exporting country is area TZCV.

Scenario 1: What If a Single Exporting Country Subsidizes?   Assume first that the exporting country under consideration is the *only* one providing export subsidies in the market for good Y. The small country's subsidy won't affect the world price of the good, P_Y^0.[10] Exporting firms receive P_Y^0 from foreign consumers *plus* the subsidy, s_1, from the government. Point G in Figure 6 represents the new equilibrium. Exporting-country production rises to Y^2 because of the higher total price received for exports. The higher price also creates an incentive for producers to sell more abroad $(Y^2 - Y^3)$ and less domestically (Y^3). Domestic consumer surplus falls to $(P_Y^0 + s_1)$MH. Domestic producer surplus rises to $N(P_Y^0 + s_1)$G. In addition, taxpayers pay RHGF to finance the subsidy. Note that import barriers must accompany export subsidies; otherwise foreign producers will bring in the good and re-export it to take advantage of the subsidy. (*Why?*)

The sum of triangles j and k measures the net deadweight loss to the exporting country. Area j is "lost twice"—once in the form of lost consumer surplus and again in the form of subsidy payments by taxpayers—and only "gained once"—in increased producer surplus. Taxpayers pay area k as part of the subsidy, but it doesn't go to producer surplus because of the high cost of producing units Y^0 through Y^2. Overall, exporting-country producers gain at the expense of exporting-country consumers and taxpayers. The welfare losses exceed the gains; thus, the export subsidy fails the compensation test from the exporting country's perspective.

Scenario 2: What If All Exporting Countries Subsidize?   Now we assume that the small exporting country under consideration isn't the only one providing an export subsidy

10.   See footnote 9.

on good Y; *all* exporting countries subsidize. In this case, a subsidy of s_2 ($= s_1$) dollars per unit on exports of Y shifts down the price exporting-country producers require for sales in the export market.[11] The downward shift represents the amount of the subsidy. Producers are willing to sell abroad at $P_Y^0 - s_2$ in Figure 6 because they also receive s_2 from their government for each unit sold abroad; therefore, the total price producers receive, including both the price paid by foreign consumers *and* the subsidy, continues to equal P_Y^0. Exporting-country production doesn't change, nor do domestic producer and consumer surplus. However, taxpayers pay TZCV to finance the subsidy. (*Why?*) The net loss to the country is simply area TZCV, transferred to importing-country consumers in the form of a lower price.

5.2 The Controversy over Export Subsidies

Export subsidies raise an obvious question: Why would any country choose to subsidize its exports, thereby providing artificially low-priced imports to foreign consumers? One possible answer lies in the redistribution of income that subsidies generate in the exporting country. If the country is alone in subsidizing (Scenario 1), export-country producers gain and therefore have an incentive to lobby for export subsidies. But if many countries subsidize in the same market (Scenario 2), the subsidies drive down the world price. Producers then cease to gain from the subsidy, but they still won't ask their governments to stop the subsidy. A producer whose government stopped subsidizing while other governments continued to do so couldn't sell any output in the world market. (*Why?*) This explains the importance of WTO negotiations for all member countries to agree to lower export subsidies simultaneously; domestic political pressure from exporters assures that no single country wants to lower its subsidies while other countries continue theirs, because that country's producers would lose their export markets.

The clustering of export subsidies in markets for agricultural products provides a clue to a second motivation for the subsidies. Most industrial economies (including the United States, the European Union, and Japan) administer complex agricultural price-support systems that keep prices for those products and farmers' incomes artificially high. When a country imposes a price floor above the equilibrium price of a good—say, wheat—the good's quantity supplied exceeds the quantity demanded. Under a price-support program, the government must prevent the natural fall in price by buying the surplus wheat. Were the government to turn around and sell that wheat domestically, the sales would undermine the domestic price-support system. However, export sales don't undermine the artificially high domestic price. The difference between the high price paid to domestic farmers and the lower world price obtained by the government for export sales represents the subsidy.

The United States and the European Union have bickered for decades over one another's agricultural subsidies. The Uruguay Round Agreement required member countries to cut their agricultural export subsidies, reduce the volume of agricultural exports receiving subsidies, and refrain from granting new subsidies to additional agricultural products. Reaching this compromise between demands for agricultural trade reform and farmers' demands for protection almost derailed the Uruguay Round talks and delayed the agreement for nearly four years. A decade later, this same issue has delayed and threatened the Doha Round of negotiations.

Each year, as part of its report on foreign trade barriers that hinder U.S. trade, the U.S. Trade Representative compiles a list of countries' export subsidies. Table 3 lists the alleged export subsidies on specific products included in the most recent report; many countries in addition to those in the table implement broad export-subsidy programs that favor all or most exports rather than exports of a specific product. Although manufactured items appear on the list, the prevalence of agricultural products among subsidized exports is striking.

---

11.   When many countries subsidize exports, they drive down the world price by the amount of the subsidy (see footnote 9).

Table 3	**EXPORT SUBSIDIES**
Country	Subsidized Products
Brazil	Regional aircraft
Canada	Softwood lumber, dairy products
China	Textiles, steel, petrochemicals, machinery, copper, corn
European Union	Aircraft, aircraft engines
Korea	Semiconductor chips, paper
Pakistan	Wheat
South Africa	Textiles, clothing, autos
Venezuela	Coffee, cocoa, fruit, seafood

Source: Data from U.S. Trade Representative, *National Trade Estimate Report on Foreign Trade Barriers* (Washington, D.C.). Available at http://www.ustr.gov.

A more complex reason for export subsidies involves the possibility that temporary export subsidies in markets with certain characteristics may allow a country to capture a larger share of the world market that it can then exploit by charging monopoly prices for the good. A full examination of this argument, part of a branch of international trade called *strategic trade policy*, must wait until Chapter Eight.

Export subsidies rarely take the form of explicit and direct payments from a government to exporting firms. WTO guidelines, even before the Uruguay Round, ruled out such payments on industrial products. Actual subsidies take less direct and visible forms. Defining precisely which actions do and don't constitute subsidies was one of the most difficult issues facing negotiators in the Uruguay Round of WTO talks. One of the most common types of subsidy involves provision of low-cost government loans to firms in certain industries. A second type of subsidy is provision of favorable tax treatment for firms involved in exporting. The Uruguay Round Agreement clarifies that forgone or uncollected government tax revenue, that is, a tax credit, does constitute a subsidy under WTO rules.

5.3 Trade-Relevant Production Subsidies

Not all subsidy controversies involve export subsidies. Some involve production subsidies for a country's export good. Remember the difference: If American Steel Company produces 5 million tons of steel of which it exports 2 million tons, an export subsidy of $10 per ton implies a total subsidy of $20 million, while a $10-per-ton production subsidy implies a total subsidy of $50 million. Why would production subsidies, which don't appear to be a trade policy, cause trade disputes? Because they can increase the quantity a country exports and, if the subsidizing country is a large exporter, push down the world price. Producers in the importing countries who face the increased competition often lobby for protection from the "unfair" subsidized goods.

Figure 7 illustrates the effects of a production subsidy on a country's export good, X. Panels (a) and (b) refer to the small- and large-country cases, respectively. In panel (a), a production subsidy of s per unit shifts the small country's domestic supply, S^d, down by that amount to $S^d + s$. The policy has no effect on the world price, P_X^0, or on domestic consumption, X^1, because the small country faces a horizontal demand curve for its exports. Domestic production rises from X^0 to X^2; and the extra production goes into exports, which rise from $X^0 - X^1$ to $X^2 - X^1$.

Panel (b) in Figure 7 illustrates the effect of a production subsidy granted by a large country to producers of its export good. This time, the country faces a downward-sloping

Figure 7   What Are the Effects of a Production Subsidy?

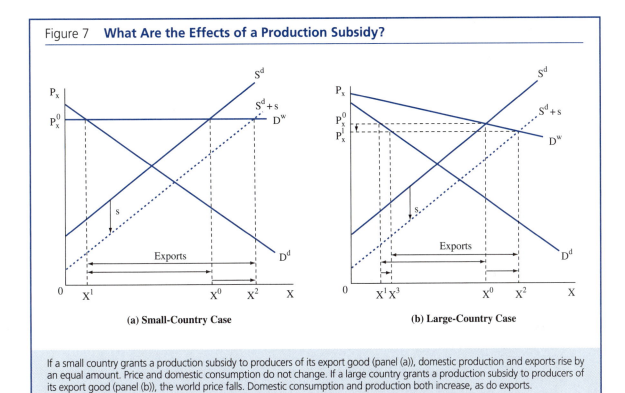

(a) Small-Country Case

(b) Large-Country Case

If a small country grants a production subsidy to producers of its export good (panel (a)), domestic production and exports rise by an equal amount. Price and domestic consumption do not change. If a large country grants a production subsidy to producers of its export good (panel (b)), the world price falls. Domestic consumption and production both increase, as do exports.

demand curve for its product. A production subsidy of s per unit shifts the country's domestic supply, S^d, down by s. The large country's subsidy does affect the world price, which falls from P_X^0 to P_X^1. Domestic consumption rises from X^1 to X^3 as consumers can buy good X at the lower price. Domestic production rises from X^0 to X^2. The extra production goes into both increased domestic consumption and increased exports. Exports rise from $X^0 - X^1$ to $X^2 - X^3$. Foreign producers of the good now face increased import competition and a lower world price, from which they are likely to seek relief in the form of a countervailing duty.

One of the world's longest-lasting trade disputes involves U.S. allegations of Canadian production subsidies for softwood lumber. The United States, pressured by its domestic lumber producers, claims that Canada subsidizes its lumber producers by charging them below-market prices to cut timber on provincially owned land. The United States periodically responds with a countervailing duty, most recently in 2002 when the United States imposed a 29 percent CVD on softwood lumber imports from Canada. U.S. consumer groups estimated that the duty would add $1,000 − $1,500 to the price of an average new house built in the United States.

6 DUMPING

Perhaps no phenomenon in international trade generates as much controversy and as many calls for protection as does dumping. **Dumping** can be defined in one of two ways.[12] According to the price-based definition, dumping occurs whenever a firm sells a good in

---

12. Many economists agree that rules against dumping should be restricted to predatory dumping (defined in section 6.3); the original 1916 U.S. law was so restricted.

a foreign market at a price below that for which the firm sells the same good in its domestic market. Under the cost-based definition, sale of a good in a foreign market at a price below its production cost constitutes dumping. The definitional distinction is important, because dumping under one definition isn't necessarily dumping under the other. In particular, whenever the domestic price of a good differs from its cost of production, the requirements for dumping differ under the two definitions.

6.1 Sporadic Dumping

Economists divide dumping into three categories. The first is **sporadic dumping**, which involves sale of a good in a foreign market for a short time at a price below either the domestic price or the cost of production. This short-lived variety of dumping resembles an international "sale." Stores sometimes sell goods for short periods at prices below their regular prices, often to eliminate undesired inventories. Sporadic dumping is the international-trade equivalent of such sales.

Sporadic dumping may disrupt the domestic market; however, it's unlikely to cause serious permanent injury to a domestic industry, just as a store's market position isn't likely to be damaged irrevocably by a competitor's occasional sales. During the brief period of dumping, domestic consumers benefit from availability of the imported good at an unusually low price.

6.2 Persistent Dumping

Persistent dumping, as the term suggests, is continued sale of a good in a foreign market at a price below either the domestic price or production cost, a practice that provides the basis for many calls for protection. The distinction between the price-based and cost-based definitions is crucial in analyzing persistent dumping.

The major cause of persistent dumping according to the price-based definition is the international version of a general phenomenon called **price discrimination**. Any firm able to separate its customers into groups with different elasticities of demand for its product and to prevent resale of the good among the groups can increase profit by charging them different prices.[13] A firm that serves both a domestic and an export market may be able to charge a higher price to domestic consumers, who typically exhibit a lower elasticity of demand than do foreign consumers. Other things being equal, the more and better the substitutes for a good, the higher the elasticity of demand; good substitutes allow consumers to be more responsive to changes in the good's price. In many industries, a firm has more competitors in export markets than in the home-country market; this implies that the elasticity of demand facing the firm in the export market typically exceeds that in the home market and creates an incentive for the firm to price discriminate.[14]

Figure 8 illustrates the relationship between international price discrimination and persistent dumping under the price-based definition. A firm producing good Y faces the situation in panel (a) in its home market and the situation in panel (b) in its export market. The demand curves reflect a higher elasticity of demand for good Y in the export market at any given price; in other words, the firm possesses more market power in the home market than in the export market—an intuitively plausible assumption.

13. A good's elasticity of demand is the percentage change in quantity demanded resulting from a 1 percent change in price (elasticity of demand = % change in quantity demanded/% change in price).

14. In Chapter Eight (section 4.2), we discuss the case of two monopolists charging high prices in their respective home markets and dumping (under the price definition) to capture part of the rival's market, a practice known as *reciprocal dumping*.

Figure 8   Persistent Dumping as International Price Discrimination

(a) Home Market   **(b) Export Market**

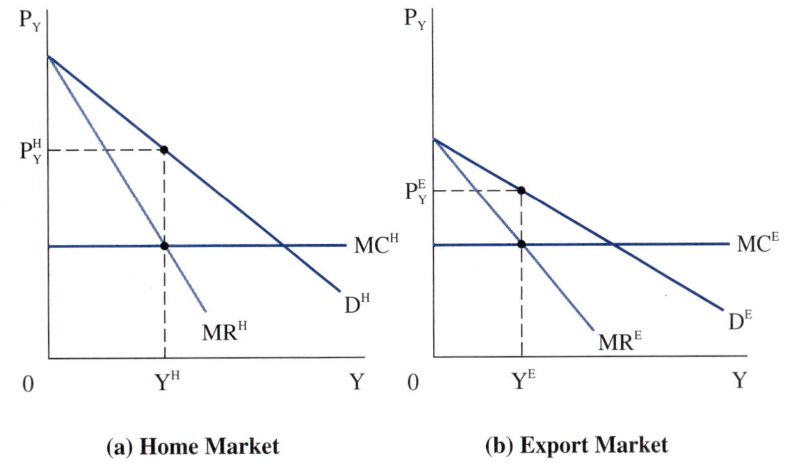

If a firm can prevent resale of its product between domestic and foreign customers, price discrimination based on different elasticities of demand by the two groups will increase the firm's profits. Because of the greater number of competitors in export markets, the firm generally will charge a higher price in the *home* market than in the *export* market (that is, $P_Y^H > P_Y^E$), generating dumping by the price-based definition.

The firm maximizes profit in each market by producing the level of output at which marginal *cost* (denoted by MC and assumed for simplicity to be constant at all levels of output and equal across markets) equals *marginal revenue* (MR).[15] The height of the corresponding demand curve at the profit-maximizing level of output reveals the profit-maximizing price. The price in the *home* market (P_Y^H) exceeds that in the *export* market (P_Y^E) because of the relative inelasticity of home-country demand. The firm dumps by the price-based definition, with a **dumping margin** of $P_Y^H - P_Y^E$. However, such price discrimination produces ambiguous welfare effects. The market power reflected in the firm's ability to charge prices above marginal cost (especially in the home market) reduces economic efficiency and harms consumers, as does any monopoly. However, the welfare effect of forcing the firm to charge equal prices in the two markets can't be ascertained without further information about the market in question. Hence, international trade theory provides no clear rationale for policies that prohibit international price discrimination or persistent dumping under the price-based definition.

What about persistent dumping under the cost-based definition? Would we expect to observe continual sales of a good below cost? The answer depends on what one means by *cost*. If *cost* is defined as the firm's marginal cost of production, economists think the general answer to the question is no: Firms won't sell a good persistently at a price below its marginal cost of production. Many industries in many countries ask for protection from foreign competition by pointing to alleged persistent dumping, but there are few documented cases of such behavior.

---

15. Marginal revenue is defined as the change in total revenue when the firm changes its output by one unit. Under the assumption that the firm has some market power and must charge the same price for all units sold in a given market, marginal revenue at any level of output is less than price. To sell an additional unit of output in any market, the firm must lower its price, and the lower price must apply to all units sold in that market. Therefore, marginal revenue from sale of the additional unit is less than the price for which the additional unit itself is sold.

Charges of dumping under the cost-based definition often use a concept of cost other than the exporting firm's *marginal* cost. For example, firms may sell in the short run at prices below their *average total* cost. In fact, we expect firms with significant fixed costs to do so in periods of low demand, such as during recessions. As long as sales bring in revenue sufficient to cover variable cost, the profit-maximizing firm will choose to produce rather than shut down in the short run—even if price falls below average total cost. This holds regardless of whether the firm sells domestically or internationally.[16]

Another problem arises because foreign production costs often are difficult to determine, presenting a temptation to use indirect measures of those costs. Careless use of the cost-based definition of dumping can allow domestic producers to accuse any foreign rival who undersells them of dumping. Assume that American Steel Company loses business to Brazilian Steel Company, which sells steel at a lower price. American Steel accuses Brazilian Steel of dumping. Since neither American Steel nor U.S. policy makers know Brazilian Steel's cost of production, American Steel argues that Brazilian Steel's prices are below *American Steel's* costs. Acceptance of such an argument as evidence of dumping sets a dangerous precedent. Domestic producers in *any* comparative-disadvantage industry could accuse foreign rivals of dumping. After all, a country with a comparative advantage always can sell the industry's product for less than a country with a comparative disadvantage. Disallowing trade based on dumping charges that involve careless use of the cost-based definition of dumping could eliminate all trade based on comparative advantage!

In practice, use of the cost-based definition in dumping cases isn't yet quite as disastrous as the previous example might suggest. When a domestic firm files dumping charges, trade law requires an effort to determine their validity using the price-based definition. If exporting-country domestic prices of the good in question aren't available (for example, if the foreign firm produces only for export), investigators must make an effort to determine the price of the good in a third market. When this fails, investigators seek production costs in the country of origin, followed by production costs in third markets.

The most famous example of this situation involved a 1974 U.S. charge that Poland dumped golf carts in the U.S. market. Poland sold no golf carts domestically, so the price-based definition of dumping proved useless. No one knew the true cost of production by Polish firms because Poland, then a centrally planned economy, didn't use market-determined prices for its inputs. To resolve the case, investigators evaluated the inputs the Polish firm used to make a golf cart at Spanish input prices. The estimated cost turned out to be very close to the price Poland charged for golf carts sold in the United States.

6.3 Predatory Dumping

Domestic firms often claim that foreign firms sell in the domestic market at prices below production cost to drive domestic firms from the industry. The alleged purpose behind this strategy of **predatory dumping** is to eliminate domestic competitors and then exploit the newly created monopoly power by raising prices. Although intuitively appealing, this story stands up poorly to scrutiny.

First, foreign firms—if indeed they sell at prices below their production cost—suffer losses while dumping. The monopoly power they hope to gain must promise future rewards high enough to compensate for current losses. Second, domestic firms (the "victims") would know that predatory dumping could only be temporary because of the losses it would create for its instigators. If the "unfair competition" is temporary, domestic firms should be able to borrow funds with which to hold out until the foreign firms give up on the attempt to drive

---

16. If sales at high prices in a protected domestic market cover the firm's fixed cost, sales in export markets can occur at any price that covers the variable cost of production.

rivals out of business. Third, even if predatory dumping drove domestic firms from the industry, the strategy would prove worthwhile only if foreign firms could then exploit their monopoly power by charging higher prices. However, once this occurred, what would prevent domestic firms (either old or new ones) from re-entering the industry and underselling the foreign monopolist? If domestic firms did this, foreign firms would have suffered losses during the dumping episode for little or no future reward. Finally, the predatory-dumping story requires a firm to perceive an opportunity to *monopolize* the industry. But large groups of firms often file dumping charges against dozens of competitors in multiple countries; the large number of firms involved on both sides of the typical dumping case gives predatory dumping claims a credibility problem.

The United States' first antidumping law, passed in 1916, applied only to predatory dumping. In the almost 80 years since, no firm has been convicted under that statute. Modern dumping cases use statutes that embody much broader definitions of dumping to include that with no predatory intent or effect.

6.4 Policy Responses to Dumping

Under U.S. trade law, when a domestic firm charges a foreign counterpart with dumping, the U.S. Department of Commerce and the U.S. International Trade Commission conduct investigations. Those investigations must determine (1) whether dumping occurred, and (2) if so, whether it materially injured or threatens to materially injure the domestic industry. If both questions are answered affirmatively, the government imposes an **antidumping duty**, an import tariff equal to the dumping margin (represented by $P_Y^H - P_Y^E$ in Figure 8).

Despite rules written into antidumping laws, many analysts argue that U.S. procedures in dumping investigations almost guarantee guilty findings for foreign firms charged with dumping. The computation of dumping margins involves many complex issues, and trading partners complain with some justification that U.S. procedures bias findings toward high dumping margins and, therefore, high antidumping duties. For example, when dumping investigations use the cost-based definition of dumping, cost calculations provide many opportunities for investigators to build in high cost estimates, which lead to finding high dumping margins.

Trading partners also complain about the U.S. practice of demanding extraordinary amounts of detailed information on short notice from firms accused of dumping. If a firm can't or chooses not to provide any piece of the requested information, the U.S. investigators can use their own "best information available" to substitute for the missing data. In practice, the "best information available" can mean data provided by the domestic firms seeking protection and, as a result, might be expected to contain a bias toward a large dumping margin.

There is evidence that these procedural issues do appear to bias findings toward high dumping margins and, therefore, high antidumping duties. In U.S. dumping cases between 1995 and 1998, those using the price-based definition found average dumping margins of 3.2 percent, those using constructed values under the cost-based definition found average dumping margins of 25.1 percent, those using surrogate constructed values for nonmarket economies found dumping margins of 40 percent, and those using "best information available" found dumping margins of a whopping 95.6 percent (indicating that foreign firms supposedly were selling products for about half of what it cost to produce them!). A similar differential of findings under the different dumping definitions and investigative procedures also exists in European Union dumping cases over the same period.[17]

17. Patrick A. Messerlin, "Antidumping and Safeguards," in *The WTO after Seattle*, edited by Jeffrey J. Schott (Washington, D.C.: Institute for International Economics, 2000), p. 169.

Figure 9   **Antidumping Actions Reported to the WTO, July 2001–June 2002**

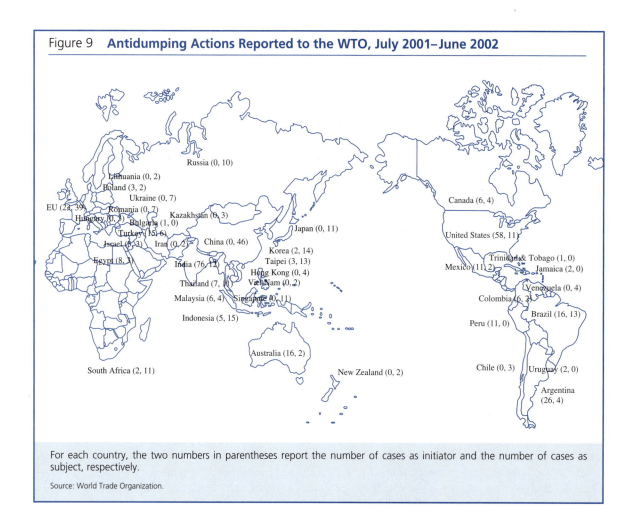

For each country, the two numbers in parentheses report the number of cases as initiator and the number of cases as subject, respectively.

Source: World Trade Organization.

Historically, the United States has used antidumping policies much more extensively than other countries. However, in recent years, trading partners have been catching up. Thirty-three member countries reported to the WTO that they had initiated 309 antidumping actions in 2002 and had 1,189 antidumping duties in force. Figure 9 indicates the cases' geographic distribution. For each country named on the map, the first number reports the number of antidumping actions *initiated* during the year and the second number reports the number of new antidumping investigations to which the country was *subject*. India (76), the United States (58), Argentina (26), and the European Union (23) reported filing the largest number of cases in 2002. China (46), the European Union and its member states (39), and Indonesia (15) were targets of the largest numbers of dumping accusations by their trading partners.

At the end of 2002, the United States had almost 300 antidumping orders in effect, covering goods from salmon to gift boxes to nails and involving trading partners as varied as Canada and Uzbekistan. Affirmative dumping and injury findings in 2002 covered goods such as folding chairs from China, frozen raspberries from Chile, and stainless steel bars from Italy. The Uruguay Round Agreement requires countries to review outstanding antidumping duties when they have been in effect for five years; these reviews can result in revocation or continuation of the duty. Table 4 reports the number of U.S. dumping cases initiated in recent years, along with the number of antidumping duties imposed and the outcome of sunset reviews.

Table 4   **U.S. ANTIDUMPING INVESTIGATIONS**

| | Investigations Initiated | Duties Imposed | Sunset Investigations | |
			Duty Revoked	Duty Continued
1986	83	26	n.a.	n.a.
1987	16	53	n.a.	n.a.
1988	42	12	n.a.	n.a.
1989	24	24	n.a.	n.a.
1990	35	14	n.a.	n.a.
1991	66	19	n.a.	n.a.
1992	84	16	n.a.	n.a.
1993	37	42	n.a.	n.a.
1994	51	16	n.a.	n.a.
1995	14	24	n.a.	n.a.
1996	21	9	n.a.	n.a.
1997	15	7	n.a.	n.a.
1998	36	9	n.a.	n.a.
1999	46	19	n.a.	n.a.
2000	45	20	57	72
2001	77	30	12	22
2002	35	27	9	2
2003	37	15	2	5

Source: Data from U.S. International Trade Commission, *Trade Policy Agenda and Annual Report*.

Like subsidy investigations, dumping investigations can lead to a protectionist outcome other than an antidumping duty. Accused exporters can stop exporting to the United States or raise their prices until the U.S. industry no longer claims injury. These actions reduce competition, lead to higher prices, and make it easier for domestic and foreign firms to engage in cartel-like behavior.

The Uruguay Round elaborated on antidumping rules negotiated as a code during the Tokyo Round. However, progress in dealing with dumping fell far short of that in many other areas. The agreement did require countries to conduct the sunset reviews and remove antidumping duties that have been in place for five years unless they can demonstrate that doing so would reinstitute the damage to the domestic industry that led to the initial finding. This provision helped curtail the practice of more-or-less permanent protection in the form of antidumping duties, a nontrivial accomplishment since many U.S. antidumping duties had been in effect since the 1970s. But 68 of the almost 300 U.S. antidumping duties in place at the end of 2002 were put in place before 1990.

7 ADMINISTRATIVE AND TECHNICAL STANDARDS

Most countries subject international trade to a variety of regulatory standards; some are protectionist by design and others unintentionally so. A few of the more common classes of restrictions include domestic-content requirements and rules of origin, government-procurement policies, technical product standards, and regulatory standards. Such policies constitute a continuing source of controversy in the international trading system because of the inherent difficulty in sorting intentionally protectionist policies from those pursued for legitimate domestic reasons but that have unintended negative effects on trade.

7.1 Domestic-Content Requirements and Rules of Origin

Modern global production makes it difficult or impossible to determine a good's "nationality," and few products exemplify this aspect of globalization as well as automobiles. A car may be assembled in England from parts produced in 20 different countries, with production coordinated by a firm owned and managed primarily by Germans and the final product sold in the United States. Such global production patterns allow firms to use different countries' comparative advantages in various aspects of production. However, the pattern can also generate protectionist pressures, as domestic industries want to keep more of the production stages for themselves and limit the competition they face. One political response to these protectionist pressures is domestic-content requirements.

Domestic-content requirements mandate that a specified percentage of a product's inputs and/or assembly have domestic origins in order for the good to be sold domestically. Worldwide, domestic-content requirements have received most attention in the automobile industry, so let's use that industry to think about what groups might support domestic-content requirements.[18] The requirements have three main constituencies. First, domestic input producers. For example, domestic auto-parts producers would support rules to require all cars sold in the country to include high percentages of domestically made parts. Second, workers in the domestic industry. A domestic-content rule on cars, for example, could require foreign auto producers to perform a high percentage of assembly tasks domestically, increasing demand for the services of domestic auto workers. Domestic-content requirements could also limit **outsourcing**, in which domestic-based automobile manufacturers buy inputs and perform assembly functions abroad. Many "American" cars—that is, cars sold by U.S.-based automobile companies—now are built abroad, much to the dismay of American auto workers. Finally, domestic producers of a good may support domestic-content requirements because such rules can raise foreign firms' costs and make them less competitive. If domestic labor and auto parts cost more than their foreign counterparts, then forcing foreign automobile producers to use more domestic-made parts and perform more assembly tasks domestically could raise those firms' costs and shift sales toward domestic-based auto producers.

Direct political pressure from protectionist-oriented special-interest groups isn't the only reason for countries' increased use of domestic-content requirements. When groups of countries negotiate reductions in their barriers to trade, those reductions sometimes apply *only* to members of the group. These agreements require a version of domestic-content rules, called **rules of origin**, to prevent nonmember countries from using the agreements to circumvent tariffs. For example, consider the North American Free Trade Agreement, which provides for tariff-free trade in most goods among Canada, Mexico, and the United States. If Canada's import tariffs exceed those of the United States, countries that export to Canada would like to ship their goods to the United States, pay the lower U.S. tariff, and then ship to Canada tariff-free from the United States under NAFTA. To prevent this, agreements such as NAFTA contain provisions that limit tariff-free access to goods that "originate" in the member countries.[19] In practice, this involves complicated and politically sensitive issues, as members of the European Union and NAFTA have discovered.

---

18. Find information on countries' domestic-content requirements for autos at http://www.ita.doc.gov/td/auto/impreq.html.

19. The alternative is to form a customs union with a common external tariff on trade with nonmembers; we'll discuss this option in Chapter Nine, section 4.1.

Under NAFTA, most goods qualify for tariff-free treatment if they *either* contain a specified percentage of North American content *or* are sufficiently "transformed" in North America to change tariff classification. Goods in politically sensitive sectors (autos, computers, and textiles and apparel) must satisfy *both* conditions. Autos, in particular, must contain 62.5 percent North American content to enter a NAFTA country tariff free. New cars sold in the NAFTA countries carry a sticker stating the percentage of the car's North American (that is, intra-NAFTA) content.

Domestic-content rules and rules of origin discourage production in the countries where opportunity costs are lowest. Therefore, such rules reduce the gains from trade. The potential losses may be particularly large in industries, such as the automobile industry, that involve many diverse manufacturing and assembly tasks. A single country isn't likely to have a comparative advantage in every aspect of automobile production, from research-and-development-intensive design to capital-intensive parts and subassembly manufacturing to labor-intensive assembly. Arrangements such as outsourcing reflect firms' attempts to perform each manufacturing and assembly stage in the country of comparative advantage. As a result, outsourcing not only contributes to efficient production of automobiles but also supports developing countries' attempts to build manufacturing sectors. A developing or newly industrializing country would find it difficult to build a complete automobile industry that could compete with established industries in the developed economies. An alternative is to specialize in the particular stages of the production process appropriate for the country's factor endowment; but domestic-content rules and rules of origin by developed countries restrict such specialization and harm developing countries. Such rules are also expensive; one study found that the cost to the EU of collecting, managing, and storing the information required to verify and administer the union's rules of origin equal about 3 percent of goods' prices.[20]

Developing countries also impose domestic-content rules.[21] For example, Vietnam offers Japanese motorcycle producers with factories in Vietnam lower tariffs on their imported components if the firms raise the percentage of Vietnamese-made components used in their bikes. In 2002, Honda claimed that approximately 60 percent of the components used in its bikes sold in Vietnam were made in Vietnam. The Vietnamese government claimed otherwise, accused Honda of overstating its use of local parts, raised the tariffs the firm had to pay on its imported components, and finally imposed import quotas on the kits used to assemble the motorcycles.[22]

7.2 Government-Procurement Policies

In our analyses of international trade, we've relied on profit-maximizing motives of firms and utility maximization by consumers. We assume that consumers and firms try to buy at the lowest and sell at the highest available prices. The interaction of buyers' and sellers' decisions in each market determines the prices of goods and, in turn, the prices of factors of production. A large amount of trade, however, is undertaken by entities that may not respond to these motives of profit and utility maximization, at least in the simple terms in which we have defined them. Governments are foremost among the trading entities with unique goals.

We've already seen several effects of government involvement in international trade: agricultural price supports and the role of government export subsidies. Two other areas involve even more direct government roles in international trade. First, governments

---

20. Cited in Hoekman, et al., p. 115.

21. See Chapter 20 in Hoekman, et al. for a cautionary tale about Australia's experience with domestic-content rules in the automobile industry.

22. Amy Kazmin, "Honda's Sweet Success Goes Sour in Vietnam," *Financial Times*, September 30, 2002.

actually buy many goods and services in international markets. Second, government-owned industries and government-run monopolies make purchases and sales. These phenomena are called **government-procurement policies**.

Most countries have **buy-domestic requirements**, which either legally or informally require governments to purchase domestically made goods on a preferential basis. The strength of the requirements varies considerably. Some prohibit government purchases of certain imports outright; for example, laws require many governments to use the domestic airline exclusively and to patronize only domestic insurers. Other laws mandate strict guidelines for giving preference to domestic over foreign producers. The U.S. Buy American Act of 1933 required a 6 percent margin of preference for domestic producers of goods bought by the government. In other words, a foreign firm would have to sell at a price more than 6 percent below the domestic firm's price to win the contract.[23] For military or defense-related goods, the margin of preference expands to 50 percent.

An interesting dispute arose in 2003 when the U.S. Congress attempted to pass legislation to increase the required U.S. content for military goods from 50 to 65 percent. We'd expect foreign governments from countries whose firms would lose business to oppose the move, and they did. Perhaps more surprisingly, the president of the United States, the Defense Department, and the Pentagon also opposed it. They argued that the more stringent domestic-content rule would lead to fights with trading partners, significantly raise the costs of many weapons systems, threaten the viability of some individual military production projects such as the Joint Strike Fighter, and erode U.S. technological superiority. In this case, the "consumer" hurt by protection was the U.S. military. So, counter to the usual pattern in which protectionist producer interests win the political battle, in this case the "consumers" won and the domestic-content requirement for military goods stayed at 50 percent.

Many of the most controversial government-procurement practices are much more subtle and informal than the provisions of the Buy American Act and its foreign counterparts. For example, governments may keep their bidding practices secret so foreign firms won't have information about the proper procedure and timing for submission of bids for government contracts. Government agencies may advertise contracts in media unlikely to be available to foreign firms and may keep bids secret to prevent scrutiny of the award process. The Tokyo Round of trade negotiations addressed some of these problems with a government-procurement code, and the Uruguay Round built on this effort. The code has only 26 signatory countries and applies only to specified government agencies and projects, but it represents a step forward in recommending that government bidding procedures be well specified and open. The Uruguay Round rules apply to procurement of services as well as goods and to some purchases by subfederal governments and public utilities. However, governments still can practice many forms of preference for domestic firms.

Even more controversy arises when the government owns sizable industries, as in the cases of postal, telephone, and telegraph services (PTTs) in Asia, Europe, and most developing economies. The governments involved often claim to maintain these monopolies for purely domestic reasons, including national security and protection of domestic consumers from exploitation by private monopolies. The complex web of restrictions on imports of goods used in these industries suggests that protection of the domestic industry from foreign competition may be another government goal. The scope of the problem varies widely across countries with the extent of public ownership of industry. National policies typically restrict imports of telecommunications equipment,

---

23. Many U.S. states have gone even further with "buy in the state" legislation, which gives preference to in-state firms for goods purchased by state and local government agencies. Los Angeles required a specified percentage of *local* value-added for purchases related to its mass-transportation system.

data processing, and computer-oriented technology by PTTs. Most governments recognize the need to privatize or deregulate their utilities, both to improve the industries' efficiency and to avoid trade disputes, but progress in this reform has varied widely across countries.

7.3 Technical, Administrative, and Regulatory Standards

Governments regulate various aspects of activity within their economies and carefully guard their rights to do so. Regulations may include health, safety, and product-labeling requirements, as well as controls over entry into certain professions and access to certain types of mass media. Domestic considerations—health, safety, or environmental ones, for example—motivate many of these **technical barriers to trade**. For example, governments require imported foods to meet hygienic standards, toys and autos to meet safety standards, and products to conform to labeling laws to prevent fraud and provide consumer information.

As in the case of government-owned telecommunications monopolies, some of the observed restrictions clearly have protectionist effects. In some instances, these effects are so strong that one must suspect the proclaimed domestic goals of the restrictions as mere covers for protectionist intent. Because of the difficulty in sorting legitimate domestic policy goals from protectionist ones, efforts at international negotiations to lower technical barriers to trade have met with relatively little success. Taken individually, the rules may seem small and rather insignificant in terms of cost, as you can see from the examples in Figure 10. When taken together, however, the costs become substantial. The proliferation

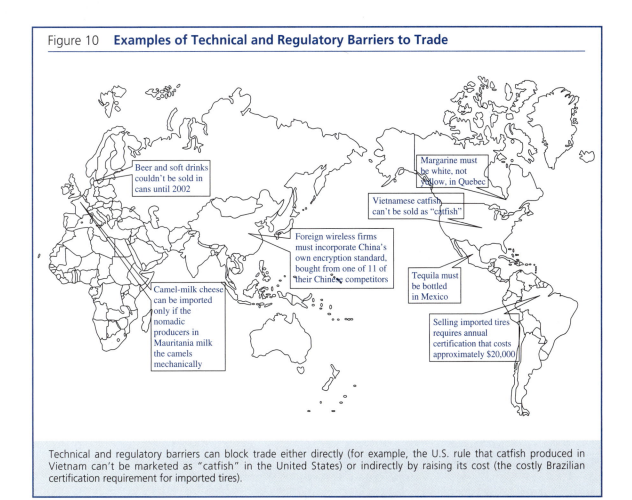

Figure 10   Examples of Technical and Regulatory Barriers to Trade

Beer and soft drinks couldn't be sold in cans until 2002

Margarine must be white, not yellow, in Quebec

Vietnamese catfish can't be sold as "catfish"

Foreign wireless firms must incorporate China's own encryption standard, bought from one of 11 of their Chinese competitors

Tequila must be bottled in Mexico

Camel-milk cheese can be imported only if the nomadic producers in Mauritania milk the camels mechanically

Selling imported tires requires annual certification that costs approximately $20,000

Technical and regulatory barriers can block trade either directly (for example, the U.S. rule that catfish produced in Vietnam can't be marketed as "catfish" in the United States) or indirectly by raising its cost (the costly Brazilian certification requirement for imported tires).

of technical and regulatory barriers to trade presents a particular problem for developing countries, which can incur high costs in their efforts to meet standards set for exporting to developed-country markets. WTO rules permit countries to use technical barriers to trade, but require that the rules be transparent, nondiscriminatory in their treatment of domestic and foreign firms, and based on sound scientific principles.

8 HOW CAN WE MEASURE NONTARIFF BARRIERS?

Nontariff barriers present major hurdles to analysts interested in measuring the range and magnitude of those barriers. Deciding exactly what should count as a nontariff barrier can be difficult in itself. Once we decide which barriers to include, at least four different measures can be calculated.

The most common empirical measure of NTBs is the **coverage ratio**, or the value of imports subject to NTBs, divided by total imports. Consider a simple example. Country A imports $60 worth of good X and $40 worth of good Y, so A's total imports equal $100. Imports of X are subject to a quota under which a maximum of $60 worth of X can be imported, and imports of Y are free of any NTBs. NTBs affect $60 out of the country's $100 worth of imports, so country A's NTB coverage ratio equals ($60/$100) = 0.6. The major problem with the coverage ratio is that *incipient* trade, shut off by trade restrictions, isn't counted. With no quota on good X, perhaps country A would have imported $5,000 worth of X; but the loss of the additional $4,940 worth of trade doesn't enter the coverage-ratio calculation. Another problem involves measuring changes in NTBs. Suppose, beginning with the situation just outlined, country A tightens the quota on good X until no imports can enter, while good Y remains unrestricted. Now none of country A's imports are covered by NTBs, so the new coverage ratio is ($0/$40) = 0. Counterintuitively, *tightening* the quota, by stopping all trade in the restricted good, *lowered* the NTB coverage ratio![24]

An alternative measure, called the **implicit tariff**, uses the equivalence between tariffs and quotas (see section 3). The idea is to calculate the tariff rate that would have the same effect on trade as the existing quota or other nontariff barrier. The Uruguay Round required that countries calculate these implicit tariffs in order to accomplish the required *tariffication*, that is, switching their agricultural protection policies from quotas to tariffs, which would then be cut according to the Uruguay Round tariff-reduction timetable. Canadian quotas on agricultural products had been so tight that their implicit tariff rates, imposed in 1995, ranged up to 335 percent. Even after the Uruguay Round phased-in tariff reductions, Canadian tariffs would still be prohibitive—285 percent on imported chicken cuts, 187 percent on eggs, and 272 percent on yogurt.[25]

The most comprehensive measures of nontariff barriers are producer- and consumer-subsidy equivalents. An industry's **producer-subsidy equivalent (PSE)** measures the difference between the income that producers in the industry receive *with* their tariffs and NTBs and the income producers would receive *with no* such barriers, and expresses that difference as a percentage of the income-without-barriers figure. If producers earn $3 million with a quota but would earn only $2 million under free trade, the producer-subsidy equivalent is ($3 million − $2 million)/$2 million = 0.5 or 50 percent. Economists have calculated producer-subsidy equivalents for many agricultural products because those products are subject to so many NTBs. Table 5 reports one set of estimates that compares agricultural PSEs for a sample of countries; Japan's agricultural producers, for example, received 138 percent more income in 1999–2001 than they would have in

---

24. Average tariff measures exhibit the same weakness; see section 3 in Chapter Six.

25. U.S. International Trade Commission, *The Year in Trade 1996* (Washington, D.C.: USITC, 1997), p. 88.

Table 5	PRODUCER-SUBSIDY EQUIVALENTS IN AGRICULTURE (PERCENT)		
	1986–1988	1995–1997	1999–2001
European Union	65.3%	28.3%	34.3%
Japan	145.4	131.7	138.1
United States	16.0	7.5	10.8
Eastern Europe	45.2	8.7	10.4
Australia and New Zealand	4.2	2.8	0.6
Norway, Switzerland, Iceland	165.9	108.1	113.0
Korea, Turkey, Mexico	31.4	38.1	42.9

Source: Data from World Bank, *Global Economic Prospects* (Washington, D.C.: World Bank, 2003), p. 121.

the absence of government assistance to the industry, including price supports facilitated by import barriers.[26]

Consumer-subsidy equivalents (CSEs) perform the same exercise for an industry's consumers. If, because of an import quota, consumers must pay $5 million for a good they could get for $4 million without the quota, the quota's consumer-subsidy equivalent is ($4 million − $5 million)/$4 million = −0.25 or −25 percent. Note the negative sign; the quota forces consumers to pay higher prices, hence in effect they receive a *negative* subsidy. Generally, protectionist policies including NTBs affect producers and consumers in an industry in opposite ways. Therefore, the producer- and consumer-subsidy equivalents for an industry have opposite signs. (*Name a trade policy with a negative PSE and a positive CSE, and vice versa.*)

CASE 1: SHOOTING DOWN THE BYRD AMENDMENT

United States

In 2000, the U.S. Congress, led by West Virginia Senator Robert Byrd, passed the Continued Dumping and Subsidies Offset Act, better known as the Byrd Amendment. The law awards the revenues from antidumping and countervailing duties to the U.S. firms that filed the corresponding dumping or subsidy cases. In 2001, the first year the law was in effect, the U.S. Customs Service distributed more than $200 million to firms in several industries. Eleven trading partners—Australia, Brazil, Canada, Chile, the European Union, India, Indonesia, Japan, Mexico, South Korea, and Thailand—filed a complaint with the WTO, claiming that the law (1) violated U.S. WTO obligations because it provides a subsidy to the firms who receive the revenues, (2) violated WTO rules that limit members' responses in dumping and subsidy cases to the imposition of duties, and (3) provided bad incentives because the lure of getting the revenues encouraged firms to file more claims alleging foreign dumping or subsidies. In July 2002, the World Trade Organization agreed and ruled the Byrd Amendment contrary to WTO rules.

The Byrd-Amendment story reveals several insights about the political process through which trade policy decisions are made.[27] First, input into the early stages of the policy-making process pays off. The two biggest payments in the bill's first year of operation went to two ball-bearing firms whose lawyers helped write the bill, Torrington Company, which got

---

26. The figures in Table 5 exclude assistance to agricultural producers in the form of direct subsidies.

27. This paragraph draws on Neil King, Jr., "Why Uncle Sam Wrote a Big Check to a Sparkler Maker," *The Wall Street Journal*, December 5, 2002.

$63 million, and Timken Company, which got $31 million. Second, the incentives provided by provisions such as the Byrd Amendment affect firms' behavior. Some firms, such as Elkton Sparkler, a maker of Fourth of July sparklers, shifted from producing their product abroad to producing domestically specifically in order to be able to file dumping charges against foreign firms and collect the tariff revenues promised by the Byrd Amendment. Third, firms aren't shy in seeking protection. Torrington Company, which received $63 million in the program's first year, had sought $23.4 *billion* (yes, that letter is a "b," not a typographical error).

The U.S. administration, never a fan of the amendment, wants Congress to repeal it, especially since it was ruled a violation of U.S. WTO obligations. As of mid-2004, the debate continues. Many of the eleven countries that filed the WTO complaint have stated their intention to retaliate against the United States if it doesn't repeal the amendment soon. Such retaliation would take the form of retaliatory tariffs on selected U.S. exports—probably selected to pressure members of the U.S. Congress who support the amendment into allowing its repeal.

CASE 2: COTTON PITS FARMER VERSUS FARMER

For decades, markets for agricultural products in the industrial economies have been among the most highly protected in the world. Successive rounds of GATT/WTO talks either neglected agricultural protection or risked failure by attempting to address it. The Uruguay Round, which took the latter course, finally made modest progress by requiring countries to replace many agricultural import quotas with tariffs. In 2002, a massive new U.S. farm bill halted several years of slow progress in reducing the support that distorts agricultural markets. That bill increased subsidies to U.S. farmers by approximately $7.5 billion.

U.S. cotton farmers receive much of the subsidy payments. Approximately 25,000 U.S. farmers, with average net worth of $800,000 each, raise cotton. Approximately half of their income comes from government subsidies. These subsidies transform the United States, one of the highest-cost cotton producers, into the world's largest cotton exporter and push down the world price of cotton (see panel (b) of Figure 7). In 2001, even before the 2002 farm bill made the subsidy program still more generous, U.S. cotton farmers received subsidy payments of approximately $3.4 billion on a 9.74-billion-pound crop. With the new farm bill, farmers are now guaranteed approximately $0.70 per pound; when the market price falls below that level, government checks make up the difference.[28] The checks allow farmers to plow their 10,000-acre cotton plantations in $125,000

air-conditioned tractors and use $300,000 mechanical pickers to harvest their crop. Other big cotton subsidizers include Spain and Greece, through the EU's Common Agricultural Policy, and China, the world's biggest producer.

Cotton farming in other parts of the world is very different. Ten million rural residents grow cotton in west and central Africa. Estimates suggest they could earn $250 million more per year if the United States stopped its cotton subsidies. Most of the African farmers plant, fertilize, and pick their cotton by hand, perhaps using an aging tractor to plow. In Mali, where per-capita income is $840 per year, cotton farmers received $0.11 per pound for their 2002 crop from the state-owned cotton company (remember, U.S. farmers are guaranteed $0.70 per pound). Other important African producers include Benin, Burkina Faso, and Chad, with annual per-capita incomes in 2002 of $1,020, $1,010, and $1,000, respectively.

In 2003, as part of the preliminary talks for the Doha round of WTO trade negotiations, African cotton producers asked their industrial-country fellow members to agree to a timetable to eliminate their cotton subsidies and, in the meantime, to pay compensation of $250 million per year to the African countries harmed by the subsidies. The talks collapsed over an impasse between the EU, which refused a demand by the United States and many developing countries to negotiate to eliminate all agricultural export subsidies, and developing countries,

28. Roger Thurow and Scott Kilman, "In U.S., Cotton Farmers Thrive; In Africa, They Fight to Survive," *The Wall Street Journal*, June 26, 2002.

who refused to talk about issues of interest to the EU without progress on agriculture.

While African cotton producers complained about the damage they suffered from subsidies and asked for compensation, Brazil filed a WTO complaint against the United States. The 2002 complaint alleged that U.S. cotton subsidies distorted international trade in cotton,

encouraged excess U.S. production, and pushed down the world price. A study by one economist found that without the subsidies, U.S. cotton exports would have fallen by 41 percent between 1999 and 2001 and that the world price of cotton would have been 12.6 percent higher.[29] In early 2004, the WTO issued a preliminary ruling in favor of Brazil. The United States announced its intention to appeal the ruling.

SUMMARY

In this chapter, we examined import and export quotas, subsidies and countervailing duties, dumping, domestic-content rules and rules of origin, government-procurement policies, and technical standards. NTBs' effects are similar to those of tariffs, but the complexity and lack of transparency typical of some NTBs suggest that their costs to the world economy may be even higher than the cost of "equivalent" tariffs. Given the WTO's success in lowering tariffs—at least by industrial economies for manufactured goods—negotiations have turned increasingly to nontariff barriers. But, unfortunately, these restrictions have been much more difficult to deal with in the context of international negotiations than the tariffs discussed in Chapter Six.

LOOKING AHEAD

Despite arguments that unrestricted trade maximizes welfare for the world as a whole, pursuit of free trade as a policy clearly is the exception rather than the rule, both now and historically. The effect of trade on the distribution of income and the adjustment costs incurred when resources must move from a comparative-disadvantage industry to one of comparative advantage provide two explanations for trade restrictions. In Chapter Eight, we examine in more detail arguments presented in favor of tariffs, quotas, and other barriers to trade.

KEY TERMS

nontariff barrier (NTB)
quota
quota rents
equivalence of
   tariffs and quotas
export quota
export subsidy
countervailing duty
   (CVD)
dumping
sporadic dumping

persistent dumping
price discrimination
dumping margin
predatory dumping
antidumping duty
domestic-content
   requirements
outsourcing
rules of origin
government-procurement
   policies

buy-domestic
   requirements
technical barriers
   to trade
coverage ratio
implicit tariff
producer-subsidy
   equivalent (PSE)
consumer-subsidy
   equivalent
   (CSE)

PROBLEMS AND QUESTIONS FOR REVIEW

1. Imports of peanuts into the United States are subject to a quota, set at about 1.7 million pounds per year.
    a. Illustrate the free-trade equilibrium in the market for peanuts. Then show the quota's effects on domestic consumption, domestic production, imports, and price. Label carefully.
    b. What are the quota's welfare effects, including both the distributional effects and the overall (net) effect on the United States? Relate the effects to your diagram in part (a).

29. Edward Alden, "Cotton Report Frays the Tempers of U.S. Farmers," *Financial Times*, May 21, 2004.

    c.   In 1990, a severe drought hit Georgia, where most U.S. peanuts are grown. Illustrate the effects of the drought, assuming that policy makers don't change the quota. What happens to domestic production, domestic consumption, imports, and price as a result of the drought?

    d.   Assume that the United States is a small country in the peanut market. Now suppose that the peanut market is subject to an import tariff *instead of* the quota. The tariff is set at a level that results in the same pre-drought level of production, consumption, and price as under the quota in part (a). Illustrate the effects of the tariff *before* the drought.

    e.   Compare the effects of the drought under the tariff with those under the quota. What are the similarities and differences?

2.   Alphaland and Betaland are identical small countries. Both have a comparative advantage in good X. Alphaland imposes an export tariff on good X, and Betaland imposes an export quota. The sizes of the tariff and quota are chosen to be equivalent. Now domestic demand for good X falls in both countries. How do the effects on the domestic price, production, consumption, and exports in Alphaland compare with those in Betaland? Why?

3.   Country A is a small country with a comparative advantage in good X. The government of country A provides X producers with a subsidy of $10 for each unit of X exported. The governments of all other X-exporting countries also subsidize exports of X by $10 per unit. Evaluate the following statement: "Producers of good X in country A don't really gain from the subsidy. Nevertheless, they are unwilling to have their government stop the subsidy."

4.   Since the mid-1990s, rules of origin in NAFTA permitted Mexican-produced apparel to enter the United States with fewer quota restrictions than those faced by clothing from non-NAFTA countries as long as the Mexican clothing is manufactured from U.S.-produced textiles. The WTO Agreement on Textiles and Clothing requires the United States to eliminate quotas on clothing imports from all WTO members by 2005. What would you expect to happen to Mexican clothing exports to the United States after 2005? How does the fact that China joined the WTO in 2001 affect your answer?

5.   The domestic demand for good X is $D^d = 100 - 20P$. The domestic supply of good X is $S^d = 20 + 20P$.

    a.   Draw the domestic demand and supply curves for good X. (Remember that price appears on the vertical axis in the graph.)

    b.   If the country allows no trade in good X, what are the equilibrium price, quantity produced, and quantity consumed?

    c.   Imports of good X are available in the world market at $P_X = 1$. Draw the total supply curve. If the country allows free trade in good X, what are the equilibrium price, quantity produced domestically, quantity consumed domestically, and quantity imported?

    d.   If the country imposes an import quota of 20 units of good X, what are the equilibrium price, quantity produced domestically, quantity consumed domestically, and quantity imported?

    e.   Who gains and who loses from the quota? Does national welfare rise or fall?

    f.   Compare your answers with those for question 6 in Chapter Six.

6.   This question continues question 7 from Chapter Six. The country of Usia has a prohibitive export tax on logs. Both Usia and Themia export lumber made from logs. Usia files a complaint against Themia alleging that the government of Themia subsidizes lumber exports and that Themia's subsidized exports steal markets from Usia's lumber producers. The government of Themia is angered by Usia's accusation and countercharges that Usia's prohibitive export tax on *logs* amounts to an export subsidy for Usia's *lumber* producers. Briefly evaluate Themia's charge.

7.   Why do WTO rules require a country that imposes a technical barrier to trade, such as a food-safety standard, to show that the standard has a scientific basis? What might happen if countries were permitted to impose technical standards with no obligation to demonstrate a scientific basis for them?

8.   In 1996, potato growers in northern Maine suffered their third year of bad harvests. They expected prices for their potatoes to rise as a result; instead, imports of Canadian potatoes rose.

    a.   Illustrate in a demand-and-supply diagram why, in the absence of imports, a bad domestic harvest would have boosted domestic potato prices.

    b.   Illustrate why the possibility of Canadian imports prevents the price increase. (You may assume that the United States is a small country in the potato market.)

c.   In which case is the sum of U.S. producer and consumer surplus greater, the case with no imports, or the case with imports?

d.   How would you expect Maine potato growers to react to the increased imports?[30]

REFERENCES AND SELECTED READINGS

Baldwin, Richard E. "Regulatory Protectionism, Developing Nations, and a Two-Tier World Trade System." *Brookings Trade Forum* (2000): 237–294.
The potential of discriminatory protectionist policies to restrict developing countries' full access to the world trade system.

Blonigen, Bruce A., and Stephen E. Haynes. "Antidumping Investigations and the Pass-Through of Antidumping Duties and Exchange Rates." *American Economic Review* 92 (September 2002): 1044–1061.
Study of how much antidumping duties affect the price of imports; for advanced students.

Davis, Christina. *Food Fights Over Free Trade.* Princeton: Princeton University Press, 2003.
A political scientist's analysis of the politics of negotiations to liberalize trade in agricultural products.

Deardorff, Alan V., and Robert M. Stern. *Measurement of Nontariff Barriers.* Ann Arbor: University of Michigan Press, 1998.
Comprehensive examination of measurement issues related to NTBs.

Engel, Eduardo M. R. A. "Poisoned Grapes, Mad Cows, and Protectionism." *Journal of Policy Reform* 4 (2000): 91–112.
When do domestic policies cross the line and become protectionism? For all students.

Graham, Edward M., and J. David Richardson, eds. *Global Competition Policy.* Washington, D.C.: Institute for International Economics, 1997.
Excellent, accessible overview of countries' competition policies and their international implications.

Hoekman, Bernard, et al., eds. *Development, Trade, and the WTO.* Washington, D.C.: World Bank, 2002.
Accessible short articles on many nontariff barriers and negotiations to reduce them.

Hufbauer, Gary C., and Kimberly A. Elliott. *Measuring the Costs of Protection in the United States.* Washington, D.C.: Institute for International Economics, 1994.
Estimates the costs of protection to the U.S. economy; for all students.

Leidy, Michael. "Antidumping: Unfair Trade or Unfair Remedy?" *Finance and Development* 32 (March 1995): 27–29.
Introductory overview of the protectionist effects of antidumping policies.

Muth, Mary K., et al. "The Fable of the Bees Revisited: Causes and Consequences of the U.S. Honey Program." *Journal of Law and Economics* 46 (October 2003): 453–478.
The U.S. price-support program for honey and its link to antidumping cases; for all students.

Organization for Economic Cooperation and Development. *Indicators of Tariff and Non-Tariff Trade Barriers.* Paris: OECD, 1997.
Good source of data on OECD members' trade barriers.

Sazanami, Yoko, Shujiro Urata, and Kiroki Kawai. *Measuring the Costs of Protection in Japan.* Washington, D.C.: Institute for International Economics, 1995.
Attempt to quantify the cost to Japanese consumers and the Japanese economy as a whole of the structure of protection; for intermediate students.

Stiglitz, Joseph E. "Dumping on Free Trade: The U.S. Import Trade Laws." *Southern Economic Journal* (1997): 402–424.
Argues for a larger role for national welfare in determining policy toward imports; for all students.

United States International Trade Commission. *The Year in Trade.* Washington, D.C.: USITC, annual.
Excellent survey of current trade issues for all students. Available on CD-ROM.

United States Trade Representative. *National Trade Estimate Report on Foreign Trade Barriers.* Washington, D.C.: USTR, annual.
Annual summary of foreign countries' trade barriers that restrict U.S. exports.

Wall, Howard J. "Using the Gravity Model to Estimate the Costs of Protection." *Federal Reserve Bank of St. Louis Review* 81 (January/February 1999): 33–40.
Investigation of how much protection distorts trade patterns; for intermediate students.

Westhoff, Frank H., Beth V. Yarbrough, and Robert M. Yarbrough. "Harassment versus Lobbying for Trade Protection." *International Trade Journal* 9 (Summer 1995): 203–224.
Examines use of protection, especially antidumping and countervailing duty policy, to harass foreign producers; for intermediate students.

World Trade Organization. *Annual Report.* Geneva: WTO, annual.
Excellent source on current international trade and trade-related issues; for all students.

---

30.   NAFTA prevented Maine potato growers from getting the quota or tariff protection they wanted. However, they did persuade U.S. officials to begin around-the-clock rigorous inspections of all Canadian potato imports. Inspectors rejected approximately 20 percent of imports based on alleged faulty labeling or grading. See "Big Potatoes," *The Economist,* January 20, 1996.

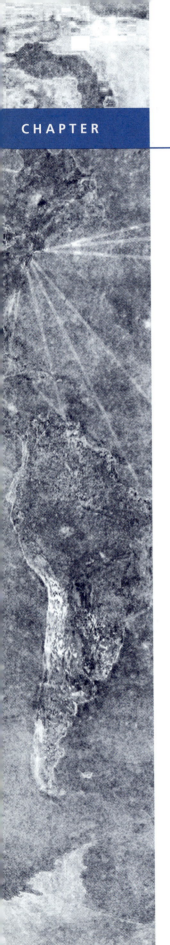

8

Arguments for Restricting Trade

1 INTRODUCTION

Chapters Six and Seven showed how international trade restrictions reduce world welfare by distorting the relationship between a good's price and its opportunity cost, causing inefficient production and consumption decisions. In this chapter, we probe the results of Chapters Six and Seven for weaknesses. Are there circumstances in which unrestricted trade isn't efficient or doesn't maximize world welfare? Can protection ever increase welfare, not just for some groups at the expense of others, but for the country or the world as a whole? Are there major aspects of the world economy that we ignored in the earlier chapters? In particular, might goals other than efficiency justify the use of protection?

2 CATEGORIES OF ARGUMENTS FOR TRADE RESTRICTIONS

In policy debates over international trade, many arguments for protection emerge. It's useful to categorize the arguments into three major groups.

Arguments that question the *assumptions* of the basic trade model comprise the first group. Assumptions frequently challenged include those of perfect competition and no externalities in either production or consumption. The situation in which all these assumptions are met is called **optimal market conditions**. A violation of one of the assumptions—for example, a monopolized industry or an externality—is referred to as a **domestic distortion**. In Chapters Two through Seven, we demonstrated that *under optimal market conditions, unrestricted trade produces an efficient result and trade restrictions reduce world welfare*. Once we relax the optimal-market-conditions assumption, the efficiency of unrestricted trade may or may not continue to hold. This chapter examines these issues.

A second category of arguments for trade restrictions focuses on trade's *distributional effects*. International trade affects the distribution of income both within each country and among countries. Both effects generate constituencies for restricting trade. Proponents of arguments in this category often couch them in somewhat deceptive terms. An explicit argument to tax domestic consumers and give the proceeds to producers in a certain industry would have scant political appeal; but an argument phrased in nationalistic terms that emphasizes preventing "them" (foreign producers) from taking something from "us" (a domestic industry) tends to meet with more success—even if it misrepresents the actual effects of the trade policy under consideration. Therefore, domestic producers seeking protection rarely claim to want to improve their own welfare at the expense of domestic consumers; instead, protection-seeking groups try to identify their own interests with those of the country as a whole to make their calls for protection seem more public spirited and less self-interested.

A third group of justifications for protection includes so-called *noneconomic arguments*. The term doesn't imply that the arguments have nothing to do with economics or that economics has nothing to say about their relative merits. This group of arguments does, however, emphasize elements beyond the narrow scope of economics by pointing out that a society typically values goals such as national security and equity along with economic efficiency. Economists have an important role to play in evaluating these justifications for protection: primarily providing information about the trade-offs between economic efficiency and other societal goals, so a well-informed policy decision can be made. If a society desires (as all do) to pursue goals in addition to economic efficiency, what kinds of policies will best achieve those goals with a minimum cost in terms of lost efficiency?

3 WHAT ABOUT "INFANT" INDUSTRIES?

One of the oldest arguments for protection, the **infant-industry argument**, makes a case for short-term protection of a new industry temporarily unable to compete with more-experienced rivals in other countries. Advocates of infant-industry protection admit that trade restrictions cause welfare losses along the lines we discussed in Chapters Six and Seven. But, they argue, those short-term losses will be more than offset when the industry matures and can compete without protection in world markets. Figure 1 illustrates the short- and long-run effects of infant-industry protection for the Y industry, where we assume for simplicity that protection takes the form of a prohibitive import tariff imposed by a small country.

Without protection, domestic production initially occurs at p_0 and consumption at c_0. (*Why?*) A prohibitive import tariff on good Y shifts production and consumption to p_1 and c_1, reducing welfare from U_0 to U_1.[1] But if temporary protection allows the infant Y industry to "grow up"—that is, to perfect its production techniques, train its workforce, and develop management skills, this improved productivity will shift the future production possibilities frontier outward.[2] At this point, policy makers would (theoretically) remove the protection, and the industry could compete with foreign rivals. The country is assumed to be small, so development of its new industry doesn't affect world prices. The new long-run equilibrium involves production at point p_2 and consumption at c_2. Welfare has increased to utility level U_2, from U_0 before the protection of the infant Y industry.

Economists generally are rather skeptical of arguments for infant-industry protection. The first reason is the difficulty in spotting good candidates for protection. Many firms and industries are born each year, and many don't survive. Successful infant-industry protection would require policy makers to recognize *in advance* industries that have a potential comparative advantage, that is, those that would, on maturing, compete successfully in world markets. A wrong decision could prove very costly, involving years of inefficiency with no reward.[3] The challenge of picking winners becomes even harder once we realize that patterns of comparative advantage change over time.

1. A prohibitive tariff shifts the country back to its autarky equilibrium. A lower tariff would place the country at some point between the free-trade and prohibitive-tariff outcomes.

2. This process often is called *learning by doing* (see section 6.3 in Chapter Five).

3. Even Japan, whose rapid growth and industrialization during the 1950s and 1960s many attribute to successful infant-industry policies, made a number of costly blunders. See Case Four and Table 2 later in the chapter.

Figure 1   **How Does Protection Affect an Infant Industry?**

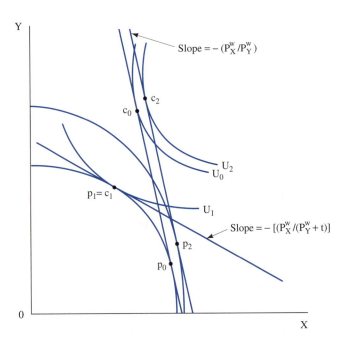

A prohibitive tariff on imports of good Y imposes a short-run welfare loss due to inefficiently high domestic production (p_1 rather than p_0) and inefficiently low domestic consumption (c_1 versus c_0) of Y. If the infant industry matures and competes in world markets without protection, the country's production possibilities frontier expands beyond the frontier that would have existed without the temporary protection afforded the Y industry. The economy then will be able to produce at p_2 and consume at c_2, a previously unattainable outcome.

Suppose that a certain industry were recognized widely as an excellent prospect. In this case, why would the industry need even temporary protection? If private investors expected the industry to succeed, they would willingly invest in it and even suffer short-run losses in return for the hope of future profits.[4] The infant-industry argument must assume that government policy makers somehow are more able than private investors to spot winners. But private investors have a big economic incentive to search out good prospects, so most economists doubt policy makers' ability to do better. Even if government policy makers somehow became aware of a new industry likely to succeed but overlooked by private investors, an alternative to infant-industry protection would be for the government to provide investors with information about the industry to encourage them to take advantage of the profitable opportunity.

A second problem with infant-industry protection is that early support of an industry that turns out successful can't prove that the protection itself constituted a wise policy. For the protection to provide *net* benefits, the industry must be successful enough to more than offset the efficiency losses incurred during the protection period. Perhaps the industry would have succeeded without protection; if so, the protection-related costs

---

4. This happens most reliably in countries with developed financial markets to channel funds effectively from savers to investors. Some developing countries still lack access to such markets, although many developing countries have integrated themselves into world financial markets. For countries that remain isolated, removing barriers to world capital markets probably represents a more promising policy than infant-industry protection justified by presence of those barriers.

incurred were wasted. Also, the resources spent in developing one infant industry could have been spent on another industry, one that might have proven even more successful.

A third problem is based on the politics of the policy-making process. The infant-industry argument justifies only *temporary* protection. Historically, removal of protection has proven very difficult. Even if changing conditions allow a now-mature industry to compete successfully without protection, maintaining the protection still permits the industry to gain at the expense of domestic consumers and foreign producers. This creates an incentive for producers in the industry to lobby for continued protection even long after any infant-industry justification fades.

Perhaps the most important basis for economists' skepticism toward infant-industry protection is the availability of superior policies for dealing with infant industries. Assume that an industry does exist that could develop successfully if it received short-run assistance. That is, ignore for the moment the problem of sorting potential winner industries from losers, and assume that future gains from protection would exceed current welfare losses. Assume also that private investors won't invest in the industry despite its promise. The policy that encourages the industry to develop at minimal efficiency cost to the economy is a production subsidy. This represents the first example of what will emerge in this chapter as a general rule: *The least-cost policy in response to a distortion is the policy that targets the policy goal directly rather than indirectly.* In the case of an infant industry, the goal is to encourage production in the industry in order to facilitate learning and the perfection of productive techniques. If increasing production is the goal, the direct policy is to temporarily subsidize production, not to restrict trade, even temporarily.

Figure 2 illustrates the superiority of the direct policy, a production subsidy, over the indirect policy, an import tariff. Panel (a) repeats the effects of a prohibitive tariff on imports of good Y, and panel (b) shows the effects of a production subsidy to Y

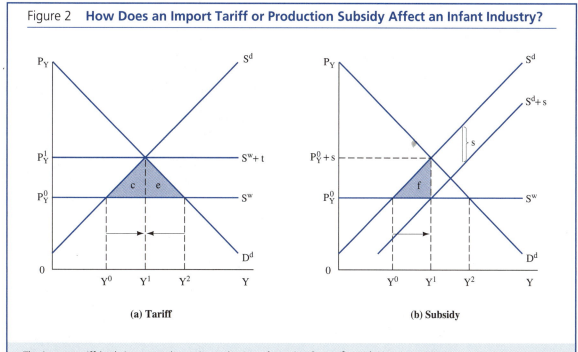

Figure 2   **How Does an Import Tariff or Production Subsidy Affect an Infant Industry?**

(a) Tariff

(b) Subsidy

The import tariff both increases domestic production of good Y from Y^0 to Y^1 (the desired goal) and decreases domestic consumption of Y from Y^2 to Y^1 (an unintended source of inefficiency). The production subsidy increases domestic production but leaves consumption unaffected.

producers. Both policies can generate equal increases in domestic production. The tariff operates by artificially raising the price of imports from P_Y^0 to P_Y^1 (where $P_Y^1 = P_Y^0 + t$), which allows domestic producers to raise their price to P_Y^1 and encourages them to expand domestic production from Y^0 to Y^1. By raising the price of good Y, the tariff also discourages consumption of Y; consumption falls from Y^2 to Y^1. The sum of the areas of triangles c and e captures the total loss of welfare to the country from the *two* inefficiencies caused by the tariff.[5]

The production subsidy of s (= t) per unit in panel (b) encourages domestic producers to produce a larger quantity of good Y at each price paid by consumers, because firms receive the subsidy payment along with that price. Domestic production rises from Y^0 to Y^1. The subsidy to producers doesn't affect the price consumers face (P_Y^0) and leaves consumption of good Y unchanged. The area of triangle f measures the net welfare loss caused by the subsidy, because for each unit of Y between Y^0 and Y^1 the opportunity cost of domestic production exceeds the cost of imports. Of course, domestic taxpayers must finance the subsidy; but the full amount of the subsidy, with the exception of area f, is transferred to domestic producers. Therefore, only area f represents a deadweight loss to society.

The import tariff and production subsidy have identical impacts on domestic production of good Y, so the two policies are equally effective in helping the infant industry develop. The production inefficiencies, represented by triangle c in the case of the tariff and by triangle f in the case of the subsidy, are identical. But the tariff involves a second inefficiency, represented by triangle e, because the tariff distorts the consumption decision by causing a rise in P_Y. The production subsidy, by targeting the policy goal more directly, encourages domestic production at a lower cost in lost economic efficiency. The production subsidy also has an additional advantage over the tariff: The visible budget cost of the subsidy makes the policy's cost transparent, allowing an informed debate in society about the desirability of supporting the particular industry in question. The tariff, on the other hand, involves costs "hidden" in higher consumer prices.

Brazil's Informatics Law provides the most infamous example of infant-industry protection that backfired. Since 1975, Brazil had informally prohibited imports of electronics products, including microchips, fax machines, and especially personal computers. In 1984, the highly restrictive Informatics Law replaced the informal prohibitions. As Brazil's secretary for science and technology put it, "It was enough for a Brazilian company to say that it was planning to develop the same thing eventually and imports were banned." The law was intended to build a domestic electronics industry by creating "market reserves," that is, reserving the domestic market for domestic firms by prohibiting imports and banning foreign companies from building local electronics manufacturing facilities. The law had unintended but predictable results: an uncompetitive and technologically outdated Brazilian electronics industry and electronics products that cost two and a half times world prices. Even Brazilian electronics firms—the supposed beneficiaries of the law—complained that it made reasonably priced, high-quality parts unavailable, thereby making it impossible for Brazilian firms to produce goods that could compete in world markets. Finally, growing opposition to the law produced change. New policies eliminated the market reserve (but replaced it with high tariffs) and allowed foreign firms to own up to 49 percent stakes in joint ventures with Brazilian partners; but government procurement of informatics and telecommunications equipment still grants complex preferences to domestic firms.

---

5. Section 4 in Chapter Six presents a more detailed treatment of the effects of an import tariff by a small country.

4 WHAT IF MARKETS AREN'T COMPETITIVE?

4.1 The Optimal Tariff: Monopoly in a World Market

We've already seen one argument for protection based on monopoly power: the optimal tariff argument in section 5.2 of Chapter Six. When a single country comprises a large enough share of the world market in a good to achieve market power, that country may be able to gain at trading partners' expense by imposing a tariff.

Figure 3 presents the graphical analysis of the optimal-tariff argument. The country is large enough that its imposition of a tariff on imports of good Y forces exporting countries to accept a lower price (P_Y^2 instead of P_Y^0). As a result, foreign producers pay a portion of the tariff revenue by accepting lower prices for their product. If the revenue gained from foreign producers (area s in Figure 3) exceeds the deadweight efficiency losses caused by the tariff (the sum of triangles m and r), the tariff-imposing country enjoys a net welfare gain *at the expense of the exporting country*. The optimal tariff rate is the one that maximizes this net gain or (area s − area [m + r]).

Note that, unlike some arguments for protection discussed in this chapter, the optimal tariff argument takes a strictly national perspective; that is, the imposing country gains, but total world welfare suffers, with imposition of an optimal tariff. Use of an optimal tariff, like any other exploitation of monopoly power, is a beggar-thy-neighbor policy. Gains come only at the expense of others, and the gains to the monopolist are smaller than the losses imposed on others (in the case of the optimal tariff, domestic

---

Figure 3   What Are the Effects of a Tariff on Imports by a Large Country?

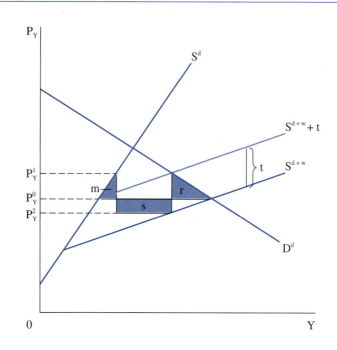

By exploiting its monopoly power, the country can gain the equivalent of area s in revenue from foreign producers. The areas of triangles m and r measure the deadweight welfare losses due to the tariff. The optimum tariff maximizes the net gain to the country from the tariff (area s − area [m + r]).

consumers and foreign producers). In addition, use of an optimal tariff invites retaliation by trading partners, which would further reduce the gains from trade.

4.2 Protection and Monopolized Industries

Another monopoly-based argument for protection focuses not on the monopoly power of a *country* in a world market, as in the case of the optimal tariff, but on the monopoly power of *firms* in a domestic industry. Recall the mechanism by which trade expands world output under perfect competition. In autarky, the opportunity cost of producing a good differs across countries. Under perfect competition, the price of a good equals its opportunity cost; thus, the relative price of a good also varies across countries in autarky. Unrestricted trade equalizes the relative price of a good across countries by allowing productive specialization and exchange. Under unrestricted trade, the relative price of a good equalizes across countries, as does the good's opportunity cost of production. Unrestricted trade satisfies the criteria for efficiency: Each good is produced at the lowest possible opportunity cost and to the point at which price equals marginal cost. The equality of relative prices and opportunity costs that follows from the assumption of perfect competition generates this efficiency result.

PRICE AND OPPORTUNITY COST FOR A MONOPOLIST   When we relax the perfect-competition assumption and allow a firm to monopolize an industry, the good's price no longer equals its marginal cost. A profit-maximizing monopolist will produce the level of output at which marginal revenue equals marginal cost, as in Figure 4. Price exceeds marginal revenue for a monopolist (see footnote 15 in Chapter Seven),

Figure 4   How Does a Monopolist Choose Its Output and Price?

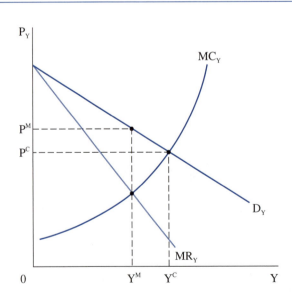

A monopolist maximizes profit by producing where marginal revenue (MR) equals marginal cost (MC). The monopolist's output (Y^M) is lower and price (P^M) higher than the perfectly competitive outcome (Y^C and P^C). Marginal revenue is less than price for the monopolist, so price exceeds marginal cost. Consumers value the marginal unit produced by the monopolist by more than the opportunity cost of producing it; thus, the monopolist's output is inefficiently low.

so marginal cost is less than price in a monopolized industry. The monopolist produces a smaller level of output and charges a higher price (Y^M and P^M in Figure 4) than if the industry were organized competitively (Y^C and P^C).

More important from the standpoint of international trade, monopoly power in a market causes relative prices to fail to reflect the true opportunity costs of production. If both the X and Y industries are perfectly competitive in country B, then $P_X^B = MC_X^B$ and $P_Y^B = MC_Y^B$, so

$$P_X^B/P_Y^B = MC_X^B/MC_Y^B, \qquad\qquad [1]$$

or relative prices reflect opportunity costs. Graphically, the autarky production and consumption decision in a country in which both industries are perfectly competitive appears as in Figure 5. The autarky price ratio equals the marginal rate of substitution along the indifference curve and the marginal rate of transformation, or relative opportunity costs, of the two goods. (For a review, see section 2.2 in Chapter Three.) Production and consumption occur at point $p_0 = c_0$ on indifference curve U_0. This outcome is efficient in the restricted sense that U_0 represents the highest level of utility attainable *without trade*.

If one industry—say, Y—is monopolized in country A, then $P_X^A = MC_X^A$ but $P_Y^A > MC_Y^A$; so,

$$P_X^A/P_Y^A < MC_X^A/MC_Y^A, \qquad\qquad [2]$$

and relative prices don't reflect opportunity costs. In Figure 5, monopolization of the Y industry causes country A to locate at point $p_1 = c_1$ on indifference curve U_1.

Figure 5   How Does a Monopoly Affect Production and Consumption in Autarky?

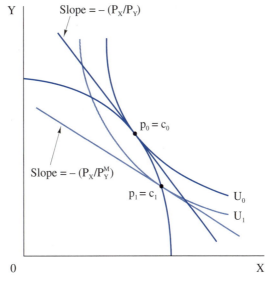

With two perfectly competitive industries, production and consumption occur at $p_0 = c_0$. The relative production costs of the two goods (represented by the slope of the production possibilities frontier) equal both the goods' relative price (represented by the slope of the price line) and consumers' marginal rate of substitution between the goods (represented by the slope of the indifference curve). The introduction of a monopoly in Y raises the relative price of good Y to P_Y^M, which is greater than its opportunity cost. Production and consumption occur at point $p_1 = c_1$, where the slope of the production possibilities frontier exceeds that of the price line and indifference curve. The monopoly lowers the level of utility attainable in autarky from U_0 to U_1.

The monopoly price charged for good Y restricts both production and consumption of that good. This outcome is inefficient for two reasons: Not only does country A fail to realize the potential gains available through international trade; the monopoly causes utility even in autarky to be lower than if both industries were competitive.

TRADE WITH A MONOPOLIZED INDUSTRY IN BOTH COUNTRIES Suppose that monopolies characterize the Y industry in both countries A and B. In autarky, both countries suffer from the monopoly-induced inefficiency illustrated in Figure 5. Allowing international trade can improve the welfare of both countries. Forced to compete with its foreign rival, each firm, formerly a domestic monopolist, lowers its price and increases its output.

Actual international trade may or may not occur. If the two countries are identical and the monopolized industry produces a homogeneous good, there's no need for actual trade. The important point is that just the *possibility* of trade forces the firms to compete by lowering price and expanding output. A firm that failed to respond in this way to the opening of trade would find itself undersold in its domestic market by its foreign rival.[6] Lowering barriers to international trade in a monopolized industry can produce gains even greater than those from opening trade in a competitive industry, because gains come from undermining monopoly power in the market as well as from the usual specialization and exchange. Although the welfare of each country improves as trade enhances efficiency, the new rivalry harms the (former) monopolists by restricting their ability to act as monopolists. This is just one of many cases where it's important to remember that *a country's welfare and the welfare of a particular firm or group of firms are not the same.* Restrictions on international trade may help firms, but almost always at the expense of consumers and the rest of the economy.

TRADE WITH A MONOPOLIZED INDUSTRY IN ONE COUNTRY Now suppose that the Y industry is monopolized in country A but competitive in country B. Intra-country competition among the country B firms results in a price of good Y equal to Y's opportunity cost in country B. The monopoly in A, however, charges a price for good Y above the opportunity cost of production. Therefore, if the cost of producing good Y is the same in both countries, B firms will offer the good for sale at a lower price than will the A firm. With no restrictions on trade in good Y, the B firms can export to A, breaking the A firm's monopoly. So, *given similar costs of production, countries tend to export goods produced by industries that are structured competitively compared to their foreign rivals.*

Maintaining a domestic monopoly in an industry structured competitively in other countries requires import barriers to prevent the monopoly, with its artificially high price, from being undersold. This provides a useful explanation for several long-standing trade disputes between the United States and other countries, including members of the European Union, over trade in utility-related goods, such as telecommunications and power-generating equipment. In the late 1970s and 1980s, the United States deregulated many of its utilities industries, such as telephone, airlines, railroads, and trucking, making them more competitive. (*Deregulation* refers to the policy process through which governments withdraw the special privileges they've granted that make firms monopolies.) Prices fell dramatically in the United States following deregulation as the affected markets became more competitive. Other countries have engaged in some utility deregulation, but the pace of the process has been slower than in the

6. A monopolist's efforts to maintain the monopoly price in the domestic market and capture a share of the rival's market by cutting price there can result in dumping charges. Such behavior is called *reciprocal dumping.*

**Figure 6   International Trade Causes a Monopolist to Behave
as If Its Industry Were Competitive**

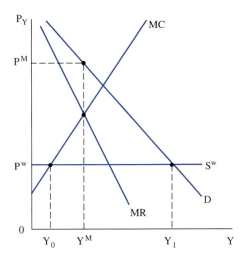

A monopolist in a small country can't ignore the competitive nature of the worldwide industry under free trade. With no trade, the monopolist produces Y^M and charges P^M. With trade, the monopolist produces Y_0 and charges the world price, P^W.

United States, so prices remain high abroad. The trade disputes involve U.S. firms' complaints about trade barriers that other countries maintain to block access of the now-cheaper U.S. goods.

More generally, unrestricted international trade, along with antitrust policy or regulation, can be a powerful tool in limiting monopoly power. The size of a country's domestic market may support only a small number of firms and, as a result, allow them significant monopoly power. By allowing foreign firms to enter the domestic market, international trade can limit domestic firms' ability to raise price above marginal cost. In fact, free trade can force a monopolist to act as if its industry were perfectly competitive!

Figure 6 illustrates the situation facing a domestic monopolist that produces good Y in a small country. With no trade, the firm would choose to produce the level of output, Y^M, at which marginal revenue equals marginal cost, and to charge the monopoly price, P^M. But if the small country allows international trade in Y, foreign producers would undersell a monopolist who followed that strategy. The importing country is small; so, with trade, consumers can import as much good Y as they want at the world price of P^W, which isn't affected by the small country's monopolized industry. With trade, if the monopolist tries to charge any price above P^W, it can't sell its product. Therefore, the monopolist will charge P^W and produce Y_0, the output at which the firm's marginal cost equals the world price. Consumers will import $Y_1 - Y_0$. Unrestricted trade forces the monopolist to behave as if the industry were perfectly competitive. This happens because trade makes the scope of the relevant industry worldwide, and the worldwide industry *is* competitive, despite the small country's monopoly firm.

TARIFFS AND QUOTAS WITH MONOPOLY   Panel (a) in Figure 7 illustrates that a tariff on a good produced by a small country's monopoly firm generates exactly the same effects as if the industry were competitive and subject to a tariff. The tariff raises the price

Figure 7   A Monopolist Behaves Differently under a Tariff and a Quota

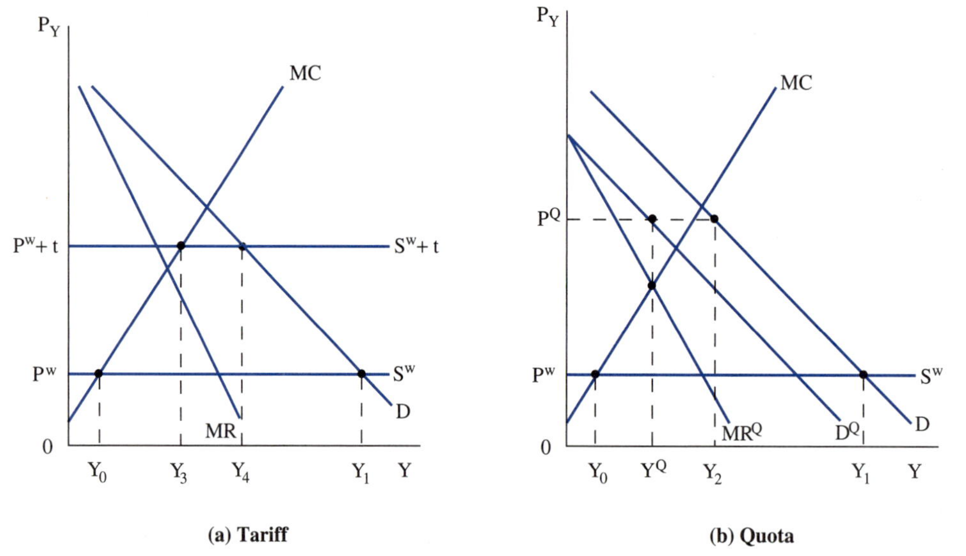

(a) Tariff

(b) Quota

The quota allows the monopolist more market power. The firm produces less output ($Y^Q < Y_3$) and charges a higher price ($P^Q > [P^W + t]$) under an import quota (panel (b)) than under a tariff (panel (a)).

the monopolist can charge by the amount of the tariff, t, to $P^W + t$. The monopolist produces a higher level of output, Y_3; and consumption falls to Y_4. Unless the tariff is prohibitive, the possibility of international trade still limits the monopolist from charging the full monopoly price.

Panel (b) shows the same monopolist's price and output choices when protection takes the form of a quota rather than a tariff. The quota shifts the demand curve facing the monopolist to the left by the amount of the quota, from D to D^Q. The marginal revenue curve corresponding to D^Q is MR^Q. The monopolist produces the level of output at which marginal cost equals this new marginal revenue, or Y^Q in panel (b), and charges price P^Q, which we read off the quota-adjusted demand curve. Consumers purchase Y_2 units, of which they import $Y_2 - Y^Q$.

Comparing panels (a) and (b) in Figure 7, note that the tariff and the quota cause the monopolist to behave differently, even when we define the two policies to allow the same quantity of imports. The tariff does allow the monopolist to produce more and charge a higher price than under unrestricted trade; but the monopolist knows that raising price above $P^W + t$ will cause consumers to buy from foreign suppliers. This constraint on the monopolist's behavior evaporates under the quota. No matter how high the monopolist raises price, consumers can't shift to imports. So quotas allow monopolists to act more like monopolists; they produce less and charge higher prices than under equivalent tariffs.

When domestic firms sell in export markets, any monopoly power they have allows them to raise prices at the expense of foreign rather than domestic consumers. This idea of capturing monopoly profits on foreign sales provides the basis for a branch of international-trade theory known as strategic trade policy.

4.3 Strategic Trade Policy

Strategic trade policy focuses on trade policy among small interdependent groups of players—firms and governments—in which any action brings a reaction, leading to games of strategy. For example, when can a firm deter a foreign rival from entering a profitable export market; or when can country A, through its choice of trade policy, cause country B to pursue a policy more favorable to A than the policy B otherwise would follow? Here we examine the strategies firms use and whether government policies can or should be used to help domestic firms fare well in international markets. There are two basic types of strategic trade policy models, based on the concepts of *profit shifting* and the *learning curve*. We'll examine each and then address practical problems and dangers related to strategic trade policy.

PROFIT-SHIFTING STRATEGIC TRADE POLICY Firms behave strategically in international markets when the number of firms is small enough to confer on them some degree of market power. Then, firms treat one another as rivals and respond to one another's actions. If the world market for a good is one in which economic profits exist, individual firms will enact strategies designed to capture the largest possible share of those profits.[7] In designing its strategy, each firm will take account of rivals' reactions.

From a national perspective, each country wants its firms in the international market to capture the largest possible share of available profits.[8] This goal coincides with the goal of the firms themselves. Typically, when the goal of individual firms matches that of policy makers, there's little need for active government policy; individual firms, acting in their own self-interest, accomplish the policy makers' goal as well. In situations involving games of strategy, however, this intuitive result can break down. Even though firms and policy makers have the same goal (shifting profits in an international market from foreign firms to domestic ones), there may be a role for an active policy to accomplish this. In other words, government policy may be able to accomplish **profit shifting** that domestic firms, either individually or as a group, can't.

Assume that a market consists of one firm in country A and one in country B.[9] Now suppose that the A firm wants to capture a larger share of the international market and its profits. If the A firm expands production with no output reduction by the B firm, the market price will fall and both firms will be worse off. Obviously, what the A firm wants is for the B firm to cut production and allow the A firm to expand its market share; however, the B firm has no incentive to go along.

One possibility is for the A firm to try to bluff the B firm into reducing output. For example, the A firm might threaten, "If you don't cut your production, I'll expand mine and drive the price of the product so low that you'll suffer losses." From the B firm's perspective, the question is whether that threat is credible; that is, should the B firm expect the A firm to carry out the threat? The answer is no. The threat isn't credible, because carrying it out obviously would impose losses on the A firm, whose own price would fall. Thus, the B firm, unimpressed with the threat, carries on business as usual, thwarting the A firm's effort to capture a larger share of the market.

Now enter the country A government. Can it devise a policy that will make the country B firm take the A firm's threat seriously? If so, the A firm can force the B firm to

---

7. Recall that economic profits exist in the long run only in markets characterized by some degree of monopoly power. In perfectly competitive markets, any positive economic profits lead to entry by additional firms, which eventually drives economic profit to zero.

8. Of course, monopoly profits come at consumers' expense. The perspective taken in the strategic trade policy literature is that, assuming an international monopoly exists along with its burden on consumers, each country wants its firms to capture the largest possible share of worldwide profits. The only alternative is to allow foreign firms to capture them.

9. Economists call markets that consist of two firms *duopolies*, a special case of oligopoly.

cut production, allowing the A firm to take up the slack and the accompanying profits. Suppose, for example, that the government of country A promises its domestic firm an export subsidy so the firm will find it still profitable to export even if the market price of the good falls to a very low level (as it would if the A firm carried out its threat to increase production). Then the A firm's threat becomes credible; carrying it out no longer will impose losses on the A firm but still will do so on the B firm. Without any retaliatory intervention by the government of country B, the B firm will respond by cutting production, allowing the A firm to expand its market share. The promised export subsidy facilitates the A firm's success by giving it the ability to credibly threaten the B firm.

The country A *firm* clearly gains; it captures a larger share of the world market and can charge a higher price thanks to the foreign rival's retreat. Whether country A *as a whole* gains is more complicated. Domestic A taxpayers must pick up the tab for the export subsidy, so the subsidy payment itself can only transfer income from taxpayers to the subsidized firm. But, depending on the number of firms in the market and on consumption patterns, the increased monopoly profits earned by the domestic firm in foreign markets may allow the subsidizing country to enjoy a net gain from its profit-shifting policy. This is possible *only* if the government can alter the strategic interaction between the two firms, causing them to make different choices than they would in the absence of the government's policy. The country as a whole can gain *only* if the subsidy causes the domestic firm to behave more aggressively, which, in turn, causes the foreign firm to retreat and produce less. This scenario is possible only in markets with a small number of firms, each of which possesses market power. Profit-shifting strategic trade policy can't work in competitive industries.

THE LEARNING CURVE AND STRATEGIC TRADE POLICY   Learning-curve models of strategic trade policy are similar to infant-industry models. As we saw in section 6.3 of Chapter Five, the basic idea is that firms in some industries learn by producing, a phenomenon known as *moving down the learning curve* or *learning by doing*. As the firm accumulates production experience, its average costs fall, making it more competitive in world markets. If the industry is one in which the presence of economic profits characterizes the world market, domestic firms' ability to capture a larger share of export markets means an ability to capture a larger share of those profits. The goal of government policy in such a scenario is to provide domestic firms with large enough markets to allow the firms to move down their learning curves.[10]

One obvious way to provide domestic firms with a large market is to restrict imports to reserve the domestic market for domestic firms. Tariffs, quotas, or other import restrictions can accomplish this task. If the domestic market is large enough to allow domestic firms to move down their learning curves, protection of the domestic market may, by making domestic firms more competitive, allow those firms to capture larger shares of export markets. Such a policy has the secondary effect of making foreign rivals less competitive by reducing their scale of production and raising their average costs. Protection of the domestic market thus becomes a tool to expand domestic firms' exports.

Domestic *firms* clearly gain from export-promotion policies. Domestic *consumers*, however, must pay higher prices in the protected home market. Thus, the country *as a whole* enjoys a net gain only if the domestic firm sells a large share of its output abroad so that foreign rather than domestic consumers bear most of the burden of the high prices. Once again, there's little doubt that protection can help the firms receiving protection; but the overall net welfare effects, even domestically, still are likely to be negative.

---

10. The learning-curve argument for protection applies only if firms can learn from domestic but not foreign firms' production. Evidence suggests that this isn't the case, at least in some industries; see section 6.4 in Chapter Five.

PROBLEMS AND PRECAUTIONS   What are the practical problems and possible dangers in using strategic trade policies? One of the most basic problems in trying to apply such a policy is defining the nationalities of firms. Given the spread of multinational enterprises, joint ventures, partnerships, and foreign stock ownership, firms' nationalities have become much less clear. Determining exactly which firms a government would want to assist with the tools of strategic trade policy becomes problematic. If the U.S. government wanted to shift economic profits toward "American" firms, exactly which firms would it assist? Firms whose stock is owned primarily by U.S. citizens, firms with production plants located in the United States, or firms that use inputs manufactured in the United States?

A second problem centers on the sensitivity of strategic trade policy recommendations to the precise assumptions of the model. For example, in profit-shifting models, if we assume that firms practice their rivalry by setting prices (and allowing quantities to be determined by market conditions) rather than by setting quantities (and allowing prices to be determined by market conditions), the optimal strategic policy recommendation switches from an export subsidy to an export tax.[11] Similarly, changes in assumptions about the number of domestic firms in the industry can shift the policy prescription from an export subsidy to an export tax, similar to the optimal export tax of section 10.2 in Chapter Six. Monopoly profits—the competition for which forms the basis for all strategic trade policies—may disappear if entry occurs in response to the policies; thus, strategic trade policies prove useless or counterproductive in industries without substantial entry barriers. All these considerations contribute to the difficulty of pinpointing industries that satisfy the requirements for successful strategic trade policy. Studies suggest that the commercial aircraft industry probably satisfies the criteria as well as any existing industry.

Like all beggar-thy-neighbor policies, strategic trade policies rely on the assumption that rival governments don't retaliate. If, in the profit-shifting case, both governments subsidize their respective firms, both countries end up worse off than in the no-subsidy case. Taxpayers in both countries bear the burden of the subsidies, but neither firm gets to enjoy the increased monopoly profits that come with increased market share, because neither firm will back down in the face of the other firm's government-backed threat.

Another issue concerns the distributional effect of such policies. As noted earlier, the pool of profits over which firms and governments fight the strategic-trade-policy battle comes from higher prices paid by consumers. Therefore, even though some may see it as preferable for "domestic" rather than "foreign" firms to capture those profits, the issue of government-assisted redistribution from consumers to (large, profitable, multinational) firms remains.

Finally, but perhaps most important, when a government chooses to become involved in an active policy of trade intervention, the system is subject to abuse by special-interest groups. In spite of stringent industry-characteristic requirements for successful strategic trade policy, producers in virtually all industries have an incentive to lobby for trade restrictions, in the guise of strategic trade policy, to gain protection from foreign rivals.

5 WHAT IF THERE ARE EXTERNALITIES?

Among the assumptions we used in deriving the result that unrestricted trade maximizes world welfare was the absence of externalities in either production or consumption. An **externality** exists when a good's production or consumption generates effects on bystanders not taken into account in the production or consumption decision.

---

11. In the formal language of strategic trade theory, price-setting behavior characterizes models having Bertrand assumptions and quantity-setting behavior characterizes models having Cournot assumptions.

Pollution provides the most common example of an externality. Without anti-pollution laws, a chemical firm may just dump its waste into a river. The resulting pollution imposes costs on individuals outside the firm (such as families who want to use the river for recreation or firms downstream that want clean river water to use in their plants). The chemical firm, meanwhile, has little incentive to take these external costs into account in making its decisions about how much output to produce. Pollution generates a **negative externality**; it imposes *costs* on others. When production of a good involves negative externalities, output of that good tends to be inefficiently big from society's point of view. The chemical firm produces too much output because it fails to consider a portion of the cost of producing the chemicals, that is, the cost of pollution to individuals outside the firm.

Production also may involve **positive externalities** by generating *benefits* for third parties not considered in the decision-making process. In this case, a firm will tend to produce too little of the good from society's perspective. Suppose that a firm, in the process of producing its output, teaches workers skills also useful in other firms. The other firms get benefits from the original firm's production. The original firm has no incentive to weigh the benefits of its training to other firms in deciding how much to produce or how many workers to train.

Consumption also can involve either negative or positive externalities. Consumption of cigarettes, for example, imposes costs on nonsmokers. As long as smokers ignore these costs in deciding how much to smoke, too much smoking occurs from society's perspective. Education generates positive consumption externalities. An education clearly benefits the individual obtaining it; but, by producing a more informed voter and citizen, it also benefits others. If individuals ignore these external benefits, they will choose inefficiently low levels of education.

Economic efficiency requires that each activity be conducted to the point at which its marginal benefit equals its marginal cost. The relevant benefits and costs include those enjoyed or suffered by individuals *other than* the consumers or producers of the good. Externalities represent costs and benefits that may be ignored in the decision-making process, so they can cause inefficient outcomes. Many government policies seek to eliminate or reduce the inefficiencies caused by positive and negative production and consumption externalities. Proponents of protectionism or trade-restricting policies often cite externalities as justifications for their proposed policies. The next two sections examine trade restrictions as ways to deal with externalities.

5.1 Production Externalities

Increasing (decreasing) production in industries that involve positive (negative) production externalities may raise welfare. We begin by considering the case of a positive production externality where the policy goal is to increase production to capture the external benefits associated with a higher level of output. Chapters Six and Seven explored several restrictions on international trade that have the effect of increasing domestic production.

Suppose production in the Y industry provides valuable worker training that benefits firms outside the industry. In Figure 8, D^d and S^d represent domestic demand and domestic supply of good Y. Recall that the height of S^d represents the opportunity cost to Y firms of producing each unit of output. The S^d curve is upward sloping because of Y firms' increasing costs. But besides the cost borne by the Y-producing firms, each unit of Y output now generates external training benefits for other firms. These *marginal external benefits* (MEB) must be combined with the Y firms' costs to ascertain the full opportunity costs to society of producing an additional unit of Y, given by $S^d + MEB$.

The country under consideration has a comparative disadvantage in production of Y and therefore imports a large percentage of the Y consumed. Under free trade, the country would consume Y_0 units and produce only Y_1 domestically. This outcome

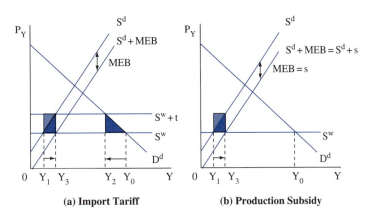

Figure 8 An Import Tariff and a Production Subsidy by a Small Country in Response to a Positive Production Externality

(a) Import Tariff

(b) Production Subsidy

Panel (a) represents the standard analysis of the effects of a tariff. The Y industry generates marginal external benefits of MEB. By increasing domestic production of good Y from Y_1 to Y_3, the tariff allows the country to capture external benefits equal to the shaded rectangle in panel (a). The shaded triangles in panel (a) represent the standard deadweight welfare losses from the tariff. The difference between the shaded rectangle and the sum of the darker shaded triangles in panel (a) gives the tariff's net welfare effect. The production subsidy in panel (b) increases domestic production without distorting prices and consumption. The country captures the same external benefits as under the import tariff (the shaded rectangle), but avoids the welfare loss caused by inefficient consumption.

ignores the external training benefits and would be efficient with no externality; but, with the externality, production of Y_1 is inefficiently low. Efficiency requires production of Y_3—the level at which the value consumers place on the last unit produced (given by the height of D^d at the world price given by the supply of imports, S^W) equals the full opportunity cost to society, which now includes the cost borne by the Y firms plus the external training benefits (given by the height of $S^d + MEB$). Now let's consider two policies that could shift output from the inefficiently low Y_1 to the efficient level of Y_3.

Imposing a restriction on Y imports, such as a tariff or quota, would allow the country to increase domestic production of Y and capture the external benefits of the additional training. Figure 8 panel (a) assumes that the (small) country chooses to impose a tariff on imports.[12] The tariff increases domestic production of Y from Y_1 to Y_3, which leads to an increase in external benefits equal to the shaded rectangle. The tariff also imposes the standard welfare losses represented by the two darkly shaded triangles.

The net welfare effect of the import tariff depends on the relative sizes of the shaded areas. If the standard welfare losses from the tariff (the two triangles) exceed the external benefits of expanded production (the rectangle), the tariff reduces welfare. If the external benefits of increased domestic production more than offset the welfare losses, the tariff increases net welfare.

Although we can't be certain whether a tariff would improve welfare compared with the case in which policy makers simply ignore the positive production externality, we can be sure that a superior policy for dealing with the externality exists. The tariff confronts the production externality *indirectly*—by restricting imports. A policy that *directly* encouraged increased production of Y

---

12. Neither the assumption that the country is small nor that the trade restriction takes the form of a tariff affects the general result; the assumptions are for simplicity only.

would be an improvement. One such policy would be a production subsidy to the Y industry. Just as in the infant-industry case, the direct production subsidy would encourage production without introducing a distortion of prices affecting consumption.

Panel (b) of Figure 8 shows the effect of a subsidy to Y producers. The domestic supply curve shifts down by the amount of the subsidy to $S^d + s$, and domestic production rises from Y_1 to Y_3. We chose the amount of the subsidy (s) to have precisely the same effect on domestic Y production as the tariff (t) in panel (a) and chose each to match the size of the marginal external training benefits (MEB). Therefore, the external benefits generated by the increased production in response to the subsidy are identical to those in response to the tariff. However, the welfare losses are smaller under the production subsidy (panel (b)) than under the import tariff (panel (a)). The tariff causes domestic consumption of good Y to fall, while the production subsidy leaves the consumption decision unaffected. The efficiency loss from the subsidy consists of the single darkly shaded triangle in panel (b). By creating the same external benefits at lower welfare cost than with the tariff, the subsidy constitutes a superior policy for handling the positive production externality.

In the preceding example, we assumed that the positive production externality took the form of worker training. If this were the case, an even better and more direct policy involves a subsidy on employment in the Y industry. A subsidy to employment rather than production would have a greater effect on employment. A production subsidy gives firms an incentive to increase output by increasing use of both labor and capital. An employment subsidy creates a more direct incentive for firms to hire and train more workers, thereby producing more external benefits. The superiority of an employment subsidy over a production subsidy for dealing with this particular type of externality is just another application of the general rule that *direct policies generate more efficient outcomes than indirect ones*. A production subsidy increases employment indirectly by increasing output; an employment subsidy increases employment directly.

What happens if production of a country's import good results in negative rather than positive externalities? In this case, the industry's output will be too high from society's point of view because firms ignore part of the production cost. One policy to discourage production is an import subsidy (that is, a negative tariff), but this is indirect and alters consumption as well as production. A better policy would be a domestic production tax that would reduce domestic production and the associated external costs without altering consumption. *(Draw diagrams similar to those in Figure 8 that compare an import subsidy and a production tax as responses to a negative production externality.)*

The good a country exports also may involve either positive or negative production externalities. Trade-oriented solutions, such as export subsidies (to encourage production in cases of positive externalities) or export taxes (to discourage production in cases of negative externalities), introduce a new source of inefficiency by distorting prices and interfering with efficient consumption decisions. Direct production subsidies or taxes avoid these effects and take account of the externality at a smaller cost in lost efficiency.

5.2 Consumption Externalities

When consumption of a good generates positive or negative externalities, consumption subsidies or taxes lead to more efficient outcomes than do trade restrictions. The reason is analogous to the production-externality case: If the problem concerns the level of consumption, the best policy is one that alters consumption directly without interfering with production. Consumption subsidies or taxes accomplish this; trade restrictions don't.

Consider the case of a negative consumption externality: cigarette smoking. Figure 9 represents conditions in the domestic market for cigarettes. We assume that cigarettes are the country's import good. D^d and S^d represent domestic demand and supply, respectively. With no externality, the free-trade outcome, with the country consuming Y_0 cigarettes and

---

Figure 9   Effect of a Tariff as a Policy Response to a Negative Consumption Externality

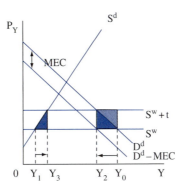

An import tariff reduces consumption, allowing the country to avoid the marginal external costs (MEC) represented by the shaded rectangle. The tariff also imposes the welfare losses associated with the two darker shaded triangles. The tariff's net welfare effect is uncertain. However, a consumption tax would be a superior policy, since it could reduce consumption by the same amount as the tariff does (from Y_0 to Y_2) but without leading to inefficiently high domestic production as the tariff does.

---

producing Y_1 domestically, would be efficient. But consumption of cigarettes imposes a *marginal external cost* (MEC) on nonsmokers that smokers fail to take into account when they decide how many cigarettes to consume. Y_0 represents an inefficiently high level of smoking from society's point of view. With the externality, Y_2 is the efficient level of cigarette consumption. At that level, the opportunity cost of producing the last cigarette (given by the world price or the height of S^W) equals the benefit to society of the last cigarette, which includes the benefit to the smoker minus the cost imposed on nonsmokers (the height of $D^d - MEC$).

The small country can discourage consumption of cigarettes by imposing an import tariff. The society suffers the usual two deadweight welfare losses from altered consumption and production, represented by the two darkly shaded triangles in Figure 9. Society also avoids the external costs represented by the shaded rectangle (in other words, this area illustrates *benefits* of the tariff policy—the costs nonsmokers avoid because the tariff causes smokers to smoke less). Whether the tariff improves welfare depends on the relative magnitudes of these effects.

Again, a superior policy exists in the form of a consumption tax. Such a tax could reduce consumption of cigarettes by the same amount as the tariff in Figure 9 does, but without creating the inefficient increase in domestic production the tariff causes. (*Demonstrate this result with a diagram.*)

When a country's import good creates a positive consumption externality, policy makers can choose between an import subsidy and a consumption subsidy. The import subsidy lowers domestic production, while the more direct policy leaves production unaffected.

The same logic applies when a country's export good exhibits externalities in consumption. In the last few years, controversy has surrounded U.S. export policy regarding tobacco and cigarettes. Policy makers, as we'll see later in the chapter (see section 10), have taken aggressive steps to open foreign markets to U.S. products in these industries. The markets in question include those in the former Soviet Union, Eastern Europe, and Asia. Antismoking activists charge policy makers with hypocrisy for forcing open export markets at the same time that they discourage smoking at home for health-related reasons. Policy makers respond that foreigners already smoke cigarettes, usually those produced by foreign governments' tobacco monopolies, and that aggressive U.S. market-opening efforts merely allow U.S. firms to capture their fair share of those markets.

Externalities on a larger scale lead to one of the hot topics in current international trade policy debates: the environment.

5.3 International Trade and the Environment

Growing concerns about the environment have made environmental issues a source of increasing controversy in international trade policy. There are three basic issues: how to conduct international trade while allowing countries to choose their own preferred levels of environmental protection, how to encourage international cooperation in safeguarding and improving the environment, and how to prevent feigned concern over the environment from serving as a cover for protectionism.

The World Trade Organization doesn't provide environmental rules, but leaves member countries free to enact their own environmental-policy choices. The WTO does require that countries' environmental policies apply equally to domestic and foreign products. For example, WTO rules permit a country to ban all automobiles because of the pollution they generate, but don't permit a country to exclude foreign automobiles on pollution grounds while allowing sale of equally polluting domestically produced cars. Countries are free to exclude *products* that fail the import country's standards. For example, the WTO permits a country to ban food products if they fail to meet hygienic standards—as stringent as the country chooses—that apply to both domestic and imported foods. However, WTO rules generally discourage countries from excluding imports based on the environmental consequences of the *process* used to produce them. For example, a country that excluded food imports by claiming that the foreign factories where the products were packed generated air pollution that exceeded the import-country's standards could face a challenge at the WTO. The reasons for tighter WTO control over process-based environmental rules than product-based ones are two: First, process-based rules can more easily be used as a cover for protectionism. Second, process-based rules are more likely to involve one country (often a wealthy developed one) attempting to force its environmental standard on an unwilling trading partner (often a poor developing one).

The most famous case revolving around the "product versus process" distinction involved the United States, Mexico, and tuna. The United States banned tuna imports from Mexico because Mexico used purse-net fishing techniques that killed dolphins. Mexico protested to the WTO, which ruled the U.S. ban illegal in 1991. Nothing about the tuna product violated U.S. standards, and the WTO generally doesn't allow one country to impose its regulations concerning production processes, such as fishing techniques, on other countries. The ruling outraged many U.S. environmentalists—never fans of the WTO or an open international trade regime. In 1994 the European Union filed another WTO complaint against the U.S. tuna ban. The WTO again ruled the ban illegal and stated that, while the United States had every right to protect dolphins, it should address the fishing-technique issue through international negotiations, not through a unilateral ban on imported tuna. U.S. legislation in 1997 ended the ban once a legally binding international dolphin conservation program—the Panama Declaration, signed by 11 countries including the United States and Mexico—was in place. Most U.S. major retail chains stock only "dolphin safe" tuna. Between 1986 and 2001, recorded average dolphin deaths per tuna net used fell from 15 to 0.16.[13]

Another case along the same lines involved shrimp and turtles. The United States banned shrimp imports from countries that catch shrimp with nets that also trap sea turtles. India, Malaysia, Pakistan, and Thailand protested the ban to the WTO.

---

13. John Authurs, "Tuna Dispute Runs Deeper Than the Death of Dolphins," *Financial Times*, June 23, 2003.

The organization's initial ruling went against the United States, which later appealed. The WTO appeal decision recognized the U.S. right to protect sea turtles, but said the protection should come through negotiation of nondiscriminatory international agreements rather than a discriminatory and unilateral import ban.

Many environmentalists claim that trade liberalization harms the environment by encouraging commercial development and facilitating firms' moves to countries of least-stringent regulation. For example, opponents of the North American Free Trade Agreement claimed it would erode U.S. progress on the environment by allowing firms to serve the U.S. market by producing in Mexico, where some regulations are less strict. However, empirical studies support some strong counterarguments. Evidence indicates that the cost of environmental compliance, even in countries with stringent regulations, comprises too small a share of total costs to provide much incentive to relocate. Evidence also suggests that the main determinant of demand for environmental protection is income; wealthy countries can afford it while poor ones can't.[14] Hence, supporters claim that free trade, by raising income, increases demand for environmental protection. Trade also spreads newer, cleaner technologies, both directly and by raising income to pay for them. Growing evidence also shows that the price-support schemes and elaborate protection granted to agriculture by most developed countries, especially within the European Union, lead to overclearing of land, overuse of fertilizers, pesticides, and water, and other negative environmental consequences. Agricultural trade based on comparative advantage rather than complicated price-control and export-subsidy schemes would generate far less environmental degradation.

Arguments for a positive relationship between trade openness and the environment received new empirical support in the early 1990s when revolutions swept Eastern Europe and revealed environmental messes the Iron Curtain had concealed. The centrally planned economies of Eastern Europe had isolated themselves from the trading system, denied firms access to new and cleaner technology, and provided firms with artificially cheap energy. The result: massive environmental problems that the countries' poorly performing economies couldn't afford to clean up.

Some types of environmental problems call more strongly for international cooperation than others. Many types of pollution have primarily local effects and, thus, reasonably are subject only to domestic rules. Other types, such as air pollution, greenhouse gases with climatic consequences, acid rain, and deforestation, can have international or even global effects and are more reasonably subject to mutually agreed international rules. Often, what is needed is not so much new environmental rules but changes in existing domestic or international policies that have adverse environmental consequences. For example, Borneo has been a prime offender in rapid cutting of its tropical rain forest. Part of the reason is its policy of short-term logging concessions that give a firm rights to log a piece of land for only 20 to 25 years. With no future rights to the land's productivity, concessionaires have little incentive to manage the forest with environmentally responsible techniques; instead, they cut as much as possible as quickly as possible and move on to the next piece of land. These issues, particularly deforestation, often pit richer industrialized countries (many of whom cut most of their forests decades ago) against poorer developing ones. One proposed solution is for developed countries to pay developing nations for the carbon-absorbing services of their forests, thereby providing a financial incentive for poor countries to maintain rather than cut their forests.

Sound environmental policy requires insulating it from protectionists who disguise their self-interested arguments as concern for the environment. In the guise of environmentalism, Germany passed legislation (the "Töpfer Law") requiring firms that sell in Germany to collect

---

14. For example, urban pollution appears to decline sharply with income after a country attains an income level of approximately $5,000 per capita per year. Chapter Eleven contains more discussion of environmental issues between developed and developing countries.

their used packaging and recycle it. While such a policy may provide some environmental benefits, it also discriminates against foreign firms that, because of transportation costs and lack of established local distribution networks, have a much harder time complying with the regulation. To cite another example, South Korea passed a Toxic Substances Control Act that required any firm selling a chemical product in South Korea to provide a list of ingredients, their proportions, and the manufacturing process used. Foreign chemical companies were suspicious of the law's true intent, because South Korea has a growing chemical industry and has been trying to move into specialty chemicals, which require technologies the country doesn't yet have. U.S. chemical firms claimed that the new disclosure rules use environmentalism to disguise South Korean chemical firms' attempt to obtain trade secrets from foreign firms.

6 SHOULDN'T THE "PLAYING FIELD" BE LEVEL?

Explicit calls for prohibitive tariffs are rare, but policy debates resound with arguments for "scientific" tariffs, which have the same effect as prohibitive ones. A **scientific tariff** is specifically designed to offset the cost advantage enjoyed by foreign producers of the tariffed good. For example, if auto makers in Japan can produce a subcompact car for $1,718 less than the cost of an equivalent American-made car, the scientific tariff on each imported Japanese subcompact car will be $1,718.[15]

Proponents of scientific tariffs argue that international trade is inherently unfair if domestic producers must compete with foreign producers who enjoy lower production costs. Domestic producers seeking protection often cite the need for a "level playing field." They argue that trade can be fair only when all producers begin on an equal footing by having equal costs.

The primary fallacy in the argument for a scientific tariff lies in its failure to recognize across-country cost differentials as a reflection of comparative advantage. Every country will be the low-opportunity-cost producer of some goods—those in which it has a comparative advantage—and the high-cost producer of other goods—those in which it has a comparative disadvantage. International trade's potential to increase world output and welfare comes from exploiting these very cost differences. Across-the-board scientific tariffs would eliminate all trade based on comparative advantage. The result would be a return to autarky and a significant reduction in world welfare.

7 HOW CAN WE COMPETE WITH LOW-WAGE COUNTRIES?

In high-wage developed countries such as the United States, one of the most commonly heard justifications for protection is labor's supposed inability to compete with low-wage foreign labor. How can it be fair to expect goods produced in the United States to compete with those produced in developing countries using labor that is paid subsistence wages for work in sweatshop conditions? Proponents of this argument assert that American labor can compete under these conditions only by accepting a significantly lower standard of living.[16] The fact is that products in many U.S. industries *do* compete successfully in world markets against goods produced using foreign labor that is paid only a small fraction of the wages earned by U.S. labor. High wages don't render an industry uncompetitive *so long as labor's productivity justifies them*.

The United States, with its highly skilled labor force and abundant capital stock relative to the rest of the world, has a comparative advantage in industries that involve

---

15. Robert B. Cohen, "The Prospects for Trade and Protectionism in the Auto Industry," in *Trade Policy in the 1980s*, edited by William R. Cline (Washington, D.C.: Institute for International Economics, 1983), p. 553.

16. See Case Two in Chapter Four.

intensive use of human capital and research-and-development skills. By world standards, U.S. workers in these industries are highly paid but also highly productive. On the other hand, the United States suffers a comparative disadvantage in goods involving intensive use of unskilled labor, which is relatively scarce in the United States. Trade according to comparative advantage moves these industries to low-wage countries—those with abundant unskilled labor. The result is more output and a higher standard of living for residents of *both* the United States and labor-abundant countries.

As productivity rises in a country, so do wages. In a world where production facilities are increasingly mobile, firms are attracted to countries with workers who are highly productive relative to the wages they earn. As firms relocate to take advantage of the high ratio of productivity to wages, they bid up those wages.[17] Taiwan, Hong Kong, South Korea, and Singapore, often referred to as the "Four Tigers" because of their impressive success in industrialization and exporting during the 1970s and 1980s, provide an outstanding example. As recently as 25 years ago, wage rates there were very low by world standards, and firms from all over the world moved labor-intensive tasks there. Then wages in the four countries began to rise rapidly; firms now shift instead to Indonesia, Malaysia, Thailand, China, the Philippines, and other unskilled-labor-abundant countries where wages remain low.

High wages *not* justified by high productivity *do* make industries uncompetitive. The U.S. automobile and steel industries, for example, lost their ability to compete in world markets largely because of increases in union wage rates far in excess of productivity gains.[18] When workers in an industry succeed in raising wages above the value of the productivity of labor, the industry loses its ability to export and also must have protection from foreign competition in the domestic market. Although firms and workers in such industries typically rationalize protection on the grounds of saving domestic jobs, evidence from the steel and auto industries doesn't support this view. The increased profitability based on protectionism in those industries tended to go to even higher wages; hence, layoffs continued. The United Auto Workers union membership, for example, fell by more than half during the 1980s and 1990s, from 1.5 million members in 1979 to fewer than 672,000 in 2000. Stringent union work rules that hinder flexibility and productivity, combined with high wages, continue to hamper the domestic industry even after three decades of protection.

8 HOW DO WE HANDLE NATIONAL SECURITY AND DEFENSE?

Some industries have particular strategic importance, making countries hesitant to depend on imports. Two examples are the food and steel industries. The strategic importance of food is obvious, and the military applications of steel make that industry crucial during periods of conflict. Another industry in which the United States has used a national security argument to limit imports is petroleum.

The national security and defense argument for protectionist policies has several weaknesses. First, in the event of war or other catastrophe, it may be more effective to build new capacity for production of needed goods than to rely on outdated and inefficient plants. During World War II, for example, the United States built many new plants, including some to produce goods previously supplied by Germany. During the Gulf War, the United States chartered on the world market half the ships used to carry equipment to the Gulf—despite the Jones Act, which has protected the U.S. shipping

17. See Case One in Chapter Four.

18. Mordechai E. Kreinin, "Wage Competitiveness in the U.S. Auto and Steel Industries," *Contemporary Policy Issues* 4 (1984), pp. 39–50. The same argument has been made about management compensation in the two industries.

industry since 1920 by requiring that all domestic maritime trade be conducted on ships that are U.S. owned, built, and staffed.[19]

Even in industries that require continuous maintenance of productive capacity, trade restrictions represent inefficient means for doing so. Production subsidies can encourage domestic production of strategic goods without altering consumption patterns. Why should consumers have to pay higher prices for all goods containing steel in order to maintain capacity for steel production in the event of war? A direct production subsidy to the steel industry avoids the effect of higher prices on consumers. Taxpayers must finance the subsidy, but all taxpayers presumably benefit from the national security provided.

We can illustrate another common fallacy in the national security argument using U.S. policy toward the petroleum industry. When imported oil was cheaply available from the Persian Gulf (before 1974), the United States chose to limit imports. The logic behind the policy was to avoid becoming dependent on imported petroleum, the supply of which could be cut off in war. The import restrictions kept U.S. petroleum prices artificially above world prices with the stated goal of encouraging the search for oil reserves in the United States. The strategy worked, but with unfortunate consequences. The United States searched for, found, and used a large share of its oil reserves during a period when low-cost imports were freely available. Once the OPEC oil embargo of 1974 ended the availability of low-cost imports, the United States sorely missed its already-used reserves. A better strategy—and one that several countries, including the United States, gradually have adopted—would have been to buy imported oil and stockpile it for emergencies. Not only would the stockpiles have been relatively inexpensive, but also domestic reserves would have been saved for the day when imports ceased to be available.

A wide range of industries, including some surprising ones, use the national security argument for protection. Of course, industries have an incentive to use any politically successful argument to obtain protection. The U.S. footwear industry, for example, argued in 1984 that national security dictated protection for shoes because in time of war, soldiers must have boots for combat. The national security argument's vulnerability to special interests asking for self-interested protection represents a serious problem.

9 AREN'T GOODS *AND* MONEY BETTER THAN JUST GOODS?

The "goods versus goods *and* money" argument for protection appeals to "common sense." When a consumer buys a domestic good, both the good and the money paid for it remain in the country; but when a consumer buys an import, the good comes into the country and the money leaves. Proponents of this protectionist argument claim that it must be better to keep both the good and the money than just the good, so a country must be better off producing everything domestically than engaging in international trade.

The fallacy in this argument lies in its failure to recognize that the country loses something when a consumer buys a domestically produced good—even though both the good and the money remain in the country. It loses the resources used up in producing the good. Whenever these resources have a higher value than the price that would have been paid for importing the good, the country is better off importing. This is just another way of stating the principle of comparative advantage. (*Why?*) Also, dollars spent on imported goods don't disappear forever; they return in the form of foreign demand for domestically produced goods or foreign capital flows into the domestic economy.

---

19. "Ruling the Waves," *The Economist*, March 23, 1991, p. 81.

10 CAN WE THREATEN OTHER COUNTRIES INTO TRADE LIBERALIZATION?

An argument heard often (especially in the United States) supports protectionism, or, more precisely, *the threat of* protectionism, as a means to lower foreign trade barriers. If domestic special-interest groups in a foreign country succeed in winning protection from competition, how can trading partners overcome the influence of those interest groups to achieve liberalization? One possible answer is "with the threat of retaliation."

A case involving the Japanese tobacco and cigarette industry illustrates this idea. For years, import tariffs and marketing restrictions closed the industry to foreign competition. In 1987, Japan Tobacco, a government-owned monopoly since 1898, held 98 percent of the Japanese cigarette market (then the second-largest market in the world at 300 billion cigarettes per year, where 60 percent of men and 15 percent of women smoked). The United States threatened to restrict imports from Japan in retaliation under Section 301 of the 1974 Trade Act, which provides for retaliation against U.S. trading partners' "unfair" trade practices. The threat worked: Japan removed its tariffs and other restrictions on imported cigarettes. In the first two years, U.S. cigarette sales in Japan rose by about 500 percent. Japan Tobacco, forced by continuing Japanese restrictions on imports of raw tobacco to buy domestically grown tobacco at two to three times world prices, found it increasingly difficult to compete. However, a study of the cost to Japanese consumers of protection found that, as of 1989, tobacco products still enjoyed nontariff barriers equivalent to a 241 percent tariff.[20] Although Japan Tobacco has since been privatized, the Japanese government still holds a two-thirds stake in the firm.

Similar stories apply in other Asian cigarette markets, among the world's fastest-growing ones as smoking declines in the United States and Western Europe. For example, Thailand formerly banned imported cigarettes as well as cigarette advertising. The United States filed a case with the World Trade Organization, claiming that the Thai bans violated WTO rules. The WTO panel ruled the import ban illegal because it discriminated between foreign and domestic cigarettes (thereby making Thailand's claimed public-health justification implausible), but upheld Thailand's right to ban cigarette advertising for health reasons so long as the ban applied equally to domestic and foreign products. Four years later, imports still accounted for only about 3 percent of Thai cigarette sales.

Several bilateral agreements between the United States and Asian countries have been renegotiated to allow those countries to restrict tobacco-product advertising for public-health reasons, with the United States retaining the right to monitor the restrictions to ensure that they don't discriminate against imported products. The United States exports more than 150 billion cigarettes annually. In addition, U.S.-based firms such as Philip Morris produce billions more cigarettes abroad, particularly in Eastern Europe, where the firms have purchased most of the formerly state-owned tobacco monopolies. U.S. cigarette export policies remain controversial for two reasons. First, they represent cases of the United States using its size and power to threaten other countries into changing policies that run counter to U.S. commercial interests. Second, many individuals argue that the U.S. government shouldn't aid U.S. firms' foreign tobacco sales at the same time that public policies in the United States discourage smoking for health reasons. Public pressure has led to some policy changes. In mid-1998, new guidelines to all U.S. embassies ordered that embassy personnel shouldn't promote the sale of tobacco or tobacco products and that diplomats should support rather than oppose local antismoking laws, so long as those laws apply on a nondiscriminatory basis to both domestic and imported tobacco.[21] And in 2003,

---

20. Yoko Sazanami et al. *Measuring the Costs of Protection in Japan* (Washington, D.C.: Institute for International Economics, 1995), p. 24.

21. Carla Anne Robbins and Tara Parker-Pope, "U.S. Embassies Stop Assisting Tobacco Firms," *The Wall Street Journal*, May 14, 1998.

the United States announced it would support a global antismoking treaty, despite tobacco-industry opposition.[22]

Despite apparent "success" stories such as the cigarette cases, many economists remain skeptical of protectionist threats as a tool for trade liberalization. Supporters insist that threats are the only way to eliminate foreign trade barriers supported by deeply entrenched and politically powerful special-interest groups. Detractors insist that the United States should concentrate on reducing its own trade barriers before issuing threats to trading partners about theirs. Skeptics also point out the danger of introducing a world trading system based on who has the power to issue effective threats rather than on the multilateral, nondiscriminatory framework of the World Trade Organization.

The Omnibus Trade and Competitiveness Act of 1988 increased the scope for protectionist threats by the United States, especially in the form of so-called **301 cases**. Under this provision, the U.S. Trade Representative must issue an annual report on policies designed to facilitate U.S. exports. Most years the report contains a list of countries that maintain "priority" unfair trade barriers with the most harmful effects on U.S. exports. Negotiations follow; and, if the named country refuses to make policy changes acceptable to the United States, retaliation can follow. Recent episodes of U.S. retaliation include 100 percent tariffs on $117 million in imports from the EU in response to the EU's refusal to drop its ban on imports of hormone-treated beef and 100 percent tariffs on $75 million of imports from Ukraine for that country's refusal to stop pirating CDs.

A related provision of the 1988 trade act, called **special-301**, provides a framework for the United States to threaten retaliation against countries that don't enforce to U.S. satisfaction copyrights, patents, trademarks, and other intellectual property rights. Many countries don't have or enforce laws that limit firms' ability to copy other firms' inventions or products without paying fees to the innovating firm. U.S. firms, especially producers of pharmaceuticals, chemicals, plant varieties, computer software, movies, and books, claim to lose millions of dollars in sales each year because illegal copies produced abroad replace those sales. In 2004, the U.S. Trade Representative had 34 countries including Canada, Israel, and Mexico on its Watch List, and 15 including the European Union, India, and Russia on its Priority Watch List. Without improvement, countries on the Priority Watch List move to the Priority Country List, which means that they must enter negotiations with the United States and that they run the risk of retaliation. Ukraine became a Priority Foreign Country in 2001 because of its continued production and export of pirated "optical media"—primarily CDs—and remains on that list in 2004.

Supporters of protectionist policies use many variations of the arguments presented in this chapter. Our primary aim has been to look logically at the arguments and evaluate their merits and demerits. The general conclusion: Protectionism isn't the best policy response to most of the problems discussed in the chapter. Regardless of the guise in which the argument appears, it's wise to approach any demand for trade-restricting policies as a request for protection from foreign competition. The most common motive underlying such requests, whether stated or not, is an effort to improve the welfare of the industry seeking protection at the expense of other groups both in the domestic economy and abroad. There's no doubt that protection can bring additional revenues to firms in protected industries; but such benefits rarely match, much less exceed, the losses to domestic consumers. One commonly used indicator of the effect of protection is the loss of consumer surplus for each job added in the protected sector. Table 1 reports this indicator for several cases of highly protected U.S. industries. U.S. consumers lost almost $150,000 in consumer surplus for each job created by protection of the U.S. textile and apparel industries, over $500,000 in consumer surplus for each job created by the bilateral agreement with Japan on semiconductor trade, and over $800,000 for each job created by applying antidumping and countervailing duties in the steel industry.

---

22. "U.S. Supports Global Anti-Smoking Treaty," *USA Today,* May 20, 2003.

Table 1 COST TO CONSUMERS PER U.S. JOB GAINED IN PROTECTED SECTORS

Sector (Date)	Loss of Consumer Surplus per Job Gained by Protection
Textiles and apparel (1990)	$144,751
U.S.–Japan semiconductor agreement (1989)	$525,619
Steel antidumping and countervailing duties (1993)	$835,351

Source: Data from Gary Clyde Hufbauer and Kimberly Ann Elliott, *Measuring the Costs of Protection in the United States* (Washington, D.C.: Institute for International Economics, 1994), pp. 15, 20.

CASE 1: STICKY BUSINESS IN SINGAPORE

Singapore

Singapore is famous for its high standards of tidiness and for the stringent policies that support public cleanliness. Large fines of over $500 for even first offenses of littering or marking buildings with graffiti keep the city in shape. Chewing gum had long been unpopular with Singapore's policy makers. Then, in the early 1990s, an event spurred those policy makers, known for their fastidiousness, into action. Someone stuck a piece of chewing gum in the door of a high-speed commuter train. The door stuck and caused a delay in the usual punctual service. Beginning in 1992 policy makers, anxious to prevent an embarrassing repeat of the train delay, as well as to avoid the messy and unsightly problem of improperly disposed used chewing gum, banned the sale of gum. Residents of Singapore who traveled abroad could return with gum for personal use, but none could be sold domestically.

U.S. gum manufacturers missed the opportunity to sell their products to 4 million Singaporeans. Wrigley, maker of several leading chewing-gum brands, pressured U.S. legislators and trade representatives to do something. The ban didn't discriminate against foreign gum because no producer existed in Singapore, nor did it violate any of Singapore's other WTO responsibilities. So the only way for the United States to get Singapore to remove or loosen the anti-gum policy was to negotiate. In 2001, the two countries began talks to reach a broad U.S.–Singapore Free Trade Agreement. Wrigley made sure that the agenda included an unlikely item that turned out to be quite sticky: the chewing-gum ban.

At first, Singapore agreed to allow in only medicinal-purpose gums prescribed by a doctor (for example, products to help stop smoking or to treat conditions such as chronic dry mouth). Wrigley and its supporters weren't satisfied. More negotiations followed. Finally, Singapore agreed to permit sales, but only of gums with proven health benefits, only by a licensed dentist or pharmacist, and only if the customer gave his or her name to the seller. This sufficed to gain entry for Wrigley's sugar-free Orbit brand of gum, which claims to strengthen tooth enamel. Singapore's stiff penalties for gum-related littering remain. Fines of over $200 plus a trip to court are common. Some pharmacists seem a bit puzzled. After all, they sell more serious drugs with fewer restrictions.

CASE 2: *NO*, THE *OTHER* TYPE OF DUMPING

Usually, when the word *dumping* arises in a trade-policy discussion, it refers to sales of a good in an export market at a price below the price charged in the home market. Recent discussions between the United States and China, however, involved *dumping* in the more everyday sense, as in garbage.

China buys large quantities of discarded material from industrial countries to reclaim the metal, plastic, and other recyclable materials using the country's abundant, cheap labor force. However, falsified documents sometimes facilitate entry for huge container ships of pure garbage, which can be hidden in China's vast, sparsely populated northwest countryside and go undetected by lax environmental-law enforcement.

Most African and Latin American countries banned garbage trade in 1991. Now China's rapid growth, which results in large quantities of domestic waste, is forcing the country to strengthen its own laws and enforcement. New rules require a license from the National Environmental Protection Agency (NEPA) to import trash; and both the NEPA and customs officials must certify that each shipment contains high recyclable content and doesn't contain certain toxic materials. But enforcement is difficult and costly. When unacceptable shipments arrive, false documents often impede a "Return to Sender" solution. In 2002, China imported 23 percent of the United States' $5.2 billion of scrap and waste exports, making scrap the third largest U.S. export to China, after airplanes and semiconductors.[23]

The relevant international rules on exporting garbage constitute the Basel Convention, a 1994 agreement among 100 countries that bans export of hazardous waste from rich countries to poor ones. Administering the Basel Convention has proven less straightforward than anticipated. In fact, some of the developing countries that originally promoted the agreement now believe it harms them. Most signatories are happy with a ban on international shipment of waste for

disposal. The controversial part of the agreement is its ban on exports of hazardous materials for *recycling*. Many developing countries, including Malaysia, India, and China, rely heavily on imported scrap to produce steel, paper, aluminum, lead, copper, and zinc, among other raw materials. The scrap is cheaper than virgin materials and requires less processing. Firms that perform the recycling as well as those that use the recycled materials worry that the Basel ban will shut off their supplies of scrap, since many of the scrap products, such as old auto batteries, are at least potentially hazardous. The outcome—and whether the agreement helps or hurts the developing countries that wanted it—depends in part on how strictly the ban is interpreted. If defined broadly, the term *hazardous* could include many products widely used in developing countries' recycling industries. A narrower definition could keep those industries viable while preventing wholesale dumping in poor countries of materials with no economic use but much potential for environmental damage.

International garbage trade isn't limited to shipments from rich countries to poor ones. Canada exports millions of cubic yards of trash to the United States each year, much of it to Michigan; and the United States exports waste to Canada. Besides China and Canada, the United Kingdom, Korea, and Mexico import large quantities of U.S. scrap.

CASE 3: SPAWNING A TRADE DISPUTE

U.S./Canada

Canada and the United States share the Pacific salmon fishery, one of the world's most valuable and biologically complex fish resources. The fishery extends through Washington, Idaho, Oregon, and Alaska and through British Columbia and the Yukon, along the Fraser, Skeena, and Thompson rivers. The most important fish include chinook, sockeye, pink, chum, and coho salmon, several subspecies of which are classified as threatened or endangered under the U.S. Endangered Species Act.

Managing a salmon fishery is complicated by the salmon life cycle. The fish migrate for hundreds or thousands of miles, from U.S. and Canadian rivers to the middle of the northern Pacific, and then back to their original river to spawn and die. The commercial harvest along the U.S.–Canada border inevitably involves U.S. boats catching "Canadian" fish, and vice versa, because fish from U.S. and Canadian rivers mingle in the ocean and on the return trip to their respective rivers.

When fish were plentiful, disputes were rare. But now, salmon stocks are in severe decline. High harvest rates, industrial development along rivers and coastlines, and more dams and reservoirs mean the salmon no longer reproduce at the rate of the harvest. The decline in the number of available fish has generated increased tension between U.S. and Canadian fishing boats—and between trade policy makers in the two countries.

The United States and Canada signed the Pacific Salmon Treaty in 1985 after 14 years of negotiations. Under the treaty, the two countries negotiated total allowable salmon catches and allocated the catch between boats from the two countries so that U.S. interceptions of "Canadian fish" and Canadian interceptions of "U.S. fish" balanced. But Canadians perceived as unreasonable U.S. demands that Canada reduce its catch of Snake River chinook and, in 1994, imposed a fee of C$1,500 on U.S. fishing boats passing

23. Jon E. Hilsenrath, "How Your Trash Helps Fuel Boom in China's Economy," *The Wall Street Journal*, April 9, 2003.

through Canadian waters. The United States declared Snake River chinook endangered in response. Unable to settle the dispute themselves, the two countries hired an arbitrator who, though agreeing with the Canadian position, resigned in frustration over the split in the parties' positions.

Canada continued to claim in 1997 that U.S. boats were catching many more Canadian salmon than the U.S. salmon caught by Canadian boats. The Canadian government warned the United States and then seized several U.S. fishing boats on their way through Canadian waters from Washington to Alaska, and British Columbian fishing boats temporarily blockaded a U.S. ferry bound for Alaska.

In 1998, while negotiations continued, Canada banned fishing of coho salmon in Canadian waters due to the specie's declining numbers, especially in the Skeena River run where Canadians claim Alaskan boats netted 600,000 coho in 1997. Canada also announced a buyback of fishing licenses to reduce the number of Canadian boats fishing both the Pacific and Atlantic coasts. But Canada acknowledged that its cutbacks would do little to improve

fish stocks if the United States didn't follow along and stop fishing practices that allegedly included taking 35 million more Canadian-spawned salmon than allowed under the 1985 treaty. The week before the opening of the 1998 salmon season, Canada and Washington State reached two agreements to cover catches of coho, chinook, and sockeye. Under the new agreements, Washington State boats must cut their catch of coho headed for British Columbia's Upper Thompson River by 22 percent, while Canadians must catch 50 percent fewer Washington-bound chinook. The sockeye agreement limits Washington State boats to 24.9 percent of the year's allowable catch of (Canadian) Fraser River sockeye. Talks between Canada and Alaska failed to lead to an agreement.

A year later, in 1999, the two countries reached a new 10-year agreement. New provisions include abundance-based management (that is, flexible catch limits based on a specie's abundance or scarcity in a particular year) and $140 million worth of spending by the United States on habitat restoration and other efforts to rebuild fish stocks.

CASE 4: **MITI MIRACLES?**

Japan

For years, in debates over the desirability of strategic trade policies (STP) of the type discussed in section 4.3, proponents of STP pointed to the Japanese economy's postwar growth and attributed it to strategic trade policies by Japan's Ministry of Trade and Industry (MITI). Many took MITI's success for granted and focused their attention on how other countries might emulate that success. In particular, how could bureaucrats in charge of STP pick winning industries for support and avoid political pressures to support losers?

A study by economists Richard Beason and David Weinstein examines Japanese industrial policy and sectoral growth between 1955 and 1990 to see if MITI in fact succeeded in promoting industrial growth to the extent widely believed. Unlike anecdotal stories that pick out a rapid-growth industry in Japan (say, autos or semiconductors) and then look for any past government support of that sector, the Beason and Weinstein study compares 13 different industries and asks whether those that got lots of government largesse performed better than those that got less. Beason and Weinstein ranked each of the 13 industries according to the amount of four different types of government support it received: subsidized loans, subsidies, effective rate of trade protection, and tax relief. Table 2 reports the rankings for each industry. Mining

got the most government support in three of the four categories, and processed food got the most trade protection.

Several patterns stand out in Table 2. First, rather than a coherent policy of supporting some sectors and not others, most industries got help on some margins and not on others. Textiles, for example, got lots of subsidies, trade protection, and tax relief, but little access to loans. Processed food got lots of trade protection, but little support in the other areas. Second, and more important, the sectors that received the *most* government help had the *lowest* growth rates. Such a pattern is discernible through casual inspection of the table; but statistical tests by Beason and Weinstein confirm it: Government support went primarily to slow-growth industries, and industries that grew quickly typically did so with relatively little government help. The authors also divided the 1955–1990 interval into two subperiods: 1955–1973, when most analysts conclude that the Japanese government and MITI in particular were most actively involved in the economy, and 1973–1990, when such involvement occurred on a lesser scale. In each subperiod, the same result holds; more government support was associated with slower growth. It appears that, despite MITI's public-relations success at convincing many otherwise, Japanese policy makers did

Table 2   **JAPANESE GOVERNMENT SUPPORT OF INDUSTRY, 1955–1990**

Sector	Annual Growth of Output (%)	Sector Ranking (1 = Most Support; 13 = Least Support)			
		Loans	Subsidies	Protection	Tax
Electrical machinery	12.2%	8	9	8	8
General machinery	11.4	12	4	11	8
Transport equipment	10.8	7	11	4	8
Fabricated metal	10.1	10	6	12	7
Oil and coal	9.8	2	13	7	3
Precision instruments	9.3	13	10	6	8
Ceramics, stone, glass	8.7	5	8	9	3
Pulp and paper	7.7	6	5	10	13
Chemicals	7.6	3	7	5	3
Basic metals	7.2	4	2	3	6
Processed food	6.3	9	12	1	12
Mining	3.8	1	1	13	1
Textiles	2.7	11	3	2	2

Source: Richard Beason and David E. Weinstein, "Growth, Economies of Scale, and Targeting in Japan (1955–90)," *Review of Economics and Statistics* (May 1996).

exactly what policy makers in most other countries tend to do: They granted support to declining industrial sectors in response to political lobbying. In 2002, Japan's Ministry of Finance made the new view official by stating that, "The Japanese model was not the source of Japanese competitiveness but the cause of our failure."[24]

CASE 5: **SCIENCE, OR POLITICS?**

U.S./E.U.

The World Trade Organization allows member countries to ban food products for safety reasons. However, to prevent protectionism in the guise of food-safety concerns, all restrictions must apply equally to domestically produced and imported products and must be based on sound scientific evidence.

In 1989, the European Union banned imports of U.S. beef based on the common U.S. industry practice of using growth hormones to increase cattle's leanness and growth rates. The United States issued a WTO challenge of the ban and won in 1997. The EU appealed the WTO decision and lost again in 1998. The WTO ruled that the EU ban lacked the necessary scientific evidence and that the EU must remove the ban by mid-1999 in order to comply with the union's WTO obligations. The EU refused, citing European consumers' concerns over growth hormones' health effects, despite the lack of hard scientific evidence. The United States offered to label all its exported beef as "Made in America," so consumers could decide whether they wanted to consume it. European policy makers refused the offer, demanding that beef be labeled as hormone treated. In 1999, faced with the EU's repeated refusal to lift the ban as ordered by the WTO, the United States requested and received WTO permission to retaliate by imposing 100 percent tariffs on $117 million worth of European exports. In late 2003, the European Union claimed to have produced scientific evidence sufficient to allow the hormone ban to continue without violating WTO rules. The United States disagreed.

24. Issei Morita, "Japanese Explode the Myth of MITI," *Financial Times,* June 27, 2002.

What constitutes "scientific evidence" in such disputes? Usually the standards set by the Codex Alimentarius, established by the United Nations Food and Agricultural Organization and the World Health Organization in 1962 to recommend, based on scientific assessments, food-safety standards. But European Union trade policy makers aren't satisfied with those rules. In the upcoming round of WTO negotiations, the EU wants to incorporate a "precautionary principle," which would allow the union to restrict access for food products about whose safety consumers have concerns but no clear scientific evidence. Agricultural exporters, on the other hand, see in the union's new demands only a continuation of EU agricultural protectionism.[25]

SUMMARY

In this chapter we analyzed the merits of many arguments for international trade restrictions, including those based on infant industries, monopolies, strategic trade policy, externalities, scientific tariffs, competition with low-wage foreign suppliers, national security, "goods versus goods and money," and protectionist threats to open markets. Several of the arguments contain valid elements, but more direct policies (such as production or consumption taxes or subsidies) generally produce results superior to those from restricting international trade. Restrictions on trade aren't the most effective policies for dealing with domestic distortions.

LOOKING AHEAD

A tension between the self-interested, nationalistic policies pursued by individual interest groups and countries and the broader perspective of the gains from an open and liberal trading system dominates the history of international trade. In Chapter Nine we explore this tension, focusing on the history of international trade policy and on the development of regional trading groups that extend beyond the boundaries of a single country. We also examine the role of national borders and the differences between interregional and international trade.

KEY TERMS

optimal market conditions	profit shifting	positive externality
domestic distortion	learning-curve models	scientific tariff
infant-industry argument	externality	301 cases
strategic trade policy	negative externality	special-301

PROBLEMS AND QUESTIONS FOR REVIEW

1. Small country Dismalia "imports" education by sending its students to school abroad. Education generates positive consumption externalities for Dismalia. As the new Dismalian Minister of Education, you must develop policy proposals for dealing with this issue.
    a. First, present to the Dismalian Minister of Trade a proposal for how trade policy might be applied to the problem. Explain the economic logic of your proposal and illustrate graphically the policy's effects.
    b. For the Dismalian Minister of the Budget, you must present a proposal for how domestic policy might be applied to the problem. Explain the economic logic of your proposal and illustrate graphically its effects.
    c. Given the choice of policies outlined in (a) and (b), what is your recommendation, and why?
2. Evaluate the following comment: "Economists have estimated that protection of the U.S. textile and apparel industry results in 169,000 more jobs in that sector than would be the case with no protection. Clearly, this is a case in which protection is justified because it works; Americans are better off."

25. See "Is EU's Environmental Push Protectionism?" *The Wall Street Journal,* August 8, 2001.

3. Analyze the following statement: "If an American buys a car produced in the United States, both the car and the money stay in the United States. If an American buys a car produced in Japan, then the car comes to America, but the money goes to Japan. Clearly, the first case is better for America because Americans get both the car and the money."

4. Good X exhibits a negative production externality, all effects of which are local; that is, production of X imposes costs on third parties, but only those who live near the production site.
   a. Good X is country A's import good, and the country also produces some good X domestically. From a national perspective, would you recommend an import tariff, a production tax, a consumption tax, or none of the above?
   b. Good X is country A's import good, and country A can't produce good X domestically. From a national perspective, would you recommend an import tariff, a production tax, a consumption tax, or none of the above?
   c. Good X is country A's export good, and some domestic production of good X is consumed domestically. From a national perspective, would you recommend an export tax, a production tax, a consumption tax, or none of the above?

5. Residents of country B consume good Y, but none is produced domestically. Good Y is characterized by a positive consumption externality. Compare the effects of an import subsidy and a consumption subsidy.

6. Explain why WTO rules permit a country to establish its own standards for health, safety, and the environment but still require that the country's rules not discriminate between domestic and foreign firms. How does this general stance apply to the Singapore chewing-gum policy?

7. Explain why an "optimal tariff" by a country with monopoly power in a market is called a *beggar-thy-neighbor policy*.

8. Small country Alpha exports lumber products obtained by cutting Alpha's forests. Cutting the forests creates negative external effects in Alpha (soil erosion, loss of wildlife habitat, and so forth). As the new Alphan Minister for the Interior, you are charged with devising policy proposals for dealing with the problem.
   a. First, you must present to the Alphan Minister of Trade a proposal for how trade policy might be applied to the problem. Explain the economic logic of your proposal and use graphs to illustrate.
   b. For the Alphan Minister of Domestic Agriculture, you must present a proposal for how domestic policy might be applied to the problem. Explain your proposal, and use graphs to illustrate.
   c. Given the choice of policies you outlined in (a) and (b), what is your recommendation, and why?
   d. Suppose now that Alpha's cutting of its forests has negative externalities abroad as well as domestically (for example, the worldwide climatic effects of destruction of forests). What are the implications for the economic efficiency of free trade from a worldwide perspective? What policy problems might such a situation present? Why?

REFERENCES AND SELECTED READINGS

Aaronson, Susan Ariel. *Taking Trade to the Streets*. Ann Arbor: University of Michigan Press, 2001.
Fascinating history of public resistance to open international markets.

Acheson, Keith, and Christopher Maule. *Much Ado about Culture: North American Trade Disputes*. Ann Arbor: University of Michigan Press, 1999.
Excellent, readable treatment of trade policy toward cultural or entertainment industries.

Antweiler, Werner, et al. "Is Free Trade Good for the Environment?" *American Economic Review* 91 (September 2001): 877–908.
Empirical study suggesting that free trade may lead to environmental improvement; for advanced students.

Bagwell, Kyle, and Robert W. Staiger. "The WTO as a Mechanism for Securing Market Access Property Rights: Implications for Global Labor and Environmental Issues." *Journal of Economic Perspectives* (Summer 2001): 69–88.
Discusses the WTO as a forum for countries to exchange property rights in market access.

Baldwin, Robert E. "Are Economists' Traditional Trade Policy Views Still Valid?" *Journal of Economic Literature* 30 (June 1992): 804–829.
Assesses free trade considering strategic trade policy arguments; for all students.

Basu, Kaushik. "Child Labor: Cause, Consequences, and Cure, with Remarks on International Labor Standards." *Journal of Economic Literature* 37 (September 1999): 1083–1119.
Accessible overview of a controversial issue.

Bhagwati, Jagdish. *Free Trade Today*. Princeton: Princeton University Press, 2002.
Readable examination of many of the arguments for protection.

Bhagwati, Jagdish, and V. K. Ramaswami. "Domestic Distortions, Tariffs, and the Theory of Optimum Subsidy." *Journal of Political Economy* 71 (February 1963): 44–50.
A classic paper comparing tariffs with other policies as responses to domestic distortions; for intermediate students.

Brown, Drusilla K. "Labor Standards: Where Do They Belong on the International Trade Agenda?" *Journal of Economic Perspectives* (Summer 2001): 89–112.
Argues against imposition of universal labor rules through the WTO; accessible to all students.

Copeland, Brian R., and M. Scott Taylor. "Trade, Growth, and the Environment." *Journal of Economic Literature* 42 (March 2004): 7–71.
Survey of the theoretical and empirical literature on links between trade and the environment; for intermediate and advanced students.

Coughlin, Cletus. "The Controversy over Free Trade: The Gap between Economists and the General Public." Federal Reserve Bank of St. Louis *Review* 84 (January/February 2002): 1–22.
Why economists are more skeptical than others about arguments for protection.

Cowen, Tyler. *Creative Destruction: How Globalization is Changing the World's Cultures*. Princeton: Princeton University Press, 2002.
Readable treatment of how trade affects culture.

Davis, Lance, and Stanley Engerman. "History Lessons: Sanctions—Neither War nor Peace." *Journal of Economic Perspectives* 16 (Spring 2003): 187–198.
Overview of trade sanctions as a tool of foreign policy.

Golub, Stephen S. "Are International Labor Standards Needed to Prevent Social Dumping?" *Finance and Development* (December 1997): 20–23.
Accessible discussion of the relationship between labor standards and trade.

Graham, Edward M., and J. David Richardson, eds. *Global Competition Policy*. Washington, D.C.: Institute for International Economics, 1997.
Excellent, accessible overview of countries' competition policies and their international implications.

Irwin, Douglas. *Against the Tide*. Princeton: Princeton University Press, 1996.
Excellent history of arguments for protection; for all students.

Irwin, Douglas A. *Free Trade Under Fire*. Princeton: Princeton University Press, 2002.
Accessible examination of many of the arguments for protection.

Jha, Prabhat, et al. "Death and Taxes: Economics of Tobacco Control." *Finance and Development* 36 (December 1999): 46–50.
Controversies over domestic and international tobacco policies.

Johnson, Harry G. "Optimal Trade Intervention in the Presence of Domestic Distortions." In *Trade, Growth, and the Balance of Payments*, edited by Richard Caves, Harry Johnson, and Peter Kenen. New York: Rand McNally, 1965.
The classic paper on the theory of protection with domestic distortions; for intermediate students.

Krugman, Paul. "What Should Trade Negotiators Negotiate About?" *Journal of Economic Literature* (March 1997): 113–120.
Arguments for and against harmonization; for all students.

Lomborg, Bjorn. *The Skeptical Environmentalist: Measuring the Real State of the World*. Cambridge: Cambridge University Press, 2001.
Professor of statistics and former Greenpeace member refutes many of the doomsday statistics widely cited by environmental activists.

Session on "Ineffectiveness of Economic Sanctions." *American Economic Review Papers and Proceedings* 89 (May 1999): 403–420.
How effective are trade sanctions in changing target countries' behavior? For all students.

Steer, Andrew. "Ten Principles of the New Environmentalism." *Finance and Development* (December 1996): 4–7.
Accessible overview of trade and the environment.

Thomas, Vinod, and Tamara Belt. "Growth and the Environment: Allies or Foes?" *Finance and Development* (June 1997): 22–24.
Introduction to the relationship between growth and environmental issues.

Uimonen, Peter, and John Whalley. *Environmental Issues in the New World Trading System*. New York: St. Martin's Press, 1997.
Interaction between environmental and trade issues.

Winters, L. Alan, et al. "Trade Liberalization and Poverty: The Evidence So Far." *Journal of Economic Literature* 52 (March 2004): 72–115.
Survey of the theoretical and empirical literatures on links between trade and poverty; for intermediate and advanced students.

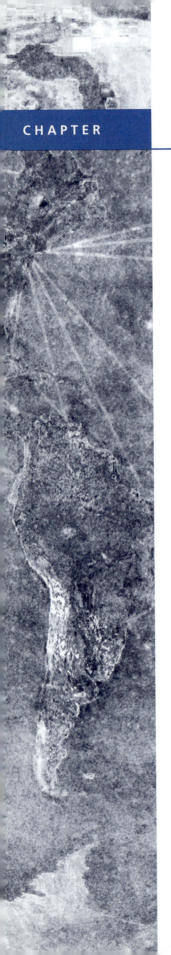

The Political Economy of Trade Policy and Borders

1 INTRODUCTION

The history of international trade and trade policy perhaps is best characterized as a reflection of countries' ambivalent feelings toward trade. On one hand, since the decline of mercantilism in the early nineteenth century, many countries have lauded free trade as an ideal. On the other hand, during the same two centuries, countries' actual trade policies have been littered with relics of mercantilist thought and with protectionist policies won by inefficient domestic industries in the political lobbying battles that determine trade policies.

From the viewpoint of world welfare as a whole, the national character of trade policy has advantages and disadvantages. On the positive side, the constitutional prohibition against tariffs among U.S. states undoubtedly has contributed to the United States' remarkable growth and stability over the last two hundred years. On the negative side, trade policy's national character tends to perpetuate the erroneous mercantilist view of trade as a zero-sum game—that one country's gains come at its trading partners' expense rather than from improved efficiency.

The fact that most trade policy is nationally determined draws our attention to the existence, definition, and economic significance of national borders, as well as to those cases in which policy making occurs at levels other than a national one. First, we recognize that sometimes countries form themselves into groups and determine jointly a range of economic policies. The European Union (EU) and the North American Free Trade Agreement (NAFTA) represent the best-known of many examples. By extending beyond the boundaries of a single country, these groups internationalize both economic activity and decision making. Trade among group members takes on some, but not all, the characteristics of a country's internal trade.

Second, regions within a single country may differ in their factor endowments, market sizes, or economic policies. Differences between the northern and southern United States, for example, have played an important role throughout the country's economic history. The same holds true for Italy, Mexico, Brazil, and many other countries. In other cases, policy makers subject subnational regions to different policies, as in the special economic zones (SEZs) along China's southern coast, where economic activity follows a more market-oriented path than in the country's interior. Trade between distinct regions, called *interregional trade*, exhibits both similarities to and differences from international trade. Understanding these similarities and differences helps illuminate the role of international trade and highlights more precisely the economic significance of national borders.

Finally, recent events in the world economy remind us that even the definition of countries can change. At the same time that some groups of countries join to coordinate their economies and trade policies, other nations disintegrate or threaten to. Examples of the first trend include the former East and West Germanys, the members of the European Union, and the NAFTA trio. The demise of the Soviet Union, civil war in the former Yugoslavia, the breakup of Czechoslovakia, and tensions between Quebec and the rest of Canada represent just a few examples of the opposite tendency of nation-states to break into smaller policy-making units. For much of the post-World War II period, trade between East and West Germany constituted inter*national* trade, while that between the Czech and Slovak regions of Czechoslovakia was inter*regional* trade. Now, the situation has reversed; trade in the Czech and Slovak case now crosses a national border while German trade no longer does.

In this chapter, we address the domestic political processes that determine national trade policies, the history of the world trading system, and some cases of supranational and subnational trade policies.

2 THE POLITICAL ECONOMY OF NATIONAL TRADE POLICY

In Chapter Eight, we saw that, despite the many guises of arguments for protection, almost all could be met with a superior policy that wouldn't sacrifice the gains from trade. The problems best solved by trade protection are few. Nonetheless, protectionist policies are numerous, diverse, and widespread. Thus far, we've explained protection's overwhelming presence in the world economy based on trade's distributional effects: International trade alters relative prices, thereby helping some groups, hurting others, and creating a natural constituency for protectionist policies. Chapters Two and Three, however, demonstrated that the benefits of unrestricted international trade outweigh the costs—in the sense that the winners can compensate the losers and still enjoy net gains. So why does unrestricted trade remain the exception rather than the rule? The keys to solving this puzzle lie in understanding the *distribution* of trade's costs and benefits and its implications for the political process through which most countries make trade-policy decisions.

The costs of international trade (for example, the decline of comparative-disadvantage industries) tend to be concentrated on a relatively small number of individuals. The benefits of international trade, on the other hand, come primarily in the form of lower prices for consumers and are spread over a large group, with each individual capturing only a small portion. This implies that in a direct referendum in which individuals costlessly voted on the question, "Should the country impose a tariff on imports of good X?" the vote should be a resounding no, because consumers of X typically outnumber producers of X by a wide margin. If it were costly to vote (perhaps because each voter must take time to gather information on the issue and go to the polling place), the referendum's outcome would be less certain. Each producer of good X would have a larger stake in the issue than each consumer, making producers likely to vote. Consumers, although they have a larger stake *as a group*, might find *as individuals* that the cost of voting exceeded the potential benefits of avoiding the tariff.

But countries rarely make trade policy decisions by direct referendum. In such a referendum, each individual votes on a specific issue, not on a list of candidates, one of whom then "represents" the voter on a number of questions. This turns out to be an important distinction. Rarely is a voter lucky enough to find a candidate who perfectly represents that voter's views on all issues; typically, picking a candidate requires trade-offs. Each voter has a priority regarding issues. For producers of good X, the tariff question is likely to decide which candidate gets their vote. For consumers of good X, the small effect the tariff would have on each individual makes the tariff a lower-priority issue. As a result, a vote-maximizing candidate will more likely follow the wishes of X producers and support the tariff.

A related phenomenon that also pushes policy in a protectionist direction concerns the costs of organization. The fact that a small number of individuals bear the costs of trade while the benefits are much more widely dispersed implies that pro-protectionist supporters will be more successful in organizing an effective lobbying force than will supporters of unrestricted trade. Suppose Congress holds a hearing in Washington, D.C., that will influence members' votes on the tariff. Who will undertake the inconvenience and expense to go to Washington to make their feelings known—workers and producers in the X industry or consumers? Workers and producers will, because failure to get a tariff will impose a cost on each individual high enough to justify the expense of the trip. An individual consumer, on the other hand, has too small a stake in the issue to make the trip worthwhile even though consumers' stake as a group may be very large. Members of Congress see a biased sample of their constituents and may respond by voting for the tariff.

This systematic pro-protection bias in the policy-making process carries over to the laws that govern the making of trade policy. One of the clearest examples is **Section 201** of the Trade Act of 1974, the "escape clause" that allows the United States to abandon its tariff-reduction obligations under the WTO whenever imports are a substantial cause of serious injury or threat to a domestic industry. Under the law, the U.S. International Trade Commission (ITC) investigates an industry's claim of injury. If the ITC finds that imports indeed injure or threaten to injure the domestic industry, the commission must recommend to the president relief in the form of a tariff, quota, or Trade Adjustment Assistance eligibility for the industry.[1] Nowhere does the law require that the ITC take the interests of consumers into account. The president, having instructions to weigh a broader set of considerations, may accept the ITC's recommendation or reject it in the national economic interest.

Of course, opening trade injures a country's industries of comparative disadvantage, as predicted by the specific-factor model and the Stolper-Samuelson theorem derived in Chapter Four. But the benefits of trade in terms of lower prices and improved efficiency more than offset these losses. The wording of Section 201, by limiting ITC consideration to the interest of domestic producers, biases trade policy toward protectionism. This bias has become stronger as successive amendments to the original Section 201 have restricted the freedom of the ITC and the president to refuse to recommend or implement import relief, part of an overall tendency by Congress to acquire more control over the making of trade policy.

Given the pro-protection bias in the policy-making process, how does trade liberalization ever get accomplished? One way is by informing voters of the often-hidden costs of protection. Even though an individual consumer may lose a relatively small amount from a single protectionist measure, such as the U.S. sugar quota, antidumping duties on foreign steel, or countervailing duties on Canadian lumber, such measures taken together impose enormous costs on consumers as a group, particularly low-income ones. Laws that require the hidden costs of protection to be spelled out can help voters make more informed decisions and pressure their political representatives to do likewise. For example, as we saw in Chapter Eight, most arguments for protection can be met with alternate policies that provide equivalent benefits at lower efficiency costs.

---

1. Before the Uruguay Round agreement, escape-clause cases often culminated in negotiation of a voluntary export restraint (VER); but the agreement limits this source of VER proliferation.

Since World War II, international negotiations through the GATT/WTO have persuaded many countries to lower their trade barriers. One reason negotiations may succeed in cases where countries aren't willing to liberalize unilaterally is that the reciprocity involved in negotiations creates another pro-liberalization constituency: export industries. In the context of reciprocal negotiations, a country lowers its trade barriers in exchange for trading partners lowering theirs. Therefore, the opposition of import-competing producers can be balanced by support from exporters who benefit from increased openness of foreign markets.

3 HOW DID WE GET HERE? A BRIEF HISTORY OF INTERNATIONAL TRADE POLICY

3.1 Before Smith, Ricardo, and Hume: Mercantilism

The first dominant theory of international trade was **mercantilism**, which prevailed from the Renaissance until the early nineteenth century. This was the era of nation-building and consolidation of power by emerging nation-states. Rulers raised armies, built navies, and went to war to protect their newly formed territorial dominions—an expensive process. These rulers viewed international trade primarily as a way to finance the expenditures involved in building their nation-states.

The use of paper money (dollar bills, euro notes, and paper yen) hadn't yet spread during the mercantilist era. "Money," or the means of payment, consisted of precious metals, primarily gold and silver, called specie. Policy makers' goal for trade was to accumulate as much specie as possible, because ownership of gold and silver provided the wherewithal to pay armies and build ships. Policies that encouraged exports and restricted imports contributed to this specie accumulation. Whenever a nation exported more than it imported vis-à-vis another country, the deficit country (the one for which the value of imports exceeded the value of exports) paid the balance of its account to the surplus country (the one for which the value of exports exceeded the value of imports) in gold or silver.[2]

Mercantilism dominated thought on trade for a remarkably long period. Eventually the Classical economists in England began to point out critical weaknesses in the mercantilist view.[3] One important point was that nations couldn't all conduct successful mercantilist policies simultaneously. One country's exports are by definition another's imports, so one country's "success" necessarily implied another's "failure." In fact, mercantilists viewed trade as a zero-sum game: Whatever specie one nation accumulated necessarily came at the expense of another. As we learned in Chapter Two, Adam Smith's and David Ricardo's work on absolute and comparative advantage transformed the perspective on trade into a positive-sum view.

David Hume continued the critique of mercantilism by arguing that even when one country "succeeded" from the mercantilist viewpoint, that "success" couldn't last. The accumulation of specie or money had the effect of raising prices in the "successful" mercantilist country. As prices rose relative to those in other countries, imports became relatively cheaper and more attractive while the desirability of the country's exports waned. The very success in accumulating specie caused imports to rise and exports to fall, eliminating the surplus that had facilitated the accumulation process. So any mercantilist "success" was short-lived at best.

---

2. Section 2 in Chapter Two discusses mercantilism in more detail.

3. Section 3 in Chapter Two contains more discussion.

Finally—and perhaps most important—specie was useful only insofar as it represented purchasing power, or the ability to buy goods and services that generate consumer satisfaction. If a country exported to the limits of its ability and imported nothing, it would accumulate specie but would have little in the way of goods and services.

3.2 Britain and the Rise of the United States

At the close of the eighteenth century, world events combined with the effects of the Classical economists' work moved trade policy away from mercantilism and toward more open trade. The Industrial Revolution created British textile, iron, and steel industries that, because of their technological superiority and scale economies, could serve the entire world. Opening export markets and locating foreign sources of raw materials became British policy priorities. Invention of railroads and steamships provided the inexpensive land and sea transport needed to expand world trade. All these events edged Britain toward a policy of relatively unrestricted trade throughout the first half of the nineteenth century, although wars and recessions interjected temporary periods of renewed trade restrictions.[4]

Before the American Revolution, the colonies used import tariffs to generate government revenue. Protection of domestic industries wasn't a major issue, because British law prevented the colonies from developing manufacturing to compete with British industry. During the Revolution, American manufacturing emerged to replace no-longer-available British imports. In what has become a common historical pattern, the end of the war coincided with demands for protection by these new American industries that had enjoyed insulation from foreign competition during the Revolution. The protection of domestic manufacturing joined revenue generation as a major reason for the tariffs instituted by the United States, which passed its first comprehensive trade legislation in 1789.

Strong disagreement over the proper course of international trade policy characterized the first half of the nineteenth century in the United States. The North, with dominant manufacturing interests, favored protective tariffs. The South, on the other hand, was still an agricultural economy and favored unrestricted trade. The South exported raw materials, primarily cotton and tobacco, in exchange for manufactures from Britain and Europe. The North might have pushed for export taxes as well as import tariffs, but the South had inserted a clause into the Constitution prohibiting export taxes. Disagreement continued up to the Civil War of the 1860s, when the North used tariffs to finance its victorious war effort and then continued to impose tariffs to protect its manufacturing interests after the South's defeat.

During the late 1800s, tariffs rose in both Britain and the United States. Germany and France were growing and industrializing rapidly, eroding Britain's technological advantage from the Industrial Revolution. During the first decade of the twentieth century, tariffs' negative effects on world growth and trade were gaining recognition. Policy makers laid plans for tariff reductions, but World War I intervened before any serious liberalization could take place. As usual, the war and its aftermath created renewed demands for protection in most countries, and tariff levels continued to rise. The U.S. economy enjoyed phenomenal growth relative to the rest of the world during this period, and U.S. trade policy became increasingly important as a worldwide model.

---

4. On Britain's nineteenth-century trade liberalization, see Beth V. Yarbrough and Robert M. Yarbrough, *Cooperation and Governance in International Trade*, in the chapter references.

Figure 1   What Happened to World Trade, 1929–1933? (Millions $)

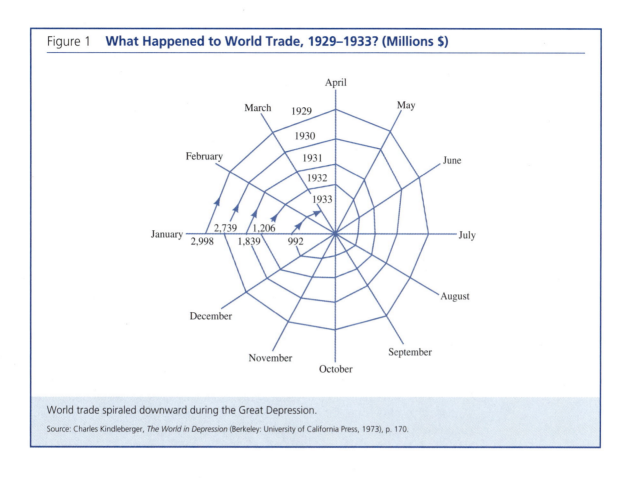

World trade spiraled downward during the Great Depression.

Source: Charles Kindleberger, *The World in Depression* (Berkeley: University of California Press, 1973), p. 170.

Unfortunately, the model set by the United States rested on the **Smoot-Hawley tariff bill of 1930**, which raised tariffs to an average of 53 percent. Other economies retaliated by raising their own trade barriers, and the volume of world trade plummeted as the world economy entered the Great Depression. Figure 1 summarizes the downward spiral of world trade during 1929–1933. Countries tried to "export" their unemployment problems by blocking imports, a classic example of a beggar-thy-neighbor policy. Economic historians disagree over the precise degree of blame for the Great Depression's duration and severity that rests on the Smoot-Hawley bill, but clearly the bill didn't help solve the severe economic problems of the time.

3.3 The Reciprocal Trade Agreements Act of 1934

Despite the dubious value of U.S. leadership in the Smoot-Hawley episode, the United States soon recognized the need for trade liberalization as a way to emerge from the Great Depression. In 1934, a radical change in U.S. trade policy produced the **Reciprocal Trade Agreements Act (RTAA)**, which set the stage for a half-century of liberalization. Not only did the act reduce the Smoot-Hawley-level tariffs; it also changed the institutional arrangements for making U.S. trade policy.[5] Previously Congress had sole responsibility for tariffs and determined, on a unilateral product-by-product basis, U.S. tariff levels. The RTAA

---

5. Political scientist I. M. Destler argues in *American Trade Politics* that this institutional change was a key element in the liberalization that followed.

Table 1 **TARIFF REDUCTIONS, 1934–2004**

GATT/WTO Conference	Average Cut in All Duties	Remaining Duties as a Proportion of 1930 Tariffs	Number of Participants
Pre-GATT (1934–1947)	33.2%	66.8%	23
First Round (Geneva, 1947)	21.1	52.7	23
Second Round (Annecy, 1949)	1.9	51.7	13
Third Round (Torquay, 1950–1951)	3.0	50.1	38
Fourth Round (Geneva, 1955–1956)	3.5	48.9	26
Dillon Round (Geneva, 1961–1962)	2.4	47.7	26
Kennedy Round (Geneva, 1964–1967)	36.0	30.5	62
Tokyo Round (Geneva, 1974–1979)	29.6	21.2	99
Uruguay Round (Geneva, 1987–1994)	38.0	13.1	125
Doha Round (Geneva, 2001–)	n.a.	n.a.	147

Source: Data from Real Phillipe Lavergne, "The Political Economy of U.S. Tariffs" (Ph.D. thesis, University of Toronto, 1981); reproduced in Robert E. Baldwin, "U.S. Trade Policy Since World War II," in *The Structure and Evolution of Recent U.S. Trade Policy*, edited by R. E. Baldwin and A. O. Krueger (Chicago: University of Chicago Press, 1984), p. 6; updated to include the Uruguay and Doha Rounds.

switched authority over tariffs to the executive branch of government and authorized tariff negotiations with other countries. For the first time, countries could negotiate, coordinate, and cooperate in their (still nationally determined) international trade policies.

The RTAA remained the backbone of U.S. trade policy through 11 revisions and extensions until the Trade Expansion Act of 1962 replaced it 28 years later. Table 1 documents the success in tariff reduction under the RTAA and summarizes the reductions achieved in negotiations between 1934 and 1962 as well as more recent events.

Another innovative aspect of the RTAA was its recognition of the interdependence of trade policies by the United States and its trading partners. The argument that U.S. tariff reductions would encourage reciprocal reductions by other countries and thereby stimulate U.S. exports (important to agricultural interests) was critical to passage of the 1934 act.

3.4 Post–World War II Trade Policy

Soon war again interrupted world trade. Emerging from World War II as the only major industrial economy with its capital stock intact, the United States took a strong leadership position in pushing for trade liberalization. The policy resulted from a combination of economic and political interests. Clearly the dominant country in technology and industrial strength, the United States had vast export opportunities it could exploit only in a relatively open trading environment. American intellectual and political leaders also believed that building economic linkages through trade could promote world peace. A related concern was the desire to help Europe reunite and rebuild quickly, to limit the spread of Soviet influence through Europe.

The United States demonstrated its commitment to open trade through its support of a strong institutional framework for international economic and political interaction. That framework included the **International Monetary Fund (IMF)**, responsible for helping member countries with short-run balance-of-payments problems; the **World Bank** to deal with economic development issues; and the **General Agreement on Tariffs and Trade (GATT)**, predecessor of today's **World Trade Organization (WTO)**. These institutions still form the basic structure for international economic relations in the monetary, development, and trade spheres, although each has evolved and others have emerged in the intervening decades.

Even in the postwar heyday of trade liberalization, the United States continued to exhibit ambivalence toward trade. The GATT was intended as a preliminary to formation of a more extensive and formal International Trade Organization (ITO), but the U.S. Congress refused to ratify the ITO because of fear of losing control over U.S. trade policy to an international organization. As a result, the GATT became the basis for international trade-policy negotiations.[6] Congress repeatedly authorized the president to seek reciprocal tariff reductions through negotiations with trading partners, but at the same time imposed increasing restrictions on the liberalization process. Perhaps the clearest example of these restrictions was the insistence in 1947 that a formal escape clause be included in all tariff treaties. The **escape clause** permits cancellation of tariff reductions shown to cause injury to a domestic industry. As earlier chapters of this book show, the gains from international trade come from specialization and exchange according to comparative advantage and exploitation of economies of scale. The process of specialization inherently involves shrinkage or elimination of some industries. The idea of an escape clause, if carried to its logical limit, could eliminate trade, because trade always injures a nation's comparative-disadvantage industries. The escape clause represents just one of a number of **safeguards** imposed by Congress in an effort to avoid the adjustment costs involved in trade's reallocation of resources.

In the United States, Congress has alternately tightened and loosened safeguard provisions with evolving perceptions of international trade. We can see these changing views by briefly examining the main trade acts passed since the 1950s: the Trade Expansion Act of 1962, the Trade Act of 1974, the Trade Agreements Act of 1979, the Trade and Tariff Act of 1984, the Omnibus Trade and Competitiveness Act of 1988, and the Uruguay Round Agreements Act of 1994.[7] Each attempted to reclaim for Congress a portion of the control over international trade policy delegated to the president during the Depression and World War II.

3.5 Trade Policy in the 1960s and 1970s

THE TRADE EXPANSION ACT AND THE KENNEDY ROUND The trade policies of the 1940s and 1950s involved extensions of the Reciprocal Trade Agreements Act. Congress had authorized the president to negotiate tariff reductions with trading partners, but throughout the period it gradually tightened restrictions on the president's actions, particularly through changes in safeguard provisions. Partly as a result of this increased protectionist sentiment, President Kennedy sought to regain momentum in trade liberalization by designing a comprehensive trade bill to replace, rather than merely revise and extend, the RTAA. The result was the Trade Expansion Act of 1962 (TEA).

In addition to granting the president authority to negotiate tariff reductions of up to 50 percent through the GATT, the TEA contained three provisions important for their lasting effect on world trade policy. The first resulted not from the bill itself but from the political process necessary to obtain its passage. To gain the political support of representatives from

---

6. The Jackson book in the chapter references includes an excellent treatment of the history of the GATT.

7. Robert E. Baldwin, *The Political Economy of U.S. Import Policy* (Cambridge, Mass.: MIT Press, 1985), provides a useful account of the ebb and flow of support for pro-trade and protectionist policies and the reflections of those sentiments in the postwar trade bills. Most provisions of each bill take the form of amendments of earlier bills; thus, U.S. trade law is cumulative. For example, Section 201 of the Trade Act of 1974, as amended by the later acts, still forms the basis of U.S. escape-clause law.

the southern states (site of the U.S. textile industry), Kennedy agreed to impose quotas on cotton textile imports and to partially exempt textiles from the negotiations to take place under the proposed bill. These quotas and exemptions grew through the years, in the form of the **Multifiber Agreement (MFA)**, into one of the world's most far-reaching and restrictive sets of trade barriers and probably the most damaging to developing economies.

The Trade Expansion Act also introduced two rather sweeping changes into the institutional arrangements for tariff negotiations. The form of negotiations shifted from a *product-by-product format* to an *across-the-board,* or *linear, format.* Before the TEA, countries had negotiated tariffs for each product separately. The process was slow and tedious, and countries often proved unwilling to consider reductions on many goods. Under the TEA, a single negotiated tariff-cutting formula would apply to all products. Each country then could submit a list of exceptions, or products on which it would not cut tariffs. The new approach speeded up the negotiation process somewhat; however, arrival at the tariff-cutting formula was slow as each country tried to fine-tune the formula to its own advantage. In the end, the Kennedy Round of tariff reductions conducted under the GATT by authority granted by the TEA achieved a tariff cut of approximately 36 percent by the major industrial countries (see Table 1).

The other institutional innovation introduced in the Trade Expansion Act was the addition of the **Trade Adjustment Assistance (TAA)** program to U.S. safeguard provisions. Before the act, if imports resulting from a tariff reduction injured an industry, the only remedy was reinstitution of the tariff. Trade Adjustment Assistance constituted an alternate way to deal with injury: directly compensate injured firms and workers for their losses. Compensation could take the form of extended unemployment benefits, retraining, and relocation assistance for workers; low-interest loans and other assistance to help firms move into new product lines; and even restitution to whole communities harmed by an industry's decline. Trade Adjustment Assistance provided a way to capture the benefits from unrestricted trade while assisting those harmed by it; in other words, the program attempted to provide the compensation discussed in earlier chapters on the distributional effect of trade.[8]

Following the success of the TEA and the accompanying Kennedy Round talks, protectionist pressures rose in the United States. U.S. industries claimed that other countries, especially members of the European Community (the smaller predecessor of today's EU), violated the spirit if not the letter of the GATT agreement by replacing their tariffs with nontariff barriers. The Trade Adjustment Assistance program, expected to reduce pressure by domestic industries for protection, had little effect during the 1960s, due to its stringent eligibility requirements. For eligibility, an industry had to prove that a tariff reduction had injured it and had been the primary cause of injury (that is, had caused at least 51 percent of the industry's problems). These requirements were interpreted strictly, and essentially no assistance was paid under the TAA program until 1969. The politically powerful AFL-CIO labor group, dissatisfied with the adjustment assistance program, reversed its historical support of trade liberalization in favor of import restrictions. Not until 1974 was Congress willing to pass another trade bill authorizing a round of tariff negotiations.

THE TRADE ACT OF 1974, THE TOKYO ROUND, AND THE 1979 TRADE AGREEMENTS ACT   The Trade Act of 1974 resembled the 1962 TEA in several respects. The 1974 bill granted the president an impressive 60 percent tariff-reduction authority, but at the same time placed additional constraints on the president's liberalization efforts and continued Congress's campaign to reclaim its power over trade

---

8. See the discussion of Trade Adjustment Assistance in section 5.4 of Chapter Four.

policy. As in 1962, obtaining adequate support for the trade bill required major concessions to the textile industry. The United States extended the existing set of import quotas from cotton textiles to cover wools and synthetics. Congress specifically excluded several items from the president's tariff-cutting authority, including footwear, an industry of particular interest to developing countries.

The bill strengthened the role of the International Trade Commission, then known as the Tariff Commission, relative to the president in the interpretation and enforcement of safeguards against injury to domestic industries. Rules requiring stronger enforcement against "unfair" foreign trade practices such as subsidies and dumping were included. The president received authority to negotiate reductions in nontariff trade barriers as well as tariffs, but only with the specific approval of Congress.

Finally, the act loosened eligibility requirements for compensation under the Trade Adjustment Assistance program in two important ways. Injury to a domestic industry no longer had to be directly linked to a government policy (tariff reduction) but only to increased imports. And increased competition from imports had to represent an "important" cause of the injury but no longer the "primary" one.

These rules set out in the Trade Act of 1974 laid the groundwork for U.S. participation in the Tokyo Round of GATT talks, which lasted from 1974 to 1979 and reduced the major industrial economies' tariff rates by approximately 30 percent. On other issues, the Tokyo Round, which was more ambitious than earlier talks in addressing problems associated with nontariff barriers, had mixed success. Because of the price-support systems we discussed in the context of export subsidies (see section 5 in Chapter Seven), trade barriers on most agricultural products proved immune to progress. Developing countries' concerns received somewhat more attention than in earlier rounds of talks, but lack of progress in the crucial agricultural, textile, apparel, and footwear industries continued.

The Tokyo Round broke controversial ground by reaching several agreements accepted by only a subset of the then more than 90 GATT member countries. Nine such **codes** were negotiated, with additional signatories free to join later. Areas covered by the codes included subsidies and countervailing duties, government procurement, standards or technical trade barriers, import licensing, customs valuation, antidumping, trade in civilian aircraft, trade in dairy products, and trade in bovine meat. Some of the codes proved more successful than others, but the idea of codes or mini-agreements remains controversial, because they represent a move away from the more traditional multilateral approach of the GATT.

The Tokyo Round left the international trading system with important unresolved issues, including developed-country barriers against developing-country exports, mutually acceptable interpretations of safeguard provisions, and procedures for settling disputes within the GATT. The United States ratified the results of the Tokyo Round negotiations in the Trade Agreements Act of 1979. That act also further limited the executive branch's discretion over trade policy by requiring more extensive monitoring of trade agreements and reporting to Congress.

3.6 Trade Policy in the 1980s and 1990s

THE TRADE AND TARIFF ACT OF 1984 The Trade and Tariff Act of 1984 is best known for its approval of an historic shift in U.S. trade policy: It gave the president authority to negotiate *bilateral* trade treaties. Since World War II, the United States had insisted that trade liberalization be accomplished *multilaterally* through the GATT to ensure that all member countries benefited from liberalization on a nondiscriminatory basis. Throughout the early 1980s, the United States promoted a new round of multilateral GATT trade talks and sought support from its trading partners for the venture. The world economy was mired in both a global recession, which increased protectionist pressures, and a developing-country debt crisis; this unfortunate combination of circumstances threatened to stymie progress toward opening trade. Other countries resisted U.S. appeals to support a new round of GATT talks. So U.S. policy makers turned to bilateral agreements for two reasons: as an alternate path to liberalization and as an attempt to pressure trading partners to support a new GATT round or risk being left out of the liberalization process.

THE OMNIBUS TRADE AND COMPETITIVENESS ACT AND THE URUGUAY ROUND AGREEMENTS ACT
Finally, a 1986 meeting of trade ministers in Uruguay launched a round of GATT talks known as the **Uruguay Round**. Goals included complete elimination of tariffs by the major trading partners; extension of GATT rules to previously neglected areas such as trade in services and agriculture; clarification of GATT's institutional role, especially in dispute settlement; better enforcement of property rights in intellectual property such as computer software and movies; and limiting use of nontariff trade barriers, particularly voluntary export restraints.

Although the Uruguay Round talks began in late 1986, it wasn't until 1988, in the Omnibus Trade and Competitiveness Act, that Congress actually granted the executive branch the formal authority to participate and to negotiate tariff reductions of up to 50 percent. The 1988 act also required domestic industries seeking import relief under the Section 201 escape clause to show that they were prepared to make "positive adjustment" to import competition. Although subject to a range of interpretation, this change at least provided the opportunity to halt the trend toward long-term, permanent protection for the country's comparative-disadvantage industries.

Despite the provision for participation in the GATT talks and the modification of Section 201 to take some account of patterns of comparative advantage, the origin of many of the 1988 act's elements lay in concern over the U.S. trade deficit and in the often-cited decline in the country's "competitiveness." As a result, many parts of the 1,000-page bill represented moves toward protectionism. Under the amended Section 301, domestic industries found it easier to claim (sometimes falsely) that they were injured by imports facilitated by foreign unfair trade practices, thereby justifying relief or retaliation.[9] The 1988 bill transferred responsibility for initiating Section 301 cases from the president to the U.S. trade representative, a move expected to make firms more likely to obtain affirmative findings in unfair trade cases.

The Uruguay Round talks were scheduled for completion by the end of 1990. If submitted to Congress by May 1991, the results of the round could have been approved under a special **fast-track** process that expedites congressional action by prohibiting amendments and limiting the time Congress has to consider the bill.[10] However, a deadlock between the United States and the European Community over always-controversial agricultural export subsidies prevented agreement, and talks broke down in 1990. The United States wanted the agreement to eliminate agricultural subsidies, and the EC wanted to keep intact its subsidy-based Common Agricultural Policy.

The Uruguay Round continued past its original deadline under a two-year extension of the president's negotiating authority granted by Congress in 1991. Key countries had reached tentative agreement in many areas, including industrial subsidies, antidumping duties, foreign investment, dispute settlement, safeguards, and bringing textile trade into

---

9. Recall that Section 301 of the Trade Act of 1974 is the foundation of U.S. trade law dealing with "unfair" trade practices of foreign countries. See also section 10 in Chapter Eight.

10. The *fast-track* terminology for Congressional authorization of trade negotiations has since been changed to *trade-promotion authority*.

the GATT system. Negotiations, however, follow a format in which no part of an agreement becomes final until the entire agreement becomes final. Continuing disagreement between the EC and the United States over the depth of cuts in farm subsidies threatened the whole negotiation, after five years' work.

Congress extended fast-track authority for the Uruguay Round for the final time in 1993, but only until December 15 of that year. U.S. policy makers took a risk that, by signaling that they would walk away from the entire venture if talks didn't conclude by the end of the year, they could pressure recalcitrant Europeans to compromise on agriculture. The gamble paid off, and GATT members approved the Uruguay Round agreement in 1994.

In the end, the Uruguay Round accomplished many of the tasks on its ambitious agenda. The major results included the following:

1. The agricultural provisions significantly reduced export subsidies and imposed some discipline on domestic subsidies. The agreement also required tariffication of existing nontariff barriers and made the resulting tariffs subject to cuts averaging 36 percent. In agricultural markets completely closed to imports, the agreement required reduction of trade barriers sufficient to allow minimum access for imports.
2. In textiles, the bilateral quotas of the Multifiber Agreement were slated to be removed for all WTO members by the end of a 10-year transition period in 2005. Most of the protection would remain in place until then, and high tariffs would remain in many textile and apparel sectors even after the quotas disappeared.
3. Overall progress on tariffs included cuts averaging almost 40 percent plus complete elimination of tariffs by industrial countries in several important sectors. A much higher percentage of world trade would occur duty free after the Uruguay Round, and many developing economies agreed to bind (that is, promise not to raise) tariffs on a large share of their imports.
4. The agreement clarified the distinction between acceptable and unacceptable subsidies. Developing countries' subsidies were subject to discipline for the first time.
5. The new General Agreement on Trade in Services began the task of developing a framework of rules for trade in services comparable to existing rules for trade in goods.
6. The agreement strengthened international rules for enforcement of intellectual property rights including patents, trademarks, copyrights, and industrial secrets. After specified transition periods, the rules would apply to developing as well as developed countries.
7. Most important, the agreement strengthened the structure of the GATT framework itself by establishing the World Trade Organization (WTO). The new organization brought together the 50-year accumulation of GATT rules and agreements under one umbrella. The WTO would exist as a "single undertaking," so member countries would subscribe to all rules and responsibilities, rather than picking and choosing as in the past. An improved dispute-settlement procedure would handle all disputes and improve members' compliance with their obligations.

THE DOHA ROUND   The eight-year Uruguay Round negotiations exhausted participants. But the history of trade policy has caused many observers to suggest the "bicycle" theory: If the liberalization process stops moving forward, it tends to fall over. So, exhausted or not, negotiators agreed at the end of the Uruguay Round to a schedule of future talks on specific issues. New talks on trade in agriculture and services started in early 2000. Many WTO members hoped to launch a new round of comprehensive negotiations; but early talks bogged down. In addition to issue-specific disagreements, WTO members faced the nontrivial task of agreeing on a strategy for approaching the new round. Most members agreed that the Uruguay Round's eight-year length overtaxed everyone's patience, suggesting that the new round should aim for a more reasonable three-to-four year completion schedule. But this raised a problem: A short time horizon required a limited and manageable agenda. But constraining the number of items on the agenda limits countries' ability to negotiate trade-offs among issues (for example, giving up something you want in agriculture in order to get something you want in services).

Finally, in late 2001, WTO members agreed, in Doha, Qatar, on a draft agenda for a new round of trade talks. Items on the agenda include (as always!) difficult and controversial ones. The United States and many developing countries want drastic changes in the European Union's Common Agricultural Policy, which turns Western European countries that would import agricultural goods under free trade into heavily subsidized exporters. Almost everyone wants the United States to stop its aggressive use of import-blocking antidumping policies; and many countries (including the United States) hope to stop the further spread of antidumping laws. Labor and environmental groups in the rich industrialized economies hope to make future trade agreements contingent on developing countries' adherence to high labor and environmental standards; but developing countries view these demands as thinly disguised protectionism on the part of the developed world. And developing economies that face public-health crises, such as the AIDS epidemic, wanted and won more generous provisions for exemptions from patents that protect the property rights of pharmaceutical firms.

After several years of starts and stops, including some spectacular negotiation breakdowns in Seattle in 1999 and Cancun in 2003, the Doha Round won't meet the hoped-for deadline. Negotiations have been unwieldy with the participation of the WTO's many new member countries. Developing countries continue to push for liberalization of developed countries' stubbornly protectionist policies in agriculture. Developed countries want developing ones to recognize that most of the gains from trade must come from developing countries' liberalization of their own trade policies.

The ongoing work of the WTO is just one of the paths by which governments have addressed many of the economic goals expressed at the end of World War II. As mentioned earlier, one of those goals was a quick rebuilding of Western Europe. The United States encouraged not only the rebuilding of individual European economies but also the economic and political unification, or *integration*, of Western Europe as a means of preserving the peace. Policy makers saw the nationalistic character of prewar political and economic policies as a cause of the war that devastated both sides.

The integration of Europe greatly affected postwar trade policy, providing one example of institutions' role in transcending the strictly national character of economic policies. Ironically, some policy makers now cite Europe's integration as a danger sign for the world trading system. European success in moving toward an open market within the European Union, along with the formation of NAFTA and many other integration groups, raise fears that the trading system will break into blocs, or regional areas *within* which trade is relatively free but *between* which protectionism dominates. To understand and evaluate these concerns, we must analyze economic integration's impact on the world trading system.

4 ECONOMIC INTEGRATION AND REGIONAL TRADING

The combination of countries' variation in economic size and the importance of economic size in determining a country's role in world markets provides a powerful incentive for nations to form themselves into groups. At the same time, the unique situation each country faces forms a barrier to smooth coordination and cooperation within such groups. Each country wants to retain its national economic goals and its power over policies for pursuing them, while capturing the ability to make decisions that transcend national boundaries. One attempt to obtain the benefits of both nationalism and supranationalism involves the creation of groups of countries that explicitly agree to coordinate certain aspects of their policies.

4.1 Stages of Integration

Integration, or the formation of countries into groups, can be either political or economic, and the distinction between the two often blurs. Five stages of economic integration represent increasing degrees of unification, as illustrated in Figure 2.

The lowest level of integration is formation of a **preferential trading arrangement (PTA)**.[11] Under this system, member countries agree to maintain lower barriers to trade within the group than to trade with nonmember countries. Each country continues to determine its own policies, but the trade policy of each includes preferential treatment of group members. One simple example of such an arrangement would be a differential tariff whereby each member placed a tariff on imports from member countries equal to half its tariff on imports from nonmembers. Panel (a) of Figure 3 illustrates such an arrangement in a three-country world where countries A and B form a PTA while C remains a nonmember.

The next stage of integration is a **free-trade area**, which involves eliminating barriers to intra-group trade while allowing each country to maintain its own nationally determined barriers to trade with nonmembers; NAFTA is an example. A free-trade area may apply to all goods or to only a specified list.[12] Free-trade areas have the advantage of requiring agreement among member countries on only a narrow range of issues. One disadvantage of this limited form of integration lies in the area of enforcement. Panel (b) in Figure 3 depicts a free-trade area in which country A maintains a 10 percent tariff on

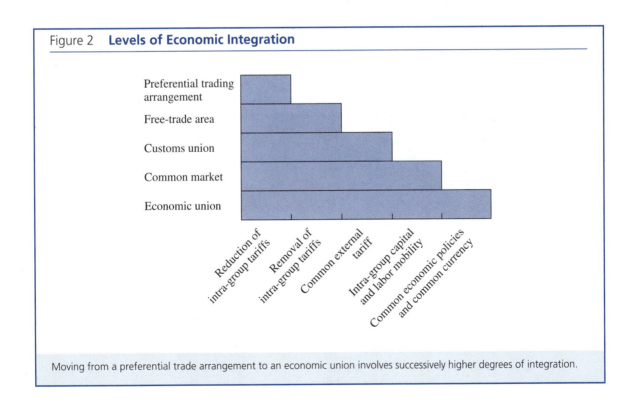

Figure 2   **Levels of Economic Integration**

Moving from a preferential trade arrangement to an economic union involves successively higher degrees of integration.

---

11. In the literature on economic integration, the terms *preferential trade arrangement* (PTA) and *regional trade arrangement* (RTA) also are used as generic names for all five stages of integration.

12. In order not to violate the WTO nondiscrimination requirement, a free-trade area or customs union (discussed shortly) must remove the barriers to all or almost all trade between members.

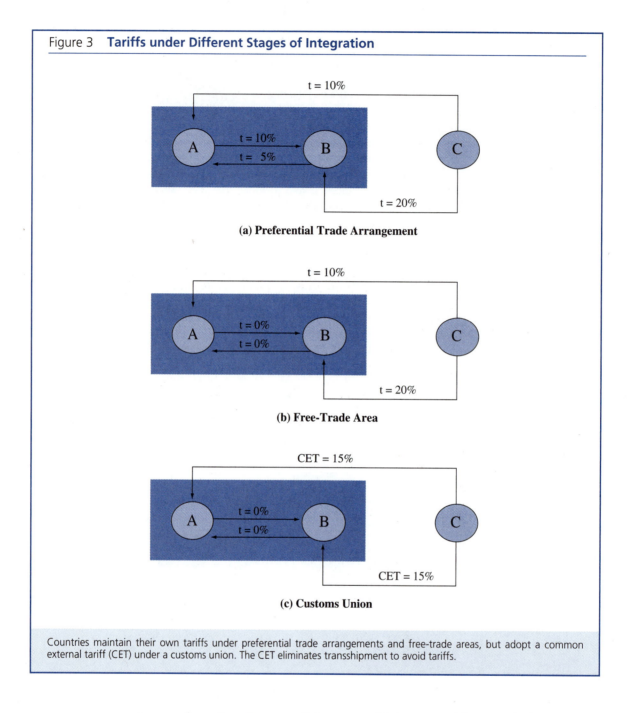

Figure 3   **Tariffs under Different Stages of Integration**

(a) Preferential Trade Arrangement

(b) Free-Trade Area

(c) Customs Union

Countries maintain their own tariffs under preferential trade arrangements and free-trade areas, but adopt a common external tariff (CET) under a customs union. The CET eliminates transshipment to avoid tariffs.

imports from C, and country B imposes a 20 percent tariff on goods from C. This situation produces an incentive for C to ship goods ultimately destined for B through A, paying the 10 percent tariff and then shipping duty-free from A to B, thereby avoiding B's 20 percent tariff. Transshipment problems arise whenever member countries try to maintain different tariff levels on trade with nonmembers.[13]

13. Preferential trade arrangements such as the NAFTA seek to avoid transshipment by restricting tariff-free treatment to goods produced in the partner country. These restrictions require rules of origin (see section 7.1 in Chapter Seven).

One way to ameliorate the transshipment problem involves moving to the next level of integration by forming a **customs union**. With this arrangement, intra-group trade faces no barriers and members maintain a **common external tariff (CET)** on trade with nonmembers. If countries A and B from the previous example formed a customs union, a uniform tariff would apply to goods from C; it could be 10 percent, 20 percent, or a compromise, perhaps 15 percent, as in panel (c) of Figure 3. In the case of the most successful economic integration, the European Union, CET levels equal the average of members' pre-integration tariff rates. The CET eliminates the incentive for transshipment that happens under a preferential- or free-trade agreement.

The fourth stage of economic integration is a **common market**, which extends free trade among members to factors of production (labor migration and capital flows) as well as to goods and services. In addition, common-market members typically maintain fixed exchange rates among their national currencies.[14] The European Union refers to the "four freedoms" that make it a common market: free intra-group movement for labor, goods, services, and capital, although several of the freedoms remain less than perfect.

The most extensive form of economic integration, an **economic union**, means common, group-determined economic policies as well as a common currency or money. Economic union proves very difficult to achieve and maintain, because it requires member countries to agree on a very wide range of issues and policies. Even politically, economically, and culturally similar countries find differences in their individual situations that make such agreement difficult. While political boundaries have economic significance, economic barriers have political implications as well. Historically, countries have been extremely reluctant to forgo the exercise of their national sovereignty in the interest of an economic union; this is one reason why the European Union's efforts to become a true economic union have been so controversial and have attracted so much attention.

4.2 Trade Creation and Trade Diversion: Integration and Welfare

The overall welfare effects of economic integration are ambiguous and require case-by-case judgment. We can see the reason for this ambiguity by recognizing integration as simultaneously a policy of protection (against nonmembers) and a move toward free trade (with members). The protectionist element of integration is called **trade diversion**. This refers to the diversion of trade from nonmembers to members caused by the discrimination inherent in integration. The trade-liberalization element of integration is called **trade creation**. Integration reduces or eliminates protection among member countries and allows them to specialize and trade according to comparative advantage and to exploit potential economies of scale. If trade creation exceeds trade diversion, economic integration increases member countries' welfare. If trade diversion dominates trade creation, members' welfare falls.

Figure 4 illustrates integration's trade-creating and trade-diverting effects. We take the point of view of a small country considering elimination of trade barriers on good X with a group of countries (that is, the formation of a free-trade area in good X). D and S, respectively, represent the country's domestic demand for and supply of good X. S^M denotes the supply of exports of good X from other countries that would be *members* of the free-trade area; S^{NM} is the supply of exports of X by countries that would be *nonmembers*.

Before integration, imports of good X from all countries are subject to a tariff of t per unit; thus, $S^M + t$ and $S^{NM} + t$ represent the effective supply curves for imports from the

---

14. An exchange rate is the price of one country's currency (for example, the U.S. dollar) expressed in terms of another country's currency (for example, the Chinese yuan). When a country fixes its exchange rate, as China does as of 2004, this price is held constant by policy makers rather than allowed to change in response to market forces of supply and demand.

Figure 4   Welfare Effects of a Free-Trade Area in Good X

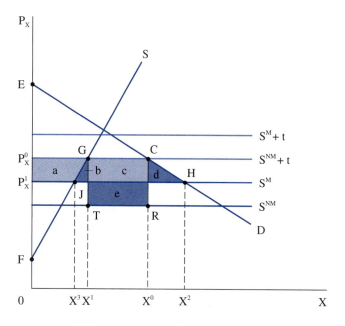

S^M denotes the supply of good X by *member* countries and S^{NM} the supply by *nonmember* countries. Formation of a free-trade area causes a move from point C to point H. Trade increases as imports rise from $X^0 - X^1$ to $X^2 - X^3$. Trade also is diverted from nonmember countries toward member countries, causing an efficiency loss represented by the area of rectangle e.

two possible sources. Point C represents the initial equilibrium. Residents of the country consume X^0 units of X at price P_X^0, of which X^1 are produced domestically and $X^0 - X^1$ are imported from countries that, if integration occurred, would be nonmembers. No imported X comes from would-be members, because nonmembers supply the good at a lower price than do members. Graphically, this is reflected by the fact that S^{NM} lies below S^M, or—equivalently—$S^{NM} + t$ lies below $S^M + t$. Consumer surplus is given by the area of triangle $P_X^0 EC$, and the surplus of domestic producers by area $FP_X^0 G$. The government collects the equivalent of the area of rectangle TGCR in tariff revenue.

After formation of a free-trade area, the relevant supply curves are S^M (because imports from member countries no longer are subject to the tariff) and $S^{NM} + t$ (because imports from nonmembers remain subject to the tariff). The new equilibrium is at point H. Residents consume X^2 units of X at price P_X^1, and X^3 units are produced domestically. The remainder ($X^2 - X^3$) are imported, but now from member countries. (*Why?*) Consumer surplus rises by area a + b + c + d, and domestic producer surplus declines by area a. The government no longer collects any tariff revenue, because all imports now come tariff-free from member countries. Area c, which previously went to the government as tariff revenue, now goes to consumers in the form of a reduced price for good X. Area b is a net gain from increased efficiency; the units of X between X^3 and X^1 previously were produced domestically at relatively high costs (represented by the height of the domestic supply curve) but now are imported at lower costs (represented by the height of S^M). This efficiency gain captures one part of integration's trade-creation effect. Area d denotes the other trade-creation effect. As the free-trade area makes lower-cost imports available, consumption increases from X^0 to X^2. For each additional unit of consumption, the value to consumers (represented by the height of the demand curve) exceeds the opportunity costs of production (represented by the height of S^M). The total trade-creating effect of the free-trade area equals the sum of triangles b and d.

Area e in Figure 4 illustrates integration's trade-diverting effect. Notice that before integration, all imports came from nonmember countries, the low-cost producers of good X. After integration, all imports come from higher-cost member-country producers. This switch from low-cost to high-cost sources of imports represents trade diversion. Before integration, area e was a portion of the tariff revenue going to the domestic government. After formation of the free-trade area, e becomes a deadweight loss. Each unit of imports between X^1 and X^0 now is being produced at an opportunity cost represented by the height of S^M rather than the lower opportunity cost given by the height of S^{NM}.

We can determine the free-trade area's overall effect on the small member country's welfare by comparing the trade-creation and trade-diversion effects. If trade creation dominates, formation of a free-trade area enhances welfare; if trade diversion exceeds trade creation, the group reduces welfare. Note that if member countries include the low-cost producers of good X, there will be no trade-diversion effect and integration will unambiguously increase welfare. (*To see this, switch the labels of S^M and S^{NM} and of $S^M + t$ and $S^{NM} + t$ in Figure 4.*) Note also that if the tariff is low enough to make the tariff-inclusive price of nonmember imports still lower than the price of tariff-free member imports, the free-trade area will have no trade-creating or trade-diverting effects—because no trade will occur with member countries even if the group does form.

We can formulate some general rules about when trade creation will be likely to dominate trade diversion or vice versa. First, the higher member countries' initial tariffs, other things equal, the more trade creation induced by integration and, therefore, the more likely integration will improve members' welfare. Second, lower member barriers against trade with nonmembers translate into less trade diversion and make welfare-enhancing integration more likely. Finally, the more members the better, because the group will more likely include low-cost producers. As noted earlier, when the low-cost producers of the good are group members, no trade diversion occurs. Another way of viewing this last rule is to notice that a free-trade area that included *all* countries couldn't generate any trade diversion, because the good's lowest-cost producers would, by definition, be members.

Economists estimate the overall impact of integration by calculating the effects corresponding to areas a, b, c, d, and e in Figure 4 for each good traded. In the case of the European Union, most analysts agree that trade creation outweighs trade diversion for most manufactured goods. However, the opposite holds for the group's highly protected agricultural sector.

4.3 Additional Considerations

The analysis of economic integration in Figure 4 is static, focusing on the reallocation of resources caused by elimination of barriers to intra-group trade over a short time period. Integration may also have dynamic effects—that is, it may cause the member economies to evolve differently over time. A complete analysis of integration's welfare effects must include an examination of the effects of these dynamic changes.

Economic integration increases the size of the "domestic" market. In industries that exhibit economies of scale, the increased market size may allow firms to achieve the economies necessary for them to become competitive in export markets, as we saw in Chapter Five.

Increased market size also may allow a group of countries to exercise some monopoly power in world markets. A group of "small" countries may, by banding together, be able to act as a "large" country and impose an optimal tariff or export tax (see sections 5.2 and 10.2 in Chapter Six). This pooling of power also may be important within international organizations and in other bargaining situations. One often-cited reason for the formation of the European Community in 1957 was to present the United States with a more nearly equal partner in terms of bargaining strength.

An additional source of dynamic benefits from economic integration takes the form of increased competitive pressures on industries within the integrated group. Once intra-group trade barriers fall, industries face competition from their counterparts in other member countries. If the group allows market forces to determine success and failure, intra-group specialization will develop along the lines of comparative advantage. Monopolization and the associated inefficiencies will be less likely to develop and persist. Groups forgo these potential benefits if they "assign" industries to the various members or otherwise prohibit competition within the group. The question of distribution of industries across member countries has proven troublesome, especially among groups of developing countries whose members are eager to industrialize.

Besides the static and dynamic welfare effects of any particular integration group, the trend toward the formation of such groups affects the fundamental norms of the international trading system. The postwar GATT/WTO system rests on a foundation of multilateral nondiscriminatory liberalization that treats all trading partners equally, in principle if not in practice. Many policy makers and economists express concern that this system may lose out to one based on bilateral arrangements and discriminatory treatment of trading partners, in which regional trading blocs partition the world trading system into a small number of groups, each practicing discriminatory protection against nonmembers.

Supporters of regional trading groups point out that more progress on difficult issues may be possible when participants are a small group of like-minded countries.[15] As the GATT/WTO membership has grown from 23 members to almost 150 (see Table 1) and become more diverse, negotiations there have become more unwieldy. At the same time, changes in the nature of trade policy and of protection have complicated the negotiation process. Tariffs have fallen substantially, and the most important issues in the world trading system now include much more complex policies—subsidies, antidumping policies, trade in services, and competition policy. These developments, taken together, may suggest a role for small-group trade agreements, along with the WTO.

4.4 Efforts at Integration: Success and Failure

Since World War II, attempts at economic integration have come in two waves. The first, in the 1960s, included numerous groups of developing economies that attempted to follow the European Community model. The definition and goals of economic integration suggest that we might expect groups of small developing countries to be most likely to choose integration as a policy. However, most early attempts at integration among developing countries met with only mediocre success, and many arrangements throughout Africa and Latin America collapsed within a few years of initiation.

The second wave of economic integration began in the mid-1980s and continues today. The United States has, for the first time, entered bilateral trade arrangements; and the European Community has expanded its membership and its integration agenda. Developing countries also are participating in this second wave of integration. Some groups that formed

---

15. See Beth V. Yarbrough, "Preferential Trade Arrangements and the GATT: EC 1992 as Rogue or Role Model?" in the chapter references.

earlier have been revived, and new groups have formed in Africa, Latin America, the Middle East, and Asia. Outside the European Union and the North American Free Trade Agreement, the groups that have received the most attention, because of their rapidly growing and industrializing economies, are the Southern Common Market (Mercosur), which includes Argentina, Brazil, Paraguay, and Uruguay, and the Association for South East Asian Nations (ASEAN, composed of Brunei, Cambodia, Indonesia, Laos, Malaysia, Myanmar, the Philippines, Singapore, Thailand, and Vietnam).

WTO member countries that form integration groups must report their actions to the WTO, because such groups don't apply the most-favored-nation and nondiscrimination principles that underlie the WTO. Article 24 of the original GATT agreement does permit economic integration so long as (1) trade liberalization applies to "substantially all" intra-group trade and (2) group barriers to trade with nonmembers aren't higher than before the group formed. Since 1948, about 300 integration groups have notified the GATT/WTO of their existence; but only about 200 remain in effect (of which many are bilateral agreements between the European Union and one nonmember country), and only a handful of those have had a substantial and sustained impact on trade.[16] Almost half of all world trade now occurs under a preferential agreement.[17] Figure 5 reports recent shares of intra-group trade for the EU, NAFTA, AFTA (the preferential trade agreement associated with the ASEAN group), and Mercosur.

The history of failed and only moderately successful attempts at economic integration testifies to the strong desire for national sovereignty in economic policy making—even though political boundaries are largely arbitrary from the standpoint of the organization of economic activity. Generally speaking, integration efforts among developed economies

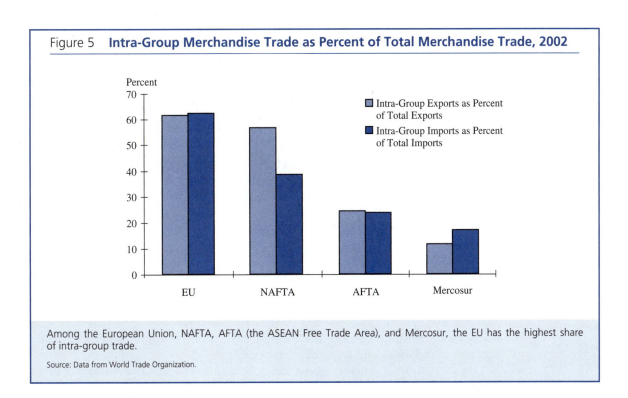

Figure 5   Intra-Group Merchandise Trade as Percent of Total Merchandise Trade, 2002

Among the European Union, NAFTA, AFTA (the ASEAN Free Trade Area), and Mercosur, the EU has the highest share of intra-group trade.

Source: Data from World Trade Organization.

---

16. For lists, see the World Trade Organization, *Annual Report*.

17. World Trade Organization, *World Trade Report 2003*, p. 48.

have enjoyed more success than those among developing ones. Some reasons for this pattern emerge from the simple graphical analysis of a free-trade area in Figure 4. Several African integration groups, for example, included economies with highly similar factor endowments and trade stemming almost exclusively from factor-endowment-based comparative advantage. Prior to integration, members imported largely the same goods from the same nonmember countries. Such a pattern provides little scope for trade creation. *(Why?)* In addition, the first wave of integration among developing economies coincided with the height of popularity of import-substitution development strategies based on extensive import restrictions.[18] Therefore, much of the trade liberalization envisioned in the integration treaties never actually occurred.

Among developed economies, especially in the European Union, beneficial effects of integration came largely from intra-industry trade based on economies of scale. So trade creation was possible despite the similarities of members' factor endowments.

The second historical wave of integration differs from the first in its inclusion of groups that encompass countries at widely divergent levels of development. NAFTA provides one example, as does the repeated expansion of the EU to include countries increasingly less developed than the original members. Developing economies can achieve two major bene-fits from integration with developed ones. The first is market access on a preferential basis. The "Europe Agreements," for example, grant many countries of Eastern and Central Europe extensive access to the EU market, although sensitive industrial sectors and agriculture remain restricted; most of the countries covered by the agreements hope to qualify eventually for full EU membership. The second benefit is a means of credibly committing the developing-country government to market-oriented reforms and open economic institutions. Mexico, eager to guarantee that it would not reverse its dramatic economic reforms of the late 1980s, saw NAFTA as a way of making a public commitment to that effect.

The developed members of developed–developing integration groups, on the other hand, often hope to discourage labor migration and to support the developing economies' commitments to market-oriented reforms. Both these elements play a large role in the relationships between the EU and the transitional economies of Central and Eastern Europe and between Mexico and the United States.

THE EUROPEAN UNION   The 1957 Treaty of Rome established the six-member European Community—Belgium, Luxembourg, the Netherlands, France, Germany, and Italy. The treaty's goals included formation of a common market with shared agricultural policies and aid programs to facilitate development of the less-developed areas within the community. More fundamentally, the goal was a unified Europe, both to prevent the intra-European rivalries that had resulted in two world wars in 30 years and to present the United States with a more equal economic and political rival.

The group satisfied its customs-union goals within about a decade of the original treaty, but efforts at further integration stalled. In 1971, the EC agreed to a 10-year plan to achieve a full economic union. An incomplete common market evolved; however, many nontariff barriers and impediments to labor and capital flows remained, most of them intimately connected to issues of national sovereignty over economic policy making. Decision-making complexity grew as membership expanded. With the addition of Spain and Portugal in 1986, the EC became the world's largest market in terms of population and the second largest in terms of GDP.

In 1987, the EC passed the Single Europe Act, an amendment to the Treaty of Rome designed to recapture momentum toward integration and to complete the open internal

---

18.   Section 4 in Chapter Eleven compares import-substitution and outward-oriented development strategies.

market by 1992. The act facilitated achievement of these goals by limiting the ability of a single member country to veto EC proposals. It also expanded the EC bureaucracy in Brussels and the scope of EC policy making in areas such as the environment, monetary policy, health and safety standards, and foreign policy.

In 1991, the EC made another major commitment toward moving to an economic union and changed the group's name from the European Community to the European Union. The Maastricht Treaty pledged member countries to coordinate their monetary, foreign and security, and immigration and policing policies. Most important, the treaty outlined a schedule and procedure by which the members would move to a common currency (the euro) and a common European central bank to conduct monetary policy for the group.

In 1994, the EU and the European Free Trade Association (EFTA), minus Switzerland and Liechtenstein, signed an accord to form the European Economic Area (EEA), which grants all members free trade in goods, services, capital flows, and labor flows, except for agriculture. Since, three EFTA members—Austria, Finland, and Sweden—have moved to full EU membership.

After years of negotiations, the EU undertook its biggest expansion in 2004 when it admitted ten new members from Central and Eastern Europe. This enlargement posed many challenges: The new members were much less developed, most having recently undergone transition from central planning. The larger group size meant finding new mechanisms for reaching and enforcing decisions. The very different income levels within the newly enlarged group raised questions about how to allocate membership's cost and benefits fairly.

In Figure 6 the 25 current EU members are indicated by light shading. Country names in all capital letters indicate the ten new members as of 2004. The darker-shaded countries have applied for membership but failed to gain entry with the "class of 2004."

Many of the most controversial issues that face Europe's integration efforts also face the world trading system: trade in services, agricultural policy, government procurement, technical barriers to trade, and capital mobility. These issues present difficulties because they involve a delicate balance between international cooperation and national sovereignty.

In general, the issues facing the European Union highlight the fundamental dilemma confronting the world economy: how to capture the gains from international cooperation and trade while maintaining politically acceptable levels of national control over economic, political, and social policy making. This dilemma becomes even more apparent as EU members move beyond a common market toward the goal of an economic and political union, with a common currency and common macroeconomic policies, and as the union encompasses a larger and more diverse membership.

THE NORTH AMERICAN FREE TRADE AGREEMENT   The North American Free Trade Agreement (NAFTA), linking the United States, Canada, and Mexico, exhibits several unique characteristics. First, an unusual process led up to the agreement. Mexico approached the United States about a free-trade agreement after launching a series of economic reforms, which included the elimination of its long-standing program of import substitution, in 1987. Shortly thereafter, the United States signed the Canada–United States Free-Trade Agreement. When the United States consented to talks with Mexico, Canada asked to join in a three-way agreement to reach "from the Yukon to Yucatan." Talks began in 1991, and the three countries initialed a 2,000-page agreement in 1992, subject to legislative approval in each country. After a long and controversial approval process, the agreement took effect on January 1, 1994. Figure 7 illustrates the pattern of trade among the three NAFTA members.

Figure 6   **European Union Members and Applicants, 2004**

More countries still want to join the European Union, which expanded in 2004 from 15 to 25 members.

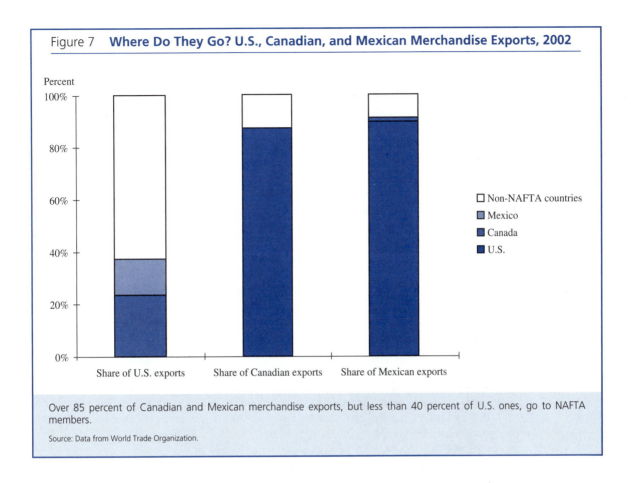

Figure 7 **Where Do They Go? U.S., Canadian, and Mexican Merchandise Exports, 2002**

Over 85 percent of Canadian and Mexican merchandise exports, but less than 40 percent of U.S. ones, go to NAFTA members.

Source: Data from World Trade Organization.

NAFTA broke ground for free-trade agreements because of its members' very different levels of economic development. Mexico had two primary reasons for desiring such an agreement with the United States. As illustrated in Figure 7, over 80 percent of Mexican exports go to the United States, so assured access to the market of Mexico's large neighbor plays a big role in the long-run viability of Mexican reforms and growth. Economic reforms in Mexico have an erratic history, and many such attempts have failed. The agreement with the United States helped demonstrate the Mexican government's commitment to reform and to open trade; such government credibility improved Mexico's ability to attract foreign investment and reestablish creditworthiness after the country's debt problems of the 1980s. In return for these benefits, Mexico made politically difficult concessions, including opening its markets for financial services, securities, and insurance as well as many parts of its oil industry—a politically sensitive move because the oil industry's nationalization coincided with Mexico's revolution. Mexico also improved the transparency of its trade laws, which, like those in many developing countries, tended to be opaque, *ad hoc*, and arbitrary.

As a large economy, the United States had a substantially smaller stake in an agreement than Mexico, because the bulk of the gains from trade between a large and a small economy go to the smaller economy, as we learned in Chapters Two and Three. Nonetheless, over 80 percent of U.S. exports to Mexico were subject to Mexican tariffs (at an average rate of 10 percent), which the agreement would eliminate. By 1996, Mexican tariffs on U.S. exports had fallen to 2.9 percent.

Under the terms of NAFTA, tariffs on approximately half of members' trade were removed immediately. Remaining tariffs will be phased out by 2010. The most sensitive items, on which some tariffs will remain until 2010, include sneakers, ceramic tile, household glassware, orange juice concentrate, peanuts, broccoli, asparagus, and melons. In agriculture, existing quotas were converted to equivalent tariffs, and those tariffs will be reduced by 2010.

One of the stickier negotiating points in NAFTA involved rules of origin that specify how much North American content a product must contain to qualify for duty-free treatment, especially in the automobile, textile and apparel, and television industries.[19] The U.S. auto industry pressed for very high (70 percent) content rules. Canada and Mexico resisted, fearful that such rules would inhibit Japanese auto producers from investing in plants in Canada and Mexico to serve the U.S. market—because such plants typically import many auto parts from Japan. A last-minute compromise set the rules of origin for autos at 62.5 percent of value. In textiles and apparel, textiles had to be woven and processed in North America to qualify for duty-free movement until 2004; apparel made from qualifying textiles also qualified.

These stringent rules of origin probably represented the biggest threat for substantial trade diversion from NAFTA, because they excluded low-cost Asian suppliers of textiles and auto parts. If the Uruguay Round agreement succeeds in eventually dismantling the worldwide web of protection in textiles and apparel, freer worldwide trade in textiles will reduce NAFTA's trade diversion, but high textile tariffs that will remain still imply a potential for substantial trade diversion. *(Why?)*

In any free-trade agreement, procedures for settling disputes and escape-clause provisions are two of the key elements. NAFTA created the North American Trade Commission, consisting of three cabinet-level officials, to hear disputes. If a member country claims that another member's exports injure one of its industries, the country can stop its tariff reduction or return to the pre-NAFTA tariff rate for that industry. Each country can do this only one time per industry, and for a maximum of three years.

Opposition to NAFTA from pro-protection forces in the United States centered on three issues: the agreement's environmental impact, the effects of differences between labor standards and wages in the United States and Mexico, and the possibility of sudden large import surges from Mexico, particularly in a few agricultural products. To gain the domestic political support necessary for passage through Congress, the United States negotiated three "side agreements" to cover some of these concerns. The environmental and labor-standard side agreements provide mechanisms to monitor members' compliance with their respective national laws and regulations and procedures for disputes. The side agreements encourage transparency and voluntary compliance and allow fines and trade sanctions only as last resorts and only for certain classes of violations. In the case of sudden and large import surges, the side agreement provides a monitoring system to allow governments to anticipate problems in import-competing industries.

NAFTA's success, like that of the European Union, has created a waiting list of would-be members throughout the Western Hemisphere. On an even larger scale, the 34 Western Hemisphere countries with democratically elected governments (all countries except Cuba) pledged in 1994 to begin work toward a Free Trade Area of the Americas, to be completed no later than the end of 2005. The initiative was formally launched in 1998, but the group's large, diverse membership makes concrete progress in reducing trade barriers difficult. Latin American countries emphasize the importance of disciplining U.S. antidumping policies and agricultural subsidies; the United States, to the extent it will address these issues at all, prefers to do so in the context of the WTO.

---

19. Section 7.1 in Chapter Seven introduces domestic-content rules and rules of origin.

MERCOSUR   Brazil, Argentina, Paraguay, and Uruguay agreed in 1991 to form a trade area called Mercosur (or the Southern Cone Common Market). In the group's first five years, intra-group trade increased by a factor of four; and in 1996 Chile and Bolivia signed agreements with Mercosur, making them associate members. In 2003, Mercosur signed an agreement with the Andean Community, another South American integration group including Colombia, Peru, Ecuador, Venezuela, and Bolivia. Despite early successes, the group hasn't been without problems (including high average tariffs against nonmembers). Its members have histories of high rates of protection, military dictatorships, and erratic trade liberalization. Auto and auto-parts trade between Brazil and Argentina remains restricted and will until 2006. Economic crises, in Brazil in 1999 and Argentina in 2001, strained relations with the group, as the two imposed unilateral restrictions on one another's exports.

Important sectors such as capital goods, informatics, telecommunications, and sugar remain outside Mercosur's liberalization at least for the short term. Perhaps more important, some analysts have questioned how much of Mercosur's increased internal trade represents trade creation and how much represents trade diversion. The fastest-growing sectors of intra-group trade include capital-intensive items such as autos, buses, and agricultural machinery, in which none of the Mercosur members may be low-cost producers relative to nonmembers.

AFTA/ASEAN   So far, formal economic integration groups have been less common in Asia than in other regions. The Association of South-East Asian Nations (ASEAN) functioned for most of its life primarily as a forum for political and economic discussion and cooperation. Members are Singapore, Indonesia, the Philippines, Thailand, Malaysia, Brunei, Cambodia, Laos, Vietnam, and Burma. In 2002, the group took steps to form the ASEAN Free Trade Area (AFTA), with the aim of reducing trade barriers. Some progress has been made on tariffs, but important nontariff barriers continue to limit intra-group trade and discourage foreign direct investment in the area. Rules of origin for the tariff reductions are complex and opaque, leading to disputes that the group, as yet, has no effective mechanism for resolving. Several members have long histories of protectionist policies, so it remains to be seen how successful this group of small economies will be in forming an effective regional area of free trade.

5 INTERREGIONAL TRADE

National boundaries distinguish inter*regional* from inter*national* trade. When boundaries change, formerly interregional trade becomes international, or vice versa. Trade between Russia and Ukraine, interregional during the Soviet Union's existence, now goes in the international ledger. And in 1997, when Hong Kong became part of China, trade between the two switched from international to interregional. Historically, most periods of widespread changes in national boundaries have coincided with major wars; for example, the end of World War II brought dramatic changes to Europe's map. More recently, an unusual number of border adjustments have occurred more peacefully, including the unification of Germany and the breakup of Czechoslovakia.

National boundaries are somewhat arbitrary from the perspective of the organization of economic activity.[20] Economic interaction between Toronto and Detroit dwarfs that between Toronto and Vancouver, or between Detroit and Seattle. Although economic activity across national borders sometimes exceeds the level of activity within borders,

20. Sometimes, however, economic considerations help explain changes in national boundaries; see, for example, Beth V. Yarbrough and Robert M. Yarbrough, "International Contracting and Territorial Control" and "Unification and Secession" in the chapter references.

political boundaries do have major economic consequences. Economic policies, laws, tastes, currencies, and economic and political systems are just a few of the dimensions on which political borders matter.

Trade barriers, in particular, influence the spatial organization of economic activity. Regions within a country (that is, areas between which relatively free trade prevails) typically exhibit greater specialization than do countries themselves, in part because national trade barriers preclude countries' further specialization.

5.1 The Role of Factor Mobility

Another dimension of economic policy that distinguishes interregional from international trade patterns is factor mobility.[21] Labor and capital move more easily within than between countries because of both natural and policy-induced barriers to intercountry mobility. The high rate of factor mobility within a national economy carries an important implication: Factors tend to flow out of the low-productivity regions within an economy, so reduced wages or returns to capital can't offset low factor productivity.

Consider a simple example in which labor is the only input. There are two geographical areas, A and B. First, assume that A and B represent countries, between which labor can't move. Labor in country A is more productive than labor in country B. This results in a situation identical to Chapter Two's Ricardian model. B's relatively unproductive labor still can compete with country A's more productive labor, at least in some goods, by accepting lower wages that reflect the lower productivity.[22] This is just comparative advantage again. Even if B's labor is less productive than A's in every industry, B still can export those goods in which B's labor is *relatively* productive.

Now, introduce one seemingly minor change. Areas A and B now represent regions within a single country, so labor can move easily between the two. But labor in A remains more productive than labor in B. A wage differential no longer will allow area B to produce and export goods to area A, because labor will flow from B to A in response to A's higher wages. Factors migrate from the low-productivity to the high-productivity area, instead of remaining in the low-productivity area and accepting a lower wage. This mobility improves efficiency because the labor moves to the area where it can be more productive, but less productive regions are abandoned.

Of course, factors of production are neither perfectly immobile between countries nor perfectly mobile within countries. Given a pattern of productivity differences across two geographic areas, the higher the factor mobility between the two, the more equal the wages and the more unequally dispersed the population. The lower the degree of factor mobility, the bigger the wage differential and the more equally dispersed the population.

5.2 The Role of Economic Policy

The majority of government policies with greatest relevance for trade are defined at the national level. U.S. imports pay the same tariff whether they land at New York or Seattle. Occasionally, however, governments show their ambivalent feelings toward trade by applying different trade rules in different regions of a country. Such policies are used most often by policy makers with histories of relatively closed, inward-looking economic policies who recognize the need to allow more trade to improve economic performance but are hesitant to give up the control that closed borders imply.

---

21. Jacob Viner, writing in 1937, emphasized the role of factor immobility in distinguishing international trade.

22. On the role of wage differentials in Ricardian comparative advantage, see sections 5.3 and 6.3 in Chapter Two.

The most common forms of subnational trade policy are special economic zones or export-processing zones. **Special economic zones (SEZs)** typically allow more generous rules for trade and for inward foreign direct investment than apply in the rest of the country. The goal is to encourage such investment, which brings access to foreign technology, manufacturing expertise, and knowledge of world export markets. Foreign firms that invest in such zones may receive exemption from taxes or minimum wage laws, as well as reduced site-rental charges, help with infrastructure, and other inducements. **Export-processing zones** concentrate on attracting firms that assemble products for export. These zones provide low-cost infrastructure such as port facilities, power supplies, and rail connections. Tariff exemptions, particularly on imported inputs, also play an important role.

Some of the most dramatic examples of special economic zones come from China, where they enjoy considerably more administrative autonomy than other areas and have been encouraged by the central government to serve as laboratories for economic and social policy experiments, including investment not covered by the country's central economic plan.[23] The Chinese SEZs are particularly interesting because they link particular provinces of China with more open nearby economies such as Taiwan. Fujian and Guangdong provinces, on China's south coast, received designation as experimental reform regions in 1978, when China first began opening up to the world economy. Since, the Chinese government has created several additional zones; their economic success, along with their rapidly rising incomes, has created popular pressure to allow the trade reforms to spread to the rest of the economy. Widespread smuggling also constrains the central government's ability to maintain divergent policies in different areas.

The most successful zone is the Greater South China Economic Region, which encompasses Guangdong and Fujian provinces, Hong Kong (now part of China), and Taiwan. Businesses in the zone combine China's cheap labor and land with Hong Kong's marketing links and transportation network, and with Taiwan's capital, manufacturing technology, and management skills. Shoes and toys comprise large shares of production in the region. The income consequences of the zones are apparent in the map in Figure 8. In 1999, as part of a package designed to lure investment funds to the economically lagging interior, China announced that every province would be allowed an economic and technological development zone.

In 2003, after its entry into the WTO, China announced that foreign firms locating in the SEZs no longer would receive lower national tax rates but would be charged the same rates as Chinese firms. At the same time, the country announced that some SEZs would be permitted to liberalize foreign investment in some service sectors—including financial services, securities, and tourism—several years ahead of the schedule contained in China's WTO accession agreement.

Latin American and other Asian economies created many special economic zones and export-processing zones during the 1980s. The zones played an important role in demonstrating the potential of open international trade to raise incomes and allow developing economies to move into manufacturing. As we mentioned in the case of China, the success of open regions within the economy typically creates political pressure for national policy reform. As many developing and transitional countries open their economies to international trade, the significance of their special zones declines. For example, the liberalization of Mexico's trade policy and the provisions of the NAFTA reduce the special role for the *maquiladora* program.

India has also announced plans for 17 SEZs as part of a plan to reduce stifling regulation and help the country compete more successfully against China for foreign investment.

---

23. On China's SEZs, see World Bank, *China: Foreign Trade Reform* (Washington, D.C.: World Bank, 1994), pp. 221–251.

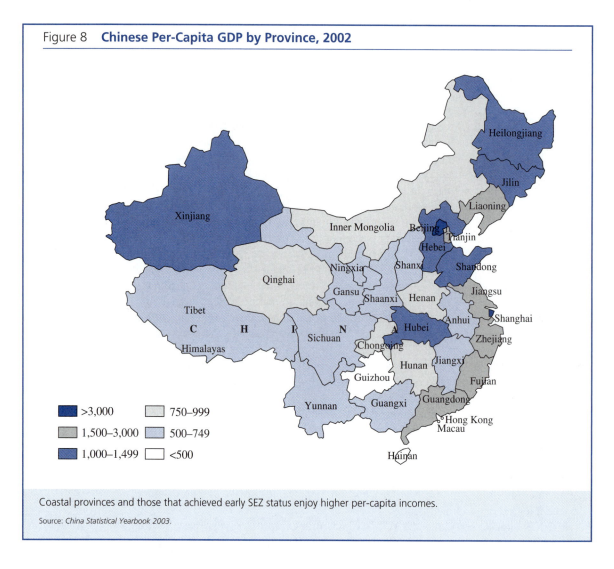

Figure 8   **Chinese Per-Capita GDP by Province, 2002**

Legend:
- >3,000
- 1,500–3,000
- 1,000–1,499
- 750–999
- 500–749
- <500

Coastal provinces and those that achieved early SEZ status enjoy higher per-capita incomes.

Source: *China Statistical Yearbook 2003*.

South Korea hopes to use three special low-tax zones, in Incheon, Busan, and Gwangyang, to encourage foreign investment. Even some of the world's very closed economies, including North Korea and Iran, use special economic zones to try to capture some of the benefits of openness without allowing foreign political ideas and culture to reach their populations.

CASE 1: NAFTA TRAFFIC JAMS

U.S./Mexico

Before the NAFTA agreement, U.S. trucks could travel only 20 miles into Mexico and Mexican trucks only 20 miles into the United States. Products destined for points farther away had to be reloaded onto domestic trucks for the rest of the trip. NAFTA was supposed to change all that. According to the agreement, by late 1995, trucks from both countries would have access to all the border states: four in the United States (California, Arizona, New Mexico, and Texas) and six in Mexico. State and federal transportation and law enforcement officials of both countries spent a lot of time preparing for the change, especially ensuring that Mexican trucks could meet U.S. safety and insurance regulations and that those regulations would be enforced. After five years under the border-state system, all limits on access to international traffic would end in 2000.

Just two weeks before the scheduled 1995 implementation, the U.S. Teamsters Union (with 1.5 million members) cited safety concerns and unfair competition from Mexico's lower-paid truckers and pressured the United States to renege, which it did. Mexico claimed that the United States violated the NAFTA agreement. The four U.S. border-state governors reaffirmed their states' ability to conduct the necessary safety inspections and patrols, since they had already hired extra officers and built extra inspection stations. Mexican truckers repeatedly blockaded busy border crossings in Laredo, Brownsville, and McAllen, Texas, in protest. Finally Mexico filed a case under NAFTA's dispute-resolution provisions. In early 2001, a five-member binational panel ruled in Mexico's favor, but not before the Clinton administration had succeeded in stalling the issue past the 2000 U.S. presidential election, in hopes of winning Teamster Union support for candidate Al Gore. The new Bush administration expressed its intention to comply with the NAFTA ruling, allowing in Mexican trucks that passed U.S. safety inspections and whose drivers were certified for

English proficiency; but a year later, political pressure from the Teamsters still stymied the plan.

In 2002, consumer and environmental groups, along with the Teamsters Union, filed a lawsuit to stop Mexican trucks from certification, claiming that the U.S. government had failed to conduct adequate studies of their potential environmental impact. The groups won in the initial court decision, but the U.S. Supreme Court overturned the decision in 2004, ruling that Mexican trucks would finally have the access promised them in 1994.

Americans and Mexicans are frustrated with border delays at major U.S.–Mexico border crossings, especially Laredo, Texas. It often takes 12 hours for a truck to cross the Rio Grande on the way from Detroit or Chicago to Mexico City, or vice versa. Few rail lines cross the border, so most goods (around 85 percent) must move by truck. And NAFTA's very success in boosting North–South trade in North America has strained the border's ability to cope with so many trucks. The Laredo crossing, built to handle about 750 trucks per day, sees about 4,000, carrying an average of $65 million worth of goods every day. As Table 2 reports, rail and air transport also shows dramatic increases between pre-NAFTA 1990 and post-NAFTA 1996.

Table 2 MONTHLY LAREDO, TEXAS, BORDER TRAFFIC, PRE- AND POST-NAFTA

Traffic Type	July 1990	July 1996
Tractor-trailer trucks	28,000	88,000
Rail cars	5,100	11,700
Air cargoes	630	2,800

Source: Data from U.S. Customs Service.

CASE 2: I.D. CARDS FOR AVOCADOS

U.S./Mexico

NAFTA implementation hasn't meant an end to trade disputes among the member countries, but post-NAFTA talks did end an 81-year-old trade fight between the United States and Mexico. U.S. officials detected avocado-seed weevils in Mexican avocados in 1914 and banned them (the avocados, along with the weevils) to

avoid pest infestation of the U.S. crop. During the 1970s, Mexico repeatedly requested an end to the quarantine; but U.S. officials continued to report finding weevils, both in growing areas of the Mexican state of Michoacan and in illegal fruit confiscated at border crossings.

After investing heavily to improve its production, packing, and shipping processes and pest control, Mexico tried again in the 1990s to end the U.S. avocado quarantine. A tiny victory came in 1993 when the U.S. altered rules to allow imported Hass avocados into Alaska—a state that while geographically very large isn't famous as a major guacamole consumer.

With the advent of NAFTA, U.S. non-avocado agricultural interests began to fear that if the U.S. avocado quarantine stayed in place, Mexico might respond with standards to keep out U.S. wheat or fruit. Finally in 1997, after several scientific studies of the alleged risks and several rounds of public hearings, the U.S. Department of Agriculture approved imports of Mexican avocados from specifically approved groves in Michoacan, but only from November through February each year, only into 19 northeastern U.S. states plus the District of Columbia, only under an elaborate system of multilayered anti-weevil safeguards, and subject to a quota of 12,000 tons. Avocados shipped to the permitted northeastern states must be sent in sealed containers. Each individual avocado must have its own "sticker of origin." States that still quarantine Mexican avocados watch out for the stickers, which would indicate illegal avocado trade.

How does the ban affect avocado prices? Fruit that sell in Mexican supermarkets for $0.30 per pound sell for $4.00 a pound just three miles north, across the Mexico–California border.[24] The quarantine on fresh avocados also generates some other interesting trade effects. If you eat guacamole in a restaurant chain or buy it in a grocery store, chances are it was made in Mexico. "For discount chains like Taco Bell, Simplot [the Mexican producer] prepares a squirtable avocado paste used as a condiment. For Chili's and TGIF, chains targeting more affluent diners, Simplot ships a watery mash, into which kitchen workers add avocado chunks to give the guacamole more of a made-on-site look. Diners shouldn't be fooled, though. Simplot also provides the chunks—which are frozen at the same facility that makes the paste."[25]

CASE 3: **ALL IN THE FAMILY**

China/Hong Kong

Most preferential trade agreements, such as the EU and NAFTA, are signed by sovereign nation-states. But, in 2003, China and Hong Kong signed a free-trade agreement (called CEPA—the Closer Economic Partnership Arrangement), even though Hong Kong had become a Special Administrative Region (SAR) of China in 1997. Despite Hong Kong's accession to China, the former British colony maintains its own trade policy, separate from that of the rest of China.

Since China entered the WTO, Chinese import tariffs on goods from Hong Kong average almost 10 percent, with much higher rates on some goods. The CEPA removed Chinese tariffs on almost 300 Hong Kong products, covering about two-thirds of Hong Kong's exports to China. But much of Hong Kong's manufacturing capacity had already moved to China, so winning exemption from the Chinese tariffs would have relatively little direct effect on Hong Kong's exports of goods to the mainland. More important, the agreement also included 18 service sectors such as banking, advertising, and movies; so Hong Kong hoped for big long-term gains for these as they achieve a preferential advantage in serving the Chinese market. The agreement also relaxed travel rules, allowing individuals from mainland China to visit Hong Kong.

24. "Bitter Fruit: Spats Persist Despite NAFTA," *The Wall Street Journal*, June 19, 2000.

25. "That Order of Guacamole Was Probably Mashed Up South of the U.S. Border," *The Wall Street Journal*, January 19, 2000.

CASE 4: IS JAPAN BEING LEFT OUT?

Japan

As of June 2002, Japan was one of only four WTO members not a party to any preferential trade agreement. Since then Japan has concluded agreements with Singapore and Mexico, and negotiations are underway with Thailand, the Philippines, Malaysia, and South Korea. The Singapore agreement was relatively easy because of Singapore's lack of agricultural production, the most sensitive and protected sector of the Japanese economy. The other agreements are more challenging. Mexico and Thailand, for example, clearly want access for their agricultural products to the highly protected Japanese

market. The Philippines wants Japan's notoriously tight immigration restrictions relaxed for Filipino nurses and maids.

Japan's sudden interest in preferential trade agreements, after two decades of shunning the growing trend, suggests that the country might be worried about being "left out." This raises an important question: How have the major preferential trade agreements of which Japan is not a member affected Japan's trade?

Figure 9 presents economist Howard Wall's estimates of six major trade groups' effects on Japanese trade.[26] For

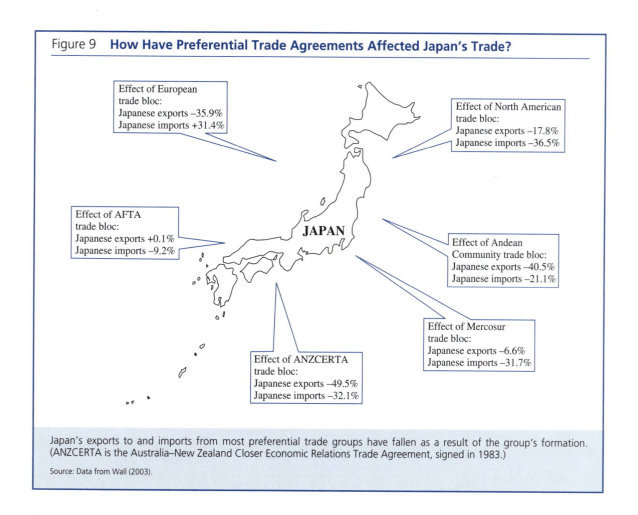

Figure 9   How Have Preferential Trade Agreements Affected Japan's Trade?

Effect of European trade bloc:
Japanese exports –35.9%
Japanese imports +31.4%

Effect of North American trade bloc:
Japanese exports –17.8%
Japanese imports –36.5%

JAPAN

Effect of AFTA trade bloc:
Japanese exports +0.1%
Japanese imports –9.2%

Effect of Andean Community trade bloc:
Japanese exports –40.5%
Japanese imports –21.1%

Effect of Mercosur trade bloc:
Japanese exports –6.6%
Japanese imports –31.7%

Effect of ANZCERTA trade bloc:
Japanese exports –49.5%
Japanese imports –32.1%

Japan's exports to and imports from most preferential trade groups have fallen as a result of the group's formation. (ANZCERTA is the Australia–New Zealand Closer Economic Relations Trade Agreement, signed in 1983.)

Source: Data from Wall (2003).

each group, the figure indicates two percentage changes: the change in Japan's exports to a trade group's members calculated as a percentage of Japan's trade with that group and Japan's imports from group-member countries also calculated as percentages of Japan's trade with that group. Most of the numbers are negative, indicating that the trade groups studied tended to reduce members' imports from and exports to Japan. The major exception is the large increase in Japanese imports from Europe. So far, the Asian economic integration group, AFTA, has had the smallest effect on Japanese trade. These results should be interpreted with caution. Data for the Wall study ended in 1997, at which time the ASEAN/AFTA countries had made little progress in reducing trade barriers, especially when compared with progress in the European Union and NAFTA.

SUMMARY

Within each economy, a complex political bargaining process determines national trade policy. The history of international trade relations chronicles the interaction of nations' political and economic self-interests. Despite the dominance of nation-states in the world economy, political boundaries remain somewhat arbitrary from the standpoint of organization of economic activities. This has resulted in the evolution of economic institutions, such as economic integration groups, that extend beyond the boundaries of a single nation.

LOOKING AHEAD

In Chapter Ten, we relax the assumption that each country contains a fixed quantity of capital and labor to be allocated among industries. We examine the implications of economic growth, international labor migration, and capital flows. Free movement of factors of production generates distributional effects similar to those of free movement of goods and services. These distributional consequences create pressures for policies that restrict the international mobility of both capital and labor.

KEY TERMS

Section 201	codes
mercantilism	Uruguay Round
Smoot-Hawley tariff bill of 1930	fast track (trade promotion authority)
Reciprocal Trade Agreements Act (RTAA)	integration
International Monetary Fund (IMF)	preferential trading arrangement (PTA)
World Bank	free-trade area
General Agreement on Tariffs and Trade (GATT)	customs union
World Trade Organization (WTO)	common external tariff (CET)
escape clause	common market
safeguards	economic union
Multifiber Agreement (MFA)	trade diversion
Trade Adjustment Assistance (TAA)	trade creation
	special economic zone (SEZ)
	export-processing zone

PROBLEMS AND QUESTIONS FOR REVIEW

1. We have seen that trade policy has predictable distributional effects. In particular, protection of a domestic industry tends to help domestic producers in that industry at the expense of domestic consumers. In almost any industry, the number of consumers outweighs the number

of producers; and we know that the loss in consumer surplus as a result of protection outweighs the gain in producer surplus. How, then, can we explain the success of domestic producers in winning protection through the political process?

2. What is fast-track (or trade-promotion) authority? Using the political economy of trade policy argument, why might such authority be important to the process of trade liberalization?
3. Country A exports $500 worth of components to country B, where workers assemble the components into a finished product, the world price of which is $1,000. Country B exports the finished good to country A.
   a. If country A imposes a 5 percent ad valorem tariff on imports and country B imposes a 10 percent ad valorem tariff on imports, how much tariff will be paid at each stage of the transaction?
   b. If the two countries have special tariff provisions that allow (1) components intended for assembly and re-export and (2) the component–re-export share of finished goods to enter tariff-free, how much tariff will be paid at each stage of the transaction?
4. Country A is a small country considering joining a free-trade area for trade in good X. The cost of importing a unit of good X from countries that would *not* be members of the potential group is $10 per unit. The cost of importing a unit of good X from countries that would be members of the potential group is $20 per unit. Currently, country A applies a $5-per-unit tariff on imports of good X from all sources. If the free-trade group forms, will there be any trade creation? Any trade diversion? Why?
5. Use the illustration of trade creation and trade diversion in Figure 4. Under what conditions is trade creation likely to outweigh trade diversion? Under what conditions is trade diversion likely to outweigh trade creation?
6. Under the Uruguay Round Agreement completed in 1994, WTO member countries agreed that their quotas on textiles and apparel imported from other members would end in 2005. Explain why this change would be expected to reduce the trade-diversion effects of agreements such as the NAFTA.
7. Suppose a labor-abundant economy that does *not* engage in international trade creates a special economic zone with free trade with the rest of the world. If labor were immobile geographically within the country, what would you expect to happen? If labor were mobile geographically within the country, what would you expect to happen? Why?
8. Consider two trends in the post–World War II world economy: (a) the number of independent countries rose from 74 in 1946 to 192 in 1995, and (b) barriers to international trade fell dramatically. How does the theory of international trade suggest these two trends might be related?

REFERENCES AND SELECTED READINGS

Alesina, Alberto, and Enrico Spolaore. "On the Number and Size of Nations." *Quarterly Journal of Economics* (November 1997): 1027–1056.
The economics of national boundaries; for intermediate students.

Alesina, Alberto, et al. "Economic Integration and Political Disintegration." *American Economic Review* (December 2000): 1276–1296.
Argues that open trade policies allow countries to be geographically smaller.

Anderson, James E., and Eric van Wincoop. "Gravity with Gravitas: A Solution to the Border Puzzle." *American Economic Review* 93 (March 2003): 170–192.
How much do national borders reduce trade? For advanced students.

Bagwell, Kyle, and Robert W. Staiger. *The Economics of the World Trading System.* Cambridge, Mass.: MIT Press, 2002.
Excellent summary of economic models of trade agreements; for advanced students.

Baldwin, Richard E., and T. Venables. "Regional Economic Integration." In *Handbook of International Economics*, Vol. 3, edited by G. M. Grossman and K. Rogoff, 1597–1644. Amsterdam: North-Holland, 1995.
Advanced survey of the literature on the causes and implications of regional trade groups.

Crowley, Meredith A. "An Introduction to the WTO and GATT." Federal Reserve Bank of Chicago *Economic Perspectives* (Fourth Quarter 2003): 42–57.
Readable overview of the history and rules of the GATT and WTO.

Destler, I. M. *American Trade Politics.* Washington, D.C.: Institute for International Economics, 1995.
A political scientist's analysis of American institutions that make trade policy and how their evolution has affected policy outcomes; for all students.

Folsom, Ralph H., et al. *NAFTA: A Problem-Oriented Coursebook*. St. Paul, Minn.: West Group, 2000.
Everything you could ever want to know about the nitty-gritty of NAFTA rules.

Grossman, Gene M., and Elhanan Helpman. *Special Interest Politics*. Cambridge, Mass.: MIT Press, 2001.
Theoretical models of how special-interest groups affect the political process through voting and financial contributions; for intermediate and advanced students.

Hoekman, Bernard, et al., eds. *Development, Trade, and the WTO*. Washington, D.C.: World Bank, 2002.
Collection of short, readable articles on many aspects of trade, including preferential agreements and multilateral negotiations.

Irwin, Douglas A. *Free Trade Under Fire*. Princeton: Princeton University Press, 2002.
Readable overview of the case for free trade, including discussions of preferential trade agreements and the WTO.

Jackson, John H. *The World Trading System*. Cambridge, Mass.: MIT Press, 1997.
Introduction to the history and structure of the GATT by a leading legal scholar of that institution.

James, Harold. *The End of Globalization: Lessons from the Great Depression*. Cambridge, Mass.: Harvard University Press, 2001.
History of the world trading system.

Krueger, Anne O. "Are Preferential Trading Arrangements Trade-Liberalizing or Protectionist?" *Journal of Economic Perspectives* 13 (Fall 1999): 85–104.
Balanced assessment of PTAs' potential effects by one of the strongest proponents of open international trade.

Leitner, Kara, and Simon Lester. "WTO Dispute Settlement 1995–2003: A Statistical Analysis." *Journal of International Economic Law* 7 (March 2004): 169–181.
Summary of disputes taken to the WTO since its formation.

Lipsey, Richard. "The Theory of Customs Unions: A General Survey." *Economic Journal* 70 (1960): 496–513.
A survey of the classic papers that developed the theory of customs unions; for intermediate students.

Magee, Stephen P., William A. Brock, and Leslie Young. *Black Hole Tariffs and Endogenous Policy Theory*. Cambridge: Cambridge University Press, 1989.
A recent classic on the political economy of protection; for intermediate and advanced students.

Panagariya, Arvind. "Preferential Trade Liberalization: The Traditional Theory and New Developments." *Journal of Economic Literature* 38 (June 2000): 287–331.
Intermediate-level survey of the implications of PTAs.

Rodrik, Dani. "Political Economy of Trade Policy." In *Handbook of International Economics*, Vol. 3, edited by G. M. Grossman and K. Rogoff, 1457–1494. Amsterdam: North-Holland, 1995.
Advanced survey of the literature on distributional aspects of trade policy and their implications for the policy process.

Rose, Andrew K. "Do We Really Know that the WTO Increases Trade?" *American Economic Review* 94 (March 2004): 98–114.
Evidence that the WTO may not explain the rapid postwar growth in trade; for intermediate and advanced students.

Shiue, Carol H. "Transport Costs and the Geography of Arbitrage in Eighteenth-Century China." *American Economic Review* 92 (December 2002): 1406–1419.
How well developed was intra-country trade in eighteenth century China? For advanced students.

Spruyt, Hendrik. *The Sovereign State and Its Competitors*. Princeton: Princeton University Press, 1994.
Political scientist's analysis of the development of the modern territorial nation-state; for all students.

United States International Trade Commission. *The Year in Trade*. Washington, D.C.: USITC, annual.
Accessible source of recent developments in the WTO and PTAs; available on CD-ROM.

Wall, Howard J. "Has Japan Been Left Out in the Cold by Regional Integration?" Federal Reserve Bank of St. Louis *Review* 84 (September/October 2002): 25–36.
Evidence that Japan's trade has declined as a result of other countries' formation of preferential trade areas.

Wall, Howard J. "NAFTA and the Geography of North American Trade." Federal Reserve Bank of St. Louis *Review* 85 (March/April 2003): 13–26.
How NAFTA has affected members' trade.

Westhoff, Frank H., Beth V. Yarbrough, and Robert M. Yarbrough. "Preferential Trade Agreements and the GATT: Can Bilateralism and Multilateralism Coexist?" *Kyklos* 47 (1994): 179–195.
Interaction of bilateral and multilateral trade-liberalization agreements; for intermediate students.

Yarbrough, Beth V. "Preferential Trade Arrangements and the GATT: EC 1992 as Rogue or Role Model?" In *The Challenge of European Integration*, edited by Berhanu Abegaz et al., 79–117. Boulder, Colo.: Westview Press, 1994.
Overview of the effects of preferential trade agreements on the world trading system; for all students.

Yarbrough, Beth V., and Robert M. Yarbrough. *Cooperation and Governance in International Trade: The Strategic Organizational Approach*. Princeton: Princeton University Press, 1992.
An analysis of bilateralism, minilateralism, and multilateralism in trade policy; for all students.

Yarbrough, Beth V., and Robert M. Yarbrough. "International Contracting and Territorial Control: The Boundary Question." *Journal of Institutional and Theoretical Economics* 150 (March 1994): 239–264.
Examines the role of economics in disputes over national boundaries; for all students.

Yarbrough, Beth V., and Robert M. Yarbrough. "Unification and Secession: Group Size and 'Escape from Lock-In,'" *Kyklos* (1998): 171–195.
The economics of national unifications and secessions; for intermediate students.

10

Growth, Immigration, and Multinationals

1 INTRODUCTION

Chapters Two through Nine examined international trade's effects on production, consumption, output and input prices, and the distribution of income under the assumptions of fixed factor endowments and fixed technology. In terms of the schematic diagram in Figure 9 in Chapter Four, factor endowments and technology, along with tastes, form the "fixed" foundation on which the basic trade model rests. These assumptions seem appropriate for many countries and time periods in which endowments and technology, while not really constant, change slowly. For other periods and countries, however, changes in endowments and technology lie at the very heart of events. Many examples come to mind: the Industrial Revolution in late eighteenth-century Britain, the massive European immigration to America during the nineteenth century, the worldwide spread of multinational corporations since World War II, the increased pace of foreign investment in the United States since the 1980s, the computer and information-technology revolutions, and recent immigration waves to both the United States and Western Europe.

Trade represents just one type of international interaction that countries find beneficial. We've seen, for example, that a labor-abundant country can exploit its comparative advantage by specializing in and exporting labor-intensive goods. However, such a country might also borrow abroad to increase its capital stock or allow its workers to emigrate. If the country is too small for domestic firms to achieve economies of scale, policies that permit inward and outward foreign direct investment might allow both domestic and foreign firms to produce at large enough scale to achieve gains from trade based on scale economies. In other words, *factor flows between countries represent another way countries can use economic interaction to benefit from their differences.*

In this chapter, we extend our basic trade model to consider issues related to economic growth and factor mobility. Thus far, we've viewed trade in static terms—that is, we've compared a country's situation under unrestricted trade with its situation at the same time and in the same circumstances but without trade. When we introduce more dynamic considerations such as economic growth, the basic characteristics of the world economy, including the pattern of comparative advantage, can change over time.[1] These changes can

---

1. Our analysis of economic growth actually provides an example of comparative-static rather than dynamic analysis. Comparative-static analysis compares the pre-growth and post-growth equilibria in the economy. A dynamic analysis also would examine the path along which the economy moves from the old equilibrium to the new one. Dynamic analysis lies beyond the scope of this book.

dramatically alter both the pattern of trade and governments' policies toward trade. For example, Britain, which came to dominate the world textile industry through the technological advances of the Industrial Revolution, lost that industry to the United States because of changing patterns of comparative advantage. The United States, in turn, lost the textile industry to the labor-abundant countries of Asia. In fact, many U.S. industries now asking for protection from the rigors of foreign competition once were industries of U.S. comparative advantage—not just textiles, but steel, automobiles, televisions, and semiconductor memory chips.

During the past few years the study of economic growth has become, literally, a growth industry within economics. To keep the scope of the discussion manageable, we'll limit our attention to the relationship between economic growth and international trade. Economic growth is a complex phenomenon, particularly when viewed as an objective of economic policy making. The debate among economists and policy makers over what types of policies promote economic growth has been long and lively, going back to Adam Smith and the founding of economics. In this chapter, our perspective differs from that of a policy maker interested in promoting economic growth. We are interested primarily in the trade-related *effects* of growth rather than how to bring it about. In Chapter Eleven, we'll examine the pursuit of growth from the viewpoint of developing countries.

For our purposes, we can define **economic growth** simply as a shift outward of a country's production possibilities frontier. Any change that allows the economy to produce a larger quantity of goods (that is, more of one good and no less of any other) represents economic growth. Recall from the discussion of production possibilities frontiers in Chapters Two and Three that the position of a country's frontier depends on the endowment of resources and on the technology with which the country can transform those resources into goods and services. The major sources of economic growth, then, are (1) increases in the quantities of resources available to the country and (2) technical progress, or improvements in available production technology. Empirical evidence suggests that increases in resources have accounted for somewhat less than half of economic growth in the modern period, and technical progress for somewhat more than half.[2]

Early economic growth theory focused on increases in stocks of labor and capital, but more recent work emphasizes the role of knowledge, education, and ideas in the technical progress that generates ongoing economic growth.[3] Called **endogenous growth theory**, these new approaches to growth recognize knowledge or ideas as an input, along with capital and labor, into an economy's ability to produce goods and services. An economy produces knowledge by investing in education and research, which requires forgoing current consumption, just as investing in physical capital does. Unfortunately, economists' understanding of the growth process, especially the role of knowledge creation, still has a long way to go. Growth rates among countries differ dramatically (see Figure 1) for reasons not fully understood, although most economists agree that governments' basic policy choices play a major role in explaining countries' different growth experiences.

As we noted in Chapters One and Nine, the assumption that factors of production move much more freely within than among countries seems realistic. A significant amount of inter-country factor movement does occur, but it remains small relative to

---

2. Case One provides more information on this issue.

3. The key citations are Robert M. Solow, "A Contribution to the Theory of Economic Growth," *Quarterly Journal of Economics* 70 (1956), pp. 65–94; and Paul M. Romer, "Endogenous Technological Change," *Journal of Political Economy* 98 (1990), pp. S71–S102, respectively.

Figure 1   **Growth Rates for 116 Countries, 1960–1985**

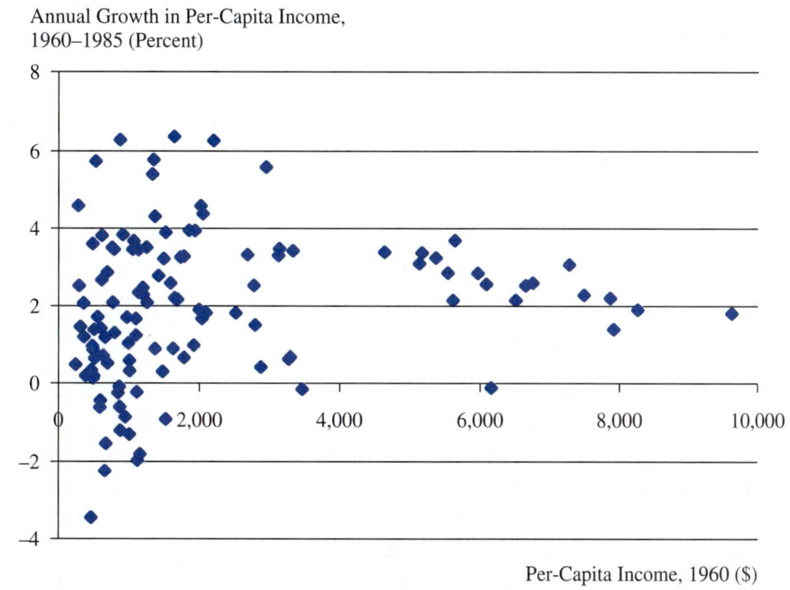

Annual Growth in Per-Capita Income,
1960–1985 (Percent)

Per-Capita Income, 1960 ($)

Countries' annual growth rates between 1960 and 1985 ranged from −4 percent to +7 percent. Countries with low relative incomes in 1960 (those on the left in the figure) experienced more diverse growth rates over the next quarter century than did countries with high relative incomes in 1960 (those on the right in the figure).

intra-country movement for two basic reasons. First, most governments maintain at least some restrictions on flows of both capital and labor across their national boundaries. The United States, for example, restricts immigration; and Mexico imposes limits on foreign-owned production facilities in some industries. Second, even without such government restrictions, the differences in costs involved in inter-country versus intra-country mobility would produce differential rates of movement. In the case of labor, some of the additional costs of inter-country mobility include the costs—both financial and psychological—of overcoming language and cultural barriers. In the case of capital, additional costs take the form of risks associated with owning capital in a foreign country, such as the risk of expropriation or of unfavorable changes in the value of the foreign country's currency. Technology can lower some of these costs. For example, e-mail and low-cost phone cards now allow immigrants to keep in touch with family back home; and those same tools help foreign investors keep up with economic developments abroad that might affect their investments. So these technological improvements are associated with increased international mobility of both labor and capital. But, as long as political boundaries continue to have economic significance, inter-country mobility will remain less than intra-country mobility.

Factor mobility among countries raises issues similar to those surrounding economic growth. In fact, we can view factor mobility as simultaneous positive growth in one country (the country of immigration, or host) and negative growth in another (the country of emigration, or source). But factor mobility also raises additional distributional issues, so we'll separate the discussions of growth (sections 2 and 3) and factor mobility (section 4), despite the close relationship between the two.

2 ECONOMIC GROWTH I: MORE INPUTS

Economists classify economic growth resulting from increased factor endowments according to the relative changes in the capital and labor endowments. A country's labor endowment can grow in three ways. The population can grow because of an increase in the birth rate relative to the death rate; the population can grow because of immigration (discussed below in section 4.1); and the labor force can increase due to a rise in *labor-force participation*, or the working portion of the population. A country's capital stock is its accumulation of durable factors of production such as machines and buildings. Capital accumulates when residents choose to consume less than the total amount of current production, setting a portion of output aside to increase future productive capacity.

2.1 More Labor *and* Capital

Economists refer to a proportional increase in a country's endowments of both labor and capital as **balanced growth**. Such growth generates an outward shift of the production possibilities frontier that maintains the frontier's original shape, as Figure 2 illustrates. The country in the figure is small in the sense that it can't alter the international terms of trade. When both goods exhibit constant returns to scale, balanced growth shifts the production possibilities frontier outward in the same proportion as the increase in the factor endowment, because constant-returns-to-scale production means that output increases proportionally with a proportional increase in all inputs. For example, after a doubling of the endowments, the new frontier intersects

Figure 2   What Are the Effects of Balanced Growth?

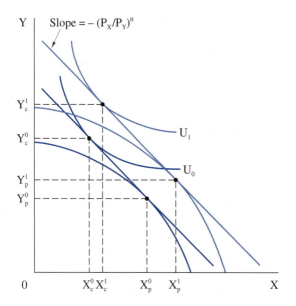

Balanced growth increases production and consumption of each good, imports, exports, and the volume of trade in the same proportion as the factor endowments. The country superscript is omitted for simplicity. Subscript p refers to production, c to consumption, 0 to pre-growth, and 1 to post-growth.

both axes at points twice as far from the origin as the original frontier. Balanced growth increases production of both goods, consumption of both goods, imports, and exports proportionally with the endowment.

How does balanced growth affect welfare, both of the growing country and of its trading partners? First, what about the growing country itself? It's tempting to answer quickly that welfare increases—based on the rise in consumption of both goods. Such a reply, however, would ignore the fact that the country's population also may have increased. *Total* consumption of both goods has risen, but that bigger total may be spread across a larger population. If the increased availability of labor that led to growth was due to an increase in population, then *per-capita* consumption (that is, total consumption divided by population) wouldn't change. *(Why?)* But if the increased availability of labor resulted from increased labor-force participation, then per-capita consumption would rise. Individuals who previously had consumed but not produced (labor-force nonparticipants) now would produce as well as consume, allowing per-capita consumption to rise.

Economists call growth's effect on per-capita consumption at unchanged terms of trade the **income effect** of growth. Balanced growth's income effect equals zero if the labor growth comes from population growth but is positive if the labor growth comes from increased labor-force participation. For a small country, the income effect captures growth's entire impact because the country can't, by definition, change its terms of trade. So the overall effect of balanced growth in a small country can be zero (if due to population growth) or positive (if due to increased labor-force participation), as summarized in Table 1's first two columns.

What about growth's effects on the growing country's trading partners? They experience no income effect because growth abroad doesn't shift their production possibilities frontiers. They also experience no terms-of-trade effect since the growing country is too small to generate any. Therefore, balanced growth in a small country leaves the country's trading partners unaffected.

For a country large enough to affect the international terms of trade, the income effect is only one of two components of growth's effect on welfare. The second

Table 1   **HOW DOES BALANCED GROWTH AFFECT WELFARE?**

	Small-Country Case	Large-Country Case
Effect on growing economy:		
Income effect	0 if population⇑; + if labor-force ⇑	0 if population ⇑; + if labor-force ⇑
Terms-of-trade effect	0	−
Change in export price	0	⇓
Change in import price	0	⇑
Net effect on per-capita consumption	0 if population ⇑; + if labor-force ⇑	Depends on magnitudes of income and terms-of-trade effects
Effect on trading partner:		
Income effect	0	0
Terms-of-trade effect	0	+
Change in export price	0	⇑
Change in import price	0	⇓
Net effect on per-capita consumption	0	+

component, the **terms-of-trade effect**, captures the effect of changes in relative output prices. A country's terms of trade equal the price of its export good(s) relative to the price of its import good(s). If country A exports X and imports Y, its terms of trade are $(P_X/P_Y)^{tt}$. Decreases in this ratio represent deterioration in the terms of trade, while increases represent improvement. If country B exports Y and imports X, its terms of trade are $(P_Y/P_X)^{tt}$, or the reciprocal of A's terms of trade. Deterioration in a country's terms of trade reduces its total consumption, because the country receives fewer units of its import good in exchange for each unit of its export good. Balanced growth causes a country to want to engage in a larger volume of trade at the original terms of trade, so the relative price of the country's import good rises (because of increased demand) and that of its export good falls (because of increased supply). This change in relative prices represents a deterioration in the terms of trade from the growing country's perspective and an improvement from the perspective of the trading partner. Note this implies that balanced growth in a large country improves the trading partner's welfare: The trading partner experiences no income effect and a positive terms-of-trade effect.

Figure 3 shows the effects of a deterioration in the growing country's terms of trade. At constant terms of trade, given by $(P_X/P_Y)^{tt}_0$, balanced growth would move the country from U_0 to U_1. Remember that the increase in total consumption doesn't necessarily translate into an increase in per-capita consumption, because U_0 and U_1 may be drawn for different population sizes. For a large country, balanced growth increases the desired volume of trade at the original terms of trade and causes the

Figure 3   **What Are the Effects of a Deterioration in a Country's Terms of Trade?**

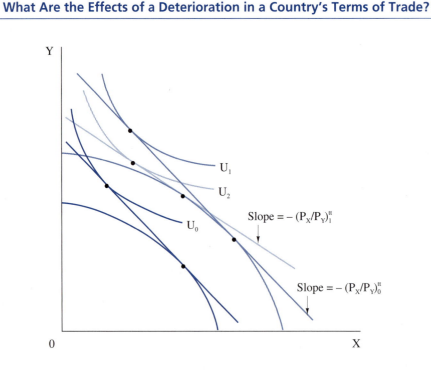

Balanced growth shifts the production possibilities frontier outward, increasing utility from U_0 to U_1 at unchanged output prices. The increased volume of trade deteriorates the terms of trade from $(P_X/P_Y)^{tt}_0$ to $(P_X/P_Y)^{tt}_1$ and lowers utility to U_2.

terms of trade to deteriorate to $(P_X/P_Y)_1^{tt}$. This terms-of-trade effect moves the country to U_2. Thus, the welfare effects of balanced growth are less encouraging for a large country than for a small one. The net effect of balanced growth on per-capita consumption in a large country depends on (1) the source of the growth in the labor endowment (population versus labor-force participation), and (2) the relative magnitudes of the income and terms-of-trade effects, as summarized in Table 1's right-hand column.

2.2 Just More Labor

An increase in a country's labor endowment with a constant capital endowment shifts the production possibilities frontier asymmetrically. The shift exhibits a bias toward production of the labor-intensive good, assumed in Figure 4 to be good X. The intersection of the new production possibilities frontier with both axes shifts outward, because the additional labor could be used to produce more of either good; but the shift along the X axis is larger. The economy's overall capital-labor ratio falls. The effect of a decline in the capital-labor ratio on the economy and its international trade depends on whether the country imports or exports the labor-intensive good and on the terms-of-trade effect.

First, consider the effect on a small country. In Figure 4, the increased labor endowment causes such a country to increase production of the labor-intensive good and reduce production of the capital-intensive one, as represented by the move from point I to point II. This somewhat peculiar-sounding result provides an example of the **Rybczynski theorem**. The theorem states that when the terms of trade are constant (as in a small country), an increase in the endowment of one factor with the other

---

Figure 4   What Are the Effects of Labor Endowment Growth?

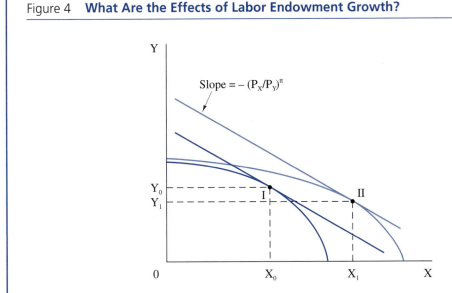

Good X is the labor-intensive good. With a constant capital endowment, output of the labor-intensive good rises more than proportionally with the labor endowment and output of the capital-intensive good falls; this provides an example of the Rybczynski theorem.

factor endowment held constant *increases* production of the good intensive in the increased factor and *decreases* production of the good intensive in the constant factor.[4]

Why would economic growth cause a country to reduce production of one of the goods? To take advantage of the increased availability of labor and increase output of the labor-intensive good, the labor-intensive industry must obtain some additional capital, because even the labor-intensive industry uses some capital along with labor. With the country's capital endowment held constant, the only source of additional capital is that already employed in the capital-intensive industry. Therefore, the capital-intensive industry must shrink—to facilitate the expansion of the labor-intensive industry made possible by the increased labor endowment.

You may be tempted to view the Rybczynski theorem as theoretical curiosity, but it actually carries important policy implications. For example, suppose a country undergoes a large-scale inflow of labor, such as those from the former Soviet Union to Israel, from Mexico to the United States, or from Eastern Europe to Germany. If the growing country's product mix didn't change, the labor inflow would reduce wages (more on this in section 4.1 below). But the country's output mix will change. The Rybczynski theorem tell us that production of the labor-intensive good rises and output of the capital-intensive good falls. Therefore, the demand for labor rises, and the economy can absorb the new labor without a reduction in the wage.

Growth of a country's labor endowment increases output of the labor-intensive good relative to the capital-intensive one. If the country exports the labor-intensive good, this increases the desired volume of trade and is referred to as *export expanding*. If the country imports the labor-intensive good, increased domestic production of it reduces desired imports and is *import replacing*.

The pattern of domestic consumption of the two goods also influences labor growth's net effect on trade. When domestic consumption of the import good rises relative to that of the export good, the effect is export expanding—that is, it represents a force that tends to increase the volume of trade. If consumption of the export good rises relative to that of the import good, the volume of trade falls and the effect is import replacing. The total effect of labor-endowment growth on the volume of trade depends on the combination of the effects on production and consumption; the volume of trade can rise, fall, or remain unchanged.

Economic growth based on increased population coupled with a constant endowment of capital generally creates a negative income effect. The increased population implies that each worker now has less capital with which to work, so labor's marginal product falls. Total consumption rises, but at a lower rate than the population growth; thus, per-capita consumption falls. As in the case of balanced growth, the income effect changes if the increased availability of labor comes from greater labor-force participation rather than increased population. Increased labor-force participation results in positive income effects, or increases in per-capita consumption.

A small country's labor growth doesn't affect its trading partners. They experience no income effect; and growth in the small country doesn't alter the terms of trade, so partners experience no terms-of-trade effect either. Table 2 summarizes the welfare effects of small-country labor growth.

---

4. Using more advanced techniques, we could demonstrate a much more general form of the Rybczynski theorem. For any change in factor endowments at unchanged output prices, the output of the labor-intensive commodity always changes in the same direction and more than proportionally with the endowment of labor. If the endowment of labor increases, output of the labor-intensive good increases by a larger percentage. If the endowment of labor decreases, output of the labor-intensive industry shrinks by a larger percentage. Similarly, output in the capital-intensive industry changes in the same direction and more than proportionally with the capital endowment. If X is the labor-intensive good, $\hat{X} > \hat{L} > \hat{K} = 0 > \hat{Y}$. In Figure 4, output of good Y must shrink because the rate of growth of the capital endowment is zero. This phenomenon provides another example of the magnification effect discussed in Chapter Four.

Table 2	HOW DOES LABOR-ENDOWMENT GROWTH AFFECT WELFARE?	
	Small-Country Case	Large-Country Case
Effect on growing economy:		
Income effect	− if population ⇑; + if labor-force ⇑	− if population ⇑; + if labor-force ⇑
Terms-of-trade effect	0	− if export-expanding; + if import-replacing
Net effect on per-capita consumption	− if population ⇑; + if labor-force ⇑	Depends on signs and magnitudes of income and terms-of-trade effects
Effect on trading partner:		
Income effect	0	0
Terms-of-trade effect	0	+ if export-expanding; − if import-replacing
Net effect on per-capita consumption	0	+ if export-expanding; − if import-replacing

For a large growing country, the impact of labor-endowment growth on the terms of trade is uncertain. If the growth expands exports, it worsens the terms of trade by increasing the supply of the export good and demand for the import good. On the other hand, if the growth replaces imports, the terms of trade improve as the supply of the export good falls along with the demand for imports. Therefore, the total effect of labor growth on per-capita consumption in a large country is ambiguous for three reasons: (1) The sign of the income effect depends on whether the labor growth comes from a growing population or increased labor-force participation; (2) the sign of the effect on the desired volume of trade, and therefore on the terms of trade, is ambiguous; and (3) if the income and terms-of-trade effects work in opposite directions, either effect may dominate. When a large country grows, its trading partners experience a terms-of-trade effect but no income effect. Therefore, export-expanding growth in one country helps its trading partners, while import-replacing growth harms them.

2.3 Just More Capital

The overall effects of growth due to an increased endowment of capital in a large country are ambiguous, as in the case of labor-based growth. The major change in the analysis is a definitely positive income effect in the case of capital-based growth. Total consumption rises; and, because the population doesn't change, a rise in per-capita consumption follows. For a small country, in which growth generates no terms-of-trade effect, capital-based growth must increase per-capita consumption. Again, growth in the small country has no effect on its trading partners.

In a large country, the terms-of-trade effect can be either positive or negative, making the overall effect of growth on both countries uncertain. If growth is import replacing, the growing country's terms of trade improve and the overall effect on its welfare is positive, while the trading partner suffers a deterioration in its terms of trade. If the growth is export expanding, the growing country's terms of trade deteriorate and the overall effect of

Table 3   HOW DOES CAPITAL-ENDOWMENT GROWTH AFFECT WELFARE?

	Small-Country Case	Large-Country Case
Effect on growing economy:		
Income effect	+	+
Terms-of-trade effect	0	− if export-expanding; + if import-replacing
Net effect on per-capita consumption	+	Depends on sign and magnitudes of income and terms-of-trade effects
Effect on trading partner:		
Income effect	0	0
Terms-of-trade effect	0	+ if export-expanding; − if import-replacing
Net effect on per-capita consumption	0	+ if export-expanding; − if import-replacing

growth on its welfare is ambiguous, while the trading partner gains from the improvement in its terms of trade. Table 3 summarizes these results for both the small-country and large-country cases.

2.4 An Extreme Case: Immiserizing Growth

For many years, economists recognized the theoretical possibility that, in some cases, increased production could lower welfare through growth's effect on the terms of trade. In 1956, Jagdish Bhagwati rigorously analyzed this situation and named it **immiserizing growth**. Sections 2.1, 2.2, and 2.3 covered several cases in which economic growth lowers per-capita consumption. We might expect such a result when growth takes the form of a larger population. The case of immiserizing growth as developed by Bhagwati is somewhat more surprising in its implication that growth could lower per-capita consumption even if population remains constant. The source of immiserizing growth is a strongly negative terms-of-trade effect. Therefore, the problem can affect only large countries, which have some influence on international terms of trade.

The possibility of immiserizing growth is illustrated in Figure 5, drawn under the assumption that growth doesn't result from an increase in population. The move from U_0 to U_1 represents growth's income effect. The growth is biased toward production of the export good (X), so the country's terms of trade deteriorate sharply, from $(P_X/P_Y)_0^{tt}$ to $(P_X/P_Y)_1^{tt}$, reducing welfare from U_1 to U_2 and leaving the country worse off than in its pre-growth situation (U_0).

Many conditions must be satisfied for the immiserizing-growth result to emerge. First, growth itself must be relatively modest; if it is substantial, the positive income effect (represented in Figure 5 by the move from U_0 to U_1) will swamp any negative terms-of-trade effect and growth will enhance welfare. Second, growth must significantly increase supply of a country's exports and demand for its imports, to generate a large terms-of-trade effect. Third, the elasticity of trading partners' demand for the country's exports must be sufficiently low for increased exports to lower their price substantially. Finally, the country must depend heavily on foreign trade so that

Figure 5 Immiserizing Growth

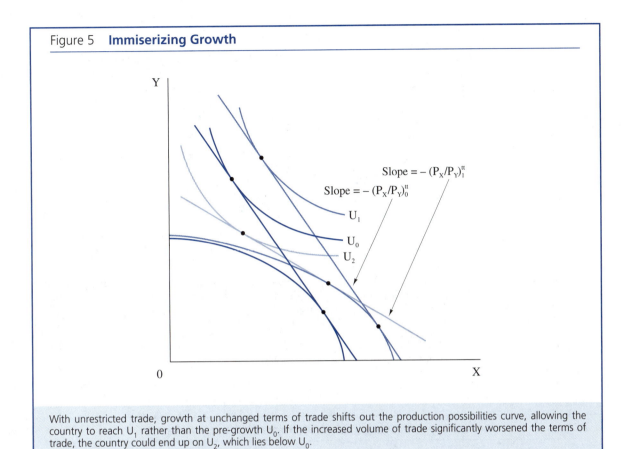

$\text{Slope} = -(P_X/P_Y)_1^{tt}$

$\text{Slope} = -(P_X/P_Y)_0^{tt}$

U_1

U_0

U_2

With unrestricted trade, growth at unchanged terms of trade shifts out the production possibilities curve, allowing the country to reach U_1 rather than the pre-growth U_0. If the increased volume of trade significantly worsened the terms of trade, the country could end up on U_2, which lies below U_0.

changes in the terms of trade exert a large impact on its welfare. In Chapter Eleven, where we discuss problems facing developing countries, the possibility of chronic deterioration in the terms of trade will play a role. Little evidence, however, suggests that immiserizing growth actually occurs; the phenomenon appears to be more a theoretical possibility than an empirical reality.

Historical periods involving rapid economic growth based solely on increases in factor endowments have been rare. More commonly, periods of growth have followed technological advances or technical progress. Of course, one frequent outcome of technical progress is to turn something not previously viewed as an important resource into a valuable factor of production (for example, development of the internal combustion engine and the subsequent importance of petroleum).

3 ECONOMIC GROWTH II: MORE PRODUCTIVITY

Economists refer to an increase in productivity as **technical progress**. Defining and measuring it is notoriously difficult. In general, technical progress occurs whenever more goods can be produced from a given quantity of resources or, equivalently, a given quantity of goods can be produced from fewer inputs. Technical progress involves an increase in the *productivity* of capital, labor, or both. For small countries, technical progress generates an unambiguously positive welfare effect; per-capita consumption rises. For large countries, the income effect of technical progress is unambiguously positive, but the terms-of-trade effect may be negative.

3.1 Types of Technical Progress

Nobel prize winner Sir John Hicks provided the classification system commonly used by economists for the various types of technical progress. Hicks classified technical progress according to its effect on the cost-minimizing capital-labor ratio that firms choose to use at unchanged factor prices.

Neutral technical progress leaves firms' chosen capital-labor ratio unchanged. It increases the productivity of both capital and labor proportionally such that at any given capital-labor ratio (K/L), the marginal rate of technical substitution (MRTS) between the two inputs remains unchanged.[5] Figure 6 panel (a) represents neutral technical progress in production of good X. (The reader may want to review the use of isoquants and the firm's choice of the cost-minimizing capital-labor ratio in section 2.1 of Chapter Three.) After the technical progress, smaller bundles of capital and labor than before can produce output X_0, but the new isoquant representing X_0 retains the same shape as the old one—just shifted in toward the origin. At the same relative factor prices, the firm chooses the same capital-labor ratio as before.

Capital-saving technical progress raises the marginal productivity of labor relative to that of capital. At unchanged factor prices, firms choose a lower capital-labor ratio, hence the term *capital-saving*. Graphically, such progress implies that for any given capital-labor ratio (along any ray from the origin), the new isoquant is steeper than the old one because the slope, given by $-(MP_{LX}/MP_{KX})$, is greater (see Figure 6 panel (b)).

Figure 6   **Neutral and Capital-Saving Technical Progress in the X Industry**

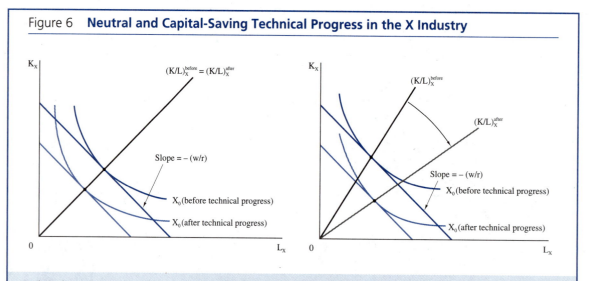

Technical progress shifts the isoquant that represents production level X_0 in toward the origin. With neutral progress (panel [a]), the isoquant retains its original shape, and firms' capital-labor ratio is unchanged at the old relative factor prices. In panel (b), capital-saving technical progress raises the marginal productivity of labor relative to that of capital. At unchanged factor prices, firms use a lower capital-labor ratio. Along any ray from the origin (for any given K/L), the new isoquant is steeper than the old one.

---

5. By definition, the MRTS equals the ratio of the *marginal products* of the two inputs $(-[MP_L/MP_K])$, where an input's marginal product equals the increase in output made possible by use of one additional unit of the input with the quantity of the other input held constant. Neutral technical progress raises MP_L and MP_K proportionally, leaving MRTS unchanged.

Note two sources of potential confusion. First, *capital*-saving technical progress makes an industry more *labor* intensive. Second, capital-saving technical progress doesn't save just capital; it saves *both* capital and labor in the sense that good X now can be produced using less of both resources than before. The term *capital-saving* indicates only that firms will employ less capital per unit of labor.

Similarly, **labor-saving technical progress** involves an increase in the marginal product of capital relative to that of labor. The cost-minimizing capital-labor ratio rises. (*We leave construction of a diagram representing labor-saving technical progress to the reader.*)

3.2 How Does Increased Productivity Affect Welfare?

The fundamental effect of any type of technical progress on the production possibilities frontier is clear: The frontier shifts outward. The precise shape of the shift, however, depends on several considerations. The frontier represents two industries, each of which can enjoy technical progress of any type and at any rate. For example, industry X might experience rapid capital-saving progress and industry Y slow neutral progress. Because of the many possible combinations, we'll restrict our attention to the case of neutral progress.

In the event that both industries enjoy neutral technical progress at the same rates, the production possibilities frontier shifts out at the rate of the increased productivity while maintaining its original shape. Figure 2, drawn to represent balanced factor growth, also can represent neutral technical progress in both industries.

The welfare analysis of balanced growth also carries over to neutral technical progress, with one important exception. Recall that balanced growth's income effect equaled zero when population grew at the same rate as output, leaving per-capita consumption unchanged.[6] Neutral technical progress involves productivity growth rather than population growth, so the increased output raises per-capita consumption. Therefore, neutral technical progress in both industries exerts a definitely positive income effect. For a small country, this income effect constitutes the only component of the welfare change, and thus the overall effect is favorable. The welfare change due to neutral technical progress in a large country depends on the relative strengths of the positive income effect and the negative terms-of-trade effect, identical to that in the case of balanced growth.

What if neutral technical progress occurs in only one industry? The intersection of the production possibilities frontier with the axis representing the static industry remains unchanged, while the intersection with the axis representing the progressive industry shifts outward at the rate of the increased productivity. A small country would reduce output in the static industry and increase output of the progressive one.

Figure 7 captures the effect of single-industry neutral progress in a small country. The production point after technical progress must lie southeast of the original production point. How do we know? The production possibilities frontier's slope represents the opportunity cost of good X in terms of forgone good Y. Neutral technical progress in the X industry reduces the amount of resources required to produce a unit of good X and, therefore, the opportunity cost of good X in terms of good Y. At the point on the new frontier directly to the right of the original production point, the new frontier must be flatter than the old one to capture the new lower opportunity cost of good X; and the point on the new frontier with a slope equal to that at the original production point must lie to the southeast.

---

6. Balanced growth creates a positive income effect if increased labor availability comes from greater labor-force participation rather than population growth.

Figure 7   What Are the Effects of Neutral Technical Progress in the X Industry?

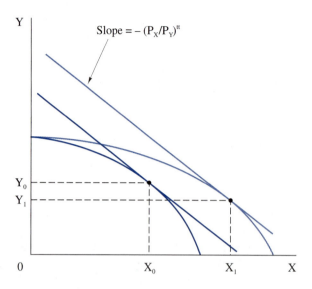

Slope $= -(P_X/P_Y)^{tt}$

With neutral technical progress in industry X, a small country reduces production of good Y and increases production of good X.

Again, the welfare effect on the small country is unambiguously positive. Total consumption rises with an unchanged population, implying increased per-capita consumption. For a large country, the total welfare effect is ambiguous because of the possibility of a deterioration in the terms of trade. In theory, technical progress could cause immiserizing growth in a large country. If the progress were strongly biased toward the export good, increased production of that good might lower its price sufficiently to offset the positive income effect on welfare. But the strict conditions discussed in section 2.4 as necessary to the immiserizing-growth result apply here, too. Again, little empirical evidence suggests actual occurrence of immiserizing growth.

For the trading partner of a large country that experiences technical progress, the welfare effect depends on what happens to the terms of trade. If the terms of trade turn in favor of the country experiencing progress, the trading partner suffers. If the progressive country experiences a deterioration in its terms of trade, the trading partner benefits from the technical progress.

Thus far, we've analyzed the effects of economic growth in one country, assuming that the fundamental situation in the other country remains unchanged, although we've seen that factor-endowment growth or technical progress in a large country affects its trading partners through the terms-of-trade effect. When factors of production can move between countries, we must extend the analysis to include the direct impacts in both countries.

4 WHAT IF FACTORS CAN MOVE?

The basic trade model of Chapters Three and Four assumes that factors of production are completely immobile between countries. Nonetheless, with unrestricted trade, factor prices tend to equalize across countries according to the factor price equalization theorem (see section 3 in Chapter Four). Trade in goods substitutes for trade in factors, because exports of a capital-intensive good are equivalent in their effects to exports of capital itself.

The link between factor mobility and international trade in goods and services lies at the center of several current international policy debates. Consider the North American Free Trade Agreement (NAFTA) implemented by the United States, Canada, and Mexico in 1994. Proponents argued that the agreement would enlarge the U.S. market for Mexican goods, raise incomes in Mexico, and decrease Mexican migration, especially illegal migration, to the United States. This view presents trade in goods and services as a substitute for factor mobility. On the other hand, opponents of the agreement claimed that firms would move from the United States to Mexico to "exploit" its low-wage labor. Along similar lines, the governments of Western Europe debate whether to lower trade barriers and admit the cheaper products from Eastern Europe or to maintain trade barriers in goods and services, especially agriculture, and risk more migration from East to West.

Achievement of complete factor price equalization would remove the major incentive for inter-country factor movements: obtaining higher factor rewards. We'll see that some reasons for factor movement persist even with complete factor price equalization, but the primary cause of factor movements is differences in factor prices across countries. As long as capital or labor earns a higher reward in one country than in another, the differential provides an incentive for factor movements.

Section 3 in Chapter Four indicated the relatively stringent requirements for complete factor price equalization. For example, the presence of either trade barriers or nontraded goods (such as haircuts) can prevent complete equalization. Trade barriers play a particularly strong role in generating factor movements. The development of U.S. production facilities by Japanese automobile producers provides one outstanding example. The United States imposed quotas on imports of Japanese automobiles in 1981, and the Japanese feared even stronger trade restrictions. One way to guarantee continued access to the U.S. market was to build production facilities in the United States—and firms, especially Toyota and Honda, did just that. Today "Japanese" auto firms produce hundreds of thousands of cars each year in the United States. A more recent version of the same story is occurring in China. Despite lowering many of its tariffs in order to join the World Trade Organization, China still imposes high tariffs on imported automobiles. So firms such as Volkswagen, General Motors, and Audi have built production facilities in China that give the firms access to Chinese consumers without facing Chinese auto tariffs.

The welfare analysis of factor movements involves four questions. First, how does factor movement affect total world output; can factor mobility increase the efficiency of the world economy as trade in outputs does? Second, how does factor movement affect the division of welfare between the two countries? Third, how does factor movement affect the distribution of income within each country? And fourth, how does the movement affect the factors that move? The answer to the fourth question is the easiest to predict: Assuming factor movements take place voluntarily, the owners of the factors that move must expect to be better off, or they wouldn't move.

Inter-country movements of capital and of labor generate similar effects. However, the particular motivations and some of the issues that arise differ between the two classes of factors; so we'll analyze separately the effects of labor mobility (section 4.1) and capital mobility (section 4.2).

4.1 Inter-Country Labor Mobility

Labor generally flows less easily than capital across national boundaries. This reflects the special character of labor as a factor of production: A unit of labor is embodied in a human being. The person has tastes and preferences, a culture, a language, and friends and family.

Individuals don't feel indifferent about where they work or the conditions under which they work; many considerations other than the wage rate enter into the location decision. The owner of a machine, on the other hand, probably doesn't care about the machine's location or working conditions so long as the equipment isn't abused in such a way as to reduce its productivity or useful lifespan.

Despite the financial and personal costs involved, growing numbers of individuals have chosen to immigrate. The International Organization for Migration estimates that, as of 2000, 175 million people, or 2.9 percent of the world population, lived outside their country of birth. Immigrants comprise 19 percent of Canada's population, 74 percent of the United Arab Emirates', and 25 percent of Switzerland's. In the first few years after the Berlin Wall opened in 1989, 1 in 16 residents of the eastern German states moved to the western states.[7] North Africans comprise a growing share of the population in Europe; the many Algerians in France provide one example. Singapore employs hundreds of thousands of foreign workers, including many from Malaysia who cross the border daily to work. Malaysia, on the other hand, also hosts foreign workers, of whom many are undocumented and come from Indonesia and Bangladesh. Approximately seven and a half million Filipinos work abroad as nurses, nannies, maids, teachers, and crew aboard the world's merchant ships. The United States, which takes in more immigrants each year than any other country, apprehends more than 1.5 million individuals illegally crossing the border from Mexico each year, and perhaps only 10 to 50 percent of those who cross illegally are caught. Experts think that about 10 million individuals live in the United States illegally.

INCENTIVES FOR MIGRATION   When labor moves between countries, the reasons can be economic or noneconomic, and often the two are interconnected. The periods of mass migration to America during the nineteenth and early twentieth centuries reflected immigrants' desire for religious and political freedom and for economic freedom to better themselves and improve opportunities for their children. These motives remain important today. A complex web of influences determines an individual's decision to move to another country, but we'll focus on economic motivations and assume that an individual tries to move when the reward paid to labor is higher in the destination country than at home.

Figure 8 provides a convenient guide for analyzing labor mobility's effects. We assume a world with two countries, A and B. The length of the horizontal axis (distance 0^A0^B) represents the total quantity of labor in the world. The two vertical axes measure the wage paid to labor in the two countries (w^A on the left axis and w^B on the right). L_0 represents the initial allocation of labor between countries A and B; so 0^AL_0 units of labor work in A, and 0^BL_0 in B.

In each country, labor earns a wage rate (w) equal to the value of the marginal unit of labor's productivity. The value of the *marginal product of labor* (VMP_L) equals the marginal product of labor (the number of units of additional output produced when 1 additional unit of labor is employed) multiplied by the price of the good produced.[8] As the quantity of labor employed in a given country increases, the marginal product of labor declines and, with it, the value of that productivity and the wage rate. The curves VMP_L^A and VMP_L^B represent the values of the marginal product of labor in countries A and B, respectively. With the initial allocation of labor between countries at L_0, workers in A earn w_0^A and workers in B earn w_0^B. The higher wage in A reflects labor's higher marginal productivity in A (point E) relative to B (point J).

---

7. Greg Steinmetz, "West German Riches Are Luring Easterners Desperate for Work," *The Wall Street Journal*, July 7, 1997.

8. An input's value marginal product is sometimes called its marginal revenue product. Marginal revenue product is defined as the input's marginal product multiplied by the firm's marginal revenue. For perfectly competitive firms, price equals marginal revenue, so value marginal product ($VMP = MP_L \cdot P$) and marginal revenue product ($MRP = MP_L \cdot MR$) are equal.

Figure 8   What Are the Effects of Labor Mobility?

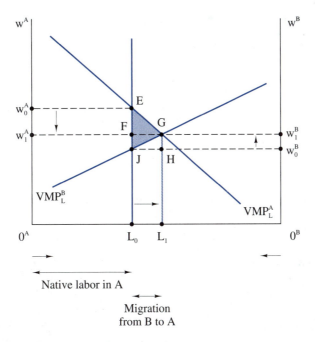

Labor's ability to move from country B to country A in response to a wage differential raises total world output by an amount represented by the area of triangle EGJ. Country A gains, and country B loses. In A, capital owners gain relative to labor; in B, workers gain relative to capital owners.

If they can, workers from country B will migrate to A to obtain higher wages. This incentive will cause the workers represented by the distance between L_0 and L_1 to move. Once sufficient migration has occurred to reach the new labor allocation at L_1, wage rates in the two countries equalize at $w_1^A = w_1^B$. If we take into account the cost of moving, which can include actual transportation costs plus the unpleasantness of leaving home, then migration may not completely eliminate the wage differential. If transportation and communication costs are high, so migration is expensive and means no future contact with home and family, we might expect a substantial wage differential to persist. In fact, if the cost of moving were as high as $w_0^A - w_0^B$, no workers would want to move and the allocation of labor would remain at L_0. If transportation and communication costs are low, so migration can be temporary and staying in touch with home and family is easy, then we'd expect more migration and a smaller equilibrium wage differential between the two countries.

LABOR MIGRATION'S EFFECTS   Our first task is to determine how labor movements in response to wage differentials affect the efficiency of the world economy. Does such mobility increase or decrease total world output? The shaded area (triangle EGJ) in Figure 8 represents an increase in total world output from the mobility of labor. Each unit of labor between L_0 and L_1 produces more in country A than in country B; that the VMP_L^A curve is higher than the VMP_L^B curve throughout the L_0 to L_1 range reflects this productivity differential. Higher wages in A signal to workers the greater value of labor's marginal product in A, attracting them to the area where they will be more productive. As immigration allows labor to be used more efficiently, total output rises.

Table 4   EFFECTS OF LABOR MIGRATION FROM COUNTRY B TO COUNTRY A

Effect on:	
Capital owners in A	+
Native labor in A	−
Immigrants	+
Net effect on A	$+(\text{area } EGL_1L_0)$
Capital owners in B	−
Labor remaining in B	+
Net effect on B	$-(\text{area } JGL_1L_0)$
Net effect on world	$+(\text{area } EGJ)$

How are the gains represented by area EGJ divided between countries A and B? The controversial nature of emigration and immigration policies leads us to suspect— correctly—that the gains aren't divided equally among all interested parties. Country A as a whole gains from the immigration. The net gain is the sum of gains by capital owners in A, losses by native country-A workers, and gains by the immigrants themselves. Country B as a whole loses from its emigration, but workers in B gain relative to owners of capital. As we predicted earlier, the immigrants themselves gain.

The net gain to country A equals the sum of the value of the marginal product of all labor between L_0 and L_1, or area EGL_1L_0. The original workforce from A loses area $w_0^A EF w_1^A$ because of immigration's negative effect on the wage rate. Area FGL_1L_0 represents the income earned by the new immigrants in country A. Area JHL_1L_0 just replaces the income they could have earned in country B; area FGHJ shows the net increase in their income that provided the incentive for migration. Owners of capital in A gain as the marginal product of capital rises because of the availability of more labor for use along with the capital.[9] Country B's output falls by JGL_1L_0 as a result of the emigration. Workers who remain in B gain area $Gw_1^B w_0^B H$ in increased wages, but B's capital owners lose as the marginal product of capital falls. Table 4 summarizes these effects.

OPPOSITION TO IMMIGRATION POLICIES   The preceding analysis makes clear why labor groups typically favor strong limits on immigration: Open immigration can lower wages of domestic workers (including earlier immigrants) who compete with new immigrants in labor markets. When immigrant workers are unskilled, the negative impact on wages affects primarily unskilled domestic workers and other recent immigrants. In recent waves of immigrants to the United States, for example, many individuals possess skill levels below those of earlier immigrants.[10] Empirical evidence suggests that in developed countries, unskilled migrants sometimes fill jobs not wanted by domestic workers, minimizing immigration's effect on wages. Overall, most empirical studies find only small effects of immigration on wages.[11] Of course, there also can be

---

9.   Recall that an input's marginal product measures the change in total output resulting from use of one more unit of the input, with the quantities of all other inputs held constant. An input's marginal product is increased by availability of a larger quantity of other inputs used together with it; a reduction in the use of other inputs lowers the marginal product.

10.   Recent immigration to the United States includes more workers with little education (elementary school or less), more workers with lots of education (college and postgraduate school), and fewer workers with intermediate levels of education (high school) than the U.S. workforce overall.

11.   We'll see one important reason why later.

noneconomic reasons for opposing open immigration, including cultural prejudice or racism, but even these seemingly noneconomic arguments may reflect fear of immigration's economic effects.

Another reason for opposition to open immigration has emerged in recent decades as governments have taken on larger roles in assuring residents minimal levels of food, housing, medical care, education, social services, and income—even if the immigrants are unable or unwilling to work. Countries that provide generous levels of such social benefits may fear an influx of immigrants who won't work and produce, as did the immigrants in Figure 8, but instead will live on government-provided benefits at the expense of domestic workers and working immigrants. Some policy makers and residents in the European Union fear that EU moves to make migration within the EU easy will result in large flows of nonworking migrants to countries with generous welfare benefits.[12] It's already the case that foreign-born individuals constitute a share of the unemployed more than twice the foreign-born share of the overall population in Sweden, Finland, Denmark, Belgium, the Netherlands, and France. In the United States, immigrants during the 1950s and 1960s didn't avail themselves of public assistance at rates exceeding those for domestic residents; however, this no longer is the case. Recent U.S. arrivals have drawn public assistance at high rates relative to earlier immigrant arrivals, and immigrants' use of public assistance appears to be growing over time. The rate of dependence on public assistance varies widely across source countries and with immigrants' age. Table 5 lists the five countries from which the United States accepted the most legal immigrants in 2002. Legal immigration to the United States totaled 1.1 million persons in 2002, and the top five countries accounted for 40 percent of that total.

Another issue that adds controversy to immigration policies is developing countries' concerns about **brain drain**, the tendency of the most highly skilled, trained, and educated individuals from developing countries to migrate to the industrialized countries. Developing countries argue that they expend scarce resources to educate and train these individuals only to lose the return on their investment to other countries, particularly the United States. Africa, according to a 2001 report by the International Organization for Migration, loses 23,000 college graduates annually, mostly to Europe and the United States. India produces approximately 100,000 engineers each year from the country's technical institutes and colleges; usually between 50,000 and 60,000 go to the United States; and for each 1,000 who leave, only one or two return.[13]

Table 5 IMMIGRATION TO THE UNITED STATES BY TOP SOURCE COUNTRIES, FISCAL YEAR 2002

Country	Immigrants (Thousands)
Mexico	219.4
India	71.1
China	61.3
Philippines	51.3
Vietnam	33.6

Source: Data from U.S. Bureau of Citizenship and Immigration Services (at http://www.uscis.gov).

12. See, for example, Hans-Werner Sinn, "Europe Faces a Rise in Welfare Migration," *Financial Times*, July 13, 2004.

13. "Soaring Indian Tech Salaries Reflect the Country's Brain Drain," *The Wall Street Journal*, August 21, 2000.

Brain-drain flows do impose costs on developing economies. But there are some positive results, too. When skilled workers leave the country, salaries there rise for the skilled workers who remain. The possibility of working abroad, even temporarily, can increase incentives for education. Recently, lower transportation and communication costs due to technological advances have reduced the costs of the brain drain to many developing countries. Now, workers who go abroad can return for frequent visits, keep in touch with acquaintances, send funds to family, and even keep up with home-country events and politics via the Internet and satellite television. These internationally mobile workers serve as important conduits for information about the rest of world and about state-of-the-art business practice, technology, and political institutions used abroad; the migrants' taste for home-country goods can also act as a political force for liberalizing trade. Groups of emigrants from specific towns and villages get together (often through Internet sites), pool their funds, and provide financing for schools, roads, and other needed investments back home. And, increasingly, the brain drain flows both ways. Taiwan, China, and India enjoy large numbers of returnees who, after spending years or even decades abroad, come home with valuable experience and funds to support new businesses.

THEORY, EVIDENCE, AND THE POLITICS OF IMMIGRATION: AN IMPORTANT CAVEAT   As noted earlier, empirical evidence suggests that any negative effect of immigration on wages is small. This may seem puzzling, given our analysis of Figure 8. However, notice something important about that analysis. It assumes, albeit implicitly, that the country produces only *one* good. What if, instead, we incorporate the idea from earlier chapters that countries produce at least two goods, a labor-intensive one and a capital-intensive one, and that those goods can be traded internationally? Then, an inflow of labor makes a country more labor abundant and causes it to shift toward producing labor-intensive goods and away from producing capital-intensive ones. The result is an increase in the demand for labor to match the increased supply.

In fact, this is what the Rybczynski theorem tells us. *The country's product mix changes with changes in its factor endowment. Therefore, factor prices needn't change in response to factor inflows and outflows.* One way to remember this important caveat is to note that the Rybczynski theorem says that changes in factor *quantities* (that is, changes in a country's endowment) lead to changes in the *quantities* of different goods produced (that is, changes in the product mix), *not* to changes in factor *prices*. This is a cousin to the Stolper-Samuelson theorem from Chapter Four, which states that changes in product *prices* lead to changes in factor *prices*.

Of course, if the world practiced complete free trade in all goods, factor-price equalization would remove much of the economic incentive for migration. Similarly, complete factor mobility would equalize factor prices and eliminate the cost differentials that form the foundation for comparative-advantage-based trade in goods. When both trade in goods and factor mobility occur, but each imperfectly, it becomes difficult to predict the relative magnitudes of the two. Nonetheless, it's important to keep in mind that the product-mix response to changing factor endowments mitigates much of the factor-price response we might expect in the simple one-good world analyzed in Figure 8.

IMMIGRATION POLICY   Over the last century, U.S. immigration policy changed dramatically four times, affecting both the overall magnitude and composition of immigration flows. In the late nineteenth century, the United States restricted many classes of immigration, including an almost total ban on people from Asia. Beginning in the 1920s, national-origin quotas severely limited entry from Southern and Eastern Europe by allocating visas to maintain the ethnic balance of the 1920 U.S. population. By 1965, the national-origin quotas had become politically unacceptable, and immigration policy shifted to a system that provided easy entry for people with family ties to U.S. residents or to earlier immigrants.

By the 1980s, U.S. immigration controversies centered squarely on Mexico. The 1986 Immigration Reform and Control Act aimed to eliminate illegal foreign workers, especially those from Mexico, from the U.S. labor market in two ways. First, the bill granted amnesty to foreign workers who had been in the United States illegally since before 1982 and could document their residence or who had worked in U.S. perishable-crop agriculture for at least 90 days during the previous year. By the end of the program, 3.2 million individuals, 90 percent from Mexico, had gained permanent-resident status through the amnesty program. Second, to reduce the demand for illegal labor, the bill imposed penalties on firms that hired illegal workers. U.S. agricultural interests incorporated provisions into the bill for temporary admission of foreign workers during the harvest season since foreign workers, most from Mexico and other parts of Central America, harvest many U.S. crops.

Predictably, based on our graphical analysis in Figure 8 and on the results in Table 4, U.S. labor unions found the 1986 bill too weak, believing that it allowed too much competition from foreign workers for U.S. jobs. Firms, on the other hand, particularly in industries such as the Los Angeles-based garment industry, found their operations threatened by the reduction in the supply of illegal labor. Many leaders of the Hispanic community also opposed the bill's provisions for penalties on firms that hire illegal workers, fearing that firms would choose to avoid the risk of hiring improperly documented workers by refusing to hire Hispanics. The number of illegal entrants apprehended along the U.S.–Mexico border declined for a few years after the 1986 bill, but the decline was short-lived. Immigration specialists think 10 million illegal immigrants live in the United States, most of them from Mexico.

In 1995, immigration-law adjustments cut legal immigration to 675,000 per year, of which up to 465,000 would go to family members of U.S. residents; up to 140,000 to individuals with special skills needed in U.S. labor markets; up to 10,000 to investors (individuals who invested at least $1 million in a business to employ at least 10 workers or $500,000 in a rural area); and up to 55,000 to "diversity immigrants"—visas to be awarded by lottery to individuals from countries other than the principal sources of current U.S. immigration.

Shortages of high-tech workers during the U.S. technology boom of the late 1990s created political pressure to raise the number of temporary skilled-based visas. Congress obliged in 2001 by raising the number of workers admitted on up-to-six-year H1-B visas from 65,000 to 195,000 per year. In 2002, 98 percent of H1-B visa holders possessed at least a bachelor's degree. Professions with the highest numbers of H1-B visas include systems analysts, computer programmers, higher education, and health care. India, China, Canada, the Philippines, and the United Kingdom send the most H1-B visa holders to the United States. In 2004, the earlier Congressional expansion of the H1-B visa program expired. Employers wanted the expansion extended, but U.S. technology workers, stung by the downturn in the information-technology sector, lobbied to let the number of H1-B visas drop back to 65,000.

AN INTERNATIONAL ISSUE   The United States isn't alone in its ongoing debate over immigration policy. Current controversy in developed countries over immigration policy centers around their desire to both encourage inflows of skilled workers and limit inflows of unskilled ones. Norway needs more doctors and seeks immigrants from Germany, France, and Austria. Much of Europe, especially Britain and Germany, joins developing countries such as China, India, and South Africa in worrying about a brain drain of their skilled workers to the United States. German immigration law makes it very difficult for German firms to hire skilled workers from outside the European Union; only 884 permits were granted in 1999.[14] In 1986, when the European Union granted membership to Spain, Portugal, and Greece, residents of those new members had to wait seven years before becoming eligible to work in another member country. After admission of ten new member countries in 2004, existing members have the option to prohibit worker migration for a transition period that can last until 2010.[15] For the countries achieving and seeking EU membership, the delays on free intra-EU immigration sound like an offer of second-class standing in the group. Many workers from Eastern and Central Europe already work illegally in the EU; for example, Albanians and Bulgarians who cross the border into Greece. Experts estimate that at least 500,000 illegal immigrants enter the European Union annually.

Canada grants well over half of its legal entries to workers with special skills needed in Canada, whereas in the United States most legal entries (two-thirds in 2002) go to individuals with family ties to people already in the country, regardless of skills or employability. Even Japan, whose resident foreigners constitute barely 1 percent of the population, faces pressure to allow more immigration, both to attract more skilled workers and to offset the demographic effects of the country's rapidly aging population. Japan already tolerates small numbers of illegal immigrants willing to do hard, dirty, or dangerous jobs; and, anticipating the need to care for rapidly increasing numbers of elderly Japanese, the government has proposed admitting more low-skilled nursing assistants.[16]

At the same time that South Africa expels each year about 100,000 illegal unskilled immigrants from the rest of Africa, still leaving between 2 million and 8 million undocumented individuals, the country loses many of its skilled workers to developed countries. In parts of the former Soviet Union, the emigration situation is even more striking. Experts estimate that the former Soviet republic of Armenia lost between 800,000 and 1.5 million people (between one-quarter and one-half of the population) between the breakup of the Soviet Union in 1991 and 2001.[17] Between a tenth and a fifth of Moldova's labor force is estimated to work, mainly illegally, in the European Union.[18]

LABOR MOBILITY WITHOUT IMMIGRATION?   As part of the trend toward increased international economic integration, firms have begun to use several arrangements that amount to labor mobility without migration. The first arrangement is manufacturing **outsourcing** or offshore assembly, in which a firm performs each step in a manufacturing process in the country with a comparative advantage in that particular stage. Components for a finished product may be produced in many countries, and labor-intensive assembly of the components often occurs in labor-abundant developing countries. Such offshore assembly operations make up a large share of manufactured imports into the United States from developing countries, especially Mexico. In many cases, including Mexico's, special tax and tariff arrangements have encouraged firms to use offshore assembly.[19] Low tariffs and low transport and communication costs facilitate outsourcing by reducing the costs of performing tasks in multiple countries. Hewlett-Packard recently designed a new small-business computer server in Singapore, approved the product in Texas, engineered it in Taiwan, and assembled the server in Singapore, Australia, China, and India. Such a fine-tuned use of worldwide comparative advantage would have been infeasible in earlier days of high tariffs and costly international transport and communication.

---

14. "Germany Faces Storm Over Tech Staffing," *The Wall Street Journal,* March 7, 2000.

15. See Figure 6 in Chapter Nine for EU membership, including the "class of 2004."

16. "The Door Opens, a Crack," *The Economist,* September 2, 2000.

17. "At Last a State, Armenia Loses People," *The Wall Street Journal,* July 6, 2001.

18. "Outsiders Aren't Helping," *The Economist,* February 15, 2003.

19. See section 9 in Chapter Six.

Sometimes technology makes possible even more innovative ways of accomplishing labor mobility without migration. U.S.–India satellite linkups permit U.S. computer firms to use Indian computer programmers for programming tasks. The U.S. firms send software design specifications to India by satellite link; the Indian software engineers develop and test the software in India and then transmit it back to the United States. Indian programmers earn more than they would otherwise in India but less than programmers in the United States. Highly trained programmers remain in India (along with their earnings), instead of migrating to the United States as part of the brain drain; as a result, India now exports billions of dollars worth of computer software each year.

Another sector moving rapidly to utilize labor abroad—to "offshore"—is remote services, which includes call centers and back-office operations. Again, India, along with Ireland and the Philippines, leads in provision of many of these services. Mortgage, credit-card, and insurance companies increasingly rely on the staff of foreign call centers to handle customers' e-mail and telephone questions, perform data-entry operations (such as keeping up with airline customers' frequent-flier miles), transcribe medical and legal dictation, and conduct basic background research and statistical analysis for financial firms and investment banks. Countries in which a large share of the population speaks English well have a big advantage in attracting these jobs. Many of the tasks involved don't require highly skilled workers, so firms can avoid paying high developed-country wages; but the tasks aren't routine enough to be performed by machines. Training often includes understanding American regional accents as well as lessons on American culture, so U.S. callers won't realize that the person answering their question isn't in the United States.

European firms often turn to Central and Eastern Europe for outsourcing because of proximity and the availability of workers proficient in Western European languages. The Czech Republic, Hungary, Poland, and Slovakia are popular call-center and back-office support sites, and Romania has become a significant international supplier of freelance software services.

Constraints on the growth of such operations in some countries include low-quality utility infrastructures (for example, local power failures are common), expensive telephone services because of not-yet-deregulated national phone monopolies, restrictive labor laws, and poor foreign-language skills. But even some developed countries with modern utility infrastructures and strong telecommunications networks are getting in on the trend. The Canadian Maritime provinces, for example, suffer high rates of unemployment after losing their traditional fishing and mining industries but have attracted several call centers, including those of Staples, Xerox, and AT&T.

Outsourcing and offshoring can be politically unpopular with workers whose jobs migrate to other countries. But both phenomena represent a use of comparative advantage, which allows the world's scarce resources to produce the largest possible quantities of goods and services. Entry-level job opportunities increase in recipient countries—along with wages. And prices of the outsourced goods and services drop, which benefits consumers.

4.2 Inter-Country Capital Mobility

Capital mobility among countries exceeds labor mobility largely because it doesn't require people to move; a capital owner can stay in one place while the capital flows from country to country in response to differences in available returns, risk, and other relevant considerations. The term *capital mobility* is somewhat deceptive. In economic discussions of international trade, *capital* typically refers to durable productive inputs such as factories, machines, and tools. But *capital mobility* refers not to literal international movement of such inputs but rather to international investment, borrowing, and lending.

There are two main categories of international capital mobility. The first is international **portfolio investment**, or the flow across national boundaries of funds to finance investments in which the lender doesn't gain operating control over the borrower. For example, when an individual, firm, or government buys bonds issued by a foreign firm or government, the transaction transfers funds between countries and represents an international portfolio investment. This type of transaction involves very low transaction costs, so portfolio investment represents the most mobile component of capital. Often all that's involved is an electronic transfer of funds, accomplished almost instantaneously at very little cost using modern electronic technology.

If a U.S. firm issues bonds (borrows) and sells some of those bonds to a resident of Germany (who thereby makes a loan to the U.S. firm), the transaction represents a **capital outflow** or an **international purchase of assets** from Germany's perspective and a **capital inflow** or **international sale of assets** from the U.S. perspective. The U.S. firm can use the borrowed funds to buy a piece of physical capital such as a new factory building; so the U.S. capital stock rises and the German capital stock falls relative to what it would have been had the German resident lent his or her funds domestically to a German firm—even though no one packed up a factory and shipped it from Germany to the United States.

The other component of international capital flows is foreign **direct investment**, which gives the investor operating ownership of and control over the borrower. For example, if a U.S. firm buys a German firm or establishes a subsidiary in Germany, the transaction represents an outward foreign direct investment from the U.S. point of view and an inward foreign direct investment from the German perspective. The line between portfolio and direct investment is somewhat fuzzy. If a U.S. firm buys stock in a Japanese corporation, the buyer may or may not gain operating control—depending on the magnitude of the purchase relative to the Japanese firm's outstanding stock shares. U.S. government statistics assume that ownership of 10 percent or more of a firm's outstanding stock gives the holder operating control and therefore classifies the investment as a direct one.

RECENT PATTERNS IN INTERNATIONAL CAPITAL MOBILITY   Worldwide, two trends characterize foreign direct investment patterns. The first is rapid, if erratic, growth. In 1980, the value of the stocks of inward and outward foreign-direct-investment assets in the world economy equaled 4.9 percent and 5.4 percent, respectively, of the value of world gross domestic product (output) at the time. By 2000, those percentages had risen to 20.0 and 19.6. Between 1982 and 2001, the total value of annual world exports grew by three times (from $2,041 billion to $6,127 billion) and annual outflows of foreign direct investment grew by more than 16 times (from $37 billion to $621 billion).[20] The late 1980s and late 1990s were characterized by dramatic surges in the rate of foreign direct investment, which had grown much more slowly from 1973 to 1984 and during the recession of the early 1990s. Outward FDI flows actually rose to $1,379 billion in 2000 before falling back due to the cyclical slowdown in the world economy and the rise in terrorism.

The second notable trend is a diversification of the source and host countries. In 1980, the value of the stocks of inward and outward foreign-direct-investment assets for developing economies as a group equaled 5.4 percent and 0.9 percent, respectively, of the developing countries' output. By 2000, those percentages had risen to 30.9 and 11.9 percent.

While foreign direct investment flows to developing countries have risen, the flows remain relatively concentrated. Of all the foreign direct investment flows into developing

20.   United Nations, *World Investment Report*.

Figure 9 Top Source and Host Countries for Foreign Direct Investment, 2001

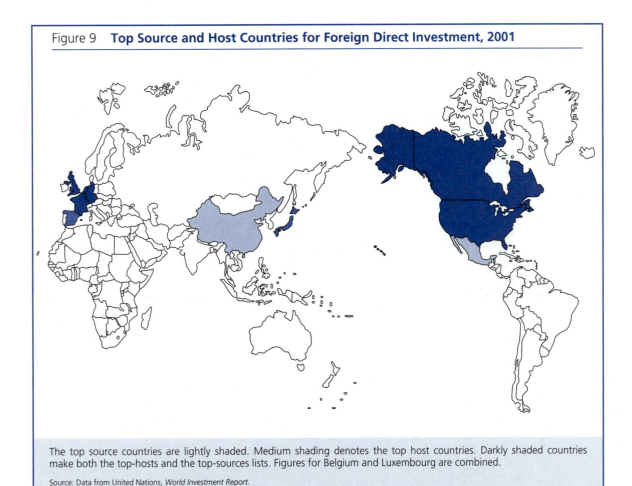

The top source countries are lightly shaded. Medium shading denotes the top host countries. Darkly shaded countries make both the top-hosts and the top-sources lists. Figures for Belgium and Luxembourg are combined.

Source: Data from United Nations, *World Investment Report.*

economies in 2001, $102 billion went to Asia, $85 billion to Latin America and the Caribbean, $27 billion to Central and Eastern European economies, and $17 billion to Africa. However, those flows were concentrated toward a few countries. Five countries took over 60 percent of the approximately $200 billion total; China alone (including Hong Kong) accounted for about a third of the total.

Figure 9 illustrates the top host and source countries for foreign direct investment flows in 2001. Countries making the source list but not the host list are shaded lightly in the figure. Countries making the host list but not the source list are denoted by medium shading in the figure. Seven economies make both lists; they are shaded darkly. Note that the most active participants in foreign direct investment, both hosts and sources, continue to be industrial economies.

Table 6 shows the relative sizes of the total international portfolio and foreign direct investment assets held by private U.S. residents in recent years. As the table makes evident, U.S. foreign direct investment dominated U.S. international portfolio investment for much of the post–World War II period. This pattern contrasts with that of British investment during Britain's economic dominance in the late nineteenth century. Britain's foreign assets consisted largely of portfolio investment, exemplified by British purchases of bonds to finance worldwide railroad construction, particularly in the United States. Since 1990, however, U.S. portfolio investment in foreign stocks has risen sharply, pushing the total of U.S.-owned foreign portfolio assets past the total of

Table 6 **PRIVATE U.S. INVESTMENT ABROAD, ASSETS AT YEAR END, 1950–2003 (BILLIONS $)**

Year	Direct Investment[a]	Bonds	Stocks	Total[b]
1950	$11.8	$3.2	$1.2	$17.5
1960	31.9	5.5	4.0	44.4
1970	78.2	13.2	6.4	105.0
1980	388.1	43.5	18.9	692.8
1990	616.7	144.7	197.6	1,920.0
2000	1,531.6	532.5	1,852.8	6,017.7
2003	2,069.0	502.1	1,972.2	6,934.3

[a]Valued at current cost.
[b]Total includes categories besides direct investment, bonds, and stocks; therefore, components don't necessarily sum to total.

Sources: Data from William H. Branson, "Trends in United States International Trade and Investment since World War II," in *The American Economy in Transition*, edited by Martin Feldstein (Chicago: University of Chicago Press, 1980), p. 237; *Survey of Current Business*.

U.S.-owned foreign direct assets. Note that Table 6 reports private investment; it doesn't include holdings of foreign assets by the U.S. government. In evaluating the overall investment position of the United States, government holdings as well as private holdings matter, but government borrowing and lending respond to different motivations than do private borrowing and lending. We'll focus on the voluntary transactions undertaken by the private sector.

The rate of foreign investment in the United States during the 1980s exceeded that of U.S. investment abroad. The result was a net capital inflow, implying that the United States borrowed abroad more than it lent abroad, as a comparison of Table 6 and Table 7 reveals. In the mid-1980s, the stock of U.S. assets held by foreigners surpassed the stock of foreign assets held by private parties in the United States. The United States became, for the first time in 70 years, a debtor.[21] As the comparison of Tables 6 and 7 documents, the rapid change in U.S. status from creditor to debtor resulted not from a decline in U.S. investment abroad but from a rapid increase in foreign investment in the United States. Note that U.S. direct investment assets held abroad still exceed foreign direct investment assets in the United States.

The most politically controversial aspect of foreign investment in the United States involved Japanese direct investment during the 1980s. Japanese firms invested heavily in the United States and made highly visible purchases such as Rockefeller Center in New York, Columbia Pictures, the Beverly Wilshire Hotel, Firestone Tire and Rubber, the Seattle Mariners baseball team, and Pebble Beach golf course. Many pundits extrapolated that pace of investment into the future and concluded that the United States soon would be owned and controlled by the Japanese. But, as happens with many economic trends, the 1990s brought a sharp reversal; the rate of foreign investment in the United States declined, including that by Japan.

Not only did the Japanese buying trend not last forever, but many of the transactions of the 1980s also turned out to be great deals for the U.S. sellers, because Japanese investors bought just before the early-1990s plummet in U.S. real estate values.

---

21. This statement isn't without controversy. Because of measurement difficulties and differences in accounting procedures, no single number can claim to represent the net investment position of the United States. In particular, measures are sensitive to how assets are valued—at historical cost, at current cost, or at market value.

Table 7 **NONOFFICIAL[a] FOREIGN INVESTMENT IN THE UNITED STATES, ASSETS AT YEAR END, 1950–2003 (BILLIONS $)**

Year	Direct Investment[b]	Bonds	Stocks	Total[c]
1950	$3.4	$0.2	$2.9	$8.0
1960	6.9	0.6	9.3	18.4
1970	13.3	6.9	18.7	44.8
1980	127.1	25.6	64.6	392.9
1990	505.3	391.3	221.7	2,051.0
2000	1,421.0	1,450.2	1,554.4	6,589.3
2003	1,554.0	2,395.5	1,538.1	8,159.2

[a]As reported by the Department of Commerce and reproduced in Tables 6 and 7, the U.S. and foreign investment positions aren't precisely comparable, because foreign assets in the United States include nonofficial assets held by foreign governments, while U.S. assets abroad exclude all government-held assets, whether official or nonofficial.
[b]Valued at current cost.
[c]Total includes categories besides direct investment, bonds, and stocks; therefore, components don't necessarily sum to total.

Sources: Data from William H. Branson, "Trends in United States International Trade and Investment since World War II," in *The American Economy in Transition*, edited by Martin Feldstein (Chicago: University of Chicago Press, 1980), pp. 239, 245; *Survey of Current Business*.

For example, a Japanese investor bought the Los Angeles Hotel Bel-Air in 1989 for $110 million and sold it in 1994 for $60 million. Similarly, the Japanese investor who bought Pebble Beach Golf Links in Pebble Beach, California, paid $841 million in 1990 and sold the course in 1992 for $500 million. Even the Rockefeller Center purchase didn't turn out well for the buyer. A Japanese firm paid $1.4 billion for 80 percent ownership of the complex between 1989 and 1991; the owners later were in bankruptcy.[22]

In the past few years, foreign investors have snapped up assets in Asia, particularly in the economies hardest hit by the Asian financial crisis. Japan's decade-long economic slump also attracted buyers. French Renault bought Nissan, Japan's second-largest auto maker. A British company bought J-Phone, Japan's third largest mobile phone firm. And Japanese assets bought by U.S. investors include many of Japan's golf courses, such as Golf Seiyo and Forest Miki.[23]

Panels (a) and (b) of Figure 10 indicate the regional allocation of U.S. outward and inward direct foreign investment for 2003, respectively. The United Kingdom, the Netherlands, Switzerland, and Canada were the top four recipients in 2003 of U.S. foreign direct investment. Although in the 1980s Japanese investment in the United States captured most of the political attention, Japan always ranked behind Europe as the largest source of foreign direct investment in the United States.

INCENTIVES FOR INTERNATIONAL CAPITAL MOVEMENTS Several incentives exist for capital owners to move their capital across national boundaries. We focus first on incentives for portfolio investment; section 4.4 will consider multinational enterprises as a vehicle of foreign direct investment. The primary incentive for capital movements, of course, is the opportunity to earn a higher rate of return. Different tax laws among countries also affect capital flows, as we'll see in section 4.3.

---

22. "Japan's U.S. Property Deals: A Poor Report Card," *The Wall Street Journal*, June 9, 1995.

23. "Fair Game for Buyers at Japan's Golf Clubs," *Financial Times*, May 19, 2001.

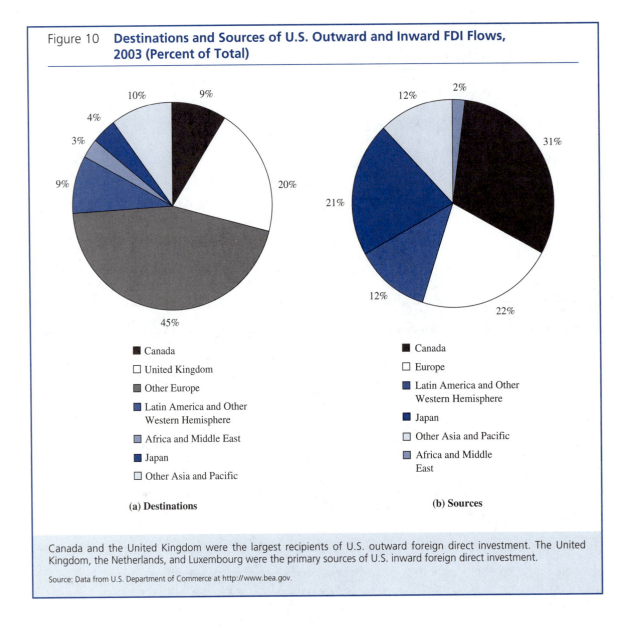

Figure 10   **Destinations and Sources of U.S. Outward and Inward FDI Flows, 2003 (Percent of Total)**

(a) Destinations

- ■ Canada
- □ United Kingdom
- ▨ Other Europe
- ■ Latin America and Other Western Hemisphere
- ▨ Africa and Middle East
- ■ Japan
- □ Other Asia and Pacific

(b) Sources

- ■ Canada
- □ Europe
- ■ Latin America and Other Western Hemisphere
- ■ Japan
- □ Other Asia and Pacific
- ▨ Africa and Middle East

Canada and the United Kingdom were the largest recipients of U.S. outward foreign direct investment. The United Kingdom, the Netherlands, and Luxembourg were the primary sources of U.S. inward foreign direct investment.

Source: Data from U.S. Department of Commerce at http://www.bea.gov.

Another major reason for capital mobility is individuals' and firms' desire to diversify their assets to reduce risk. Evidence suggests that most individuals are risk averse. This just means that given a choice between two assets, one with a certain return and the other with a return that is uncertain but expected to equal, on average, the certain return on the other asset, most individuals will choose the certain return.[24] Most investment decisions involve a trade-off between the rate of return and the level of risk; by tolerating more risk, an investor often can earn a higher rate of return.

To reduce the riskiness of a portfolio or group of assets, an investor need not hold only low-risk, low-return assets. One can do better by diversification. **Diversification**

---

24. *If offered a choice between (1) $5 with certainty and (2) a gamble with a 50 percent chance of winning $10 and a 50 percent chance of winning nothing, which would you choose?* If you chose (1), you exhibited aversion to risk, because the expected value of the two offers is equal (at $5) while offer (1) involves no risk.

refers to holding a variety of assets, chosen so that when some perform poorly, others are likely to perform well. An owner of an orange grove in Florida and a hotel on a Florida beach wouldn't be very well diversified. A severe freeze, for example, would both kill the orange trees and ruin the hotel business. Owning an orange grove in Florida and a New England ski resort would provide better diversification. A severe winter might kill the orange trees, but it would help the ski business; a warm winter, on the other hand, might mean no skiing but a big orange crop. Diversification just means owning assets that any given set of circumstances would affect differently.

A role for international capital mobility in diversification is obvious. Holding all one's assets in a single country heightens risk because it subjects all the assets to common events. A political disturbance, a natural disaster, or an economic recession in the country could cause all the assets to perform poorly. Holding assets in several countries, on the other hand, can diversify these risks. If one country pursues a policy that turns out to be disastrous, the policy would harm only a subset of the portfolio of internationally diversified assets. Asset holders' risk aversion creates a motivation for capital mobility even under conditions of full factor price equalization.

Yet another motivation for capital mobility focuses on mobility as a way of trading goods across time, called **intertemporal trade**. Without international borrowing and lending, each country must divide its current production between current consumption and investment in tools to improve future output; the sum of consumption and investment must equal output each period for each country. Intertemporal trade, however, relaxes this constraint. A country with a net capital inflow borrows from the rest of the world. Residents of the country consume and invest more than current production by borrowing, but they will have to consume and invest less than production later when they repay the loans. Such borrowing by a developing country, for example, might allow the country to take advantage of productive investment opportunities that its current low level of production couldn't fund. A country with a net capital outflow, on the other hand, lends to the rest of the world. Residents consume and invest less than current production, lend their savings to foreigners, and can consume and invest more than production in the future when borrowers repay the loans with interest. In the 1970s, for example, oil-exporting countries suddenly found themselves with more current income than they could consume or invest profitably in their home economies; therefore, they used the savings to buy assets abroad.

Such intertemporal exchange in assets can be mutually beneficial in much the same way as ordinary trade in goods and services. In fact, we can even phrase the story in terms of comparative advantage. Countries with an abundance of current production and a scarcity of domestic investment opportunities exhibit a comparative advantage in "current goods" relative to "future goods." Such countries can specialize in producing current goods by lending abroad and import future goods when the borrowers repay. On the other hand, countries with a scarcity of current production and an abundance of domestic investment opportunities hold a comparative advantage in future goods relative to current goods. They can import current goods by borrowing abroad and export future goods when they repay their loans.

CAPITAL MOBILITY'S EFFECTS   Analysis of the effects of capital mobility is very similar to that for labor mobility. Figure 11 modifies the labor-mobility diagram from Figure 8. From an initial allocation of capital between the two countries represented by K_0, capital flows from country B to country A in response to the higher rate of return in A, $r_0^A > r_0^B$. Area EGJ measures the positive effect on world output from capital's shift from B to A. This gain comes from using the units of capital between K_0 and K_1 in the country with the higher value marginal product of capital (VMP_K).

The allocation of capital mobility's benefits differs from the case of labor mobility. With labor mobility, not only the labor power itself migrated but also the owner of the labor. When capital migrates to country A, its owner typically stays in B. The migrant

Figure 11   What Are the Effects of Capital Mobility?

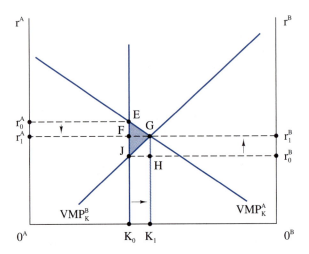

Beginning at point E, capital flows, in response to the higher rate of return in country A, improve efficiency and increase output by EGJ. Both countries gain because ownership of the migrant capital remains with country B. In A, workers gain relative to capital owners; in B, capital owners gain relative to workers.

capital earns FGK_1K_0 in A, a gain of FGHJ over what it earned in B. This represents a gain to country B, which enjoys the income from the capital because its owner still resides there. Country A gains EGF, the productivity of the migrant capital above the return paid to its owner. The emigrant country loses in the case of labor mobility but gains from capital mobility, because it retains the ownership of and rights to the income from the migrant capital. Therefore, both countries enjoy a net gain; as usual, however, some groups within each country gain while others lose.

Owners of "native" capital in A suffer a reduction in their rate of return from r_0^A to r_1^A because of the capital inflow. Workers in A gain as the marginal productivity of labor rises from the availability of additional capital with which to work. Owners of capital that remains in country B benefit from the rise in the return to capital that occurs after the capital outflow. Workers in B have less capital to work with, suffer reduced marginal products, and earn lower wages. Therefore, it's not surprising most labor groups favor restrictions not only on labor immigration but on capital outflows. Table 8 summarizes these results.

So far we've considered only factor mobility in response to inter-country differentials in the rewards paid to factors of production. An additional consideration arises when governments tax the rewards paid to inputs.

4.3 Taxation and Factor Mobility

Most governments levy taxes on income earned by both workers and owners of capital. The rates of taxation and the precise rules that define taxable income vary widely from country to country, creating additional incentives for inter-country factor mobility. Ireland, for example, attracted many writers and poets by exempting from taxation all income earned from such activities. Several movie stars, rock stars, and athletes (including David Bowie, Michael Caine, Roger Moore, and Sean Connery)

Table 8	**EFFECTS OF CAPITAL FLOW FROM COUNTRY B TO COUNTRY A**
Effect on:	
Owners of native capital in A	−
Laborers in A	+
Net effect on A	+ (area EGF)
Owners of capital remaining in B	+
Laborers in B	−
Owners of migrant capital	+
Net effect on B	+ (area FGJ)
Net effect on world welfare	+ (area EGJ)

left England to avoid its high tax rates, formerly as high as 83 percent. England responded by lowering its top income tax rate dramatically and lured most of its tax exiles home.

Our analysis so far suggests that factor mobility increases world efficiency by drawing resources to the locations where they can be most productive. This conclusion *doesn't* apply, however, to mobility motivated solely by countries' differing tax rates and rules. Although such mobility clearly benefits the migrant labor or capital, it doesn't contribute to the efficiency of the world economy.[25] On the other hand, it does raise some interesting policy issues.

Taxation of wages and capital income have similar effects. The following discussion focuses on taxation of wages. The results carry over, with minor modifications, to taxation of capital. Figure 12 resembles Figure 8, which illustrated the effects of labor mobility. To keep the analysis simple, Figure 12 assumes that the initial allocation of labor between countries A and B (represented by L_0) is the efficient one; that is, at L_0 the values of the marginal productivity of labor and wage rates are equal in the two countries. Now suppose country A imposes a tax on wages at a rate denoted by t^A, where $0 < t^A < 1$.[26] For each dollar of wages earned, a worker must pay t^A in taxes, leaving a net reward or "take-home pay" of $\$1(1 - t^A)$. At any wage rate w^A, labor suppliers get to keep only $w^A(1 - t^A)$. Workers no longer choose between countries A and B by comparing $VMP_L^A = w^A$ with $VMP_L^B = w^B$; now the relevant comparison from the individual worker's point of view is between net or after-tax wages in the two countries, or $VMP_L^A(1 - t^A) = w^A(1 - t^A)$ in A and $VMP_L^B = w^B$ in B. At L_0, $w_0^A(1 - t^A) < w_0^B$; thus, country A's taxation of wages causes the units of labor between L_1 and L_0 to migrate to country B to avoid the tax. Remember that L_0 represents the efficient, or output-maximizing, allocation of labor between the two countries. The workers who migrate in response to country A's tax are less productive in B than in A (reflected in the fact that VMP_L^A lies above VMP_L^B between L_1 and L_0); but because of the tax in A, workers earn higher *net* wages by working in B. Area EGJ measures the total *loss* of world output from the tax-migration effect.

---

25. This statement ignores supply-side or incentive arguments that, for example, individuals work more when they face low marginal tax rates because the after-tax return to working is higher.

26. For simplicity, we assume a constant tax rate; that is, the tax system is proportional. The tax liability equals a constant proportion (t^A) of the wage. Systems in which the tax rate rises with income are progressive, while those in which it falls with rising income are regressive. In Figure 12, for simplicity, we depict the tax by a parallel shift of the VMP curve. In reality, the new curve would be steeper than the original one.

Figure 12   What Are the Effects of Wage Taxation by Country A?

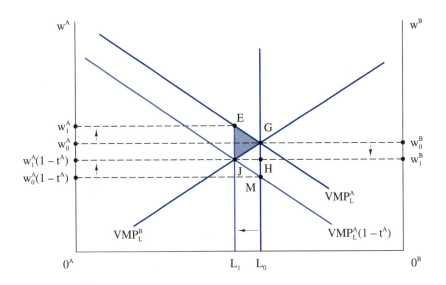

Beginning with an efficient allocation of labor between A and B, taxation of wages by A reduces total output by EGJ. Workers between L_1 and L_0 migrate to B in response to a differential in wages net of taxes, but gross returns reflect true labor productivity. Immigration harms workers in B. Workers in A are better off than they would be in the presence of the tax and with no labor mobility.

Total output in A falls by EGL_0L_1. Workers who remain in A earn w_1^A but get to keep only $w_1^A(1 - t^A)$. They're worse off than before the tax (because $w_1^A[1 - t^A] < w_0^A$) but better off than if the tax had occurred with restrictions on labor mobility, in which case net wages would have fallen all the way to $w_0^A(1 - t^A)$. (*Why?*) Capital owners in A earn less because their capital has less labor with which to work than before the imposition of the tax. The country-A government collects $w_1^A EJ w_1^A(1 - t^A)$ in tax revenue. Note, however, that labor's ability to move to avoid the tax reduces the government's ability to raise revenue by taxing wages. With completely immobile labor, the same tax rate depicted in Figure 12 would have raised $w_0^A GM w_0^A(1 - t^A)$ in revenue.

Total output in country B rises by JGL_0L_1. Native workers in B lose $Gw_0^B w_1^B H$ because of the inflow of workers, and owners of capital gain. The mobility of labor drives the wage rate in B down to equality with the *net* wage in A, even though wages in B remain untaxed.

Country A's taxation of wages distorts the labor market and results in inefficient labor migration from A to B. Workers flow to the country in which they can earn the higher net wage, but gross rather than net wages reflect true productivity.

Figure 12 assumes that only country A taxes wages. In reality, most countries do; and the size of the distortion created by those taxes depends on relative tax rates. If countries A and B tax wages at the same rate and use the same definitions for taxable income, the taxes don't create any incentive for labor migration, because workers face the same taxes no matter where they live and work. (*How would you represent this case in Figure 12?*)[27] As long

---

27. Add a $VMP_L^B(1 - t^B)$ curve to represent the net return to labor in country B. If $t^B = t^A$, the new curve will intersect $VMP_L^A(1 - t^A)$ at point M. No labor will migrate. Gross wages will be equal at $w_0^A = w_0^B$, and net wages will be equal at $w_0^A(1 - t^A) = w_0^B(1 - t^B)$.

as the only choice labor has is whether to live and work in country A or country B, taxation has no net migration effect when countries impose equal taxes.[28]

Because of the importance of *relative* tax rates, governments worry about other countries' tax policies. During the 1980s, top income tax rates trended downward in the major industrial economies. That the trend was in the same direction for many countries limited incentives for migration in response to the tax changes. Even with the downward trend, substantial differences in tax rates remain. Simple comparisons can be misleading, however. For example, in some countries much of the relevant taxation occurs at the provincial or state rather than the federal level, and overall tax liability always depends on definitions of taxable income and allowable deductions as well as tax rates.

The pattern in corporate tax rates, or taxes on capital, is similar to that in personal income taxes. Differences in tax rates remain a source of controversy, particularly among members of the European Union. Despite the distorting effects of differences in taxes on capital, rates in 2004 ranged from Hungary's 16 percent to Germany's 38.3 percent. Some older EU member countries with high tax rates such as Germany and France have pressured new members, including low-tax Central and Eastern European transitional economies such as Poland and Slovakia, to raise tax rates in the interest of "harmonization." The new members, eager to attract capital inflows to their still-transitional economies, resent the pressure and accuse the older high-tax countries of seeking to eliminate competition for capital.

So far, our examination of taxation's effects has maintained one subtle but important assumption: Income was subject to taxation by only one country at a time. By moving from A to B, workers could avoid paying the tax levied by A but became subject to any tax levied by B. Luckily for tax attorneys, the real-life situation is much more complex. A citizen working or investing abroad or a firm earning income abroad often faces taxation by both the domestic and foreign governments. This raises several policy issues.

Double taxation, or taxation of the same income by two governments, creates a strong disincentive for factor mobility. Many governments agree, through tax treaties, to eliminate or reduce double taxation by granting either tax credits or tax deductions for taxes paid to foreign governments. A tax credit reduces the tax liability to country A by the full amount of the tax paid to country B. A tax deduction reduces the income subject to taxation in A by the amount of the tax paid to B. The tax credit eliminates double taxation, leaving a total tax liability equal to the higher of the two countries' tax rates. The tax deduction, on the other hand, reduces but doesn't eliminate double taxation. The negotiation of bilateral tax treaties reflects a delicate balancing of costs and benefits in terms of the revenue of the governments involved. Even with tax treaties, international mobility of factors of production reallocates the world's tax base, providing another source of controversy over policies toward factor mobility.

Most industrial countries, including the United States, use a residence-based tax system that taxes U.S. residents' income—even if earned outside the country—but doesn't tax interest income paid to foreigners. Many developing countries, on the other hand, use a source-based tax system that taxes any income originating in the domestic economy but not domestic citizens' income earned abroad. The combination of the two systems creates an incentive for capital flows from developing countries to industrial countries. (*Why?*) India recently changed its tax laws to make the global earnings of Indians who return to India after living abroad subject to taxation.[29]

28. Taxation may cause some individuals to choose not to work; in that case, it will lower the total quantity of labor available. Even if taxation has no effect on total world output, distributive effects remain. The tax transfers the revenue raised from workers to the government, and the overall outcome depends on how government chooses to use the revenue.

29. "Indian Tax Change Will Close Expatriate Loophole," *Financial Times*, August 12, 2003.

4.4 Multinational Enterprises and the World Economy

One of the major economic trends of the postwar period has been the growth of firms across national boundaries, a source of both political and economic controversy. Estimates indicate that intra-firm trade within multinationals accounts for about one-third of all world trade, and that multinationals' exports to non-affiliates account for another third, leaving only one-third of all trade to national rather than multinational firms.[30] The world's top 100 non-financial multinational enterprises employ more than 14 million workers and have annual foreign sales of $2.5 trillion.[31]

DEFINITION   We can define **multinational enterprises (MNEs)** simply as firms that manage and control facilities in at least two countries. This simple definition, however, doesn't clearly separate multinational enterprises from other firms; the main source of ambiguity is the meaning of "manage and control." Would a firm based in country A, which owns half the shares of stock of a firm in country B, be an MNE? From the standpoint of economic theory, the primary issue in establishing whether an enterprise qualifies as an MNE is whether decisions made in one country direct and allocate resources located in another. This transcending of national boundaries makes MNEs both economically important and controversial.

Multinational enterprises can be classified into three groups based on the pattern of organization of their production. Some MNEs produce the same or similar goods in several countries; these are called *horizontally integrated MNEs*. For example, Intel produces semiconductor chips in the United States, Ireland, Israel, Malaysia, the Philippines, China, and Costa Rica. Other enterprises produce inputs in one country that they then use to produce another good in another country; these are referred to as *vertically integrated MNEs*. For example, the General Motors plant in Tonawanda, New York, produces engines to supply GM auto plants worldwide. The third possibility involves production of different or even totally unrelated goods in various countries; such arrangements are called *diversified* or *conglomerate MNEs*. For example, Japanese electronics firms such as Toshiba, Matsushita, and Sony manufacture a wide range of electronics products around the world. Early MNEs clustered in agricultural and mining sectors, where industrial economies invested in developing countries' raw-materials sectors; but the bulk of multinational activity now occurs in manufacturing, especially in the electronics, automobile, chemical, and pharmaceutical industries.

The MNE phenomenon isn't new, but the multinationalization of production has grown rapidly since World War II. Advances in transportation and communications technologies have increased the feasibility of global production. U.S. intra-MNE trade, that between U.S. parent firms and their foreign affiliates, comprises about 40 percent of all U.S. merchandise exports and imports.

The central questions to be answered concerning multinational enterprises include the reasons for their existence, their welfare implications, and the policy issues they raise for both parent and host governments. We now turn to each of these issues.

WHY GO MULTINATIONAL?   For years, most analysts of multinational enterprises viewed them as vehicles for spreading capital from one country to another, a perspective known as the **capital arbitrage theory of multinationals**. In capital-abundant countries, capital tends to earn a low return compared with that in capital-scarce countries. This difference in returns creates an incentive for capital owners to shift their resources from

---

30.   WTO (1996), p. 44.

31.   United Nations, *World Investment Report 2002*.

low-return to high-return countries, as discussed in section 4.2. Such activity increases total world income because it moves capital from areas of low productivity to those of higher productivity. However, at least three aspects of observed MNE behavior suggest that capital arbitrage can't be the sole explanation for MNEs. First, MNE capital doesn't flow solely or even primarily from capital-abundant to capital-scarce countries. A large share of inward foreign direct investment goes to developed, capital-rich economies, not to developing capital-scarce ones. Second, in many countries inflows and outflows of MNE capital occur simultaneously. Figure 9 revealed that 7 of the 10 leading FDI *host* countries also number among the top 10 *source* countries. Third, although MNEs often do move capital from one country to another, such movements aren't necessary because MNEs can borrow funds locally for their subsidiaries. Rather than simply moving capital, multinationals change where goods get produced and who controls the production. Overall, the capital-arbitrage hypothesis appears incomplete as an explanation of the MNE phenomenon.

When seeking to understand the observed location of production facilities around the world, economists think first of the low-cost way to serve markets. The theories of comparative advantage and trade based on scale economies are, after all, theories of the *location* of production: Industries tend to locate where they can produce a product at the lowest possible opportunity cost. However, this rule alone can't explain the existence of multinational enterprises, because all firms in each country could be locally owned and controlled. For example, the fact that Honda sells automobiles in both Japan and the United States doesn't imply that the firm must own and control separate production sites in Japan and Marysville, Ohio. Alternatives include (1) production just in Japan with export to the U.S. market and (2) licensing by Honda of a U.S. company to produce and sell Hondas in the United States in exchange for a license fee. That Honda now also exports automobiles from its U.S. plants to Japan further complicates the picture!

A theory of the MNE phenomenon must explain why an enterprise chooses multinational production over exporting or licensing. Why does the firm choose to produce abroad *and* to maintain domestic ownership and control of that production? In other words, why does the enterprise choose to have its decision making and control of resources cross national borders? After all, multinational operation clearly involves costs. The firm must move resources, goods, employees, and information around the world and learn the laws and customs of multiple countries. The headquarters in the parent country must monitor the activities of its foreign affiliates. Occasionally hosts even expropriate investor assets. For example, when China's First Automobile Works' license to build Audi automobiles expired in 1997, the firm simply expropriated the technology and put its own Red Flag logo on the cars.[32] Given these costs, an MNE must expect significant benefits from centralized control of foreign facilities.

In choosing between exporting and producing abroad as alternate methods to serve a foreign market, the presence or absence of trade barriers is one important determinant of strategy. If the foreign market is protected by tariffs, quotas, or other restrictions on imports, exporting becomes less attractive relative to producing abroad. Statistical studies have confirmed that trade barriers encourage MNE activity. Even during the Great Depression, U.S. firms set up production facilities behind the Smoot–Hawley retaliatory tariffs passed by many countries. More recently, some developing countries have used this response as a strategy for attracting foreign investment. The tactic involves imposing import restrictions high enough to force foreign firms that want to sell in the market to establish local production facilities.

---

32. Craig S. Smith and Rebecca Blumenstein, "In China, GM Bets Billions on a Market Strewn with Casualties," *The Wall Street Journal,* February 11, 1998.

Some Japanese investment in the United States, such as that in the auto industry during the 1980s, also fits this pattern, sometimes called *tariff-jumping*, or *market-access*, *foreign direct investment*. Foreign direct investment can also defuse protectionist political sentiment in the host country; this is called *quid pro quo investment*.

Empirical evidence indicates that deliberate use of high trade barriers to attract inward foreign direct investment can work but has some negative consequences. Most important, the investment attracted tends to be simply production to serve the domestic market, not technology transfer or export-oriented production. Also, high trade barriers can make the domestic MNE affiliate less competitive by raising the cost of imported inputs it uses.

The nonexport alternative to forming an MNE is to license a foreign firm to serve the foreign market. Examination of this alternative takes us closer to the frontiers of MNE research. Empirically, MNEs cluster in industries with large research-and-development or technological-innovation components, such as electronics, chemicals, and pharmaceuticals. The special character of information, technology, and other outputs of the research-and-development process provide a key to understanding the choice between licensing and multinational production. Suppose that a firm in country A, through a costly research-and-development program, discovers a lower-cost technology to produce good X. The firm adopts the new technology in the domestic market and wants to use it to sell in country B. The firm has no production facilities in B, and B's trade barriers against imports make exporting there infeasible. The firm can either acquire or build production facilities in B, thereby becoming an MNE, or license the right to use the new technology to an existing firm in B. Consider the second alternative, licensing. How much would the A firm charge for the license, and how much would the firm in B be willing to pay? The character of new technology makes it difficult to arrive at a mutually acceptable price. The firm in B has no incentive to accept the A firm's word on the new technology's worth—because of the A firm's incentive to exaggerate it. But if the A firm reveals the technological secret to the firm in B to establish the innovation's value, the B firm may steal the design and use it without paying any license fee. The combination of the A firm's incentive to overstate the new technology's value and the B firm's motive to steal the underlying information can make a licensing agreement difficult to achieve.

These problems may be particularly acute in developing countries that have weak or nonexistent systems of patent and trademark protection for inventions. For these reasons, firms in technologically innovative or research-and-development-intensive industries tend to choose multinational production over licensing. By forming an MNE, the firm maintains *control* over its technology while using it to serve foreign markets. Figure 13 reveals that U.S. foreign direct investment tends to be higher in industries, such as chemicals, that involve high levels of research and development.

SUBSTITUTE FOR OR COMPLEMENT OF TRADE?   We've seen that both international trade and foreign direct investment by MNEs are growing rapidly—more rapidly, in fact, than overall production. How might the two trends be related? In particular, does more MNE activity tend to be associated with more international trade, or less? Existing empirical evidence suggests that the tentative answer is *both*. Some types of foreign direct investment substitute for trade in goods, while other types encourage more such trade.

When firms go multinational primarily to locate their production according to comparative advantage, international trade tends to increase. If, for example, U.S.-based auto firms produce cars for the U.S. market in Mexico rather than in the United States because of Mexico's comparative advantage, then more international trade in cars occurs. On the other hand, some firms may go multinational to gain better access to local

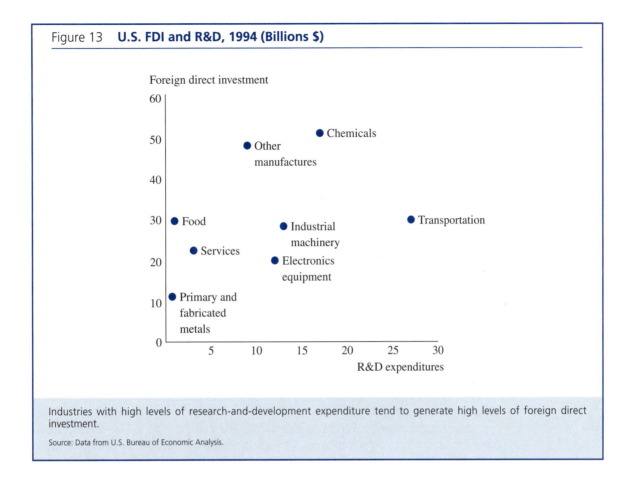

Figure 13   **U.S. FDI and R&D, 1994 (Billions $)**

Industries with high levels of research-and-development expenditure tend to generate high levels of foreign direct investment.

Source: Data from U.S. Bureau of Economic Analysis.

markets. Japanese auto firms use their U.S. production facilities primarily (although no longer exclusively) to serve the U.S. market. To the extent that this production replaces U.S. car imports from Japan, international auto trade falls.

MNEs' EFFECTS   The effect of multinational enterprises, both overall and on parent and host countries separately, is a subject of disagreement. Insofar as MNEs play a role in moving production to its least-cost locations and contribute to the spread of technological improvements, total world output increases. This makes possible an increase in total world welfare and potentially (though not necessarily) improves welfare in parent and host countries alike. MNEs may facilitate achievement of scale economies by handling some functions, such as research and finance, centrally while continuing to adapt to local conditions in other areas of operation, such as labor relations and marketing. By handling many transactions internally, the MNE may be able to guarantee supplies of raw materials (by owning its own) and build more reliable distribution networks.

Most of the controversy surrounding multinationals relates to the division of their benefits and costs between parent and host countries. U.S. labor organizations, for example, claim that multinational production by U.S. firms "exports" jobs. Because of the scarcity and relatively high wages of unskilled labor in the United States, firms tend to move abroad production that involves intensive use of unskilled labor. Assembly tasks, such as those in apparel, consumer electronics, and some high-technology products, often are conducted for U.S. companies by operations in labor-abundant and low-wage countries, from Mexico to China.

Claims by labor groups that this constitutes export of jobs that rightly belong to U.S. workers are subject to several important qualifications. The movement of production to low-cost areas maximizes total world output and income. In many cases firms face a choice between moving abroad or stopping production completely; that is, solely domestic production may cease to be viable due to comparative disadvantage. If foreign production operations make inputs cheaper for U.S. producers, the competitive positions of those producers improve. Increased foreign production also increases employment in management and research within the parent country. To the extent that foreign production raises foreign incomes, demand for U.S. exports increases, raising employment in export-oriented industries. Multinational enterprises play important roles in spreading training, as well as norms of corporate governance, accounting, and law. And firms' ability to leave a country may constrain governments' abilities to pursue bad policies without accountability.

The proliferation of multinationals also tends to spread the technology developed in parent countries to the rest of the world. Developing countries have complained that MNEs keep research-and-development operations clustered in the industrialized countries rather than spreading facilities that would allow developing countries to become more self-sufficient in research and development and technological innovation. Most empirical studies, however, find both that MNEs do transfer advanced technology to their hosts and that the presence of MNEs enhances the efficiency of local firms. The trend of increased technology transfer through MNEs reflects the firms' growing globalization, in which the full range of firm activities occurs in locations throughout the world. General Motors, for example, has five state-of-the-art factories—in Argentina, Poland, China, Thailand, and Brazil. The five utilize advanced technologies not present in any of the firm's U.S. plants, and local engineers played central roles in the design of all five.

Developing countries also charge that MNEs' sheer size and economic strength allow them to exploit their host countries. This alleged exploitation takes a variety of forms: bargaining with the host government for excessive tax concessions, paying unfairly low prices for raw materials removed from the host country, and issuing deceptive financial statements to repatriate all the benefits from the operation to the parent country. *(Refer back to Figure 11. What area represents the amount MNEs would need to extract to leave the host country no better off than before the investment?)* An additional concern is MNEs' general domination of the host's economy and culture, which can cause a loss of indigenous values and damage to local enterprises.[33] Local firms in the host country, of course, have an incentive to block the entry of MNEs that would compete in the local market.

A final source of contention between MNEs and their parent and host governments arises not because of the multinationals themselves but rather because of governments' policies toward them. An MNE exists under the jurisdiction of several governments, and one of the most controversial questions surrounding these arrangements concerns those governments' rights to tax the MNE.[34] By moving production facilities around the world, multinationals reallocate the tax base among countries, as we saw in section 4.3, sometimes with significant distributional consequences.

GOVERNMENT POLICIES TOWARD MNEs   Historically, government policies toward multinationals have been erratic. Countries vacillate between explicitly encouraging foreign investment and legally forbidding it. Current policies toward both inward

---

33. More generally, MNEs can act as powerful instruments of social change. For example, MNEs often provide jobs and economic opportunities in countries where traditional cultural values have limited women's access to activities outside the home.

34. The discussion of taxes and factor mobility in section 4.3 applies to multinational enterprises as well as labor.

investment (as viewed by the host country) and outward investment (as viewed by the parent country) differ widely across countries, although the last few years have seen a general move toward greater encouragement of foreign investment. In 2001, 71 countries worldwide made 208 changes in laws covering foreign direct investment; and the United Nations characterizes more than 90 percent of those legal changes as having created a more open environment for foreign direct investment.[35]

However, despite the desire, particularly by developing countries, to attract foreign capital, many countries continue to restrict the entry and behavior of MNEs. Common host-country policies include bans from MNE participation in certain industries, limits on dividend payments and repatriation of profits to the parent country, requirements that MNEs buy specified percentages of inputs locally, local ownership requirements, minimum export limits, and ceilings on royalty payments for technology owned by parent-country firms. Industries in which governments often restrict MNE participation include banking, insurance, telecommunications, pharmaceuticals, computers, and advertising.

At the same time such restrictions make foreign investment less attractive, many host-country governments offer tax incentives to multinationals to locate in their countries. Other incentives include government provision of infrastructure such as roads, ports, railroads, and other facilities, as well as exemption from tariffs on imported inputs. Host countries end up using these incentives to compete for investments by firms such as General Electric, Intel, Microsoft, and Toyota. For example, after several episodes of tightening restrictions on foreign firms, China announced in 1999 that it would provide firms that transferred technology to China with exemptions from income and sales taxes.[36] To the extent that the *total* amount of investment remains unaffected by these fiscal incentive packages, such competition merely reallocates investment among host countries and transfers resources from the "winning" hosts to the MNEs that benefit from the incentives.

Parent-country governments generally place far fewer restrictions on MNE behavior than do hosts. As mentioned earlier, labor groups often argue that multinational production leads to job loss, despite a lack of empirical evidence of such economy-wide effects. In the United States there have been union-backed efforts to pass domestic-content legislation for the automobile industry, but the attempts have failed so far, except for NAFTA's stringent rules of origin.

CASE 1: GROWTH MYTHS AND MIRACLES

We've seen in this chapter that a country's output can grow in two basic ways—more inputs or higher productivity. Either shifts the country's production possibilities frontier outward. We can make the growth relationship a bit more precise by stating it as an equation, often referred to as the *growth-accounting equation*:

Rate of growth of output =

Rate of growth of labor inputs	+	Rate of growth of capital inputs	+	Rate of growth of productivity

The last term on the right-hand side of the equation is called **total factor productivity (TFP)** and refers to organizational

---

35. United Nations, *World Investment Report 2002*.

36. "China Takes Steps to Increase Investment," *The Wall Street Journal*, September 10, 1999.

and technological advances that allow the country to produce more output from the same amount of labor and capital inputs. In other words, TFP captures changes in the effectiveness with which labor and capital resources are used.

Much of the recent increase in economic research on the subject of growth has taken the form of empirical studies of the growth-accounting equation to discover how much of observed growth should be attributed to the equation's various right-hand-side terms for different countries and time periods. Table 9 presents results from one study. The table reports the percentage of output growth attributable to labor, capital, and productivity for seven industrial countries during 1960–1989. With the notable exceptions of the United States and Canada, TFP accounted for very large shares of growth. Unfortunately, the data that underlie such studies are subject to significant measurement error, and the findings of different studies vary significantly.

The division of economic growth into its input and productivity components took central stage in a debate over Asia's (pre-financial-crisis) growth experience. The growth of several Asian economies since the 1960s was widely touted as a "miracle"—often attributed by noneconomists and even by a few economists to a unique combination of Asian cultural values and government industrial policies. Economist Paul Krugman triggered the debate in 1994 by arguing that the Asian

"miracle" was in fact a "myth."[37] He suggested that Asian economies had experienced such high growth rates mainly by utilizing more resources—that is, working harder and forgoing consumption to invest more—not by increasing productivity. In fact, he even compared the Asian experience to that of the Stalinist era in the former Soviet Union. The USSR achieved very high growth rates during the 1950s and 1960s by reducing consumption and investing at unprecedented rates. Output grew, but only so long as the unsustainable level of investment continued. Much of the investment went to unproductive projects, as directed by central planners; and growth collapsed (as, eventually, did the Soviet Union itself). No one suggested—even later in light of their severe financial crisis—that the Asian economies would suffer Soviet Union-like collapses. The question was whether they would again reach the dramatic growth rates they had experienced during the past couple of decades or whether their growth rates would settle down to a couple of percentage points faster than those in the industrial market economies. Once the region recovers fully from its late-1990s financial crisis, will the countries' emphasis on education generate rising productivity to sustain rapid growth? Or will the rapid increases in their rates of labor and capital utilization simply come to an inevitable end, leaving growth rates much like those in the rest of the world?

Table 9 **PERCENT OF OUTPUT GROWTH ATTRIBUTABLE TO LABOR, CAPITAL, AND PRODUCTIVITY, 1960–1989**

	Percentage of output growth						
	U.S.	CANADA	JAPAN	FRANCE	U.K.	ITALY	GERMANY
Labor input per capita	32.2%	27.5%	37.5%	−5.9%	−7.1%	−0.6%	−11.3%
Capital input per capita	41.7	50.6	12.7	46.4	49.8	44.8	53.7
Productivity	26.2	21.8	49.8	59.6	57.3	55.8	57.6
Output per capita	100.0	100.0	100.0	100.0	100.0	100.0	100.0

Source: Data from Chrys Dougherty and Dale W. Jorgenson, "International Comparisons of the Source of Economic Growth," *American Economic Review Papers and Proceedings* (May 1996), p. 26.

37. "The Myth of the Asian Miracle," *Foreign Affairs* (1994).

CASE 2: HOW BIG ARE THEY?

It's common to read comparisons of the sizes of MNEs and national economies. One such recent comparison found that on a "biggest 50" list, 14 entries were multinational firms and 36 were national economies. These comparisons do point out something important about the structure of international production, but they're also definitionally flawed and therefore misleading. Each country's output, as measured by its gross domestic product (GDP), is a value-added measure; that is, GDP sums the market value of all final goods and services produced in the economy in a year. This measurement technique avoids double counting: If the economy produces a sweater, we count the sweater's value in GDP, but not the value of the wool, because the sweater's value already embodies the value of the wool. A firm's annual sales, in contrast, allow goods to be double- or triple-counted as they're sold, rebought, and resold in a multistage production process. So, a "fair" size comparison between national economies and firms requires that we adjust the measure of firm size to reflect just value-added and avoid double-counting; this gives us

a measure that is conceptually more comparable with countries' GDP.

What's the result? Using data for 2000, a "biggest 100" list included 29 multinational firms and 71 countries.[38] The U.S. economy held the top spot with a GDP of $9,810 billion, followed by Japan, Germany, the United Kingdom, France, and China. A multinational firm doesn't appear until number 45: ExxonMobil with a value-added of $63 billion, placing it between Chile (GDP = $71 billion) and Pakistan (GDP = $62 billion). So 44 national economies, including several developing ones, outrank the largest multinational firm in terms of value-added. In the ranks between 50 and 100, approximately half the entries are multinational firms and half are national economies.

How much difference does it make that we adjust firms' rank to reflect their value-added rather than their sales relative to countries' GDPs? In a 2000 ranking by sales, the largest multinational, again ExxonMobil, would have ranked number 22 instead of number 45. Its sales of $206 billion would have placed it just behind Belgium and just ahead of Turkey.

CASE 3: SAVING, INVESTMENT, AND INTERTEMPORAL TRADE

With no international capital mobility, each country's investment must equal its saving, because the only way to obtain funds to finance an investment project is to forgo current consumption, that is, to save. In such a world, a graph with national investment rates plotted on the horizontal axis and national saving rates on the vertical one would show countries as a series of dots on an upward-sloping 45-degree line. Countries with low saving and investment rates would appear as dots on the lower, left-hand end of the line, and those with high saving and investment rates on the upper, right-hand end of the line.

Of course, capital isn't completely immobile. Most countries have removed many (but not all) of their legal

barriers to capital flows, at least in the industrialized world. But a graph of countries' actual saving and investment rates looks remarkably similar to the 45-degree line we just described. Of the 23 industrialized countries included in a famous study by economist Martin Feldstein, not a single one paired low saving and high investment or high saving and low investment; the maximum difference between the two rates for any country equaled about 4 percent.

Countries' saving rates differ for several reasons. Cultures place different levels of importance on thriftiness. A country's age, demographic, and labor-force participation patterns affect saving because individuals' saving behavior varies over their life cycle. Tax systems can encourage or

---

38. United Nations Conference on Trade and Development, *World Investment Report 2002,* p. 90.

discourage saving. Countries with generous public and private retirement systems may experience lower levels of nonretirement saving than those in which individuals feel more responsible for their own retirement income.

The close relationship between a country's saving and investment rates has at least two possible interpretations. The first takes the relationship as evidence of a lack of international capital mobility. Countries' saving and investment rates match closely, just as we argued would be the case if mobility were zero. This suggests that capital may not flow from countries with poor investment opportunities to those with good ones.

The second interpretation argues that perhaps countries with high saving rates happen to be the same countries that also offer good investment opportunities, while countries with low saving rates offer few or poor investment opportunities. Countries that experience rapid economic growth, for example, tend to both save and invest at high rates. Countries whose economic policy makers follow policies that lead to stability foster both saving and investment in their economies. Other countries' policy makers cause uncertainty and instability that discourage both saving and investment.

Unfortunately, economists don't have enough information about the potential gains from intertemporal trade to choose confidently between these two quite different interpretations. We do know, however, that international capital mobility has risen in recent years and that countries' saving and investment rates diverge more now than in earlier years.

CASE 4: SEND MONEY

We saw in section 4.1 that labor mobility's effects on the country of emigration depend on whether workers who move send any of their earnings back home. Officially, foreign workers in developed countries sent $93 billion back to their home countries in 2003; and experts estimate that another $15 billion – $45 billion was sent through unofficial—and uncounted—channels. A study by the Inter-American Development Bank found that migrants from Latin America sent $38 billion home in 2003, mostly from the United States, but also from Europe and Asia. Remittances to Latin America help support more than 50 million people. The 7.5 million Filipinos working abroad in 162 countries (mostly the United States, Saudi Arabia, and Japan) sent $6.2 billion in worker remittances to family members in the Philippines in 2001.[39] Experts estimate that another $3 billion was sent outside the banking system, thereby escaping measurement.

Countries that receive the highest total amount of remittances include India, Mexico, and the Philippines; but remittances as a percent of GDP are higher for other countries such as Lesotho, Jordan, and Albania (see Figure 14). Regionally, Latin America and the Caribbean are the largest recipients, but remittances to South Asia equal a larger share of that region's GDP.

While total remittances amount to huge sums, the individual transactions typically are quite small. Family members abroad send an average of about $250 eight to ten times per year. So the $93 billion in total remittances mean approximately 350 million separate transactions. Most go by Western Union, MoneyGram, or Orlandi Valuta; typical fees take more than 10 percent of the sum remitted. In addition, 5 percent of the sum remitted usually goes to foreign-exchange fees.

After the September 11, 2001, terrorist attacks on the United States, information surfaced that the perpetrators had used an informal and unregulated international money-moving network called *hawala* to handle their financial needs. Several *hawala* operations had their funds frozen as part of the anti-terrorism campaign. Unfortunately, while having the beneficial effect of making it harder to finance terrorism, loss of this network also left many foreign workers with fewer alternatives for sending remittances home to countries with poorly developed banking systems.

To combat the combination of high remittance fees and the vulnerability of informal transfers to terrorism funding, the United States Treasury has gotten involved in encouraging competition among official financial institutions

---

39. "One Nation, Overseas," *Wired,* June 2002.

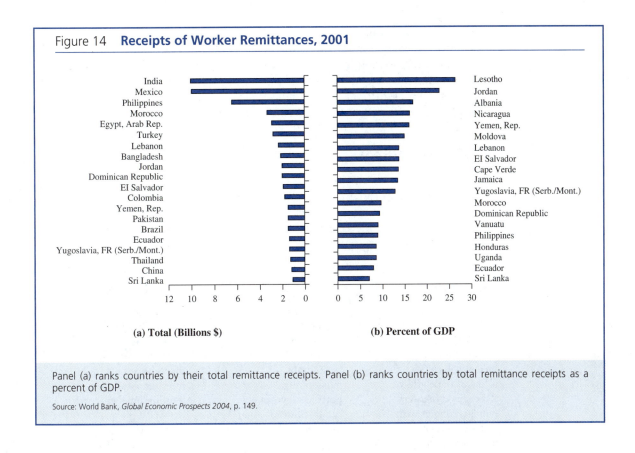

Figure 14 **Receipts of Worker Remittances, 2001**

(a) Total (Billions $)

(b) Percent of GDP

Panel (a) ranks countries by their total remittance receipts. Panel (b) ranks countries by total remittance receipts as a percent of GDP.

Source: World Bank, *Global Economic Prospects 2004*, p. 149.

(for example, commercial banks) to create secure low-cost financial channels for remittances. Several commercial banks have started new programs to facilitate basic banking and remittance services for migrant workers and recent immigrants. Remittance fees have started to come down, particularly for transfers to Mexico. Some banks now offer accounts that can be accessed easily on either side of the border as well as a remittance system that makes funds deposited in the United States available instantaneously to family members in Mexico through ATMs.

SUMMARY

Economic growth's effect on welfare is more complex than a first glance suggests. The two components are the income effect (which applies to both small and large countries) and the terms-of-trade effect (which applies only to large countries). When growth results from increased factor endowments, the direction of the income effect depends on the relative increases in total consumption and population. If total consumption rises at a faster rate than population, per-capita consumption rises. The terms-of-trade effect can be either positive or negative, depending on growth's impact on the desired volume of trade at the original terms of trade. The overall effect of factor-endowment-based economic growth on welfare is uncertain for both large and small countries.

Economic growth due to technical progress improves the welfare of small countries by raising per-capita consumption. For large countries, the terms-of-trade effect can be either positive or negative. The possibility of a strongly negative terms-of-trade effect outweighing the positive income effect implies that growth can be immiserizing, although little empirical evidence supports this view.

International mobility of factors of production increases the efficiency of the world economy when it is based on differential productivity across countries. Mobility can also alter the distribution of income in each country between capital owners and labor, making policies that promote or restrict mobility controversial. When artificial incentives such as differential tax rates cause migration of capital or labor, the migration reduces the efficiency of the world economy.

LOOKING AHEAD

Chapter Eleven focuses on special trade-related problems facing developing countries. It examines the role of international trade in growth and development, as well as the use of trade restrictions for dealing with the special problems of development. We also explore the experience of a new class of developing economies—those in transition from central planning.

KEY TERMS

economic growth
endogenous
   growth theory
balanced growth
income effect
terms-of-trade effect
Rybczynski theorem
immiserizing growth
technical progress
neutral technical
   progress

capital-saving
   technical progress
labor-saving
   technical progress
brain drain
outsourcing
portfolio investment
capital outflow
international
   purchase
   of assets

capital inflow
international sale
   of assets
direct investment
diversification
intertemporal trade
multinational enterprise
   (MNE)
capital arbitrage
   theory of multinationals
total factor productivity (TFP)

PROBLEMS AND QUESTIONS FOR REVIEW

1. Technological advances in computer hookups and satellite communications have allowed U.S.-based computer software development firms to "offshore" tasks—to use computer programmers in India for programming projects. The firms send program specifications to India via satellite; the Indian programmers do the programming (at wages below those of U.S. programmers) and transmit the completed programs back to the United States via satellite.
   a. Explain whether you expect the following groups to support or oppose the new arrangements and why: U.S. computer software development firms, U.S. computer programmers, computer programmers in India.
   b. What effect might such policies have on the brain drain?
2. How would you expect each of the following to affect the brain drain and its implications?
   a. Worker remittances.
   b. Temporary visas such as the U.S. H1-B program.
   c. Lower transaction costs for worker remittances.
3. U.S. automobile manufacturers took a variety of positions on U.S. limits on auto imports from Japan in the 1980s. Ordinarily, we would expect domestic producers to favor such restrictions. What might explain the observation that some domestic producers didn't favor the import restrictions?
4. a. Illustrate an equilibrium situation with an efficient allocation of capital between two developing countries, A and B, and with no taxation of capital income in either country. Be sure to label carefully and explain.
   b. Illustrate the effects if country A imposes a tax (at rate t^A) on capital income. What are the tax's implications for capital mobility, efficiency, and country A's government budget?

    c.   Illustrate the effects if country B also imposes a tax at rate $t^B = t^A$ on capital income. What are the tax's implications for capital mobility, efficiency, and for the two countries' government budgets, compared with the situation in part (b)?

    d.   Developing countries often grant tax concessions (that is, partial or complete tax exemptions) to multinational firms in an effort to attract capital inflows. What happens if country A grants concessions and country B doesn't? What happens if both countries grant concessions? Why might countries want to negotiate agreements that limit concessions they can grant to multinational firms?

5.   Explain the similarities between balanced growth and neutral technical progress. Can the welfare effects of the two differ? Why, or why not?

6.   Countries A and B, the only two countries in the world, follow free trade in goods X and Y. Country A has a comparative advantage in good X, which is labor intensive.

    a.   Compare the wage rates in the two countries under free trade.

    b.   Now country B imposes a tariff on X imports. If labor can move between countries, will the tariff create an incentive to move from A to B, from B to A, or neither? Why?

7.   Each year, labor flows from Mexico to the United States. If the United States and Mexico eliminated barriers to trade in goods and services, would you expect the migration to increase or decrease? Why? Might your answer differ for the short run and the long run? Why?

8.   Country A and Country B use labor and capital to produce a single good. Each country has the same amount of capital and the same technology. The value marginal product of labor in each country depends on how many workers are employed according to the following schedule:

Number of Workers Employed	Marginal Product of Last Worker	Price of Output	Value Marginal Product of Last Worker
1	10	$10	$100
2	9	$10	$90
3	8	$10	$80
4	7	$10	$70
5	6	$10	$60
6	5	$10	$50
7	4	$10	$40
8	3	$10	$30
9	2	$10	$20
10	1	$10	$10

Initially, there is no labor mobility, and 8 workers are employed in country A and 4 workers in country B. If labor mobility were allowed, what would happen to employment, production, and wages in each country?

REFERENCES AND SELECTED READINGS

Aghion, Philippe, and Peter Howitt. *Endogenous Growth Theory.* Cambridge, Mass.: MIT Press, 1998.
Advanced textbook on the theory of economic growth.

Barro, Robert J. *Determinants of Economic Growth.* Cambridge, Mass.: MIT Press, 1997.
Accessible overview of the recent empirical literature on economic growth.

Bhagwati, Jagdish N. "Immiserizing Growth: A Geometrical Note." *Review of Economic Studies* (June 1956): 201–205.
The original demonstration of immiserizing growth.

Bhagwati, Jagdish, and T. N. Srinivasan. "Trade and Poverty in the Poor Countries." *American Economic Review Papers and Proceedings* 92 (May 2002): 180–183.
Short version of the arguments for open trade as an antipoverty tool.

Carrington, William J., and Enrica Detragiache. "How Extensive Is the Brain Drain?" *Finance and Development* 36 (June 1999): 46–49.
How much do developing countries lose as a result of skilled workers emigrating to developed countries?

Easterly, William. *The Elusive Quest for Growth: Economists' Adventures and Misadventures in the Tropics.* Cambridge, Mass.: MIT Press, 2001.
Easy-to-read but highly informative tour of development policies.

Forbes, Kristin J. "A Reassessment of the Relationship between Inequality and Growth." *American Economic Review* 90 (September 2000): 869–887.
Advanced; finds a short-run positive effect of inequality on growth.

Frankel, Jeffrey A., and David Romer. "Does Trade Cause Growth?" *American Economic Review* 89 (June 1999): 379–399.
Strong evidence that open trade contributes to growth, not the other way around.

Graham, Edward M. *Fighting the Wrong Enemy: Antiglobal Activists and Multinational Enterprises.* Washington, D.C.: Institute for International Economics, 2000.
Readable treatment of the benefits of multinational enterprises.

Graham, Edward M., and Paul R. Krugman. *Foreign Direct Investment in the United States.* Washington, D.C.: Institute for International Economics, 1995.
Measurement and implications of foreign direct investment in the United States; for all students.

Gropp, Reint, and Kristina Kostial. "FDI and Corporate Tax Revenue: Tax Harmonization or Competition?" *Finance and Development* 38 (June 2001): 10–13.
Global patterns in tax rates.

Jones, Charles I. *Introduction to Economic Growth.* New York: Norton, 1998.
Textbook on growth theory; for intermediate to advanced students.

Lerman, Robert I. "U.S. Wage Inequality Trends and Recent Immigration." *American Economic Review Papers and Proceedings* 89 (May 1999): 23–28.
A reevaluation of immigration's effects on wages.

Loungani, Prakash, and Assaf Razin. "How Beneficial Is Foreign Direct Investment for Developing Countries?" *Finance and Development* 38 (June 2001): 6–9.
Evaluating the impact of FDI on host countries.

Markusen, James R. "The Boundaries of Multinational Enterprises and the Theory of International Trade." *Journal of Economic Perspectives* 9 (Spring 1995): 169–190.
Relationship between multinational firms and patterns of international trade; for intermediate students.

Mataloni, Raymond J., Jr. "A Guide to BEA Statistics on U.S. Multinational Companies." U.S. Department of Commerce, *Survey of Current Business* 75 (March 1995): 38–55.
Detailed guide to U.S. government statistics on multinationals.

Organization for Economic Cooperation and Development. *Migration and Regional Economic Integration in Asia.* Paris: OECD, 1998.
Introduction to recent migration trends in Asia.

O'Rourke, Kevin H., and Jeffrey G. Williamson. *Globalization and History.* Cambridge, Mass.: MIT Press, 1999.
Fascinating exploration of immigration in the nineteenth-century Atlantic economy.

Rybczynski, T. M. "Factor Endowment and Relative Commodity Prices." *Economica* 22 (November 1955): 336–341.
The original statement of the Rybczynski theorem; for intermediate students.

Schuknecht, Ludger. "A Trade Policy Perspective on Capital Controls." *Finance and Development* 36 (March 1999): 38–41.
Uses the basic trade model to illustrate the benefits of open international capital flows.

Temple, Jonathan. "The New Growth Evidence." *Journal of Economic Literature* 37 (March 1999): 112–156.
Intermediate/advanced overview of the recent empirical evidence on causes of economic growth.

Trebilock, Michael J. "The Law and Economics of Immigration Policy." *American Law and Economics Review* 5 (Fall 2003): 271–317.
Good overview of the economics, politics, and philosophy of immigration policy.

United Nations Conference on Trade and Development. *World Investment Report.* New York: United Nations, annual.
Excellent source of data on foreign direct investment.

Webb, Roy H. "National Productivity Statistics." Federal Reserve Bank of Richmond *Economic Quarterly* 84 (Winter 1998): 45–64.
An introduction to measures of productivity, changes in productivity over time, and explanations for those changes.

Wong, Kar-yiu. *International Trade in Goods and Factor Mobility.* Cambridge, Mass.: MIT Press, 1995.
Advanced international textbook emphasizing factor mobility.

World Trade Organization. *Trade and Foreign Direct Investment: Annual Report 1996,* Vol. I. Geneva: WTO, 1996.
Excellent introductory survey of theory and evidence on foreign direct investment and its relation to trade.

11

CHAPTER

Development, Transition, and Trade

1 INTRODUCTION

The basic theories of international trade developed in Chapters Two through Ten apply to countries regardless of their levels of economic development. The gains from specialization and exchange exist for Belgium and Moldova and for Singapore and Eritrea. Regardless of what country imposes them, tariffs and quotas harm domestic consumers, deny the protected industries scale economies, slow the spread of new technology, and risk creating bloated and inefficient monopoly firms with the political clout to maintain their protected status at the expense of the rest of the domestic economy.

Despite the general applicability of what we've learned about international trade, developing countries undeniably face special challenges. The post–World War II development record presents a juxtaposition of dismal failures and sparkling successes. The challenge to economists and policy makers is clear: Understand the development process well enough to explain the successes and learn to apply their lessons to remedy the failures.[1]

Consider some of the failures. Eight developing countries experienced drops of more than 5 percent in their per-capita incomes during 2001–2002: Argentina, Gambia, Guinea-Bissau, Madagascar, Uruguay, Venezuela, the West Bank and Gaza, and Zimbabwe.[2] Of course, many types of disturbances can cause short-run declines in output; but even over the long run, some countries have experienced large declines in per-capita income. During the three decades from 1965 to 1998, the Democratic Republic of the Congo (formerly Zaire), Kuwait, Nicaragua, Niger, United Arab Emirates, and Zambia each experienced an average annual decline of 2 percent or more in per-capita GNP.

Annual per-capita income in Burundi, Democratic Republic of Congo, and Ethiopia in 2002 was $100. A baby born in 2002 in Sierra Leone faced an infant-mortality rate of 165 per thousand live births and a life expectancy of 37 years. Experts estimate that 48 percent of Nepali and Bangladeshi children under five years old suffered from malnutrition during 2002. Only 8 percent of Rwanda's population had access to sanitation in 2000, and only 13 percent of Afghanis had access to safe drinking water. In 2002, 92 percent of adult women in Burkina Faso could not read; only 23 percent of primary-school-age children in Afghanistan attended school. Measured by the World Bank's standard—living on less than $1 per day—1.1 billion people in 2001 endured extreme poverty.

Despite these clear indicators of past failures and future challenges, the development record isn't uniformly bleak. Five developing economies—Angola, Armenia, Kazakhstan,

---

1. See World Bank, *Globalization, Growth, and Poverty*.

2. Data come from the World Bank's *World Development Indicators*.

Serbia and Montenegro, and Turkmenistan—increased their per-capita incomes by more than 10 percent during 2001–2002. Botswana, China, Hong Kong, South Korea, Oman, Singapore, and Thailand each experienced average annual per-capita income growth of 5 percent or more for the three decades from 1965 through 1998. Between 1970 and 2002, infant mortality in the low-income economies fell from 113 per thousand live births to 79. Life expectancy at birth in the low-income economies rose from 53 years to 59 years between 1980 and 2002. Many other indicators of well-being show similar gains. Developing countries as a group, and even the 64 low-income ones, have made dramatic progress. A handful of countries have done so to the point that the term *developing* no longer seems to fit.

In this chapter, we focus on the trade-related issues facing developing countries. First, we define and evaluate the magnitude of the development task. Next, we highlight several distinct subgroups of developing countries that face somewhat different sets of problems and concerns. Finally, we outline the experience and prospects of both traditional developing economies and the economies in transition from central planning.

2 DEFINING DEVELOPMENT

The ultimate goal of a country's development process is to improve its residents' well-being, but there's neither an indisputable definition of economic development nor an unambiguous standard by which to measure a country's development status.

Per-capita gross national product or income represents the most widely used single indicator of development. **Gross national product (GNP)** measures the value of a country's yearly output.[3] International organizations divide countries into several development groups based on per-capita income, or GNP divided by population. The World Bank classifies countries into "high-income economies" with annual per-capita incomes above $9,076 in 2002, "upper-middle-income economies" with per-capita incomes between $2,936 and $9,075, "lower-middle-income economies" with per-capita incomes between $736 and $2,935, and "low-income economies" with per-capita incomes below $735. That 2.5 billion people live in low-income economies, while only 966 million live in high-income ones, highlights the magnitude of the development task.

As an indicator of development, per-capita GNP is far from perfect. First, it fails to account for variation in the scope of market transactions in different economies. Economic transactions typically count in GNP only if they occur in an organized market. As a country develops, an increasingly large share of its economic activity typically moves into organized markets; for example, commercially bought food and restaurant meals often replace home-grown and prepared food. Therefore, much of the economic activity in developing countries can fail to show up in per-capita GNP figures, causing those figures to overestimate the gap between developing and developed countries.

A second shortcoming of differences in per-capita income as an indicator of development is that such differences, dramatic as they are, fail to capture many issues relevant to development. For example, average infant mortality and life expectancy at birth in low-income countries are 79 per thousand and 59 years, respectively, compared with 5 per thousand and 79 years in the high-income countries. A third weakness of focusing exclusively on per-capita income as a development indicator is that it fails to indicate the distribution of income across the population.

Table 1 reports countries' 2002 per-capita incomes, 2002 child-mortality rates, and Gini indices, a measure of how equally income is distributed across the population. The Gini index varies from zero to one hundred; a value of zero indicates a perfectly equal income distribution (every individual has income equal to per-capita income), and a value of

---

3. More precisely, gross national product is the sum of the current market values of all currently produced final goods and services over a specified time period, such as one year.

Table 1   **PER-CAPITA INCOME, INFANT MORTALITY, AND GINI INDEX OF INCOME DISTRIBUTION**

Country	Per-Capita Income, 2002 ($)	Under-5 Mortality per 1,000 Live Births, 2002	Gini Index	Country	Per-Capita Income, 2002 ($)	Under-5 Mortality per 1,000 Live Births, 2002	Gini Index
Afghanistan	n.a.	257	n.a.	Eritrea	190	80	n.a.
Albania	$1,450	24	28.2	Estonia	4,190	12	37.2
Algeria	1,720	49	35.3	Ethiopia	100	171	30.0
Angola	710	260	n.a.	Finland	23,890	5	26.9
Argentina	4,220	19	52.2	France	22,240	6	32.7
Armenia	790	35	37.9	Gabon	3,060	85	n.a.
Australia	19,530	6	35.2	Gambia	270	126	38.0
Austria	23,860	5	30.0	Georgia	650	29	36.9
Azerbaijan	710	96	36.5	Germany	22,740	5	28.3
Bangladesh	380	73	31.8	Ghana	270	97	30.0
Belarus	1,360	20	30.4	Greece	11,660	5	35.4
Belgium	22,940	6	25.0	Guatemala	1,760	49	48.3
Benin	380	151	n.a.	Guinea	410	165	40.3
Bolivia	900	71	44.7	Guinea-Bissau	130	211	47.0
Bosnia	1,310	18	26.2	Guyana	n.a.	n.a.	43.2
Botswana	3,010	110	63.0	Haiti	440	123	n.a.
Brazil	2,830	37	59.1	Honduras	930	42	55.0
Bulgaria	1,770	16	31.9	Hungary	5,290	9	24.4
Burkina Faso	250	207	48.2	India	470	90	32.5
Burundi	100	208	33.3	Indonesia	710	43	34.3
Cambodia	300	138	40.4	Iran, Islamic R.	1,720	41	43.0
Cameroon	550	166	44.6	Iraq	n.a.	125	n.a.
Canada	22,390	7	31.1	Ireland	23,030	6	35.9
C. African Rep.	250	180	61.3	Israel	16,020	6	35.5
Chad	210	200	n.a.	Italy	19,080	6	36.0
Chile	4,250	12	57.1	Jamaica	2,690	· 20	37.9
China	960	38	44.7	Japan	34,010	5	24.9
Hong Kong	24,690	n.a.	43.4	Jordan	1,760	33	36.4
Colombia	1,820	23	57.6	Kazakhstan	1,520	99	31.3
Congo, D. Rep.	100	205	n.a.	Kenya	360	122	44.5
Congo, Rep.	610	108	n.a.	Korea, Dem Rep.	n.a.	55	n.a.
Costa Rica	4,070	11	46.5	Korea, Rep.	9,930	5	31.6
Côte d'Ivoire	620	191	45.2	Kuwait	16,340	10	n.a.
Croatia	4,540	8	29.0	Kyrgyz Rep.	290	61	29.0
Cuba	n.a.	9	n.a.	Lao, PDR	310	100	37.0
Czech Rep.	5,480	5	25.4	Latvia	3,480	21	32.4
Denmark	30,260	4	24.7	Lebanon	3,990	32	n.a.
Dominican Rep.	n.a.	38	47.4	Lesotho	550	132	63.2
Ecuador	1,490	29	43.7	Liberia	140	235	n.a.
Egypt	1,470	39	34.4	Libya	n.a.	19	n.a.
El Salvador	2,110	39	53.2	Lithuania	3,670	9	31.9

(continues)

Table 1 *(continued)*

Country	Per-Capita Income, 2002 ($)	Under-5 Mortality per 1,000 Live Births, 2002	Gini Index	Country	Per-Capita Income, 2002 ($)	Under-5 Mortality per 1,000 Live Births, 2002	Gini Index
Madagascar	230	135	47.5	Luxembourg	n.a.	n.a.	30.8
Malawi	160	182	50.3	Macedonia	1,710	26	28.2
Malaysia	3,540	8	49.2	Singapore	20,690	4	42.5
Mali	240	222	50.5	Slovak Rep.	3,970	9	25.8
Mauritania	280	183	39.0	Slovenia	10,370	5	28.4
Mauritius	3,860	19	n.a.	Somalia	n.a.	225	n.a.
Mexico	5,920	29	54.6	South Africa	2,500	65	59.3
Moldova	460	32	36.2	Spain	14,580	6	32.5
Mongolia	430	71	44.0	Sri Lanka	850	19	34.4
Morocco	1,170	43	39.5	St. Lucia	n.a.	n.a.	42.6
Mozambique	200	205	39.6	Sudan	370	94	n.a.
Myanmar	n.a.	108	n.a.	Swaziland	1,240	149	60.9
Namibia	1,790	67	70.7	Sweden	25,970	3	25.0
Nepal	230	83	36.7	Switzerland	36,170	6	33.1
Netherlands	23,390	5	32.6	Syria	1,130	28	n.a.
New Zealand	13,260	6	36.2	Tajikistan	180	116	34.7
Nicaragua	710	41	55.1	Tanzania	290	165	38.2
Niger	180	264	50.5	Thailand	2,000	28	43.2
Nigeria	300	201	50.6	Togo	270	140	n.a.
Norway	38,730	4	25.8	Trinidad/ Tobago	6,750	20	40.3
Oman	7,830	13	n.a.	Tunisia	1,990	26	39.8
Pakistan	420	101	33.0	Turkey	2,490	41	40.0
Panama	4,020	25	56.4	Turkmenistan	n.a.	86	40.8
P. New Guinea	530	94	50.9	Uganda	240	141	43.0
Paraguay	1,170	30	56.8	Ukraine	780	20	29.0
Peru	2,020	39	49.8	U. Arab Emirates	n.a.	9	n.a.
Philippines	1,030	37	46.1	United Kingdom	25,510	7	36.0
Poland	4,570	9	31.6	United States	35,400	8	40.8
Portugal	10,720	6	38.5	Uruguay	4,340	15	44.6
Romania	1,870	21	30.3	Uzbekistan	310	65	26.8
Russia	2,130	21	45.6	Venezuela	4,080	22	49.1
Rwanda	230	203	28.9	Vietnam	430	26	36.1
Saudi Arabia	8,530	28	n.a.	W. Bank and Gaza	1,110	n.a.	n.a.
Senegal	470	138	41.3	Yemen, Rep.	490	114	33.4
Serbia	1,400	19	n.a.	Zambia	340	182	52.6
Sierra Leone	140	284	62.9	Zimbabwe	n.a.	123	56.8

Source: Data from World Bank, *World Development Indicators.*

one hundred denotes the extreme of unequal distribution (one individual receives all the income). For the countries reported, the Gini index varies from Hungary's 24.4, where the highest-income 20 percent of the population earns 38 percent of all income, to Namibia's 70.7, where the highest-income 20 percent of the population earns 79 percent of all income.

Table 1 reveals that individual countries often fare quite differently in terms of different indicators of well-being; some enjoy high per-capita income although other indicators of well-being lag, while others exhibit the opposite pattern. Compare, for example, Botswana and Brazil. Per-capita incomes are very similar, yet Botswana's infant-mortality rate is almost three times as high as Brazil's. Or, consider Kazakhstan and Laos. Although Kazakhstan's income equals almost five times Laos's, the two countries have almost identical infant-mortality rates.

Lumping all low- and middle-income economies together under the rubric "developing countries" conceals important differences, both in the well-being of their residents and in the trade-related issues of primary concern to policy makers in the various countries. Table 2 divides the low- and middle-income economies by region and reports their basic development indicators.

Note the differences revealed in Table 2. Sub-Saharan Africa suffers low per-capita GNP, negative long-term growth rates, short life expectancy, and high illiteracy. The East Asia region, on the other hand, although per-capita GNP remains low, has enjoyed very rapid long-term economic growth along with life expectancy that approaches that in high-income economies; but illiteracy remains high. Latin America and the Caribbean enjoy the highest incomes among developing countries, as well as long life expectancy and low rates of illiteracy, but their low long-term growth rate reveals continuing economic difficulties. The Middle East and North Africa stand out for their lack of growth and high illiteracy rates.

Increases in per-capita income are essential to the development process. Even small differences in rates of economic growth can substantially alter the length of time required to, say, double a country's per-capita income. Table 3 provides a rough rule for the relationship between growth rates and length of time required to double income: To find the years required to double income, divide the growth rate (measured in percent per year) into 70. Consider the implications. The growth rate of 2.2 percent recorded by low- and middle-income developing countries as a group between 1965 and 1998 (from Table 2) produces a doubling of income in approximately 32 years. Growing instead at the 5.7 percent rate

Table 2   LOW- AND MIDDLE-INCOME ECONOMIES' DEVELOPMENT INDICATORS

Country group	GNP per Capita 2002 ($)	Annual Growth, 1965–1998 (Percent)	Life Expectancy, 2002	Adult Female Illiteracy, 2002 (Percent)
All low income	$ 430	3.7%	59	47%
All middle income	1,850	1.9	70	17
Lower middle income	1,400	n.a.	69	18
Upper middle income	5,110	2.2	73	8
All low- and middle-income	1,170	2.2	65	30
Sub-Saharan Africa	450	−0.3	46	44
East Asia and Pacific	960	5.7	69	18
South Asia	460	2.7	63	56
Europe and Central Asia	2,160	n.a.	69	4
Middle East and North Africa	2,240	0.2	69	45
Latin America and Caribbean	3,280	1.3	71	11

Source: The World Bank, *World Development Indicators.*

Table 3	**GROWTH RATES AND LENGTH OF TIME REQUIRED TO DOUBLE INCOME**		
Growth Rate (%)	Approximate Years to Double Income	Growth Rate (%)	Approximate Years to Double Income
1%	70	6%	12
2	35	7	10
3	24	8	9
4	18	9	8
5	14	10	7

experienced by the East Asian and Pacific economies doubles incomes in about 12 years. Achieving even the more modest goal of boosting growth from 2.2 percent to 3.2 percent would cut the doubling period from 32 years to 22. With a life expectancy in the mid-60s, this is enough to change an individual's life experience from one in which per-capita income increases by a factor of four to one in which it increases by a factor of eight.

3 DEVELOPMENT ISSUES

Since the 1940s, when developing economies began to achieve political independence in large numbers, policies to foster economic development have been an area of active research, both theoretical and empirical. Individual countries have followed a variety of policies in their efforts to develop; as we've seen, the results have been mixed. Some, such as Taiwan, South Korea, Hong Kong, and Singapore, have achieved economic success that even the high-income economies envy. Others, including many in sub-Saharan Africa, continue to suffer severe economic deprivation.

Nonetheless, developing countries as a group have shared some commonalities. Historically, most followed policies that favored the industrialized sectors of their economies over primary-product production, for reasons we explore later. Most isolated themselves, at least to some degree, from the international trading system. And the state dominated the typical developing-country economy, enforcing elaborate protection and trade-control schemes, managing huge state-owned enterprises, deciding which firms got funds for new investment projects, and administering detailed "plans" for the country's development.

Many economists and policy makers believed during the 1950s and 1960s that the fundamental results of international trade theory didn't apply to developing economies as they did to developed ones, because the basic structure of developing economies was different. Policy makers from most developing countries argued that their undeveloped status warranted special assistance from the developed economies and fundamental changes in the international trading system. These calls for change became known as the **North–South debate**, because most developed economies lie in the Northern Hemisphere temperate zone.[4]

The developing economies' divergent experience during the past 25 years, especially the impressive growth and industrialization of several Asian economies, has made developing countries' policy concerns and interests more diverse, as the more successful economies have come to hold more in common with the high-income economies than

---

4. Bloom and Sachs (1998) argue that a tropical location presents a very high hurdle to economic growth.

with the least-developed ones. In addition to these changes, advances in economists' understanding of the development process have produced a new consensus that, despite lively disagreements over details, accepts two basic points: (1) International trade theory *does* apply to developing countries, and (2) the market-based international trade system benefits developing countries that choose to participate and contributes in many complex and subtle ways to successful development.

We can organize our discussion around five basic trade-related issues that have played central roles in policy debates. As the developing countries' experiences have diverged, some of the issues remain more salient for some countries than for others.

1. What is the proper role of agriculture and other primary-product sectors in a developing economy, and what are appropriate policies toward those sectors? Until the 1970s, most developing countries specialized in primary products, including agriculture, metals, and minerals; a large number still do.
2. What is the appropriate role of industrialization in development, and what policies can achieve the desired goals? Historically, most developing-country policy makers viewed economic development as synonymous with industrialization. We'll see that, in their attempts to industrialize, economies have followed two alternate strategies: inward-oriented import substitution and outward-oriented development, which differ dramatically in their focus on industrialization and in their policies toward trade.
3. How can countries with modest resources gain access to new productivity-enhancing technologies? Developing countries' low incomes limit the resources available to spend on research and development. One possible shortcut involves borrowing and adapting technology from more advanced economies, but the international system of patents and the monopoly power held by some technologically innovative firms constrains such borrowing. On the other hand, industries in the industrialized economies—semiconductors, movies, and computer software, for example—claim that they lose millions in revenues as a result of unauthorized copying of their products by counterfeiters based in developing economies.
4. How can developing countries borrow to gain the advantages of intertemporal trade without encountering debt crises of the type that made the 1980s a "lost decade" in terms of growth for many borrowers? Many developing countries continue to exhibit very low saving rates, making them dependent on foreign borrowing to finance investment. They still face the problem of how to maintain policies that create enough confidence in their economies' future performance to allow them to borrow to finance development-related investment.
5. To what extent is there an inevitable trade-off between economic growth and environmental quality? High-income developed economies (not to mention vocal "anti-globalization" activists) press the developing economies to adopt more stringent environmental protections. Developing countries guard their right to exploit their resources as they see fit, despite developed countries' wishes to restrict practices, such as cutting of tropical rain forests, which may have global climatic consequences.

4 AGRICULTURE, INDUSTRY, OR BOTH?

There are few areas of economics in which the views held by most economists have changed more than in the field of development.[5] During the 1950s and 1960s, certain stylized facts about developing economies and the nature of the world economy, now recognized as erroneous and misleading, were widely accepted. Also, many important elements of the

---

5. This section draws on Krueger (1997) and Bruton (1998).

relevant international economic theory (for example, the effective rate of protection, the superiority of subsidies over protection for dealing with domestic distortions, and the analysis of trade policy with economies of scale) had not yet been discovered.

4.1 Views on Development, Circa 1950–1965

The central stylized fact of development economics during the 1950s and early 1960s was the belief that poor developing economies were fundamentally and structurally different from rich developed ones. The two primary aspects of difference centered on the relationships between agriculture and manufacturing and between capital and labor.

Developing economies were seen as prisoners of their dependence on agriculture and other primary products and their corresponding dependence on imported manufactured goods from the developed countries. All agriculture was perceived as labor intensive and all manufacturing as capital intensive, while developing economies typically were labor abundant and developed ones capital abundant. Many economists and policy makers drew the inference that specialization and trade according to comparative advantage would make developing economies permanent agricultural producers. Developing countries also claimed that their terms of trade deteriorated over time as prices of the primary products they exported fell relative to those of the manufactured goods they imported.[6] Given these views, the conclusion was that international trade according to comparative advantage would condemn developing economies to permanently low and erratic export earnings and incomes because of their specialization in agriculture and other primary products.

Developing countries were also thought to have far too much labor—so much that its marginal product was low or even zero—and far too little capital. Economists believed that the traditional structure and culture of labor-abundant, agriculturally oriented economies made them unresponsive to prices, incentives, and other market forces. This implied that development, which was thought to require an escape from dependence on agriculture, could only be brought about by dramatic government policies that forced the economies out of their traditional *status quo*. Most important were government policies to encourage capital-good imports that could support domestic manufacturing at the expense of agriculture and thereby change the fundamental structure of developing economies to one more like that of the developed economies—capital abundant and dominated by manufacturing.

4.2 Import Substitution

Economic historians often call international trade the "engine of growth." Historically, periods of rapid growth in international trade have corresponded with periods of rapid increases in world output. Nonetheless, until recently most developing countries sought to limit their exposure to the world trading system by following an **import-substitution** development strategy, which involved extensive use of trade barriers to protect domestic industries from import competition. Import substitution focused on eliminating imported manufactures and encouraging the growth of domestic manufacturing. Many developing countries followed import-substitution policies during the 1950s and 1960s, and a few continue to do so.

The policies' logic followed directly from the stylized facts discussed earlier. If industrialization was necessary for development and if free trade would leave developing countries specialized in agriculture, then government policy had to generate investment in new manufacturing industries. The infant-industry argument for protection, outlined in Chapter Eight, also played an important role in import substitution. If mature

---

6. A country's terms of trade consist of the price of the country's export good(s) relative to the price of its import good(s). A rise in this ratio is an improvement in the terms of trade and a fall is a deterioration.

manufacturing industries already existed in the developed countries, potential entrants from developing economies couldn't compete in the short run with those established competitors. Temporary infant-industry protection, however, might support new developing-country firms; those firms could eventually become competitive, at which time government could remove the protection.

The precise form and extent of import substitution differed from country to country. Brazil's "Law of Similars" declared that firms that imported goods similar to ones produced domestically would lose their access to government credit, tax privileges, and right to bid on government contracts. In India, all imports required a license (the so-called "License Raj"), and firms petitioning for one had to provide a letter from all potential domestic suppliers explaining why the domestic firms couldn't meet the specifications. Turkey maintained a list of goods for which import licenses could be granted; once domestic production of an item began, the good was removed from the list. In other words, imports that competed with domestic goods were effectively banned.

Because the import-substitution policy package emphasized production of manufactured goods for the domestic market (that is, to substitute for imports), the policies penalized the agricultural and export sectors of the economy. These sectors were often taxed, denied access to credit, and refused permits for imported inputs they needed. In many cases, for example, import barriers restricted farmers' access to new agricultural technology and to productivity-enhancing improvements such as tractors and improved seed varieties. Governments maintained monopolies in farm products and forced farmers to sell to those monopolies at prices far below market levels, discouraging production. Again, the logic could be found in the accepted stylized facts about developing economies, the nature of markets, and the development process. If the structure of agriculture made it a dead end, and if the static nature of traditional societies made them unresponsive to prices and other incentives, then development policy needed to shrink that sector and shift resources into manufacturing. Domestic politics also contributed to these counterproductive agricultural policies in many countries because small-scale rural farmers typically possessed little political influence compared with urban elites who benefited from low food prices and generous government assistance to manufacturing.

4.3 As The World Learns: Changing Views on Development

Since about 1965, the views of most economists and policy makers on the development process have changed dramatically. Many of the stylized facts accepted earlier have now been recognized as incomplete, irrelevant, or just plain wrong.

Developing economies do differ from developed ones—in their capital-labor ratios, their histories and political institutions, and their endowments of expertise and entrepreneurship. However, *developing economies respond to prices and incentives and can benefit from international trade based on comparative advantage or economies of scale just as developed economies do.*

Countries' comparative advantages evolve over time, and developing economies can and do specialize in manufacturing. The agricultural and manufacturing sectors each contain goods whose production is labor intensive (for example, rice and apparel) and products whose production is capital intensive (for example, wheat and aircraft). The comparative advantage for labor-abundant developing economies lies in labor-intensive agricultural products *and* labor-intensive manufactures; the comparative advantage for capital-abundant developed economies is in capital-intensive agricultural products *and* capital-intensive manufactures. Therefore, labor abundance doesn't imply a comparative advantage in agriculture and a comparative disadvantage in manufacturing, as had been thought earlier. Similarly, investment in education, skills, and human capital allow developing economies to alter their factor endowments and shift their comparative advantage toward more skill- and technology-intensive products.

The presumed long-run deterioration of developing countries' terms of trade also turned out to be wrong. Empirical investigations have demonstrated that developing countries' terms of trade exhibit little or no long-run tendency to decline. Periods of decline, such as the 1980s, certainly do occur and make the development process more difficult. Countries that depend on one or a few export products, such as the oil-exporting developing countries, can experience dramatic shifts in their terms of trade. But the earlier presumption of a permanent downward trend in the terms of trade for all developing countries involved in primary-product markets was simply mistaken.

THE FAILURE OF IMPORT SUBSTITUTION   Evidence suggests that forgoing gains from trade to develop domestic manufacturing industries through import substitution does *not* constitute a promising development strategy; in fact, the results of import substitution disappointed, exactly as our basic trade model would lead us to expect.

Several problems contributed to the apparent failure of many import-substitution programs. Most important, the infant-industry argument, as we saw in Chapter Eight, suffers from serious weaknesses. A period of temporary government support is no substitute for comparative advantage, and an industry without comparative advantage will remain an infant forever. In many developing economies, shortages of skilled labor, experienced management, clear and well-enforced property rights and contract law, and entrepreneurship hampered the emergence of successful industrial enterprises. Under these circumstances, an import-substitution policy based on import barriers simply guaranteed the continued existence of an inefficient domestic industry, often a monopoly—at the expense of domestic consumers and taxpayers. To make matters worse, many of the developing countries that pursued import substitution most aggressively were small, so their attempts to develop manufacturing based solely on the domestic market doomed firms to produce at inefficiently small scale.

Import substitution also failed for reasons having as much to do with politics as with economics. The strategy's emphasis on manufacturing tempted many developing economies to pour vast resources into building highly visible and symbolic national industries, such as steel, autos, chemicals, and national airlines, without regard for comparative advantage or economies of scale. Active involvement by governments in favoring some sectors of the economy over others asked governments to predict which industries would succeed. Such predictions run a high risk of failure as patterns of comparative advantage change. Even in Japan, a success story overall, the industries that proved most successful often weren't the ones favored by the government during the years of import substitution in the 1950s and 1960s, as we saw in Case Four in Chapter Eight. Governments often failed in the task of choosing industries to support because they picked in part based on special-interest groups' political pressure for protection rather than on economic analysis. Political factors also made the switch away from import substitution difficult, even after the strategy's failure became apparent. Capital owners and workers in industries created by import-substitution policies were potent political forces to block a shift toward other development strategies. And, since import-substitution policies placed so much power in the hands of government planners and bureaucrats, they often proved understandably reluctant to move toward more market-oriented policies that would reduce their control and prestige.

Somewhat more surprising than its other shortcomings is the fact that import substitution failed to decrease dependence on imports. By artificially encouraging industrialization even in areas of comparative disadvantage, import substitution actually increased dependence on the imported inputs and capital goods required to keep production going in the protected industries. Because of the inefficient nature of many of the manufacturing processes, the value of these imports often exceeded that of the finished manufactured goods imported before institution of an import-substitution policy. The inefficiencies of import-substitution policies multiplied when the chosen industries exhibited economies of scale, because the domestic market typically was too small to support production at a scale sufficient to achieve those economies.

The import-substitution blueprint for development involved an attempt to replicate developed economies with their high capital-labor ratios and dominant manufacturing sectors. When developing countries emphasized *capital*-intensive production despite their *labor* abundance, they suffered high unemployment and chronically low wages and incomes. Low domestic income, in turn, limited the domestic market for the manufactured goods that governments so carefully cultivated. The protected industries couldn't export—because of their comparative disadvantage, but had little domestic market.

LESSONS FROM THE NEWLY INDUSTRIALIZING COUNTRIES Some developing economies switched away from import substitution early (Taiwan was among the first) and opened their economies to trade. Details differed from country to country, but common elements included reducing import protection, removing policy biases against exports and agriculture, and allowing manufacturers to produce for export as well as for the domestic market. Economies that made these policy shifts enjoyed remarkable rates of economic growth and industrialization. Some, including Taiwan, South Korea, Hong Kong, and Singapore, earned the name **newly industrializing countries (NICs)** for their swift move along the development path.

Most indicators suggest that these economies now have more in common with the developed countries than with the low-income developing ones, as Table 4 reports. They built major export industries including steel, shipbuilding, chemicals, semiconductors, and computers. They undertook foreign investment projects in Asia, as well as in the United States and Europe. They even started financing foreign-aid projects in less-developed economies. Observing these countries' successes helped to change attitudes about development, because their experience challenged old assumptions—such as the ones about developing countries' alleged permanent condemnation to agriculture and inability to build export industries.

Scholars and policy makers debate the precise reasons for the NICs' successes. In particular, disagreement persists concerning the extent to which the governments directed investment to specific industries (that is, "picked winners"). Most analysts agree, however, that the key was the shift away from import substitution toward policies that opened the economy to international trade, foreign investment, foreign competition, and new technology and know-how. The new policies respected patterns of comparative advantage, the importance of achieving economies of scale, and the role for exports.

Table 4 **NEWLY INDUSTRIALIZING COUNTRIES' ECONOMIC INDICATORS, 2003**

Country	Per-Capita GDP, ($ at Purchasing Power Parity)	Exports (Billions $)	Imports (Billions $)	Male Life Expectancy at Birth
Hong Kong	$28,700	$225.9	$230.3	79
Singapore	23,700	142.4	121.6	79
South Korea	17,700	201.3	175.6	72
Taiwan	23,400	143.0	119.6	74

Source: Central Intelligence Agency, *World Factbook* (available at http://www.cia.org).

4.4 Outward-Oriented Development

As we've seen, industrialization traditionally has been viewed as a crucial step in the process of economic development. The record of success in industrialization varies. The United States and Japan were, not too many years ago, developing countries and now are industrial giants in the world economy. More recent years have seen other success stories, including Taiwan, South Korea, and Brazil. The experiences of other countries, such as India and many in sub-Saharan Africa, have been less encouraging, sometimes for obvious reasons and sometimes for less obvious ones. Overall, the developing countries' shares of production and export of manufactures have increased significantly over the past three decades; but most of the early growth has come in middle-income developing countries rather than low-income ones.

One of the most dramatic events in the world economy during the 1980s was the shift of many developing countries from inward-looking import-substitution policies to more outward-oriented policies that recognized a role for exports. **Outward-oriented growth** is best characterized as open to the world economy. This development strategy involves exploiting comparative advantage and economies of scale and importing goods costly to produce domestically. Industrialization for its own sake receives less emphasis here than under an import-substitution policy. Countries specialize production along the lines dictated by their comparative advantage, which may be resource based, and in sectors where export success can allow them to achieve economies of scale. Industrialization is a natural outcome of the overall development process rather than a goal pursued for its own sake.

To understand the differential success of import-substitution and outward-oriented development strategies, recall how early chapters of this book emphasized the importance of market-determined prices in guiding resources to their highest-valued use. An inward-oriented strategy, or import substitution, involves circumventing market forces to alter prices and encourage domestic manufacturing regardless of the pattern of comparative advantage and without regard to the prospects for achieving economies of scale. Such a strategy typically involves extensive use of tariffs, quotas, and import-licensing schemes, often justified by appeals to the infant-industry argument for protection (see section 3 in Chapter Eight). The second strategy, an outward-oriented one, stresses specialization according to comparative advantage and reliance on sectors where firms can achieve economies of scale rather than an attempt at artificially induced industrialization.

4.5 Lessons

Few economists today expect or recommend a return to policies like import substitution. Most now agree that openness plays complex and essential roles in development: It provides access to consumer goods, new technology, and managerial and entrepreneurial resources; and it provides domestic firms with market discipline, incentives to reduce costs, and motivation to innovate as they face competition from foreign firms.

Despite these broad areas of new consensus, areas of disagreement remain. Critics of the enthusiasm for outward-oriented development strategies emphasize the daunting difficulty of the development task and caution that mere openness to international trade, while it may facilitate that task, can hardly transform it into a quick and simple one. Successful development requires sound policies, implemented effectively from a base of good information. Important resources include not just labor and capital, but human skills, policy competence, entrepreneurship, the ability to learn and adapt, credible and trustworthy business and government institutions, and an understanding of each economy's unique history, politics, and culture. Given this demanding recipe, in which openness to international trade is just one of many important ingredients, it seems likely that the development record will continue to be a mixed one.

5 NORTH–SOUTH ISSUES

Thus far, we've focused on developing countries' own policies and how they affect the prospects for successful development. But, of course, external considerations such as the health of the overall world economy and the policies followed by developed countries and international organizations also affect developing economies. Sometimes developing countries want developed ones to change their policies or want international organizations to allow them special privileges because of the difficult development tasks they face. Three specific areas of ongoing disagreement and negotiation concern agricultural policy, technology-transfer and intellectual-property issues, and the environment.

5.1 Agricultural Policy

Recall that the main goal of import substitution involved shifting resources out of the traditional agricultural sector and into manufacturing. Import-substitution policies discriminated against agriculture in many ways. Agricultural prices were kept artificially low, which discouraged production. It also kept incomes low for the majority of the population, which limited domestic demand for new, domestically produced manufactured goods. Workers who lacked the skills to work in industry became unemployed as the agricultural sector stagnated or shrank. As the severe long-run distortions caused by import-substitution policies came to be recognized, developing economies and their advisors also began to appreciate the important roles for agriculture in a developing economy—even one that hopes eventually to become more involved in manufacturing.

When developing economies switched their policies to ones that respected their comparative advantage in agriculture and began to try to export agricultural products, they found that developed countries' agricultural policies limited the developing countries' abilities to export primary products. In the developed countries, agricultural policies have primarily domestic goals, including raising agricultural prices and supporting domestic farmers' incomes. However, as we saw in Chapters Seven and Eight, these domestic policies often require trade-policy supplements, especially import quotas and export subsidies. Unfortunately, these developed-country agricultural policies seemed to ignore the impact on developing countries.

A second aspect of developed countries' agricultural policies makes it more difficult for developing-country agricultural producers to move into refining and processing of their agricultural products. We saw in section 8 of Chapter Six that the **effective rate of protection (ERP)** provided by a given nominal tariff on a finished product depends on the tariffs levied on inputs used in producing it. The lower the tariffs on inputs, other things equal, the higher the rate of protection on the finished good. The developed countries' practice of **cascading tariffs**, or **tariff escalation**, imposes increasing tariff rates as a good moves through the stages of production; tariffs are lowest on raw materials and highest on finished goods. The result is often an effective rate of protection on processed and finished goods several times their nominal tariff rates. In reaching developed-country markets, developing countries face increasingly high barriers as they attempt to move into processing and manufacturing.

These agriculture-related issues have ranked high on developing countries' lists of concerns about the world trading system since the 1980s. The beginning of the Uruguay Round of GATT talks in 1986 involved special attempts to encourage active participation by developing countries, and the debates over agricultural policy played a key role. Earlier GATT rounds had ignored agricultural trade, although it was a major concern of developing countries and a major source of trade disputes, because the developed economies didn't want to face the domestic political consequences of changing their highly protectionist agricultural policies. Early in the Uruguay Round, developed countries promised to include agriculture in the talks in exchange for developing countries' active participation and their consent to include trade liberalization in services on the agenda as well.

In the end, the Uruguay Round made progress in agricultural reform. Several of the changes enhanced developing countries' access to export markets in the developed countries. WTO members no longer could grant new export subsidies on agricultural goods. Developed countries were given six years to cut their existing export subsidies by 36 percent, and each country's volume of subsidized exports had to fall by 21 percent. Developing countries were required to institute similar changes, but at rates of 24 percent and 14 percent on the amount and volume of subsidies, respectively. Countries were required to reduce their aggregate domestic subsidies to farmers by 20 percent.

The Uruguay Round agreement also required developed member countries to convert all nontariff barriers into their tariff equivalents, which then became subject to the negotiated schedule of tariff reductions—of 36 percent over six years. However, it is clear that even after the 36 percent reductions, agricultural tariffs by developed countries are still very high, much higher than those on manufactured goods. The Uruguay Round agreement required developing countries to convert their nontariff barriers to tariffs and then cut those tariffs, but with cuts of 24 percent over 10 years. For the least-developed economies, the agreement required binding agricultural tariffs at current levels, but no cuts. Markets subject to prohibitive quotas, such as the Japanese rice market, had to provide minimum access to imports. In addition, the agreement reduced cascading tariffs.

Developing countries' agricultural wish list for the ongoing Doha round of WTO negotiations hasn't changed much since the Uruguay Round: reduce developed-country barriers against agricultural imports and cut developed countries' agricultural export subsidies. The political opposition to these changes hasn't shifted much either. European Union opposition to changes in its subsidy-based Common Agricultural Policy remains strong, especially in France; and a recent U.S. farm bill, passed in 2002, moved U.S. agricultural policy in a pro-protection direction, reversing several years of progress in liberalizing American farm trade. Doha Round talks already have broken down at several points due to impasses between developing-country demands for freer international agricultural trade and developed-country reluctance to reduce protection. Developing economies got an important boost for their Doha demands in 2004 when the World Trade Organization, in two high-profile disputes, ruled that U.S. cotton subsidies and EU sugar subsidies violated WTO commitments. Midway through the negotiation process, the tentative framework for a Doha agreement includes elimination of agricultural export subsidies and substantial cuts in developed countries' agricultural production subsidies and other policies that distort trade in agriculture.

5.2 Technology, Intellectual Property, and Development

Technology, viewed from the economist's perspective, is simply the set of rules that govern how inputs can be transformed into goods and services. Improvements in technology allow more goods and services to be produced from the same quantity of inputs, or the same quantity of goods and services to be produced from a smaller quantity of inputs. Technological improvement contributes to economic development by increasing the output a country can produce given its resource endowment.[7]

The research and development (R&D) process that leads to technological innovations is long, expensive, risky, and skill intensive. It's also subject to economies of scale, implying that R&D on a small scale is inefficient. These characteristics of the R&D process make it difficult for developing countries to create their own indigenous technologies, resulting in dependence on the developed world for technological innovation.

---

7. Section 3 in Chapter Ten analyzed the effect of technical progress on economic growth.

TECHNOLOGY TRANSFER AND APPROPRIATENESS Developing economies point to two aspects of current technology arrangements that they believe work to their disadvantage. The first is the terms on which developing-country firms can gain access to new technologies, often through multinational enterprises. The second issue concerns the nature of the technology itself and its appropriateness for developing countries.

In the industrial market economies, where most technological innovation historically has taken place, private firms typically conduct most research, spurred by the promise of profit from any forthcoming innovations. An international system of patents—legal restrictions on uncompensated use of technology developed by others—protects technology from being freely copied, a protection that allows firms engaged in research to capture the return necessary to justify their costly R&D efforts. If a newly developed innovation were freely available to all, research might slow as the incentive to innovate evaporated.

The prices firms charge for licenses to use their new technologies do slow the spread of technology from developed to developing countries. In the past, many multinational enterprises maintained their technologically innovative research-and-development divisions in their home countries and restricted the degree of **technology transfer** to their foreign subsidiaries. Critics of multinationals claimed that these policies prevented developing countries from using the technologies to advance the rest of their economies. However, as we saw in Chapter Ten, multinational firms increasingly use their newest techniques in foreign plants and conduct research there. The distinction between typical parent-country activities and typical host-country activities is fading for most multinationals as they move toward true global production, at least in countries with policies in place to control counterfeiting and piracy.

The more relevant question isn't whether developing economies would benefit if given free access to all technology created by developed-country firms (an unlikely scenario), but whether developing countries that open themselves to trade gain access to useful technologies and grow faster than countries that insulate themselves from the world trading system. Recent experience provides a clear answer to this question.[8] Although the most successful developing economies differ widely in the extent to which they've welcomed foreign direct investment by multinational enterprises, virtually all have imported and exported relatively freely and used their trade to learn about and master technologies created abroad.

Most major technological advances have occurred in physical-capital-abundant and human-capital-abundant countries, where firms' goals for technological improvement include substitution of abundant capital for relatively scarce unskilled labor. Developing countries, however, claim that they need a different type of technology, because they tend to have abundant unskilled labor and little physical or human capital. The appropriate technologies in such situations typically would be more labor intensive. Thus, multinational enterprises often receive blame for introducing inappropriate technology. But firms, whether multinational or domestic, respond to the incentives they face in choosing technologies and production processes. In the past, many developing economies' import-substitution policies encouraged firms to use highly capital-intensive technologies, because capital-intensive industries gave the appearance of successful industrialization. Without such artificial incentives, multinational firms producing in labor-abundant countries have an incentive to use technologies that take advantage of the availability of low-wage labor. Thus, labor-abundant developing countries must recognize that the production techniques that use their labor and, thereby, raise wages, may not correspond to the symbolically important capital-intensive industrialization typical of industries such as steel and chemicals. And within any given industry, production techniques in labor-abundant countries will be more labor intensive than those used in other countries. Recall the example from Chapter Three

---

8. See, for example, Edwards (1998) and Frankel and Romer (1999).

of General Motors' two state-of-the-art production facilities. The plant in Germany, a capital-abundant, high-wage country, is 95 percent automated, while the plant in Argentina, a labor-abundant, low-wage country, is 45 percent automated.

INTELLECTUAL PROPERTY   Trade disputes over **intellectual property** involve trade in goods that infringe on foreign copyrights, trademarks, industrial secrets, and patents, including counterfeit goods. Industries in which intellectual-property issues play a large role include pharmaceuticals, computer software, music recordings, computers, books, and movies.[9] These issues have only recently earned a prominent role in international trade negotiations. Earlier, developed economies tended to ignore whatever losses their firms sustained due to unauthorized copying, and developing economies openly claimed the right to copy at will in order to diffuse the benefits from technological advances and to avoid the monopoly prices charged by innovating firms for their technologies.

More recently, trade in goods containing important intellectual-property elements has grown much faster than trade overall. This trend has caused firms in developed economies to take their lost revenues more seriously, since the developed economies exhibit strong comparative advantage in most of the relevant industries. In addition, the growth of developing economies' markets has made innovating firms eager to sell there, but some developing countries' weak intellectual-property laws and enforcement have limited the profitability of doing so.

Several developing economies have moved unilaterally to strengthen their intellectual-property protection. Although this trend represents in part a response to pressure from developed countries, especially the United States, other reasons exist as well. Some of the more successful developing economies have begun to innovate and shift into industries where they themselves desire intellectual-property protection. Other countries hope, by strengthening their rules, to encourage inward foreign direct investment and foreign firms' willingness to share new technologies with their local affiliates.

Several factors complicate international negotiations over intellectual-property rules. One is the difficulty in determining the optimal level of protection. Any system of intellectual-property rules represents a trade-off between the incentives to innovate (which rest on strong protection) and the benefits from rapid diffusion (which come from weak or nonexistent rules). Probably a more important impediment to successful negotiations is the obvious distributional consequence of rule changes. Unlike negotiations to lower most trade barriers, which produce gains for all countries, strengthening intellectual-property protection is likely to generate gains for some (developed and a few advanced developing economies) and losses for others (most developing economies), at least in the short run. Each country knows into which group it falls, so gaining consensus is difficult. Countries that expect to be technology importers for the foreseeable future have little incentive to enforce stronger intellectual-property rules, and countries that are or expect to become technology exporters have every incentive to push for strong rules and enforcement.

The Uruguay Round produced an agreement on intellectual property. Members granted *national treatment*, which means that foreign intellectual property receives protection equal to that granted to domestic intellectual property. Countries must grant any protection given to one trading partner to all under the agreement's most-favored-nation provision. Members also agreed to respect copyrights, trademarks, industrial-design secrets, and patents, with rules phased in over a 1-year period for developed countries, 5 years for developing countries and economies in transition, and 11 years for the least-developed economies.

---

9. One example: China imposes an import quota that allows in only 20 foreign films annually (up from 10); but less than a week after the film's U.S. release, counterfeit DVDs of *Harry Potter and the Sorcerer's Stone* sold on Beijing streets for 5 yuan ($1.20) complete with Chinese subtitles.

During the agenda negotiations to begin the new Doha Round, WTO members clarified that existing WTO intellectual property rules allow countries to engage in compulsory licensing of pharmaceuticals necessary to respond to public health crises. This clarification had been sought by poor countries facing large-scale AIDS infections and by pharmaceutical firms in countries such as India and Brazil, which specialize in copying existing drugs. U.S.-based drug companies claimed that the clarification would do little to alleviate the AIDS crisis in poor countries, since lack of treatment resulted more from poverty, lack of basic medical infrastructure, and poor health policies than from lack of access to state-of-the-art medicines. We'll see more about the pharmaceutical issue in Case Four.

5.3 Debts for Development

In 1982, Mexico announced that it could no longer afford to make the scheduled payments on its debt, and the debt owed by developing economies moved to the front page of newspapers worldwide. A full decade passed before policy makers declared the "end of the debt crisis." During that decade, developing countries' inability to make interest and principal payments on their debt periodically threatened the stability of the world financial system and continually strained relations between developed-country creditors and their developing-country debtors. Since the crisis decade of the 1980s, countries from Korea to Russia to Argentina have endured debt-related economic crises.

DEFINING AND MEASURING EXTERNAL DEBT   Developing economies have long relied heavily on borrowing from abroad to finance the domestic investment that plays a vital role in development. The extent and exact nature of the borrowing have varied through time. Before World War I and again between World War I and World War II, British private investors financed much of the investment in the then-developing world (including the United States) by buying bonds. After World War II, the newly created international organizations, the International Monetary Fund and the World Bank, began making development-oriented loans. At the same time, private investors from developed countries undertook large-scale foreign direct investment in the developing world, at first in mining and mineral industries and later in manufacturing. Newly independent developing economies in the 1960s often viewed these foreign direct investors as exploiters and sought alternate sources of funding that would maintain more local control. They found such a source in the mid-1970s when members of OPEC lacked adequate domestic investment opportunities to absorb their burgeoning oil revenues. The OPEC countries deposited their funds in banks, mostly in the United States, which then made bank loans to developing economies.

All these sources of borrowing—bonds sold abroad to private investors, official lending, foreign direct investment, and foreign bank loans—together constitute **external debt**, that is, borrowing from abroad.[10] Developing countries' sources of borrowing vary greatly in their importance over time, but all four types continue to be used. Table 5 divides developing countries' recent borrowing into its main components. Note that private capital flows grew rapidly up until 1998, while flows of official assistance, from developed-country governments and international organizations, have fluctuated with little long-term change. Private capital flows go primarily to middle-income rather than low-income countries. In middle-income developing economies, private investors now fund even infrastructure projects such as power plants, once a mainstay of official development assistance. Official assistance goes to low-income countries and, increasingly, to humanitarian assistance and aid to countries in crisis.

Developing countries' external debt now totals well over $2.6 trillion. However, in analyzing debt, knowing the total quantity owed—even when the amount is measured

---

10. With the "end of the debt crisis," stock markets in "emerging" economies began to attract investment funds from abroad. This represents a fifth component of external debt, but it was trivial during most of the crisis of the 1980s.

Table 5 **NET CAPITAL FLOWS TO DEVELOPING COUNTRIES, 1990–2002 (BILLIONS $)**

Type of Flow	1990	1991	1992	1993	1994	1995	1996	1997	1998	1999	2000	2001	2002
Official flows	$ 55.9	$ 62.3	$ 54.0	$ 53.4	$ 45.9	$ 53.9	$ 31.0	$ 39.7	$ 62.3	$ 42.9	$ 23.4	$ 57.5	$ 49.0
Private flows	42.6	61.6	99.7	165.8	174.5	203.3	282.1	285.1	205.2	194.7	191.8	152.8	143.3
Portfolio flows	18.5	26.4	52.2	99.8	85.7	98.3	151.3	26.7	7.4	15.0	26.0	6.0	9.4
Debt flows	15.7	18.8	38.1	48.8	50.5	62.2	102.1	84.0	87.4	21.9	14.5	-8.6	2.9
Bank lending	3.2	5.0	16.4	3.5	8.8	30.4	37.5	43.1	51.4	-5.9	2.6	-11.8	-16.0
Bond financing	1.2	10.9	11.1	36.6	38.2	30.8	62.4	38.4	39.7	29.6	17.4	10.1	18.6
Other	11.3	2.8	10.7	8.7	3.5	1.0	2.2	2.5	-3.6	-1.8	-5.5	-7.0	-5.5
Equity	2.8	7.6	14.1	51.0	35.2	36.1	49.2	26.7	7.4	15.0	26.0	6.0	9.4
Foreign direct investment	24.1	35.3	47.5	66.0	88.8	105.0	130.8	169.3	174.5	179.3	160.6	171.7	143.0
Private flows' share (percent)	43.2	49.7	64.9	75.6	79.2	79.0	90.1	87.8	76.7	81.9	89.1	72.7	74.4

Source: Data from World Bank, *Global Development Finance* (available at http://www.worldbank.org).

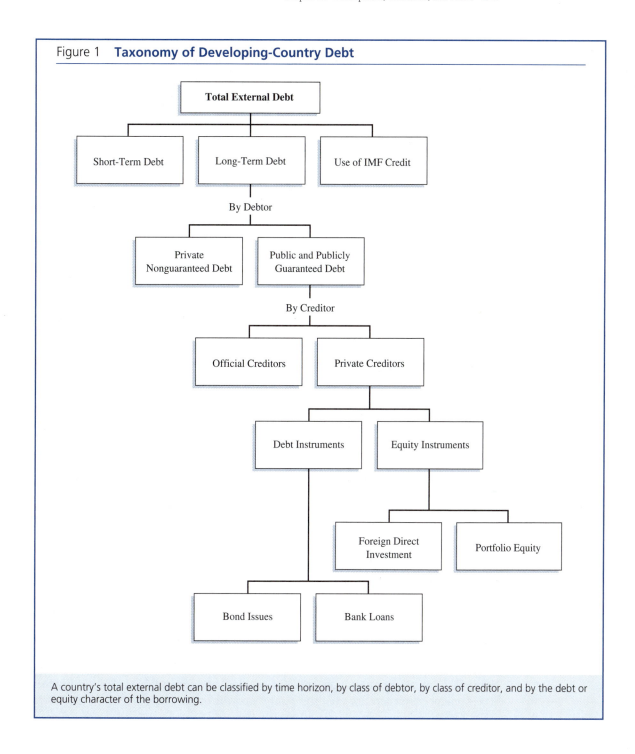

Figure 1   **Taxonomy of Developing-Country Debt**

A country's total external debt can be classified by time horizon, by class of debtor, by class of creditor, and by the debt or equity character of the borrowing.

in trillions—isn't sufficient; different types of debt carry different implications. Figure 1 diagrams a useful taxonomy. Total debt can be divided into short-term debt, long-term debt, and use of credit from the International Monetary Fund (IMF). The bulk of developing-country debt (over 88 percent as of 2003) falls into the long-term category. This means the principal needn't be repaid until at least one year in the future; only interest payments are required in the short term. Long-term debt is classified by the identity of the debtor—the private sector or the public sector. Public-sector debt refers to amounts either owed by or guaranteed by the developing-country government; private-sector debt is owed by individuals and firms and not guaranteed by government. The majority of total long-term developing-country debt is public or publicly guaranteed. For short-term debt (loans with maturities of one year or less), available statistics don't distinguish between public- and private-sector debt.

The distinction between public and private debtors is important because of its implications for the remedies available when repayment problems arise. Governments owed or guaranteed almost all the developing-country debt during the 1980s (around 90 percent), so the defaults feared during that debt crisis would have been **government** or **sovereign defaults** rather than defaults by private firms or individuals. This effectively ruled out the legal remedies a bank normally would pursue against a firm or individual who failed to make loan payments. However, even governments have incentives not to default on their loans. The primary reason: Such behavior can result in inability to borrow in the future, at least for several years.[11] Loss of borrowing privileges, in turn, limits access to trade by eliminating a major source of trade financing. An additional incentive rests on the threat of seizure by creditors of any assets that the debtor government owns abroad.[12]

Just as debt can be divided according to type of *debtor*, either public or private, it can also be classified by type of *creditor*. The main classification distinguishes between **official debt**, owed to governments and international organizations, and **commercial**, or **unofficial**, or **market debt**, owed to private sources, including commercial banks. During the 1950s and 1960s, the bulk of development loans were of the official type. Throughout the 1970s, commercial banks became more involved in making loans to developing countries. In 2003, about 38 percent of developing-country debt was owed to other governments and international organizations; the remaining 62 percent was owed to private creditors, including U.S., European, and Japanese banks as well as private bondholders.

We also can classify borrowing by the nature of the payments owed by debtors to creditors. The two main types are borrowing using **debt instruments** and borrowing using **equity instruments**. Debt instruments obligate the debtor to make payments of a fixed amount to the creditor at a specified date, regardless of the profitability of the financed project and regardless of economic circumstances. Borrowing by issuing bonds and through bank loans both fall into this category. The alternative is equity finance, in which debtor and creditor agree to share in the fortunes of a project, good or bad, with the shares determined in advance. Historically, equity finance in developing economies occurred primarily through foreign direct investment, which also facilitates technology transfer and provides access to international export markets. Only recently have stock markets in some developing economies evolved to the point that they attract significant flows of portfolio equity finance from investors in developed economies.[13] Borrowing through equity has the advantage that when an investment project turns out badly, the payments owed by the debtor to its creditors automatically fall, eliminating the risk of default. One reason developing countries encountered problems with their accumulation of borrowing in the 1980s was that most of the debt took the form of bank loans and bonds rather than equity. When projects failed and debtors' economic circumstances deteriorated, the same loan payments still came due. The same phenomenon occurred during the Asian financial crisis in 1997–1998. More

11. History reveals that punishment for debt repudiation doesn't last forever. Most of the countries of Latin America, for example, defaulted on loans during the 1930s. But by the early postwar years, those countries were borrowing again in international capital markets. Likewise, the defaulters of the 1980s soon were able to borrow again; in fact, less than two decades later, Brazil and Argentina once again experienced crises.

12. During the summer of 2001, Russia pulled its military jets out of the Paris Air Show early to avoid having them impounded in retaliation for Russia's nonpayment of a multimillion-dollar debt to a Swiss firm. See "Russian Fighters Dodge Swiss Creditors," *Financial Times,* July 23, 2002.

13. Recall that direct investment gives the buyer operating control, while portfolio investment doesn't.

recently, private debt flows to developing countries have slowed (at least partly in response to debt crises), while foreign direct investment has continued; so current developing country borrowing contains fewer debt instruments and more equity ones. In 2002, foreign direct investment and portfolio equity investment comprised virtually all of private net capital flows to developing countries, as Table 5 reveals.

GENERAL RULES OF DEBT   That many developing countries face large external debts doesn't necessarily signal a problem. We've seen that intertemporal trade, in which countries with low current saving but plentiful investment opportunities borrow from countries with high current saving but scarce investment opportunities, generates gains from trade. We'd expect this type of borrowing by developing countries from developed countries to produce gains for both debtors and creditors. However, all borrowing, whether by individuals, firms, or governments, must conform to a few simple rules to avoid repayment and default problems.

The economic implications of debt depend on the amount of funds borrowed, the use to which the funds are put, the terms of the borrowing, and the borrower's future prospects and general economic circumstances. Only when one considers all these aspects can one appraise a particular country's debt situation. Generally, borrowing presents no problem as long as (1) the funds finance investment projects that produce returns sufficient to pay the interest on the loan (to "service the debt," in banking jargon); (2) the **maturity** of the loan, or the time over which it must be repaid, matches that of the financed investment projects; and (3) the possibility of unforeseen events is evaluated in calculating the total acceptable amount of debt.

In evaluating any debt, the most important question concerns the use of the funds. When a borrower uses debt to finance consumption in excess of income, the borrowed funds don't produce the returns to cover repayment. The debtor can't even make interest payments as they come due, much less repay the loan's principal, or the sum originally borrowed. This inability to repay is called **insolvency**. If, on the other hand, a borrower finances investment projects that produce a return sufficient to cover repayment, then both the debtor and the creditor benefit. Therefore, developing countries need an effective banking system and financial markets to channel funds to *productive* investment projects; this is essential both to avoid debt crises and to maximize the economic-growth potential from the borrowing.

A second source of potential debt problems concerns the relationship between the maturity, or time horizon, of the borrowing and the time frame of the funded projects. Many potentially productive investments undertaken in developing countries involve long-term projects that can't be expected to pay off for several years. Loans that come due before the investment projects they fund become productive can lead to a **liquidity problem**; the borrower can afford to repay eventually—but not on schedule. One common response to inability to service existing debt is to borrow more to cover the interest payments. Often these additional loans are short-term ones. The funds go to pay interest on earlier loans or, in some cases, to finance consumption-oriented expenditures, so they don't generate returns for repayment. The short-term nature of the additional debt can aggravate an already bad situation, and default becomes a serious possibility.

A final potential error by borrowers and lenders is to assume that the economic conditions prevailing at the time loans are made will continue indefinitely. An individual analogy would be to borrow an amount based on current income with no regard for the possibility of unemployment, illness, or other causes of reduction in income. A country deciding the amount it can prudently borrow must forecast not only its own economic prospects, but those of the larger world economy, since external events can exert a big impact on a country's ability to repay.

WHAT WENT WRONG IN THE 1980s?   Unfortunately, much of the borrowing by developing countries during the 1970s broke at least one of these general rules; and some of it violated all three, leading to the 1980s debt crisis. In some countries, such as Mexico (current external debt, $141 billion), the bulk of the investment funded by borrowing was undertaken by the public rather than the private sector, and a large portion went into inefficient state-owned industries. Before their recent reforms, developing-country governments typically sold food, gasoline and other forms of fuel, and basic utility services such as electricity at artificially low prices. Insofar as borrowed funds went into investment to produce goods then sold at prices below their production costs, the funds actually paid for current consumption. Venezuela (current external debt, $33 billion) tried to industrialize quickly using borrowed funds and, in the process, invested heavily in inefficient industries that produced no return. Peru (current external debt, $28 billion) also borrowed heavily and used the funds to subsidize highly inefficient state-run enterprises. Argentina (current external debt, $132 billion) spent a large share of its borrowed funds on military hardware. Many of these investments produced zero, or even negative, economic returns; so the debtors suffered crises of insolvency.

Changes in the nature of developing-country debt also led to liquidity problems that contributed to the 1980s crisis. Before the 1970s, most developing countries borrowed almost exclusively from official lenders such as the World Bank and the IMF, whose lending constituted long-term debt at concessional, or below-market, interest rates. As middle-income countries' borrowing moved to private sources of funds such as the recycled OPEC oil revenues during the 1970s, loan terms shortened and banks charged market interest rates. Many countries used these short-term loans to finance long-term investment projects that, even if successful, couldn't possibly produce returns in time to repay the loans. Venezuela, for example, incurred a large amount of short-term debt for long-term industrialization projects and encountered a liquidity crisis.

The 1980s crisis also occurred in part because both debtors and creditors failed to account for the possibility of future changes in the world economy. During the 1970s, when many of the loans that led to the crisis were made, commodity prices were booming; and developing countries guessed wrong concerning the permanence of those price increases. Countries such as Mexico and Venezuela, lucky enough to have stocks of minerals and other products enjoying rising prices, invested heavily in increased capacity designed to take advantage of the high prices. Unfortunately, by the time the investments got under way, the high prices were a thing of the past. Investments that would have been very profitable at 1974 prices turned out to be very unprofitable at the prices prevailing in 1979 and 1980, when the debt came due.

Along with faulty forecasts of future commodity prices, developing countries based their borrowing in the 1970s on the assumption that developed countries' economic policies would remain more or less unchanged. Instead, the 1980s opened with developed countries making determined efforts to reduce their high inflation rates. The resulting recession cut deeply into their demand for developing countries' exports, but the debtors had counted on revenue from exports to cover debt payments. Prices for primary products, the leading exports for many debtor economies, collapsed as demand in the developed economies fell. To make matters worse, the recession in the developed economies increased pressures by their domestic industries for protection from foreign competition, so developed-country markets became less open to developing-country exports. The dramatic changes in developed countries' economic policy also caused real interest rates to rise, and much of the developing-country debt was subject to floating interest rates, so payments on the existing debt rose. The same economic forces that cut demand for their exports and raised interest rates on their outstanding loans also caused the value of many debtors' national currencies to fall (or *depreciate*) against the U.S. dollar. Most of the debt was denominated in dollars, so the amount of debt rose sharply when measured in the debtors' local currencies.[14]

---

14. Most developing countries cannot borrow abroad in their own currency because foreign lenders lack confidence that the developed countries' currencies will maintain their value; therefore, almost all developing-country external debt is denominated in a foreign currency, usually the dollar or euro.

Developing-country debtors hoped that the painful combination of recession, reduced export demand, higher interest rates, and currency depreciations was temporary. In an effort to avoid the painful adjustment to these adverse circumstances, many borrowers simply borrowed more to finance spending at current levels. Such decisions contributed to both the liquidity and solvency problems facing debtors. The burgeoning debt-service burdens faced by several middle-income developing countries (especially Argentina, Brazil, and Mexico) began to dry up the sources of private borrowing. The OPEC oil-revenue surpluses disappeared as OPEC fell victim to internal cheating; and banks, so eager to lend in the 1970s, sharply curtailed their lending to developing-country governments. Additional loans were required to prevent default on existing loans; official lenders, especially the IMF, found themselves acting as lenders of last resort and playing an increasing role as arbitrators between debtor countries and creditor banks.

LEGACY OF A CRISIS: WHAT SHOULD WE HAVE LEARNED, AND DID WE LEARN IT?   The day-to-day threat of simultaneous major sovereign defaults by large developing countries no longer hangs chronically over the international financial system as it did throughout the 1980s. Flows of much-needed private capital are under way to many debtor countries, eloquent testimony to investors' confidence in those countries' economic potential. Nonetheless, serious debt problems remain in at least two senses: the continuing high levels of debt in the low-income economies and the continuing heavy reliance by most developing countries on external capital flows to fund development-related investment. The first puts a drag on low-income economies' growth. The second creates periodic macroeconomic crises, such as those in Asia in 1997–1998, Brazil and Russia in 1998, and more recently in Turkey and Argentina.

The debt crisis of the 1980s centered on middle- rather than low-income developing countries for two reasons. First, low-income developing economies—because of their civil wars, poor governance, weak macroeconomic policies, inadequate infrastructures, and unskilled workforces—never gained access to the large-scale private commercial bank lending that played a key role in the debt crisis of the 1980s. Figure 2 locates the heavily indebted poor countries. They receive aid flows from official development agencies that also provide long-term loans at concessional interest rates. As a result, low-income economies escaped the sudden inability to repay that hit the middle-income countries who borrowed from commercial banks during the years of plentiful OPEC funds. Second, because the low-income economies remain small relative to the world economy as a whole, their financial difficulties don't threaten the stability of the world financial system as simultaneous difficulties in Brazil, Mexico, and Argentina did.

The debt crisis of the 1980s was a crisis of the middle-income economies, so the responses focused on those economies as well. The heavily indebted poor countries continue to face huge external debts with little prospect of repayment; their external debt totaled $147 billion in 2003. Burundi, Liberia, Rwanda, Serbia and Montenegro, Sudan, and Zambia each owe debt more than 400 times their respective annual export earnings. Moreover, many poor countries lack the basic institutional structures essential for economic growth and development. Some have suffered decades-long government policies that produce income insufficient to feed their populations, much less repay debt. Most long ago stopped making payments on their medium- and long-term debt to private creditors and fell behind in payments to governments and international agencies. Much of these countries' debt has been forgiven already. A 1996 IMF/World Bank HIPC (*Heavily Indebted Poor Countries*) Debt Initiative promises to forgive more for countries that institute the macroeconomic, structural, and social reforms necessary to facilitate growth, avoid future debt problems, and alleviate poverty.

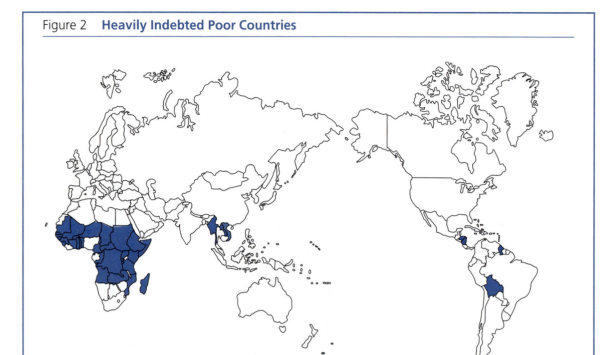

Figure 2   **Heavily Indebted Poor Countries**

Official flows still comprise the bulk of capital flows to the 33 heavily indebted poor countries (HIPCs). To receive IMF designation as an HIPC, a country must have low income and a present value of debt equal to at least 120 percent of GDP or 400 percent of annual export revenues.

Source: International Monetary Fund, *World Economic Outlook,* April 2004.

Most analysts agree that some debt forgiveness is essential to provide incentives for reform. Countries with huge debt accumulations know that if they reform and grow, most of the benefits will go to their foreign creditors; this can weaken the incentives for good policies and growth. But debt forgiveness also carries costs. It can adversely affect the debtors' future ability to borrow and reduce pressure on debtor governments to alter the policies that led to debt problems of such magnitudes. In the long run, only fundamental reforms to build institutions that can support economic growth, combined with continued help from creditors, will allow these countries to overcome their debt.

A second, more general legacy of the 1980s debt crisis is developing countries' continued heavy reliance on capital flows from abroad to finance investment. As noted earlier, the post-crisis renewal of capital flows into developing economies during the early 1990s represented the most often-cited basis for proclamation of the debt crisis's end. A substantial portion of these early inflows represented the return of flight capital that flowed out during the crisis; this repatriation was a one-time phenomenon and couldn't be counted on as a permanent method of external finance. The revival of capital flows to developing economies in the 1990s differed in several ways from earlier flows. *Private* capital flows accounted for a much larger share of the total. On the debtor side, private borrowers played a bigger role; large-scale sovereign borrowing was somewhat less prevalent than in the 1970s, in part because developing countries' reforms had assigned governments more limited roles in the economy. The post-crisis flows also included more equity instruments, both foreign direct investment and portfolio equity, than the bank-loan-heavy flows of the 1970s.

Recurrent debt-related crises—Mexico, Thailand, Brazil, Russia, Turkey, Argentina—continue to remind both economists and policy makers that foreign capital inflows are reversible; so economies dependent on such flows face particular pressures to maintain policies that support investor confidence. Those same policies can encourage domestic saving and provide a domestic source of funds for development-related investment.[15] Private investors watch developing countries' policies closely for signs of trouble. The recent growth of private capital flows to these countries has been uneven, as investors look for sound economic policies and good growth prospects and attempt to avoid crises. Table 6 reports the regional breakdown of private capital flows and their division between low- and middle-income recipients. The table also lists the top five recipient countries, which together account for 56 percent of the total, but for a smaller share now than in 1990.

Some of the 1980s debt crisis's legacies take the form of even more general lessons about the world economy. The successful growth of many developing economies over the past three decades has rendered them an important force in the world economy. Trade and capital flows between developed and developing economies are substantial, so problems in either area no longer can be ignored in the other. The debt crisis forced recognition of this increased interdependence. The crisis also forced many developing economies to undertake structural reforms and to support institutional structures such as the WTO and NAFTA for codifying those reforms, thereby helping to ensure that they remain in place. The crisis reinforced the importance of the different implications of various types of external borrowing. The large role of bank loans in the 1980s crisis reminded debtors and creditors of the appropriate roles for debt instruments and equity instruments in foreign borrowing. Debtors and creditors alike were reminded of the importance of competent domestic institutions, especially a sound banking system and other financial markets, in assuring that borrowed funds are used effectively to facilitate economic growth and development (not to mention repayment). Finally, the crisis highlighted the futility of debtor–creditor deadlock once a crisis erupts. Only when debtors and creditors worked together, with support from other governments and international organizations, did the worst of the crisis end. Unfortunately, the recurrent crises since the 1980s suggest that participants in international capital markets, both lenders and policy makers in borrower countries, have yet to incorporate these lessons fully into their decision making.

5.4 Economic Development and the Environment

Scholars and policy makers long have recognized links between international trade and environmental policies, but recent increased concern with environmental issues has moved the trade–environment link to center stage.[16] This applies especially to developing countries, because environmental quality represents an essential element in the improved quality of life that is development's ultimate goal, and because some forms of environmental degradation hinder productivity and development prospects.

Several characteristics of environmental issues combine to produce controversy and difficulties in international policy making. First, a lack of scientific consensus on the physical effects of some classes of pollution (for example, "greenhouse gases" and the extent and implications of any accompanying global warming) makes agreements difficult to reach because each side of the debate can point to reputable scientific studies that support its position. Second, countries with different income levels demand different levels of environmental quality or protection, just as they demand different qualities of housing, food, or transportation. Again, this greatly complicates international agreements. Low-income developing countries fear having the high-income developed countries' relatively stringent

15. Case Three in Chapter Ten examines the continued correlation between domestic saving and investment.

16. Chapter Eight section 5.3 contains a more general discussion of international trade and the environment. Here, we restrict our attention to issues of particular concern to developing economies.

Table 6 **NET PRIVATE CAPITAL FLOWS TO DEVELOPING COUNTRIES, 1990–2002 (BILLIONS $)**

Country Group or Country	1990	1991	1992	1993	1994	1995	1996	1997	1998	1999	2000	2001	2002
All developing countries:	$44.4	$56.9	$90.6	$157.1	$161.3	$184.2	$243.8	$256.0	$267.7	$216.8	$180.0	$174.2	$153.8
Sub-Saharan Africa	0.3	0.8	−0.3	−0.5	5.2	9.1	11.8	8.0	3.5	17.6	9.6	13.4	7.0
East Asia and the Pacific	19.3	20.8	36.9	62.4	71.0	84.1	108.7	89.0	67.2	41.4	34.4	37.2	47.5
South Asia	2.2	1.9	2.9	6.0	8.5	5.2	10.7	9.0	7.6	3.4	10.1	5.1	5.7
Europe and Central Asia	9.5	7.9	21.8	25.6	17.2	30.1	31.2	41.0	53.3	48.2	42.1	38.9	53.7
Latin America and Caribbean	12.5	22.9	28.7	59.8	53.6	54.3	74.3	95.0	126.9	103.0	80.5	71.5	34.5
Middle East and North Africa	0.6	2.2	0.5	3.9	5.8	1.4	6.9	14.0	9.2	3.2	3.2	8.0	5.4
Income group:													
Low-income countries	11.4	12.1	25.4	50.0	57.1	53.4	67.1	88.7	52.4	3.0	4.7	6.5	7.2
Middle-income countries	32.0	44.0	64.8	107.1	104.2	130.7	176.7	210.0	215.3	213.8	175.3	167.7	146.7
Top country destinations (2002):													
China	8.1	7.5	21.3	39.6	44.4	44.3	52.0	60.8	42.7	36.5	40.6	41.1	47.1
Czech Republic	n.a.	n.a.	n.a.	3.2	2.0	6.4	5.4	2.3	6.6	5.1	3.7	5.8	10.4
Mexico	8.2	12.0	9.2	21.2	20.7	13.1	28.1	20.5	23.2	31.3	10.1	28.2	10.3
Brazil	0.5	3.6	9.8	16.1	12.2	19.1	14.7	43.4	54.4	20.0	38.3	23.2	9.9
Russia	5.6	0.2	10.8	3.1	0.3	1.1	3.6	12.5	19.3	2.9	1.4	1.4	8.0

Source: World Bank, World Development Indicators.

environmental standards imposed on them. Third, environmental restrictions provide an easy disguise for protectionism. For example, a developed country that wants to protect its vegetable producers from competition might justify a ban on imports by claiming that producers in developing countries use environmentally unacceptable chemicals or pesticides.[17] Finally, different population densities, geography, and past pollution levels imply that countries' *assimilative capacities* (that is, their abilities to absorb new pollution with minimal damage) vary widely. A factory whose air pollution might impose heavy health costs if placed in the Los Angeles basin might pose few costs in North Dakota. The Los Angeles basin has a relatively high population density, a geographical configuration in which sea winds trap pollution against the mountains that ring the basin, and a high existing level of many pollutants; North Dakota's situation, and hence its assimilative capacity, is quite different.

Differences among types of pollution also complicate the link between international trade and the environment. Some types (for example, water pollution) have primarily local effects and can be dealt with through domestically financed local policies. Others have cross-border, or even global, effects and require more international coordination of policies as well as more cooperative financing. For example, habitat destruction that reduces biological diversity and deforestation that leads to global climatic consequences impose costs on the entire world. Solving these problems requires international cooperation. Potential approaches include payments by wealthy countries to developing countries for the "species-diversity services" and "carbon-absorption services" provided by their forests. Such payments would provide incentives for developing countries to conserve their habitat and forests.

The environmental priorities of developed and developing countries differ. If you ask an individual in a high-income, developed country about environmental problems, his or her response probably would deal with issues such as carbon dioxide emissions from automobiles, depletion of the ozone layer by chlorofluorocarbons, global warming, and hazardous waste disposal. The same question posed to a resident of a low-income developing country would more likely elicit concern over unsafe drinking water, lack of sanitation facilities, soil depletion, and indoor smoke from burning wood or dung for cooking. These understandable differences in priorities, along with inevitable controversy over who pays for cleanup, go a long way toward explaining the difficulties in international discussions about the environment.

Increasingly, specialists in the environment recognize that the logical first step toward improvement involves curtailing policies that actually encourage environmental damage. Examples of such policies include subsidized use of fossil fuels and water, lack of private-property rights for poor farmers in their land, insulation of state-owned industries (which tend to be heavy polluters) from competitive forces, and rewarding aggressive land clearing by awarding ownership of land to those who clear it.[18] All these policies are prevalent in developing countries, and all take a heavy toll on the environment. Fortunately, elimination of these policies would improve economic efficiency, facilitate international trade liberalization, *and* raise incomes as well as improve the environment. Therefore, the commonly held idea that economic development and international trade necessarily come at an environmental cost clearly is wrong. The truth is much more complex, and sound policy making requires a strong grounding in both science and economics.

6 DEVELOPING MARKETS: ECONOMIES IN TRANSITION

Between 1989 and 1991, the breakup of the Soviet Union and the overthrow of Communist governments in its Central and Eastern European satellite states revealed a new group of developing economies. Forty years of central planning had left a zone of

---

17. Section 5.3 in Chapter Eight outlines WTO rules on environmental protection through trade policy.

18. See section 5.3 in Chapter Eight for specific examples.

outdated technology, environmental disasters, dilapidated factories, and stifled citizens. Even areas such as East Germany, industrialized and modern before coming under Soviet domination at the end of World War II, had declined into backwardness compared with the Western market economies. The most fundamental task facing the formerly centrally planned countries was the shift to market-oriented economies, so they came to be called **economies in transition**.[19] As a group, they have much in common with other developing economies, but face some unique problems and opportunities. To understand the special character of the trade-related aspects of their development prospects, we must briefly turn back the clock and return to central planning.

6.1 International Trade and Central Planning

A **market-based economic system** relies on *prices* to allocate resources, signal trends, and provide incentives. If a good's price rises, this signals increased scarcity and gives consumers an incentive to consume less of the good and producers an incentive to make more of it. Similarly, a rise in an input's price informs firms that the input has become scarcer and gives them an incentive to use less of it and more of other relatively cheaper inputs. A **centrally planned economy**, in contrast, relies instead on government *planning* to decide what and how much to produce and how much to pay factors of production. When government bureaucrats rather than market forces set prices, no automatic mechanism exists to equate quantity supplied with quantity demanded, and shortages and surpluses are more the rule than the exception.

Market-determined prices play a central role in international trade theory (for example, as the basis for the definition of comparative advantage), so that theory says little about how centrally planned economies conduct their international trade policies. In practice, autarky, or self-sufficiency, often was an explicit policy goal. Planners viewed trade as a necessary evil whereby export goods were produced to obtain only those imports impossible to produce domestically. Like policy makers in many other developing economies, central planners also placed great weight on industrialization as a policy goal.

The Soviet Union moved to a system of central planning in the 1920s, approximately a decade after the 1917 revolution brought the Communists to power. From the late 1920s until the end of World War II, the Soviet state pursued national self-sufficiency and industrialization, accompanied by a disastrous collectivization of agriculture. Following World War II, the Soviet Union extended its power into Central and Eastern Europe and integrated those economies into its self-sufficient industrial system. The countries formed the **Council for Mutual Economic Assistance (CMEA, or COMECON)** to manage and coordinate their intra-group trade. Original CMEA members were the Soviet Union, Poland, Hungary, Czechoslovakia, Bulgaria, and Romania; later, East Germany, Vietnam, Cuba, and (temporarily) Albania joined.

Trade within the CMEA grew rapidly, expanding from less than one-third of members' total trade to over three-fourths in just the first five years. The Soviet Union exported oil to other members in return for manufactured goods such as tractors, buses, and forklifts. Although the planners didn't believe in international trade according to comparative advantage, they did believe in specialization and economies of scale. Many goods were produced in a single enormous plant that served the entire CMEA market.[20] Even basic goods such as steel and automobiles came from a mere handful of factories.

19. Other economies throughout the world, including many in Africa, also abandoned central planning during the 1980s and early 1990s. These countries typically aren't included in "economies in transition," although they face many of the same challenges.

20. In the Soviet Union, of 5,884 product lines, 77 percent were supplied by a single producer ("Remaking the Soviet Union," *The Economist,* July 13, 1991, p. 23).

As a result, the CMEA countries traded heavily with one another even though they traded relatively little with the West, especially during periods of heightened Cold War tensions. The Soviet Union linked its own republics even more tightly; only the Russian Republic exported less than 30 percent of it output in 1988, and 10 republics exported more than 50 percent. In 1989, 90 percent of Belarus's trade was with other Soviet republics; 80 percent of all Soviet trade occurred among the Soviet republics themselves.

The CMEA trading system, inefficient as it was (for reasons we'll see in a moment), did allow the centrally planned economies to escape some of the negative effects of their isolation from the rest of the world trading system.[21] Unfortunately, the pattern of trade established under the CMEA made the 1989–1991 revolutions more painful and complicated some countries' transitions to market economies. Bulgaria, for example, conducted approximately 80 percent of its trade with CMEA members, so the sudden collapse of the Soviet Union abruptly halted most of Bulgaria's trade.

The CMEA economies' isolation from the rest of the world wasn't just a matter of ideological refusal to accept the theory of comparative advantage or of political tensions with the West. To be feasible, a centrally planned system *must* insulate itself from contact with market economies; otherwise, trade at market-determined world prices will erode the government's ability to impose its artificial prices and centrally planned resource allocation. For example, the Soviet Union's central plans emphasized production of capital and military goods and left little productive capacity for consumer goods. The results were predictable: queues, waiting, rationing, and high black-market prices for consumer goods. If the Soviet government had allowed free trade, at least some Soviet consumers would have purchased Western consumer goods and Western firms would have bought the capital goods on which the Soviet government kept prices artificially low (that is, a fraction of the opportunity cost of producing them). To avoid these deviations from the state's economic plan, a centrally planned economy must prevent a free flow of goods between itself and market economies.

CMEA countries achieved this separation primarily through monopoly state bureaucracies to handle all foreign trade.[22] Typically the state planning ministry worked with a ministry of foreign trade to decide which goods the country would need but not be able to produce domestically. To obtain these needed imports, they made plans to use other "surplus" goods as exports. The foreign-trade ministry then informed the official state-trading bureaucracy of the necessary imports and exports. This bureaucratic process greatly interfered with the efficiency of trade. Goods often failed to arrive as planned. Firms, under political pressure to meet their state-imposed output quotas, hoarded inputs so they could continue to produce when input shipments failed to appear. The result was an economy of enormous enterprises, each of which tried to maintain self-sufficiency to the greatest extent possible within the central-planning system.

The nature of centrally planned economies imposed several other barriers to efficient international trade. First, planners didn't allow their currencies to be traded in foreign-exchange markets; in particular, the currencies weren't *convertible* into other currencies. If a Czechoslovakian firm exported machinery to the Soviet Union and received payment in rubles (the Soviet currency), Czechoslovakia could spend the proceeds only on imports from a country willing to accept rubles in payment, most likely the Soviet Union itself. If the ruble had been freely convertible, Czechoslovakia could, for example, have exchanged the rubles for Japanese yen in the foreign-exchange market and used the yen to import goods from Japan.

---

21. Ignoring the political barriers to East–West trade, most intra-CMEA trade represented trade diversion (see section 4.2 in Chapter Nine). However, during the Cold War and Soviet domination of Eastern Europe, trade with the West was severely limited, so the only real choice was between no trade and intra-CMEA trade.

22. Lenin imposed a state monopoly on foreign trade shortly after the 1917 revolution in Russia; most other socialist economies followed.

But the centrally planned economies maintained artificial exchange rates for their currencies just as they maintained other artificial prices, so unrestricted trade in currencies had to be avoided. The result was bilateralism in trade; that is, each country had to import and export approximately equal amounts with each trading partner, because the proceeds from exports took the form of nonconvertible currencies useful only on imports from the currency-issuing country. This bilateralism ignored patterns of comparative advantage and led to inefficient trade flows at prices that bore little resemblance to market-determined world prices.

The planning system presented an additional barrier to trade with market economies by giving producers no incentive to make the types of high-quality goods demanded in world markets. Under central planning, the rewards producers earned were only weakly connected to the quality or desirability of their product. Producers couldn't keep any profits that resulted from a superior product, so quality tended to be low and erratic. Such products couldn't compete with Western-made goods in world markets, but traded in CMEA transactions at prices that ignored the goods' shoddy quality.

The CMEA amounted to a trading system that ignored comparative advantage, overemphasized regional specialization and economies of scale, channeled trade to group members at the expense of potential trade with the West, and ignored market prices and product quality. Needless to say, this historical legacy didn't facilitate transition.

6.2 The Painful Transition from Central Planning

Even before the massive political and economic change that swept Central and Eastern Europe and the Soviet Union between 1989 and 1991, some of the centrally planned economies liberalized their trade procedures to allow firms that wanted to import or export to deal more directly with foreign firms. Most notably, as part of the Soviet Union's economic restructuring or *perestroika*, new trade laws allowed Soviet firms to trade directly with foreign firms as of 1989. The Soviet Union also expressed interest in joining GATT, forerunner of today's WTO, but Western nations were skeptical about the feasibility of applying GATT's market-oriented rules to an economy so insulated from world markets.[23] In efforts to improve product quality and upgrade their technology, several countries including the Soviet Union started to encourage joint ventures with Western firms.

Between 1989 and 1991, economic and political reforms in Eastern Europe and the Soviet Union grew from a trickle to a torrent. One by one, authoritarian regimes fell, and new governments pledged themselves to the difficult task of transition to market-oriented economies. As this process continues well into its second decade, each country faces unique problems and challenges, but there are elements common to all.

Although analysts agree that the economies of the former Soviet Union and Central and Eastern Europe will perform much better under market systems than under central planning, things got worse before they got better. With the threat of Soviet military intervention gone, so was the incentive to accept the system's poor-quality goods. Consumer demand shifted to better, Western-made goods. The massive state-owned factories lost their only markets. The CMEA disbanded as members shifted their trade to the West. Countries such as Hungary and Czechoslovakia that had relied on exports of manufactured goods saw the (artificial) prices of those goods collapse when confronted with world market prices for higher-quality goods. Some economies tried to shift exports to the West, but their outdated technology and trade barriers in developed-country markets limited this ability in the short run.

Several economies in transition instituted large-scale reforms early, signaling a dramatic shift to a market orientation. For these countries—including Albania, the

---

23. Russia currently is negotiating to join the WTO. A key aspect of those accession negotiations was whether Russia would be recognized as a market economy. In 2004, both the United States and the European Union agreed that Russian transition had proceeded sufficiently for the country to have official "market economy" status; see Case Six.

Baltic republics, the Czech Republic, Mongolia, Poland, the Slovak Republic, and Slovenia—the worst of the short-run shock of transition seems to be over, and growth rates are climbing, albeit erratically. For others, late or overly timid reforms or special difficulties such as massive corruption or armed conflicts have their economies still mired in the downturn phase of transition.

One additional problem in evaluating the early performance and prospects of the transitional economies was the lack of reliable data on key economic variables such as gross national product. Existing data from the central-planning era had two problems. First, GNP calculations in centrally planned economies often included only the state-owned sector of large industries. Typically, this represented the least productive sector, especially as reforms removed the subsidies that had kept these "dinosaur" industries alive. As reforms took hold and small, privately owned firms appeared, this dynamic sector of the economy provided a growing share of income and employment but failed to find its way into official accounts. The second data problem reflected the effect of inconvertible currencies. Cross-country comparisons of GNP figures require that data be "translated" from domestic currency units (the Soviet ruble, or the Polish zloty) to a common unit, usually the U.S. dollar. This translation process uses the exchange rate, or the value of one currency expressed in units of the other currency. But, as we've noted, the centrally planned economies maintained highly artificial exchange rates. This implies that economic data calculated using such rates were highly suspect at best. At least a portion of the dramatic declines in reported income levels in the transitional economies after 1989 reflected the use of more realistic exchange rates for the calculations. Table 7 reports estimates of GNP per capita during transition for the former Soviet Republics and the Central and Eastern European economies; however, the World Bank cautions that the early figures, especially those for the former Soviet Union, must be regarded as tentative.

The transitional economies as a whole grew in 1997 for the first time in seven years. On average, an economy suffered three years of falling output after introducing sustained reforms. Industry's share of output has fallen in most of the countries, while services have grown and agriculture has grown in some and declined in others. By the end of transition's first decade, the countries' economic and policy performances had become highly differentiated. Some had built impressive track records of reform and had realistic hopes of joining the European Union (achieved by eight transitional economies in 2004); others had hardly started down the road to reform and recovery.

6.3 The Reform Agenda and Prospects

The list of major transition tasks included eliminating price controls and introducing market-determined prices, cutting government subsidies to industry, removing restrictions on private ownership and market activities, cutting military spending and the role of government in the economy, assuring macroeconomic stability, providing incentives for improved productivity and quality, privatization, designing systems for effective corporate governance, and creation of independent central banks to administer monetary and foreign-exchange policies. In the former Soviet Union, even more fundamental reforms such as building a legal system to protect private property, a framework for enforcement of contracts, and a transparent accounting system were (and still are) needed; some of the economies of Central and Eastern Europe, with their shorter histories of central planning, were luckier in these regards.

Most analysts and policy makers agreed on most items on the reform list. However, there were two controversies. The first concerned the proper speed and ordering of reforms. Faced with such a daunting list, should one attempt all the reforms simultaneously and as quickly as possible? Or should one concentrate on a few elements at a time and allow for lengthy adjustment periods? History provides few models of such broad political and economic change; therefore, substantial disagreement remains on this question. Poland followed the

Table 7   **PER-CAPITA GNP FOR THE ECONOMIES IN TRANSITION, 1989–2002 ($)**

Country	1989	1990	1991	1992	1993	1994	1995	1996	1997	1998	1999	2000	2001	2002
Albania	n.a.	n.a.	n.a.	n.a.	$340	$380	$670	$820	$750	$810	$870	$1,220	$1,400	$1,450
Bulgaria	$2,320	$2,250	$1,840	$1,330	1,140	1,250	1,330	1,190	1,140	1,230	1,380	1,510	1,650	1,770
Czechoslovakia	3,540	3,140	2,470	n.a.	n.a.	n.a.	n.a.	n.a.	n.a.	n.a.	n.a.	n.a.	n.a.	n.a.
Czech Rep.	n.a.	n.a.	n.a.	2,450	2,710	3,200	3,870	4,740	5,200	5,040	5,060	4,920	5,260	5,480
Slovak Rep.	n.a.	n.a.	n.a.	1,930	1,950	2,250	2,950	3,410	3,700	3,700	3,590	3,700	3,770	3,970
Hungary	2,590	2,780	2,720	2,970	3,350	3,840	4,120	4,340	4,430	4,510	4,650	4,740	4,820	5,290
Poland	1,790	1,690	1,790	1,910	2,260	2,410	2,790	3,230	3,590	3,900	3,960	4,200	4,350	4,570
Romania	n.a.	1,640	1,390	1,130	1,140	1,270	1,480	1,600	1,420	1,390	1,520	1,670	1,720	1,870
Yugoslavia	2,920	3,060	n.a.	n.a.	n.a.	n.a.	n.a.	n.a.	n.a.	n.a.	n.a.	n.a.	n.a.	n.a.
Bosnia	n.a.	n.a.	n.a.	n.a.	n.a.	n.a.	n.a.	800	1,020	1,190	1,240	1,270	1,280	1,310
Croatia	n.a.	n.a.	n.a.	n.a.	n.a.	2,560	3,250	3,800	4,610	4,520	4,580	4,510	4,330	4,540
Macedonia	n.a.	n.a.	n.a.	n.a.	n.a.	820	860	990	1,090	1,290	1,690	1,710	1,690	1,710
Slovenia	n.a.	n.a.	n.a.	n.a.	n.a.	7,040	8,200	9,240	9,680	9,760	9,890	10,070	10,160	10,370
Soviet Union	n.a.	n.a.	n.a.	n.a.	n.a.	n.a.	n.a.	n.a.	n.a.	n.a.	n.a.	n.a.	n.a.	n.a.
Armenia	n.a.	2,380	2,150	780	660	680	730	630	530	480	490	650	700	790
Azerbaijan	n.a.	1,640	1,670	740	730	500	480	480	510	490	550	610	660	710
Belarus	n.a.	3,110	3,110	2,930	2,870	2,160	2,070	2,070	2,150	2,200	2,630	2,990	1,300	1,360
Estonia	n.a.	4,170	3,830	2,760	3,080	2,820	2,860	3,080	3,330	3,390	3,480	3,410	3,930	4,190
Georgia	n.a.	2,120	1,640	850	580	n.a.	440	850	840	930	620	590	600	650
Kazakhstan	n.a.	2,600	2,470	1,680	1,560	1,160	1,330	1,350	1,340	1,310	1,230	1,190	1,350	1,520
Kirgizstan	n.a.	1,570	1,550	820	850	630	700	550	440	350	300	270	280	290
Latvia	n.a.	3,590	3,410	1,930	2,010	2,320	2,270	2,300	2,430	2,430	2,470	2,860	3,260	3,480
Lithuania	n.a.	3,110	2,710	1,310	1,320	1,350	1,900	2,280	2,230	2,440	2,620	2,900	3,340	3,670
Moldova	n.a.	2,390	2,170	1,300	1,060	870	920	590	540	410	370	400	400	460
Russia	n.a.	3,430	3,220	2,510	2,340	2,650	2,240	2,410	2,740	2,300	2,270	1,660	1,800	2,130
Tajikistan	n.a.	1,130	1,050	490	470	360	n.a.	340	330	350	290	170	170	180
Turkmenistan	n.a.	1,690	1,700	1,230	n.a.	n.a.	n.a.	940	630	n.a.	660	840	1,090	n.a.
Ukraine	n.a.	2,500	2,340	1,820	2,210	1,910	1,630	1,200	1,040	850	750	700	720	780
Uzbekistan	n.a.	1,340	1,350	850	970	960	970	1,010	1,010	870	720	610	320	310

Source: World Bank, World Development Indicators; United Nations, Human Development Report.

sudden or "big bang" approach on January 1, 1990, when it cut tariffs and moved its zloty currency toward convertibility. Many economists argue that opening international trade supports the other needed reforms by providing information about market prices, putting competitive pressure on domestic firms to improve quality, and providing access to new technology, an area in which most of the economies in transition lag seriously behind the West. The former Soviet Republics have, with few exceptions, taken more gradual approaches, but have met with only erratic success. China's gradualism, in which liberalization began in agriculture during the late 1970s and only gradually extended to industry, has been somewhat more successful; but China's political liberalization lags behind its economic reforms. Table 8 reports the transitional economies' status on the major margins of reform.

The data in Table 8 highlight the countries' diverse policies and progress. Some, such as the Czech Republic, Hungary, and Poland, show substantial reform on all margins, with scores of 3 or 4 on all aspects of reform. Others, such as Belarus and Turkmenistan, have hardly begun their reform tasks. Still others, such as Bosnia, Bulgaria, Romania, and Tajikistan, show substantial progress on some margins of reform and much less on others. Generally, the countries of Central and Eastern Europe have undertaken the most complete reforms; the former Soviet republics in Central Asia, on the other hand, lag behind.

A second debate over reform concerns how (and how much) to cushion the effects of transition on individuals and firms. On the one hand, failure to provide social cushions generates social and political discontent that may threaten the reform process. On the other hand, too much cushioning removes the essential incentives to adjust and prolongs the inevitable pain of transition. As price controls are removed, particularly for key goods such as energy, food, and housing, citizens can bring tremendous political pressure to raise wages to maintain their purchasing power. But the low productivity in many sectors doesn't justify those higher wages, so yielding to the political pressure prolongs the transitional period of increased unemployment.[24]

Different initial conditions meant that the short-run economic prospects at the time of transition varied substantially across Eastern Europe and the former Soviet Union. In some countries, such as Hungary, central planning was never complete and substantial market expertise existed within the population. In others, such as the former Soviet Union, a longer and more exclusive history of socialism meant that few citizens possessed significant market experience. The share of the state sector in the economies varied substantially before reforms began. For example, in the mid-1980s, 97 percent of value-added originated in the state sector in Czechoslovakia, East Germany, and the Soviet Union, but only 65 percent in Hungary.[25] So the magnitude of the privatization task— a slow and difficult aspect of reform—differed across countries. In some countries, the population strongly supported reform; other countries faced more troubling and unstable domestic political situations or even civil or interstate conflict.

The former Soviet republics faced several additional problems. The breakup of the country severed long-standing supply relations, leaving factories without supplies and component producers without customers. Unlike most Eastern European economies, the Soviet planning system encompassed agriculture as well as industry, so both sectors had to undergo the transition process. Separated from the national framework of the Soviet Union, the republics lacked the institutions of a typical nation-state, including central banks and legal frameworks to deal with the bankruptcies that constitute an inevitable part of the transition process. The republics had to decide how closely to cooperate and what functions to share within the Commonwealth of Independent States, a loose

---

24. See Cases One and Two in Chapter Four and section 7 in Chapter Eight on the relationship among wages, productivity, and competitiveness.

25. *The Wall Street Journal*, July 23, 1991.

Table 8 **TRANSITIONAL ECONOMIES' REFORM, 2003 (4+ = MARKET ECONOMY, 1 = LITTLE PROGRESS)**

Country	Private-Sector Share of GDP (Percent)	Enterprises			Markets and Trade			Financial Institutions	
		Privatization		Governance and Restructuring	Price Liberalization	Trade and Foreign-Exchange System	Competition Policy	Banking Reform and Interest-Rate Liberalization	Securities Markets & Non-Bank Financial Institutions
		Large-Scale	Small-Scale						
Albania	75	2+	4	2	4−	4+	2−	2+	2−
Armenia	70	3+	4−	2+	4+	4+	2	2+	2
Azerbaijan	60	2	4−	2+	4	4−	2	2+	2−
Belarus	25	1	2+	1	3−	2+	2	2−	2−
Bosnia/Herzegovina	50	2+	3	2	4	4−	1	2+	2−
Bulgaria	75	4−	4−	3−	4+	4+	2+	3+	2+
Croatia	60	3+	4+	3−	4	4+	2+	4−	3−
Czech Rep.	80	4	4+	3+	4+	4+	3	4−	3
Estonia	80	4	4+	3+	4	4+	3−	4−	3+
FYR Macedonia	60	3	4	2+	4	4+	2	3	3+
Georgia	65	3+	4	2	4	4+	2	2+	2−
Hungary	80	4	4+	3+	4	4+	3	4	4−
Kazakhstan	65	3	4	2	4	3+	2	3	2+
Kirgizstan	65	3	4	2	4+	4+	2	2+	2
Latvia	70	3+	4+	3	4+	4+	3−	4−	3
Lithuania	75	4−	4+	3	4+	4+	3	3	3
Moldova	50	3	3+	2−	4+	4+	2	2+	2
Poland	75	3+	4+	3+	4+	4+	3	3+	4−
Romania	65	3+	4−	2	4+	4	2+	3−	2
Russia	70	3+	4	2+	4	3+	2+	2	3−
Serbia/Montenegro	45	2+	3	2	4	3+	1	2+	2
Slovak Rep.	80	4	4+	3	4+	4+	3	3+	3−
Slovenia	65	3	4+	3	4	4+	3−	3+	3−
Tajikistan	50	2+	4−	2−	4−	3+	2−	2−	1
Turkmenistan	25	1	2	1	3−	1	1	1	1
Ukraine	65	3	4	2	4	3	2+	2+	2
Uzbekistan	45	3−	3	2−	3−	2−	2−	2−	2

Source: Data from European Bank for Reconstruction and Development, *Transition Report 2003.*

confederation joined by most former Soviet republics. Prospects for economic growth and development varied widely among the republics based on different size, resource endowments, international linkages, damage from broken supplier relationships, environmental problems, ethnic tensions, and degrees of political instability.

Like other developing countries, the economies in transition also faced the hurdle of developed-country trade barriers. Industries in which the emerging economies have comparative advantage—such as agriculture, textiles, and steel—are precisely those industries in which many developed countries erect the highest trade barriers. The Uruguay Round reforms improved market access for the economies in transition. In addition, for transitional economies with WTO membership, the reforms required them to continue to dismantle their own trade barriers, although the agreement permits a slower liberalization schedule for developing and transitional economies than for developed ones. As of 2004, many transitional economies had attained full WTO membership; most of the others, including Russia, had requested membership.

For all but the least reformed transitional economies, divergent performance increasingly reflects policy choices rather than initial conditions. Difficult work remains, especially in the areas of capital- and financial-market reforms, enterprise restructuring and governance, government reform of tax systems, and corruption. There are reasons for optimism. All the economies should be able to attain substantial productivity gains from restructuring their enterprises. And most enjoy highly educated and skilled workforces. However, everyone now recognizes that building market institutions and policies is a long-term job that requires persistence and, sometimes, resourcefulness and stamina in the face of opposition by vested interests. Countries' differing current positions along the transition path can be summarized by their relationships with the European Union, their nearest high-income trading partner. In 2004, the Czech Republic, Estonia, Hungary, Latvia, Lithuania, Poland, the Slovak Republic, and Slovenia joined the EU as full members. Bulgaria and Romania hope to do so in 2007. Albania, Bosnia and Herzegovina, Croatia, Macedonia, and Serbia and Montenegro participate in the EU's Stabilization and Association Process, an association agreement that could eventually lead to membership. As more transitional economies join the EU and complete the reforms that comprise that process, trade and investment flows will tend to shift toward those countries; other transitional economies will have to press forward on their own institutional reforms or risk significant economic isolation.

CASE 1: DOES AID AID GROWTH?

Developing countries have received billions of dollars in aid over the past several decades. Most studies, however, have found virtually no relationship between the amount of aid a country receives and growth of its per-capita income. Recently, economists Craig Burnside and David Dollar set out to take a more careful look, using better data and statistical techniques than earlier studies. The investigation covered 56 developing countries from 1970 until 1993. What did the investigators find?

First, they confirmed a finding of many other studies that a developing country's growth depends heavily on its own economic policies. This led Burnside and Dollar to wonder if perhaps aid does affect growth, but only in countries that follow growth-conducive policies. What if aid acts basically as an income transfer? When the recipient government invests the additional income in productive projects, income will rise. This will be likely to happen in countries where governments choose their own policies with an eye toward growth. But when governments simply consume the additional income, aid won't enhance growth; this is most likely to occur in countries whose governments follow distorting policies that discourage investment and growth.

Policies found in many studies to be conducive to growth include low inflation, an absence of government budget deficits, and openness to trade. For countries meeting these conditions, Burnside and Dollar find that aid does help growth.

Burnside and Dollar also investigated a follow-up question: Have donors responded by giving more aid to countries whose governments follow good policies? Apparently not. Bilateral aid in particular (that is, aid from a single donor government to a recipient government) seems unaffected by the economic wisdom of the recipient government's policy choices. Such aid appears to lead to a rise in government consumption, not to a rise in investment or growth. Multilateral aid, on the other hand (that is, aid administered by international organizations and regional development banks), responds somewhat more to

recipient policy and is less likely to go toward increased government consumption.

With the end of the Cold War—which had created political and security reasons for particular aid patterns regardless of growth goals—donors may start to focus aid where studies suggest it will have the strongest growth-enhancing effect: in countries whose own governments follow good economic policies. Such a shift in aid allocation might also nudge bad-policy governments to reconsider their policy choices. One new U.S. aid program asks potential recipient governments to "compete" for aid by submitting proposals documenting their growth-conducive policies. And some multilateral aid agencies now allow non-governmental groups to apply for aid, opening up new channels for aid to reach the population of countries with corrupt and ineffective governments.

CASE 2: DOES POLICY MATTER? THE TWO KOREAS

North Korea/South Korea

No country in the modern world exists in complete autarky. Some, however, come much closer than others.[26] Since Korea split into the Republic of (South) Korea and the Democratic People's Republic of (North) Korea during the Korean War of the early 1950s, the North's philosophy has been one of *juche,* or self-sufficient industrialization. The government of the North, one of the world's last centrally planned Communist regimes, strictly controls foreign trade, along with other contact with the outside world. In fact, experts have called North Korea the "world's most autarchic economy." The South, on the other hand, has pursued outward- or trade-oriented development policies. So the two countries, side by side, provide a dramatic example of inward- versus outward-oriented development strategies.

The difference in results is remarkable, as summarized in Table 9. The South's per-capita gross domestic product exceeds that of the North by a factor of 17; despite the setbacks caused by the Asian financial crisis of 1997, the South's economic growth dwarfs the North's. In fact, North Korea's output shrunk by an average of about 5 percent per year during the 1990s; exports fell by about two-thirds during the decade. Estimates indicate that 1999 was the

only year during the 1990s during which North Korean GDP grew rather than shrunk.

Of course, North Korea's attempts at self-sufficiency aren't the only cause of its economic problems. Estimates place North Korea's army at 1.2 million people; and military expenditures absorb up to a quarter of the economy's meager output. Until 1990, the small amount of trade in which the country engaged took the form of oil imports from the Soviet Union to fuel huge state-owned industrial plants and exports of low-quality goods to Eastern Europe. Since the demise of the Soviet Union, North Korea's factories now run far below capacity because the country lacks the foreign currency to buy oil at world prices on the open market. The decline of central planning in Eastern Europe eliminated the markets for North Korea's few exports, whose low quality made them noncompetitive in world markets. These problems led to idle fuelless factories, power outages, famine, and rumors of fatalities of up to 2 million North Koreans from starvation. Floods and a failed rice crop in 1995 and 1996 forced the country to seek food aid abroad.

North Korea responded to its growing economic problems by opening a tiny crack in the door to the outside

---

26. Similarly, no country practices perfectly free trade. In May 1997, Mongolia became the only country in the world to levy no taxes on trade; see "Those Free-Trading Mongolians," *The Economist,* April 26, 1997.

Table 9 COMPARISON OF NORTH AND SOUTH KOREA, 2002–2004

Indicator	North Korea	South Korea
Territory (1,000 square kilometers)	120	98
Population (million persons)	22.7	48.6
GDP (billions $)[a]	22.9	855
Per-capita GDP ($)[a]	1,000	17,700
Economic growth (percent)	1.0	2.8
Exports (billions $)	1.0	201.3
Imports (billions $)	2.0	175.6
Telephones (millions)		
Main lines	1.1	23.2
Cellular	n.a.	32.3
Internet		
Hosts (thousands)	n.a.	407.3
Users (thousands)	n.a.	26,207
Paved highways (kilometers)	1,997	64,808
Military expenditure (percent of GDP)	22.9	2.7

[a]Converted to U.S. dollars at purchasing-power-parity exchange rates.

Source: Central Intelligence Agency, *The World Factbook* (available at http://www.cia.gov).

world. The government encourages foreign firms to take advantage of North Korea's low wages by investing in a special economic zone, the Rajin-Sonbong Free Economic and Trade Zone, modeled on China's coastal economic zones. But the government keeps that area (strategically placed to handle South Korea–China trade) isolated from the rest of the country to prevent the spread of political ideas; investors have been wary, despite generous tax incentives and relaxed rules that permit 100 percent foreign ownership of new enterprises in the zone. Several firms have pulled out, and a Hong Kong-run casino comprises the primary remaining draw.

Talks have been underway for years on several major projects involving North Korea. The first is the reunification of the two Koreas, with the obvious hope that the South could revitalize the North. The costs, however, could be enormous; one estimate placed the cost to bring the North's per-capita income up to 60 percent of the South's (the minimum level thought to keep North-South migration manageable) at $1.7 trillion.[27] A second project is the Tumen River Economic Development Area, a free-trade zone among North Korea, China, and Russia, along with Mongolia and South Korea, at the mouth of the Tumen River. The zone could allow North Korea to capture at least a portion of the potential gains from trade. The original idea was to process Russian and Mongolian raw materials with Chinese labor and then export the products through the North Korean port of Rajin. However, despite the area's strategic and commercial importance, strong support from the United Nations Development Program, and over $900 million already invested over 10 years, the project seems to have stalled.

In May 1995, a South Korean firm won government approval for the first joint venture with a firm from the North since the Korean War. North Korea allows Hyundai, in exchange for $1 billion over six years, to operate a tourist service that allows South Koreans to visit—under carefully restricted conditions—the Diamond Mountains in the north. South Korea's state-owned Tobacco and Ginseng Corporation now sends tobacco leaves north, where they are used in One Mind cigarettes, sold in both

27. Marcus Noland et al., "The Economics of Korean Unification," Institute for International Economics, Working Paper 97–5, p. 3.

North and South Korea. South Korean firms have opened an auto plant, greenhouses, and a pig farm. A handful of international merchant banks have established joint ventures with local North Korean partners.

Experts estimate that liberalization of international trade could raise North Korean GDP by 25 to 35 percent. Given the country's resource endowment, especially abundant unskilled and semi-skilled labor, its potential areas of comparative advantage include fish, minerals, textiles, apparel, and a broad range of light manufacturing. Freed from the dictates of central planners, the agricultural and capital-goods sectors—areas of comparative disadvantage—would shrink.

In late 1999, in exchange for North Korean promises to limit its nuclear-weapons and missile-testing programs, the United States eased trade restrictions—in place since 1950—that had prohibited trade between the United States and North Korea. After shrinking between 25 and 40 percent during the 1990s, North Korea's economy enjoyed a year of positive growth in 1999. Unfortunately for the citizens of North Korea, the government withdrew once again from engagement with the rest of the world in

response to South Korea's support of the antiterrorism campaign launched after the September 11, 2001, terrorist attacks on New York and Washington, D.C.

Political and economic policy over the past few years have been erratic. Reforms have allowed farmers to sell their produce, wages have been raised, government-issued coupons are no longer required to buy food or clothing, and the government has announced a special walled free-trade zone in Sinuiju. At the same time, international ramifications of the government's pursuit of nuclear weapons have blocked trade and even limited donors' willingness to provide humanitarian aid (along with allegations that donated food goes to feed the army rather than needy civilians). Experts claim that much of the money to support the Kim Jong Il regime comes from production and sale of heroin, other illegal drugs, counterfeit currencies, and weapons.

Regardless of timetables or fates of particular projects, one thing is certain. If North Korea hopes to experience economic growth, open international trade based on comparative advantage will constitute a vital component of the necessary policy changes.

CASE 3: OPEN TO DEVELOPMENT

We saw in Chapter Ten that a country can grow in two ways: use more inputs or use inputs more productively. The latter path involves boosting total factor productivity, a measure of how efficiently an economy uses its inputs. Total factor productivity rises because of technological innovations, including organizational ones, that allow a given quantity of inputs to produce more output. Table 10 reports estimates of the contributions of the various sources of growth for developing countries as a group and for subsets of developing countries divided by their growth rates. Notice that high rates of total factor productivity distinguish the high-growth economies from the medium-growth ones and, especially, from the low-growth ones, which actually suffered a large decline in productivity between 1982 and 1991.

What contributes to growth in total factor productivity? One source of innovation, especially for poor developing economies, is borrowing technology from abroad through imports or foreign direct investment. This suggests that, in addition to providing a one-time increase in output as traditional trade models suggest, openness may raise a country's rate of growth by encouraging increases in its total factor productivity.

A recent study by Sebastian Edwards empirically examines this proposition. Do countries that make themselves open to trade grow faster? The answer appears to be yes. Edwards used a sample of 93 countries and nine different measures of openness between 1980 and 1990. He found that, for every one of the nine measures, more-open countries exhibited higher rates of total factor productivity growth.[28]

---

28. See Edwards (1998), as well as Frankel and Romer (1999).

Table 10 CONTRIBUTIONS TO GROWTH, 1971–1991

	Share in Total GDP Growth		
	1971–1981	1982–1991	1971–1991
Developing countries:			
Average GDP	100.0%	100.0%	100.0%
Capital contribution	51.7	47.6	48.1
Labor contribution	26.7	31.0	25.0
Total factor productivity	21.7	23.8	25.0
High-growth countries:			
Average GDP	100.0	100.0	100.0
Capital contribution	49.3	47.1	47.2
Labor contribution	21.3	17.6	18.1
Total factor productivity	29.3	33.8	34.7
Medium-growth countries:			
Average GDP	100.0	100.0	100.0
Capital contribution	54.5	41.4	50.0
Labor contribution	32.7	44.8	35.7
Total factor productivity	12.7	10.3	16.7
Low-growth countries:			
Average GDP	100.0	100.0	100.0
Capital contribution	57.6	75.0	57.1
Labor contribution	30.3	137.5	42.9
Total factor productivity	12.1	−112.5	0.0

Source: Data from United Nations Industrial Development Organization, *Industrial Development Global Report 1997*, p. 9.

CASE 4: REPRODUCING PHARMACEUTICALS

India

For years, firms in many developing countries have copied products created by developed-country firms. Developing countries' lack of intellectual-property laws or failure to enforce them let this copying continue with no remuneration to the innovative firms. India, for example, built a thriving pharmaceutical industry centered in Mumbai and Hyderabad. Indian law protected patents on the *process* for making a drug but not on the *product* itself, so Indian firms could copy drugs legally—so long as they altered slightly the manufacturing process for the active ingredient's molecule. Analysts estimate that this allowed Indian drug manufacturers to spend less than 2 percent of their sales revenue on research and development, compared with the 16 percent spent by the U.S. firms that develop and test most new drugs.

Intellectual-property provisions of the Uruguay Round agreement promised to change the situation for developing countries that, like India, belong to the WTO. Under the agreement, all new product or process innovations receive 20 years of patent protection from the date of application. However, the WTO gave the least-developed countries such as India up to 11 years (until 2005) to implement the new rules; innovations already in the pipeline received no protection.

The 2005 deadline created a big incentive for Indian pharmaceutical firms to copy as many drugs as possible as quickly as possible. Consider Viagra, Pfizer's popular anti-impotence pill. Within months of the drug's 1998 U.S. debut, several Indian firms were producing Viagra's active ingredient, sildenafil citrate, selling it illegally at home (where it had yet to be approved by the Indian government), and exporting it. The black market price was reported to be $13 per tablet (compared with $10 for a Pfizer tablet in the United States), but experts expected the domestic price of Indian tablets to fall to between $1 and $2 by the time government approved legalized domestic sales.

Pfizer, Eli Lilly, Warner-Lambert, and other U.S. pharmaceutical firms often don't sell their latest drugs in India (or in other piracy-prone countries such as Argentina) because the local knockoffs undercut the innovators' prices. Once the Uruguay Round agreement takes full effect, unlicensed pharmaceutical firms may find their copying of patented drugs restricted. But countries such as India and Argentina may also enjoy more foreign direct investment and technology sharing by the innovators themselves once their research activities receive some protection. In fact, Eli Lilly, AstraZeneca, and other foreign pharmaceutical firms have plans in place for more research and production in India after January 1, 2005—the date India is scheduled to begin recognition of international drug patents.

Perhaps the most visible issue concerning intellectual property rights in pharmaceuticals centers on the extent of countries' right to override patents in public-health crises by engaging in compulsory licensing, that is, by copying pharmaceuticals without the innovating firm's permission when that firm refuses to license the product. WTO rules do allow such licensing; that permission received clarification during negotiations to begin the new Doha Round. Developing countries such as India and Brazil, with large copy-based pharmaceutical industries, along with some medical and AIDS activist groups, claimed a victory. But many public-health experts pointed out that licensing issues for state-of-the-art drugs were, at most, secondary problems in treating public-health crises such as AIDS in poor developing countries; more substantial barriers to be overcome include poverty, lack of basic medical infrastructure, and poor health policies. The other major concern with allowing generous compulsory licensing is a longer-term one. If authorities can't prevent the cheaper drugs intended for poor countries from being resold in industrial countries, pharmaceutical companies will lose their profit incentive to engage in the costly research and development that leads to new drugs.[29]

CASE 5: OIL JUNKIES?

Consider the following unflattering description of oil-endowed economies: "[O]il revenues are to the Middle East what heroin is to the junkie. Day to day, shooting up keeps you from feeling sick; over time, though, it keeps you from being healthy. . . . The oil producers are addicts. They prefer the comfortable squalor of staying hooked to the work it would take to kick the habit."[30]

Economists have noted for decades that economies with abundant endowments of natural resources, such as oil, often perform poorly. Think, for example, about the economies of the Middle East and North Africa. In fact, this tendency earned a seemingly oxymoronic name: the **resource curse**. How can resources be a curse when they're, after all, what makes possible production of the goods and services we want? What's special about natural resources, as opposed to labor or capital, that might make too much a bad rather than a good thing?

First, an increase in natural resources tends to increase that sector's output at the expense of manufacturing. We can think of this as an application of the Rybczynski theorem from Chapter Ten. Recall what that theorem tells us: When a small country experiences an increase in its endowment of one input (here, oil reserves), output of the good that uses that input intensively (here, oil) will rise more than proportionally *and* output of the other good (here, manufacturing) will fall. Shrinkage of the other sector must happen to free up the labor and capital needed for expansion of the oil sector. So large natural-resource endowments can lead to lack of development of other sectors of the economy.

Second, prices and revenues from natural-resource products can be volatile. For an economy highly dependent on such products, income and government tax revenues reflect this volatility. So it's important for policy makers to manage prudently. When prices and revenues are high, policy makers must have both the foresight and the political will to put some away for the proverbial rainy day (the best-known example is Norway's Norwegian Government Petroleum Fund, a national "savings account" for oil revenues). Or, to put it differently, using up oil and gas reserves depletes the country's capital stock. So unless part of the revenues earned

---

29. See the Arrow; Kremer; Scherer and Watal; and Subramanian articles in the chapter references.
30. James Surowiecki, "The Real Price of Oil," *The New Yorker,* December 3, 2001, p. 41.

Table 11	RESOURCE DEPENDENCE OF OIL- AND GAS-RICH TRANSITIONAL ECONOMIES, 2000				
	Azerbaijan	Kazakhstan	Russia	Turkmenistan	Uzbekistan
Oil and gas exports as percent of total exports	85.2%	46.8%	50.4%	81.0%	12.3%
Oil and gas exports as percent of GDP	30.5	24.7	21.5	68.7	4.3
Oil and gas revenues as percent of total government revenues	36.2	27.5	30.1	42.0	14.8
FDI in oil and gas sector as percent of total FDI	80.5	69.7	n.a.	n.a.	n.a.

Source: Data from European Bank for Reconstruction and Development, *Transition Report 2001*.

from the oil and gas go into productive investment projects to increase other components of the capital stock, the country's ability to produce income over time will decline. Unfortunately, many poor developing and transitional economies lack the policy-making expertise and credibility to handle such prudent management of revenues.

Third, the availability of "windfall" wealth from natural resources can destroy incentives to invest in education and technological innovation—key elements for sustained economic growth. For a personal-level analogy, think how you might have behaved differently if you'd won the lottery at age 16; would you have invested in a college education? Living off a windfall is always easier than working to create something, so the availability of oil or gas resources can reduce the incentives for entrepreneurship. When there's enough oil for the entire population to live off of it, at least for a while, the lack of incentives for entrepreneurship and other economic activity can erode the basis for long-term growth.

Fourth, in many developing and transitional economies, the natural-resource sectors are dominated by the government or newly privatized monopolies. Competitive pressures are suppressed through entry or ownership restrictions. Once again, incentives to innovate disappear, even in the resource sector.

Finally, the existence of rents from natural-resource monopolies often leads to corruption and political fights over the division of those rents. Consumers want, and often get, highly subsidized energy prices, which encourage overly rapid depletion of the resource. The politically powerful spend their time fighting over access to reserves and pipelines. Promising pipeline routes lead to territorial disputes and even armed conflicts, which further drain the country's ability to produce.

Among the transitional economies, Russia, Kazakhstan, Azerbaijan, Turkmenistan, and Uzbekistan have rich oil and gas reserves; Table 11 summarizes the degree of their dependence on their resource sectors.

How will this affect their transitions and future growth? Will they avoid the resource curse, or will they follow the unfortunate economic paths of Nigeria, Saudi Arabia, Algeria, Venezuela, and Iran? So far, the evidence suggests that the resource-endowed transitional economies performed less well during 1989–2000 on the European Bank for Reconstruction and Development's indicators of progress in transition than did other transitional economies. All of the problems mentioned here have been in evidence, albeit to differing degrees in the various countries.

CASE 6: WTO MEMBER OR MARKET ECONOMY?

China/Russia

When centrally planned economies try to transform themselves through economic liberalization, two goals often loom large for policy makers: win membership in the World Trade Organization and win designation by the United States as a market economy. As of 2004, China and Russia each have reached one of the goals but failed to reach the other.

China asked to join the WTO in 1986, 36 years after the Communist government pulled out of the WTO's predecessor organization, the General Agreement on Tariffs and Trade (GATT). But reentry wasn't easy. China missed its goal of accession by 1995—in time to be a charter member of the World Trade Organization. Finally, after 15 years of off-and-on talks, accession negotiations ended successfully in 2001. But, much to China's disappointment, both the United States and the European Union refused to grant market-economy status, claiming that the state still played too large a role in the Chinese economy. Why does market-economy status matter so much even after a country joins the WTO? When firms in the United States file dumping charges against firms in a foreign country, the rules under which the merits of the case are judged are much more favorable to the "defendant" country if it is officially a market economy (see section 6 in Chapter Seven). Nonmarket economies

face antidumping rules much more likely to result in a "guilty" finding. So Chinese firms remain vulnerable to dumping charges.

Russia's story contrasts with China's. The Soviet Union announced interest in joining the GATT soon after the country's economic liberalization or *perestroika* program in 1989. As of 2004, WTO membership still eludes Russia. Talks have been held up by Russia's insistence on protecting some of its industries (such as automobiles), maintaining the right to subsidize its farmers, and keeping domestic energy prices artificially low for both residential and industrial users. However, in 2002, both the European Union and the United States granted Russia market-economy status, based on the Russian government's reduced role in production and resource allocation, the role of markets in establishing wages in Russia, and the economy's openness to foreign investment.

SUMMARY

The basic economic theory of international trade as developed in Chapters Two through Ten applies to developed and developing countries alike. But developing countries face special concerns regarding specialization in primary products, their desire for industrialization, access to new technologies, external borrowing to finance investment, environmental policies, and integration into the world economy. The process of economic development is long and difficult and offers few easy answers or quick fixes. But active participation in the world economy, based on comparative advantage and economies of scale, appears to offer a brighter future for the developing nations than the price-distorting and inward-looking policies prevalent in the past.

LOOKING AHEAD

Thus far, we've ignored the fact that economic transactions across national borders involve use of more than one currency or unit of money. If you are reading *The World Economy*, we will continue to Chapter Twelve, where we explore the mechanics of dealing in different currencies and the policies open to governments for determining the value of their currencies relative to those of other countries.

KEY TERMS

gross national product (GNP)
North–South debate
import substitution
newly industrializing countries (NICs)
outward-oriented growth
effective rate of protection (ERP)
cascading tariffs (tariff escalation)
technology
technology transfer
intellectual property
external debt
government (sovereign) defaults
official debt

commercial (unofficial, or market) debt
debt instruments
equity instruments
maturity
insolvency
liquidity problem
economies in transition
market-based economic system
centrally planned economy
Council for Mutual Economic Assistance
   (CMEA, or COMECON)
resource curse

PROBLEMS AND QUESTIONS FOR REVIEW

1. Developing countries often accuse developed ones of pursuing trade policies that impede the ability of developing countries to export to developed countries. Briefly describe two examples of trade policies that provide some support for the developing countries' position, including why the policies you cite might harm developing countries.

2. Suppose you've been called in as a consultant to a country trying to decide whether to take out a substantial amount in foreign bank loans. What basic questions would you ask the country in order to obtain information to evaluate the desirability of the borrowing? Briefly explain the importance of each of your questions and how the answer to each would affect your recommendation.

3. In India's pharmaceutical and biotechnology industries, most firms simply manufacture drugs and vaccines discovered and developed by foreign firms. However, a few Indian firms engage in research and development to develop new drugs and vaccines. How would you expect these two groups of Indian firms to differ in their views on India's intellectual-property laws? In particular, which group would you expect to support stronger patent protection?

4. Cashew nuts provide the second-largest source of export revenue for Mozambique. The country imposes a 20 percent export tax on unprocessed cashews to support a cashew-processing industry that removes the kernels from their outer shells. A World Bank study found that cashew farmers would be much better off if the government simply removed the export tax on unprocessed cashews, but the government refused. Explain the policy and its expected beneficiaries and losers. Does the export tax represent an example of import-substitution development strategy or an outward-oriented one?

5. Pharmaceutical A treats Alpha Syndrome, a disease prevalent in both rich developed and poor developing countries. Pharmaceutical B treats Beta Syndrome, a disease prevalent only in poor developing countries. Both drugs were developed through costly R&D programs in a rich developed economy. If intellectual-property rules permit generous copying (that is, if patent protection for intellectual property is weak), what long-term problem might this cause in finding new and better drugs to treat Alpha Syndrome but not in finding new and better drugs to treat Beta Syndrome?

6. Briefly describe several reasons why developing and developed countries often have difficulty reaching agreements in negotiations over environmental issues.

7. Explain why, using the theory from earlier chapters of the book, you might expect outward-oriented development strategies to be more successful than strategies based on import substitution.

8. Explain two reasons why the successor states to the former Soviet Union experienced a more painful and prolonged economic downturn from the events of 1989–1991 than did most of the formerly centrally planned states of Eastern Europe.

REFERENCES AND SELECTED READINGS

African Development Bank. *African Development Report*. Oxford: Oxford University Press, annual.
Analysis and data of development-related activities in Africa.

Arrow, Kenneth J. "New Antimalarial Drugs: Biology and Economics Meet." *Finance and Development* 41 (March 2004): 20–21.
The economics of medicines for diseases that exist only in developing countries.

Bannister, Geoffrey J., and Kamau Thugge. "International Trade and Poverty Alleviation." *Finance and Development* 38 (December 2001): 48–51.
Channels through which trade can alleviate poverty.

Bhagwati, Jagdish, and T. N. Srinivasan. "Trade and Poverty in the Poor Countries." *American Economic Review Papers and Proceedings* 92 (May 2002): 180–183.
The role of open trade in poverty reduction.

Bloom, David E., and Jeffrey D. Sachs. "Geography, Demography, and Economic Growth in Africa." *Brookings Papers on Economic Activity* 2 (1998): 207–296.
Argues for an important role of geography in Africa's slow growth.

Bruton, Henry J. "A Reconsideration of Import Substitution." *Journal of Economic Literature* (June 1998): 903–936.
Strengths and weaknesses of import substitution and outward-oriented development; for all students.

Burda, Michael C., and Jennifer Hunt. "From Reunification to Economic Integration: Productivity and the Labor Market in Eastern Germany." *Brookings Papers on Economic Activity* 2001 (Issue 2): 1–92.
How labor markets have affected the process of German unification.

Burnside, Craig, and David Dollar. "Aid, Policies, and Growth." *American Economic Review* 90 (September 2000): 847–868.
Does foreign aid contribute to recipients' economic growth?

Campos, Nauro F., and Fabrizio Coricelli. "Growth in Transition: What We Know, What We Don't, and What We Should." *Journal of Economic Literature* 40 (September 2002): 793–836.
Well-organized overview of the lessons of ten years of transition.

Clague, Christopher, ed. *Institutions and Economic Development.* Baltimore: Johns Hopkins University Press, 1997.
Collection of accessible applied papers on the roles of governance in development.

Collier, Paul, and Jan Willem Gunning. "Explaining African Economic Performance." *Journal of Economic Literature* 37 (March 1999): 64–111.
Survey of why African economic growth has lagged behind that of other regions.

Edwards, Sebastian. "Openness, Productivity, and Growth: What Do We Really Know?" *Economic Journal* (March 1998): 383–398.
More evidence on the complex relationship between trade and growth.

European Bank for Reconstruction and Development. *Transition Report.* London: EBRD, annual.
Excellent source of up-to-date analysis and data on the transitional economies.

Frankel, Jeffrey A., and David Romer. "Does Trade Cause Growth?" *American Economic Review* 89 (June 1999): 379–399.
Strong evidence that open trade contributes to growth, not the other way around.

Freeman, Paul K., et al. "Being Prepared." *Finance and Development* 40 (September 2003): 42–45.
The challenge that natural disasters pose for developing countries.

Klitgaard, Robert. *Tropical Gangsters.* New York: Basic Books, 1990.
A Harvard University economist's entertaining story of his experiences with corruption while working on a World Bank project in Equatorial Guinea.

Kremer, Michael. "Pharmaceuticals and the Developing World." *Journal of Economic Perspectives* 16 (Fall 2002): 67–90.
Excellent accessible survey of the economics of pharmaceuticals and the implications for developing countries.

Krueger, Anne O. "Trade Policy and Economic Development: How We Learn." *American Economic Review* (March 1997): 1–22.
Accessible review of recent changes in views toward development by one of the field's leading authorities.

Lougani, Prakeash. "Inequality." *Finance and Development* 40 (September 2003): 22–23.
Short overview of trends in the main measures of income inequality.

Maskus, Keith E. *Intellectual Property Rights in the Global Economy.* Washington, D.C.: Institute for International Economics, 2000.
Accessible discussion of striking a balance between incentives for innovation and spreading the benefits of new ideas.

Mitra, Pradeep K., and Marcelo Selowsky. "Lessons from a Decade of Transition in Eastern Europe and the Former Soviet Union." *Finance and Development* 39 (June 2002): 48–51.
Short overview of a World Bank study on the lessons of transition.

Mshomba, Richard E. *Africa in the Global Economy.* Boulder, Colo.: Lynne Rienner, 2000.
Excellent introduction to the role of international trade and trade policy in Africa.

Scherer, F. M., and Jayashree Watal. "Post-TRIPS: Options for Access to Patented Medicines in Developing Nations." *Journal of International Economic Law* 5 (December 2002): 913–940.
The economics of medicines for poor countries.

Session on "The Future of the International Monetary Fund and World Bank." *American Economic Review Papers and Proceedings* 93 (May 2003): 31–50.
Collection of short papers on the successes and failures of two international economic institutions.

Subramanian, Arvind. "Medicines, Patents, and TRIPS." *Finance and Development* 41 (March 2004): 22–25.
The economics of international patent rules for pharmaceuticals.

Symposium on "International Public Goods and the Transfer of Technology under a Globalized International Property Regime." *Journal of International Economic Law* 7 (June 2004): 275–482.
Collection of papers on the economic and legal aspects of international property rights.

Symposium on "Transition Economics." *Journal of Economic Perspectives* 16 (Winter 2002): 3–125.
Collection of articles on various aspects of transition, ten years into the process.

United Nations Industrial Development Organization. *Industrial Development: Global Report.* Oxford: Oxford University Press, annual.
Excellent source of analysis and data on industrialization.

World Bank. *Globalization, Growth, and Poverty.* Washington, D.C.: The World Bank, 2002.
Up-to-date analysis of economic integration's effects on poverty.

World Bank. *World Development Report.* New York: Oxford University Press, annual.
Devoted to examination of various aspects of development; accessible to all students. Also contains large collection of data.

Yarbrough, Beth V., and Robert M. Yarbrough. "Unification and Secession: Group Size and 'Escape from Lock-In.'" *Kyklos* (1998): 171–195.
Changing national borders as a way of overcoming political opposition to reform; for intermediate students.

Country or Economy Index

Subject Index